Islam in Retrospect

Islam in Retrospect
Recovering the Message

by Maher S. Mahmassani

OLIVE
BRANCH
PRESS

An imprint of Interlink Publishing Group, Inc.
www.interlinkbooks.com

First published in 2014 by

OLIVE BRANCH PRESS
An imprint of Interlink Publishing Group, Inc.
46 Crosby Street, Northampton, Massachusetts 01060
www.interlinkbooks.com

Library of Congress Cataloging-in-Publication Data

Mahmasani, Mahir.
Islam in retrospect : recovering the message / by Maher S. Mahmassani.
--
First American edition.
pages cm.
Includes bibliographical references and index.
ISBN 978-1-56656-922-4
1. Islam--Essence, genius, nature. 2. Islam--Universality. I. Title.
BP163.M328 2014
297.2--dc23
2014021489

Printed and bound in the United States of America

Dedication

This work is dedicated

1) to the fond memory of my late father Sobhi Rajab Mahmassani who dedicated his life to promote the noble values of Islam, and in particular the values of peace, tolerance, justice, and compassion that form the core of Sharia'a;

2) to my dear wife, Hania, for 40 years of love, understanding, and compassion, and whose patience, support, and strong encouragement made this work possible;

3) to my son Sobhi, my daughter Zein, and her husband Yanal; and

4) to my most precious grandchildren, Rakan and Jood.

ACKNOWLEDGMENTS

I grew up in a home where Islam was practiced with open-mindedness and tolerance. My father, Sobhi Rajab Mahmassani, was a scholar of Islamic law who over the course of his lifetime published a number of valuable books on various topics of Islam. He consistently preached the Islam of diversity, peace, justice, equity, compassion, tolerance, freedom of conscience and expression, and human rights.

Yet, despite this home environment, the influences of my social and geographic environment were somehow stronger and led me toward becoming a reasonably faithful and believing Muslim. I say *reasonably* because there were some things in the Islam that was around and within me that bothered me, and which I found difficult to reconcile with certain fundamental principles of the faith.

Among other things, I found it difficult to reconcile assumed beliefs of male supremacy with the principles of gender equality that the Qur'an promotes; calls for jihad and violence with the calls for peace and compassion heard throughout the Qur'an; the repression of questioning and discussion of matters of faith with the Qur'anic encouragement of the faithful to use the mind and seek conviction in faith; the inferior treatment of non-Muslims with the freedom of faith and other human rights that the Qur'an stresses; and the disparagement of efforts to promote democracy and secular legislation with the understanding, central to the Qur'an, that God has designated humankind as trustees on this earth.

These tensions prompted me to learn more about Islam and offered me the opportunity to become acquainted with the rich contributions of the scholars of Islam of the Enlightenment era, namely Rifa'a al-Tahtawi, Muhammad Abdu, Jamaluddin al-Afghani, 'Ali Abdel-Raziq, and Qasim Amin. I then discovered some of the modern Muslim and non-Muslim, Arab and non-Arab, scholars of Islam who dealt with various topics of Islam in the most rational and Cartesian ways, namely Khalil Abdul-Karim, Khaled Abou El Fadl, Ahmad Amin, Abbas Mahmud al-Aqqad, Muhammad Sa'id 'Ashmawi, Jacques Berque, Daniel Brown, Abdelmajid Charfi, Mohamed Charfi, Malek Chebel, Farid Esack, John Esposito, Abdou Filali-Ansari,

Yvonne Haddad, Aziza al-Hibri, Muhammad 'Abed al-Jabiri, Ann Mayer, Abdulaziz Sachedina, Muhammad Shahrour, Abdolkarim Soroush, and Muhammad Talbi. These readings led me to engage in further, in-depth research, at the end of which I discovered that what had initially bothered me was not, in fact, part of the Message, the divine word of God. Instead, it was part of history and traditions that had accumulated over time and that somehow had become a sacred part of Islam. This inspired me to proceed with this book. To all these scholars, and to others, I owe the knowledge and enlightenment that I tried to bring out in this work.

This work never would have come to light without the encouragement of my publisher, Michel Moushabeck, who thoughtfully reviewed my manuscript and provided the commitment needed to proceed with its publication. A thoroughgoing, collaborative production process shaped an extensive, complex document into clearer and more readable final form. To the entire staff at Interlink Publishing, particularly the project team of John Fiscella (editing), Jennifer Staltare (proofreading), and Pamela Fontes-May (design and layout), I owe my thanks and gratitude for their patient and diligent efforts.

CONTENTS

PREFACE

The term *Muslim* as used throughout this text refers to anyone who claims to be a Muslim—that is, anyone who professes *al-Shahāda*, or declaration of faith, that "There is no god but Allah; and Muhammad is the Messenger of Allah"—without making any value judgment about the substance of his or her belief. This book is not about prejudging who is a 'true' or 'good' Muslim and who is not, all of which falls within the jurisdiction of the Almighty.

This book is about Islam and how Islam is understood, as a religion, exclusively through the provisions of the Holy Qur'an, rather than through the commentaries, customs, habits, behavior, or public statements of Muslims, whether clergy, scholars, or laypersons. The following view of Islam expressed by Christian Makarian helps to clarify our focus.

> Reading through the biographic literature about Muhammad and his Companions...one reaches a definition of Islam of the early days as follows: it is about rallying with—or submission to—a new power paradigm established by a prophet who frames its laws in the name of God, and whose political foundations rely on a permanent military activity.[1]

Makarian's perspective does not distinguish between tradition and scripture, that is, the human and the divine. While this book is neither an apology for, nor condemnation of, the behavior of certain Muslims, it does attempt to differentiate between the accumulated heritage of Muslim peoples and societies and the original religious tenets of Islam, apart from such customs and practices.[2] The widely divergent customs and practices of Muslim societies have been commonly confused with—and made to seem an intrinsic part of—Islam. It is when a line between these elements and scripture is clearly drawn that it becomes possible to rethink one's understanding of Islam as a religion of progress and release it from constraints falsely attributed to it.[3]

Nor is this book a criticism of depictions of Islam by non-Muslims who observe and focus on the behavior of selected Muslim peoples. As with any faith, it is understandable that a non-Muslim layperson, as opposed to a scholar, might acquire impressions of Islam from observing the behavior of various Muslims and from the statements and writings of Muslim religious institutions.[4] Instead, this book is a straightforward attempt to understand Islam through a fair and open-minded reading of the Scriptures, without undue reading between the lines or looking for hidden meanings that may have been unintended in the first place. There are no codes to break to extract the *bāṭin* (intrinsic meaning) from the *ẓāhir* (external and conspicuous meaning). The early exegeses, or scholarly critical interpretations using historical and other methods, of the Holy Qur'an will not be treated as binding explanations. These early interpretations are no more than good faith renditions of each author's respective understanding of the Qur'an based on the prevailing heritage, value system, and customs. Prophetic Tradition will also be reexamined, namely the traditions of Prophet Muhammad (Peace be on Him),[5] to better appreciate its true value.

To accomplish this it is necessary to begin by reviewing common perceptions of Islam that are usually taken for granted. Themes will be thoroughly explained and examined in order to clearly distinguish between myth and actual message. Such is the intent behind the title of this book. By 'Islam in retrospect' is meant the process of stepping back and taking a clear look at the actual central underlying tenets of Islam. That examination reveals that the Islam portrayed through prevailing beliefs and behaviors is, in many cases, a distortion of Islam.

Muslim societies are currently on a path similar to that of Christian societies several centuries ago. At times throughout history, Christianity has been associated with violence and with years of bloody conflicts and wars, some religious in nature, others less so. Yet, the behavior of Christian persons or clergy involved was not necessarily an expression of the Christian faith, although some have asserted that it was. In the main, Christianity today focuses on the message of divine love that is central to the religion. For Islam, although its message is also one of peace and divine love, Islam is often perceived or portrayed as a religion of violence, stemming from the behavior or speech of persons who profess to represent or speak for it. Predictably, this creates resistance to the idea that Islam and modernity are compatible. In reality, Islam *is* modernity: *it is universal, it is secular, and it is progressive.* It glorifies the role of the mind and invites learning, and hence, modernity and change.

As perceived through aspects of its accumulated heritage and history, Islam continues to be judged severely in the light of today's generally accepted values and principles. In reality, these representations of Islam are trapped in early critical interpretations, practices, and history. Instead, Islam should be perceived, analyzed, evaluated, and appreciated in light of values and practices that were prevailing at the time that it was revealed. At that time, Islam led the way toward progress and enlightenment. It contained the seeds of a universal, secular, and progressive outlook. The problem is not simply the portrayal of Islam by non-Muslims; it is the portrayal of Islam by scholars and clergy who have maintained an inflexible approach, stifling the universal outlook inherent to Islam.

In preparing this study, twelve different translations of the meanings of the Holy Qur'an have been consulted. Verses quoted here have been carefully selected using the version that most faithfully conveys the meaning and intent of the verse in question. In some cases, my own translation is offered. With respect to verses that are simply cited without quotation, any of the twelve versions listed in the bibliography would be useful to consult. On the other hand, the reader will notice that this book focuses mostly on references from reformist thinkers.[6] This is intentional in order to demonstrate that the ideas advocated in this study are not anathema to Islam as a religious tradition, nor are they unusual, invented, or new. What is new, and what this study hopes to contribute to, is a consensus that is slowly building to restate—and reaffirm—what Islam's message in fact has been, all along.

INTRODUCTION
Myths and Changing Realities

Our understanding of Islam has been, and continues to be, stigmatized by preset ideas that have developed and accumulated over time. These ideas are only recently being reconsidered, if not challenged. In retrospect, these widely accepted ideas are in fact myths that have profoundly distorted our understanding of Islam. What are these myths? How were they constructed? What do they conceal about the nature of Islam? How might an examination of these myths illuminate an effort to recover Islam's message?

Prevalent Myths about Islam

MYTH: "The Holy Qur'an should be understood without regard to context."

Dating back to Islam's origins, the Holy Qur'an has been interpreted as a universal, self-contained text, where each verse stands on its own and is explained objectively, without regard to its context and specificity. In fact, Islam *is* universal, but it is universal in the sense that its message is global.[1] While the original audience of the Qur'an was the greater society of Prophet Muhammad, the intended audience for its underlying message is the entirety of humanity in all times and places. Throughout Prophet Muhammad's mission, God addressed Muhammad to inform him about the nature of his mission and to guide him in its day-to-day performance. God also addressed the people of Muhammad's society and those to whom Muhammad was preaching to convey the Message. That Message also contained valuable principles of morality and ethics, sufficient to extend its reach universally and to guide humanity. That is why the Qur'an addressed its first audience in their own language, Arabic, the language that they understood, and why it addressed them by reference to their own customs and practices. At times, God intervened to change hideous customs and practices, such as vengence; at other times, existing customs were tolerated temporarily to effect a gradual removal, such as slavery; or at times, customs were retained, built upon, and developed, such as the hajj.

Context is very important because Islam did not appear in a vacuum, as is implied by the use of the term *jāhiliyya* (the era of ignorance) when referring to the pre-Islamic period that preceded the revelation of the Holy Qur'an, during which the message of Islam was as yet unknown. It was a period when people were in ignorance of the divine truth and guidance revealed in the Qur'an. In this respect, *jāhiliyya* does not necessarily include the people who received, accepted, and lived the previous messages of God, namely, believing Jews and Christians. It applies to pagans, polytheists, and those Christians and Jews who did not truly adhere to the particular divine messages addressed to them.

In reality, Islam emerged within the environment of a reasonably evolved society, with a developed civilization and established traditions, aspects of which found their way into Islam. In this sense, Islam did not completely break from its past, as *fiqh* (Islamic law) would suggest. That is why certain Christian and Jewish traditions, as well, found their way into Islamic traditions.[2] The Holy Qur'an itself assumes that, prior to Islam, Muslims lived in a diverse environment, an implication that can be found in several verses where knowledge of the subject matter by the immediate Arab recipients is presumed.[3]

Understanding the nature of the pre-Islamic period leads us to reject the barrier commonly erected between Islam and the *jāhiliyya,* and the portrayal of everything in people's lives during the *jāhiliyya* as taboo.[4] That Islam did not appear in a vacuum is a theme that will recur throughout this work. In considering the intent and scope of specific verses of the Scriptures, it is necessary to place them in context, determine their raison d'être, and examine the circumstances in which they were revealed (or *asbāb an-nuzūl*)[5] before reaching a level of certainty about their meaning. This is essential in order to determine the scope of the universal nature of each verse. The Divine Message often cannot be understood apart from the geographical, historical, or social conditions at the time of the Revelation. Events and circumstances pertaining to the period preceding the revelation of Islam should not be discarded as remnants of the *jāhiliyya.* Instead, attention should be drawn to the problems inherent in confusing the divine sources of Islam with religious tradition, a key myth that has generated profound consequences.

MYTH: "The accumulated Islamic heritage is an integral part of Islam."

Ebrahim Moosa rightly points out that "no one has seen 'Islam' in its transparent glory to really judge it," but that a wide range of Muslims of all denominations, types, and characters can be observed. He concludes that "it is actually Muslims who embody Islam."[6] Identifying the actual sources of Islam enables us to define what Islam is. What differentiates various strands of Islam depends on the perception of what is or is not part of Islam.

While Islam as a culture may include the accumulated heritage and wisdom of Muslim peoples throughout the ages, the Holy Qur'an is the sole source of the binding principles of the religion. Only the Qur'an is divine, that is, infallible and perfect. Everything else that has been sacralized over time by the *fuqahā'* (scholars of jurisprudence), including Prophetic Tradition, is man-made and nondivine, bound by time and place. Unfortunately today, when Islam is taught in schools, the meanings of the Qur'anic verses are those attributed to them in the compilations written in the first three centuries following the death of the Prophet. Thereafter, commentaries focused mainly on repeating and reinterpreting the works of the early commentators. As a result, the works of those early commentators came to be viewed as sacred, almost on par with the Qur'an. For that reason, current understandings of Islam are often inconsistent with the letter and spirit of the Divine Message.

Islam is universal and the Holy Qur'an is its sole source. It is critical to reject the idea that Islam must at all times be interpreted, understood, and lived in the same way that the early companions and commentators interpreted, understood, and lived it.

MYTH: "Islam is about blind submission to God."

It is argued that the term *Islam* means "submission." This view has consistently served as a cornerstone of Islamic religious education. Indeed, we are taught that as human beings we are helpless because God is the Almighty. This view suggests that no matter how much we plan and decide on matters pertaining to our lives, those plans and decisions are meaningless unless God so desires and approves, in His absolute discretion. In that role, God is depicted as unpredictable, because to attempt to predict God's will—a pretense that we humans can attain divine knowledge—translates into the severely punishable sin of *shirk* (association). Since no one can pretend to God's knowledge, whatever we may plan can only be a modest wish, coupled with a prayer that God may, in His bounty and grace, allow that wish to be fulfilled.

Islam is not about *istislām* (or surrender), although both terms derive from the same root term in Arabic. That is why many jurisprudents have conflated Islam with *istislām* and instructed that Islam was about surrender before the Almighty. Yet, while God is the Almighty, we are not powerless, because the Almighty created humankind and endowed us with meaningful capacities, both intellectual and physical. Yes, God is infinitely more powerful than we are. But that power is not expressed to prevent us from exercising our own. God created us from His spirit. For that reason, God gave us a wide range of freedom of thought and action. In His infinite wisdom, He might use that unlimited power to redress certain situations and also for other purposes which may be beyond our grasp. One thing is certain: the unlimited power of God is not intended to be exercised solely to keep reminding us of our failures. God is not sadistic; such a behavior would be inconsistent with His infinite justice and compassion.

What, then, is Islam about? It is about the utmost personal striving toward self-improvement, with God's help and guidance. As individuals we do our utmost; we plan our best and then seek God's guidance and help. That help may manifest in the form of inspiration, strength, or determination to go about finding the opportunities that lead to the success of our plans. That assistance is also about God preempting those parts of our plans which may not be in our best interests. Islam is finally about trusting in God's judgment when human plans are prevented for reasons that are beyond our knowledge. This is what submission to God means; namely, leaving to Him what is absolutely beyond our control and judgment, trusting in His infinite wisdom and compassion, accepting the outcome of our efforts and His intervention, drawing the appropriate conclusions, and learning from our experience.

While Islam speaks of individual choice and action, it has become, in the eyes of many, a religion of complete reliance on the will of God. This study asserts that Islam promotes freedom of choice and should not be associated with determinism.

MYTH: "Divine governance is exclusive and does not recognize any other governance."

"We have revealed to you the Book, an exposition of everything, and guidance, and mercy, and glad tidings for the Muslims."[7] Holy Qur'an, Verse 16:89

This and other verses of the Qur'an are often cited to argue that God has given humanity all the laws needed to organize our lives. These laws cannot be replaced by, or supplemented with, new man-made laws. Whoever does so not only goes against the will of God but also commits the unforgivable sin of association with God. In other words, by enacting their own laws humans would be claiming powers that belong exclusively to God.[8]

This interpretation implies that, since God is in exclusive charge of governance, humanity has no choice whatsoever. God makes all choices, and humanity unquestionably submits to them. The corollary is that every aspect of human life, including choices and relations among people in daily life, has already been irrevocably determined by God. Similarly, it is not legitimate for the state to enact and administer laws because God has already enacted all the laws that are needed. Otherwise, the implication would be that God's laws are insufficient or inadequate, each of which is a sinful premise.

In reality, this verse and similar ones have been taken out of context and have no such meaning. Humans were given the freedom to determine the governance of their own social and political lives. Such governance is neither defiant of, nor in contradiction with, God's governance. When God created humankind, in His infinite wisdom and power, He granted them a wide range of freedom to organize their lives and respective environments. Not only is Islam not incompatible with secularism, it is inherently secular.

MYTH: "Islam is a comprehensive legal, economic, social, and political system."

As a corollary to the claim that divine governance is absolute and does not leave any room for human governance, the religious establishment teaches that Islam is a comprehensive system which encompasses all aspects of life.[9] It is consistently asserted that Islam contains the solutions to every issue in life and that it is sufficient to consult the works of the elders to solve any present or future problems.

According to that teaching, Islam is a body of laws of all types: it is a legal system called Shari'a that no parliament or legislative body can imitate or modify; it is also an economic system with stringent rules that govern each and every type of transaction that people may consider in their business dealings; and it is even a comprehensive body of social norms for day-to-day life that people must observe in interacting with each other. The state has the duty to ascertain that divine laws are faithfully complied with, and that God's order is established and maintained on earth. If Islam is an all-encompassing system, every act in humankind's day-to-day life becomes an act of faith, and every deviation from the ordained divine system is a sin punishable by the state in this life, and by God in the hereafter.

These unwarranted beliefs impede societies from progressing. Islam, contrary to archaic teachings, is progressive. It did not call for rigid laws of any kind, nor did it mandate any specific political system. What Islam introduced is a comprehensive value system to guide humankind's endeavors; it enables laws and systems best suited to help people lead their lives on this earth. God gave mankind the means to fully exercise human governance on earth, of which He made them trustees.

This study dispels the myth that Islam is a comprehensive legal, economic, social, and political system, a fallacy that developed from, among other causes, confusing tradition with tenets of faith. Instead it reaffirms that Islam is a comprehensive value system intended to indefinitely lead progress. Islam contains universal values that enable humanity to design legal, economic, social, and political systems that are best suited to diverse times and places.

MYTH: "Islam is a collective religion."

The claim that Islam is an all-encompassing legal, economic, social, and political system derives from another strongly held belief that Islam is a religion in which the collective interests must prevail over individual ones. As a result, a central authority becomes necessary to provide interpretations of divine laws and mandates, and monitor compliance with them. Among other tasks, this authority promotes collective prayer, ensures that the collective interests prevail over the individual ones, and organizes the collective defense of God, His prophet, and His religion. According to this belief, divine laws must be enforced on everyone, believers and nonbelievers, and jihad as a tool of such enforcement becomes perceived as a duty to fight for the cause of God. This explains how a clergy-like religious establishment came into existence in a religion that does not even recognize—let alone tolerate—intermediation between humankind and God.

Contrary to how it is frequently perceived, jihad is not about doing anything for the cause of God. Instead, it relates to a code of behavior that leads the believer on the path toward God. In fact, God has no need for people to do anything for Him, let alone defend Him, His religion, or His prophet. On the other hand, God does not allow any person or institution to intermediate between Him and humankind. Each individual has direct access to God, an access that is open and unobstructed at all times. Thus, people need no instruction manual or guidance in addressing God. Each person can do so at any time, from any place, and in any form that he or she prefers.

This study rejects the idea that Islam is necessarily a religion in which relations with God must be organized collectively, led by an expert knowledgeable in matters pertaining to God. The idea that jihad is inextricably linked to conflict and violence must be taken apart and cast aside. Islam is both humanistic and individualistic. It is a faith in which there is no room for intermediation between God and people, and in which violence is permissible in only the most limited circumstances unrelated to the spread of religion or the defense of God and His cause.

MYTH: "Islam is about divine duties, not human rights."
According to this idea, the purpose of humankind in this earthly life is to serve God in order to secure a good end in the hereafter. To accomplish this, God has prescribed a number of duties whose performance must be organized collectively so as to secure the widest observance.

However, God cannot have created humankind to be His servants, because He, perfect and almighty, has no need for anyone. God created us in order to love Him and love each other. When a human being loves God, he or she loves God's creatures. He created humankind to worship Him, where worship is equivalent to love. Thus He gave humankind rights that are intrinsic to human nature and which, if exercised and secured, ensure that humans enjoy happiness. If that is the case, what is the role of the divine duties? Divine duties are intended to be duties toward each other as humans, so that humans may live in harmony and fulfill God's purpose of creation. God imposed duties upon each individual in order to ensure that he or she can live and enjoy the rights that are innate in human nature.

In this light, the idea that Islam is about divine duties toward a jealous God, and that human rights are strictly subject to—and limited by—those duties whose stated purpose must prevail over any other consideration, should be dispelled. God created humankind with those sacred rights which we call "human rights," and divine duties were set forth for the purpose of securing the enforcement and enjoyment of these human rights.

MYTH: "Islam is the sole religious truth."
One of the most important rights that God granted to humankind is freedom of faith. God sent His chosen messenger, Prophet Muhammad, to convey the truth contained in His Divine Message. Yet, despite all the proofs that He revealed through that message, He left it to each person's judgment to accept the Message or reject it. He made sure to warn His Prophet not to force anyone into accepting it.

Many commentators on the Holy Qur'an misunderstood the Message and conveyed a corrupted interpretation of it; namely, that the Message contained in the Qur'an represents the sole truth. According to these commentators, there is no other truth and none other is acceptable. This includes any truths previously revealed by God through his previous messages. While the Holy Qur'an specifically states that Muhammad's message is a confirmation and continuation of previous divine messages, these commentators went as far as to claim that God later abrogated that statement and urged the faithful to fight and kill whoever does not accept and adopt the message of Muhammad. This misunderstanding became an integral part of a belief system perpetuated through teachings about Islam that many clerics and religious scholars spread.

Belief that the Message revealed by Prophet Muhammad is the only source of divine truth, and that whoever does not believe it is doomed and must be persecuted, is a fallacy that should be dispelled. Islam, in its strict sense as the Message revealed to Muhammad, is one among other paths that God recognizes and legitimizes as leading to the Truth. Islam, in its wider sense, is tolerant of—and encourages—diversity among people, since God is the ultimate judge in the hereafter, and none among humankind can pretend to exercise justice on God's behalf.

MYTH: "By way of abrogation, provisions of the Message are reversed and previous religions are superseded."

Two major periods mark the twenty-two years during which the Holy Qur'an was revealed to Prophet Muhammad. Revelation started in Mecca, where the Prophet was born and grew up. However, because of the nature and substance of that revelation, the Prophet faced a forceful reaction and opposition on the part of the Meccan people, which later turned violent. The Prophet managed to survive the hostility of the Meccans for twelve years, after which he fled to the city of Yathrib, later called Medina, following the Prophet's migration there (the hijra). Despite his triumphal return to Mecca in the tenth year of the hijra, the Prophet died in Medina.

The substance, scope, and tone of the Qur'anic verses revealed in Mecca differ from those of the verses revealed after the migration to Medina. In the beginning, the Message was mainly about introducing the new faith. Then, following the migration to Medina and the start of the wars against the Prophet's detractors, the Qur'anic revelation became more focused on guiding the Prophet's footsteps in organizing the daily social life of the Medinan community that was forming. The Qur'an during the Meccan period was mainly concerned with setting out the parameters of the new faith (the unicity of God, the continuity of the Abrahamic tradition, the Final Day, the attributes of God), and its basic principles (love among humankind, the worship of God by humanity, human rights, peace, tolerance, diversity, and avoidance of violence). In contrast, during the period in Medina verses of an entirely different nature were revealed. During that time, God was guiding Muhammad's steps in performing his mission of conveying the Message and defending the community that rallied behind him. In that period, the Prophet found himself facing aggression from polytheists and from peoples of other faiths. Certain verses revealed under those circumstances appeared to be inconsistent with previously revealed verses (namely, on fighting and tolerance, among others). Commentators were quick to conclude that God had abrogated the previous messages of tolerance and peace, and replaced them with the permission to use force to spread the Divine Message. They assumed that, as Muslims had gained power and strength in Medina, they no longer needed to be tolerant and peace-minded.

The concept of abrogation has also been used to claim that Islam has superseded all previous religions, namely Judaism and Christianity, on the assumption that Islam updates previous revelations, leaving no further need for them in the presence of the ultimate version.

The myth that God modified, reversed, or otherwise abrogated His earlier messages conveyed through Moses and Jesus, and that God had changed His mind about the substance of His initial message revealed to Prophet Muhammad in Mecca, should be rejected. This study argues against the concept of abrogation. Every verse of the Holy Qur'an was revealed by God for a purpose and continues to remain in full force and effect; God has not changed His mind about any injunction nor reversed any part of His message. Islam is a religion of peace and tolerance, regardless of those verses of the Qur'an which, in the abstract and taken out of their individual contexts, could be interpreted to imply otherwise. Among multiple factors, each verse must be understood and interpreted in light of the context in which it was revealed.

MYTH: "Islam is incompatible with reason."

It is often alleged that the act of faith is incompatible with reason. People must blindly trust every word in the Divine Message without questioning any aspect of any belief or obligation. Over time, this concept extended beyond the verses of the Qur'an to encompass understandings of those verses by the Prophet, his companions, and the early commentators of the Qur'an and Prophetic Tradition. As a result, rational thinking about any part of the faith, or its interpretation by early commentators, could be counted as an act of heresy.

Indeed, if a person believes that God is perfect, why would he or she then allow himself or herself to question God's word? If one questions God's word, it means that he or she is presumably placing himself or herself on the level of God to judge the relevance, irrelevance, or acceptability of what God has prescribed, all of which falls within the sin of *shirk* (association with God). As the argument goes: when a person questions any aspect of a divine prescription, it means that he or she is looking to be convinced of its purpose and relevance before accepting it; failing such conviction, a person is free to reject the faith. In such cases, using the mind would constitute an affront to God because it allows one to question divine truths and matters already decided by God.

This approach is clearly contrary to God's message to humanity in the Holy Qur'an. Throughout the Qur'an, God appealed to the minds of people and enticed them to reason so that they might appreciate the Message entrusted to Muhammad. Would He have endowed humanity with this wonderful tool and then enjoined us against using it?

Faith is not incompatible with reason and the mind. The Qur'an insists that God does not want anyone to blindly accept the Message. He wants every person to be convinced of the truth that He sent so that His judgment on the Final Day can be based on real intentions as opposed to external actions or abstentions.

MYTH: "Islam is incompatible with modernity."

Apologists often claim that Islam is compatible with modernity, then qualify that statement with provisos. Unfortunately, much of modernity is portrayed as objectionable to the extent that it originates from the non-Muslim West, whose purpose is to cut off Muslims from their traditions and religion.[10] On the other hand, modernists who stress the extent to which Islam has been kept within narrow outdated confines have set forth to change, or demand a change in, Islam. For that purpose, they advance the various tools of change, namely *ijtihād* (independent reasoning) and reinterpretation, in order to demonstrate that Islam can change. Yet, Mohammed Charfi, a rationalist modernist who studies Islam in its original form before the assimilation of sacralized traditions, points to political leaders who give modernity a bad name through their abusive use of authority in the name of modernity.[11]

This study asserts that Islam is not incompatible with modernity. Islam is intrinsically progressive and contains the engines of change. It is not Islam that needs to be changed in order to "catch up" with modernity and the West. What needs to be changed is our own understanding of Islam, because, when properly understood, Islam is no longer seen as needing to catch up with modernity. Instead Islam can be seen as an engine of change and capable of creating new pathways toward modernity.

How Did these Myths about Islam Develop?[12]

What happened to Islam? To even understand this question, it is perhaps necessary to first ask what happened to religion itself. Muhammad Sa'id 'Ashmawy argues that because religion appeared in many different places at different times, instead of becoming a universal humanistic force uniting people and fostering development, in many cases it became ethnic and local, sowing division and conflict, and instilling rigidity, inflexibility, and inaction.[13] What 'Ashmawy is referring to is the transformation of religion—including Islam—into an identity.

Islam began as a divine message, consisting substantially of: the genesis of creation; the attributes of God; the Day of Judgment; stories of past peoples and prophets; and a set of universal higher principles and values to guide people, from then till the Final Day, in their relations among each other, and in the exercise of their faith and communication with God. Early Muslims interpreted this new religion by referring to their own heritage and perceptions of the world, universe, and society. But instead of allowing interpretations to evolve in keeping with the evolution of value systems and traditions, these initial interpretations acquired a sacred status and became assimilated with the Message.[14]

Islam spoke of peace, yet it became in the minds of many—Muslims and non-Muslims, Arabs and Westerners alike—a religion associated with violence. Islam spoke of tolerance and diversity, yet many Muslims adopted faith as an identity and propagated intolerance. Islam spoke of love and justice, yet it became a "religion of the sword," the sword of justice becoming the sword of violence. Islam spoke of good governance and smooth relations among people on the basis of *al-amr bi-l-ma'rūf wa-n--nahiy 'ani-l-munkar* (enjoin the good and prevent evil); in turn, this same principle was usurped to legitimate self-help and the administering of justice based on narrow, restrictive interpretations of Islam. Islam spoke of education, yet education became limited to studying religion to the exclusion of other subjects, and studying the fixed commentaries from the early ages of Islam. As a result of these limitations in religious education, faith was relegated to secondary status, while religious loyalties replaced human brotherhood and religion became an identity.[15] In this light, from the perspective of religion, our responsibility is to acknowledge the existence of ignorance and to address it. This brings us to the realm of sociology, where our understanding should now focus.

Methodology and Key Terminology
The methodology of this study is guided by the following principles.

First, we will adhere to the Holy Qur'an, the primary divine source. While reference will be made to products of human thought, namely the works of early classical and modern-day commentators and scholars, care will be taken to avoid treating them as sources. Instead, they will be used to determine understandings of the source at different periods of history and in different parts of the world. The aim is to avoid distortions in analysis by assuring 'like comparisons.' To accomplish this, it is essential to compare sources. Islam is a source of divine revelation; not a collection of institutions. Questions having to do with implementation and enforcement, even if influenced by religious interpretation, relate to commentaries and customs, which in various instances may be outdated, or even erroneous.

Second, this methodology will rely on the *tajdīd*, or renewal approach, rather than *taqlīd*, or imitation of interpretations and solutions from the past, adhering to the Holy Qur'an as our primary text. For the sake of clarity, materials other than the Qur'an will be utilized as valuable references with respect to heritage and customs. When we return to the Holy Qur'an as sole source, our interpretations necessarily will be based on current value systems and sets of knowledge and information. Hence, only interpretations which are meaningfully relevant to present-day environments and concerns will be emphasized. The resultant understanding is likely to lead us forward instead of forcing us to lean backward, sacrificing the present to adhere to outmoded or irrelevant interpretations or understandings. When moving forward, there is always among devout Muslims a pressure and fear that reinterpretation of the Message might lead to misinterpretation of, or straying away from, the divine text. When there is doubt, there can be a tendency to fall back on the safety net of *taqlīd,* and uncritical imitation of the past. Presumably, then, blame, if any, goes to the imitated party. But the *tajdīd* (renewal) approach opens new horizons for freedom and progress, because there is then a choice to accept or reject anything which is not specifically inconsistent with a universal message or text.[16]

Third, while differentiating history and tradition from the Holy Qur'an as a principal source of Islam, this study recognizes the importance of history and tradition as means to trace the progress of Islamic societies and values, objectively and critically. Reviewing Islamic history and practice critically is neither contrary nor offensive to Islam, because, while Islam is divine, Islamic history is human. Religious teaching has often discouraged critical assessment of past and current understandings and practices, leading people to lose sight of Islam as an engine of progress and modernity. When Islam is perceived as such, the role of clerics as indispensable intermediaries can be reexamined. The past then becomes an archive of valuable experiences from which a wealth of lessons can be drawn to improve and sharpen our understanding of Islam and its potential role in our lives and relationships.[17] Unfortunately, worthwhile reformist approaches have thus far been less successful because of the perceived need to seek legitimacy from the guardians of the systems targeted for reform. Bearing in mind that the guardians of a system may have a vested interest in preserving that system from which they stand to benefit, any attempt to reform it with the blessings of its guardians seems unlikely to succeed.[18]

Fourth, this study is not an apologetic embellishment of Islam. It is about distinguishing the Divine Message from its interpretations and implementation over time. The purpose is to safeguard the universal nature of that message and to secure its continued ability to lead progress. While interpretations and implementations constitute an important part of the history and civilization of Muslim peoples of a given moment in time, they should not be confused with Islam as a divinely revealed message. In instances where a certain practice or interpretation adopted by Muslims is criticized, such criticism should not be construed as a criticism of Islam. The purpose is to improve understanding of the relevant message and thus reform practices and strive for progress. Both non-Muslims and Muslims alike receive a false perception of Islam from the behavior or rhetoric of many who claim to speak for Islam and those who commit destructive acts in the name of Islam.[19]

Fifth, given that Islam did not appear in a vacuum, anything in the Qur'an which existed in the pre-Islamic *jāhiliyya* period should be rethought. Based on a reexamination of the context in which a passage was revealed, one may conclude that it is a reference to a tolerated practice waiting to be set aside, as opposed to a universally binding religious injunction. This approach will be clearer when addressing currently controversial subjects such as the veil, slavery, polygamy, and repudiation.

Sixth, this study will strive to avoid two opposite tendencies. The first is that which ignores the context of revelation and takes Islam entirely out of its Arabian setting and heritage; the other is the tendency to conflate Islam with Arabian culture and heritage.[20] The former tendency robs Islam of its meaning, purpose, and soul; the latter tendency denies Islam its universality. The reality lies in a different perception of Islam that sees it as neither a fixed, unchangeable culture, nor an identity, both of which limit its universal nature. Viewed as a faith which guides Muslims in the path of God and in their relations among each other, Islam becomes an infinite source of light and guidance, ready to lead progress in all times, ages, and places, and among people of all creeds and races.

Seventh, it should be stressed that this book is not about the theological aspects of religion. It therefore is not concerned with any controversies relating to the existence or nonexistence of God, the unicity of God, whether or not Prophet Muhammad truly received the Message of God, or whether or not the Holy Qur'an is the word of God, all such controversies falling outside the scope of our specific purpose. This study is based on the true belief that God does exist and is one God, that the Prophet is His messenger, and that the Holy Qur'an is the true word of God. Similarly, it will not be concerned about the polemics that arose regarding the authenticity of the Qur'an, when it was recorded, and when and by whom it was assembled. This subject has been discussed at length by other researchers.[21] Commentaries in this book are based on the assumptions that: (1) the recording of the Qur'an took place substantially during the lifetime of the Prophet; (2) although certain trustworthy commentators assure us that most verses of the Qur'an were assembled during the lifetime and under the immediate supervision of the Prophet, the order in which the verses are assembled is, in reality, irrelevant, since in the first place those verses were not revealed in any specific substantive order, but as a guide to the footsteps and actions of the Prophet and sometimes in response to questions raised on specific issues; and (3) ultimately, while some scholars cast doubt on the completeness and/or accuracy of a number of verses, the areas of controversy are not related to any essential elements of the faith. By adhering to the overall sense of the Message, the details may be perceived in perspective.

Finally, following are the intended meanings of certain key terms that are consistently used throughout this study.

♦ Islam is *universal* in the sense that it is addressed and is relevant to all people of all times and all places, Muslims and non-Muslims.

♦ Islam is *secular* in the sense that it does not provide for a system for political, legal, or economic governance, nor for a clergy to intermediate the relations of Muslims with God or to perform any role in state affairs or to otherwise claim to exercise any form of governance over Muslims in any respect.

♦ Islam is *progressive* in the sense that it glorifies the mind, invites change and modernity, and calls for the respect of human rights.

♦ *Muslim societies* refers to societies of countries with a majority Muslim population and to Muslim communities in countries with majority non-Muslim populations.

♦ *Tradition* refers to everything that entered Islam over time since the Revelation and became in people's minds an integral part of Islam, namely: customs and practices; traditions of the Prophet, his companions and successors; works of early and later exegetes and commentators; *ijmā'* (consensus of people and 'ulama'); the works of *fiqh*; and the teachings and fatwas of religious establishments.

♦ *Liberal* refers to a free mindset which rejects any restrictions

on the use of the mind and is not resistant to change from
entrenched customs, practices, and prevailing interpretations.

* *Conservative* refers to a mindset that is faithfully attached
  to traditions and is resistant to change except under the most
  exceptional circumstances and then handles such change with
  the utmost care.

What Happened to the Message?

Calls to reexamine the classical sources of Islam are often triggered by
upheavals in the Muslim world and by attempts to redefine or adapt social
and legal norms to changing circumstances.[22] That struggle to confront
changing conditions with classical sources of Islamic law is an exercise
in futility. There is nothing wrong with Islam. What is wrong is our
understanding of it. It is our misperception of Islam as a comprehensive
and all-encompassing political, legal, economic, and social system that is
mistaken, because it restricts Islam to a set of rules that cannot outlast their
time; hence, the constant concern to change and modernize Islam. When
Islam is perceived as infinitely wider than a system of some kind, then it
becomes a true source of—instead of an obstacle to—human progress.
That is what this study and reaffirmation of central tenets of Islam will
strive to demonstrate; namely, its universal, secular, and progressive
nature.

PART ONE
The Universal Nature of Islam

"One reason that a primary sacred text like the Qur'an cannot be expected 'to deliver a single authoritative usage' is the difficulty of reading it conclusively."[1] —Asma Barlas

If the Holy Qur'an had delivered a "single authoritative" message, then Islam would no longer be universal. But Islam is universal[2] in the sense that it is for all times and for all peoples of every race and place, wherever their geographical locations may be. It claims relevance to peoples' lives in this incarnation and in the hereafter. All peoples of all creeds are subject to the same process of divine judgment for their acts and behaviors in this world, subject only to having received, or having had the opportunity to receive, the Message.

Indeed, God defines himself in the Holy Qur'an as the god of all humanity (*rabbu-l-'ālamīn*). His message is generally addressed to that collective humanity in the form of *ya ayyuha-n-nās,* or "O' you people," irrespective of their particular creeds. Few are the instances in which the Message addresses the believers only, and in those instances the Message is usually specific to a circumstance. In that capacity, God is the universal god, the sole god of everyone, everything, everywhere, and every time. He does not say that He is the god of the Muslims or that He does not accept being the god of the pagans.

To make clear its universality, the Divine Message of the Holy Qur'an expressly states that Islam is not solely the religion revealed to Prophet Muhammad. Islam is the religion of all those who believe in one god and in the successive messages that God revealed to his prophets and messengers, commencing with Adam and Abraham;[3] the message revealed in the Qur'an is a culmination of the previous messages and as such is declared by God to be the last and final universal revelation. This does not mean that God has ceased all contact with humanity. God in his infinite wisdom may or may not continue to communicate with individuals through individual and personal revelation. What has ended is universal revelation; namely, messages that are addressed to all humanity, beyond the final revealed message of the Holy Qur'an. By declaring Prophet Muhammad as His last and final messenger, and his mission as the last and final prophetic mission, God has announced His resolve to leave his creatures to exercise trusteeship of this earth and to organize their lives and legislate for themselves, guided by universal principles.

How could the message of Islam be universal when it has been revealed to its messenger at a particular time in history, in a specific geographical location, and in the language of the people living in that location? Moreover, the Message was revealed over a period of twenty-plus years, in response to events that were happening at that time, but most importantly, by way of guiding the footsteps of the Messenger in the performance of his mission. In other words, the Message did not appear in a vacuum. It appeared in a well-defined environment and addressed the habits, customs, and traditions of those living in that environment. This paradox perhaps explains how generation after generation, Muslims and non-Muslims alike, have understood—or perhaps misunderstood—Islam.

To perceive the Holy Qur'an as a divinely revealed scripture, it is necessary to situate it within its environment and social context. This permits us to better comprehend the reason for many of the rules included in it. Then the universal nature and scope of Islam can more clearly be seen. It is also possible then to examine the various sources of Islam, as generally accepted by Muslims at this time, to determine which of them are universal, and to what extent.

In this section, we will place the Holy Qur'an, as a divinely revealed scripture, in its social context and environment. This will serve as background which will enable us to have a better comprehension of the raison d'être for many rules set forth in the Qur'an. As a result, a better light will be shed over the true universal nature of Islam and its true scope. We can then review, discuss, and appreciate the various basic sources of Islam, as generally accepted by Muslims at this time, so as to determine which of them are universal, and to what extent.

CHAPTER 1
Islam Did Not Appear in a Vacuum

The period preceding the beginning of the Revelation at the outset of the seventh century A.D. is called the *jāhiliyya*, which in Arabic, means the era of ignorance. That era is often mistakenly regarded as an era of total darkness when tribal life was primitive, and abuse and violence prevailed. While it is true that some of the higher moral principles brought about by Islam were not present in pre-Islamic tribal life in the Arabian Peninsula,[1] history reveals that standards of knowledge and living were more varied than the prevailing literature implies. Tribal life differed from the life of the sedentary populations living in the neighboring towns of Mesopotamia and the eastern Mediterranean basin.[2] Yet, the bedouin populations of Arabia had well-established customs and cultural practices. The various tribes of the peninsula interacted and traded among one another following a tribal code of conduct. They also interacted frequently with their sedentary neighbors, many of whom were brought up in the midst of the Hellenistic, Persian, Ethiopian, and Indian civilizations.

On the peninsula, tribal life was plagued by internecine fighting based on the precepts of *ghazuw* (tribal raids) and *tha'r* (revenge), where fighting routinely took place between tribes, and among clans within tribes. Similarly, a number of customs were discriminatory or abusive. At the same time, there developed a wealth of oral literature and poetry. Cultural exchange took place regularly among tribes to the extent that they were institutionalized to revolve around specific periods of the year, during which all activities were focused on the intertribal exchanges, both trade and cultural. Tribes interacted socially to the extent that intertribal marriages were common, serving as tools to seal bonds and ties between tribes.

Beyond the peninsula, Arabian bedouins interacted frequently with their neighbors. They organized regular trade trips in every direction—to Mesopotamia, Persia, the eastern Mediterranean, Yemen, and Ethiopia.[3] Even when the Revelation began and early converted Muslims were mistreated by their kin, their first exodus was to Ethiopia, where they were well received. They did not arrive there as strangers but as returning traders with whom there were established, ongoing relations.

Not all tribal customs were reprehensible, and many found their way into Islam.[4] Some were even adapted as integral parts of Islamic worship, such as the hajj. During the pre-Islamic period, the hajj season was a key period in the life of people of the Hijaz region of the Arabian Peninsula. The period stretched over three entire months each year, during which people from all over Arabia came to Mecca to worship their respective deities. Worship took place in the same location where the Muslim hajj is performed now. Hajj was viewed and organized as a religious, business, social, and cultural event, and every year it was the subject of careful preparation. Each of the two prominent clans of *Quraysh*, the leading tribe of Mecca, took charge of an aspect of preparation.[5] In addition to worship, hajj was an opportunity for trade, with people gathering from all over Arabia and beyond to buy and sell commodities. Poets also came to conduct exchanges and to compete in poetry recitations. To ensure the annual event's success, it was collectively agreed among the participating tribes that all fighting would be suspended during the entire three months. This truce was strictly observed; any violent conflict underway would stop on the first day of hajj and resume when the three-month period ended.

Following the Revelation, hajj continued to take place every year, except that the idols representing the deities were destroyed, and God was worshipped instead. Hajj remained a time for intense trade and for social and cultural exchange. The prohibition on violence continued during the commonly known sacred months of Islam, namely, Dhu-l-Qi'dah, Dhu-l-Hijja, Muharram, and Rajab, namely the eleventh, twelfth, first, and seventh months of the Muslim lunar calendar, respectively.[6] The belief in resurrection and final judgment, the fast during the month of Ramadan, the practice of circumcision, the prohibition of *riba,* the consumption of pork and alcoholic drinks, and other matters, all of these predate the revelation of the Qur'an.[7]

Secular institutions and culture that already existed around the Arabian Peninsula also found their way into the Holy Qur'an and Islam, such as the *jizya,* the head tax that was imposed in the Islamic state on Christians and Jews, as Peoples of the Book, presumably according to Qur'anic

Verse Q9:29. The *jizya* had apparently been known to the Byzantines, but it was mainly imposed by the Persian Sassanids on Christians in return for peace.[8] In pre-Islamic bedouin society, countless stories were told related to ghouls, djinns, and demons, many of which became part of the early Islamic writings,[9] including the books of *Sira* and Prophetic Tradition.[10]

Even the term Allah, as a designation of the supreme deity, was in use prior to the revelation of the Holy Qur'an.[11] At the same time, one finds in the Qur'an names of deities most popular among the tribes of the region.[12] Yet, not all Arabian bedouins were polytheists and idol worshippers; many of them were Christians[13] and Jews. Others, though neither Christians nor Jews, were nevertheless monotheists, otherwise known as *ḥanīfs*.[14] While they may not have found a detailed faith with a theory of God, Arabian bedouins were generally against idol worship and believed in the existence of a unique deity or force that created the universe and controls it. Even those who were polytheists and idol worshippers were familiar with the monotheistic religions through their interaction with Christians, Jews, and Sabeans during their trading voyages to areas surrounding the Peninsula.[15]

The Holy Qur'an contains abundant material about the Christian and Jewish faiths.[16] In some cases, it even goes into several controversial details.[17] It is clear that Prophet Muhammad was not unaware of those faiths and the cultures relating to them. He had been a close friend and companion of his first wife's cousin, Waraqa Ibn Nawfal, a Christian cleric. From Ibn Nawfal he learned the essentials of the Christian faith. Prophet Muhammad also made contact with the monks living in the Christian monasteries located along the trading routes between the Hijaz and *Bilād al-Shām*, the current Levant region bordering the eastern shore of the Mediterranean.[18] In addition, because Islam is portrayed in the Holy Qur'an as a revised iteration of the Abrahamic faiths, countless concepts common to Christianity and Judaism are found in the Qur'an and the *fiqh* (Islamic jurisprudence). This explains, for example, how the death penalty for apostasy found its way from Judaism into Islamic law.[19]

Therefore, the revelation of the Divine Message to Prophet Muhammad, and its spread among the Arabian bedouins, did not start with an empty slate. It was not a set of rules and precepts intended to fill a vacuum where none had existed, or where rules had no place. The new revelation appeared within a specific historical context and social heritage, including prevailing myths.[20] It also appeared within a diverse religious environment where crude and primitive polytheism coexisted with the religious experience of Jews and Christians.[21] Islam should be understood with such an environment in mind. The interactions of Islam with the past, with previous cultures, and with the other peoples and their cultures, are inherent to Islam and should be kept in mind in interpreting and living it.[22]

As a result, the Holy Qur'an is filled with episodes reflecting the customs and moods of the times, including what many—Muslims and non-Muslims alike—have inaccurately perceived as a message of roughness and violence. A thorough reading of the Qur'an, in light of the background prevailing immediately before and during the period of the Revelation, should help refute this impression and reconcile the roughness of certain rules set forth in it with the messages of love, peace, and compassion that Islam came into being to promote.[23] For instance, in the twenty-first century corporeal punishment is perceived as excessive and cruel. Viewed in the context of seventh-century Arabia and its surroundings, it can be seen as a lesser of evils compared to the alternative of collective punishment that prevailed under tribal rules. Islam, in this case, was actually moving society in the direction of change and progress.

Mohammed Charfi points astutely to the fact that certain terms used throughout the Qur'an signal the logistics of the particular time and place in question. He rightly highlights the use of the term *sijn*, which means captivity in jail, in connection with the stories of Joseph and Moses in pharaonic Egypt. This term reflects the state structure in effect there, which provided for a place of detention in the context of state-administered justice. By contrast, this term is not used in connection with tribal life in Arabia where no state structure existed.[24]

The appropriate use of terminology reflective of the time and place of the Revelation is further illustrated by the depiction of paradise as gardens beneath which rivers flow.[25] Since the Qur'an is in Arabic and is addressed initially—though not, as some contend, *primarily*—to the people of the desert in Arabia, that depiction is appealing indeed. But it may be less appealing to peoples in geographical areas blessed with generous greenery and water who might find paradise more attractive with sun and sand.[26]

Abdou Filali-Ansari observes that Islam clearly appeared in an environment where the concept of state was unknown and in which that vacuum was filled by the tribe. He further observes that the first community of Muslims became united by a bond of common faith that they received, as opposed to the predominant tribal bonds. That faith contained principles of morality, among other things, governing relations among members, thereby replacing the power plays of tribal ties and customs.[27] This is what explains the thorough focus, during the Medinan period, on stating the socio-religious foundations of the first Muslim community, in contrast to then prevalent tribal customs.[28] The specificity of the Medinan verses would have major implications for interpreting the Holy Qur'an and determining the scope of its universality.

Without understanding the specific historic circumstances under which specific verses of the Qur'an were revealed,[29] their relevant message may not be understood. Without fully appreciating the circumstances surrounding the Revelation, the underlying message, which is intended to endure *ad infinitum eternam* and serve as a universal guiding light, may never be captured. Instead, a time-bound literal sense is often mistaken for the universal message. This study will examine cases of how bypassing analysis of the circumstances of the Revelation led to many of the ills that plague Muslim populations in the twenty-first century. The current perception and practice of political and legal governance, human rights, jihad, and violence are among the issues that will be examined to demonstrate the extent to which current perception and practice differ from the universal message. It may then become clearer that many textual statements and tolerances found in the Qur'an were not intended to constitute absolute and permanent rules, despite the circumstances that occasioned them. On the contrary, such statements and tolerances, which may appear obsolete by today's standards, carry powerful underlying messages that, in reality, energize and can serve as engines of progress.

Indeed, after noting that the Holy Qur'an is tied to its sociohistorical context and that it indicts pre-Islamic ways of ignorance, Shabbir

Akhtar questions the relevance of attributing what he calls a "normative universality" to its verses, given the specificity of the occasions of its revelation.[30] This is a useful question. The reference to circumstances of the pre-Islamic era is intended to place the Message within reach of the immediate addressees; that is the function of literal interpretation and understanding. Yet, the Qur'an was also made available and offered to the generations to come through the universal message underlying the literal one derived from local circumstances. Understanding local circumstances is an example of how the mind can be used to acquire the full benefit of the divinely revealed message. This is the essence of the *āyas*, or divine signs, intended to guide the recipient in grasping the essence of the Message.

Hussein Ahmad Amin sums up well the role played by reflection on local circumstances in reading the Qur'an.

> I realized that religion…occurs within a specific society at a specific moment; thus its teachings necessarily reflect the colors of the circumstances of the relevant society and the requirements of the relevant time. Religion is an absolute truth which is shaped by a specific historic framework and appears in a social environment and reflects its characteristics, so that it may be accepted and understood by the majority of its audience.[31]

The 'colors' of a society include not only its cultural practices and customs but also its beliefs and prevalent myths. For instance, drinking alcohol and inebriation were associated with the polytheist worship of Greek deities. Dionysus was the god of the grape harvest and wine, and his Roman successor is Bacchus. This, in part, explains Christ's instructions to his followers not to worship when they were drunk, as well as the Qur'anic injunction against going to prayers while intoxicated.[32] It also explains the extent to which local Christian and Jewish practices found their way into the verses of the Holy Qur'an, and later into Muslim practices.

The same holds for the Arabic language in which the Qur'an was revealed, and more particularly the dialect of the tribe of *Quraysh*. The Holy Qur'an was revealed to a *Qurayshi* person, for him to spread its message to the *Qurayshis* in their surroundings. In the first place, the Holy Qur'an's first recipient—Prophet Muhammad—had to understand the message properly; otherwise he would not have been in a position to pass it on to the immediate recipients. Second, the people to whom the Prophet needed to convey its message, had to be able to understand it. For that, its language and content had to be familiar; hence the references to local customs and practices and to the prevailing belief systems. This fact carries important implications, with respect to both the immediate and ultimate recipients of the Qur'anic message.

In light of their level of education and their living conditions, the immediate recipients of the Message did not need to do much interpretation. They only needed to focus on the literal meaning of the revealed text and, in case of doubt, to ask the Prophet or any of the Companions. However, that would not suffice for the ultimate recipients of the Message, namely, for the rest of humanity. Most of the ultimate recipients of the Message do not speak Arabic; and those who do, comprehend and speak an Arabic whose vocabulary has, over time, evolved in meaning and scope to reflect their respective environments in terms of cultural practices, customs, and beliefs. Yet, the Qur'an is accessible to ultimate recipients through the concept of *i'jāz*, or that which is inimitable.

However, for ultimate recipients of the Message, an understanding of the context in which the Qur'an was revealed, together with the meanings of the words in the tribal language of the time, is essential in order to elucidate the underlying message. Whenever the idea of revenge appears in the Qur'an, it is a reference to the tribal right of every individual to take immediate revenge for an act committed by another person. That understanding was perfectly legitimate for a bedouin Arab at the time of the Revelation. The Holy Qur'an, while temporarily tolerant of revenge, sought to promote tribal peace by encouraging the replacement of revenge by an indemnity, called *al-diyya*, for which the entire tribe stands guarantor. This was further justified by the lack of a state structure that could provide governance. Read in today's Arabic language and context, revenge is no longer tolerable because the tribal system of governance is no longer compatible with state-organized governance, through state institutions.[33] *Tha'r* (revenge), while still a common word in Arabic, now has different meanings than the ones associated with the ancient tribal practices of the Arabian bedouin population of the sixth and seventh centuries.[34]

The question of the original context in which the Holy Qur'an appeared acquires special importance in dealing with controversial theological and philosophical issues, such as one that has occasioned acrimony among Muslims ever since the Qur'an was revealed: whether the Qur'an is created or is otherwise inherently eternal, that is, of the nature of God, having no beginning or end. Given that the Qur'an was revealed, at times, in response to events that were occurring during the time of- and questions that were raised by- the Prophet and his companions, one could ask if, being the word of God, there is any reason why the Qur'an could not have been uttered by God—or come into existence—at a given time in history so as to remain in existence and effect thereafter *ad infinitum eternam*? Given that God is Almighty and capable of everything, would such a perception reduce the divine origin of the Qur'an and its universality?

The fact that the Holy Qur'an addressed relevant issues at the time of its revelation, and that contemporary customs, practices, and beliefs found their way into its verses, raises many issues relating to the identification of the rules cited in the Qur'an and their proper interpretation. This will be examined in defining the scope of universality of the Holy Qur'an, after first considering the sources of Islam.

CHAPTER 2
The Holy Qur'an as the Essential Source of Islam

Islam is a divinely revealed religion. God revealed it to His prophet and messenger, Muhammad, with instruction to spread the Message, commencing with his immediate people. Based on that revelation and ever since the performance by Prophet Muhammad of his divine mission, generations of Muslims have come to treat the divine text and the Prophetic Tradition as the two principal sources of Islam.

The divine text is the word of God expressed in the Holy Qur'an. Prophetic Tradition—referred to as sunna (practices) and hadith (oral traditions)—derives from the reported practices and words of Prophet Muhammad and according to some the practices of the Enlightened Caliphs.[1] These are the four caliphs who immediately succeeded the Prophet, namely, Abou Bakr al-Siddiq, 'Umar Ibn al-Khattab, 'Uthman Ibn 'Affan, and 'Ali Ibn Abi Taleb.[2] Then, following the death of the Prophet and his first four successors, the scholars of Islam, known as *fuqahā'*,[3] began preparing their commentaries on the Qur'an, building on the divine text and Prophetic Tradition. Over a period of four centuries, a body of rules and dogmas was developed which became supplemental sources of Islam. These are currently referred to as accessories to the principal sources.

The two principal sources of Islam differ inherently from one another. While the Holy Qur'an is divine, the sunna and hadith are human, being the traditions of the Prophet. The principal sources also differ substantially from the sources that are accessory to them. The principal sources are directly related to the Revelation, to the Prophet who received the Revelation, and to the people who were his close and trusted companions. By contrast, the other sources are stories, commentaries, interpretations, and analyses by ordinary human beings which began as oral tradition transmitted from one generation to the next until they found their way into written script, with all the limitations and deficiencies arising from reliance on the memories of people who come from diverse backgrounds and whose interests and objectives may differ or be incompatible.

Because the divine is perfect and infallible, and the human is imperfect and fallible, in discussing the sources of Islam it is crucial to differentiate the divine from the human. Distinguishing divine sources from historic and social accumulations over time will make it possible to rediscover the true essence and universal nature of Islam.[4]

Oral versus Written Sources: Compilation

The Holy Qur'an is the text revealed by God to Prophet Muhammad through Archangel Gabriel over a period of twenty-two years, commencing in 610 AD and ending with the death of the Prophet in 632 AD.

It is widely accepted that the Qur'an was set down in writing as instructed by the Prophet primarily as the text was being revealed.[5] Yet, the recorded documents were never stored together or dated to determine which was revealed first and which next; and, wherever they were stored, they were not kept in any particular order.[6] However, following the death of the Prophet, his first successor, Caliph Abou Bakr, faced a widespread movement of collective apostasy among tribes expecting the new religion to wither away with the passing of the Messenger. Indeed, Abou Bakr, with the strong support of 'Umar, saw in that movement a serious threat to the communal tie[7] established by Prophet Muhammad among the various peoples of the Arabian Peninsula, a tie founded on the new faith, one of whose aims was to bridge prevailing tribal divisions. Abou Bakr and his immediate companions perceived that communal tie as the seed of an emerging new state, now being seriously threatened by the collective apostasy movement. Caliph Abou Bakr was also concerned that this movement could put an end to the spread of the new faith and possibly reverse the achievements of Prophet Muhammad, as well. Abou Bakr therefore decided to confront the apostasy movement with an iron fist. He created several armies that set forth to fight the defecting tribes. These wars engaged by Abou Bakr were called the Wars of the *Ridda* (Wars of Apostasy).[8]

However, because of the widespread nature of the movement, and because fighting took place simultaneously in various locations, Muslim warriors suffered massive casualties. A number of previously close companions of the Prophet, who had memorized substantial portions of the Qur'an, lost their lives. This loss enticed 'Umar to press Abou Bakr to order the collection and compilation of the Qur'an for fear that it would be lost forever, in whole or in part, with the loss of those who had memorized it. Thus, a compilation effort began during the caliphate of the Prophet's first successor, Abou Bakr. That effort, however, was limited to putting together what could be found of the different manuscripts kept by the various scribes of the Prophet and transcriptions from the memories of those who had memorized verses among the Companions. The gathered documents were entrusted to Hafsa, wife of the Prophet and daughter of Caliph 'Umar. The collection was not, therefore, a compilation of the Holy Qur'an into a single complete document.[9] That task would not be fulfilled until the reign of the third enlightened caliph, 'Uthman.

As time passed and the Arab-Islamic Empire expanded, it appeared that certain texts of the Revelation existed in several versions, phrased in the various dialects spoken throughout the Arabian Peninsula. Some authors even claimed that versions encountered differed not only in form but also in substance. The third caliph, 'Uthman, took upon himself the task of ordering and overseeing the unification of the texts of the Holy Qur'an into a single official version, in the dialect of the tribe of *Quraysh*, that of the Prophet Muhammad. The task was entrusted to a group of people selected from the scribes of Prophet Muhammad who were still alive. Their mission was to come up with a unified version, commencing with the manuscripts of the first compilation held by Hafsa, wife of the Prophet. As the task was completed, 'Uthman ordered the distribution of the newly issued official version throughout the expanding Arab-Islamic Empire and the destruction of all other versions.[10] It is this same version that is currently recognized as the only true and authentic Qur'an, formally known as *al-Muṣhaf al-Imam*, but also more commonly known as *al-Muṣhaf al-'Uthmāni*. Dating from this primary contribution by Caliph 'Uthman, and despite polemics raised about potential discrepancies with other versions then in existence as compiled by some companions,[11] *al-Muṣhaf al-'Uthmāni* became generally accepted as the authentic and accurate version of the Holy Qur'an.[12] Muslim scholars rarely called its authenticity or integrity into question[13] in any substantive manner.[14]

Controversies Surrounding the Origins of the Qur'an

The same cannot be said of a number of Western scholars who went to great lengths to cast doubt on, or argue against, the Qur'an's divine origin, authenticity, and accuracy.[15] Was the Qur'an truly of divine origin? Were its texts the actual words of God or the words of Muhammad, as his own version of divine revelation?[16] If the actual text of the Qur'an was revealed in God's own words, was *al-Muṣḥaf al-'Uthmāni*, as the sole recognized version of the Qur'an, an accurate and complete account of God's revelation?

On the question of the Qur'an's divine origins, a number of orientalists rejected the prophethood of Muhammad and consequently the idea that anything he uttered might have originated from God.[17] In their view, the Qur'anic text had been authored by Muhammad[18] or by some poets among the Companions, following inspiration from Judaic and/or Christian sources.[19] In support of this view, these authors cite the widely reported contacts of Prophet Muhammad with the priests and monks he encountered and befriended on his various trading trips to the Levant[20] prior to the start of the Divine Revelation. They also cite his close relationship with Waraqa Ibn Nawfal, a Christian cleric and cousin of his first wife, Khadija.[21] William Muir, in *The Life of Muhammad from Original Sources*, treats the Qur'an as a kind of autobiography of the Prophet Muhammad. [22] Alfred-Louis de Prémare and Mondher Sfar, for their part, cite the circumstantial nature of the Revelation and the heterogeneity of the text to argue that the Qur'an is the work of the Prophet himself. They point to the fact that the titles of the respective suras or chapters, of the Qur'an often do not correspond with the themes discussed in them.[23]

Granting that Prophet Muhammad had indeed received divine revelations, another controversy arose around the question of the Prophet's role in phrasing the verses of the Qur'an. Is the Qur'an the verbatim word of God, or is it the word of the Prophet who phrased the Divine Revelation as conveyed to him by the Archangel Gabriel?[24] This important issue is fundamental to understanding the Qur'an's scope of application. If the Qur'an is the true and authentic word of God, divinely phrased as conveyed to the Prophet with the mission to convey it further, in its original form, then its scope is truly universal. For it is perfect, following the perfection of the Creator and untainted by the limitations of time and place. But if the text is the Prophet's own phrasing of the meanings of the Revelation, then it is a human version of a revelation as understood by the Prophet who received it. This means it is a human interpretation emanating from that person's own understanding of the message based on that person's faculties and also on the prevailing cultural environment at the time. As such, that interpretation would be limited by the human imperfections of the intermediary, as well as by the limitations of time and place.[25]

Proponents of the view that the Qur'an is Prophet Muhammad's own version of the Divine Revelation advance the following arguments: (1) the sequence of the Qur'anic verses generally does not follow a rational sequence of subjects, a sign of human imperfection; (2) repetitions of certain verses, either verbatim or with differences in phrasing, reflect imperfect, human organization; and (3) certain verses appear to be contradictory.[26]

For their part, proponents of the view that the Qur'an is the divine word itself without human intervention, prophetic or otherwise, cite that: (1) the Qur'an itself, repeatedly and in no uncertain terms confirms its origins;[27] (2) the Prophet himself could not have phrased the Qur'an because he was an illiterate;[28] and (3) most importantly, the Qur'an is written in a language which cannot be humanly imitated.[29]

Further controversy arose concerning the accuracy and completeness of the Qur'an, raising questions along several lines.[30] First, Alfred-Louis de Prémare[31] raised the issue: Could the scribes who recorded the Revelation as uttered by the Prophet have inadvertently construed the Prophet's own views as revelation and recorded them as such? In other words, is the Holy Qur'an genuinely divine revelation in its entirety, or is it possible that ordinary Prophetic Tradition, or hadith, of the Prophet could have been mistaken as Qur'an and recorded as such? In support of this, de Prémare emphasized the Qur'an's apparent fragmentation and lack of rational unity. Then he cited the formulation "the Messenger says...," which appears in Verse Q25:30, as potential evidence of manipulation, or a confusing of hadith with revelation. He also cited a French translation of Verse Q25:32 attributing to God the ritual recitation of the Qur'an, which led him to conclude that, since God does not *recite* the Qur'an, it most probably would have been the Prophet who performed such recitation, adding to the confusion over the circumstances of the Qur'an's origins. In addition, some ancient commentators during the first few centuries of Islam have reported that when 'Uthman unified the text of the Qur'an and ordered the destruction of all other circulating versions, there remained some, namely those of the Companions Abou Musa, Ubayy, and Ibn Mas'ud, that were often cited as differing in certain ways from the newly distributed official version.

Qur'anic Verses Dealing with Controversies

A thorough reading of the Holy Qur'an discloses that the controversies surrounding the divine or human origin of the Qur'an, including any possible conscious or inadvertent role that the Prophet may have taken in the recording of Qur'anic text, are not solely the recent works of orientalists and modern researchers. Such polemics started during Prophet Muhammad's lifetime, contemporaneously with the Revelation. Various claims about the nondivine origins of the Qur'an are cited and refuted in numerous verses of the Qur'an, including the following ones.

> The Prophet is a sorcerer, and the Qur'an is a work of sorcery.
> Q43:30—*"But when the Truth came to them, they said: 'This is sorcery, and we do reject it.'"*[32]

> The Prophet is a poet, and the Qur'an is a work of poetry.
> Q52:30—*"Or do they say, '[He is but] a poet—let us await what time will do unto him.'"*[33]

> The Prophet is a lunatic, and he is hallucinating by believing that he is a prophet, communicating with God's messenger.
> Q15:6— *"They say, 'O you to whom the Dhikr (the Qur'an) has been revealed, you are surely insane."*[34]

> The contents of the Qur'an are nothing more than commonly known myths about ancient peoples and times.

Q16:24—*"When it is said to them, 'What has your Lord sent down?' They say, 'It is nothing but the tales of the ancient people.'"*[35]

The Prophet was being taught and inculcated by humans about the text of the Qur'an, which he presumably uttered, claiming that it came from God.

Q16:103—*"We know indeed that they say, 'It is a man that teaches him.' The tongue of him they wickedly point to is notably foreign, while this is Arabic, pure and clear."*[36]

More particularly, the non-Muslims of Medina, who insisted on denying the prophethood of Muhammad, often claimed that the text of the Qur'an was a mere repetition of the Judaic Scriptures as taught to him by his mentors, including the Christian monk Bahira.[37]

After refuting these allegations, the text of the Qur'an states that it is the word of God. In particular, it asserts that the Prophet is not a sorcerer, a poet, a lunatic, or a priest of any kind. It attests that the Qur'an is not the work of humans, whether of Prophet Muhammad himself or of others who may have taught and inculcated it to him. It concludes that it is entirely the divine word of God, revealed and conveyed to Muhammad in its original form for him to pass on to humanity, as set forth in Verses Q25:4 to 6.

> Moreover, those who are bent on denying the truth are wont to say, "This [Qur'an] is nothing but a lie which he [himself] has devised with the help of other people, who thereupon have perverted the truth and brought a falsehood into being" (4). And they say, "Fables of ancient times which he has caused to be written down, so that they might be read out to him at morn and evening" (5)! Say [O Muhammad]: "He who knows all the mysteries of the heavens and the earth has bestowed from on high this" [Qur'an upon me]!(6).[38]

Guided by the Qur'an, several authors have endeavored to refute claims of any potential attempt by Prophet Muhammad to add, remove, or modify any verses revealed to him by God. In support of this, they assert that the Qur'an itself contains all the needed assurances that it is complete, and that it also contains instances in which God has intervened to prevent or correct mistakes made by the Prophet, whether in his personal behavior or in the reception and transmission of certain verses. All of this attests to the potential infallibility of the Prophet in the performance of his immediate mission of receiving the Message and transmitting it.

The most noted instance in which the Prophet was instructed to remove verses which he had previously transmitted was when it was brought to his attention by the carrier of the Revelation that those verses had been conveyed to him by Satan (the Satanic Verses) impersonating the Archangel Gabriel. This occurred in Mecca, where pressure against Muhammad from the city's leaders was mounting as his message was starting to gain ground. He was advised by his clansmen that if he would make a gesture of compromise, they would be willing to accept, if not adopt— or live in peace with—his message. What they requested of the Prophet was recognition, even if slight, of the existing Meccan *Qurayshi* deities, alongside the sole creator role of God himself. For the leaders of *Quraysh,* such a gesture would sufficiently enable them to maintain the traditional role of the *Quraysh* and Mecca. In particular, they wished to continue their role of hosting the annual hajj pilgrimage, which contributed to the wealth, power, and predominance of the *Quraysh* and Mecca. In response to this overture, a few verses were presumably "revealed" in which God gave to prominent deities of Mecca a role in providing intercession for humans before God. Shortly after having uttered these presumed verses, Archangel Gabriel descended to warn Muhammad that the verses were sent not by him but by Satan. As such, these verses were not part of the Holy Qur'an and should be removed from it. The Prophet promptly and faithfully complied.[39] The Qur'an closes this episode in Verse Q22:52, warning against Satan's meddling and assuring that God is watching and making sure to prevent any Satanic distortions of Qur'anic text: *"Never have we sent a single prophet or apostle before you with whose wishes Satan did not tamper. But God abrogates the interjections of Satan and confirms His own revelations. God is all-knowing and wise."*[40]

The Qur'an as the Complete and Accurate Divine Word

Throughout this book, I assume—and truly believe—that the Qur'an is the authentic, divinely phrased word of God, as revealed to Prophet Muhammad for onward transmission to his people in the performance of his mission.[41] This belief, however, does not discount the possibility that certain verses may have been added, repeated, or removed during the phases of its collection and unification, or that certain words may have been misplaced or misused. Instead, and to the extent that any such discrepancies may have occurred, it appears that only minor subjects may have been affected, leaving the essence of the Holy Qur'an unaffected.[42]

In any case, the argument that proposes the possible illiteracy of Prophet Muhammad[43] as evidence for the divine origin of the Qur'an is superfluous and unconvincing. Prophet Muhammad is often portrayed as an illiterate person based on the use of the terms *ummi* and *ummiyyūn* to describe the Prophet, as evidenced in Verse Q7:158.

> *(O Prophet Muhammad) Say, "O people, I am a messenger of Allah (sent) to you from the One to whom belongs the kingdom of the heavens and the earth. There is no god but He. He gives life and brings death. So, believe in Allah and His Messenger, the Ummiyy (unlettered) prophet, who believes in Allah and in His words, and follow him, so that you may find the right path."*[44]

The term *ummi* in the context of the Revelation is not about literacy or illiteracy. It refers to the people of the *umma*, the ordinary people. When the Qur'an describes Prophet Muhammad as an *ummi*, the idea is that he is one of us, an ordinary person. Unproven as well are the arguments drawn from the elegance and beauty of the language in which the Holy Qur'an is phrased.[45] Such semantics-based reasoning is implausible because it ignores that the Arabic-speaking recipients of the Message are only a small fraction of its wider, universal audience.[46]

De Prémare and Sfar, among others, seem to imply that the mere fact that the Qur'an restates biblical and other myths and stories reduces it to being a paraphrase of ancient Scriptures authored by the Prophet himself or by the monks and other priests with whom he had contact.[47] This implication derives from de Prémare's assertion that Prophet Muhammad never denied knowledge of previous religious Scriptures, while he affirmed that his version was divinely revealed, defying the deniers to produce a similar text.[48] Against such implications and arguments, it is important to keep in mind that the Qur'an acknowledges that its texts continue, amplify, and perfect past divine texts and do not simply copy or reiterate them. The Prophet was certainly aware of older Scriptures, as evidenced by his documented contacts with Ibn Nawfal and Levantine monastics. But that does not mean that he, or they, authored the Qur'an. The Qur'an in more than one instance attests that it is the reaffirmation of previous messages. God sends messengers and prophets to all people and addresses them in their particular languages, as seen in Verse Q14:4: *"AND NEVER have We sent forth any apostle otherwise than [with a message] in his own people's tongue, so that he might make [the truth] clear unto them"*[49] On that basis, the Holy Qur'an has been revealed in the Arabic language, as set down in countless verses; for example, Verse Q12:2: *"We have sent it down as an Arabic Qur'an, in order that ye may learn wisdom"*[50] It should be no surprise that a message substantially similar—though not identical—to the messages conveyed to Moses, and then Jesus, returned in the Arabic language through Prophet Muhammad, because he is the Prophet sent to the population of the Arabian Peninsula. This is confirmed in such passages as Verse Q46:12: *"And yet, before this there was the revelation of Moses, a guide and a [sign of God's] grace; and this [Qur'an] is a divine writ confirming the truth [of the Torah] in the Arabic tongue, to warn those who are bent on evildoing, and [to bring] a glad tiding to the doers of good."*[51]

As for the likelihood raised by de Prémare that the scribes of the Prophet may have mistaken hadith (the sayings) of the Prophet for Qur'anic verses, that would appear remote because the recorded tradition of Prophet Muhammad indicates that he strictly prohibited recording any of his sayings or acts for fear that they might have been mistaken for verses of the Qur'an. The arguments that de Prémare derived from Verses Q25:30 and Q25:32 to further support the claim that Prophet Muhammad may have been the author of selected verses of the Qur'an are not rationally evident, either. With respect to Verse Q25:30, *"The Messenger says, 'O my Lord, behold, my people have taken this Koran as a thing to be shunned,'"*[52] the use of the formulation "the Messenger says," as opposed to use of the ceremonial "we," is neither inadvertent nor a slip of the tongue. It is perfectly plausible and should be understood in the context in which it appeared. This verse is one of a series of verses describing the attitude of nonbelievers when faced with the Day of Judgment. On that day they will regret the dismissive attitude that they took toward the Prophet's call to faith, and the Prophet will explain to God that they have discarded the Qur'an that he brought to them. However, with respect to Verse Q25:32 relating to the ceremonial recitation of the Qur'an by God, de Prémare's understanding of that verse was based entirely on an erroneous French translation of it. In reality, the verse does not refer to a recitation of the Qur'an by God, ceremonial or otherwise. Verse Q25:32 refers to God telling His Prophet that He has revealed the Qur'an to him gradually in response to the doubt raised by nonbelievers enquiring about the reason why the Qur'an would not be revealed at once as a whole: "*And those who disbelieve say: 'Why is not the Qur'an revealed to him all at once?' Thus (it is sent down in parts), that We may strengthen your heart thereby. And We have* revealed it to you gradually, in stages."[53]

Finally, the arguments drawn from the facts that the verses of the Qur'an are not organized in any particular rational sequence, that certain verses are repeated in exactly the same or slightly different form, and that certain verses may imply contradictory meanings, do not prove the human origin of the Qur'an, nor do they stand up to reasonable scrutiny. In fact, all these arguments become irrelevant in light of the fact that the Qur'an was gradually revealed over a period of twenty-two years; and, during the latter part of that period, revelation became interactive, as God guided the steps of the Prophet in the performance of his mission, at times correcting his behavior or responding to his queries. Therefore, it is important to place each verse in the context of its revelation because the circumstances that occasioned a particular revelation shed light on and justify the potential repetition of, and/or contradiction with, a previous revelation.

Laurence Brown attempts to demonstrate the absence of evidence that the Qur'an is not the word of God.[54] In addition, while the relevant verses of the Qur'an were divinely revealed, their compilation was the work of humans, which may explain aspects of the rational order of verses and suras. In other words, the so-called nonrational sequencing of verses and suras in the Qur'an does not indicate their nondivine origin but only points to potential human intervention in their compilation. On the other hand, the compilation of the Holy Qur'an by humans could explain omissions or additions to the text of the Message which may have occurred in the course of the first and second compilations, as cited in the early commentaries.[55]

In any event, history did not report any instances of use or abuse of the Holy Qur'an for political purposes, similar to reports relating to the Prophetic Tradition. The jurisprudents (*fuqahā'*) of the first few centuries of Islam, who commented on the Qur'an and developed Islamic law from it, wrote from a completed Qur'an, not one still being drafted or even edited. Accordingly, it is possible to claim and assume that the text of the Holy Qur'an currently in hand is an accurate one, and that if it may include any discrepancies, such are minor.[56] It is conceivable that certain words appearing in the Qur'an, as in any of the preceding Scriptures, may not reflect the exact phrasing of the Revelation as received by the Prophet, because God has not addressed people individually but has done so through prophets. Therefore, the human intermediation in passing on the messages to the rest of us through the Companions and scribes could reasonably allow some degree of imperfection attached to human imperfection. This takes us into the realm of faith. Yet, the Qur'an does contain verses which guide the Prophet in the performance of his mission.[57] It even contains instances in which God has revealed verses correcting certain actions of the Prophet where necessary, all of which adds comfort to belief in the accuracy and completeness of the Qur'an that is in hand.

Going beyond arguments used to refute challenges to the divine origin of the Qur'an and, in addition to arguments eventually drawn from natural phenomena described in it but not explained scientifically until centuries later,[58] it is possible to concur with the argument drawn from the inimitability of the Holy Qur'an—the substantive phrasing of the Qur'an which potentially exceeds human imitation,[59] or the *i'jāz* of the Qur'an.[60]

I'jāz resides in the fact that the Qur'an is phrased in language belonging to the seventh century, yet it can be understood by, and is relevant to, all humans of any century thereafter, as if it were addressed directly to them.[61] In other words, all people can understand the Qur'an from their individual viewpoints and understandings of the meanings of words used in it, consistent with the knowledge base and value system prevailing in the relevant cultural environment. Muhammad Shahrour explains and illustrates the *i'jāz* of the Qur'an, citing the example of an accomplished scientist who, in his lifetime, has accumulated a wealth of information and theories, and made important contributions in his field. He wishes to pass on that scientific wealth in his lifetime to his son, who is only a few years old. But first the scientist must determine what type of language to use to speak to his son. Should he use language understandable to a ten-year-old child, a fifteen-year-old adolescent, an eighteen-year-old young man, or a mature, forty-year-old scholar? Perhaps his son may never reach a level that would enable him to properly understand his father's legacy. The scientist decides to write the scientific legacy in a utopic language that could be understood by any person of any age or intellectual level, from the lowest level of comprehension to the highest degree of erudition. Each reader, irrespective of age or intellectual level, would be able to benefit from the wealth of scientific information, as necessary in each case and permitted by the living environment and intellectual level of the reader.[62]

In light of the above, this study is based on the strong premise that the Qur'an is the accurate, entire, and unaltered word of God.

Chronology of the Qur'anic Revelation

Spanning a period of twenty-two years, revelation commenced in the year 610 AD while Prophet Muhammad lived in Mecca, locus of his Hashimite clan. It ended in the year 632 AD with the death of Prophet Muhammad in the city of Medina, to which he and his companions fled in the year 622 AD, avoiding persecution which had turned life-threatening. Therefore, the Meccan phase of Qur'anic revelation occurred during the first thirteen years of the Prophet's mission, while the Medinan phase took place during the last ten years of the Prophet's life.

In Mecca, prior to the Revelation, Muhammad worked as a trader in the business of his wealthy wife, Khadija. At that time, he was not yet seen by his peers as a potential religious or political leader, leadership being the exclusive domain of the elders, in accordance with prevailing tribal practice. It took him three years from the start of revelation to begin spreading the Message on any scale beyond his immediate friends and family. During that early period, the Message was general, dogmatic, and untied to specific events then taking place. It essentially concerned the nature of the new faith, its place in the context of the previous monotheistic faiths revealed to Muhammad's predecessors (from Abraham to Jesus), and its basic foundations, consisting of *tawḥīd* (the unicity of God), the Day of Judgment, life after death, hell, and paradise. As Muhammad began to spread the Message, the elders of his tribe of *Quraysh*, whose power and wealth derived from the worship of the deities of Mecca, felt threatened by the substance of that message. They made serious attempts to dissuade him from continuing with his mission. That process of dissuasion, peaceful at first, soon turned violent when they confronted Muhammad's determination, derived from his unshakable faith in God, to carry on with his divine mission, whatever the cost. Revelation was by then becoming more immediate; God was now providing Muhammad the support that he needed in the form of day-to-day guidance of his footsteps.

When Prophet Muhammad decided to move to Medina,[63] he was quick to organize the migration that became known as the hijra, together with his companions who were similarly exposed to danger and suffering oppression. The initially peaceful and welcoming atmosphere in Medina, by comparison to that in Mecca, added to the Prophet's mission the tasks of organizing the first Muslim community in Medina and fighting the wars that accompanied the performance of his mission. The focus of revelation had now to gear toward communal tasks in order to deal with, among other things, feuds and sensitivities within the new community—first among Muslims, between the Meccan companions and the *anṣār* of Medina;[64] then between Muslims and Jews.

The thorough reader of the Qur'an will notice the differing themes and tones of the Qur'an in the various Meccan phases and in the Medinan phase of revelation.[65] For example, the early suras revealed in Mecca are relatively short; they cover substantially one subject, presumably because they were not occasioned by events surrounding the Prophet's mission or affecting it. By contrast, the suras revealed in Medina are longer and treat multiple topics, dealing mainly with issues faced by the Prophet as events unfolded.[66] This explains why the book which recounts the circumstances of revelation[67] hardly refers to any of the verses conveyed during the early Meccan period, because they were unsolicited. Similarly, the various books which purported to interpret and explain the meanings of the Qur'anic verses revealed during the early Meccan period did not refer to the relevant events which occasioned their revelation.

Referring again[68] to the controversy which arose among philosophers and theologians as to whether the Qur'an is created or uncreated, in the sense that it existed ever since God existed, here it should be pointed out how scholars and theologians who adhere to the view that the Qur'an is uncreated reconcile their position with the chronological nature of revelation. They advance the argument that, while the Qur'an was in existence since the beginning of time, it was sent down in its entirety on the Sacred Night of *Laylat-ul-Qadr*,[69] but that individual verses were revealed to Prophet Muhammad gradually over the entire period of his mission.[70]

Abrogation: Nāsekh and Mansūkh

While concluding and asserting that the official version of the Holy Qur'an is the accurate and complete, divinely revealed version, yet it is necessary to identify which parts of it, if any, may have been divinely modified or removed. This brings us to the issue of abrogation, the idea that certain verses of the Qur'an have been annulled by God, and other verses have ceased to be effective as a result of some decision or utterance by Prophet Muhammad. The issue of abrogation is a very important one because its wide acceptance has placed a severe limitation on the universality of the Qur'an. According to this concept of *naskh* (abrogation), the abrogating verse is called *nāsekh* and the abrogated verse is called *mansūkh*.[71] This concept, around which general, though not entire, consensus has developed, is founded on Verses Q2:106 and Q16:101 and 102 of the Qur'an, each of which discuss the abrogation of Qur'anic *āyas* by God.

Three dimensions have generally been identified and debated in connection with the concept of abrogation: (1) the abrogation of one or more verses by more recent verses within the Qur'an itself; (2) the abrogation of certain verses of the Qur'an by subsequent statements or behaviors of Prophet Muhammad; and (3) the abrogation of Christianity and Judaism and their respective Scriptures by Islam and the Qur'an.[72] This section will consider only the first dimension, namely abrogation of Qur'anic verses by subsequently revealed verses. Abrogation of Qur'anic verses by action of the Prophet, if any, will be discussed in connection with the discussion of hadith and sunna, or the Prophetic Tradition; and the alleged abrogation of Christianity and Judaism and their relevant Scriptures by Islam will be discussed in conjunction with the relation of Islam to other Abrahamic faiths.

To illustrate the issue of abrogation, in Verses Q60:7 to 9, God tells the believers of Mecca who migrated with the Prophet to Medina that it is not necessary to feud with their Meccan relatives who did not convert to Islam and stayed behind, if they abstain from fighting the believers. He goes as far as allowing them to befriend one another, as long as the polytheists of Mecca do not fight the believers solely because of their creed.[73] In the same spirit, several verses promote freedom of faith and forbid any forceful measures to convert people to the new faith. Yet, several ancient and more recent commentaries claim that all such verses have been abrogated by subsequently revealed verses which allegedly ordered the Prophet and his companions to fight unbelievers.[74] If such views were correct, this raises serious questions. Is it possible that God changed his mind about dealing with the people of Mecca in a matter of days, weeks, or months? After all, Sūrat al-Mumtaḥina (Q60) in which Verses Q:60:7 to 9 appear, and in which the Meccan companions are advised not to feud with fellow Meccans who did not migrate with them, was revealed quite late in the life of the Prophet, just a few months preceding the conquest of Mecca and years after the alleged instruction to fight unbelievers was given. Is it logical that God changed his mind several times during the twenty-two years which the Revelation spanned, but not once before or after it? Isn't perfection the essence of God, that which makes Him different from the rest of us? It is not logical to claim that God changes His mind, because any such claim would imply that, in the first place, He made less than perfect decisions, and then decided to reverse them. This conclusion defies the essence of God. It also defies the logic and sense that He keeps reminding us of throughout the Qur'an.

The idea that God revealed Qur'anic verses, then later changed his mind about their substance and reversed them, cannot be supported. This is not because God is not capable of doing so. God is the Almighty and capable of anything and everything, without restrictions or limitations on His power. However, this concept is contrary to a perception of God who, when He issued His commands, rulings, and advice, supported all of them with *āyas*, that is, convincing proofs and signs. If He asks us to be convinced, it means that He Himself is convinced. If that is the case, how convincing is it to reverse position in a matter of days, months, or years? It is conceivable, some might say, that God, in His utmost compassion, observes the interests of the people and intervenes at times to make adjustments to their plight. That, perhaps, could have been plausible, except that God has decided that Muhammad is the last and final messenger and prophet, and consequently the Qur'an is the last and final scripture and message to be revealed by God. Given that divine assertion, how is it possible to rationally justify that He might abandon his compassionate attention to the interests of people and withhold further adjustments as He previously undertook to do during the life of Muhammad? That is not plausible either. Instead, what is rational and plausible is that God has in the first place revealed the right and correct principles, which are universal and, through gradualism and other signs, He showed us the way for change and progress.

With respect to the verses on which the concept of abrogation is based, the term *āya* as it appears in the Qur'an has been incorrectly interpreted as referring to Qur'anic text. More clearly, *āya* refers to the signs and examples provided by God to evidence the relevance of the principles that He sent through the Qur'anic revelation.[75] This explains why the term *āya*, when it appears in the Qur'an, is almost consistently coupled with an appeal to peoples' minds. God offers *āyas*[76] for people to ponder and, if convinced, to find comfort in their provisions.[77] In Arabic the term *āya* means a sublime showpiece, a noble sign and proof. This explains the use of the same term to describe the verses of the Qur'an. Each verse, by virtue of its divine origin, constitutes a sublime revealed truth and—as such—serves as a "proof" for that truth.[78] Therefore, even in the limited instances in which the term appears in the Qur'an in reference to its verses, the syntax consistently leads us to understand the term as meaning a sign or proof.

To illustrate, in Verse Q3:58, God tells His prophet about the "verses" and the Wise Remembrance that He "recites" to Muhammad. In this instance, recite is a translation for the Arabic terms *natlu* and *tilāwa,* which can mean recite or recitation.[79] But it also means "telling," such as telling a story. In this context, where this term is being used in conjunction with *āyas* and the Wise Reminder, it clearly means telling as opposed to reciting. Keeping in mind that the Wise Reminder is the Qur'an itself, and remembering also that God does not recite the Qur'an or any of its verses to the Prophet but reveals them to him through an intermediary, Archangel Gabriel, the meaning of this verse could be understood as follows: God reveals to His Prophet the Qur'an, in which He tells him about the proofs and signs contained throughout the Qur'an.[80] This verse, in particular, appears in conjunction with tales about Mary and Jesus, and—for that purpose—its context serves to confirm that the term *āya* is not about text of the Qur'an, nor any other divine book.

With these understandings of *āya* in mind, let us consider the first cited verse upon which the concept of abrogation is founded, Verse Q2:106: *"Whenever we abrogate an 'āya' or cause it to be forgotten, we bring another one which is better than it or similar to it; did you not know that God is capable of all things."* It becomes more rational to translate *āya* here as sign, proof, or example, rather than verse.[81] As God's basic message has not changed since the beginning of his revelations, commencing with Abraham, it is more likely that God may have come up with better, or simply clearer, examples and signs for each of the people to whom He sent messengers, ones better suited to their individual circumstances. The same holds for the second set of verses cited above, which serve as basis for the concept of abrogation, namely Verses Q16:101 and 102.

> *When We substitute one revelation for another and Allah knows best what He reveals (in stages) they say "Thou art but a forger": but most of them understand not (101). Say the Holy Spirit has brought the revelation from thy Lord in truth, in order to strengthen those who believe and as a Guide and Glad Tidings to Muslims (102).*[82]

In Verse 101, God tells the Prophet and his listeners that if a revealed sign (*āya*) is different from a previous one, it is not Prophet Muhammad's fault; instead, it is God's expressed will. The context of this verse is as follows: the Prophet is accused by his detractors among the polytheists and Jews of Medina of making up self-serving verses to change rules at will as necessary to manage situations of the moment. He is also accused of copying older Scriptures into the Qur'an after making certain changes of his own. These accusations came about when Prophet Muhammad announced the verse commanding that prayers be performed facing Mecca instead of facing Jerusalem. In this accusation, the implication was that prayers facing Jerusalem were performed copying the Jewish practice, and that since he was no longer on such good terms with the Jews, Muhammad decided to face Mecca instead.

The issue is clarified when we remember that Muhammad's entire message confirms and reiterates older revelations and Scriptures, with certain changes clarifying signs of God. Thus, God did not abrogate His own previous messages conveyed by Moses and Jesus. He replaced certain revelations and signs by others, without changing the Message. In reality, He conveyed an updated message more suitable to the needs and circumstances of Muhammad's audience, the immediate addressees of that message.[83]

The only abrogation-related instance in which *āya* can be interpreted as a reference to a Qur'anic verse is Verse Q22:52: *"Never have we sent a single prophet or apostle before you with whose wishes Satan did not tamper. But God abrogates the interjections of Satan and confirms His own revelations. God is all-knowing and wise."*[84] However, this verse is thought to relate to the Satanic Verses that God effectively abrogated and removed altogether from the Qur'an.[85] This is a further indication that if indeed abrogation consistently referred to verses of the Qur'an—as opposed to signs and examples, then the abrogated verses would have been ordered removed from the Qur'an following the example of the Satanic Verses.[86]

Apart from the textual foundation for the concept of abrogation, there is a practical foundation upon which advocates of the concept have relied. This foundation is derived from a modern legalistic approach, according to which the more recent legislation supersedes the older one.[87] This approach cannot be defended convincingly for two important reasons. First, Islam is not a legal system, and its verses are not to be confused with articles of a code, or even with mere legal rulings.[88] Second, there is no reliably established chronological order of revelation for the verses of the Qur'an that would allow the rule of the recent superseding the older to be even considered. While commentaries and critical interpretations have identified the context of certain verses, such identification is not sufficiently conclusive to declare the abrogation of divine revelation, let alone to justify it. Moreover, commentaries often tell contradictory stories about the circumstances which accompanied certain revelations. Also, the circumstances of revelation for verses often could not be identified. This is the case for most of the verses revealed during the early prophethood of Muhammad.

Authors, such as Farid Esack and Ahmad Amin[89] have viewed abrogation as a tool of gradualism in revelation, by which God gradually enacts rules and dogmas, commencing with the mild, then at the opportune time abrogating them when the stricter rules are thought to be appropriate.[90] While God's wisdom and compassion can be seen in replacing the tribal rules of society with just and humane higher principles, it does not follow that, in bringing forth the ultimate principle, the previous one is abrogated, because the previous solution remains valid intrinsically.[91] This point is illustrated by an example drawn from the gradual intimation to abstain from drinking alcohol. First, Verse Q2:219 offered a general value judgment with respect to alcoholic drinks, noting that while they are essentially harmful, yet they can be beneficial: *"They ask you about drinking and gambling. Say: 'There is great harm in both, although they have some benefit for men; but their harm is far greater than their benefit.'* "[92] At this stage, the verse in question does not contain any instructions of any kind as to whether people can or should, cannot or should not consume drinks containing alcohol. Second, Verse Q4:43 forbade praying while intoxicated: *"Believers, do not approach your prayers when you are drunk, but wait till you can grasp the meaning of your words."* [93] This clear command contains two dimensions; namely, that to pray while drunk is a sin that offends God because the drunk person cannot be sincere in his prayer, and that it is not a sin to get drunk as long as one does not pray or commit other sins while under the effect of alcohol. Verses Q5:90 and 91 appeared containing the final ruling.

> *O believers, wine and gambling, idols and divining arrows are an abhorrence, the work of Satan. So keep away from it, that you may prevail (90). Satan only desires to arouse discord and hatred among you with wine and gambling, and to deter you from the mention of God and from prayer. Will you desist? (91).* [94]

In these verses, God warns of tricks that Satan uses to draw people from God's graces. He distracts people from good behavior and renders them instead to hate and harm each other. Alcoholic drinks that adversely affect the functions of the mind are among those dangers, and God for that purpose urges people to stay away specifically from the work of Satan (the Verse urges to stay away "from it" as opposed to "from them").

Note here that, with respect to the ruling on alcoholic drinks, God provided a reason for it, namely that Satan -through drinking among other things- can distract people from prayer and from remembrance of God, while causing them to hate others and do harm to them. Therefore, if drink does not have the potential to cause harm, it need not be regulated. By contrast, the following verses simply set forth the prohibition as a command, as a clear-cut rule without any justification:

Q2:173—*"He has forbidden you carrion, blood, flesh of swine; also any flesh consecrated other than in the name of God. But whoever is driven by necessity, intending neither to sin nor to transgress, shall incur no guilt. God is forgiving and merciful"*;[95]

Q5:3—*"You are forbidden carrion, blood, and the flesh of swine; also any flesh dedicated to any other than God. You are forbidden the flesh of strangled animals and of those beaten or gored to death; of those killed by a fall or mangled by beasts of prey (unless you make it clean by making the death stroke yourselves); also of animals sacrificed to idols"*;[96] and

Q16:115— *"He has forbidden you carrion, blood, flesh of swine; also any flesh consecrated other than in the name of God. But whoever is driven by necessity, intending neither to sin nor to transgress, will find that God is forgiving and merciful".*[97]

Nevertheless, the majority of commentators concluded that alcohol was as prohibited as pork under all circumstances. Others, however, concluded from the difference in phrasing that alcohol was prohibited only in order to prevent the harmful outcomes set forth in Verses Q5:90 and 91, and that it would not be sinful to drink alcohol if the person in question took the appropriate precautions to prevent those harmful outcomes and was successful in doing so.

This example is typical of gradual divine ruling. It serves to refute the concept of abrogation and to reject the implication that the last ruling on an issue abrogates all previous rulings on that same issue. In our example, assuming even that Verse Q5:90 is a final and unquestionable prohibition of alcohol under all circumstances, it remains that nonetheless Verse Q5:90 did not abrogate Verses Q2:219 and Q4:43, because these two verses still retain value. With respect to Verse Q2:219, which does not contain any rulings that are by implication reversed, the value judgment and statement of fact contained in it about the potential harmful and beneficial effects of alcohol do not change, whether alcohol is permitted or not. As for Verse Q4:43, hypocrisy in prayer is a sin which is committed merely by putting oneself in a position to stand before God in a state of mind that distracts the person praying from meaning what he or she may be uttering, and that is so whether alcohol is permitted or not, and whatever may be the cause of drunkenness.

Provided that the proper chronological sequence in revelation can be sufficiently established, gradualism—including the ultimate potential reversal of prior rulings—should be perceived as relative illustrations of God's *āyas*. These are divine signals and examples of how rules can and must change following changed circumstances. Through these signals, God is enjoining humanity to modify the rules and/or their own interpretations, as needed to cope with changed circumstances. This would explain why a reversed rule is not abrogated but, instead, remains in full force and effect. In fact, in addition to its explanatory function, it is conceivable that the reversed rule might remain applicable in circumstances similar to the ones in which it was revealed. Clearly we are in the presence of an encouragement to remain open-minded and ready to progress through change.

Finally, it is necessary to always remember that revelation of many segments of the Qur'an occurred in an interactive manner to guide the Prophet in the face of adverse situations and to help him respond to queries by his companions. Therefore, the relevant context of each verse is important to attempt to understand the divine intent. What may appear as a reversal when taken out of context ceases to be as such when placed in its proper context. As a result, opposite solutions are often prescribed for different circumstances, yet each such solution remains relevant and valid under comparable circumstances.

What appears to the hasty interpreter as an abrogation is in reality a meaningful and important divine guidance to all humanity to use its judgment in order to maneuver through difficult times and to resolve problems. This principle is essential to ensure the universality of the Qur'anic message. It is critically important in framing the scope and meaning of abrogation accurately, because its misunderstanding by Muslims and non-Muslims alike has lead to deplorable consequences.[98] Non-Muslim authors have used the concept of abrogation to support claims denying the divine origin of the Qur'an. To them, it is no more than a ploy to disguise the human origin of the Qur'an or the human manipulation of the divine text by the Prophet, or through him, as an intermediary.[99]

Within Islam, the regretful early consensus[100] among Muslim commentators and clerics gave the concept of abrogation a wide scope which sadly deprived the Qur'an and Muslims of the essence and soul of Islam: the main divine commands enjoining peace, acceptance of the other, compassion, and open-mindedness were considered abrogated in favor of an intolerant and violent framework. In fact, revelation during most of the Meccan period in Prophet Muhammad's career preached a compassionate, tolerant, liberal, and progressive Islam. Then, following the migration to Medina where Prophet Muhammad set about organizing the *umma* (community) and spreading the Message, Divine Revelation enjoined him to take certain actions which appeared to be inconsistent with the earlier Meccan message. Commentators then interpreted those verses as superseding the Meccan message. That consensus regretfully was followed by later generations of 'ulama' (religious scholars) right up until today. In contrast, Mahmoud Taha noted and took into consideration the differing contexts of revelation in Mecca and Medina. He noted that the earlier Meccan message was laying the grounds for the new faith without regard to issues of daily life. As such, it constituted the core essence of the faith.[101] In Medina, however, revelation was guiding the footsteps of the Prophet in his daily endeavors to organize the *umma* and to spread the Message. On that basis, Mahmud Taha rejects the view that the context-focused revelation of Medina could have done away with the essence of the faith as revealed in the early period of Mecca. He concludes that the Medinan revelation had the effect of temporarily suspending the effects of the Meccan revelation, but then only to the extent necessary for Prophet Muhammad to fulfill his Mission.[102]

Similarly, Ibn Qayyim al-Jawziyyah understands the concept of abrogation in a tempered way where, while no verses are superseded and removed, the contradicting verses are interpreted as exceptions required by the circumstances (when the rule is inconsistent) or as a clarifying rule when the previous rule appears different from—though not totally inconsistent with—the newer one.[103]

In light of all this, it can be argued that the concept of abrogation, whereby verses of the Qur'an become obsolete and inoperative, is very dangerous for the stability of the religion.[104] It creates uncertainty in the mind of the believers. For that purpose, the scope of the concept of abrogation can be viewed in the following framework:

> Abrogation relates exclusively to the *āyas*, consisting of examples and signs that God gave to humanity in the series of His revealed messages leading to—and including—the Holy Qur'an. Abrogation then means that God over time has revealed examples relating to His truths and injunctions that are better suited to the audience of the relevant message, as each message came in a different context of time and place.

> No verse of the Qur'an has superseded a previous one. Every verse of the Qur'an has a meaning and a purpose, and remains a live, unextinguished text. The only verses truly abrogated are those that have been inspired by Satan and thus have been removed entirely from the Qur'an, as was the case of the Satanic Verses.

To the extent that a rule or command in the Qur'an may appear as different from—or even inconsistent with—a previous one, the recent rule or command should not be interpreted as having superseded the previous one. Instead, it should, first, be accepted as more suited for the relevant situation. Second it should be viewed as an encouragement by example from God to not be rigid and to adapt the rules to our needs as circumstances change. It is an invitation to be flexible and mindful of our interests. When gradualism is applied in imposing divine rules and commands, it should not be perceived as a phased abrogation. Instead, it is a further demonstration of the need to be mindful of circumstances and to not apply rules blindly.

CHAPTER 3
The Nature and Role of Prophetic Tradition

Sunna and hadith are the reported traditions of Prophet Muhammad. They collectively constitute the Prophetic Tradition. The Prophetic Tradition includes the words uttered by Prophet Muhammad, as well as his expressed and implied actions and reactions in his public and personal life, during the period of the Divine Revelation. Sunna literally means "the way" or "practice." With respect to Prophet Muhammad's tradition, sunna consists of: (1) the sunna *fi'liyya*, or the acts performed by the Prophet; (2) the sunna *qawliyya*, or what the Prophet said or uttered; and (3) the sunna *taqrīriyya*, or what the Prophet implied by keeping silent in reaction to specific occurrences, in terms of consent or otherwise, depending on the context.[1]

Some scholars have extended the scope of Prophetic Tradition to include the practices of the Enlightened Caliphs, namely Abou Bakr, 'Umar, 'Uthman, and 'Ali, because of their close companionship with Prophet Muhammad. However, throughout this study, Prophetic Tradition will be exclusively about the traditions of the Prophet consistent with the following principles: (1) Muhammad is the *messenger* and *prophet* chosen by God; and (2) divine missions are neither delegable in the lifetime of the prophet or messenger, nor transferable after the prophet's death.

Although the Qur'an is the uncontested and primary source of Islam, with sunna and hadith being sources only to the extent that the Qur'an is silent on an issue, early and later theologists of Islam have actually treated the Prophetic Tradition as a source of Islam almost equal to the Qur'an. It is understandable that in the early period of Islam, people might not remember every verse of the Qur'an but find it easier to recall the words and actions of the Prophet. No one could be blamed for emulating the Prophet. However, with the passage of time, the Qur'an could no longer be ignored as it got compiled and widely distributed. As the companions of the Prophet dispersed into the expanding empire, and thereafter grew old and died, the tradition of the Prophet risked following their fate.

Since then, the scholars of Islam have developed a specialized science to define, compile, and interpret Prophetic Tradition.[2] Conditions were designed to help determine which traditions of the Prophet would be retained and included in Prophetic Tradition as a primary source of Islam. These conditions are applied in order to: (1) determine if the subject matter of the relevant tradition is directly or indirectly addressed by provisions of the Qur'an; (2) determine the extent to which a matter is so addressed; and (3) ascertain whether the relevant Prophetic Tradition is true and accurate.

Following consideration of the theological foundation for treating the Prophetic Tradition as a source of Islam, we shall examine issues associated with the compilation of the Prophetic Tradition, and with the scope of its application. This topic acquires a wider dimension when we realize that early and later theologists and scholars have, over time, attributed a scope to Prophetic Tradition which is not commensurate with its secondary role as a source of Islam. As such, Prophetic Tradition ranks below the Qur'an, and its role is subject to the scope permitted under the Qur'an. Yet, scholars have claimed, asserted, and built a framework for Islam on the basis that just as the Qur'an can abrogate Prophetic Tradition, Prophetic Tradition can in fact abrogate Qur'anic verses.

Because Prophetic Tradition is a record of the words, actions, and reactions of Prophet Muhammad, such claims and assertions would suggest that, in addition to conveying the Message, Prophet Muhammad was required also to regulate the implementation of, and secure compliance with, that message. Such assertions imply that perhaps Prophet Muhammad was of a superhuman nature, which allowed him to edit or modify divine revelation. In view of these serious, fundamental implications, we shall first discuss the human nature of Prophet Muhammad and then examine the nature of his assigned role as it transpires from the relevant verses of the Qur'an. Based on this, we will be in a better position to assess questions related to the accuracy and authenticity of Prophetic Tradition, and to appreciate its real value as a source of Islam and as a tool for its proper understanding.

The Human Nature of Prophet Muhammad

Although no one has directly claimed that Prophet Muhammad was a god or possessed divine qualities, a number of the stories, concepts, and theories attributed to his life and activities do border on the divine or imply superhuman qualities that are squarely refuted by the Holy Qur'an. Some of these theories have been accepted by a majority of scholars and have now become an integral part of the Muslim creed, such as the conception that Prophet Muhammad, his closest companions, and their lives in the early period of Islam are perfect. Reporting and commenting on the results of widely conducted polls, John Esposito and Dalia Mogahed observe:

> Sunni Muslims look to an ideal portrait of 'the first generation' of Muslims (called the Companions of the Prophet) as their model—a common reference point by which to measure, judge, and reform society…Muslims look to the Prophet Muhammad as the perfect human example of living.[3]

In particular, bizarre stories and myths formed around the person of Prophet Muhammad. These myths of Muhammad when he was growing up and as a young man served to build an aura around him and portray one who was destined—from birth—for prophecy. One story, described in Ibn Is'haq's biography of the Prophet,[4] tells how, when Muhammad was still a young boy, several angels dressed in white came upon him, slit his throat, removed his heart, then put it back in place after removing Satan from it. Considering that, until the first revelation occurred when he was forty, Muhammad was an ordinary person who did not have the slightest clue, nor any pre-warnings, of the mission to which he would be destined, such a myth casts Prophet Muhammad free of imperfections and divine-like. Another story tells that, while resting at a Christian monastery on returning from a trading trip to the Levant, Muhammad and his party were received by the monk Bahira who is said to have noticed an aura shining over Muhammad's head and then to have discovered a mark on his skin over his shoulder, presumably a seal of prophecy.[5] But the most widely repeated myth was that Prophet Muhammad was an illiterate person, which lent credibility to his divine power to receive and transmit such a perfect and eloquent message as the Holy Qur'an.[6] This claim was based on verses of the Qur'an in which the Prophet is described as an *ummi* (common person) who has been chosen among the *ummiyyūn* (plural of *ummi*) to receive and spread the Message. Whereas in today's Arabic, *ummi* could refer to an illiterate person, the term did not have such meaning in the days of the Qur'anic revelation, especially in a document which God tells us is the continuation and culmination of the Abrahamic Scriptures. Indeed, while the Bible declares Moses to be a prophet to the Israelites, as God's Chosen People, the Qur'an—as the final Divine Message—is universal, conveyed to all people through Prophet Muhammad, himself an *ummi*, selected from the *ummiyyūn*, the common people.[7]

These and other similar stories which mystify the Prophet[8] set the stage for the various serious claims about his infallibility, called the *'isma*, which have had a long-lasting and marked impact on the scope of the Islamic religion. *'Isma*, or the alleged infallibility of the Prophet, has been assigned varying scope by different thinkers. At one end of the spectrum, the scope of infallibility of Prophet Muhammad has been limited to the reception and conveyance of the Divine Message.[9] At the other end, the scope of infallibility encompasses almost all words and deeds, including actions and reactions, of Prophet Muhammad, presumably from the start of Revelation.[10] The infallibility of the Prophet is founded on a widely advocated claim that the words and deeds of Prophet Muhammad are divine revelation to the same extent as the Qur'an. This is the line of thinking that Imam al-Shafi'i developed and established, which equates the commands of Prophet Muhammad with divine commands.[11] It was accepted at that time by prominent jurists, such as Abu Hamid al-Ghazali and Ibn Hazm al-Andalusi,[12] and thereafter it became part of the dogma, to be assiduously followed by the majority of Islamic theologians, with the severe consequences that we will discuss.[13] For example, following the positions of al-Ghazali and Ibn Hazm al-Andalusi almost verbatim, Taha Hussein asserts, "[t]his revelation which continued uninterrupted for twenty-three years descended at times as Qur'an, was pronounced by the Prophet as 'hadith' at other times, or otherwise took the form of general prophetic behavior to be followed."[14]

One might perhaps think that those who perceived, and truly believed in, the Prophetic Tradition as an extension of divine revelation may have done so with Jesus Christ and the scriptural testimony about him in mind. Indeed, Jesus Christ is described in the Qur'an as the "word of God," a concept equivalent—at least in name—to the concept of *logos* appearing in the New Testament.[15] Clearly this comparison is out of place, because Prophet Muhammad is the carrier—and not the incarnation—of the word of God, as specifically stated in the Holy Qur'an.

The first corollary of extending the scope of divine revelation beyond the text of the Holy Qur'an, so as to encompass the deeds and words of Prophet Muhammad, is the actual extension of the Message to include all those deeds and words of the Prophet. This leads to restricting the scope of the provisions of the Qur'an and severely curtailing its universal aspect. It also adds confusion from apparent contradictions or inconsistencies between provisions of the Qur'an and provisions of Prophetic Tradition. As a result, the traditional schools of *fiqh* sought to remedy the situation by extending the concept of abrogation to cross-abrogation between the Qur'an and sunna, whereby Qur'anic verses would abrogate Prophetic Tradition, and Prophetic Tradition would abrogate Qur'anic verses.[16] That solution was disastrous and unfortunate on three important counts.

First, the general and universal Divine Message of the Qur'an is a progressive message with all the ingredients enabling Islam to lead progress. By contrast, the incorporation of the human element represented by Prophetic Tradition into the Message resulted in the substantial dilution of its progressiveness. In fact, while the Holy Qur'an, as a divine revelation, is infinite in its perfection, Prophetic Tradition is human and, by its nature, limited in several respects—in time and space, to name but two.

Second, because Prophet Muhammad had made sure that his scribes recorded every verse of the Qur'an that was revealed to him, we have a reasonably complete and accurate text of it. By contrast, Prophetic Tradition was entirely oral, and its compilation did not start until decades after the death of Prophet Muhammad. Thus, its accuracy and completeness are deficient, and for this reason Prophetic Tradition is unreliable. With this in mind, the scale of the issue—and the ensuing uncertainty—acquires a grave magnitude if we truly believe that this unreliable source could have abrogated and modified the Holy Qur'an, which is the primary source of Islam.

Third, in order for the cross-abrogation to work and to be meaningful, in addition to the certainty about the accuracy and completeness of the source, we ought to be equally certain about the respective chronologies and the circumstances of revelation of each verse in the Qur'an, and about each deed and word deemed Prophetic Tradition. While there are some recorded accounts about the circumstances of revelation of certain Qur'anic verses, they relate to a fraction only of the verses of the Qur'an and are thus insufficient to allow an accurate reorganization of the Qur'anic verses by chronological order of revelation. In addition, the reliability of Prophetic Tradition is doubtful in the sense that individual traditions continued for decades in the form of oral tradition.[17]

A strong rational foundation for *'isma*, the doctrine of the infallibility of Prophet Muhammad, has been advanced by its advocates. We will critically examine this doctrine in light of the unequivocal confirmation by the Holy Qur'an itself of the full human nature of Prophet Muhammad. An important segment of medieval *fiqh* (Islamic) jurisprudents consider that the integrity of the Qur'an itself is guaranteed by *'isma*,[18] with the necessary corollary that the Prophet's traditions represent God's will. On that basis, if the words and actions of Prophet Muhammad reflect God's will, then Prophetic Tradition might "safely" be claimed to be divine revelation.

A wide segment of Muslim theologians has gone so far as to extend prophetic infallibility to most, if not all, aspects of Prophet Muhammad's words and deeds,[19] reasoning along the following lines: (1) Prophetic Tradition and the Holy Qur'an derive from the same source, namely God, and they are both divine revelation, except that the Holy Qur'an includes revelation which is meant to be recited, while Prophetic Tradition is intended to clarify and supplement the Qur'an; (2) Prophet Muhammad's behavior in his daily life represents the role model to be closely followed by Muslims, because that behavior—in terms of speech, action, abstention, and acquiescence—constitutes the substance of Prophetic Tradition; (3) unlike Christianity, Islam does not differentiate between the individual realms of

God and Caesar; (4) through the Qur'an and Prophetic Tradition, Islam extends at all times to every aspect of a person's life, without exception, including physical, spiritual, social, political, and other aspects; and (5) Divine Revelation being infallible, Prophetic Tradition as embodiment of the Prophet's comprehensive behavior is revelation, hence infallible.

Another segment of Muslim scholars found it more appropriate, in light of the Qur'anic verses about the human nature of Muhammad, to limit the sphere of that infallibility. However, there was no consensus over the delimitation of that sphere: to some, infallibility would be strictly limited to the Divine Message—meaning the Qur'an—while the majority advocated for a separation between the personal and prophetic spheres of Prophet Muhammad's activity so as to limit infallibility solely to his deeds and words which he performed and uttered in his prophetic capacity.[20] As Daniel Brown notes, "Thus the prophet's persona was divided into 'human' and 'prophetic' spheres."[21] Yet, others denied a divine character to anything the Prophet did or uttered, beyond the limited scope of receiving the Holy Qur'an, treating Prophetic Tradition as the Prophet's *ijtihād* (critical reasoning). However, they recognized the binding character of such activities and utterances of the Prophet, despite their human character.[22]

The doctrine of prophetic infallibility does not withstand scrutiny, and its consequences contradict the scriptural evidence for the absolute and undivided human nature of Prophet Muhammad. Infallibility, as an attribute of perfection, is incompatible with human nature. If God is the only perfect being, then anyone deemed or claiming to be infallible would become associated with God by virtue of being attributed divine qualities. That, Prophet Muhammad never claimed. On the other hand, the artificial theory about the dual personas of Prophet Muhammad is an awkward one because it inadvertently leads to attributing two natures to the Prophet, one derived from the human persona and the other derived from the presumed divine quality of infallibility associated with his prophetic persona. That theory is reminiscent of the theological controversies that afflicted Christianity from its early days with respect to the dual or single nature of Jesus Christ.

The absolute and undivided human nature of Prophet Muhammad is confirmed by a number of verses of the Qur'an.[23]

> Q2:151—*As also We have sent in your midst a messenger from among you, who recites to you Our verses, and purifies you, and teaches you the Book and the wisdom, and teaches you what you did not know.*[24]

This verse confirms that the Prophet is just an ordinary person like the ones to whom he carries and delivers the Divine Message.

> Q3:79—*It befits no human being that God should reveal to him the Book, the Wisdom and Prophecy, then say to mankind: 'Be my worshippers apart from God.' Rather should he say: 'Be true guides since you teach the Book and you have studied it.'*[25]

This verse is important because it addresses both Muslims and Christians. It came down initially when the Christians of Najran who visited the Prophet asked him if they should worship him in the same way that Jesus allegedly asked them to do. The verse then told them that he, Muhammad, is a human being and in that capacity is not entitled to require anyone to worship him, whether in addition to, or instead of, God. This indirectly tells those Christians of Najran that Jesus, too, could not have made any such claim, no matter the extent to which God may have endowed him with powers and blessings. At the same time, this message is addressed to those Muslims who were so attached to Muhammad that they sought to prostrate before him. That is why Verse 80 of that same sura adds: *"Nor would he enjoin you to serve the angels and prophets as your gods; nor would he enjoin you to be unbelievers after you have submitted to God."*[26]

> Q6:50—*Say: 'I do not tell you that I possess the treasures of God, nor do I know the Unseen. Nor do I tell you I am an angel. I merely follow what is revealed to me.' Say: 'Is the blind man the equal of one who sees? Will you not reflect?'*[27]

Q7:188—*Say: 'I have no power to do myself good or harm save as God wills. Had I known the Unseen I would have done myself much good, and no harm would have touched me. I am merely a warner, and a herald of good tidings to a people who believe.'*[28]

Q14:11—*Their prophets said to them, 'We are no more than a human being like you, but Allah bestows His favour upon whom He wills from among His servants. It is not for us to bring you an authority without Allah's permission, and in Allah the believers must place their trust.'*[29]

This is further confirmation that Prophets, including Muhammad, are mere humans like everyone else, and for that reason the verse goes on to command that people should rely on God and no one else.

Q17:93—*Say: 'Glory be to my Lord! Am I anything other than a human being, a Messenger?'*[30]

This verse comes in the context of the polytheist elders of Mecca, in a bid to find common ground between their faith and the new faith being preached by Muhammad, telling Muhammad that he needed to prove to them his capacity as prophet by performing some miracles.

Q18:110—*Say: 'I am but a man like yourselves, (but) the inspiration has come to me, that your God is one God.'*[31]

Q22.52—*Never have We sent a single prophet or apostle before you with whose wishes Satan did not tamper. But God abrogates the interjections of Satan and confirms His own revelations. God is all-knowing and wise.*[32]

This confirms that Satan can induce a prophet in error, the ultimate sign of fallibility.

Q62:2—*It is He that has sent forth among the Gentiles an apostle of their own to recite to them His revelations, to purify them, and to instruct them in the Book and in wisdom, though they have hitherto been in evident error.*[33]

There is no stronger confirmation of the ordinary common humanity of the Prophet than comparing him to the rest of his community.

These verses unequivocally refer to Prophet Muhammad as being human in every respect, as being a commoner chosen from the community that is the immediate addressee of the Message, without differentiating between his personal capacity and his prophetic capacity. Abou Bakr summed this up eloquently in his address to the crowds that were reacting to the news of Prophet Muhammad's death, in which he laid out the plain reality that Muhammad was no more than an ordinary human who died and no longer existed: *"If you worshiped Muhammad, Muhammad is dead; and if you worship God, God is alive and never dies."*[34]

Thus, Prophet Muhammad is fully a human being who has been entrusted with a prophetic mission, without any change in his capacity or nature.[35] That fact carries important consequences. Bearing in mind that, as a form of perfection, infallibility is a divine quality, the first and immediate consequence of the ordinary human nature attaching to Prophet Muhammad is that he is not infallible by his nature. In fact, in Sūrat al-Nasr (Q110), which was revealed shortly after the victorious return to Mecca, Prophet Muhammad is cheered by God: "(O Prophet,) When there comes Allah's help and the Victory (1), and you see people entering Allah's (approved) religion in multitudes (2), then pronounce the purity and praise of your Lord, and seek forgiveness from Him. Surely He is Ever-Relenting (3)."[36] Had Prophet Muhammad been infallible, there would be no reason for him to seek forgiveness for sins and mistakes that he could not have committed.[37]

Yet, Prophet Muhammad had a form of "limited infallibility," on a *de facto* basis only. The Qur'an assures us that, with respect to the conveyance of the Qur'anic message, the Prophet speaks out of revelation, in the sense that the words so conveyed by him are not his own but those of God. Verses Q53:3 and 4 stipulate: *"He does not speak out of his own fancy (3). This is an inspired revelation (4)."*[38] Because the Prophet is an ordinary human being like the rest of us, and as such is not perfect, he is likely to make mistakes in receiving the revealed messages and thereafter in repeating them in the course of their conveyance, in the sense that he can forget or even misunderstand. However, as far as these mistakes are concerned, we are assured by God that He corrects them as they occur, because He guides His Prophet in the performance of his mission, as confirmed in Verses Q75:16 to 19:

> *(O Prophet,) do not move your tongue (during revelation) for (reciting) it (the Qur'an) to receive it in hurry (16). It is surely undertaken by Us to store it (in your heart), and to let it be recited (by you after revelation is completed) (17). Therefore, when it is recited by Us (through the angel), follow its recitation (by concentration of your heart) (18). Then, it is undertaken by Us to explain it (19).*[39]

As an immediate and unequivocal outcome of that fact, the Divine Message that the Prophet delivers to us in the form of Qur'anic verses is free of any mistakes whatsoever.

It becomes clear that if the Message that Muhammad conveyed to us is perfect, complete, and accurate, it is not because he is infallible but because God made sure that His Prophet did not make any mistakes. This should clarify the intent of the hadith in which the Prophet confirms to his companions that he is a human and can commit errors except on matters relating to the Revelation.[40] In this statement, the Prophet was not telling his companions that, by implication, in matters pertaining to revelation he is not human. Instead, he was telling them that his infallibility was strictly limited to actually conveying the revealed message, on a strictly *de facto* basis, and that it did not extend to its explanation, interpretation or implementation. We cannot stress enough the substance of Verse Q22:52, cited earlier, according to which God intervened to remove the verses with which Satan had tampered. If the Prophet's words and deeds can be tampered with by Satan, this is the evident proof that the Prophet is an ordinary fallible human being.[41]

In addition, while that *de facto* infallibility of the Prophet can provide assurance of the authenticity of the Holy Qur'an, it has no bearing on the controversies which arose following his death with respect to the Qur'an's accuracy and completeness. They are compilation-related controversies unrelated to the integrity of the Prophet or to the integrity with which he accomplished his mission. Those controversies relate to the humans who memorized and transcribed what they memorized, the humans who held on to these records, and the humans who compiled the verses.

Another important consequence of Prophet Muhammad being an ordinary human is that his actions and words are human and not divine. Self-evidently, such actions and words that are not involved in the conveyance of the Qur'anic message may or may not have been the product of divine revelation, as many have claimed. The Qur'an itself offers us indirect proof of that conclusion when God intervened to bring His prophet's attention to certain behaviors of his in the performance of his duties.[42] Note that, because the Prophetic Tradition is not part of the Divine Message, God did not correct Muhammad in every word or behavior in his daily life. It follows that, if everything that the Prophet did and said was revelation, there would have been no need for God to correct him on anything. This should not preclude the possibility that certain actions and words of the Prophet may have been guided by revelation, but they remain limited to the Prophet's performance of his duties and are not part of the universal Divine Message.[43] This, ultimately, is the reason why, in their individual lifetimes, Prophet Muhammad and the Enlightened Caliphs, his longtime companions who succeeded him in the leadership of the *umma*, were careful not to allow any records to be made of the Prophetic Tradition.

Prophet Muhammad, being a fallible, ordinary human being, was in no position to provide the assurance and security of the Holy Qur'an's integrity, let alone the need to complement it.[44] The Holy Qur'an, as a divine message, is perfect and complete by itself, and its contents need not be validated or supplemented by Prophetic Tradition or by any other authority.

It is easy then to answer Daniel Brown's question about how to differentiate between the fallible and the infallible.[45] Only the *conveyance* of the Qur'an is infallible, because God confirmed it. All of Prophet Muhammad's other words and deeds are fallible because they are human, without any distinction between the prophetic sphere and ordinary life sphere. Yet, Muhammad's words and deeds, while not mandatory and binding, retain great value and are worthy of the most careful analysis and understanding. Even though Muhammad was an ordinary human being, he was one with noble and virtuous qualities that earned him the divine choice to convey the Message. In particular, special attention is warranted to the words he uttered and the deeds he performed in the course of fulfilling his prophetic duties. The issue then becomes how to draw a line between the Prophetic Tradition associated with the performance of prophetic duties and the rest of the words and deeds associated with the Prophet's routine ordinary life. Where to draw that line depends on the scope of the role and mission assigned to Prophet Muhammad. By extension, some commentators have viewed the primary role of Prophet Muhammad as one of witness, providing testimony that the Qur'an was in fact originating from God.[46] Such a position is untenable, because God needs no one to witness for him. On the contrary, it is God who gave Prophet Muhammad, as He gave all other prophets before him, the *hujjas* (proofs) for people to believe that they may indeed be bringing a message from God.

Hisham Jait, observing that belief is a feeling which does not depend on rational evidence but instead is founded on divine revelation, suggests, "[t]his requires, of course, that we believe the prophet and even treat him as a saint."[47] True, we believe the message brought to us by the Prophet because it is divine and was delivered under divine guidance. We can also believe in the integrity of the Prophet in the performance of his mission because God selected him from among other mortals on the basis of his high morals. Still, this falls short of sacralizing the Prophet and treating him as a saint, with all the consequences attaching to such sacralization.[48] Following the fulfillment of his mission, and like any ordinary mortal, Prophet Muhammad died and is no longer present. As a result, he no longer has any mandatory role in our lives today, except for his legacy, which continues as a shining, guiding light.

The Assigned Role and Mission of Prophet Muhammad

Having established the human, nondivine nature of Prophet Muhammad, what was he? The Qur'an told us that he was neither a poet,[49] nor a priest,[50] nor an ensorcelled lunatic,[51] nor a plagiarizer;[52] all of which were accusations made against Muhammad because he claimed the uncommon role of prophet and messenger of God. These accusations could imply an abnormal mental condition. However, with these expected accusations, God clarified what Muhammad was and provided the *āyas* (signs) to prove his status. He was a prophet and a messenger with an assigned role and a clearly defined mission.

Our understanding of the role and mission of Prophet Muhammad is based solely on the divine statements found in the Qur'an. In fact, only this divine source can enable us to appreciate the role of Prophetic Tradition, because it allows us to determine if any action, reaction, or word included in the Prophetic Tradition occurred in the performance of an assigned mission or not. Previously, we encountered the claim relating to the potential abrogation of Qur'anic verses by Prophetic Tradition. Such claim could have been based only on one of two possible explanations: (1) either the Prophet is divine and his word is equivalent to God's word, which is tantamount to the sin of *shirk,* or association with God; or (2) his assigned role included making changes to the Qur'an through his words and deeds. Having refuted the first alternative in the preceding section, it remains to determine if the role of Prophet Muhammad included anything which could explain the power to abrogate verses of the Qur'an. We will explore the verses which define the obvious role and mission of the Prophet. Then we will consider other roles that have been attributed to him through the ages and scrutinize them against the provisions of the Qur'an.

Conveying the Message

The Qur'an expressly provides that Prophet Muhammad is primarily a messenger.[53] He is the messenger of God with the clear mission of conveying the Message to his immediate community of people, as did his predecessors in their individual communities.[54] Indeed, Muhammad is one among a great number of prophets and messengers that have been sent over time by God to various peoples to spread the divine truth,[55] so that divine justice may take place. The Holy Qur'an stipulates that receiving the divine truth is a prerequisite to appearing for final judgment.[56]

That mission of conveying the Divine Message rests upon the idea of *al-balāgh al-mubīn*, which means receiving the Message and passing it on, in clearly articulated form, to the people in the Messenger's community, *verbatim* as received, without addition or subtraction.[57] This idea appears repeatedly in the Qur'an.[58] We call this the primary mission because the Divine Message is contained, in its entirety, in the Qur'an. So it is important that the Qur'an be clearly identified as the message that came from God, and in the form in which it came, without modification of any kind.

HERALDING GOOD NEWS AND WARNING

With this understanding of the primary mission, clarified and ensured through *al-balāgh al-mubīn*, the task entrusted to Prophet Muhammad of transmitting the Message to his community has three related aspects: (1) heralding the good news to those who accept the Message and believe in it; (2) warning those who refuse to hear the Message—or those who hear it but fail to accept it—of the punishment that God may inflict on them on the Day of Judgment; and (3) acting as witness before God.[59] The first two aspects, heralding the good news and warning, are primarily included together in the various verses of the Qur'an which set forth the mission of the Prophet, because ultimately they constitute the two alternative faces of the reward and punishment system for accepting or rejecting the Message.[60] Yet, we find verses in which the warning mission is spelled out separately from that of heralding good news. They are mainly instances that occurred during the Meccan period of Muhammad's mission in the face of persecution against him by his own people who adamantly rejected his mission and the Message that he brought.[61] Indeed, the mission of warning appeared with the very first verses that were revealed to the Prophet, at the start of revelation. While Muhammad was lying down, enfolded in his garments, Archangel Gabriel instructed him to get up on his feet and "warn" his corrupt and unbelieving community.[62]

The fact that the mission of Prophet Muhammad started by conveying the Message and by warning does not mean that it did not continue in that way until the end of his life. Dominique Urvoy, among other commentators, argues that Prophet Muhammad "having been for eight years in Mecca nothing more than a warner ... became after the 'hijra' to Medina an armed prophet."[63] Such a conclusion is not valid, because the Qur'anic verses of the later Medinan period continued to limit the role of the Prophet to conveying the Message and to warning.[64]

Acting as a Witness

The role of Muhammad as a witness, as part of his mission, has been most misunderstood by early commentators and by clerics of our times. That role has been mystified and construed as one where Prophet Muhammad would, on the Day of Judgment, appear before God and act as witness against nonbelievers and sinners. Based on that misunderstanding, commentators have expanded the scope of Prophet Muhammad's role as witness to include the role of intercessor, which they attributed to him according to other verses of the Qur'an.[65] They have claimed that Prophet Muhammad, while attending the "prosecution" of people on the Day of Judgment as a witness, would act as intercessor before God on behalf of believers so that God might show mercy and compassion toward them and forgive them.[66]

It is useful to view the role of witness in context. Prophet Muhammad's role as a witness should not be given any mystical, beyond-human dimensions. The role of witnessing is not a role performed exclusively by prophets in general, or by Muhammad in particular. The Qur'an mentions that ordinary people will witness against each other, and Muhammad will witness over them all.[67] But most importantly, Prophet Muhammad, on the Day of Judgment, will not be rendering any services to God by providing Him information about doers of good or evil, nor will he be providing any advice about who deserves reward and who deserves punishment. Believing that God depends or relies on the Prophet and/or his predecessors to provide Him that information, would imply that God's knowledge is less than complete or that divine justice is less than perfect. If that were the case, one may wonder about the relevance of prophets, including Muhammad, being mandated to witness on the Day of Judgment. Prophet Muhammad's testimony, like that of any other witness, will help those who stand for judgment to accept the charges against them. He will be there to face and remind those people who might claim that he did not convey the Message to them or might claim that they accepted the Message while in fact they rejected it and abused its carrier. Verses Q4:40 to 42 are clear on this point.

> *He does not wrong anyone by as much as the weight of a speck of dust: He doubles any good deed and gives a tremendous reward of His own (40). What will they do when we bring a witness from each community, with you [Muhammad] as a witness against these people? (41) On that day, those who disbelieved and disobeyed the Prophet will wish that the earth could swallow them up: they will not be able to hide anything from God (42).*[68]

It is therefore clear that this role of witness is an integral part of God's system of justice. Because divine justice is universal, it is not limited to believers. It extends to nonbelievers and offers them convincing proofs before enforcing God's judgment. This role is a service to nonbelievers because believers already know and believe in God's all-encompassing and unlimited knowledge and justice, and they trust in His unlimited Mercy.

On the other hand, Prophet Muhammad will be a true witness. His role relates exclusively to acts and events that he witnessed. It is thus a limited and circumstantial role strictly related to the performance of his mission to convey the Message, herald good news, and warn. As such, that mission ends with his death. This is what Verse Q10:46 expressly confirms: "*Whether We let you [Prophet] see some of the punishment We have threatened them with, or cause you to die [first], they will return to Us: God is witness to what they do.*"[69] In this light, Prophet Muhammad's role is entirely circumstantial, perhaps justified by the fact that he was wronged while he spread the Message; and that it was necessary to provide a witness against those who wronged him. Otherwise, God declares in more than one verse of the Qur'an that He is the ultimate witness. His knowledge is infinite and does not need to be complemented by anyone, including angels and prophets.[70] Verse Q5:117, relating to Jesus, describes this limited role of messengers as witnesses, in the sense that they act with respect to events that they have effectively witnessed and no more. Jesus tells God: "*I said nothing to them except what you commanded me: 'Worship God, my Lord and your Lord.' I was a witness to them while I lived among them, But when you caused me to die, it was You who kept watch over them. You are witness over all things*."[71]

No Intercession

The theology of intercession falls outside the scope of this work. However, because the role of witness was extended to encompass intercession, it becomes important to dispel any misunderstandings over the role of the prophets, including Prophet Muhammad, or of any other person, in interceding before God on behalf of people, whether or not they are believers.[72] While God will always hear the prayers of believers for forgiveness of self and others—including prayers of prophets, messengers, and angels because of their exemplary ethics—the scope of prayer falls short of that of intercession. While a prayer is an act of humility where the praying person makes a case in a subdued manner without prejudgment of the outcome of that prayer, intercession implies a certain authority or influence of the intercessor over the judge or person exercising ultimate authority. It is true that, because God is the sole creator and Almighty and does not share his power with anyone, He consistently encourages His Messenger[73] and all believers to pray for pardon for the self and for others. However, prayer falls short of intercession with God, the latter being entirely ruled out because there is no authority over, or equivalent to, that of God.

Qur'anic verses dealing with intercession are of three types. The first category asserts the unicity of God, where despite the warnings made by Prophet Muhammad, people still believed in the ultimate intercession powers of the deities that they worshipped. That first category of verses confirms to them that neither deities of any kind nor any other creatures are empowered, or may otherwise provide any intercession. Intercession, unlike prayer, implies wielding of power on the part of the intercessor, and God is the sole Almighty whose power cannot be shared by anyone.[74]

The second category of verses confirms the fact that not only can no one intercede for another, but that only God can do so because only He wields power.[75] The interrelation between intercession, the unicity of God, and His infinite power is summed up in Verses Q39:43 and 44: *"Have they chosen others besides God to intercede for them? Say: 'Even though they have no power nor understanding?' Say: 'Intercession is wholly in the hands of God. He has sovereignty over the heavens and the earth. To Him shall you be recalled.'"*[76]

The third category of versus dealing with intercession rejects intercession on grounds of strict and perfect divine justice and compassion. In several verses, God declares that He is all-knowledgeable of what each person has intended, done, and not done, and for that purpose the intercessor cannot contribute anything to God's knowledge. Nor can the intercessor be more compassionate than God, because God is the most compassionate. God will thus let each person make his case and, in His ultimate justice and compassion, God will render the final judgment.[77] Any other interpretation would then wrongly imply that God has two standards of justice, one for those who were lucky enough to find an intercessor and another for the less fortunate who lacked an intercessor. In other words, the judgment could then potentially differ for the same person depending on whether he or she had an intercessor. This is the essence of divine justice and, for this reason, God repeatedly reaffirms in the Qur'an that there are no intercessions on the Day of Judgment.

That said, three apparent paradoxes relating to intercession should be clarified. One arises from a Qur'anic verse which, in referring to Prophet Muhammad, presumably indicates that he will not be disgraced before his people on the Day of Judgment. A second arises from a Qur'anic verse which refers to intercession by ordinary people. A third arises from a series of Qur'anic verses in which God seems to accept intercession, but only after He authorizes it.

In the first case, Verse 66:8 states:

O believers, turn in repentance, in sincere repentance, to God. Perhaps your Lord will remit your sins and admit you into Gardens beneath which rivers flow, upon a Day when God shall not discredit the Prophet and those who are with

him. Their light will radiate before them and on their right hands, and they shall
say: "Our Lord, make our light resplendent and forgive us, for You hold power
over all things."[78]

Some commentators saw in this verse evidence that Prophet Muhammad would not be disgraced on the Day of Judgment by God's refusal of his intercession.[79] But this verse is not about intercession or any divine privileges of the Prophet. It was simply a reminder by God to the Prophet's community that if they heeded his warnings and decided to repent and accept the Message, God would be there, ready to accept their repentance and vindicate His Prophet. God would thus fulfill the promises that He mandated the Prophet to make to his people in conveying the Message, that is, the promise of reward in paradise for those who genuinely repent and believe in the Message.

In the second case, Verse Q4:85 provides: "*Whoever [recommends and helps] a good cause becomes a partner therein: And whoever [recommends and helps] an evil cause, shares in its burden: And God hath power over all things.*"[80] In the preceding quotation, the phrase "recommends and helps" represents the translator's understanding and rendition of the Arabic term *shafā'a*, which primarily means intercession. However, in this context, the term clearly was not about intercession by anyone before God. It was a purely temporal issue, exclusively among humans, that is, people encouraging others and participating with them in a good deed or a bad deed. For that purpose, the verse promises divine acknowledgment and reward for someone intervening in a good cause and divine displeasure for intervening in a bad cause. This misunderstanding was even reflected in the rendition of this verse into English by some translators of the Qur'an.[81]

In the third case, there are a number of Qur'anic verses in which intercession is rejected, except when authorized by God.[82] None of these verses refer to intercession by Prophet Muhammad or by any other prophet. They talk about intercession in general, thereby implying intercession by anyone—including angels, saints, prophets, and ordinary persons—in favor of any other person. However, that reference to intercession was not made in any context of wielding power, since it requires the precondition of God's authorization.[83] For that purpose, God's authorization must be an authorization of the intercessor and of the person in whose favor the intercession is undertaken. In either case, both the intercessor and the intercessee must be true believers in the unicity of God and His attributes, and must deserve the favor. In other words, if all the conditions of being a true believer and a good person must be fulfilled to authorize the intercession, this means that by the time the authorization is granted, God has already made His judgment, and the intercession will not have resulted in changing God's judgment. This is fully consistent with divine justice and the unicity of God, with Whose judgments no one interferes or participates. That ruling is made conclusively in Verse Q32:4: "*Allah is the One who created the heavens and the earth and all that is between them in six days, then He positioned Himself on the Throne. Other than Him, there is neither a guardian for you, nor an intercessor. Would you then not observe the advice?*"[84] What, then, does "intercession with God's permission," as used in all these verses, mean? It means no more than an ordinary prayer by a person who is himself a believer and prays for the salvation of another person whom he truly believes to be deserving of salvation.

A Divine Mercy

The Qur'an states a very specific purpose for the four-fold prophetic mission of conveying the Message, heralding good news, warning, and acting as witness. The purpose of that mission is for God to make available His mercy universally. In other words, every person should have the opportunity to receive the Divine Message embodied in the Holy Qur'an. Every person is thus made aware of the rewards of accepting the Message and living by its values, as well as of the eternal punishment for declining the offered truth.[85] That is why Prophet Muhammad was enjoined to consistently remind the recipients of the Message of its most important contents.[86]

Making divine mercy available universally is not just a purpose of Muhammad's mission; it is the sole purpose of that mission: "*We have not sent thee, save as a mercy unto all beings.*"[87] Unlike the way some people like to portray God—as a jealous being, eager to see all persons submitted to Him in subservience—God is not affected in any manner nor is His ego nurtured or offended if the divine truth conveyed in the Message is accepted or rejected by its recipients. The sole purpose of that divine truth is to give further opportunities to humans to fulfill what God destined them for, and that is to be his trustees in this world.[88]

Because Muhammad's mission is a divine mercy of universal dimensions, Muhammad was encouraged, acting as a shining light, to spread out his preaching to ensure the widest reach for the Message.[89] For that same reason, Verses Q27:91 and 92 contain a powerful message about the well-defined role of the Prophet and the freedom of choice of persons.

> *I have only been commanded to worship the Lord of this city which God has sanctified. To Him all things belong (91). And I have been commanded to be a Muslim, and to recite the Qur'an. Whoso is guided, is guided for his own good. Whoso strays into error, say: "I am merely a warner."(92)*[90]

This is further proof that the Prophet was not asked to do anything for God's own sake. God sent him solely for the sake of humanity, to convey the Message and provide reasonable guidance to his people through its implementation.[91]

Not an Enforcer

Since divine justice requires free will, Prophet Muhammad's mission did not include any duty to compel people to believe.[92] Initially, as the Prophet faced the rejection of the Message among his tribesmen of Mecca with deep disappointment, God gave him comfort with His assurances that if he fulfills his primary mission to convey the Message, he should not be concerned or otherwise hold himself responsible if anyone refuses or fails to accept it, as set forth in Verse Q2:119: *"Surely, We have sent you with the truth, as a bearer of good tidings, and a warner, and you will not be asked about the people of Hell."*[93] Indeed, it was sufficient for the Prophet to pass on the Message accurately, in its entirety, together with the frequent reminders and warnings that he was entrusted to make, and then let each individual make a choice freely to accept or reject the Message. To emphasize that right to free choice, the Qur'anic verses did not stop at stating that the Prophet's mission did not extend beyond conveying the Message. Those same verses went on to specifically confirm that the prophetic mission did not include enforcing the Message or otherwise securing that it is accepted and implemented, as set forth in Verse Q50:45: *"We know well what they say, and you are not (sent) as one who compels them. So exhort, through the Qur'an, the one who fears My warning,"*[94]

Not only did the mission of Prophet Muhammad not include the duty to compel people to believe or otherwise accept the Message and live by it, but it expressly stated that the mission in question does not actually include the authority to do it. It was not left to Prophet Muhammad's discretion to determine whether or not to enforce the Message. The rationale for excluding enforcement from the Prophet's mission was to shield him from any inadvertent attempt to exercise exclusive divine prerogatives, as set forth in Verse Q2:272 in the following terms: *"Not upon you, [O Muhammad], is [responsibility for] their guidance, but Allah guides whom He wills."*[95] In fact, enforcement consists of compelling people to comply, then punishing those who fail to do so. Since compliance consists primarily in believing the Message, punishing would imply that the enforcer has reached the conviction that the culprit is a nonbeliever. The immediate concern is then to determine how a proper judgment can be made. Could the Prophet conclusively tell what's inside the hearts and minds of people being punished? The answer is no, because the Qur'an says in Verse Q16:125 that only God has that knowledge: *"Call to the way of your Lord with wisdom and fair counsel, and debate with them in the fairest manner. Your Lord knows best who has strayed from His path; He knows best who are guided aright."*[96] Assuming the person being so punished indeed did not believe, would he not be precluded from repenting and redeeming himself if he were to be prematurely punished by other than God? In fact, God gives the chance to people until the last minute of their lives to reach the truth and believe; even sinners can hope for God's clemency and pardon.[97] By punishing them ahead of time, the person inflicting the punishment would be exercising prerogatives of God.

The rationale for denying the Prophet the authority to enforce the Message is to preserve the free will of people and the unlimited opportunity for each individual to accept the truth at any time in that individual's life.

Another rationale is to protect the enforcer from inadvertently exercising God's exclusive prerogatives. This explains that the Holy Qur'an repeatedly reminds Prophet Muhammad that God did not appoint him to act for Him as "divine guardian" or act on His behalf as "taskmaster;"[98] in fact, *ḥafīẓ* and *wakīl*, the original terms in Arabic for divine guardian and taskmaster, are listed among the ninety-nine attributes of God. And, to avoid doubt, the Qur'an further expressly draws the line delimiting the Prophet's authority by spelling out, in Verse Q13:40, that the Prophet conveys the Message and God reserves judgment: *"Whether We let you glimpse in some measure the scourge We promise them, or call you back to Us before We smite them, your mission is only to give warning: it is for Us to do the reckoning."*[99]

It is important to keep clearly in mind the rationale behind that limitation in Prophet Muhammad's mission because it has serious consequences which could adversely affect our understanding of Islam and its unlimited universal scope. Being a matter of basic faith and not of a circumstantial tactical nature, this approach did not change following the transfer to Medina and receipt of the leave to fight. These verses were not abrogated as is often claimed. Divine mercy and justice remained unchanged, and God's exclusive prerogatives were not reduced, when the Prophet and his followers' position of weakness in Mecca changed to one of strength as they moved to Medina. Divine mercy, divine justice, and divine prerogatives are of the essence; they are universal and eternal, and do not change with changing human circumstances. By way of illustration, Verses Q88:21 to 26 provide as follows: *"So [Prophet] warn them: your only task is to give warning (21), you are not there to control them (22), As for those who turn away and disbelieve (23), God will inflict the greatest torment upon them (24). It is to Us they will return (25), and then it is for Us to call them to account (26)."*[100] These verses sum up all the substantive parts of the Prophet's mission: Verse 21 sets out his primary role of spreading the Message by way of warning and reminding; Verse 22 establishes the principle that the Prophet is not mandated to compel people to believe; Verses 23 to 26 set forth the rational corollary of that principle; namely, reckoning and judgment are the exclusive domain of

God. Any claim that Verse 22 has been abrogated would logically entail that its corollaries have been abrogated as well. In other words, God will no longer have the final say on judgment and punishment. Such a claim clearly constitutes a major sin. That is why the same message was delivered unchanged in its substance to the Prophet throughout his prophetic career, that is, from its start in Mecca when Muhammad's message was being ridiculed, until almost the last day of his life in Medina when he was at the apogee of his power.[101] We even find that well into the Medinan period, Prophet Muhammad was still being reminded that even the primary duty of spreading the Message is not intended to be performed freely, but instead only with the permission of God, as set forth in Verses Q33:45 and 46: *"Prophet, We have sent you forth as a witness, a bearer of good tidings, and a warner (45); one who shall call men to God by His leave and guide them like a shining light (46)."*[102]

Throughout his life, Prophet Muhammad never pretended to enforce the provisions of the Qur'an or compel anyone into believing or performing any religious duties because he was best placed to avoid committing the sin of *shirk*, or, associating with—and purporting to exercise the powers or prerogatives of—God. In any event, whenever an inadvertent action on the part of the Prophet could have been interpreted as a potential act of compelling, he was promptly reminded of the essence of his role.[103] This is a domain of Islamic history that has been misunderstood by commentators and *fuqahā'* (jurisprudents) alike, and that misunderstanding has been perpetuated through the sacralization of their works and by treating those works as part of the Scriptures and sources of the faith.[104]

Arbitrator Role

Since Prophet Muhammad was specifically precluded from any enforcement role of the Message, this should dispel the widely accepted claim that Islam is a system of government and that Prophet Muhammad founded the first Islamic state in Medina.[105] Yet, one might legitimately ask about the purport of the Qur'anic verses which exhort believers to bring up issues to be ruled upon by Prophet Muhammad. This brings us to the temporal mission of Prophet Muhammad to act as arbitrator among the people of the *umma*, the community of believers.[106] Verse Q4:65 provides as follows: "*By your Lord they will not be true believers until they let you decide between them in all matters of dispute, and find no resistance in their souls to your decisions, accepting them totally.*"[107] This and other verses (listed below) have been wrongly interpreted as mandating Prophet Muhammad to act as judge among people and to do so by divine law.

It is often believed that Prophet Muhammad was a mandated ruler or judge, with sole authority to render judgments. That is not the case, because God is the sole and ultimate judge, and Prophet Muhammad could only act as arbitrator in disputes that were brought to his attention. When placed in its proper historical context, Verse Q4:65 should not be perceived as setting forth a divinely assigned mission to the Prophet. Recall that the prophetic mission came in the midst of a bedouin tribal society in which organized state structures, including institutionalized administration of justice, were nonexistent and where the tribal chief exercised absolute authority over the members of the tribe, including the settlement of disputes. In such an environment, a dispute between persons belonging to two different tribes could likely lead to an armed feud between the two tribes. Islam sought to change that social order: (1) by replacing tribal ties with the *umma* bond, namely, one based on the community of belief in one and the same God; and (2) by founding that new society and settling disputes among its members on the basis of the principles of fairness and justice set forth in the Holy Qur'an, as opposed to principles based on *'aṣabiyya* (blood-based tribal relations). It is on that basis that Prophet Muhammad organized the first *umma* consisting of his companions who emigrated with him from Mecca and the Muslims, Jews, and pagans[108] of Medina. That organization was evidenced by a charter that the leaders of the various groups approved to indicate their willingness to live in harmony, based on these principles of fairness and justice. Because it was the first *umma* to be organized in light of the principles of the new faith, it was normal that it be led by Prophet Muhammad, as carrier of the Message, so as to establish that the new social order was viable, while he performed the essence of his mission of spreading the Message. That arbitration role was therefore intended to enable the Prophet to demonstrate that dispute settlement could be achieved based on the principles of fairness and justice as opposed to tribal rules.

Heralding Principles of Fairness and Justice

While the role of arbitrator was circumstantial as the affairs of the *umma* were being organized, the principles of fairness and justice brought about for the new social order were of the essence of the Message. Verses Q5:48 and 50 confirm this.

> *To you We revealed the Book with the Truth, confirming previous Scriptures and witnessing to their veracity. So judge between them as God revealed and do not follow their whims, to turn you away from the truth revealed to you. For every community We decreed a law and a way of life. Had God willed, He could have made you a single community—but in order to test you in what He revealed to you. So vie with one another in virtue. To God is your homecoming, all of you, and He will then acquaint you with that over which you differed (48)... Do they truly desire the law of paganism? But who is fairer than God in judgment for a people firm of faith? (50)*[109]

Despite the circumstantial perception arising from Verse Q4:65 that arbitration is mandatory,[110] it was left to people to seek Prophet Muhammad's involvement to resolve their disputes. It was also optional for Prophet Muhammad to accept or not accept the assignment in each case, provided always that if he agreed to judge, he had no choice but to do so in fairness. This is clearly spelled out in Verse Q5:42: "If they come to you, *judge among them* or turn away *from them, they will not harm you one jot.* But if you judge, *then judge among them with fairness, for God loves those who act with fairness.*"[111]

The noble principles of fairness and justice contained in the Divine Message brought by Prophet Muhammad are the essence of the universality of that message and transcend the limited scope of the frameworks in which they have been placed. Unfortunately, these principles have been confined to a construction according to which the Divine Message carried with it a divine legal system (Shari'a). The legal system developed by the 'ulama', or religious scholars, of the early period based on these and other principles, acquired a form of sanctity and became part of the faith.

As a result, this legal system froze in time and failed to progress. For this and other reasons, it is not possible to subscribe to the view that Prophet Muhammad was a lawgiver.[112] What Prophet Muhammad brought in the Message goes beyond—and transcends the concept of—law giving, into setting forth the principles of universal fairness and justice which can potentially form the basis of any legal system, at any time and in any place.

In reflecting on the mission of Prophet Muhammad, one would ask, how the sunna and hadith—the Prophet's deeds and words—became a source of religious faith, practice and law? Did the Prophet's mission include explaining and supplementing the Qur'an?

The Potential Scriptural Foundation of Prophetic Tradition

None of the terms referring to Prophetic Tradition—namely sunna and hadith appear in the Holy Qur'an. At first view, Prophetic Tradition and adherence to it are not divinely provided for or mandated. Might this concept have developed later in light of the divinely mandated mission of Prophet Muhammad?

The mission of Prophet Muhammad is to convey the Message, as disclosed by God, to preach the rewards of accepting the Message, and to warn of the consequences of rejecting it. We have also seen that, because the Message is a divine mercy and God's justice is impeccable, Prophet Muhammad was not attributed any powers or privileges which interfered with divine justice, such as enforcement powers or intercession privileges. The recipients of the Message were thus left entirely free to accept it or reject it. Within that strict framework for his mission, the actions, reactions, and words of the Prophet are not part of the Message. On a first impression, Prophetic Tradition cannot serve as a source of religion or divine law unless the Holy Qur'an contains provisions to the contrary.

Proponents of Prophetic Tradition as a source of Islam have relied on three categories of provisions in the Qur'an to support their views: (1) a verse which presumably declares the Prophet's actions, reactions, and words as divinely inspired, and verses which mandate the belief in the Prophet; (2) verses which presumably imply that the Prophet had rule-making powers, whether by way of adding to the rules and commands of the Holy Qur'an or by interpreting, complementing, or commenting on any of its provisions; and (3) several verses expressly enjoining believers to obey the Prophet. In this section we will explore these arguments and verses which served as bases for such a role being attributed to sunna and hadith.

The Nature of Prophetic Tradition

The claim that all Prophetic Tradition constitutes Divine Revelation is based on the assumption that, commencing with the start of revelation, all behaviors of Prophet Muhammad were guided by God. That claim was first made authoritatively by Imam al-Shafi'i, leader of the school of jurisprudence that carries his name. He is the prime architect of the Prophetic Tradition as second source of Shari'a, to which a value almost equal to that of the Holy Qur'an is attributed. That position is implied in al-Shafi'i's assertion that the Qur'an, though the word of God, "cannot abrogate the Sunna because to recognize this possibility would be to nullify the explanatory role of the Sunna."[113]

Claims about the revealed nature of Prophetic Tradition have been based in part on certain verses which require believers to believe in God and His Prophet, such as Verse Q64:8: "*So, believe in Allah and His Messenger, and in the light We have sent down. And Allah is fully aware of what you do.*"[114] But clearly these verses are about believing in the role of Muhammad as prophet and messenger of God, that is, believing in what he conveys of the Message in this capacity.

The verses most cited by commentators in support of Prophetic Tradition as being divinely revealed, and to be treated as a source of Islam, are Q53:3 and 4 which provide as follows: "*He does not speak out of his own fancy (3). This is an inspired revelation (4).*"[115] While most of the commentators, in their interpretations of the Qur'an, have limited the scope of these verses to the conveyance of the Qur'an, still some thought that their scope extended to everything that the Prophet said or did. In so doing, they were echoing the views of al-Ghazali[116] and Ibn Hazm al-Andalusi,[117] among others. In this respect, it is important to examine these views to try to arrive at a reasonable conception of the nature of Prophetic Tradition.

First, the claim that everything that Prophet Muhammad did or said was divine inspiration can be ruled out in light of the fact that God occasionally cautioned the Prophet against certain behaviors. God would not have brought his prophet's attention to things he said or did or abstained from doing if, in doing so, the Prophet was consistently guided by divine inspiration.

Second, it is safe to assume that we are not qualified, nor do we have the means to determine and to rule out entirely, any potential divine inspiration associated with Prophetic Tradition. Indeed, divine inspiration is not restricted to prophets and messengers, and God can occasionally inspire ordinary people with revelation. However, that revelation remains private and is not intended as a universal message for widespread conveyance. Even when divine inspiration is addressed to prophets and messengers, not all such inspiration is intended to be conveyed universally; only the part that God specifically designates as a message is.

When Divine Revelation to Prophet Muhammad commenced, starting with Sūrat al-'Alaq, the Prophet kept it to himself and did not spread the word beyond his wife, Khadija, and her cousin, Waraqa Ibn Nawfal, who had a close relationship with Muhammad. He actually shared that inspiration with Khadija and her cousin mostly out of fear of the moment and the intense emotion it elicited. Only with the Sūrat Al-Muddathir was Muhammad directed to spread the Message, as set forth in Verses Q74:1 and 2: "*O thou wrapped up (in the mantle) (1)! Arise and deliver thy warning (2)!*"[118] Therefore, it is possible that, throughout his mission, Prophet Muhammad may have received divine inspiration which is not part of the Message. It is for that purpose that the overwhelming religious doctrine went to great lengths to identify the actions, reactions, and words of Prophet Muhammad so as to separate what was revelation from what was not. However, this exercise would not have any imperative relevance unless Prophetic Tradition so inspired was a message to be spread, and as such is binding.

Third, divine inspiration does not necessarily, by the mere fact that it is divine, carry a universal binding effect. Binding effect is presumed with respect to such inspiration which constitutes a message, and then only to the extent that it contains dogmas and other matters to be complied with. For example, the Holy Qur'an contains a great number of verses which tell tales of peoples past, stories for people to ponder in the process of their acceptance of the Message and believing it. There are also in the Holy Qur'an a number of verses intended to guide some of Prophet Muhammad's steps in performing his mission. As such, and though they are part of the Message, most of the binding instructions contained in them are exclusively practical instructions to the Prophet, and possibly to his companions. The message in those verses to the rest of the people is informative, with an implied encouragement to ponder them and draw from them the appropriate conclusions. That said, it is also possible and plausible that Prophet Muhammad may have received divine guidance in the performance of his mission outside the scope of the Message.

Finally, it is also possible and plausible that Prophet Muhammad may have received divine guidance in clarifying certain verses of the Qur'an to the recipients of the Message, advising his companions on certain rules of daily conduct and behavior, or simply with respect to his own conduct and behavior. Should these divinely inspired actions, reactions, and words of the Prophet carry any binding effect, either because they are divinely inspired or because they relate to certain parts of the Message? Before attempting to develop a convincing answer to this question, we should explore the Scriptures which mandate the need to obey the Prophet.

Potential Rule-Making Powers of the Prophet

Early and modern-day commentators have variously relied on three categories of verses to support the dogma about the binding effect of Prophetic Tradition.[119] The first category of verses refers to prohibitions enacted by Prophet Muhammad, thereby implying that he had special privileges to enact such prohibitions, as in Verse Q9:29.

> *Fight those People of the Book who do not believe in Allah, nor in the Last Day, and do not take as unlawful what Allah* and His Messenger have declared as unlawful, *and do not profess the Faith of Truth; (fight them) until they pay Jizya with their own hands while they are subdued.*[120]

In this verse, the reference to declaring unlawful by God and the Prophet induced several commentators to believe that the Prophet had been empowered to add to the list of prohibitions mandated by God in the Qur'an. Each of al-Zamakhshari,[121] al-Baydawi,[122] and al-Razi[123]—to name but a few of the early exegetes—and al-Tantawi[24] among the contemporary ones have interpreted the verse in question as a reference to prohibitions set forth in the Holy Qur'an and in the Prophetic Tradition. In reality, the reference in this verse about forbidding by God and the Prophet should not be construed as a reference to prophetic privileges, which are distinct from the infinite powers of God. It is merely about the Prophet conveying to people that which God has determined, in the Holy Qur'an, to prohibit. Any confusion about this should be dispelled by the clear language of Verse Q66:1 (*"O Prophet, why do you ban [on yourself] something that Allah has made lawful for you, seeking to please your wives...?"*[125]), in which God blames the Prophet for having vowed to impose upon himself a prohibition that God had not imposed.[126]

Indeed, the Holy Qur'an clearly spells out that the power to impose prohibitions of the haram category is the exclusive domain of God, which He does not share with anyone, including the Prophet. For that purpose, Verse Q16:116 considers those who declare any lawful thing as haram to be liars upon God: *"Hence, do not utter falsehoods by letting your tongues determine [at your own discretion], 'This is lawful and that is forbidden,' thus attributing your own lying inventions to God: for, behold, they who attribute their own lying inventions to God will never attain to a happy state!"*[127] On that basis, a review of the provisions of the Qur'an indicates that the number of haram matters, that is, strictly prohibited under any circumstance (other than for necessity with respect to some of the items) are very limited and are specifically listed in the Holy Qur'an. They are: any form of association with God (Verse Q6:151 and Q7:33); imputing to God what is not in the Qur'an (Verse Q7:33); the commission of shameful acts (*al-fāhisha* and *al-baghiy*) and sins (*al-ithm*) (Verses Q6:151 and Q7:33); eating pork, blood, and animals found dead (Verses Q2:173, Q5:3, and Q6:145 and 16:115); killing a person (Verses 6:151, Q17:33, and Q25:68); the practice of *riba,* or charging and paying usurious rates of interest on loans taking advantage of the need or inexperience of the borrower (Verse Q2:275); hunting while in *iḥrām* clothing in Mecca (Verse Q5:95); driving people out of their homes (Verse Q2:85); marriage among persons within specific ranges of close relationship (Verse Q4:23); and the marriage of a believer to a nonbeliever and to an adulterer (Verse Q24:3). Yet, in practice, the list of divine prohibitions has grown exponentially to include numerous matters rightly or wrongly attributed to the Prophet, including trivial matters such as the prohibitions of wearing gold and silk by men, the trimming of eyebrows by women and men alike, building sculptures and making paintings representing human beings, to name but a few of that long list.[128]

In the second category, we find the verses which refer to *ḥikma* as a Divine Revelation that the Prophet must teach to the people, alongside the Qur'anic message, in the course of fulfillment of his mission. Imam al-Shafi'i[129] and other advocates of treating Prophetic Tradition as a primary source of Islam have construed the term *ḥikma,* or wisdom, as a reference to the Prophetic Tradition itself, namely the religious laws, regulations, details, and clarifications arising from the sayings, actions, and reactions of the Prophet in his lifetime following the start of revelation. Several verses of the Qur'an make references to wisdom, such as Q3:164 as follows: *"Allah has surely conferred favor on the believers when He raised in their midst a messenger from among themselves who recites to them His verses and makes them pure and teaches them the Book and the Wisdom, while earlier, they were in open error."*[130] Al-Tabari,[131] al-Zamakhshari,[132] al-Qurtubi,[133] and Ibn Kathir[134] are among the early exegetes who considered wisdom to be a reference to the Prophetic Tradition. They do not give any basis for their conclusion; they merely take it for granted.[135] Among the modern exegetes, al-Sha'rawi[136] and al-Tantawi[137] follow that same route, except that al-Tantawi went to great lengths to include all the laws and jurisprudence developed based on Prophetic Tradition. Even in an English translation of the Qur'an, one translator included a bracket to provide his own interpretation of the meaning of *ḥikma* to encompass the entire Prophetic Tradition and all the rules of law and jurisprudence derived from it.[138] These views ignore the fact that the wisdom in question, otherwise called *hikma,* is revealed by God, as confirmed in Verse Q4:113: "Allah has revealed *to you* the Book and the wisdom*, and has taught you what you did not know. The grace of Allah on you has always been great.*"[139] Under Verse Q33:34, which uses the term "wisdom" along the same lines as in Verse Q3:164, al-Tabari insists on treating "wisdom" as a divinely revealed Prophetic Tradition which did not translate into Qur'anic verses. This is unacceptable because it is inconsistent with the statement by God that He has included in the Holy Qur'an his entire message, that is, all that is needed in a clearly spelled-out manner (Q16:89 says: *"And We have revealed to you the Book, an exposition of everything, and guidance, and mercy, and glad tidings for the Muslims."*)[140] This confirms that *hikma* is not some revealed wisdom outside the scope of the Holy Qur'an, but that it is an integral part of it.[141] Indeed, with respect to Verses Q54:4 and 5 in which the term "wisdom" is used, the commentators this time are unanimous that, unlike the case of the other verses cited, the wisdom being referred to is an integral part of the Holy Qur'an and nothing else. Verses Q54:4 and 5 provide as follows: *"And there has come to them as much news (of the earlier communities) as it is enough to deter (4) (containing) a perfect wisdom. But the warnings are of no avail (to them) (5)."*[142] In this light, it becomes confusing to give the same term *hikma* multiple meanings that are not related (i.e., one time as Prophetic Tradition and the other as part of the Holy Qur'an), for no reason of context or otherwise.

However, Ibn 'Ashour[143] did not subscribe to the views which equate *hikma,* or wisdom, with Prophetic Tradition. He offers a good definition of *hikma,* as mere wisdom which is an integral part of the Divine Message contained in the Qur'an and explains, "'Wisdom' *includes all the rules of Sharia'a, namely the rules of ethics and the laws of conduct, which shield the souls from evil and the social order from trouble.*" For that purpose, Ibn 'Ashour refers to Verse Q2:269, which states: *"He gives the Wisdom to whomsoever He will, and whoso is given the Wisdom, has been given much good; yet none remembers but men possessed of minds."*[144] From this verse, it is clear that Prophet Muhammad is not the sole recipient of wisdom, and that it is not incumbent on the believers to restrict wisdom to the Prophet's understanding of it, but that it is the prerogative of each person to decide how to understand and act upon wisdom.

In the third category, we refer to the verses which speak of the Prophet's potential involvement in explaining or clarifying the provisions of the Qur'an. One such example appears in Verse Q16:44: *"(We sent them) with clear signs and scriptures. And We sent down the Reminder (the Qur'an) to you, so that you explain to the people what has been revealed for them, and so that they may ponder."*[145] Among the early exegetes, al-Razi and al-Qurtubi saw in this verse a mandate to the Prophet to explain the Qur'an either because certain of its provisions are not clear or because certain other provisions are global and general. This would presumably make it necessary for the Prophet to clarify the methodology of understanding, and details of implementation of, these Qur'anic provisions and, where necessary, to complement them. Among the modern commentators, we find that M. M. al-Sha'rawi went far along this line of thinking.[146] Imam al-Shafi'i goes even further, asserting that the Holy Qur'an could not be properly understood without the Prophetic Tradition, and such a view was and continues to be echoed by others.[147]

Views such as these can be refuted because they assume that God's message is either incomplete or unclear. These views are unacceptable because they are incompatible with the perfection of God and that of the Divine Message. As Ibn 'Ashour rightly points out,[148] these views are inconsistent with the provisions of the verse under consideration, which invites people to ponder, as opposed to merely accept, the Prophet's explanation of God's revelations as received through the Prophet. Ibn 'Ashour further refers to Verse Q16:89 (*"And We have revealed to you the Book, an exposition of everything, and guidance, and mercy, and glad tidings for the Muslims"*[149]) in which God declares that He has explained everything in the Qur'an, and the rest is for everyone to ponder and understand, each in his or her own way. On that basis, God did not leave any substantive issues incomplete or unclear for the Prophet to amplify and complement or to explain. In the end, when Verses Q16:44 and 89 are read together it becomes clear that what is meant in Verse Q16:44 is that the Prophet merely puts before the people what was revealed to them in the Holy Qur'an in terms of signs and Scriptures.

An indicative observation drawn from the Qur'an helps us to sum up this examination of the potential rule-making powers of the Prophet. The Qur'an contains a large number of verses in which God addresses Prophet Muhammad and which start with the phrases "they consult you about" or "they ask you about." Each one of these verses contains a clarification relating to a specific topic on which Muhammad had sought God's guidance to provide the answer. Bearing in mind that these explanations are directly provided by God to His Prophet, the implication is that the Prophet did not have—or was not otherwise empowered to provide—an answer to the questions, which are answered by God. One would expect that if, in fact, the Prophet was mandated to explain or amplify and to complement the Qur'an, he would have provided the answers by himself without relying on God to provide each and every answer.[150] In all these verses, God expressly instructs His messenger that, if anyone seeks his fatwa (religious opinion) on any matter, such fatwas are the exclusive realm of God and not that of any human being, whether a prophet or a cleric.[151]

Obedience to Prophet Muhammad

The Holy Qur'an contains a great number of verses enjoining believers to obey the Prophet. Most of these injunctions couple obedience to the Prophet with the mandated obedience to God. While obedience to God does not create any confusion or issue in terms of accepting the principles of faith, performing the worship requirements, and complying with the rules and prohibitions contained in the Holy Qur'an, the Qur'anic requirement to obey the Prophet is somehow more problematic. Several commentators took the injunctions to obey the Prophet out of context and interpreted them as a binding mandate to follow the traditions of the Prophet. This perception of the injunction to obey the Prophet was also generally accepted by a wide range of early and modern-day jurisprudents as a strong foundation on which to base the mandatory nature and binding effect of Prophetic Tradition.

We can dismiss extreme positions which attribute to Prophet Muhammad para-human qualities and perceive him as the agent of God.

According to al-Mawdudi, while admitting that Prophet Muhammad is an ordinary person when acting in his personal capacity, his acts turn divine when he acts as a prophet. Following that argument, Prophet Muhammad in his prophetic capacity is the agent of God and acts on His behalf; hence the Qur'anic command to obey the Prophet.[152] But God does not use humans as His agents, His tools being primarily the angels. The Holy Qur'an does not contain any provision designating Prophet Muhammad as agent of God. On the contrary, keeping in mind that the agent speaks for, and exercises the powers of, the principal, namely God in this instance, God made sure to clarify that the Prophet did not speak for him but simply conveyed His message, without any enforcement powers. For the same reason, we do not subscribe to the interpretation by Imam al-Shafi'i, among others, according to which the injunction to obey the Prophet is an injunction to treat Prophetic Tradition as divine commands to be followed at all times as complements to the Message.[153]

In reality, and following a more focused, in-context reading of the relevant Qur'anic verses, obedience to the Prophet is exclusively about following his leadership in connection with the performance of his mission of conveying the Message in his capacity as prophet and messenger. It is helpful to remember that God instructed his Prophet and Companions to leave Mecca and its polytheist community and emigrate to Medina. A new community would be established there to provide him a reasonable environment of stability that would enable him to carry out the duties that he was prevented from performing in Mecca. The agreement entered into with the leaders of the Jewish and newly converted Muslim tribes of Medina[154] sets forth the principles of coexistence among the parties. However, considering the tribal nature of the Medinan environment, the agreement in question did not provide for the creation of any institutions. It solely replaced tribal justice with the Prophet's arbitration for settlement of disputes among the parties. Thus Prophet Muhammad was made the actual leader of that community of believers without, however, formally attributing to him any rule-making powers.

In this setup, there was no divine intention to establish Prophet Muhammad as a king, or a political ruler, of Medina or of any other city or region. Placed in the context of the instructions to the Prophet and his companions to leave Mecca, the purpose of the social arrangement was to create a nucleus for a new society with a faith-based culture, as opposed to a tribal-based culture. Most importantly, however, the new alignment was also intended to provide the proper environment for the Prophet to carry out his mission, that of spreading the Message. In that environment, most members of the newly created community had a role in assisting the Prophet in performing his divinely assigned duties. They had to fulfill that role, first, by contributing to the development of the faith-based culture through their obedience to God, namely by accepting the principles of faith, performing the worship requirements, and complying with the rules and prohibitions contained in the Qur'an.[155] Second, and very importantly, they were expected to assist the Prophet in his endeavors to repel aggressions aiming to disrupt the faith-based living of the believers and prevent the Prophet from fulfilling his mission of spreading the Message. These aggressions were launched early on by the Meccan polytheists against the Prophet and his new community, commencing with the battle of Badr.[156] They were followed by disputes, which led to wars, within the new community itself when a number of Jews of Medina, aided by hypocrites, nonbelievers who had pretended to have accepted Muhammad's message, took action to obstruct the Prophet's efforts in repelling aggression and spreading the Message.[157]

It is in this context that the verses requiring obedience to the Prophet should be read. Any other reading of these verses could, if taken out of context, result in unintended interpretations, that contradict, or are inconsistent with, other Qur'anic verses. The need to keep in mind the context for these verses is evidenced by the fact that all instances, except one, in which the believers are enjoined to obey the Prophet came in verses revealed following the emigration from Mecca to Medina. This was the start of the Prophet's leadership role: first, he led his companions out of Mecca; second, he organized the community of believers in Medina; and third, he led the defense against the aggressions of the polytheists and dealt with the disputes that opposed the Prophet and his followers to the Jews and hypocrites.

Instances mandating obedience to the Prophet primarily appeared in straightforward commands, in the form of "obey God and obey the Prophet" or "obey God and the Prophet."[158] Most of these instances were merely about urging followers to obey the daily instructions of the Prophet as leader of the community, particularly in dealing with aggressions and disputes.[159] The other instances of the direct command to obey the Prophet came in connection with the delivery of a certain divine command or general worship-related requirements relevant to the community as a whole.[160] Therefore, these are injunctions primarily to obey the commands of God, and the instructions of the Prophet—as carrier of the Message—for the proper performance of these commands. They are thus unrelated to any presumed rule-making privileges of the Prophet that could survive his role as Messenger.

The mandate to obey the Prophet did not come only in the form of a straightforward command using the term "obey." It came also in other forms that strongly imply the need to obey him. One such form talks about the punishments for those who resist the lead of the Prophet or who display a hostile attitude toward him.[161] In these instances, the concepts of *'Iṣyān* (rebellion and resistance) and *shiqāq* (quarrel and obstruction) are used to warn against resisting and antagonizing the Prophet, or otherwise quarrelling with him and disputing his actions. All these instances are about warnings to the hypocrites, who in appearance pretended to have accepted the Message of Islam, then showed belligerence to the Prophet. In that same context, Verse Q8:27 warns against betraying the Prophet. In one instance, a person was mandated to act as an intermediary for negotiations in the context of a dispute with Jews of Medina; this verse warns against betrayal of the Prophet by that person.[162]

However, one instance should be singled out from the ones cited here which, if taken out of context, may appear to support a potential claim for universal obedience to the Prophet. It is the instance dealt with in Verse Q33:36, which provides as follows: *"It is not open for a believing man or a believing woman, once Allah and His messenger have decided a thing, that they should have a choice about their matter; and whoever disobeys Allah and His messenger, he indeed gets off the track, falling into an open error.*"[163] This verse was simply about a certain woman who had refused the Prophet's decision to marry her to his adoptive son, and it came to scold her for refusing a decision made by the Prophet. This context is indicative of an occurrence unrelated to any rule-making prerogatives of the Prophet that survived his lifetime.[164]

In another instance, we find an equally apparent powerful form, in the Arabic language, in which people are told to accept whatever the Prophet brings them and abstain from whatever he forbids: "*Whatever the Messenger gives you, take; whatever he forbids you, give over.*" Taking this out of context,[165] several commentators quickly concluded that it was about the general command to heed the rules of action and abstention set forth by the Prophet, thereby setting the scriptural foundation for the Prophetic Tradition to be treated as a primary source of Islam.[166] However, when put in context, this verse is merely about the allocation and distribution of the spoils of war and the distribution of shares among the warriors who won the first battle of Badr when they were about to fight one another over them. Verse 59:7 reads: "*Whatsoever spoils of war God has given to His Messenger from the people of the cities belongs to God, and His Messenger, and the near kinsman, orphans, the needy and the traveler, so that it be not a thing taken in turns among the rich of you. Whatever the Messenger gives you, take; whatever he forbids you, give over. And fear God; surely God is terrible in retribution.*"[167] This verse states the rule of entrusting the Prophet with the allocation and distribution of war spoils, so that people should accept whatever he allocates to them and comply with whatever he forbids them from sharing.

Another powerful form, in Arabic, was also used to support and confirm the scriptural foundation for Prophetic Tradition as the primary source of Islam. It appears in Verse Q33:21: "*There is indeed a good model for you in the Messenger of Allah—for the one who has hope in Allah and the Last Day, and remembers Allah profusely.*"[168] However, as in the case of Verse Q59:7, this verse has a specific context. It was about the battle of the Trench, in which a large number of the Medinan companions of the Prophet failed to join. So the verse in question is blaming those who stayed behind. They are told that the Prophet is a good model to be followed, in terms of bearing all the hardships required in order to prevail against adversity and the forces of evil. So here again the verse is about the leadership of the Prophet in times of adversity, and it is unrelated to Prophetic Tradition and any other presumed universal rule-making role of the Prophet.[169]

Two other verses help us to see that the command to obey the Prophet is entirely temporary and circumstantial, stemming from his role as *de facto* leader of his community, and then for no purpose other than to enable him carry out a divine mission. The first of these two verses is Q4:64.

> *All the messengers We sent were meant to be obeyed, by God's leave. If only [the hypocrites] had come to you [Prophet] when they wronged themselves, and begged God's forgiveness, and the Messenger had asked forgiveness for them, they would have found that God accepts repentance and is most merciful.*[170]

The people being referenced in this verse by the pronoun "they" are the hypocrites who failed to bring their disputes to be resolved by arbitration by Prophet Muhammad. In other words, disputes among the believers in the community tend to disrupt the Prophet's efforts in carrying out his mission. Therefore, his followers are mandated to obey him so that he may focus all his efforts toward his mission, without being distracted from it by disputes among his followers.[171]

The second relevant verse is Q4:80: "*Whoever obeys the Messenger obeys Allah, and whoever turns away, then, We did not send you to stand guard over them.*"[172] This verse came in the context of the people who resisted and rebelled against the recently commanded duty to fight the nonbelievers and repel their aggressions. Within that context, the Prophet had presumably said, "*Whoever loves me loves God and whoever obeys me obeys God*"; so someone accused him of pretending to be and behaving like a God, namely, like Jesus Christ, and expecting to be obeyed.[173] In response to that accusation, this verse confirms that the Prophet does not require obedience, except to what God commands, because he himself obeys God and only conveys His message without adding anything from his own (Verses Q7:157 and 158).[174] This is further scriptural confirmation that Prophet Muhammad was an ordinary human being and did not have any rule-making prerogatives beyond the divinely revealed commands in the form of Qur'anic verses. However, Ibn Kathir unjustifiably links this verse to Verse Q53:3, in which Prophet Muhammad is said to speak not out of his fancy but out of divine inspiration.[175] There is no reason to make that link between the two verses because the context of Verse Q4:80 is about the order to fight and those who refuse to obey the injunction of the Prophet to participate in the fighting. Because the battle in reference was commanded or authorized by God, refusing to obey the commands of the Prophet to participate is equivalent to refusing to obey God. Therefore, and here too, this verse is not about Prophetic Tradition. Any different conclusion can be justified only by the relevant commentator having reached that conclusion after having removed the relevant verse from its proper context. This verse was gravely taken out of context by Ibn Kathir. Similarly, al-Shafi'i used this verse, taken out of context, in support of his theory about the infallibility of the Prophet and its corollary that Prophetic Tradition is entirely divine revelation, with the same binding power as the Holy Qur'an.

Obedience among humans is only to living persons if they are vested with the leadership authority, and that authority ends when they die. Islam mandates that Muslims believe in the messages brought by previous prophets and messengers. Does that mean that Abraham, Moses, Jesus, and the rest of the prophets should all be obeyed eternally? The answer is clearly in the negative. By contrast, obedience to God is eternal and universal because God is eternal and does not die.

Issues Relating to the Reliability and Nature of Prophetic Tradition

To reiterate, according to the Holy Qur'an, Prophet Muhammad is a human being, and while his actions and sayings at times may have been divinely guided by way of revelation, he was not infallible.[176] While the Qur'an mandated obedience to the Prophet, that obedience was due him as leader of the new community of the faithful that he established in Medina and was necessary for him to carry out his divinely assigned mission. Therefore, the scope of that obedience did not extend beyond his lifetime. God, in his divine perfection, gave to Prophet Muhammad a complete, accurate, and perfect Qur'an, whereupon He did not mandate him to explain, amplify, or complement the Holy Qur'an, let alone to modify it.

The first conclusion that can safely be drawn is that Prophetic Tradition, as a potential source of faith and jurisprudence, is different from the Holy Qur'an in two important respects. Initially, and contrary to the Holy Qur'an whose authenticity and integrity are substantially not subject to doubt, the authenticity and integrity of the Prophetic Tradition are clearly lacking, and they remain to our days the center of increasing controversies.[177] In addition, whereas the Holy Qur'an is the uncontested—at least by Muslim scholars and the general Muslim public alike—expression of the divine word as revealed to the Prophet, the Prophetic Tradition is the expression of the acts and words of the Prophet, an entirely human being. Yet, and notwithstanding these two basic differences, Prophetic Tradition, which is reasonably identified as true, remains a very important element of the Islamic heritage.

Authenticity and Integrity of the Prophetic Tradition

Unlike the Qur'an which was recorded, concurrently with the revelation of each verse, by the scribes designated by the Prophet to record the Message, Prophetic Tradition was not recorded at any point in time during the lifetime of the Prophet, but was compiled later on, commencing more than a hundred years following his death. Therefore, until actual compilation took place, Prophetic Tradition remained an oral tradition, transmitted from one generation to the next by word of mouth.[178]

A first attempt at a compilation and recordation of Prophetic Tradition took place during the reign of the Omayyad Caliph 'Umar Bin Abdel 'Aziz,[179] more than eighty years following the death of Prophet Muhammad; but that attempt did not materialize. It was only with the advent of the Abbasid Caliphate, over a century after the death of the Prophet, that a systematic work of compilation and drafting of Prophetic Tradition commenced. That task was undertaken by several researchers. They spread out in all directions of the Empire in search of individuals with memories of the Prophet's traditions. They also researched the entire line of transmitters through whom those memories traveled across the generations.

Because of the exceedingly long time during which Prophetic Tradition remained as an oral tradition, its authenticity and integrity were seriously cast into doubt, not only by modernist thinkers but also by early thinkers, as early as the period immediately following its compilation.[180] In addition to the inaccuracies arising from normal failings of human memories over time, there was a major concern about the authenticity and accuracy of Prophetic Tradition deriving from fraud committed on a wide scale for reasons totally alien to the faith.[181] Indeed, many social and political developments occurred after the death of Prophet Muhammad that provided a fertile ground for the fabrication of traditions and attribution of traditions to the Prophet.[182] Fabricated traditions aimed to provide support for one family against another or a tribe against another or even entire peoples against others.[183] Ahmad Amin points to a number of political feuds in which fabrication of Prophetic Tradition proliferated, namely: (1) the feud between 'Ali and Abou Bakr that surfaced following the death of the Prophet; (2) the feud between 'Ali and Mu'awiya, following which the caliphate moved to the Omayyad dynasty, thereby ending the period of Enlightened Caliphate led by the closest companions of the Prophet; (3) the feud between 'Abdul Malik, the Omayyad caliph in Damascus, and Abdullah Ibn al-Zubayr, a close companion of the Prophet, who led a dissenting movement from Medina against the transfer of the caliphate to the Omayyad dynasty and the move of the seat of the caliphate from Medina to Damascus; (4) the feud between princes from the Omayyad dynasty and notables from the Abbasid family that resulted in the transfer of the caliphate to the latter and the start of the Abbasid dynasty, which lasted for several long centuries; (5) the feuds among Arabs, Persians, and Byzantines; and (6) day-to-day feuds among loyalists of caliphs and local princes.[184]

Amin points also to several other circumstances outside the realm of politics which gave rise to active fabrication of Prophetic Tradition. He cites, in particular, philosophical controversies opposing proponents of free choice to proponents of divine predestination, and proponents of creation of the Qur'an against proponents of its uncreation, to name but a few. He also cites the attempts by clerics to create fear among the general Muslim public on matters of halal and haram, in their efforts to maintain their prominent social positions and power. Since the Prophet is the firsthand recipient of God's message and its direct transmitter, imitating the Prophet by following his traditions is a safety net for which no one could be faulted. This approach strongly motivated the fabrication process. Finally, this wave of fabrication of traditions attributed to the Prophet allowed the accumulation of numerous absurd or corrupt traditions. It also allowed the infiltration of countless presumed traditions of the Prophet copied *verbatim* from Jewish and Christian sources.[185]

The overwhelming reliance on Prophetic Tradition by rulers, clerics, and ordinary people to demonstrate their adherence to the faith was reason enough to develop a new religious science, *'ilm Muṣṭalaḥ al-hadith,* or the science of Prophetic Tradition. Its objective was to ascertain the accuracy and reliability of Prophetic Tradition through the critical analysis of compiled and recorded traditions. Indeed, as the compilations of sunna and hadith multiplied, religious scholars went about the necessary related tasks of identifying, verifying, and interpreting the contents of these compilations. The first essential task was to check the reliability of the chain linking each tradition to the Prophet by way of determining that its chain of transmitters went uninterrupted all the way to one of his companions. It was imperative to ascertain the extent to which each transmitter in the relevant chain is worthy of confidence. As a result, works of classification of Prophetic Tradition by categories based on the relevant perceived authenticity came into existence. A tradition of the Prophet would be treated as authentic if its chain of transmitters was found to be uninterrupted, and each transmitter therein was vetted as worthy of confidence. Authentic traditions which met these criteria were compiled in compendia called *Ṣaḥīḥ.*[186] This compilation process, which was done diligently and thoroughly, constituted an important and necessary first step. However, the process was not pursued beyond the reliability of the chain of oral transmitters to the logical crucial level of properly analyzing the reliability and credibility of the substantive contents of each tradition. As a result, the outcome suffered major flaws.

First, while the credibility and integrity of each transmitter in each chain was presumably verified, the credibility and integrity of the first transmitter was not verified. The argument given for that shortcoming goes as follows: (1) whoever may have heard or witnessed the relevant tradition firsthand from the Prophet is necessarily a companion of the Prophet; (2) the integrity of the Companions is by definition presumed to be beyond any shadow of doubt as to their words and deeds; and (3) their *'adāla* (integrity and virtue) and character are presumed to be testified to by Allah and His Prophet.[187] In reality, while a number of close companions of the Prophet were indeed exemplars in their probity and integrity, for many others, the case is not obvious. In fact, history books recount numerous tales about companions who do not have the *'adāla* presumed in people deemed companions of the Prophet.[188] Most importantly, the definition of the term "companion" is very wide, and there is no consensus over its scope. For many, such as the prominent compilers of Prophetic Tradition al-Bukhari and Ahmad Ibn Hanbal (leader of the Hanbali School of Jurisprudence), its scope includes almost every person who at one time or another, following the start of revelation, got the chance to see or talk to the Prophet at least once.[189] The situation could have been different if the title of "companion" was attributed by the Prophet himself to those of his followers who were selected on grounds of their ethics and high morals. That was not the case. To illustrate the magnitude of the issue, Abou Bakr, 'Umar, and 'Ali were among the closest companions of the Prophet who were most notorious for their integrity and probity, and who could have heard or witnessed most of the reported traditions because of the extent of time that they spent with him. Yet, traditions attributed to them are extremely rare. By contrast and by way of example, Abu Hurayra and Abdullah Ibn 'Abbas, two of the most prolific conveyors of Prophetic Tradition, have each told of hundreds of traditions, which are reported in the *Ṣaḥīḥ* compendia[190] (and even more in others) at a time when they had not been in the Prophet's company long enough for that purpose; the first is reported to have known the Prophet during only the last three years of the Prophet's life[191] and the second was only thirteen years old when the Prophet died.[192] In addition, the reputations of both Abu Hurayra and Ibn 'Abbas are reported to have been doubtful. During the caliphate of 'Umar, Abu Hurayra is reported to have been fired from his position as governor of Bassorah for diverting funds from *bayt al-māl*, or the public treasury. The same was reported about Abdullah Ibn 'Abbas, who presumably was discharged by Caliph 'Ali from his position as governor of Bahrain for similar reasons.[193] Moreover, Prophetic Traditions reported by companions who have not personally witnessed the occurrence of the relevant tradition have been widely—though not unanimously—accepted as true and recognized as binding. This is particularly the case of most traditions reported by younger companions, such as Abdullah Ibn 'Abbas, who did not have the opportunity to be in the company of the Prophet long enough or were not sufficiently mature to grasp the sense of the acts or words of the Prophet that they may have witnessed.

Second, no matter how good the transmitters' memories may have been, such memories were human and could have been subject to normal inadvertent failings. Any text so transmitted is bound to suffer modifications upon each transmission across generations. In reality, speaking of Prophetic Tradition as a potential primary source of religion, any outcome of compilation can be only a modest pool of anecdotes whose phrasing could not have possibly captured the exact formulation of each idea, nor the exact translation and interpretation of each action, as uttered or performed by the Prophet. Because Prophetic Tradition, by definition, is closely associated with the events affecting the day-to-day behavior of the Prophet during his lifetime from the start of revelation, the problem gets compounded when accounts relating to the Prophet's life (the *sīra*) remained an oral tradition as well for more than a hundred years following his death. That gap allowed a certain aura of sanctity to form around the Prophet; and myths were invented with respect to all aspects of his life, and not just the part associated with the performance of his divine mission.[194] Therefore, the unreliability of the Prophet's life history can only result in the unreliability of the Prophetic Tradition because the latter is derived from the *sīra*.[195]

Finally, and assuming the words and actions of the Prophet were reasonably and accurately memorized and transmitted, the immediate and overall contexts in which such words and actions were said or done would, to the extent they are reported, be subjective and reflective of the relevant transmitter's perception and understanding of the relevant context, and possibly that of the compilers' as well. On this point, Abdelmajid Charfi observes that the presumed authenticity of the Prophetic Tradition is even more problematic because it relies on recollections, gathered long after the fact itself, which tend to rephrase the fact in terms that befit the hero as opposed to the true fact.[196]

In retrospect, the issues surrounding the authenticity and reliability of Prophetic Tradition are not a sorry happening of history. The Prophet and his trusted companions had perhaps anticipated the outcome.

Perception of Prophetic Tradition by the Prophet and his Trusted Companions

During the lifetime of Prophet Muhammad and following the start of revelation, only the Qur'anic revelation was recorded, to the exclusion of anything said or done by the Prophet. More particularly, the Prophet had strictly banned the recording of any part of his speech or acts.[197] He was concerned that people might confuse the Divine Message with the Prophet's own words and deeds; his own traditions should at no time be perceived by his community as part of the Holy Qur'an. That said, on his deathbed, the Prophet was inclined to leave a written will to believers containing some final advice. 'Umar, his future successor, with whom the Prophet shared the idea, advised against it. He pointed to the full sufficiency of the Holy Qur'an and to the long-standing position of the Prophet regarding the ban on recording any of his acts or speeches. The Prophet accepted the advice and agreed that nothing should be done which could lead people to believe that the last will of the Prophet is part of the Revelation.[198]

By way of respect for the will so expressed by the Prophet, Caliph Abou Bakr destroyed all manuscripts that he and his daughter Aisha, widow of the Prophet, held in their possession containing records of certain traditions of the Prophet.[199] On his part, Caliph 'Umar, who strongly believed in the advisability of emulating the Prophet's example, and despite his earlier advice that the Prophet should not leave a written will, did briefly consider the idea of recording the Prophetic Tradition for fear that the memory of the Prophet's acts and words would be lost forever. However, he quickly decided to drop the idea because he feared, more than ever before, that the believers might one day elevate the Prophetic Tradition to the level of the Holy Qur'an, and possibly neglect the latter in favor of the former.[200]

Unfortunately, however, certain schools of thought knowingly ignored the purpose and relevance of the fact that the traditions of the Prophet, unlike the Qur'an, were not recorded in due course. They insisted on claiming that traditions of the Prophet were binding divine revelations. Al-Mawdudi, for example, insists that acceptance of Prophetic Tradition as a primary and binding source of Islam is "a necessary test of faith" of true believers. In addition, he considers that the reliability and authority of the Qur'an itself depends on the fact that it is "attested to by reliable witnesses."[201] This argument by al-Mawdudi is flawed. Prophetic Tradition as human behavior can be witnessed by humans. Instead, the Holy Qur'an is a divine document whose acceptance as authentic is not dependent on human witness. God sent it together with its proof, the latter being in the form of *i'jāz*, its incomparability and inimitability, among other attributes.

In retrospect, had the Prophet really believed his deeds and words to be binding divine revelation, a message to be conveyed, he would have dealt with them and recorded them in the same manner as he dealt with, and secured the recording of, the Holy Qur'an. However, the Prophet—*al-Amīn*, the trusted—left no room for guessing as he affirmed the exact opposite when he banned the recording of his deeds and words.

The Word of God and the Tradition of Man

As the word of God, the Holy Qur'an is perfect. By contrast, the Prophetic Tradition is less than perfect because it is human, and the Prophet, as a human being, was neither divine nor infallible. On that basis, and contrary to the claims of early exegetes and many of their followers among contemporary scholars, Prophetic Tradition cannot abrogate Qur'anic provisions. Similarly, Prophetic Tradition is not a necessary tool for understanding the Qur'an[202] because to claim otherwise would imply that the Holy Qur'an, as a Divine Revelation, is imperfect and can be improved on by way of abrogation, among other forms of intervention. It would even imply that Prophetic Tradition is superior to the Holy Qur'an if without it the Qur'an is unclear, insufficient, and incomplete. Moreover, to the extent that Prophet Muhammad is the one credited with such improvements and clarifications, if any, the further implication then would be that the Prophet is, at least, the equal of God. Both of such implications involve the major sin of *shirk* (association with God), which Prophet Muhammad never committed nor attempted to commit but, on the contrary, strove very hard to avoid throughout his exemplary behavior, including that of prohibiting the recording of his traditions.[203]

Prophet Muhammad and all of the caliphs that succeeded him in the hundred years following his death perceived Prophetic Tradition as a living example of the implementation of the rules brought by the new faith. Their continued ban on recording Prophetic Tradition is a testimony to their strong and express endeavor to prevent any attempts to equate the Prophetic Tradition and the Qur'anic revelation, or to impute one to the other. They all remembered the admonition by God, set forth in Verse Q2:79, against allowing anything to be done which might imply that human words are the words of God: *"So, woe to those who write the Book with their hands and then say, 'This is from Allah,' so that they may gain thereby a trifling price. Then, woe to them for what their hands have written, and woe to them for what they earn."*[204]

This is consistent with the intent by God, incorporated in verses of the Qur'an, to provide a Qur'an which is comprehensive, self-contained, and understandable to all. By way of confirmation, the Qur'an expressly says in Verse Q7:52: *"Surely We have brought them a book that We have elaborated with knowledge, as guidance and mercy for a people who believe"*; and in Verses Q17:105 and 106: *"With truth We have sent it (the Qur'an) down and with truth it descended, and We did not send you but as a bearer of good tidings and as a warner (105). We have divided the Qur'an in portions, so that you may recite it to the people gradually, and We have revealed it little by little (106)."*[205] Having confirmed that the Qur'an is clear, understandable, and comprehensive, God goes on to warn against making any changes to it.[206] We thus find numerous verses in the Qur'an which confirm that neither the Qur'an nor any of its verses may be abrogated, and no one, including the Prophet, may change the words of God.[207]

Q6:34—*"No one can change the words of Allah, and of course, some accounts of the messengers have already come to you."*

Q6:115—*"The Word of your Lord is perfect in truth and justice. None is there to change His words."*

Q10:15—*"Say, 'It is not possible for me to make changes in it on my own. I follow nothing but what is revealed to me. If I disobey my Lord, I fear the punishment of a terrible day.'"*

Q10:64—*"For them there is the good news in the worldly life and in the Hereafter: there is no change in the words of Allah. That is the great achievement."*

Q18:27—*"And recite what has been revealed to you of the Book of your Lord. There is no one to change His words, and you will never find a refuge beside Him."*

The proponents of the concept that the Qur'anic revelation can be abrogated by Prophetic Tradition justify their views on the grounds that Prophetic Tradition is Divine Revelation to the same extent as the Qur'an itself. As such, any abrogation of the Qur'an by Prophetic Tradition would in reality be an abrogation by God, except that it is provided through the medium of Prophetic Tradition.[208] This view is expressed by Abu Hamid al-Ghazali.

> There is no dispute that the Prophet does not abrogate the Qur'an on his own initiative but, instead, by way of revelation from above without necessarily that revelation taking the form of Qur'anic message. And if we granted that abrogation could take place by way of prophetic *ijtihād*, it remains that such *ijtihād* is in fact inspired by God in such a way that, in reality, the abrogator is God using his Prophet as mouthpiece.[209]

This argument and conclusion are inconsistent with the divine injunction that people should ponder God's commands and make sense out of them. Abrogation of the Qur'an by a medium which is neither the Qur'an, nor defined or otherwise alluded to in the Qur'an, is not consistent with divine justice. God himself, in the Qur'an, asserts that He sent the books so that people may behave accordingly and so that they may be aware of the bases on which He will render His Final Judgment. He even confirmed that he would not punish people for their behaviors if they did not receive a divine message. It would therefore defy divine justice to believe that God would send the Qur'an, then modify it in an inconspicuous manner that leaves people at risk of remaining unaware of any such modification. Such an outcome is inconceivable, since the Prophet, as the trusted *al-Amīn*, would have spread the word to that effect. Not only did the Prophet not specifically mention any potential changes to the Qur'an resulting from his traditions, he expressly instructed against mixing his traditions with the words of God to prevent any such unwanted implications. It is not wise to accept the principle that the Qur'an can be abrogated by Prophetic Tradition because it throws much confusion into the stability of the Holy Qur'an and defies the divine assertions that appear repeatedly in it about its clarity and comprehensiveness.

While the current form of the Holy Qur'an is generally accepted as authentic and accurate, Prophetic Tradition is questionable and has been the subject of serious controversies. Numerous prophetic traditions have been fabricated and controverted to suit political and power games. If the Qur'an is allowed to be abrogated and superseded by Prophetic Tradition, the way to challenge the entire stability of the Qur'an becomes wide open. This should not lead to the hasty conclusion that Prophetic Tradition is of no value and should be discarded, because while the Prophetic Tradition is not binding, yet it is very important. However, whatever the value attributed to a tradition may be, it must first be reasonably established and determined to be true and reliable.

Conditions Necessary for the Reliability of Prophetic Tradition

We indicated earlier that a whole science, *'ilm Muṣṭalaḥ al-hadith,* has developed to identify authentic Prophetic Tradition. Unfortunately, and because Prophetic Tradition was primarily transmitted orally over several generations, the science of *'ilm Muṣṭalaḥ al-hadith* focused almost exclusively on retracing each tradition to Prophet Muhammad, or to any of his companions, without further scrutinizing the substance.

As a result, Prophetic Tradition was categorized from solid and trustworthy to average and weak, depending on: (1) whether the chain of transmitters is complete, commencing from the relevant companion, as primary source, all the way down to the person from whom the tradition in question is received by the relevant compiler; (2) the reported reputation and integrity of each transmitter in the relevant chain of the tradition; and (3) the number of companions to whom the tradition may be traced. Accordingly, the tradition that has an unbroken chain is stronger than the one where one or more transmitters in the chain could not be identified; and if that tradition is reportedly told by more than one companion, it is a stronger tradition in terms of its chances of being true than if it is told by just one source.

Certain schools of thought accepted Prophetic Tradition as reliable and binding, irrespective of any of the stated conditions of form, on the basis that any doubt cast on any part of the prophetic mission is equivalent to a doubt cast on its entirety, including the Holy Qur'an.[210] Such an approach seems unreliable. First, it is clearly possible to draw a line between Divine Revelation to the Prophet and human tradition emanating from the Prophet, because God did draw that line, and the Prophet did so, as well, in his trustworthy approach. Second, issues relating to the reliability of Prophetic Tradition have nothing to do with the trustworthiness of the Prophet. The problem is with the trustworthiness of the compilers and transmitters.

The compilation works yielded a large number of compendia, each made up of several volumes containing thousands of traditions, of different categories in terms of strength and reliability.[211] Of all these references, there are two compendia, namely Sahih Muslim and Sahih al-Bukhari, which contain all of the traditions of the Prophet that are "deemed" strong in accordance with the criteria set forth above. For that purpose, these two compendia were, and continue to be, almost universally recognized and accepted as the ultimate authority on Prophetic Tradition. However, because the compilers of the Prophet's traditions focused solely on form, the records that they created—including Sahih Muslim and Sahih al-Bukhari—were, in terms of substance, filled with wide-scope traditions and tales attributed to the Prophet, some potentially serious and meaningful, some at best neutral and irrelevant,[212] and many more totally unrealistic and irrational.[213] For example, Prophet Muhammad is reported to have proscribed giving alms to anyone from the *Quraysh* tribe and their followers because they are presumably too far above the rest of the people for them to accept alms. The Prophet is said to have described the alms as the Muslims' dirt.[214] Clearly, such a tradition is not plausible because (1) the Holy Qur'an describes the alms as a soul and property cleansing tool (Q9:103); (2) God is the one who accepts repentance and accepts the alms (Q9:104); and (3) people are enjoined to direct their alms to the Prophet by way of getting closer to him (Q58:12). In addition, with criteria limited to form only as previously noted, the fabrication and forgery of traditions wrongly attributed to the Prophet became very easy. It was enough to invent the relevant story and make up the chain of transmitters using trustworthy names; and that story then becomes a tradition that finds its way into any one of the two authoritative compendia.

Over time, scholars and historians realized that reliance on traditions compiled without any attention to substance hampered progress and created confusion. It was found necessary to extend the criteria beyond mere form to include scrutiny of the substance of each tradition. As a result, to be considered as authentic and reliable, each tradition had to meet the further criteria that it not be inconsistent with any provisions of the Qur'an or with rational thinking.[215] There was no general consensus as to the relevance and necessity of these additional criteria for scrutiny of the substance. A large number of 'ulama', namely among the adherents to the *ahl al-hadith* (scholars reliant primarily on hadith) school of thought as opposed to *ahl al-ra'y* (scholars reliant on rational thought) school of thought, were more comfortable with reliance on hadith of any strength than with reliance on the fruit of the mind. Apparently, they were not interested in substantive criteria.

No general consensus could even be gathered around the scope of these substantive criteria. Regarding the condition of consistency with rational thinking, reason and rationality are subjective: what is reasonable and realistic to some may not be so for others. However, the condition of consistency and compatibility with the provisions of the Holy Qur'an, in appearance a reasonably objective criterion, became corrupted through subjective interpretations of the provisions of the Qur'an. While countless examples can be given, one will serve to illustrate this point. Indeed, for all those who believe that Prophetic Tradition is divine because presumably all behavior of the Prophet was divinely inspired and guided through revelation, this condition became superfluous: whenever they found a tradition of the Prophet inconsistent with a Qur'anic provision, they ruled the relevant Qur'anic provision abrogated by that tradition. This is how Islamic law came to prohibit wills being made to any person who is otherwise among the heirs of the deceased, notwithstanding that the Qur'an expressly enjoins people to make wills to their closest family members, that is, persons who are typically heirs by virtue of the proximity of the family tie. The Holy Qur'an, in Verse Q2:180, stipulates: "*It is prescribed, when death approaches any of you, if he leave any goods that he make a* bequest to parents and next of kin*, according to reasonable usage; this is due from the God-fearing.*"[216] Despite the clarity of this verse, there is a general consensus that wills may not be made in favor of heirs, because this provision has been abrogated. Imam Malik and the adherents to his school of *fiqh*, among others, consider that this verse has been abrogated by a tradition of the Prophet which provides that "*There shall be no will in favor of an heir.*"[217] Unfortunately, instead of analyzing that tradition and placing it in context to determine its true scope, especially that it is directly inconsistent with a provision of the Holy Qur'an, it was decided to let that tradition prevail over the Qur'an through abrogation.

In addition to the above criteria, Imam Malik[218] added a further condition for reliability of prophetic traditions, namely that the transmitters must be knowledgeable; they must have mastered the learning being transmitted.[219] This condition is superfluous and serves only to create a nonexistent role for a self-proclaimed elite because, unless the transmitter is expected to edit or otherwise sanitize the substance of the transmission, his knowledge is irrelevant to the truthfulness of the material being transmitted. God used the Prophet, an ordinary person with no prior knowledge of the subject matter of that transmission, to receive and convey His message, and the Prophet, in turn, relied on his companions for its onward conveyance.

Despite all the conditions of form and substance devised over the years to analyze and screen Prophetic Tradition, there is no definitive consensus over the authenticity and reliability of any specific set of prophetic traditions. Even given all the issues outlined in this section that tainted the authenticity and reliability of Prophetic Tradition, we find a general consensus that developed in the early days of Islam that Prophetic Tradition is a primary source of Islam, second only to—and for some equal to—the Holy Qur'an. It is also generally accepted that the traditions found in the two authoritative compendia (Sahih Muslim and Sahih al-Bukhari) are, with some exceptions, substantially reliable. However, that consensus is recently being shaken by modern thinkers whose thoughts, supported by powerful evidence, have opened the door for rethinking the role of Prophetic Tradition. Zakaria Ouzon has devoted one work[220] to prove that even the most revered compendium of al-Bukhari is filled with unrealistic traditions imputed to the Prophet, some that defy logic and reason, and many others that defy the clear provisions of the Holy Qur'an. We thus find scores of traditions which wrongly attribute to the Prophet views that are in clear contradiction with the provisions of the Holy Qur'an such as, without limitation, traditions which: (1) demean women; (2) are offensive to the other Abrahamic faiths in terms of their inadequacy to achieve salvation for their respective believers; and (3) tend to reinstate reprehensible tribal fanaticism, such as the claim that only *Qurayshis* can lead the Muslim nation.

The True Role and Scope of Prophetic Tradition

Before considering the potential theological role and scope of Prophetic Tradition, it is essential to stress and value its role in providing a vivid and lively account of the social life, customs, and traditions prevailing during the period of revelation and the conduct of the Prophet's mission. The cultural environment substantially contributes to the understanding of the circumstances of revelation and the immediate purposes sought from it. From this perspective, that of the historian and the anthropologist, one can understand and agree with the strong reaction of Khalil 'Abdul-Karim against the views which deny any role for Prophetic Tradition.[221] From the theologian's perspective however, the importance and value of Prophetic Tradition lies in its role of providing guidance, as model for *ijtihād*, and as methodology for deriving maximum benefit from the universal and progressive nature of Islam.

Prophetic Guidance

Bearing in mind the context of the Revelation, and although there is not a single verse in the Holy Qur'an which specifically mandates Prophet Muhammad to interpret the Qur'an, it is conceivable that the recipients of the Message reasonably expected its carrier to be qualified to explain it. More particularly, since the Message did not appear in a vacuum, its primary objective, after reiterating the substance of previous divine messages about God's unicity and compassionate sovereignty, was to replace reprehensible tribal relations and customs with universal divine principles of social and individual ethics.[222] Within that framework, people were reasonably entitled to believe that Prophet Muhammad, as carrier of the Message, would be qualified to guide them in its implementation, and that his behavior would, relatively and to a certain extent,[223] exemplify the substance of the Message. People could therefore reasonably expect the Prophet to answer questions, clear up confusions, and regulate for the new circumstances.

In addition, the continuous intervention of the Prophet was an essential necessity, for several reasons. Primarily, the Message was descending with time intervals between revelations, and—at times—in an interactive manner, in response to specific circumstances. Moreover, from a practical perspective, whatever had been conveyed of the Message could not have been heard by everyone at the same time and, for those who may have heard it at one point or another, the Message was not readily available for them to reread it, if they did not memorize it. Most importantly, it was an entirely new message, intended, among other things, to reform their habitual way of life. Therefore, it was inconceivable that the Prophet would deliver the

Message, and then abstain from any involvement in its implementation. That is precisely why the Prophet was frequently present among his companions and followers, answering their questions and providing them the necessary guidance in living their new faith. This explains why numerous verses throughout the Qur'an mandate obedience to the Prophet and emulation of his example. They were necessary to enable him, while revelation was taking place, to carry out his much needed leadership role in spreading the Message being revealed, establishing the detailed rules and procedures relating to worship-related duties, and setting forth the roots and foundations for the new social order brought about by the new faith. In this respect, one view by the Amritsar school of thought dismisses any such role of the Prophet, comparing his function to that of a postman whose sole duty is to deliver the message.[224] This is an extreme, unfounded view because, while the postman delivers the mail and does not read it, Prophet Muhammad read and understood the Message to be delivered and, in the process of spreading it, he gave the example of its implementation through his *ijtihād*.

Prophet Muhammad, very eloquently, told believers in no uncertain terms what to make of his traditions.

> *If I direct you to do anything which is directly related to your faith, take it, and if I direct you to do anything else from my own initiative, I am only a human being and you know better the things that relate to your own life; What is suggested to you as coming from me, compare it to the book of God (the Qur'an); if it is consistent with its provisions, I could have said it, otherwise I surely did not say it.*[225]

In this manner, the Prophet directly refuted and condemned potential attempts at sacralizing his traditions.

Worship-Related Prophetic Tradition

With respect to worship, the Qur'an mandated a limited number of practices that each good Muslim is expected to perform, some on a regular basis, such as prayer (salat), pilgrimage (hajj), payment of alms (zakat), and fasting the month of Ramadan (*ṣawm*). The Qur'an, though, left open certain details relating to performance of these worship-related duties.[226]

For example, the Qur'an did not specify the prayer or hajj performance procedures, nor did it prescribe the number of daily prayers that Muslims are expected to perform. One might conclude from the silence of the Qur'an on these and other worship-related matters that God had intentionally given to each individual the freedom to determine, in his or her discretion, how best to perform the assigned duties and communicate with God. God is indeed always available to hear the prayers of the believers, as much as He is aware of their true intentions in performing the assigned duties. Yet, because there is merit in the collective performance of worship-related duties, the example of the Prophet becomes of utmost importance in setting forth the procedures for such performances. The rituals created could then be followed uniformly by all believers across continents and constitute a bond of faith among them.

Prophetic *ijtihād*

Following the completion of Prophet Muhammad's mission and his death soon thereafter, his traditions could no longer remain eternally binding. As a result, and except for traditions setting forth the detailed practice of worship-related duties, Prophetic Tradition cannot be treated as an integral part of the faith. The Qur'an said so, and Prophet Muhammad confirmed it, in words and deeds. That conclusion has a very good purpose, that of securing the continued universal acceptance of Islam and the uninterrupted progress of Muslim communities. In other words, the exclusion of Prophetic Tradition as a primary source of Islam is essential to the universality of Islam: God declared Muhammad as the final messenger and confirmed having completed and perfected His message for all humans for eternity.[227] In that light, God could not have mandated that limitations be placed on the universality of the Divine Message by way of framing it within the bounds of the human Prophetic Tradition and those of the culture and traditions of the short span of Prophet Muhammad's and his companions' lifetimes following the start of revelation.[228] This explains why any traditions imputed to the Prophet which are inconsistent with the Divine Message should be rejected upfront, no matter how solidly they may be traced to the companions of the Prophet, and no matter how trustworthy the ultimate companion(s) to whom they are imputed may have been: the Prophet, being the most trusted, could not have called for anything which modifies, neutralizes, or cancels the word of God. By way of example, Khalil 'Abdul-Karim reports a tradition of the Prophet in which he has presumably forbidden his companions to read religious Scriptures other than the Qur'an;[229] while in all likelihood such tradition is not true and accurate, yet the fact remains that, because it is directly inconsistent with the Qur'anic provisions requiring Muslims to believe in the messages of Moses and Jesus, that tradition cannot be relevant to Muslims irrespective of whether the Prophet has indeed said it or not. The same principle applies, for the same reason, to any tradition of the Prophet which is inconsistent with the Qur'an.

A rereading of the Prophet's tradition in which he proscribed writing of his traditions is clear.

> *The Prophet of God (Peace Be Upon Him) said: "Do not write anything which is imputed to me; whoever may have so written anything other than the Qur'an should immediately erase it; however, you may discuss verbally any matter without limitation, except that whoever has knowingly imputed anything to me which is not true will surely find his seat in hell waiting for him."*[230]

In essence, the prohibition to record traditions indicates that the Prophet did not intend to give his sayings a scope extending beyond his own lifetime. In other words, and aside from the fear of mix-up with Qur'anic text, the Prophet is telling his people that, unlike the Qur'an, his traditions are not universal. They are good for their time because they represent the best of the Prophet's *ijtihād*, and that *ijtihād* is time- and location-bound. That is an acknowledgment by the Prophet that his tradition may not be useful for a different context. It remains true that people who knew the Prophet could talk about him and imitate him, but then such imitation may become irrelevant for later generations.[231] It also explains why the Prophet allowed that his traditions be repeated and discussed orally but made sure that they not be written lest they become binding universally.

It is important to stress the fact that the value of Prophetic Tradition does not derive from any presumptive binding effect. It derives primarily from the qualities of the person chosen by God to be His prophet and messenger, and from the context in which Prophet Muhammad went about fulfilling his mission. Indeed, all the issues affecting the integrity, accuracy, and authenticity of the Prophetic Tradition notwithstanding, the fact remains that the traditions of the Prophet, no matter the extent to which some of such traditions may be unreliable, are of great value in various respects.

Prophetic Tradition as a Methodology

Ijtihād is by definition a product of the human mind and, as such, that product is framed by the circumstances of the time and place of the person producing that *ijtihād*. It is a process by which a person uses his or her mind in applying or otherwise adapting certain existing rules in order to resolve problems being faced, in the best interests of the community as perceived by that person. Because problems and interests are typical of their time and place, any suitable solution, however well it may resolve the problem and safeguard the interests of the community, may not be suitable to resolve similar problems occurring in a different location or time. However, despite that *ijtihād* is a human—as opposed to divine— product and is thus less than perfect, yet the fact that it is the *ijtihād* of Prophet Muhammad, the person chosen by God to carry His message, gives that *ijtihād* a special value and importance. Prophet Muhammad was specifically chosen by God from among his peers, in recognition of his integrity and good judgment, with the expectation that such integrity and judgment would be necessary to deliver the Message, guide his people through its implementation, and, to certain reasonable extents, exemplify it through his behavior.

Such being the case, one may legitimately ponder what makes the Prophet's *ijtihād* valuable and important if at best that *ijtihād* is good only for its time and place. In particular, fifteen centuries have lapsed since the Revelation, and our problems are different from those faced and resolved by the Prophet. Consequently, the solutions that the Prophet strove to devise for the problems of his time may not be relevant for our time. The answer to this concern becomes clear when we acknowledge the difference in nature between the Divine Message and the human Prophetic

Tradition, and nevertheless perceive the complementarity between the two. There is no rational complementarity between the Message and the Tradition in terms of the latter supplementing or otherwise modifying the former. Complementarity instead becomes obvious when the Message is accepted as the perfect, comprehensive, and complete universal truth, and then the Prophetic Tradition is viewed, together with the traditions of the Companions who succeeded the Prophet, as the methodology for implementing the Message and living the new faith.[232] In that sense, the methodology, if applied with the same open-mindedness and rationality as applied by the Prophet and his enlightened successors, should yield the relevant solutions for the relevant problems that arise from time to time.

In other words, when the Prophet applied his mind to the implementation of the rules brought about by the new faith or to resolve problems as they arose, he exercised a rational process of *ijtihād* which brought about the relevant solutions; and it is this rational process that is important to believers of all times and places, as opposed to the substance of the relevant solutions. Consequently, the real value in Prophetic Tradition is in the principles of humanity, tolerance, flexibility, and progress—among other values—that the Prophet consistently applied,[233] and which believers are called upon to emulate in applying the Message for their relevant times and resolving the issues of their specific time and place.[234] If it is irrelevant to imitate the specific action exemplified in the relevant tradition, emulating the process which led to that action is relevant and remains relevant at all times and in all places.[235]

The range of general doctrinal positions that were expressed over time regarding Prophetic Tradition can be summarized. In the first place, and until relatively recently, substantially all early and later jurisprudents generally concurred on the unchallenged authority of the Prophet and the duty of Muslims to obey him. They differed only on the scope of these statements: (1) some jurisprudents required more stringent conditions than others to ascertain the accuracy and reliability of the relevant prophetic traditions; and (2) some jurisprudents attributed the adjective of binding tradition to certain actions of the Prophet to the extent they concern major religion-related issues, excluding other issues relating to less major or otherwise futile matters of daily life.[236] At the other extreme, more recent jurisprudents opted for setting Prophetic Tradition totally aside as irrelevant, or at best recognizing some jurisprudential and historic value in it.[237] In between these positions, revivalists and contemporary thinkers who feel uncomfortable with Prophetic Tradition as a source of religion have been reluctant to expressly say so. They have, instead, tried to approach the issue indirectly through the generally accepted challenges to the authenticity and reliability of Prophetic Tradition, rather than challenging the principle of its binding effect.[238] In this manner, the issue is presumably avoided by casting doubt over the authenticity rather than on the binding effect. This would mean that whatever of the Prophetic Tradition could be proven authentic would then be accepted as binding for that reason only, an unwanted conclusion as set forth above. In reality, by rejecting *taqlīd* (blind imitation) while maintaining commitment to Prophetic Tradition as a primary source of Islam alongside the Qur'an, revivalists have not achieved the intended purpose, because seeking flexibility and progress within a limited binding framework dating back to the seventh century is an impossible task. As a result, the revivalists, on substance, did not advance beyond the classical approach; they only polished the facade. They sought, though in vain, to modernize sunna but only by rethinking their validation process.

Finally, Daniel Brown interestingly points to the fact that the early Muslims did not draw distinctions between the provisions of the Qur'an and the traditions of the Prophet, his companions, and successor caliphs, all of which were implicitly placed under the "aura of revelation."[239] Simply speaking, at that time the Qur'an had not yet been compiled, and therefore it was not widely distributed. However, one thing is clear: no one considered it important to compile anything other than the Holy Qur'an. Also, because the Companions knew the Prophet closely, they considered him a good example to follow, not from a religious perspective but from a social viewpoint. The importance of the methodology derived from analyzing the thought processes leading to the particular traditions of the Prophet and those of his most trusted companions who succeeded him by far exceeds the substantive contents of these traditions or their jurisprudential value. To recover the Message, it is the importance of that process that must be illustrated and brought into clear focus.

CHAPTER 4
The Scope of the Universal Nature of Islam: Issues of Interpretation

The "Qur'anic Imperative" mode has only one tense: the Present. "Read ('iqra') the Qur'an as if it was revealed to you" is what a prophetic tradition enjoins us to do. The Space-Time of Revelation is not that of a pause, but that of a dynamic continuum. God never ceases to reveal Himself in the omnipresent Present. —Mohamed Talbi[1]

An entire spectrum of views can be found about the universal nature of Islam. At one extreme, Islam is universal in every respect. It extends to all people, to all times and places; it encompasses all facets of life, in its minutest details; and it extends to all the components of Islam, meaning to the Message, including every verse of the Holy Qur'an, the Prophetic Tradition, and the history of their implementation over the centuries. At the other extreme, Islam, at best, is a paraphrase of the Judeo-Christian Scriptures taught, or perhaps dictated, to Prophet Muhammad by some priests and rabbis with whom he had contact. As such, his message is no more than another presentation of previous revelations, reformulated and repackaged for his audience in the Arabian Peninsula, namely the several tribes that spread across the land, starting with his own, the *Quraysh* tribe.[2]

Fundamentalists, Islamophobes, and to an extent revivalists, perceive Islam exclusively through its iteration during the first few centuries after the Revelation. Fundamentalists believe that the grandeur of Islam in history was made possible by the "true" Islam, as conveyed and taught by Prophet Muhammad, and as lived and implemented by him, the Companions, and their successors. For them, that grandeur faded, and Muslim societies regressed and fell into ignorance—that is, turned back toward *jāhiliyya*—following their deviation from that early iteration of Islam. That is why Muslims who are nostalgic about their past believe they can reclaim their former grandeur if they could restore early Islam in all its purity and candor.

On their part, Islamophobes have a similar perception of Islam as defined by its early iteration. Instead of the Fundamentalists' nostalgia, they fear that the spread of Islam in the West might be the way to recreate the past. They place in that context the attempts by Muslims of the diaspora to modify Western civilization through creeping state recognition of religious particularities and imported customs and traditions.

Finally, though ironically, certain modern-day revivalists have also perceived Islam through its early iteration but have striven instead to call for "reform" of Islam, substantially from within, using the recognized tools of interpretation. They substantially believe that the continued imitation of the Islam of the early days is responsible for many of the obstacles to progress that a number of Islamic societies face. Yet, they believe also that the situation can be reversed through the reinterpretation of the collective heritage of Islam, especially the Islam of the early days.

Besides the extremes of the spectrum, traditional Muslim scholars and clerics have variously included in Islam some dose of historical heritage, that which incorporates their living experience of Islam. This explains the lengthy discussions that have taken place, in vain it would seem, about whether the political and legal systems brought about by Islam can be applied with or without adaptation, and whether or not they are adaptable in the first place. These discussions have not borne any fruit, and no results appear to be looming on the horizon. An explanation that can be advanced for such failure to move the discussion from the realm of concept to implementation lies in the fact that the solutions to issues and problems of today and tomorrow were being formulated using the tools of the past.

Islam, in its universal nature, is not constructively discussed by reference to any particular historical phase of Islam nor to any particular interpretation of it. In this study, the universal Islam that is examined is the one that transcends all localities and historicity, the one that was revealed and transmitted in the Holy Qur'an, and no other source. Even as far as the Qur'an is concerned, it is essential to be selective in order to distinguish the specific from the general, the local example from the guiding principle, the publicly addressed message from the message addressed to the Prophet, and, most importantly, the human from the divine. Thus, when the need for reform is discussed, it is not the reform of Islam that is sought because Islam is perfect. What must be reformed is our understanding of Islam, through its primary divine source, uncontaminated by special circumstances or history. True reform should be brought about through restoring the universal nature of Islam, which has been usurped over time.

To start, the scope of Islam's universal nature should be defined: first, in terms of identifying the audience to whom the Message is relevant and to whom it is addressed; and second, in terms of time and space. Then it will be possible to identify, among the divine and human components of Islam, which one or more qualify as universal. The structure of that component can then be analyzed in order to determine the scope of universality.

Islam is for All People

Islam is universal in the sense that it is for all people. Yet, the Holy Qur'an was revealed in the Arabic language, and Muhammad was selected to receive the Message and convey it within his community.[3] The first issue then is to determine the extent to which the universality of the Message may be adversely affected by the fact that the immediate addressees of the Holy Qur'an were the people of the Arabian Peninsula, and that it was delivered in their language, through a person selected from their midst. Another issue arises from the fact that, even among those who speak the Arabic language, claims were made about the Qur'an containing a large number of verses whose understanding is stated in the Qur'an itself to be beyond the comprehension of the majority of people. In this section, we will first consider any reservations about Islam's universality in the sense that it is for all people. We will also examine the Arabic language paradox to determine if it is any indication that non-Arabic-speaking people are excluded from the reach of Islam. We will then deliberate whether or not the message of Islam requires an elite with specialized capabilities to mediate people's access to understanding that message.

Unrestricted Scope

Islam is for all people without any limitations. Islam is not limited to the believers who have accepted the Message brought by Prophet Muhammad. It is addressed to all humanity, to all people irrespective of their actual creeds.[4] God expressly revealed this. First, He described himself as the

God of all the worlds and all beings that He created,[5] and not as God of the believers or some other category of persons. He is even the God of the disbelievers who rejected the Message, and of the pagans who may or may not have received the Message. Then, because He is the God of all humankind, He has over the ages sent countless messengers to peoples in countless locations carrying the truth about, among other things, the unicity of God and His attributes, the duties of people to each other for a harmonious society, and life after death.[6] While all or some of the previous messages may have been specifically addressed to their immediate audiences, the Message of the Holy Qur'an carried by Prophet Muhammad was addressed to all people without any discrimination or exclusion of any kind. The Qur'an specifically confirms this in a series of verses.

Q7:158—"*Say: 'O* mankind, *I am the Messenger of God* to you all, *of Him to whom belongs the kingdom of the heavens and of the earth. There is no god but He. He gives life, and makes to die.*'"[7]

Q21:107—"*We have not sent thee, save as a mercy* unto all beings."[8]

Q25:1—"*Blessed be He who has sent down the Salvation upon His servant, that he may be a warner* to all beings."[9]

Q34:28—"*We did not send you (O prophet,) but to the* entire mankind, *as a bearer of good news and as a warner, but most people do not know.*"[10]

Although the Message was revealed in the Arabian Peninsula, to a messenger there, yet it is a universal message addressed to all of humankind and not just to the people of the Arabian Peninsula, as one might otherwise expect. This is set forth in straightforward terms in the above verses of the Holy Qur'an. It is further confirmed by the widely used Qur'anic form *ya ayyuha-n-nās*, meaning "O people" which is found in countless verses, instead of the form *ya ayyuha-l-mu'minūn*, meaning "O believers." Then, in terms of the reach of the Message, the term *people*, as primary audience of the Message, is mentioned 182 times in the Qur'an. There are certainly ample messages for the believers and the disbelievers. For the believers there are loads of rewards, and for the disbelievers there are dire threats of punishment. Yet, even those messages addressed to the believers and the disbelievers are indirectly destined as well to all people by way of encouragement to believe and dissuasion from disbelief. Verse Q10:2 is an example where the message is primarily addressed to people in general, with references to both the believers and disbelievers among them.

> *Is it surprising for the people that We have sent the divine revelation to a man from among them to direct him that he should warn the people (who are heedless), and give happy news to those who believe that they will have a truly excellent footing at a place near their Lord? The disbelievers said, "Surely, he is an open sorcerer."*[11]

The Arabic Language Paradox

Islam has been adopted by, and has become an integral part of the fabric of, many ethnic groups, such as—other than the Arabs of the Peninsula—the inhabitants of the Levant, the Indian subcontinent, Persians, Turks, and many others. Yet, it cannot be identified exclusively with any of these groups, nor can any such group claim Islam as its national identity. Indeed, in the words of Abdullah Khalayfi,

> Islam is counted among the great historic creeds and universal religions; and notwithstanding its spread across national and cultural boundaries, it nevertheless reflects the particularities of the various national groups over which it extends. Therefore, the universality of Islam and its exposure to all national entities is, according to certain scholars, a living proof that loyalty to Islam and loyalty to the relevant national identity constitute two different bonds...The differing natures of the Islamic bond and the national bond indicate that each such bond has its own field and its own impact.[12]

On that basis Islam is universal, in spite of the fact that the Arabs of the Arabian Peninsula were its first and immediate audience and claim Islam as their identity.

How do we reconcile the fact that Muhammad's message is universal and yet that it is expressed through the Arabic language?[13] This question is frequently and legitimately raised by non-Arabic-speaking Muslims and non-Muslims alike.[14] On the other hand, it is at times used by Arab Muslims to boast about Islam being first and foremost their religion and that if it came in their own language, it constitutes a divine tribute to them and to their cultures.[15] In fact, humankind has no universal language, divine or otherwise, which all people can understand. We have noted earlier that Islam did not appear in a vacuum but in the midst of a specific society and that it used as its starting point the prevailing tribal heritage of the Arabian Peninsula.[16] Still, its having been revealed in the Arabic language should not justify the disqualification of the Qur'an as a universal message, because divine messages are always expressed in a human language, that of the relevant messenger and people, as stated in Verse Q14:4.

> *AND NEVER have We sent forth any apostle otherwise than [with a message] in his own people's tongue, so that he might make [the truth] clear unto them; but God lets go astray him that wills [to go astray], and guides him that wills [to be guided]—for He alone is almighty, truly wise.*[17]

Accordingly, the language of the Message is not the criterion for its universality or specificity.

What makes the Qur'anic message universal is the presence of direct divine statements to that effect. In spite of the fact that the *Quraysh* and the other Arab-speaking tribes of the Arabian Peninsula and its surroundings were its initial audience, the primary and ultimate addressees of the Qur'anic message are all of mankind and not just the Arabic-speaking peoples of the Arabian Peninsula. Above all, what makes the Qur'anic message universal is its substance. Indeed, since God has sent that same message previously to countless other peoples, the Message brought by Prophet Muhammad is a reminder of, and encompasses, all previous messages brought by the various prophets and messengers of God, starting with Abraham and including Moses and Jesus. A logical reason for the same message to be resent countless times in different languages is to assure that substantially all of humankind gets an opportunity to be made aware of it—that it be conveyed universally. The concept of Islam as the universal and comprehensive religion, which encompasses all previous divine messages, is expressed in the following terms in the Qur'an.

> Q2:2 to 5—*"This Book is not to be doubted. It is a guide for the righteous (2), who believe in the unseen and are steadfast in prayer; who give in alms from what we gave them (3), who believe in what has been revealed to you and what was revealed before you, and have absolute faith in the life to come (4). These are rightly guided by their Lord; these shall surely triumph (5)."*[18]

> Q3:84 and 85—*"Say: 'We believe in God, and in what has been revealed to us and what was revealed to Abraham, Isma'il, Isaac, Jacob, and the Tribes, and in (the Books) given to Moses, Jesus, and the prophets, from their Lord: We make no distinction between one and another among them, and to God do we bow our will (in Islam)' (84). If anyone desires a religion other than Islam (submission to God), never will it be accepted of him; and in the Hereafter He will be in the ranks of those who have lost (All spiritual good) (85)."*[19]

> Q42:13—*"He has ordained for you of religion what He enjoined upon Noah and that which We have revealed to you, [O Muhammad], and what We enjoined upon Abraham and Moses and Jesus—to establish the religion and not be divided therein. Difficult for those who associate others with Allah is that to which you invite them. Allah chooses for Himself whom He wills and guides to Himself whoever turns back [to Him]."*[20]

Regarding the language of the Holy Qur'an, deniers of the divine origins of the Qur'an, such as Gabriel Sawma and Christoph Luxenberg, have made strong claims about its Aramaïc origins, including the assertion that the Qur'an's true language is Aramaïc.[21] They argue for the necessity of interpreting the Holy Qur'an in light of the meaning, in the

Aramaïc language, of the Arabic terms which share common roots with corresponding terms in that language. In reality, there is no reason to interpret the Qur'an based on the meaning of the Aramaïc terms which resemble Arabic ones. Firstly, all Semitic languages, including Arabic, Hebrew, Aramaïc, and others share a substantive stock of common-rooted vocabulary. While this may explain that a number of terms in the Qur'an have homonyms and perhaps synonyms in Aramaïc, it does not constitute sufficient reason to give the Arabic terms Aramaïc meanings. It is also true that, in the period preceding and following the Revelation, there were continuous contacts and exchanges among the Aramaïc speaking and Arabic-speaking peoples of the region. But again, this interaction is insufficient reason to justify that the Qur'an be interpreted and understood in light of the state of the Aramaïc language at that time.

There is no need to borrow tools from the Aramaïc language to interpret the Qur'an for important reasons, namely: (1) the Arabic language had long existed as the spoken language of the majority of the tribes in the Arabian Peninsula, even though its script had not yet been refined with the full array of diacritic signs; and (2) the Qur'an was indeed revealed in the Arabic language, as repeated time and again in countless verses,[22] following the divine tradition of sending messages to individual messengers in their own languages for the benefit of their peoples.

Moreover, the claims brought by Luxenberg and Sawma echo accusations which go back to the period of revelation, made by pagans against Prophet Muhammad in rejecting any originality attributed to the Qur'an.[23] Arthur Jeffery has addressed the issue of the potential foreign vocabulary of the Qur'an from the perspective of its strict interpretation. He rightly observes that foreign terms may certainly have entered the Arabic-language vocabulary and through it found their way into the Qur'an; and that is the natural outcome of the interaction of the Arabs with the diverse peoples surrounding them such as the Persians, Byzantines, Greeks, Indians, Ethiopians, and other African peoples.[24]

The fact that the Qur'an was received in the Arabic language is no indication that the Arabic language should prevail over other languages or that God has any preference for that language or for the people who speak that language.[25] On the contrary, God told us in Verse Q49:13 of the Holy Qur'an that all people, irrespective of gender, race, color, or language are equal except for their individual degrees of *taqwa,* or piety and righteousness: *"O mankind, We created you male and female, and made you into nations and tribes that you may come to know one another. The noblest among you in God's sight are the most pious."*[26]

Most of those who looked for earthly origins of the Holy Qur'an outside the Divine Revelation in the Arabic language were attempting to trace those origins in Christian and/or Jewish Scriptures.[27] They were forgetting, or perhaps even ignoring, that the Qur'an itself has asserted that it is a reminder of the Christian and Jewish Scriptures and that ultimately those Scriptures, commencing with the Abrahamic faith, belonged to one and the same origin, God.

Islam is for All Times and Places

Islam is universal not only because it addresses humankind as a whole, including all people of all creeds, but also because it addresses all people of all times and in all places. We have already seen that the message conveyed by Prophet Muhammad contains substantially the same fundamentals found in all previous divine messages. As confirmed in Verse Q40:78, universal Islam has been revealed to countless people in countless locations and not just to the peoples of the known prophets and messengers whose stories are narrated in the Qur'an.

Islam is also universal in the sense that, in addition to the people who received divine messages before the time of Prophet Muhammad, the Holy Qur'an addresses, and is relevant for, all people, wherever located, who are yet to come till the end of humanity and the Day of Judgment.[28] This is clear from the provisions of the Qur'an in which God confirms, shortly before Prophet Muhammad's death following completion of his final hajj, that He had by then completed the Message of Islam.[29] This explains that Muhammad is declared as the last and final prophet and messenger of God.[30] One might reasonably wonder why the succession of prophets and string of divine messages should end with Prophet Muhammad and the Qur'an, respectively. One answer flows from the text of Verse Q5:3, namely that, having finished with the conveyance of the religion of Islam which He had started with Abraham, God's Message was now perfect and complete. There was no further need for more prophets and messengers.

One might wonder also whether or not the Message is truly universal, knowing that no further prophets and messengers will be called to spread the word to future generations and in other lands.[31] In response to this concern, universality is primarily a statement of potentiality as opposed to a statement of actuality: universality is not necessarily about whether or not the Message was universally delivered to every person of every region and race in this world. The Message can be universal irrespective of the scope of its actual distribution and spread. That scope would ultimately determine the level of accountability and the judgments that God renders on the Day of Judgment, as confirmed by God in Verses Q17:15, Q26:208 and 209, and Q36:70. From that perspective, it is not important for us to know the detailed history of every message that God has sent, because what truly matters is whether individual persons got a reasonable opportunity to receive any such message.

Finally, universality is also about the continued ability of the Message to inspire with the passage of time. Daniel Brown, summarizing the views of modern thinkers from the Indian subcontinent, observes that, while Islam's core message does not change, our own understanding of its teachings changes as our capacities grow with time, hence the ability of each new generation to find in it new treasures.[32] Muhammad Shahrour attributes the universality of the Qur'anic message, in terms of its validity for all times and places, to an inherent characteristic of the Qur'an which serves as witness to its divine origin, that of *i'jāz*, its perfection and inimitability, both in form and substance, which served as Prophet Muhammad's miracle.

That said, universality is about the validity, soundness, and relevance of the Message at all times and in all places.

No Elitism in Islam

Elitism in Islam has been advanced on two important grounds. The first ground is based on an implied pairing of Islam and Arabism so as to support the notion of the apparent and necessary superiority of Arab Muslims over other Muslims. The second ground of elitism is based on the implied inability of the common mind to comprehend the Qur'anic message so as to conclude with the need to depend on learned scholars and to justify the indirect creation of a "clergy," nowhere called for in Islam.[33]

The advocates of pairing Islam and Arabism[34] invoke the repeated assurances made in the Meccan verses about the Qur'an having been revealed in the Arabic language, thereby setting forth what Shaykh Sobhi al-Saleh calls "the basic guidelines of a policy of Arabization." On that basis, al-Saleh asserts, "[t]he revelation of the Qur'an in the Arabic language must have inspired to the Arabs sentiments of great glory and pride... and to the non-Arabs sentiments of deep veneration and honor for everything Arab, in terms of language, descendence, perspective and birth."[35] In this statement, al-Saleh echoes the views of Shaykh Muhammad Rashid Rida who carries the argument so far as to (1) limit the right of *ijtihād* (the adaptation and implementation of the Qur'anic provisions by way of applying reason and judgment) to those who master the Arabic language exclusively; (2) require that the head of the Islamic state be an Arab who masters the Arabic language, because in that capacity he acts as the supreme imam who carries out the duty of ensuring the continued spread of the Message and retains the ultimate authority in performing *ijtihād*.[36]

However, such views are limiting because the Arabs among the Muslims are but a small fraction, and God—in His infinite Compassion—has not excluded the non-Arab Muslim masses from direct access to the Holy Qur'an and its understanding. In fact, the New Testament was originally recorded in Greek and Aramaïc, yet Christianity was not exposed to any risk of loss over time because of the masses who did not learn these languages.

Similarly, it is often claimed that, because the Qur'an can be understood only by people well versed in the Arabic language, such is reason enough that no translation into any language may be called a translation of the Qur'an but a translation of its meanings. This is not a convincing argument to justify any form of Arab elitism or to deny the ability of non-Arab Muslims to fully understand and live Islam just like any Arab Muslim.

That is why a non-Arab Muslim such as Abdennour Bidar is fully entitled to his views when he writes, "Islam must reform its 'arabocentric' vision of itself." Indeed, and from his own experience with understanding the Qur'an after having learned it both in French and Arabic, Bidar rightly observes that the Arabic version did not add anything to his understanding because God speaks all languages.[37]

The focus on the Arabic language which can be observed in the Meccan verses of the Qur'an is not related to what al-Saleh calls a "politics of Arabization." Instead, the divine focus is on addressing people in their own language for the purpose of enabling them to understand the Message. To avoid any doubt, the Message asserts that there is no preference for Arab over non-Arab peoples: divine preference is exclusively based on piety and righteousness, and no other consideration of language or race.[38]

Concerning the second ground of alleged elitism, an important measure of the universality of a message is its accessibility to all people, and their ability to understand it, both in substance and form. With respect to substance, it has been alleged that the Qur'an contains truths that go beyond the ability of the ordinary mind to grasp, citing for that purpose several verses of the Qur'an, such as, *"We cite these examples for people, but no one understands them except the knowledgeable ones."*[39] Prophetic Tradition is also relied on to make that same point, citing two traditions, namely, *"We, Prophets, have been commanded to address people in accordance with what their brains can handle,"* and *"You should not address people in a language that their minds cannot comprehend lest it causes trouble."*[40] For that purpose, these truths must presumably be diluted and presented in simple doses to render them accessible to the minds of the wider masses of people.[41]

Such perceptions of the Qur'anic message and of the mental capabilities of its receivers should be rejected. They are unduly discriminatory on several counts: (1) they underestimate the intelligence of people; (2) they ignore that God has endowed humankind with a mind so that they may act as God's trustees; and (3) most importantly, to the extent that the Message must filter through intermediaries other than the initial messenger in order to reach its addressees, the universal nature of Islam would thereby be undermined. Bearing these reasons in mind, the quoted verse is not about the superior powers of experts in religious science or in any other science. It is simply about the knowledge of the basics of the faith and the truths brought about by the Qur'anic message— namely the truth about the unicity of God, that He is sole creator and Almighty, and has the final say on the Day of Judgment. As for the cited prophetic traditions, they are both classified among the weak traditions, with doubtful authenticity.

With respect to form, a wide spectrum of people, including scholars, clerics, and others, have asserted that the language of the Holy Qur'an is not understandable to the common person, let alone to all people. They proclaim that, in order to properly understand and interpret the Holy Qur'an, a person must master the Arabic language as opposed to being able to speak it and read it only. That person must also be conversant with the various religious sciences, including the Prophetic Tradition and the works of the commentators and scholars.[42] Such views are at times motivated by a genuine belief that the language of the Qur'an is difficult to comprehend, and at other times it is motivated by a concern to justify a role for a class of learned people, including clergy. On this subject, Farid Esack recounts the experience of a group of young people in South Africa who decided to learn the Arabic language in order to directly access to the Holy Qur'an. They were seeking self-confidence and freedom from the domineering influence of the clergy who monopolized control over understanding the Qur'an by virtue of, among other things, being able to speak and read Arabic. It is no surprise that the decision by the young South Africans to learn Arabic triggered the anger of a clergy threatened with losing its status as guardian of the holy text.[43]

God affirms in the Qur'an that the Message is for the common folk, and for that reason he made it easy and intelligible to all people, and not just to the scholars and the learned. More specifically, He states:

"It is He that has sent forth among the Gentiles an apostle of their own to recite to them His revelations, to purify them, and to instruct them in the Book and in wisdom, though they have hitherto been in evident error."[44]

"Surely We have brought them a book that We have elaborated with knowledge, as guidance and mercy for a people who believe."[45]

"By the Book that makes things clear."[46]

"So, We had made it (the Qur'an) easy in your tongue, so that they may take lesson."[47]

On that basis, the Qur'an is not only for Muslims, whether learned or not. It is for everyone, without exception, and all people have equal opportunity to access the Qur'an and its understanding.[48] It is true that people are enticed to learn and strive in their education. It is also true that people who learn are better able to benefit from the signs and examples that the Qur'an offers and thereby get a better grasp of the Qur'an's wisdom. Yet, as far as the basic faith and the fundamental truths contained in the Qur'an are concerned, these are accessible to all without any need for intermediaries. Therefore, the Qur'anic verses which apparently discriminate between the knowledgeable and the ignorant, and between the blind and the person who can see, are in reality verses which praise reading and learning the Qur'an. As a result of such process, those who are ignorant and blind about the divine truths will begin to see and to acquire the needed knowledge.[49]

There is however an intriguing verse of the Qur'an over which heated arguments and counterarguments have been exchanged about the potential need for expert intermediation of accessibility to the Qur'an, and it is Verse Q3:7.

He is the One who has revealed to you the Book (the Qur'ān). Out of it there are verses that are muHkamāt (of established meaning), which are the principal verses of the Book, and some others are Mutashābihāt (whose definite meanings are unknown). Now those who have perversity in their hearts go after such part of it as is mutashābih, seeking (to create) discord, and searching for its interpretation (that meets their desires), while no one knows its interpretation except Allah; and those well-grounded in knowledge say: "We believe therein; all is from our Lord." Only the men of understanding observe the advice.[50]

Those who support the elitist requirement to master the Arabic language and those who deny the universal nature of Islam, or at least its wide scope, equally advance this verse in support of their claims, from three related perspectives.

From the first perspective, the adjective *mutashābihāt* has been given several meanings by interpreters. The term has been interpreted as: (1) a reference to abrogated verses that have been replaced by relevant abrogating verses, the so-called *muḥkamāt* verses;[51] (2) a reference to allegories that need to be interpreted, hence the need for learned scholars to provide appropriate interpretations; (3) following the root term *shabah* (or resemblance) from which *mutashābihāt* derives, a reference to verses which resemble one another in form but which may have different interpretations depending on the circumstances of revelation of the respective verses;[52] and (4) verses whose meaning is not known precisely or definitively enough.[53]

An interesting approach is advanced by Jalal al-Din al-Suyuti and Jalal al-Din al-Mahalli, in which the term *mutashābihāt,* as used in the Qur'an, has two meanings. In Verse Q3:7 it refers to the unintelligible signs appearing at the beginning of certain verses in the form of loose letters, such as Ṣad (for the letter Ṣ), Ṭaha (for the letters Ṭ and H), Alif Lam Mim (for the letters A, L, and M), and so on. On that basis, all the verses of the Qur'an are of the *muḥkamāt* category, that is, verses whose meaning is clear and unambiguous, as confirmed in Verse Q11:1: *"(This is) a book the verses of which have been made firm, and elaborated by the One who is All Wise, All Aware."*[54]

The other meaning of the term *mutashābihāt* appears in Verse Q39:23, which declares the entire Qur'an to be *mutashābihan.* This would imply that all verses of the Qur'an are *mutashābihāt,* but in reality it means that substantially all the verses of the Qur'an are similar to each other in terms of their authenticity of origin and their truth. Or as al-Tabari suggests, "[T]he provisions of the Qur'an resemble one another, confirm one another, and witness one another."[55]

This latter approach appearing in Tafsir al-Jalalayn holds credibility. Any explanation of *mutashābihāt* verses which is based on mystery and mere interpretation is implausible because it is inconsistent with the divine statements in the Qur'an that God has made the Holy Qur'an accessible to all, as part of a system of divine justice, and where all that is needed is for people to read or listen to the verses and ponder them, which is substantially within the abilities of most people. On that basis, (1) *muḥkamāt* verses are the ones which deal with the rules of worship and the principles governing relations among humans in their day-to-day activities; and (2) *mutashābihāt* verses are the ones which are mainly about the stories of ancient peoples, the Day of Judgment, the afterlife, signs and examples offered in the Qur'an; and any other matters which an ordinary human cannot see and has no means to verify.[56] This explains that "those who are well-grounded in knowledge" have no option but to acknowledge their trust in the substance of those verses which they cannot verify for the sole reason that these verses come from God.

From the second perspective, since the Arabic script of the seventh century, in which the Qur'an descended and was compiled, did not contain punctuation signs, deniers of the universal reach of Islam read the second sentence of the verse in question—which follows the categorization of verses into *muḥkamāt,* whose meaning is clear, and *mutashābihāt,* whose definite meaning is elusive—into two sentences.

> *Now those who have perversity in their hearts go after such part of it as is mutashābih, seeking (to create) discord, and searching for its interpretation (that meets their desires), while no one knows its interpretation except Allah and those well-grounded in knowledge. Say: "We believe therein; all is from our Lord."*

By moving the punctuation sign from "Allah" to "those well-grounded in knowledge," an understanding of *mutashābihāt* verses—otherwise beyond the reach of ordinary persons—becomes accessible to the scholars in addition to God, instead of remaining the exclusive realm of God. In addition, such a shift in the punctuation renders the rest of the verse meaningless.[57]

From the third perspective, the meaning of the last sentence of the verse in question (*"Only the men of understanding observe the advice"*) should not be stretched to imply that only scholars observe the advice because they are the only ones, as opposed to ordinary people, who are capable of understanding it. In reality, this sentence mainly refers to the wise persons among ordinary people who take seriously the truths and higher principles revealed by God.

Finally, the meaning of Verse Q3:7 cited above becomes clear when placed in its context in light of its circumstance of revelation. This verse was revealed in connection with the event in which Prophet Muhammad received a delegation of Christians from Najran who came to debate with him, intending eventually to embarrass him over a few basic faith issues related to Islam's perception of the birth of Jesus Christ, his divinity or humanity, the status of his mother Mary, and the role of the Holy Ghost, among other thorny topics. This verse thus accuses the delegation from Najran of not acting in good faith because they were giving to *mutashābihāt* verses meanings that suited them to make their point and thereby create discord among Muslims.[58]

Boundaries of Universality—The Qur'anOnly

Which Islam is universal? Is it Islam the message, Islam the civilization, or Islam the history? This question is germane because there is an important difference between these Islams. Islam the message is the only one whose origin is exclusively divine. The Holy Qur'an is the word of God and does not contain any human input. On the other hand, Islam the history, in addition to its message as a starting point, consists of the implementation of Islam throughout the evolution of Muslim societies, starting with the society in which Islam was revealed and extending to our modern days, including the glorious days of the vast empire built following the death of the Prophet. In addition to its message and the historical data, Islam the civilization consists of the Islamic heritage, including intellectual and scientific heritage. In other words, Islam the history and Islam the civilization include, in addition to its Divine Message, the human heritage of particular times and places, or accumulated over time.[59]

Because the Qur'an, being the word of God, is perfect and contains all the truths that humankind needs to strive toward ultimate truth and achieve salvation, God made it His last message to humanity, based on which the Final Judgment will be conducted.[60] The Message must therefore be sufficient to remain relevant for all people, at all times, and in all places to achieve that purpose. From this perspective, the Message as contained in the Holy Qur'an is universal.

Can the same be said of the human heritage that accompanied the revelation of the Qur'an and thereafter accumulated over the years? That heritage in question starts with the Prophetic Tradition and the tradition of the four rightly guided companions of the Prophet. It also includes all the intellectual efforts that went into explaining, interpreting, and elaborating the religious science that developed over time, such as the commentaries, compilations, and doctrines brought about by the various schools of jurisprudence.

Unfortunately, that heritage is often confused with the divine as the result of a conscious reluctance to draw a line between the two. Ebrahim Moosa expresses a genuine concern when he observes that God never spoke to humans directly, other than to prophets through revelation, and concludes that whatever we know about Islam consists of claims made by fellow Muslims.[61] While it is true that God revealed the Qur'an to mankind through Prophet Muhammad, yet, Prophet Muhammad made sure to clearly distinguish between the Divine Revelation and his own tradition in order to prevent any confusion between them. The flaw here is that, except for accepting the word of the Prophet about the divine origin of the Qur'anic Message, Muslims have a direct, unmediated access to Islam through the Holy Qur'an. Everything else and all others are guiding lights. Thus the line is very clear between Islam the message and Islam the civilization, because the former is divine and the latter is human.[62] In addition, the persons listed as sources of Islam are not equal. While the Prophet can possibly be classified as a source, everyone else is a layperson and his/her views do not form part of Islam. Even as far as the Prophet is concerned, and apart from certain worship-related procedures discussed previously, everything else he said or did is a most valuable guidance which Muslims, in the post-revelatory period, are free to follow or not to follow.

To other thinkers, the divine's own existence becomes contingent on the human. For al-Shatibi,[63] the certainty of any divine ruling contained in the Qur'anic Message is contingent on corroboration by Prophetic Tradition and *ijmā'* (consensus). No wonder then that the human work product, as shaped by the circumstances of days long passed, became part of religion, having been sacralized for no purpose whatsoever. In addition to its being insensitive to the perfection of the divine, such an attitude implies the insufficiency of the divine unless associated with the human.

Without prejudice to the wealth of that heritage and the high quality of the thought that went into it, that heritage is necessarily marked with the prejudices, issues, problems, and solutions that are characteristic of specific times and places. Being a human heritage, it reflects the level of instruction and education of the particular thinker, the level of sophistication of the environment that inspired that thought, and the nature of the issues that concerned society and motivated thinkers to find appropriate solutions. This, for example, explains the wide differences in approach and outcome observed between one school of jurisprudence and another. For example, the Maliki and Hanbali schools of thought came about in the Hijaz, in Medina, the city in which Prophet Muhammad strove to carry out his mission, whereas the Hanafi school of thought originated in Baghdad, following the expansion of the Islamic empire into the Near East and Mesopotamia. Indeed, since the primarily tribal social environment of Medina and its Hijaz surroundings, as experienced by Prophet Muhammad, changed only marginally following his death, the problems faced in that area could for centuries forward continue to be resolved based substantially on Prophetic Tradition. The same could not be said of Baghdad, which had achieved a high level of sophistication as a result of the interaction among the Persian, Hellenistic, and Byzantine cultures.[64] In such an environment, Prophetic Tradition could not constitute a source sufficient to provide solutions for problems which would never be conceivable in a tribal environment. This explains that the Hanafi School of Jurisprudence resorted to tools based on intellectual effort to extract most of its doctrines and solutions.

From the perspective of a thinker striving to analyze his/her environment and devise solutions to its problems, general theories and special solutions could be relevant only for that environment because no two environments are identical, for the solutions of one to be transposed into the other. Unfortunately, this is what happened in Muslim societies generally. In fact, in the three centuries following the death of the Prophet, scholars started compiling the traditions of the Prophet, including any stories which—when put together—could serve as biography of the

Prophet. Muslims felt safer solving their problems by imitating a reported example of the Prophet or that of a companion of the Prophet. Instead, venturing into what is considered the risky process of inventing a solution exclusively through the works of the mind, could lead into the realm of the punishable, if a solution should inadvertently be inconsistent with the principles of the new faith. In this respect, we bring to attention a tradition of Prophet Muhammad in which he is presumed to have warned against any form of innovation: *"The most evil thing is innovation; every innovation constitutes a* 'bid'a' *or heresy, every* 'bid'a' *is* 'ḍalāla' *or error and strayance from the right path, and every* 'ḍalāla' *leads to the fire of hell."*[65] As with all Prophetic Tradition, that tradition is unreliable because of the fabrication and tampering that accompanied its compilation and recording, over the few centuries that followed the death of Prophet Muhammad, and the political and other interests which motivated such fraud.Assuming the accuracy of that tradition, it was certainly not the Prophet's intention to prevent people from having their own understanding of the faith, by which they would live and be judged. He intented to warn against recontaminating the purity of the new faith and the worship of God with reprehensible practices brought back from the *jāhiliyya*. He meant to protect and shield the fundamentals of the faith from extraneous factors and contaminants, such as, for example, canceling the fast of Ramadan or the prayer, and/or replacing them with some other rituals, pagan or otherwise.

As a result, fear of God and his punishment, as consistently and skillfully advocated by clerics and rulers to maintain control over their peoples, prevailed over the countless appeals in the Qur'an for people to use their minds. The minds of the people were disregarded, while those of the rulers and clerics raced to create the framework within which the minds of the people could be controlled and neutralized. In such an environment, the common people obediently followed the lead of "learned" ones who claimed deep knowledge of the Prophetic Tradition and the traditions of the Companions, and the implied interpretations of the Qur'an arising from them. This fear, nurtured and manipulated by many in the name of religion, led and continues to lead to the swelling of the Islamic "heritage" and to the overloading of the Message with issues and matters that are alien to it.[66] This approach is the natural corollary of the claims that religion regulates all facets of life and holds ready-made solutions to every problem and issue of all times.

Over time, the scholarly works of the early compilers of traditions, interpreters, and exegetes of the Holy Qur'an and of Prophetic Tradition, became an integral part of the faith to which people turned more easily than to the presumably "unintelligible" or difficult to understand language of the Qur'an. This has led to the *de facto* sacralization of the human heritage and to stagnation within the community to the detriment of the infinite wealth of the original Qur'anic Message.[67] Abdolkarim Soroush pertinently describes it as "a moment in which sanctity (taqaddus) is sought in petrification or fossilisation (tajahhur). The very notion of thinking things through becomes an abomination, an audacity in the face of the 'law-giver' (*shāri'*)."[68]

Unfortunately the sacralization of that heritage continues to weigh heavily on Muslims— ordinary people and scholars alike—where the Holy Qur'an is abandoned in favor of the works of commentators and exegetes.[69]

Daniel Brown recounts how the behavior of the Companions came to be perceived as the live practice of the Prophet's traditions, to be imitated by their successors and their individual communities.[70] It is a process which sacralizes the Prophet in the first place, emphasizes *taqlīd* (blind imitation), and renders immaterial the need to ascertain the veracity of individual traditions. Along the same lines, Fazlur Rahman draws a global picture of how Prophetic Tradition evolved beyond what the Prophet may or may not have done to include the traditions of the Companions and the consensus of their communities, which are believed to represent what the Prophet would have done or said under various circumstances.[71] This is a destructive approach which erodes religion, as Muslims gradually cease to submit to the Message of God and true traditions of the Prophet, and embrace instead the practice of the Prophet's companions, their successors, and their own communities. Such an approach ignores that communities have been frequently manipulated by caliphs, rulers, "clergy," and others, and opens the door to incorporating adverse elements into religion by bringing history into Prophetic Tradition.

Furthermore, even the countless scholars who sought to differentiate religion from religious thought for fear that the human heritage might supersede the Divine Message often failed to include Prophetic Tradition within religious thought. As a result, potential progress was inhibited by the withdrawal of Prophetic Tradition from the sphere of the profane and by its inclusion in the realm of the sacred.[72] This is perhaps what Muhammad Arkoun meant by describing the sacralization of Prophetic Tradition as a transformation of the thinkable into unthinkable.[73] It is precisely the fear of sacralization that must have motivated Prophet Muhammad to strictly prohibit any recording of his traditions. He was concerned that people would abandon the Qur'an to imitate him. Abdelmajid Charfi refers to the phenomenon when he writes, "Contemporary Muslims abstain from any direct contact with the Qur'anic text, and they continue to read it through the works of the fuqahā'and the commentators of the past."[74] Moreover, Prophet Muhammad is reported to have even recommended that the Qur'an be read by each person as if it was directly revealed to him/her. Isn't such advice the essence of the universal nature of Islam?

It can be concluded that, since God has no associates, and since no human being participates with Him in framing religion, the entire religion must be found exclusively in the Holy Qur'an. Then, a desacralization of the human heritage of Islam is called for in order to reactivate the universal nature of the Message. Desacralization will take root when Muslims are ready to accept that religion is distinct from the people's understandings of it.[75] In particular, human understanding of religion is not, and cannot be, universal because it is necessarily a representation of a particular environment in which that understanding took shape. Accordingly, how Prophet Muhammad and the Companions who succeeded him understood and implemented the Qur'anic Message is relevant only for their environment; that is, for their time and place. It is not part of Islam the Message, but it is certainly part of Islam the history and the Islamic heritage. The Holy Qur'an remains at all times and in all places the sole divine source of Islam, with everything else produced over the years by the human mind being seen as nonuniversal,[76] but serving nevertheless as guiding lights from historical and jurisprudential perspectives.[77]

Identifying the Message

Which parts of the Qur'an are universal?

The question is crucial, since the Holy Qur'an is filled with messages that are very specific to the initial addressees of that Message, namely the Arabic-speaking tribes inhabiting the Arabian Peninsula. Could that Message, which deals very deeply with tribal issues and problems of the seventh century in Arabia, using their language, be of interest—let alone be relevant—to all people, at all times, and in all places?[78] How can a message which addresses issues of sorcery, revenge among tribes, and other tribal customs help to address problems arising—if not lead progress—in the age of high technology and the global environment of the twenty-first century?

The Holy Qur'an deals with a wide range of topics, including stories about peoples historically, principles of the faith and worship, and rules of conduct among humans. Some of these topics may acquire more relevance for some people at some point in time while being intended for all people, at all times and in all places.

The Holy Qur'an was revealed to Prophet Muhammad over a period of more than twenty years, in an interactive manner, where a large number of verses were intended to guide his steps in the performance of his prophetic mission, and those verses would have served their purpose upon the complete fulfillment of that mission.

In this section we will consider the extent to which the verses of the Qur'an, which on the surface may appear to focus on specific purposes or address the seventh-century tribes of the Arabian Peninsula, in fact can be universal.

External Message and Underlying Message

For a message to be universal it must be relevant to all people, at all times and in all places. In order for it to remain relevant *ad infinitum eternam*, it must remain alive and survive from one generation to the next. This means that, from the start, that message must be sufficiently understandable and relevant, primarily to the initial addressees. If rejected, it would fade into obsolescence and miss the opportunity to reach subsequent generations.[79]

Therefore, surviving the first generation of the initial addressees is a crucial hurdle to cross. A message that has been accepted spreads geographically, and its survival becomes easier to assume if the basic seeds of relevance exist in the first place.

This explains the core of the Prophet's mission, expressed in Verse Q62:2: *"It is He that has sent forth among the Gentiles an apostle of their own to recite to them His revelations, to purify them, and to instruct them in the Book and in wisdom, though they have hitherto been in evident error."*[80] This verse requires that the Message be conveyed to the people by someone coming from their midst and who speaks their language—two important conditions if the Message is to take hold and be accepted wholeheartedly. Only then would the Message have any chance to spread. It also explains the nature of the language used in the Qur'an, a language very deeply rooted in the day-to-day tribal life of the *Quraysh*, the Arabian Peninsula, and their immediate surroundings.[81] It explains the interactive sequence of revelation so as to guide the footsteps of the Prophet in this prophetic mission. Placed in this context, most Qur'anic verses had an external, conspicuous message corresponding to its immediate purpose, that of guiding the steps of the Prophet and dealing with the current environment of the Muslims. However, they also have another underlying, continuously adapting universal message for the rest of humankind until the end of time.

Because the Holy Qur'an was revealed in the language of the time and place of the Revelation, it was readily understood. It triggered the entire spectrum of reactions, from immediate acceptance or rejection of the obvious to hesitation over the suspicious and/or uncertain. This enabled the Prophet, with the help of the Companions, to go about the fulfillment of his mission. As a result, and following a long, arduous and protracted process, the Message spread and continues to do so to our day. Yet, a review of the immediate meaning of the external message makes it clear that its essence may not appeal or be relevant to later generations or to populations elsewhere, in the same manner as it appealed or was relevant to the people of Mecca and the Arabian Peninsula at the time of revelation. This explains the need to transcend a meaning as it became obsolete with the disappearance of the initial audience to which it was addressed, in search for the universal message addressed to the rest of humankind of all times and places, for them to consider and benefit therefrom.[82]

The Qur'an depicts the end of the world signaling the advent of the Final Day, together with the punishment and reward system following the Final Judgment in the afterlife, in vivid terms intended to entice humankind to accept and observe the new faith. It promises decadent material pleasures of paradise for the blessed, and threatens eternal fire in hell for the noncompliant. It depicts paradise in a setting of lush gardens surrounded with abundant waters, where the blessed can enjoy unlimited food, drinks, and all the material pleasures of life that anyone could think of, let alone wish for. Clearly, this depiction of paradise is one which particularly appealed to the people of the Arabian Peninsula of the Prophet's time, who suffered from the scorching heat of the desert, where food was a scarce commodity, where society was characterized by male chauvinism, and where contact between men and women fell in the realm of the prohibited and strictly sanctioned, and over which tribes could go to war in revenge for tribal honor.

However, had the Message been initially revealed in a different location of the globe blessed with water and greenery and where food was plentiful, or had it been revealed in the twenty-first century when segregation of the sexes has been lifted and social norms governing contacts between men and women have been relaxed, the particular depiction of heaven in the Qur'an might not have been sufficiently appealing. Moreover, the focus on the exclusive pleasures of the male population in the depiction of paradise could, in our age, even serve as a disincentive for women to live a good life in order to seek paradise.

That said, it remains that in this particular example there is a universal and eternal message for humankind which underlies the material depictions of the primary message that was addressed to the initial audience of the Prophet. That underlying message is substantially about the existence of life after death, whose quality for each person is determined by God, in His infinite justice and without discrimination of any kind among people— male and female—after an overall assessment and evaluation of that person's character and actions in the span of his/her worldly life. Thus, the particular material depictions of paradise become irrelevant, leaving what essentially counts, namely that people who live a virtuous life will receive a generous divine reward.

Another example, illustrating a worship requirement, is about the details of timing governing the fast of the month of Ramadan. Among other rules, the Qur'an provides that the duration of the fast, each day, is from the time that "*the white thread of the dawn becomes distinct from the black thread*" until "*the night.*"[83] Here, too, the measure of time is phrased in language readily meaningful to the primary audience of the Prophet, one that every person can easily monitor by looking toward the sky and verifying the thread lighting test. In addition, the time span included in that depiction is a reasonable period for that location, where the difference in daylight duration between the longest and shortest day of the year is negligible. That depiction would have been different had the Revelation descended in some other location, further north, where continuous daylight could extend from hours to days, making it eventually hard and dangerous for any person to fast, no matter how well-intentioned and healthy that person may be. In this case, the underlying message is that each person is required to fast for a period sufficient to benefit that person's health and make that person feel the hardships endured by the poor people whom he/she is enjoined to feed and help. Thus the time span, as specifically depicted in Verse Q2:187 to run from dawn to sunset, becomes irrelevant and at times impractical. Accordingly, since the dawn-to-sunset criterion is just a measure of time and has no particular spiritual connotation, it becomes possible for people living in other geographic locations to adopt different, more reasonable schedules in keeping with a substantially comparable time span.

There are serious and inherent risks associated with an understanding of the Qur'an limited to the external meanings of its verses, whether the reader is a fundamentalist or a modernist. At one extreme, attributing universality to the external meaning of verses to the exclusion of the underlying message results in social and scientific stagnation and lack of progress. At the other extreme, holding to the external meaning of the verses in order to negate their universal scope could lead to deconstruction, destruction, and obsolescence of the Message,[84] an outcome perhaps even more harmful than the former extreme.

What is universal in the Holy Qur'an is substantially the corpus of underlying messages arising from the various verses of the Qur'an, to the exclusion of the external messages destined primarily to convince and appeal to the initial audience of the Prophet. Only through elucidation of these underlying messages can the universal nature of Islam and its continued relevance be preserved. It is necessary, then, to explore the manner in which the Qur'anic Message should be approached and understood.

Interpretation versus Explanation

If the underlying messages in the Qur'an are the ones that matter, those underlying messages need to be identified by way of interpretation. Why should the Qur'anic Message be interpreted and not simply explained? After all, doesn't the Qur'an assert that it is revealed in plain, humanly easy-to-understand Arabic language, accessible to all? Indeed, the Qur'an was revealed in Arabic, the language commonly spoken and understood by the people of the Arabian Peninsula at the time of revelation. However, in this case, the issue is not about the understandability of the language used; instead, it is about two different levels of understanding of the same text. For the initial audience of the Prophet, which needs to accept the Message so that it may survive and spread, it is sufficient for them to understand the external immediate meaning. It addresses itself to them using terms, concepts, and figures of speech that are familiar to their environment and that reflect their customs and concerns.[85] However, each subsequent generation that reads the same message will transcend that immediate meaning of the Message, and any other previously extrapolated meanings of it, and seek for the relevant underlying message, that is, the one which is relevant for their time and place. By doing so, the person reading the Message would be performing an interpretation which should lead him/her to the relevant underlying message.

That act of interpretation, which is required to identify the universal message, acquires a greater importance if we clarify what it means for the underlying message of a Qur'anic verse to be universal. Contrary to the general perception arising from long-standing jurisprudence, it is the Message itself that is universal and valid for all times and places rather than its understanding in the early days of Islam and its later interpretations at any point in time. That is why the exegetes of the older days never contemplated legislating for the future and for other than their own societies.[86]

"Read and Listen to the Qur'an as if it was revealed to you," said Prophet Muhammad.[87] This prophetic tradition, assuming its authenticity, means that the Message was not revealed exclusively to Prophet Muhammad so that he might, in his discretion, convey his understanding of it or otherwise be selective in what he conveys. The Message was instead revealed to all of humanity, through Prophet Muhammad, as a transmitter. His mission was to convey the Message exactly as received, without addition or subtraction.[88] When he was asked to clarify or explain any part of the Revelation, he often abstained from answering until he received the divine answer.[89] The difference between Prophet Muhammad's receiving the Message as the sole addressee and his receiving it as a transmitter is significant. In the former case, it means that the Message is not universal because it would be addressed to him only. Thus its relevance to his people would be relative to the extent to which he elects to share the Message, and its relevance to us becomes historical. However, in the latter case, the Message is truly universal because every person, without exception—from then until the Day of Reckoning—is a primary recipient of it. As primary recipient, each person is equally entitled to the manner in which he/she understands the Message and elects to make use of it. The logical corollary of the Message being revealed for the benefit of each and every person is that no one is entitled to impose a particular understanding, whether his/her own understanding or someone else's.

Because people vary, whether they live in the same environment or in different environments separated in time and space, their particular understandings of the Message should not be expected to be similar. Accordingly, there is not a single underlying message that expresses an ultimate truth or that lasts *ad infinitum*, because that underlying message is an expression of human understanding of the relevant message. Above all, however, it reflects the specific understanding of the particular person who, through his/her own interpretation, extracted that message. Thus, the underlying message would in all likelihood differ from one place to another, from one age to another, and from one person to another. It is from this perspective that the commentaries and exegeses that have accumulated over the years and found their way into the sacred heritage of Islam should be perceived and considered. These commentaries and exegeses, though they constitute a valuable historical and jurisprudential heritage, are nevertheless not universal and, for that reason, should at no time be confused with, or otherwise be made a part of, the faith.

This leads to the conclusion that, in searching for and elucidating the underlying message, it is essential for each individual as a primary recipient of the Message to remain free from the burdens of commentaries and exegeses of others which impose or propose the authors' own specific interpretations.[90] Mohamed Talbi eloquently illustrates the universal nature of the Holy Qur'an by describing it as an infinite revelation that does not stop revealing itself.[91] It follows that the richness of that universal message would be severely reduced if any interpretation is universalized or is otherwise given a reach extending beyond its own time and place. This is precisely why the same is said of Prophetic Tradition, it being a human interpretation reflective of the Prophet's own specific environment, as opposed to the original message, which is universal and adaptive to every environment till the end of time. What makes Islam universal is that it invites multiple understandings and interpretations of the underlying message. As long as these understandings and implementations keep changing, the original message remains relevant and able to inspire progress, answers, and solutions.

It is unfortunate that, to the detriment of Muslim communities, the universality inherent in the Holy Qur'an was substantially diluted, while universality was extended to Prophetic Tradition. Daniel Brown articulates the claim, proposing, "[t]he Sunna is universal because it is applicable in all times and places, rules every aspect of life, and encompasses every kind of relationship...The simplicity of Sunna lies in its tolerance, convenience, and ease; it imposes no undue burden."[92] In this respect, it should be clarified that simplicity and tolerance were the qualities of Prophet Muhammad. Thus the simplicity, tolerance, and convenience of the Prophetic Tradition are derived from those same qualities of the Prophet and are only so with respect to that part of the tradition which is proven authentic. As such, it is a tribute to the wise, enlightened, and rational methodology that the Prophet applied in living the faith. As for the statement that Prophetic Tradition "imposes no undue burden," in fairness, it is true that, it does not. However, when it is unfairly claimed to rule every aspect of life and encompass every kind of relationship, then such an unsubstantiated claim would wrongly make it appear as being itself the burden. Such a perception not only restricts but entirely obstructs the universality inherent in the Qur'an and all freedom that the Qur'an came to promote.

Clear perception of the Qur'an's universality is further weakened by assertions, such as the following by Daniel Brown, which contend, "[t]he Sunna distinguishes what the Qur'an combines, it disentangles what the Qur'an intertwines, and it specifies what the Qur'an deals with in general terms."[93] Unfortunately, such sacralization of Prophetic Tradition is harmful to the Holy Qur'an in its universality. God in his infinite wisdom had intentionally left matters combined, intertwined, or written in general terms for Muslims in all places and at all times to distinguish, disentangle, and specify in light of their circumstances of time and place, just as Prophet Muhammad so wisely taught when he did so for his own time and place in the performance of his prophetic mission. Prophet Muhammad never contemplated taking away our freedom through his example, and it is for this reason that he made sure to prohibit any recordation of his traditions. Any assertion to the contrary would imply that God had done an incomplete job in the Qur'an and that Prophet Muhammad came to finish it. Did the Prophet ever make any such a claim?

Basic Principles of Interpretation

To achieve a meaningful interpretation of the text and extract the underlying message, a few basic principles may be suggested for consideration. First, the given text for interpretation should be analyzed together with all other provisions of the Qur'an that deal with the same subject. Otherwise, a meaning could be derived which contradicts other provisions dealing with the same subject.[94] This requirement is set forth in Verse Q25:32. For example, exegetes have interpreted Verse Q66:9[95] about jihad as a final, unrestricted order from God to the Prophet and the Companions to fight the disbelievers and hypocrites for no reason other than for being disbelievers. It is an obvious interpretation reached when the verse in question is taken on its own, without reference to the other Qur'anic provisions on jihad and fighting. However, when read in conjunction with the overall body of verses dealing with jihad and fighting, as it is only rational to do, the interpretation changes entirely. In that case, jihad is then perceived as a noble act of worship which can take the form of fighting only under the most compelling circumstances and against persons who prevent Muslims from striving in the path of God, and then only as necessary to remove the obstruction in question. Another good example can be found in the verses dealing with the crime of murder, where a number of verses may imply that it is a private matter between the family of the killer and that of the victim. As such it is resolved by way of capital punishment, blood money, and/or simple pardon, as the family of the victim may determine. However, when Verse Q5:32 is brought together with the other verses on the matter, murder then becomes a crime against humanity that may no longer be resolved solely with the involvement of the victim's family.[96]

It is also necessary to treat the relevant text as a live text, in the sense that its environment must be taken into consideration, with its geographic, social, historical, and cultural characteristics.[97] In other words, since the Message did not appear in a vacuum, it must be placed in context so that a rational cause, reasonably justified by the circumstances surrounding the relevant event, could be attributed to the message.[98] Only then can the external message be understood, and the underlying message made manifest to observe and record. For example, on the strength of Verses Q7:157 and Q62:2, Prophet Muhammad was, during the performance of his divine mission, described as an illiterate individual. This description, which is contrary to all evidence derived from his early and later life, has been and continues to be used as a cornerstone to demonstrate the divine origin of the Holy Qur'an. According to that theory, an illiterate person could not possibly have composed the Qur'an using the powerful language in which it was revealed, a humanly impossible task. Placed in context, these verses did not allude to the illiteracy of the Prophet. Instead, they portray him as a commoner, as opposed to one who belongs to the chosen people, selected to bring a message to the commoners. In this respect, the confusion arose because in the Arabic language the same term, *ummi,* is used for commoner and illiterate. Thus, it is a message which confirms God's approach of selecting His messengers among the intended audience of the relevant message. When a verse is taken out of its context, the interpretation becomes contrary to the logic of things. We need to caution here against confusing between the context and circumstances of revelation on the one hand, and the context and circumstances of the interpreter on the other. While the context and circumstances of revelation are relevant to extract the underlying universal message in the first place, the context and circumstances of the interpreter help to progress the relevant interpretation and implementation of the universal message in different times and locations.

Interpretation of a verse in context has two aspects. First, a Qur'anic text must be interpreted bearing in mind the geographic and social context of the time when that verse was revealed. In reference to the social and geographic context of the time of revelation, reconsider Verse Q59:7: "*Whatever the Messenger gives you, take; whatever he forbids you, give over. And fear God; surely God is terrible in retribution.*" Read independently and outside its context, this text can be understood as conferring upon Prophet Muhammad a normative authority, that of specifying rules which at times supplement the Qur'an. Indeed, the exegetes have advanced this text as basis for the binding nature of Prophetic Tradition. However, placed in its social and historical context, this verse means something entirely different, totally unrelated to Prophetic Tradition or the mission of Prophet Muhammad. The entire verse reads as follows:

> *Whatsoever spoils of war God has given to His Messenger from the people of the cities belongs to God, and His Messenger, and the near kinsman, orphans, the needy and the traveler, so that it be not a thing taken in turns among the rich of*

you. Whatever the Messenger gives you, take; whatever he forbids you, give over.
And fear God; surely God is terrible in retribution.[99]

In context, this verse deals with the distribution of the spoils of war in a bid to change tribal behaviors of fighting over these spoils and is unrelated to Prophetic Tradition.

Second, a verse must be interpreted in light of the circumstances on the occasion of which that verse has been revealed. In Verses Q18:23 and 24, God tells His Prophet, *"Do not say of anything: 'I will do it tomorrow,' (23) without adding 'If God wills.' When you forget, remember your Lord and say: 'May God guide me and bring me nearer to the Truth' (24)."*[100] Taken at face value, this verse appears to be telling humankind that God is the one who has decided on everything people do, irrespective of their own wills. Accordingly whatever any person elects to do remains subject to God's having allowed or decided it in the first place.

These verses have served as scriptural foundation for the theory of predestination so widely accepted and advocated in mainstream Islam, past and present. However, when placed in context, these verses are totally unrelated to humankind's freedom of choice. Instead, they refer to an inadvertence on the part of the Prophet as he was prompted to answer certain difficult questions by antagonistic people of his tribe in the hope of embarrassing him. He promised to bring an answer the following day, in the expectation that God would reveal it to him. However, following a fifteen-day interruption of revelation, God warned him against making any promises about things that are not within his own reach or control. He was thus cautioned that promises whose fulfillment falls within the realm of God may only be made subject to God's will.[101]

Finally, any interpretation of a Qur'anic text must not contradict any other provision of the Qur'an. As indicated earlier, use of the theory of abrogation to justify or bypass contradictions should be rejected. Otherwise, the implication is that God changes His mind on short notice, which in turn implies that God is not perfect. Unfortunately, when Prophet Muhammad, as leader of his community, ruled over a certain matter in a manner inconsistent with a Qur'anic verse, exegesis provides that the ruling abrogates the contradicting Qur'anic verse instead of crediting the Prophet with providing the proper methodology for the wise implementation of the underlying universal message. The following example illustrates this point. Verse Q2:180 enjoins every person with some wealth to make a will to his or her closest of kin as he or she approaches death: "*It has been ordained upon you, when death is near to one of you, leaving wealth behind, to make a will in favour of parents and close relatives, impartially. This is incumbent upon the pious.*"[102] This verse was initially interpreted as mandating, by way of religious obligation, that a will be written to dispose of wealth. Then the early exegetes[103] decided that this verse had been abrogated, at least partially, with respect to wills in favor of relatives who are otherwise natural heirs of the deceased person, thus leaving it legal to allow wills made out in favor of non-heirs.[104] However, they were divided over the manner in which the rule in question was abrogated. Some claimed that it was abrogated by subsequent verses that set forth the rules of distribution of the estate among the heirs.[105] Others[106] considered that Verse Q2:180 was abrogated by Prophetic Tradition when Prophet Muhammad decreed, "*No will is permitted in favor of an heir.*"[107] In this example, while there is a consensus that Verse 2:180 has been partially abrogated, the disagreement among the majority of exegetes and scholars is only about the manner in which it was abrogated, namely by another verse or by Prophetic Tradition. Instead, a closer look at each position brings out the reality.

First, the meaning of Verse Q2:180 cannot be inconsistent with that of the verses relating to the allocation of estates because each set of rules deals with different ways of devolution of estates (wills versus *ab intestat* inheritance), where one does not exclude the other. To confirm it, Verse Q4:11, which allocates the shares in an estate to the heirs, specifies that the stated allocation applies after setting aside the necessary assets to give effect to wills.

Second, the tradition of the Prophet quoted in the instance is deemed weak and unreliable following the rules of assessment of Prophetic Tradition. Despite the fact that the divine output cannot be abrogated by human output, the tradition in question—if authentic—holds far-reaching methodological and historical importance. As discussed earlier, the Holy

Qur'an sought to revoke and replace reprehensible tribal practices. In this particular case of estate devolution, the Qur'an sought to change the unjust tribal system under which estates pass almost exclusively to the older of the male descendants of the deceased. It decreed that male and female close kin—children, parents, and siblings of the deceased person—are entitled to a fair share of the estate. Bearing that in mind, the Prophet acted in the spirit of the Qur'an when he took it upon himself to prohibit the will to any person in the category of heirs, in obvious contradiction of a Qur'anic provision. His initiative in this case had a wise purpose: to prevent people from using wills to revert to the tribal system and circumvent the Qur'anic principle of fair distribution to all children, males and females, instead of the eldest male descendant. That measure by the Prophet was therefore wise,[108] at least temporarily, until people accepted the revolutionary principle brought about by the Qur'an.[109] Didn't all systems of inheritance at that time, Christian and others, follow the principles of devolving the estate to the eldest male in order to retain large productive estates in the family? This guides us to pause and confront a serious impact of the theory of abrogation.

Meccan Verses and Medinan Verses

The Qur'an was revealed to Prophet Muhammad in both Mecca and in Medina, where he went about performing his prophetic mission. Given that the circumstances in which that mission was performed were substantially different in Mecca and Medina, the style and substance of the Qur'anic text reflects those differences. In Mecca, the Qur'anic verses were more focused on the fundamental principles of the new faith and on related worship requirements. By contrast, the Qur'anic verses of Medina added another dimension, consisting of organizing the community of Medinans which formed under the leadership of Prophet Muhammad, following the conclusion of what is commonly known as the Charter of Medina.

The Charter of Medina was an agreement entered into among the principal inhabitants of Medina—namely the large Jewish community, the Medinan Muslims and pagans, and the Meccan immigrants (the Prophet and his companions). Its purpose was to settle the peace following the internecine wars among the tribes in Medina, and to secure peaceful coexistence and the settlement of disputes among them in an environment of religious diversity and freedom. Noting the absence of a state structure in pre-Islamic Arabia, Abdou Filali-Ansari proposes that Prophet Muhammad went about creating a state structure to organize the community among the spectrum of people newly converted to Islam on the basis of the new common faith, with ties founded in higher ethics which transcended narrow, feud-breeding tribal ties.[110] While it is clear that it was Islam's vocation to replace tribal ties with faith-based ones, the view that the Prophet had set forth to create a state in Medina, as expressed by Filali-Ansari and many other scholars, should be rejected. The Prophet set forth to lay the ground for a basic organization, sufficient to enable him to carry out his prophetic mission, which did not include a political component.

In addition to the frequent reminders about the fundamentals of the faith, the unicity of God, and life after death following the Final Judgment, the Qur'anic verses revealed in Medina dealt with organizational issues of public life arising in the new community of Medina. The Medinan verses also dealt with a new thrust in the performance of the prophetic mission, which involved fighting—first against the Meccans, then against other tribes throughout the Arabian Peninsula, including the Jewish tribes of Medina. Therefore, by contrast to the Meccan verses whose scope was general, the scope of Medinan verses was specific and issues-related. For that reason, some solutions revealed in Medina appeared to be inconsistent with the general principles revealed in Mecca. For example, it is in Medina that Prophet Muhammad received the direction to fight the pagans and other nonbelievers, whereas Meccan verses had preached peace and avoidance of violence, but also precluded the Prophet from imposing the faith on anyone. It is also in Medina that apostasy was treated as a sin, then a temporal crime, whereas the Meccan verses preached the freedom of faith.

This prompted the exegetes to treat the Medinan verses and related Prophetic Tradition as having precedence over the Meccan verses, thereby deeming the latter to have been abrogated by the more recent Medinan verses. This approach rallied the consensus of scholars of the early years, and indeed we find countless works identifying Meccan verses which have been reversed by more recent Medinan verses. However, more recently, the late Mahmoud Taha came up with a theory that the essence of Islam was revealed in the Meccan verses, which he calls the First Message of Islam. According to him, and since the essence of the faith had already been conveyed, the verses revealed in Medina were no longer about the faith per se. They were more concerned with housekeeping matters related to the new community organized in Medina, together with the spread of the Message and the wars that had to be conducted in connection with it. Taha called the Medinan verses the Second Message of Islam. Because of the general nature of the Meccan verses and the special purpose of the Medinan verses, Taha concluded that only the Meccan verses, that is, the First Message of Islam, were universal.[111] These views of Mahmoud Taha cost him his life: a court in his native country, the Sudan, condemned him to death and executed him for apostasy.

Neither of these two approaches with respect to the perceived inconsistencies between Meccan and Medinan verses should be accepted. First, the concept of abrogation of any Qur'anic verse by another Qur'anic verse should be rejected. Second, it is also necessary to reject any theory which distinguishes between Qur'anic verses based on their particular places or circumstances of their revelation so as to set aside some as not being universal in their scope. Instead, it should be affirmed that each and every Qur'anic verse is universal, some based on their general affirmation of the faith and the duties of worship, and others based on their underlying message, regardless of their immediate purport and the specific circumstances that they address.[112] Even the verses which appear to be inconsistent with previous verses are as universal and important as the ones which they appear to contradict. They are the shining light which provides a guiding example of the need to exercise wisdom and flexibility in living the new faith and implementing its basic principles—the proper methodology to give full effect to, and fulfill the intent of, the Qur'anic Message.

Viewed as a divinely revealed methodology, the Message is telling us that the principles, wherever stated, are not to be blindly implemented. Instead, each rule, each principle, must be implemented with due regard to the circumstances of the time and in light of the interests of the people concerned. They can even be set aside when their implementation is likely to cause more harm than their temporary suspension.[113] This is how Medinan verses, which appear to be in contradiction with principles set forth in Meccan verses, should be perceived.

Universality and *Fiṭra*

It can be concluded that the universality of the Qur'anic Message is an embodiment of divine *fiṭra*. The term *fiṭra* comes from the root verb *faṭara,* which means to create, as used in Verse Q6:79.[114] The term *fiṭra* means the innate attributes inherent in creation.[115] With this in mind, Verse Q30:30 manifests the full magnitude of the claim that the faith brought by the Qur'anic Message is innate in humankind and inherent in human nature as God created it, and is thus universal: "*So [Prophet] as a man of pure faith, stand firm and true in your devotion to the religion. This is* the natural disposition God instilled in mankind—*there is no altering God's creation—and this is the right religion, though most people do not realize it.*"[116]

As such, the faith is universal in the sense that it is a reference to the instinctive sense of security that people search for in religion.[117] It has existed and been relevant ever since God created humankind, as opposed to having been decided by God at some point in time, then revealed to a messenger to be conveyed to people. It will therefore remain in existence and relevant until the Final Day. This, for Sir Sayyid Ahmad Khan, constitutes the prime benchmark to assert the veracity of religion.[118] That is why, time and again in the Holy Qur'an, God asserts that Prophet Muhammad's message is, among other things, a reminder of what people already know.

When the Message speaks of the unicity of God, that unicity is indeed innate and inherent in human nature. That concept did not appear with the rise of the monotheistic religions. In the words of Shabbir Akhtar, "Man is naturally inclined to worship his unique creator, Allah: man is homo Islamicus."[119] It was there even since the inception of what we perceive as polytheistic religions, such as the religions involving the Egyptian, Greek, Roman, and Phoenician deities. Indeed, the fact that these religions had each its grand, controlling deity, such as Osiris for the Egyptians, Zeus for the Greeks, and Jupiter as king of the Roman gods, is a witness to the innate concept of unicity. This was the mythological expression of the ultimate One.[120] Even in the Qur'an itself, the polytheists are depicted as conceding the existence of a one-and-only transcending deity.[121] It is also important to note that the principles of morality,[122] of right and wrong,[123] and the basic values conveyed by the Message, such as the values of diversity,[124] justice, equity, charity, freedom, and reason, are all innate and inherent in human nature, and as such are universal.[125]

Universality being an attribute of *fiṭra*, Islam is universal because its essential principles— the concept of God's unicity and the principles of ethics and morality brought by religion—are inherent in human nature in the form of *fiṭra*. They are not a byproduct of one religious message or another.[126] Yet, divine revelation is nevertheless necessary as it brings awareness of, and consciousness toward, what is already in us, as part of God's creation. Perceived in this manner, the secular nature of Islam is clearly highlighted in what Abdulaziz Sachedina calls "the profound secularity of the fiṭra."[127]

Unfortunately, the religious discourse still attached to the works of the early exegetes usurped the universal nature of Islam when it confined Islam to its early iteration during the seventh and eighth centuries and universalized that time period's interpretation and implementation of it. In other words, what humans built up around Islam resulted in the covering over of its divine intent as a religion which is simple and understandable by way of innate knowledge (*fiṭra*). Instead Islam's divine intent became shrouded in complexities fabricated by people intent on controlling the religion and its adherents for political and other purposes. This is the process described earlier as the sacralization of human thought, which resulted in the suffocation of the universal call of the Divine Revelation. Therefore, to restore to Islam its universal nature it is necessary to desacralize what was wrongly sacralized in the first place. This process begins with recognizing the secular nature of Islam.

PART TWO
The Secular Nature of Islam

It is often claimed, as a fundamental aspect of Islam's universality, that Islam encompasses and regulates all facets of life. This claim reflects a narrow perception of the universal nature of Islam. Those who maintain such a narrow perception of Islam's universality try to impose the rigor of what Islam purportedly encompasses and regulates. To that effect, many Muslims, over the ages, have been concerned about their day-to-day lives and activities being scrupulously carried out and performed as prescribed by religion. Often attendant to any social innovation is a concern about what position religion will take regarding it, for fear of deviating from strict compliance with the faith. Especially from the perspective of many learned scholars, Islam is first perceived as a body of laws, before acknowledging its primary goal of leading us onto the path of God through *īmān* (faith) and *al-'amal al-ṣāliḥ* (good deeds).[1] As a result, Muslim societies have seen a sharp rise in the importance of the role of 'ulama', that is, individuals learned and versed in religious science who are qualified to determine, with respect to each facet of life, what complies and what does not comply with the "laws" which complement the faith. As a result, fatwas and fatwa-issuing clerics have been on the rise, as well.[2]

On that basis, a number of expressions are commonly used to express the wide-ranging scope of Islam as a religion: for example, *dīn wa dunia,* or religion and day-to-day life; *dīn wa dawla,* or religion and state; *dīn wa shari'a,* or religion and legal system. Essentially, Islam has been portrayed as a religion that comprises a system of state governance and organization, a legal system, an economic system, and a comprehensive social order which requires expertise in religious science in order to secure compliance with the faith, bring blessings and happiness, and avoid the wrath of the Almighty. That is what justifies the historical rise of a class of clerics[3] whose job is to keep everyone—ruler and ruled—honest.

This situation is not peculiar to Islam and Muslim societies. The Christian societies of Europe had a long history of dominance by the Catholic Church and its clergy, some of whom—in the name of

Christianity—amassed wealth and committed atrocities. That dominance led to protracted wars between Catholics and Protestant reformers in the sixteenth and seventeenth centuries, followed by periods of instability, until the separation of church and state was gradually implemented in the eighteenth century under the influence of the rising intellectual and philosophical movements.

In part, secularization contributed to the widespread progress that the West witnessed since then. In Muslim societies, secularization was viewed by some as tantamount to rejection of Divine Governance and as an abandonment of faith. Even worse, leading religious voices today target secularization as being a primary *cause* of a number of challenges that Islamic nations face. It is claimed that conditions in Muslim nations have deteriorated because these societies abandoned religion in favor of secularization. Religion should therefore be revived and more strictly implemented as the sole engine necessary to run the state, the economy, and every facet of life.

This view of Islam perpetuates a narrow understanding of Islam's universal nature. Scholars have addressed this issue of secularization in Islam in order to attempt to draw the boundaries within which Islamic nations could consider secularizing aspects of life. At one end of the opinion spectrum, Shaykh Yusuf Qaradawy, among others, calls attention to the evils of secularism and concludes that secularism was exported to, or imposed upon, Muslim nations by the West.[4] For his part, leading Moroccan scholar Abdou Filali-Ansari attempts to create a platform for discussing the issue constructively by simply asking if Islam is compatible with secularism.[5] Filali-Ansari's question is long overdue.

Islam was in essence secular long before secularism was put forward in the West. The issue is not *if* Islam is compatible with secularism, but *how* to restore to Islam its secular nature. The capacity of Islam to tolerate the stresses associated with secularism has been continually doubted and questioned, when Islam should be recognized as a vital instrument of learning and change. Western nations that adhere to other monotheistic faiths became secularized through a separation of church and state. In the case of Islam, the inherently secular nature of its central tenets renders it universal and a leader of change and progress. This aspect of Islam has been severely misunderstood.[6]

What is the meaning of secularism? How is Islam inherently secular? If Islam is inherently secular, what should be the role of the clergy? In this section, it is argued that Islam is neither a system of government nor a legal or economic system. Instead, Islam is an individualistic[7] and deeply humanistic religion, a way of life, serving as a guiding light and a path to God. Abdelmajid Charfi eloquently describes Islam's individualistic and humanistic character in this way.

> By professing the unicity of a transcendent and universal God, Islam has eliminated most channels of mediation with the sacred. Having stripped religion of the sacred's most powerful accessories, such as the mysteries, the miracles, and magic, it has for the first time in history, referred man to himself and to his individual responsibility.[8]

CHAPTER 5
Defining Secularism

The term "secularism" means different things to different people. Over time it has been implemented in different ways from one country to another. Manifestations of secularism have ranged from state opposition to religion, to state neutrality despite official state endorsement of religion, to everything in-between, including atheism, separation of religion and state, or separation of church and state.[1] For instance, Marxist regimes historically have been associated with the violent repression of religious expression, rooted in philosophical perceptions of religion as a destructive force in society. At the other extreme, tens of countries, while branding secularism among the qualifiers for their political systems, still maintain an official state religion and church. This is the case in Norway, Denmark, Iceland, Finland, and England in the primarily secular Christian West, and of Syria, Egypt, and Malaysia in the secularly inclined Muslim East.

Similarly, in literature, sociology, political science, and philosophy, the terms secularism and atheism have been used sometimes interchangeably and at other times to indicate nuances within the respective frameworks of these concepts in reflecting their attitudes toward religion, God, the clergy, or other religious institutions.[2] However, among the religious establishment, the opponents of secularization are almost unanimous in attributing to secularists an attitude of belligerence toward religion.[3]

For example, Fazlur Rahman asserts, "Secularism is necessarily atheist."[4] Similarly, Shaykh Yusuf Qaradawy[5] compares secular systems to the idols of the *jāhiliyya,* because in both cases people thought them to be useful, while in reality they are insignificant in their essence. He considers secularity of any kind as the worst enemy of—and a threat to—religion. In the words of Shabbir Akhtar, "The confrontation is about secularism's bold bid to change from being subordinate to any religion to being autonomous of and from all religion."[6] For that purpose, the late Muhammad 'Abed al-Jabiri offers a brief historical outline of the emancipation of the Arab nations from Ottoman rule and the rise of the terms "laicity" and "secularism." He prefers instead to set these terms aside and use the expression "democracy and rationality."[7]

In reality, secularity is not concerned with accepting, rejecting, supporting, or opposing religion, because Islam and secularity are completely different concepts, neither of which is hostile to—or in conflict with—the other.

Secularism continues to be resisted, and at times rejected outright, simply because it is a product of the West.[8] In fact, secularism is blamed for the demise of the family in the West. It is also blamed for the investment of Western technology in weapons of mass destruction following an erosion of religious morals and values.[9] Citing the *de facto* antagonism between Islam and Western modernity, Shabbir Akhtar has observed, "The resurgence of Islam as a political force opposing western political designs has inspired a conservative scholarship which rejects issues such as secularism and religious pluralism as western issues and dismisses western criteria of rationality and plausibility as 'occidentric.'"[10] This demonstrates what happens when religion is perceived as an identity: the dilemma becomes the Islamization of the West versus the Westernization of Islam. The problem with such an approach is that it is one-dimensional, whereby the choice is narrowed to a single alternative: Western modernity, versus a nonsecular religious system based on centuries-old interpretations.

In reality, the issue is not as black-and-white as it appears. Such an approach reflects an abandonment of autonomy, a capitulation to the thoughts of others. It displays a relinquishment of one's own right, and duty, to think critically. Western secularism is not about specific solutions adopted in the West. It is about the proper use of the mind and the rational thinking required to freely create solutions that are suitable to diverse environments. Many continue to reject secularism as a tool of Western imperialism for controlling other nations, namely Muslim nations. But by doing so, they abdicate the right to think, for no reason other than the fact that those who developed secular thought processes came from the West.

Approaches to secularism adopted by those various thinkers fall beyond the scope of our subject. Instead, here we will identify the basic criteria of secularism which characterize Islam as an essentially secular religion. These criteria concern harmony among groups in society, as well as the rights of the individual in living his or her faith.

Group-Related Criteria

History has traced the evolution of state structure from the tribal system, in which a tribe's leader, counseled by the tribe's elders, organizes and administers the tribe's affairs and resolves disputes among its members, in accordance with unwritten tribal rules and traditions accumulated over time. Relations between tribes, and among people of different tribes, are governed by tribal traditions when the tribes involved in a dispute are essentially equal in riches and strength. Otherwise, the rules set forth by the stronger and richer tribe prevail, and often disputes are settled by way of self-help, revenge, and war.

Alternatively, when society was made up of one homogeneous group belonging to the same religious creed, as was the case with much of Christian Europe, church and state were somewhat in accord. The church provided the divine blessing and recognition of the political power of the ruling party (person or family), while the ruling party provided the state with protection and a framework for the church's social and worship-related activities. They would at times engage in strife against each other, but overall the system continued as long as the group was homogeneous in terms of their basic faith. Christianity has often expressed a relationship to secularism based on the saying attributed to Jesus Christ: "Give to Caesar what is Caesar's, and to God what is God's."[11] Yet, because divine governance is all-encompassing and the church represents God in this life, the church had a natural say in state affairs and—more often than not—exercised the upper hand over the state structure. However, this harmonious tandem could not continue when social homogeneity faltered with the increase in social, religious and political diversity. Freethinkers were starting to question the wisdom of continuing to allow religion to influence state action. Also, the rise of alternative brands of Christianity (such as Protestantism and its challenge to the power of the Catholic Church) and the ensuing religious wars contributed to the eventual separation of church and state. It also resulted in what would be wrongly perceived as the separation of religion and state. Secularization became a compelling priority.

For the purpose of defining—and framing the scope of—the secular nature of Islam, it is important to avoid the use of the terms "separation of church and state" or "separation of religion and state." This is crucial because avoiding these terms (1) prevents potential negative connotations, such as any notion of belligerence toward Islam and its religious establishment; and (2) helps us to avoid the potential implication that the state can or should promote atheism,[12] supersede religion and its institutions, or prevent any role for religion and its institutions.

The Religious Neutrality of the State

We start from the premise that secularism means that the state is neutral on matters of belief, in the sense that: (1) the state has no mandate or right to influence the personal beliefs of people, including whether or not those beliefs are about the existence or nonexistence of God, and in the affirmative what God's role is or might be; (2) the state has one set of laws, rules, and regulations that every person, including the state itself, must comply with, irrespective of creed, or religious affiliation; (3) people's rights and duties to the state and among each other are not influenced by any particular creed, irrespective of the number of people who share that creed; (4) the state administers the state organization, including justice, in strict compliance with the laws and regulations duly adopted, without discrimination of any kind based on creed or religious affiliation; (5) the government of a secular state is accountable exclusively to its constituency from which it derives its legitimacy and, unlike a theocratic government whose powers are presumably divine, it can be critiqued, deposed, and replaced;[13] and (6) the citizens of a secular state are not subjects who seek and expect the generosity and compassion of a divinely vested ruler; instead they are equal participating partners who enjoy rights and are entitled to demand them.

From this perspective, Abdullahi An-Na'im rightly asserts, "People cannot truly live by their convictions according to their belief in and understanding of Islam if rulers use the extensive coercive powers of the state to impose their view of Shari'a on the population at large, Muslims and non-Muslims alike." With such a statement, An-Na'im is subscribing to the humanistic nature of Islam and to an individualistic understanding of religion. However, he perhaps overstates the case when he defines secularism as "the institutional separation of Islam and state," and explains the rationale behind that separation as being "necessary for Shari'a to have a proper positive and enlightening role in the lives of Muslims and Islamic societies." It is preferable to speak of the *neutrality* of the state toward religion—any religion—rather than *separation*, which might imply hostility toward religion. As for its rationale, secularism is essential in order to secure freedom of faith for all and not just to improve the role of Shari'a in the lives of Muslims.[14]

Filali-Ansari concisely describes secularism as: "a political conception which implies the separation of civil society and religious society, and where the State exercises no religious power and the Church wields no political power."[15] In other words, as the state is a legal entity, and not a physical person, it is impractical to conceive of the state itself as having a religion. A state religion would be unnecessary unless it referred to the religion of the majority of a state's citizens or to a religion which was favored by the state, and whose adherents enjoyed certain privileges or rights under the laws of that state.

Religion is essentially a faith, consisting of a body of creeds which typically define the relationship of humankind to God and set forth ethical principles and moral values necessary to secure a harmonious relationship among people. No religion should ever be used or abused for political purposes. Instead, it should be possible for religion to be observed and lived, individually and collectively.[16]

Freedom of Faith and Worship

In a secular environment and as a neutral entity, the state nevertheless acknowledges the right of its citizens to select the religion of their choice. The state also recognizes the rights of its citizens to live their faiths and to worship freely. Those rights should be not only recognized but guaranteed by the state. The only potential limitations to these rights and freedoms would be the ones required to comply with the laws, rules, and regulations in force, including the guarantee of the rights of adherents to other faiths to believe and worship.

In such a secular environment, the public display of religious beliefs and performance of acts of worship is allowed when related clearly to religious purposes and not when being employed as tools of political expression, or to interfere with the freedom of faith and worship of others. Subject to these same limitations, people should also be guaranteed the right to spread their faith by all reasonable and lawful means.

Finally, in a secular environment, it is possible for adherents of different faiths, or denominations of the same faith, to build their own places of worship (mosques, churches, synagogues, temples, etc.), without political or other illegal strings attached.

The Interaction of Religion and Church[17] with the State

Opponents of secularism have concluded that secularism is a tool for setting religion aside from the lives of people, individually and collectively, and for precluding God from ruling over his creation. Secularism thus leads to the replacement of God's rule by ephemeral human social and political organization.[18] Such a perception of secularism, in which humankind is perceived as competing with God, is demeaning to the concept of God, because God does not manifest and exercise His power through man-made institutions. No one can pretend to prevent God under any pretext, including secularism, from ruling over His creation because He is the Almighty.

A state is not necessarily expected to ignore religion or to prohibit official involvement in religious activities, or even to avoid any such involvement, for it to be considered a secular state. What is important is that religion does not constitute the basis of the legitimacy of its government or serve to motivate its actions.[19] A truly secular state should find no embarrassment in recognizing the value of the diversity of creeds in its midst, or in encouraging or even sponsoring constructive interaction among those creeds for their respective benefits and that of the community as a whole. A state can even be deemed to exercise constructive secularism when it celebrates religious holidays as public holidays and sponsors religious charitable, educational, and cultural activities or encourages the self-fulfillment of all the adherents of each creed and faith by creating for them the proper environment and securing equal opportunities for that purpose.[20]

Nor is secularism about repudiation of religious heritage. On the contrary, a secular environment is a necessary condition for individuals—whose rights are guaranteed by secular law—to enjoy the freedoms of faith and worship, in accordance with the practices of their religion. Yet, it is important to caution against what Abdullahi An-Na'im describes as "maintaining the connection between Islam and politics" which "allows for the implementation of Islamic principles in official policy and legislation."[21] In a secular state that is neutral toward religions, it is not conceivable that a connection is allowed between Islam and politics without allowing similar connections involving other religions too. Similarly, allowing for the implementation of Islamic principles in official policy and legislation would pave the way for the implementation of other religions' principles, as well. As a result, the state loses its neutrality while the relevant religious establishments regain a foothold in state affairs and thus begin to guide and oversee the implementation of the particular religious principles in policy and legislation.[22]

In a secular environment, no religious establishment has the vested right to run state organizations or influence the exercise of any state functions and duties. Similarly, neither the state nor any of its institutions is allowed in a secular environment to interfere in the organization and day-to-day activities of, or exercise any oversight on, religious establishments, other than to secure their compliance with the applicable laws and regulations in effect. Yet, these establishments, whether as individuals or as organized legal entities, enjoy the full and unreduced civil rights of ordinary citizens. It is even possible for the state to cooperate with religious establishments to facilitate the exercise of civil rights by adherents of such establishments. By way of example, in a secular state, marriages celebrated between any two persons, irrespective of their creeds and faiths, should be governed by the same laws and regulations and be subject to the same judicial system for resolution of disputes. But a secular state can recognize a marriage which is officiated by a religious authority that would also ensure that all statutory requirements, as are applicable to all, are duly complied with. Similarly, a state institution which implements social policies through institutions affiliated with religious establishments would not be breaching the principles of secularity.

With this in mind, the claim that secularism is tantamount to atheism and war against religion[23] is unsubstantiated (except perhaps certain practices of regimes which were particularly hostile to religion), because then the only logical alternative is to adopt a religious system. In reality, secularism is the guarantee of freedom of faith. It is the formula which guarantees bringing religion back into the life of people who so desire, to each person the religion that he or she chooses. The example of Marxism given by opponents of secularism in support of their views is irrelevant because Marxism does not fall under secularism, or even under atheism; instead Marxism can be categorized as "anti-theism." Opponents of secularism go on to raise fears about a secular regime being hostile to religious preachers, as in a Marxist regime. This fear is irrelevant, because hostility toward preachers is not equivalent to hostility towards their religion. In a true secular environment where freedom of faith prevails and the religious establishment does not interfere with the affairs of state, there is no fear of official state hostility against preachers and clerics, as long as the latter do not adopt behaviors which may lead to abuse of religion or the secular public order.

In this light, secularism does not require that the state ignore or negate the existence of God or enforce the treatment of religious faith and worship strictly as a matter of personal spirituality. The state can be perfectly secular as long as it acknowledges, respects, and guarantees freedom of faith and worship for all people on an equal basis (including the right to reject all faith), and organizes its interaction with religions and religious establishments in strict observance of applicable laws and regulations and without discrimination of any kind.

Individual-Related Criteria

From the individual's perspective, a secular framework is one where a person's day-to-day life is regulated by humanly enacted laws, and where the spiritual aspect of one's life is not mandatorily organized by the church as a statutory religious authority and establishment.

Regulation of Day-to-Day Life

From an individual perspective, a secular state system would have legislation duly adopted by the legitimate decision-making power, which does not necessarily regulate every facet of the life of its citizens. Legislation, however, could be expected to regulate specific activities involving interaction among people and to resolve disputes as they arise. The statutes would also set forth general principles of conduct to ensure social peace and harmony among people, together with certain prohibitions and limits not to be exceeded.

That secular system does not, *a priori*, accommodate a role for religious laws, nor allow religious authorities to impose binding requirements that are inconsistent with the secular statutes in effect, or interfere with the smooth administration of justice on the basis of creed or religious traditions. However, with that principle firmly recognized and acknowledged, statutes of civilized nations usually, though not universally, are not inconsistent with ethical and moral religious values because statutes and religious principles often are inspired by the same source, namely natural law which, in Islam, corresponds to *fiṭra*.

Interaction of God and Humankind

Recalling again the famous statement by Jesus Christ about the separation of church and state: "give to Caesar what is Caesar's, and to God what is God's,"[24] even in the sphere of "what is God's," interaction with God is not entirely free and direct. In certain denominations, the church holds divine powers conferred on it by Jesus Christ, and therefore individual interaction with God often must go through the church, which acts as an intermediary between God and humankind.

In a secular environment, the church (in the general sense of the term as a reference to any religious establishment) and its clergy can have a major, important role in the lives of the believers. However, while that role may be religiously mandatory, depending on the particular faith, it remains from the state's perspective entirely optional and complementary—never essential or mandatory—for the proper interaction with God or the performance of a person's religious duties and worship requirements. Therefore, from a statutory perspective, the church is not a necessary medium in order for any person to interact with God, and clerics have no statutory preassigned role to that effect.

On the basis of the criteria described above to determine the secularity of a system, it is necessary then to examine the extent to which Islam inherently is secular, not only whether or not Islam is consistent with secularism. However, for that purpose, it is important to caution against comparing secularism and Islam: Islam is a religion, and secularism is not. Instead, secularism is a political system in which the state is administered collectively by society, rather than by religion.

CHAPTER 6
Divine Governance and Human Government

Islam has been consistently portrayed as a comprehensive religion which encompasses a state as an indispensable tool for the performance of religious duties. According to this perception—and as John Esposito rightly observes—early Islamic society followed the lead of the major religions that preceded Islam in associating religion with political power, namely, "Judaism in the kingdoms of Judaea and Israel, Christianity in the Roman (Byzantine) empire, Zoroastrianism in the Persian (Sassanid) empire."[1] Islam is a comprehensive religion, we are told, because it regulates all facets of life, including every aspect of daily life. The argument continues that this comprehensiveness of Islam's scope is an attribute of Islam's universal nature, and derives from the all-encompassing divine governance that the Qur'an provided for. Because God, as the absolute sovereign, has created humankind and has enacted for them all the regulations that they may ever need in their day-to-day life, there is neither need nor room for any governance other than God's governance.

Yet, human government is required to the extent necessary to implement God's rules and ensure that believers comply with them.[2] For that purpose, human government should be made up of people who are learned in religious science and can use that science to elucidate the divine rules that regulate humankind's life and secure the *umma*'s safe transition to the hereafter.

When the scope of divine governance is clearly defined it can be convincingly argued that divine governance was not intended to regulate all facets of life. Instead, it gave people the freedom to organize their own lives and in effect left no real need or role for clergy. This is part of the essence of Islam's being secular.

The Scope of Divine Governance

Opponents of secularism in Muslim societies claim that Islam, as a comprehensive religion, makes no distinction between the spiritual and the temporal and the only sovereign ruler is God. Thus, there can be no state structure under which humans can exercise any kind of governance because governance is exclusively divine, and no one can participate with God in exercising sovereignty.[3] Borrowing the comparison from Christianity, Shabbir Akhtar describes this nonsecular depiction of divine sovereignty in the following terms: "Everything belongs to God... nothing should belong to Caesar. God is the measure of all things."[4] The problem with this view is that it compares Caesar with God, as if they were likes. God as the absolute and Almighty sovereign does not share His sovereignty and powers with anyone. In fact, it is a grave sin to assign spheres of sovereignty between God and humanity. However, in his absolute sovereignty, God has assigned a certain scope of action for humankind, and that scope is large enough to include state organization and government. Opponents of secularism claim there are several verses of the Holy Qur'an that substantiate their view of divine governance:

Q4:65—*"By your Lord they will not be true believers until they let you decide between them in all matters of dispute, and find no resistance in their souls to your decisions, accepting them totally."*[5]

Q5:3—*"Today, I have perfected your religion for you, and have completed My blessing upon you, and chosen Islam as Dīn (religion and a way of life) for you."*[6]

Q6:57—*"The Decision belongs to none but Allah."*[7]

Q12:40—*"Whatever you worship, other than Him, are nothing but names you have coined, you and your fathers. Allah has sent down no authority for them. Sovereignty belongs to none but Allah. He has ordained that you shall not worship anyone but Him. This is the only right path. But most of the people do not know."*[8]

Q24:51—*"The only reply of the (true) believers, when they are summoned to Allah and His messenger that he (the messenger) may judge between them, is that they say, 'We listen and obey.' Such people are the successful.'*[9]

Q33:36—*"It is not open for a believing man or a believing woman, once Allah and His messenger have decided a thing, that they should have a choice about the matter; and whoever disobeys Allah and His messenger, he indeed gets off the track, falling into an open error."*[10]

Q42:10—*"And in anything over which you disagree—its ruling is [to be referred] to Allah. [Say], 'That is Allah, my Lord; upon Him I have relied, and to Him I turn back.'"*[11]

In fact, however, none of the verses quoted above support the interpretation of divine sovereignty as a micromanagement system which God exercises either directly or through agents. For example, the meaning and intent of Verse Q4:65 is different from the one given to it. Verse Q4:64, which immediately precedes it, says: *"All the messengers We sent were meant to be obeyed, by God's leave. If only [the hypocrites] had come to you [Prophet] when they wronged themselves, and begged God's forgiveness, and the Messenger had asked forgiveness for them, they would have found that God accepts repentance and is most merciful"* (64).[12] Read together then, these two verses refer to the powers conferred upon the Prophet to lead his community and fulfill his prophetic mission of spreading the Message. As disputes among the members of the community are likely to distract the Prophet from his mission, the Prophet is empowered to arbitrate such disputes in order to avoid such distractions, and the members of the community are ordered to obey the Prophet. The Arabic term *yuḥakkimūka* used in Verse Q4:65, being derived from the root term *ḥukm*, was erroneously understood by opponents of secularism as a reference to governance rather than its actual meaning of settlement of disputes by the Prophet, acting as arbitrator.[13] Bearing in mind that arbitration is optional for the parties, it is noteworthy that the Prophet was designated as arbitrator and not as judge, a specific indication that his role is not part of any statutory governance.

With respect to Verse Q5:3, the text quoted above is taken out of context because it is only an extract from Verse Q5:3, and, if read independently of its context, could imply that the perfection of religion cited therein is a reference to a comprehensive code for day-to-day human needs under the watchful divine eye. However, that meaning and implication cease to be obvious when read in conjunction with the full text of the verse (from the same translation used above), including the context that it provides.

> *Prohibited for you are: carrion, blood, the flesh of swine, and those upon which (a name) other than that of Allah has been invoked (at the time of slaughter), animal killed by strangulation, or killed by a blow, or by a fall, or by goring, or that which is eaten by a beast unless you have properly slaughtered it; and that which has been slaughtered before the idols, and that you determine shares through the arrows. (All of) this is sin. Today those who disbelieve have lost all hope of (damaging) your faith. So, do not fear them, and fear Me. Today, I have perfected your religion for you, and have completed My blessing upon you, and chosen Islam as Dīn (religion and a way of life) for you. But whoever is compelled by extreme hunger, having no inclination toward sin, then Allah is Most-Forgiving, Very-Merciful.*

It is clear that the extract in question, presumably supporting the concept of exclusive[14] divine governance, is not about divine governance in the first place. It is about the basics of halal and haram, (permitted and prohibited foods). This is confirmed in the last sentence of the verse which provides an exception to the principle set forth in the previous sentences with respect to waiver of the sin when committed under the duress of hunger.

Similarly for Verse Q6:57, the text quoted above is an extract taken out of context; and that context is totally alien to the concept of divine governance.[15] It is again the Arabic term *ḥukm* that has been wrongly portrayed as a reference to divine governance when it merely refers to a divine decision.[16] The entire verse reads: "*Say, 'I am on clear guidance from my Lord, and you have cried lies to it. That which you demand to be hastened is not up to me. The Decision belongs to none but Allah. He relates the Truth and He is the best of all judges.'*" This verse was revealed when certain persons among the nobility of the *Quraysh* challenged Prophet Muhammad on his threats of God's wrath against nonbelievers and dared him to solicit that wrath if he was truly a messenger of God. The answer, as conveyed in Q6:57, is that God is the one who will decide on the timing of his wrath.[17] Again this context is not related to divine governance in the sense attributed to it by opponents of secularism.

Verse Q12:40, among all the verses listed above, is perhaps the only one which refers to divine sovereignty. However, the reference does not imply that humankind should have no role in governance. Instead, the verse was intended to convince polytheists that their idols are powerless and they should not be worshipped. For whereas these idols were never able to create anything, God has created all things. Therefore, the sovereignty referred to in this verse is an attribute of creation, in the sense that God is sovereign over his creation.[18]

Verse Q24:51 falls within a series of verses, commencing with Verse Q24:47,[19] which describe the hypocrites and their behavior. While the hypocrites declare belief in Prophet Muhammad's message, they fail to confirm that belief with the appropriate behavior, namely, compliance with the Message. As indicated previously, accepting the arbitration and judgments of the Prophet was an expedient necessary to resolve disputes among the members of the community who were likely to disrupt the performance by the Prophet of his prophetic mission. Here too, the Arabic term *ḥukm*, which means judgment or decision, has been misinterpreted as divine governance administered by the Prophet. This misunderstanding is further aggravated by an unsubstantiated quotation attributed to a prominent companion of the Prophet, 'Umar Ibn al-Khattab, which presumably says: "The main bond of Islam lies in the acknowledgment that there is no god but Allah, performance of prayers, payment of zakat, and obedience to those whom God has placed in charge of Muslims."[20] In reality, God has never placed, nor required the placing of, any person in charge of the Muslims, except for Prophet Muhammad (and then only for the specific purpose of performing his prophetic mission).

As far as Verse Q33:36 is concerned, it is one of a number of Qur'anic verses that are strictly limited to the Prophet, relevant only during his lifetime. Its context has already been discussed in connection with the nature and effect of Prophetic Tradition. It is another example of a verse being removed from its context and then wrongly presented as the basis for a major issue like divine governance. It is true that this verse addresses an aspect of divine governance, but it is a specific aspect that ended with the death of the Prophet.

Verse Q42:10 is another example of misinterpretation. Verse Q42:10 concludes a string of verses which start with Verse Q42:7, in which God tells Prophet Muhammad that He has given him the Qur'an in the Arabic language so that he might warn the people of Mecca against persisting with polytheist creeds. God goes on to remind the Prophet that, had He wanted, He could have made them all believers but preferred to leave them free to believe or not believe. However, anticipating that disputes may therefore arise among believers and nonbelievers on matters of religious creed, God reminds the Prophet that such disputes would ultimately be resolved by God on the Day of Judgment.[21] So it is no longer a worldly dispute to be resolved by the Prophet but is instead a fundamental faith-related issue that can only be settled by God on the Final Day.

The above discussion provides vivid examples of secularism being wrongly portrayed as an affront to divine sovereignty, that is, a sinful aggression on the infinite prerogatives of God. It also provides an illustration of how willful or inadvertent misreading can occur when the sacred text is taken out of context. When human interpretations are sacralized, a misinterpretation can have long-term adverse effects on all adherents of Islam.

The above verses, as cited by opponents of secularism, do not prove their point and are not about divine sovereignty in the first place, yet divine sovereignty does exist and is not to be ignored or denied; and its existence does not preclude secularism. Divine sovereignty is the direct corollary of God's oneness and of his role as sole creator of everything in the universe. It is also the logical corollary of everything in the universe belonging to God. This is set forth clearly in the following Qur'anic verses:

Q2:115—*"To Allah belongs the East and the West. So, whichever way you turn, there is the Face of Allah. Indeed, Allah is All-Embracing, All-Knowing."*[22]

Q20:5 to 8—*"(God) Most Gracious is firmly established on the throne (of authority) (5) To Him belongs what is in the heavens and on earth, and all between them, and all beneath the soil (6). If thou pronounce the word aloud, (it is no matter): for verily He knoweth what is secret and what is yet more hidden (7) God! there is no god but He! To Him belong the most Beautiful Names (8)."*[23]

Q22:64— *"Unto Him belongs all that is in the heavens and all that is on earth; and, verily, God—He alone—is self-sufficient, the One to whom all praise is due."*[24]

Q34:1 and 2—*"Praise be to Allah, to whom belongs all that is in the heavens and all that is on the earth; and for Him is the praise in the Hereafter, and He is the Wise, the All-Aware (1). He knows all that goes into the earth and all that comes out from it, and all that comes down from the sky and all that ascends thereto. He is the Very-Merciful, the Most-Forgiving (2)."*[25]

Q39:62 and 63—*"GOD is the Creator of all things, and He alone has the power to determine the fate of all things (62). His are the keys [to the mysteries] of the heavens and the earth: and they who are bent on denying the truth of God's messages—it is they, they, who are the losers! (63)."*[26]

Because God has created everything, His creation remains at all times under His control and sovereignty under the so-called Divine *wilāya*. This divine sovereignty is further illustrated in the various attributes of God, otherwise known as the Beautiful Names of God, ninety-nine in number, the most prominent of which in exemplifying sovereignty are the attributes of perfection, infinite knowledge, infinite might, infinite wisdom, and, most importantly, infinite justice and compassion. In addition to numerous verses addressing God's attributes, Verses Q59:22 to 24 exemplify the Beautiful Names illustrative of divine sovereignty.

> *He is Allah, besides whom there is no god, the Knower of the unseen and the seen. He is All-Merciful, Very-Merciful (22). He is Allah, besides whom there is no god, the Sovereign, the Supreme-in-Holiness, the Safe (from all defects), the Giver-Of-Peace, the Guardian, the All-Mighty, the All-Repairer, the Sublime. Pure is Allah from what they associate with Him (23). He is Allah, the Creator, the Inventor, the Shaper. His are the Most Beautiful Names. His purity is proclaimed by all that is in the heavens and the earth, and He is the All-Mighty, the All-Wise (24).*[27]

Finally, the concept of divine sovereignty is enshrined in one of the most famous verses of the Qur'an, known as the Verse of the Chair (*Āyat al-Kursiyy*), namely, Verse Q2:255.

> *Allah: There is no god but He, the Living, the All-Sustaining. Neither dozing overtakes Him nor sleep. To Him belongs all that is in the heavens and all that is on the earth. Who can intercede with Him without His permission? He knows what is before them and what is behind them; while they encompass nothing of His knowledge, except what He wills. His Kursiyy (Chair) extends to the Heavens and to the Earth, and it does not weary Him to look after them. He is the All-High, the Supreme.*[28]

Divine sovereignty is therefore absolute, infinite, and exclusive. However, while it is not shared with Caesar or with anyone else, it is also not exclusive of human government on earth. Perhaps secularism, as exemplified by human government, is a witness of divine sovereignty and an exercise thereof, through God's determination when he created Mankind.

The Trusteeship by Humankind

When God completed His creation of the universe, both heavens and earth (Verse Q2:29), He told the angels that He was creating men and women for the purpose of making them trustees of the earth (Verse Q2:30).[29] A conversation then ensued between God and the angels about the wisdom of putting humankind in charge of the world. To the angels who thought otherwise, God said that the decision to empower humans was a considered decision, made for good reasons that are unknown to the angels and after having taught Adam what is needed to exercise the power that God entrusted to him (Verses Q2:31 to 33).[30]

The decision by God to install a trustee on earth is not limited to Adam and the first generation of men and women; it is a legacy that is entrusted to each subsequent generation of humankind. This is set forth in Verse Q35:39: *"He is the One who has made you successors (of the past generations) on the earth."*[31] Therefore, it is very important to note and keep in mind that the trusteeship was not granted by God to the believers exclusively. Instead, it was granted to all of humankind, irrespective of creed. Accordingly, those whom God—in the exercise of His Governance—removed and replaced from time to time were not punished because of the quality of their beliefs but because of their mischievous behavior and the corruption that they created.[32]

God's decision to make humankind trustees of the earth is an example of God exercising His divine governance. By making and implementing that decision, despite claims to the contrary made by some Islamists,[33] God did not relinquish any part of His Governance to the men and women He created. Nor did He share any part of His Governance with them. Indeed, the power that God entrusted to humankind was not a divine power to act on His behalf: first, for the reason that humans are fallible and make mistakes, which is inconsistent with the exercise of divine power; and second, because any claim to the contrary implies an association of humankind with God. Instead, the role of trustee is a freedom that God bestowed on humankind so that they might live their lives under His watchfulness, while he retained full judgment over how that freedom was exercised. Again, this is set forth in the Qur'an, in Verse Q6:165, as follows: *"It is He who made you the vicegerents of the earth and raised some of you in ranks over others, so that He may test you in what He has given you. Surely, your Lord is swift in punishing, and surely He is Most-Forgiving, Very-Merciful."*[34] From this perspective, there is no inconsistency between the infinite divine sovereignty and the "limited" human sovereignty, ordained by God under the trusteeship. The human sovereignty is described as "limited" only in order to reserve the magnitude of God's infinite nature relative to the finite nature of humanity.

Human sovereignty over what God entrusted to humankind is very wide: God has granted humankind, equally among each of them until the end of times, the entire freedom in the performance of the trust, commensurate with—and by way of *quid pro quo*—for the accountability to which humankind will be held. That sovereignty of humankind over what God entrusted to them is almost absolute, subject only to occasional interventions by God—in His divine governance and utmost Compassion—to offer help in answer to human prayers or otherwise to guide a good deed or even redress a wrong. It is true that God is Almighty, and His intervention, in the specific relevant instance, can potentially be perceived as negative, neutral, or positive. However, He has made clear that—consistent with divine justice—He would not intervene if people do not make negative changes in their behavior as to deserve it, as follows: "*All this is because Allah is not the one who may change a favour He has conferred on a people unless they change their own condition, and that Allah is All-Hearing, All-Knowing.*"[35]

Thus, people are not just spectators to what God has created. Their role as trustees is an active one upon which depends their happiness and progress in life. Humans can even "create" within the sphere of their trusteeship, for didn't God breathe His own Divine Spirit into humankind?

This should serve to dispel any potential misconception about the alleged divine guidance of the Muslim community through the process of *ijmā'* or consensus. By way of example, Bernard Lewis accurately reports on the doctrine of consensus, as portrayed by *fiqh*, as follows:

> The Doctrine of consensus, according to which divine guidance passed to the Muslim community as a whole after the death of the Prophet, gave a religious significance to the acts and experience of that community, in which could be seen the revelation of God's will on earth. God, it was believed, would not allow His community to fall into sin. What the community as a whole accepted and did was right and was an expression of God's purpose.[36]

While it is true, as Lewis states, that the doctrine of consensus has been perceived by generally accepted jurisprudence (*fiqh*) as a reliable source because it expresses the infallible general wisdom of the community, in reality this doctrine is nowhere stated in the Holy Qur'an. We do not find in the Qur'an any implication that the consensus of the community is sanctioned by God, or that God has delegated any of His divine prerogatives to any humans, individually or collectively. That is why no human being is infallible, whether individually or collectively.

It becomes irrelevant to distinguish between rights of God and rights of people because these two categories of rights are not of the same type. Sovereignty does not consist of a pool of rights from which God chose and retained a portion and left the rest to humankind. All rights belong to God. God's rights are infinite, and whatever rights people have derive from God. God's Governance has no limitations. If it did, we would be mixing divine governance with human government. In reality, the discussion about the rights of God is superfluous because God has no need for rights. God wields a power derived from His Almighty attributes. Similarly, in their relations with God, humans have no rights that they can claim from God. Instead, humans have freedoms that God Has bestowed on them under the scope of the trusteeship. The rights of people exist in their relations among each other, for rights and obligations can only be exercised among equals.[37]

Even as God empowered humankind to freely organize their lives on earth, He did not step aside to just observe humanity in action and keep a balance sheet of their good deeds and misdeeds for the Day of Judgment. On the contrary, He remained active and involved. The Qur'an states: "*To Allah doth belong the dominion of the heavens and the earth, and all that is therein, and it is He Who hath power over all things* (Q5:120)."[38] While God gave humans the power to take charge of their lives, He nevertheless encouraged them to call on Him, and He promised to listen.[39] He also indicated that He would involve himself by sending in the rain, and bestowing riches and bounties.[40] Finally also, God reaffirmed countless times in the Qur'an that "*It is in Allah alone that the believers must place their trust.*"

God exercising his own governance does not reduce the freedom that God gave to humankind, and thus does not contradict or in any manner restrict the organization and exercise of human government. The concept of exclusive divine governance, which ignores human trusteeship, has plagued the Muslim people for centuries. By way of example, religion is expected to address all emerging situations that Muslim communities encounter at any point in time and in any place.[41] This concept of divine governance derives from the erroneous belief that religion must solve our problems as they arise. In reality, that task is not incumbent upon religion but, instead, is incumbent upon humankind. God has given humankind the means—that is, mind and reason—and the freedom to act; and religion has given us the principles and the ethics, leaving it to us to enact the rules, the laws, and the processes to solve our problems, then to adapt them and change them as needed. In retrospect, the lethargy that certain environments continue to experience is the result of misunderstanding, the consequent refusal to act, and the insistence on waiting for God to act on their behalf.

Unfortunately, the association of religion and state, derived from these misperceptions of fundamental tenets of Islam, has been construed as a necessary tool for fulfillment of divine governance. It further implies that divine governance is exercised through the state, or that the state is vested with some divine agency which it exercises through the clergy.[42] These are the claims made by critics of Turkey's secularization, which they perceive as the total disintegration of the Islamic religion.[43] The response to such "outrage" is that Islam was not revealed as an "authority" to be exercised by human agents but as a faith and message of love and peace. Mahmoud Ayoub rightly observes how, in the Middle East, religion has consistently been perceived not merely as a set of beliefs and a theological system but rather as a "framework of a sociopolitical identity: a culture and way of life, a communion of worship and liturgy."[44] This may explain why progress has been slow in these societies. In fact, divine governance has been relied on exclusively while ignoring the important component of trusteeship, whereby people simply abdicated the role and duties that God assigned to them.

Thus divine governance is just the opposite of what fundamentalist—and some traditional—Islam has called for: the concession of leadership to the clergy in accordance with their interpretation of the Qur'an. Instead, humankind should (1) organize their lives as they wish, under the trusteeship concept, guided—if they so desire in their free will—by the Qur'anic principles; then (2) leave matters to God for his judgment on the Final Day, or for any earlier action according to His attribute as the Almighty. In this respect, God's judgment is based on criteria that are different from ours: God, who knows the true intentions of people, will judge them accordingly.[45] Therefore, divine governance is in reality an injunction for secularism, where humankind is invited to do its part without, however, usurping and exercising God's prerogatives of reward and punishment on His behalf.

Islam Does Not Regulate All Facets of Life

Those who reject secularism claim that God has regulated every facet of life, leaving no room for any form of governance other than divine governance. To them, the global and comprehensive coverage, which extends to every detail in our day-to-day life, is an attribute of the universal nature of Islam.[46] Even less extreme and liberal thinkers are comfortable with the concept of Islam having regulated all facets of life and find it reasonable that all our actions must first be screened in order to determine whether or not they are compatible with Islam.[47]

Islam is thus perceived as an integrated life system which, in all facets of life, including political governance, makes no distinction between the religious and the secular.[48] In other words, Islam is perceived at once as both religion and state—*dīn wa dawla*. According to such a perception, no state structure should dictate any aspect of life lest it trespasses on the jurisdiction of divine governance. Similarly, no human government should pretend to control what is otherwise under God's control lest it commits the sin of association. The obvious result is that secularism is not acceptable, because it prevents Islam from being the center and focus of all activities in life. For in a secular environment, a good Muslim would be unable to live out his faith and fully comply with his "divine" obligations.[49]

In reality, the Holy Qur'an does not contain such norms regulating all facets of life. Instead, there are verses containing rich values to be observed in relations among people, as well as basic and fundamental principles of morality and ethics. These values and principles are phrased in general terms so that they may be universally understood and adapted by each generation in the manner most befitting the relevant environment and its circumstances. Unfortunately, what are portrayed as divine comprehensive rules for all facets of life are just man-made rules that were passed down by the early scholars of Islam.[50] They undertook a systematic approach, commendable for its time, so that they might foresee potential future circumstances and design rules to address them when the time came. Unsurprisingly, rulers and clerics took advantage of that situation. Secularism is thus not an attempt to usurp or restrict the rulership of God so much as a measure to redress and remove the autocratic power forcefully claimed by temporal rulers, at times in association with the "clergy," in the name of religion.

Going further, Shabbir Akhtar[51] observes what he considers to be a decline of Islam as a religious and political force and blames it on what he calls the "increasing threat of secularity." That threat is thus incumbent on an Islam, which is perceived as a theocratic doctrine in which religious prescriptions extend to everything which might fall under secular existence. In reality, it is not secularism that is harming the welfare of Muslim peoples and nations. Instead, it is the perception of Islam as necessarily including a theocratic state and government which has led to decline. The rejection of the theocratic state implied in the call for secularism is unfortunately perceived as a rejection of Islam itself.

Shabbir Akhtar points to certain effects of secularization in the West, especially as people tend to forget God in their day-to-day lives, then remember him on occasions that he refers to as the "rites of passage," namely, at birth, marriage, and death.[52] But it is not necessary to institutionalize God's remembrance by creating a theocracy; nor is it necessary that the observance of religious duties be enforced by state institutions. Shaykh Yusuf Qaradawy adopted this very argument in order to refute the concept of secularism. According to him, secularism deprives Islam of its essence and vocation to lead, and confines it to a ceremonial role for special occasions such as birth, marriage, divorce, death, and the like.[53] In reality, given the universal nature of Islam, God is the god of the Universe and of all people and not just the god of Muslims; and God's

Message, the Holy Qur'an, is addressed to all people, including believers and nonbelievers. This explains why the Qur'an makes room for pluralism and diversity, which in turn shows that Islam is inherently secular, not just merely tolerant of secularity.[54]

Two Qur'anic verses have been advanced as the scriptural foundation for the perception of Islam as an all-encompassing message that regulates all facets of life:

> Q6:38—*"There is not an animal (that lives) on the earth, nor a being that flies on its wings, but (forms part of) communities like you.* Nothing have We omitted from the Book, *and they (all) shall be gathered to their Lord in the end."*[55]

> Q16:89—*"And (think of) the day We shall send to every people a witness from among them (to testify) against them, and We shall bring you (O prophet) as witness against these. And We have revealed to you the Book,* an exposition of everything, *and guidance, and mercy, and glad tidings for the Muslims."*[56]

These two verses, when read in their proper context, are not about all facets of life having been divinely regulated by the Qur'an.[57]

In Verse Q16:89, the subject of discussion is actually about the Day of Judgment, when people will be judged following the utmost divine justice, based—among other things—on witness accounts. Because divine justice leaves no room for injustice, people are informed of their religious duties and requirements before being held accountable. Therefore, the highlighted reference in Verse Q16:89 is intended to educate people so that they might avoid committing the haram (the religiously proscribed), prevent the *'iqāb* (the ultimate punishment), and instead, achieve the *thawāb* (the ultimate reward).[58] The erroneous interpretation of this verse as a reference to all facets of life is based on an explanation attributed to Ibn Mas'ud, a companion of the Prophet. Later on, certain exegetes further added to the scope of the verse in question the elucidations of the 'ulama' of the various schools of Islamic jurisprudence, as extracted from the above sources. This extension of the scope of Verse Q16:89 is totally unwarranted because the sacred text clearly refers to the Qur'an as having already exposed everything, and thus being a text that needs no further extrapolative interpretation. However, later commentators justified the extension of the scope of Verse Q16:89 on the grounds that Prophetic Tradition and other expert interpretations of, and extrapolations from, the Qur'an are as legitimate as what was originally revealed in the Qur'an.[59] This explanation does not stand up to the basic religious creed that equating human work with the Divine Message constitutes an association with God. On this basis, the reference to the Revealed Book in Verse Q16:89 should never extend to any human output, irrespective of who that person is and of how learned his or her mind might be.

The second verse, Q6:38, comes in the context of a series of verses which advise the Prophet about the mocking attitude of people toward prophetic messages in general, including the attitude of Meccans toward the Message brought by Prophet Muhammad. In particular, with respect to the pagan Meccans' disdain for the Qur'an's warnings about the Day of Judgment, God informs us that He keeps track of his creatures' actions, humans and animals, in their minutest details; and every creature, by the end of its lifetime returns to God to face divine justice on the Day of Judgment. The phrase *"Nothing have we omitted from the Book"* appearing in Verse Q6:38 has been the subject of two interpretations by commentators, both taken out of context: (1) that no facet of life has been left unregulated by the Qur'an (in that same context, the term "Book" was taken as a reference to the Qur'an);[60] and (2) that God has presumably predestined every movement and action of every one of His creatures, human and animal (in such a context, the term Book from the root term *kataba* is a reference to the end product of God's decision-making process, which in the instance is about decisions made by way of predestination).[61] However, when placed in context, the verse in question means that God keeps track, and has complete records, of every act of all of His creatures.[62] Therefore, rather that the regulation of every facet of life, this verse is about the wide and unlimited knowledge and awareness of God needed to administer divine justice on the Day of Judgment.

In light of all the above, it can now be established that secularity is an attribute of Islam: God has given humanity, as trustees, the entire freedom to legislate the relevant rules and regulations for their lives; and such rules would in most likelihood be consistent with the principles of morality and values set forth in the Holy Qur'an, which in turn are part of the *fiṭra* upon which God has fashioned His Creation.

No Role for Clergy in Islam

The fact that the Holy Qur'an has not regulated all facets of life, nor provided ready-made solutions for all of the problems of humanity, is not an indication of its insufficiency. Instead, it is a tribute to humanity, whom God installed as trustee of the world that He created. As a universal message embodied primarily in the underlying messages of its verses, the Qur'an provides lasting inspiration to each person so that they might learn the lessons; but also learn to *continuously* devise relevant and appropriate solutions throughout their lives. However, certain *fuqahā'*, clerics, and commentators have wronged the Qur'an by limiting its scope to offering ready-made solutions based on artificial extrapolations from Qur'anic verses. As a result of the perpetuation of outdated solutions, progress was impeded.

Throughout the Holy Qur'an, Islam does not provide nor leave space for any role to be performed by a member of the clergy, whether organized in the form of a structured institution or acting on an individual basis.[63] In this respect, 'Ali Shari'ati asserts that the relationship of humankind with God is direct and unmediated.[64] Nevertheless, over time the role of religious clerics, howsoever called (*fuqahā'*, 'ulama', mullas, or shaykhs), developed into a role almost similar to that of the clergy in Christianity. Many, though not all, evolved into an organized authority that claimed authoritative understanding of the Qur'an and other sources of religious science[65] and of the conduct of the Muslim worship. They also claimed authority to formulate—and rule on—religious law and the administration of justice, and fundamentally to *speak for* Islam.[66] Such churchlike organization and practice even came to be sponsored by the state and in many areas became a state function.

The Evolution of an Institutionalized Muslim Clergy

Clerics were initially useful when the Qur'an was not yet generally available in written form. Those who had not memorized the Qur'an relied on clerics to teach them its contents and guide them in observing its requirements, for worship and otherwise. Most often, the clerics taught the Qur'an with particular focus on their own or some other received interpretations, as opposed to just reciting the text and letting the recipient interpret its verses according to his or her own understanding. Many could not even distinguish the interpretation from the original text. As a result, since very few could read and write, there developed a class of learned clerics, otherwise known as *fuqahā'* and 'ulama', who dominated access to the Qur'an, with the exception of the few from the nonlearned class who memorized the Qur'an.

A segment of that same class of learned clerics also associated itself with people in power and those aspiring to seize power. They contributed their learning toward the recitation of verses, identification of Prophetic Tradition, and interpretation of the Qur'an and Prophetic Tradition in support of the case of their associates. As a result, they found their way into lucrative positions of power in public office, and over time they took charge of education, the judiciary, and religious affairs. That sort of joint venture among rulers and clerics, which developed in the early days of the caliphate, has been a trademark of Islamic history and continues to exist in many parts of Muslim nations.[67] Under that well-established— though unwritten—joint venture, and by bringing the clerical class into the government functions, rulers were generally successful in controlling religion and religious establishments, and preventing the rise of an autonomous power with political clout, similar to the power of the Christian church in medieval Europe.[68] For its part, the religious establishment was able, through the prerogative of telling the ruler what the law is,[69] to achieve a monopoly over the implementation and administration of religion, develop a powerful popular base under the direct protection of rulers, and thereby wield state power.

While the class of clerics may have dominated the administration of religion and the development of religious thought, that dominance was not limited to clerics associated with the state structure, that is, those allied with the rulers. Religious thought continued to develop outside the scope of state functions. Several schools of thought were founded, in Arabic called *madhāhib* (or *madhhab,* singular). They formed schools of thought, independent from each other, with their particular methods of interpretation of the Qur'an and views of Prophetic Tradition. In Sunni Islam, there developed the four major schools—namely the Hanafi, Shafi'i, Maliki, and Hanbali schools. Also there developed other, less widespread schools, such as the Ẓāhiri and Awza'i schools.

The institutionalization of the clerics' role first got a boost when, toward the end of the fourth century after the hijra, a general consensus formed among the ranking jurisprudents of the four major Sunni schools of thought to limit the proliferation of *ijtihād.*[70] That consensus, intended initially to limit the proliferation of lightly rendered religious interpretations, became the starting point of an institutionalization process in which clerics placed themselves in one of the four major official boxes, corresponding to the four permitted schools of thought. However, the formal and final institutionalization of the religious establishment came with the advent of the Ottoman Empire which created the institution of *iftā'.*[71] Once the Ottomans, who had recently converted to Islam, invaded and occupied the Arab Muslim nations, they created the *iftā'* to act as the official reference authority to ensure that the new state properly followed the prescriptions of Islam. In that function, the *iftā'* as an institution was officially mandated to issue binding interpretations of religion in its widest meaning as an all-encompassing system exercising authority over all facets of life, including law and government. The clerics charged with the duties of the *iftā'* institution were empowered to pronounce and interpret the law, advise all sectors of government on compliance with the various religious aspects of their duties, appoint clerics and imams for mosques and education establishments, and administer the assets of the religious endowments. The *iftā'*, headed by the grand mufti, became one of the pillars of the Ottoman Sultanate's state structure, ranking just after the sultan in the administrative hierarchy, alongside the prime minister and head of the armies.[72]

Following the collapse of the Ottoman Empire, at the end of World War I, the *iftā'* did not follow the fate of the empire that gave rise to it in the first place, but continued to function in each of the nations that emerged from the demise of the empire. While that institution did not sustain its previous clout in terms of dictating the law and overseeing compliance of state action with religious precepts, it remained a part of the state structure, that is, a public function benefiting from state protection in return for providing an umbrella of popular legitimacy. Moreover, while the role of the *iftā'* institution may have declined following the efforts on the part of each Muslim nation to secularize part of their legal and judicial systems, the *iftā'* as an institution persisted nevertheless as the official and unchallenged authority, speaking in the name of Islam and on behalf of the practicing peoples of the Muslim nations. It thus became another churchlike institution, similar to traditional ecclesiastic establishments which exercise religious authority over their constituencies, with the exception that the *iftā'* institution remained part of the state structure.

M. Charfi says that over time, Muslim clerics became an obstacle to progress and modernity. He observes that at the beginning of the twentieth century, the efforts of Islamic revivalists,[73] such as Muhammad Abdu, Jamaluddin al-Afghani, Muhammad Rashid Rida, Muhammad Chaker, and Tahar Haddad, have been opposed and condemned by conservative clerics because they endangered the centuries-old closure of the doors of *ijtihād*, called for the emancipation of women, and encouraged the demise of cult-like traditions.[74]

Scriptural Foundation

The verses of the Holy Qur'an make no reference whatsoever to clerics and specialists of religion or religious science, howsoever called, whether as *fuqahā'* or 'ulama'; nor is any role specified for them.[75] Many of these scholars can certainly provide guidance and help to less educated people; however, no matter the extent of their erudition in religious science, they are not indispensable for the ordinary person to understand the Divine Message. The Qur'an is described in Verse Q41:3 as "*A Book whose verses have been detailed, an Arabic Qur'an for a people who know.*"[76] Therefore, basic understanding of the Arabic language was sufficient to understand the Qur'an without any divinely nominated or assigned intermediaries.[77] Nasr Hamid Abizaid describes the Qur'an as a message "of a divine origin but formulated in a human language."[78] This explains why our understanding of any verse of the Qur'an does not necessarily reflect the divine truth. In other words, our understanding is based on language, which is a human phenomenon, and that understanding can change from one place to another and from one person to another. Furthermore, because the Message is divine and our understanding of it is not divine, no human being, no matter how learned, can claim to have attained any truth or perfection in its interpretation. All of this denies any role for a clergy in Islam. It also explains why human beings should be tolerant of the views of others, and avoid imposing their own views.

This should not be taken to mean that anyone who is not versed in the Arabic language needs a learned intermediary for access to the Divine Message, because numerous versions of the Holy Qur'an are available to everyone in almost every major language. Even as far as the Arabic language itself is concerned, some people may be more versed than others in the techniques of the language or may simply be illiterate, and unable to read and write. In such cases, if a person finds a text which is difficult to understand, then that person may have recourse to dictionaries and similar tools, or may seek help from a person who can read and explain. However, while a role for 'ulama' may be welcome to assist those who cannot read or those who may seek specific help, or even to provide guidance in general, the person who provides that help need not be a clergy mandated intermediary.

Thus it becomes clearer that the frequent references in the Qur'an to those who know and those who do not know are not references to any form of learned knowledge acquired through religious study and specialization similar to the knowledge and erudition often claimed by clerics. The knowledge in question is merely the knowledge about the basic divine truths contained in God's Message, acquired from simply reading, understanding and pondering the verses of the Qur'an.[79] This is further confirmed in verses which mention knowledge in connection with *"a people who have knowledge"*[80] where the reference in question is to a community or a group of people who have received the Message, rather than to specific individuals who have acquired deep knowledge of certain aspects of the Message or of religious science. This leaves the few instances in which learned people are mentioned either in the form of *"those who are firmly grounded in knowledge"* (*al-rāsikhūna fil-'ilm*)[81] or in the form of *"those who have been given knowledge"* (*alladhīna ūtu-l-'ilm*).[82] In the former case, *"those who are firmly grounded in knowledge"* is a reference to the learned leaders in Christianity and Judaism (in the case of Verse Q3:7) and those who have read and understood the Divine Message (in the case of Verse Q4:162). In the latter case, *"those who have been given knowledge"* refers—save for one exception—to those who are aware of the messages of God among the People of the Book or the companions of the Prophet. The only exception is the one appearing in Verse Q58:11 where *"those who ... have been given knowledge"* may be construed as a reference to a privileged category of learned people, but then without any implication of an indispensable or necessary role for them.

If the understanding of the Divine Message contained in the Holy Qur'an does not require an intermediary, then a Muslim's relation with God is direct and unmediated by anyone,[83] including the Prophet. The fact that God has specifically directed the Prophet to announce that he is no guardian over the believers constitutes God's express intent to keep the relationship with the believers a direct one.[84] This is further confirmed in the several instances in which God encourages people to rely on Him,[85] which implies that no one else may be relied on . This is true of all aspects of the believers' day-to-day lives, including in matters of worship. God, in Islam, has established a direct relationship with mankind, without intermediary. A person can talk, pray, and communicate directly with God on any matter whatsoever. Muslims are even encouraged to do so, as set forth in Verse Q40:60 *"And your Lord says, 'Call upon Me; I will respond to you'. Indeed, those who disdain My worship will enter Hell [rendered] contemptible,"*[86] and in Verse Q2:186 *"And when My servants question you concerning Me, I am near; I answer the call of the caller when he calls to Me; so let them respond to Me, and let them believe in Me that they might go aright."*[87] Thus, Muslims do not need any interpreter to relate the substance of communication with God. Prayer does not involve any leader's role. Any person is entitled to act as imam, to lead the collective prayer, provided he or she[88] knows how to pray.

As the first Muslim conquests were being conducted outside the Arabian Peninsula inside the lands of the Levant (Syria, Lebanon, and the Holy Land of today), the inhabitants of those lands, mainly Christians, converted to Islam in large numbers because—among other reasons and contrary to the prevailing version that Islam spread under duress by the sword—they were attracted by the fact that Islam had no clergy and man's relation to God could be simple, direct, and unmediated. In addition, conversion to Islam relieved the converted from the *jizya* head tax.[89] These mass conversions were not always welcomed by the conquerors, because conversion to Islam meant the loss by the caliphate of the permanent head tax income, otherwise known as *jiziya*, which was imposed on non-Muslims in return for living in peace among Muslims.

Unfortunately, shortly following the disappearance of the last companions of the Prophet and the rise of the first few generations of clerics, the secular nature of Islam was blurred by the rise of an overwhelming role for clerics and its institutionalization into a clergy-like setup that continues to this day. In this respect, Mohamed Talbi cites an instance in which a journalist exclaimed, "Laicity without God, it is so much more relaxing! By eliminating God, we can achieve total freedom...."[90] This statement has been pushed too far; it is not laicity without God that should be contemplated, but instead laicity without the self-appointed agents of God. Indeed, on more than one occasion in the Holy Qur'an, God made sure to dispel any implication that He may have appointed—or would tolerate self-appointed—human agents to interpret God's rules or otherwise regulate on His behalf those areas left unregulated by God. In Verse Q4:127, God tells the Prophet: "*They ask you [Prophet] for a ruling about Women. Say, 'God Himself gives you a ruling about them....*"[91] While the immediate message relates to women, widows, and orphans, the more important and universal underlying message rises to the very principle of the role of the Prophet and whether or not he is empowered to interpret the rules of Shari'a. The clear, straightforward answer is that God declines sharing divine governance with anyone. The verse tells the Messenger that if anyone seeks his formal interpretation, or fatwa, on this or any other subject, he should tell them that he has no such power, such being the exclusive realm of God. So if even the Prophet did not have that power, there can be no chance that anyone else among clerics at any level, learned or otherwise, might have powers or claims to exercise prerogatives that the Prophet himself did not have in the first place.

There is a very good reason for God's denial of any role for anyone, including clergy. In his lifetime, any question received by the Prophet was answered by God, and God continued to provide answers until the entire message has been fully conveyed. That occurred shortly before the Prophet's death, when Verse Q5:3 was revealed, confirming the end of the Message.[92] Beyond that time, each person will be left to his or her own good faith efforts to strive to understand the Qur'an and advance in the path of God; and in all cases, God judges the intentions and not the results. A. Charfi rightly notes that to attribute a prominent role to people in the clergy is equivalent to the sin of association with God, otherwise known as *shirk*.[93]

The above should serve to clear up the misunderstanding about the relationship between secularism and divine governance: (1) secularism is not inconsistent with divine governance; and (2) secularism is not inconsistent with a role for learned clerics to provide guidance and teach what they believe to be their understanding of religion and of the Message of God, provided that they do not speak for God or otherwise behave as His agents; and provided further that the freedom of their audience to accept or reject the substance of that teaching is at all times fully respected without any implied consequences of divine sanctions. This same misunderstanding is unfortunately repeated when we read that secularism, following the Renaissance, won a victory over religion because of the practices and abuses of the Christian churches against people, in particular against scientists and thinkers.[94] In reality, secularism did not win any victories against religion but against the abusers of religion. But religion should not be eliminated solely because there are people who abuse it.[95]

Two differing perceptions are often expressed regarding the absence of a role for clergy. Some see it as an advantage, while others see it as a vacuum, the lack of any authority vested with the power to speak for Islam.[96] While this situation may create a degree of confusion and uncertainty as to what is or is not consistent with Islam, yet, the benefits outweigh the drawbacks. In a secular environment which does not contemplate or accept coercion in the implementation of religious law, God is the sole authority, and each person is free to understand religion as he or she pleases. This is the essence of Islam. And to the question of who speaks for Islam, the simple answer is that only God speaks for Islam, and that He already did through the Divine Revelation of the Holy Qur'an.[97]

Abou El Fadl warns that the absence of a widely recognized mainstream authority leads to the rise of extremist and fundamentalist movements, because mainstream authority has historically acted to marginalize extremist creeds.[98] But are our choices truly limited to extremism versus traditionalism, thereby foregoing modernity and progress? Unfortunately, the institutions of the so-called traditional mainstream authorities, perceived under the current circumstances as the legitimate authorities, have failed to lead toward progress and have generally resisted it instead. Concern about the rise of extremism can be substantially alleviated in a secular environment where God is left to exercise His authority, where no one speaks for God, and where extremist, moderate, traditionalist, progressive, conservative, and liberal Muslims are all equally subject to the laws of the land, as adopted by the legitimate legislative authority.[99] In such an environment, the self-enforcement of any law, let alone religious law, is strictly prohibited, and the administration of justice belongs exclusively to state institutions.

Reflections on Secularization Experiments in Muslim Nations

Two prominent experiments with total secularization in the Muslim world have been undertaken during the twentieth century, and both experiments have drawn criticism from antisecularists. They are the secularization projects widely implemented by President Mustapha Kemal Atatürk in Turkey following the end of World War I[100] and by President Habib Bourguiba in Tunisia following independence of that nation from French rule.

A common starting premise in the critique of these experiments is that the importation of any ready-made political system is evil, and that secularity is a ready-made system imported from the West. While any stigmatization based solely on origin is to be rejected, even so, secularism is not a political system. It is merely a concept which preserves and respects the attributes of the individual realms of divine governance and human government, and precludes church intervention in state affairs. As such, and as demonstrated in the previous sections, Islam is itself secular and not merely tolerant of secularity.

A second line of critique is the nostalgic observation that at no time in the history of Muslim nations has there been any dichotomy between religious education and secular education, religious justice and civil justice, religion and day-to-day life. Therefore, secularity is bound to create a destructive divide for no valid reason. Another nostalgic observation claims as well that a secular environment ignores the traditions of chastity and covering of women which are typical of Islamic decency.[101] These observations are entirely unwarranted. In the first case, the nonsecular system being deplored does not recognize and respect diversity, where Muslims and non-Muslims alike may enjoy equal rights, leaving differences of opinions and faith to the realm of divine governance. In the second case, the nonsecular system is credited with the enforcement of religious rules and traditions, whereas in reality Islam posits faith and practice of worship as an entirely free option for humankind, sanctioned only by God on the Final Day. On that basis, a secular political system is more consistent with Islam because of its secular character.

With respect to the Turkish experiment in secularization, that experiment is deemed by its critics to have failed because, after a century of attempts to Westernize Turkish society, the people succeeded in electing an Islamist majority to parliament, with the victory in 1995 of Mr. Nejmeddine Arbakan and his party in national elections.[102] This statement is lacking on several counts. First, even though the West may exemplify certain advances achieved in secularity and modernity, secularization and modernization are not about the imposition of Western characteristics on Turkish identity. Second, relative to other nations in the Middle East that did not secularize, Turkey has surpassed its neighbors in terms of education levels, economic advancement, and human rights. Finally, the political successes of Arbakan's—and nowaday's Erdoğan's—parties constitute a witness to the success of the secular system in providing the proper environment for a true democracy.

With respect to the Tunisian experiment in secularization, the government's justification for keeping religion out of politics and prohibiting the formation of religious parties is considered by the antisecularists as a deceitful attempt to eradicate religion under a secret plan implemented by the secular government. In support of this view, the Tunisian religious movements and their leaders are credited with having been instrumental in opposing the French colonial power—they issued fatwas declaring collaboration with the occupier or acceptance of French citizenship as tantamount to apostasy and betrayal of Islam, the Muslims, and the Prophet of Islam. Thus, the successes of the Islamists have consistently been stolen and claimed by the secularists and atheists.[103] For its part, the Tunisian government advanced convincing arguments to justify its action, as follows: (1) religion should remain above politics to avoid its being abused by the individual parties as a tool of political strife; and (2) if religion becomes an integral part of a political party's program, it could potentially result in the return of the caliphate, the reinstatement of a role for the clergy, and a reduction of the sphere of people's sovereignty over the state's affairs, all of which adversely affects the rights of non-Muslims and hinders the exercise of democracy in a diversified society. These are all legitimate objectives of secularism that can be described as direct objectives of Islam, as well.

The Tunisian Government is blamed for adopting a policy of resisting the efforts deployed by the religious establishment to remind people of the concept of enjoining good and prohibiting evil, inciting them to observe religious commands, promoting jihad for the cause of God, and encouraging the mobilization of all available power to terrorize and fight the enemies of God and the nation.[104] What antisecularists find objectionable is precisely the effort to set aside what has stifled the emancipation of Muslims and contributed to their failure to achieve progress over the ages.

But enjoining good and prohibiting evil is not a religious duty exercisable by each Muslim at his or her discretion. It is a collective principle that the community implements in the manner that best serves its interests. On the other hand, defending one's own country against potential enemies is a collective interest of Muslims and non-Muslims alike, unrelated to the cause of God or the path toward God. Thus it does not qualify as jihad. In any event, this is a function that the state performs in the best interests of the nation, as determined by the representatives of that nation, away from any other considerations, religious or otherwise.

In sum, secularism is neither an alternative nor a hindrance to Islam because secularity itself is an attribute of Islam. Secularism is not about the fulfillment of the desire for separation of the religious from the political, because the ethical principles and moral values brought about by Islam are substantially founded in *fiṭra*, the innate component inherent in the divine creation of humankind. In any event, the Scripture does not deal with affairs of state because Islam is neither a system of government nor a legal system.

CHAPTER 7
The Evolution of the Islamic State

"Political Islam" has come to the forefront of our perceptions of Islam as one of the religion's key components. The notion is based in the belief that Islam is a global system which encompasses the temporal and the religious, that is, *dīn wa dawla*, or religion and state. Political Islam exemplifies claims that Islam is an all-inclusive code for all aspects of life, namely a sociopolitical order involving a state constitution, with its legal and judicial systems.[1] In support of such a claim, in addition to the verses of the Qur'an discussed in Chapter 6, reference is made to the state that Prophet Muhammad presumably founded in the oasis of Yathrib, later known as *al-Madina al-Munawwara* (Medina), following his exit from Mecca.[2] Then, following the death of the Prophet, his successors went about the task of building a state and expanding its reach, while spreading the Message of God. The state system so created is what is now commonly known as the "caliphate," the generally acknowledged Islamic state that lasted until the first quarter of the twentieth century.

In reality, political Islam has nothing to do with Islam because Islam is not a political system. Attesting that the subject of the Islamic state is not dealt with in any of the Holy Qur'an's provisions, Mohammed Charfi states concisely, "State and politics are not part of religion."[3] Political Islam is just ordinary politics, practiced by Muslim individuals and groups—otherwise known as Islamists—and claimed to be an expression of Islam.[4]

The Community of Medina

Although the facts clearly indicate otherwise, it is widely believed that Prophet Muhammad founded a state in Medina as part of his mission to spread the Message of Islam, on the assumption that Islam includes a system of government.[5] According to Roger Caratini, "[i]n the same time, he was founding what we can call the Islamic society whose political, legal and economic system is defined in the Qur'an, that is a system founded on religious bases."[6] Similarly, Shaykh Muhammad al-Ghazali contends, "[n]o prophet carrying a previous message got the opportunity to found a state using his book,"[7] whereas in fact less than one-third of the Qur'an had by then been revealed, and the founding charter of that "state" contains not a single mention of, or reference to, the Holy Qur'an. For his part, Khalil Abdul-Karim even claims that the Prophet had the personal ambition of creating an *umma* which had no relations or ties to its predecessors. Here, too, such a claim is not plausible because it is contrary to the provisions of the Qur'an which place Islam in the lineage of the Abrahamic faiths and encourage diversity and interaction among cultures.[8] Further it is claimed that what the Prophet founded was a theocracy headed by him, because he was continuously connected to God through revelation, and God kept that link active in His bid to oversee and manage everything said and done by the Prophet.[9] Such extremist views notwithstanding, it remains a widely accepted view among Muslims and non-Muslims alike, conservatives and liberals, that Islam introduced a set of rules that define a comprehensive political, legal, and economic system for founding and running a state based on religion.[10]

This perception of Islam has garnered a wide consensus and become an integral part of the faith, to the extent that its denial could be interpreted as a departure from the faith, and to some perhaps tantamount to apostasy.[11] Witness to this observation is the episode that took place in Egypt in 1925 around the publication by Shaykh 'Ali 'Abdel Raziq, a prominent Azharite Islamic court judge, of his famous book entitled *al-Islam wa Usul al-Hukm* (*Islam and the Principles of Government*). In this work, Shaykh 'Ali 'Abdel Raziq advanced the view that at no time was Prophet Muhammad a king or a state founder and that the authority that he enjoyed was an absolute authority, different in nature from that of a mere state ruler, conferred by God to His Messenger as an attribute of prophecy and a tool for performance of his mission.[12] That controversy remained at the theological level of the basic faith, without thorough analysis of the various actions undertaken by the Prophet in Medina which could be construed as acts of statesmanship. However, other thinkers[13] reached the conclusion that the Prophet had indeed founded the first Islamic state in Medina. They based that conclusion on the empirical observation of the Prophet's activities in organizing the community of believers, administering justice, and waging wars, among other activities.

The most important action by the Prophet to be regarded as an act of statesmanship is the constitutive agreement negotiated and executed among the Prophet, his companions from Mecca, and the tribes inhabiting the Medina region—Muslims and non-Muslims.[14] That document is commonly referred to in historical texts as the Charter (or Constitution) of Medina.[15] Later on, historians and political scientists would consider the Charter of Medina as an act of statesmanship by Prophet Muhammad[16] and describe the community of Medina that he organized as the first Islamic state. Citing Article 23 of the Charter, 'Ali Bulaç concludes that the Prophet assumed the role of absolute ruler, thereby confirming that in Islam, religious practice, belief, and law cannot be separated from one another.[17]

However, the circumstances in which that community was formed indicate that the intended purpose was merely to create a framework within which the Prophet and his companions from Mecca could live in peace with the inhabitants of Medina. Prophet Muhammad and his companions decided to leave Mecca when mounting pressure on them became intolerable following the death of Abu Taleb, the Prophet's uncle and powerful protector, in his capacity as leader of the Prophet's Banu Hashim clan. With this context in mind, a closer look at the provisions of the Charter of Medina and the circumstances in which it was prepared clearly indicate that it was not a state setup that the Prophet sought to achieve.[18] In fact, God had a message to convey. He selected Muhammad and made him His prophet and messenger. He revealed the Message to him in stages so that he might perform the mission as best he could over the period of revelation. God did not install Prophet Muhammad as ruler, whether over the people to whom the Message was addressed or any other peoples. He did not want him to be distracted from the main mission of conveying the Message, and that message does not include a theory of state. That is why God carefully defined the Prophet's mission in the Qur'an and made sure to exclude from it any coercive role. Prophet Muhammad was expressly informed that his mission did not include imposing the faith or ruling over people.

In order to devote his entire time to the divine mission entrusted to him, the Prophet needed an environment of normalcy and peace where he and his companions could operate without being distracted and sidetracked by issues and strife with the tribes of Medina. The Charter of Medina had specifically that purpose and no other. A careful review of the Charter reveals that it did not contain any state structural provisions or ones indicative of a new political order.[19] It did not, as a normal constitution would, regulate the exercise of power. All it did was to set forth the principles of peaceful coexistence among diverse tribal and religious communities based on equality, mutual recognition and respect, freedom of faith, and sanctity of life and property.[20]

Because it is not a constitutional document, in the sense of nation building, the Charter reaffirms certain tribal customs designed to reserve the jurisdiction of the individual tribes and rules concerning relations of people belonging to each tribe, but excluding customs associated with blood revenge which led to the killing of believers. The only other aspect in which the Prophet was attributed a public role was that of dispute settlement, by way of arbitration, between people of different tribes or faiths. Placed in perspective, this dispute settlement mechanism was nowhere to be perceived as a state-like mechanism. Instead, it was an expedient to prevent personal disputes from developing into major tribal conflicts which could derail the mission of the Messenger of God. This is also what the various Qur'anic verses refer to in using the term *hukm* to describe the Prophet's role of settling disputes by arbitration.[21]

In view of the context of the founding of the community of Medina, the conclusion advanced by Roger Caratini that Prophet Muhammad was founding an "Islamic society whose political, legal and economic system is defined in the Qur'an, that is, a system founded on religious bases," cannot be substantiated. That community was established at the outset of the Prophet's stay in Medina, before the verses considered by religious scholars to be of a nation-building nature were revealed. It is very likely that the Shari'a-related organizational verses may have been revealed in the course of guiding the footsteps of the Prophet in resolving issues that arose from time to time which could threaten the peace of the community.

However, it cannot be said that the system founded by the Prophet was based on religious grounds. What the Charter of Medina established was solely a secular environment which recognizes and acknowledges diversity and sets forth the basic principles for a multi-faith community.

On the other hand, the Prophet did not, during his tenure as leader of the community of Medina, carry out any of the duties of state. He did not appoint administrative heads for the various regions that submitted to him. Instead, he appointed companions who had memorized parts of the Qur'an to go out and teach the new converts the essentials of the new faith. Nor did he create a tax regime and tax collection system to fund state activities. Rather, he set aside the defined share of spoils of war and, from time to time, collected zakat and charities that he used to help the poor and for other social purposes. His war ventures were funded by the warriors themselves, each one defraying his individual costs for weapons, clothes, food, and other needs.

Finally, the Prophet's role could have been perceived as that of a political leader and statesman as a result of the various wars that he waged in the performance of his divine mission. Such wars were perhaps viewed as actions designed to expand the nation of Islam that he founded, as a prerequisite for spreading the Message of God.[22] In reality, at no time did the mission of Prophet Muhammad include the use of the sword as a tool to spread God's Message. Despite all claims to the contrary made by religious scholars and clerics, at no time did God instruct the Prophet to take up the sword to spread the Message and force people to adhere to the faith or else face death or enslavement. What God instructed the Prophet and his companions to do in Medina, which previously was proscribed in Mecca, was to take up the sword in self-defense and protection of the faith. That license to fight in self-defense was denied in Mecca because God knew that the Muslims would be substantially outnumbered. In any event, during the lifetime of the Prophet's uncle and protector, Abu Taleb, there was no need for fighting. Then as that protection faded with the death of Abu Taleb, the Prophet and his companions were guided toward migrating from Mecca to Medina where they could build up their strength and fight in self-defense, if attacked to prevent fulfillment of the divine mission.

In the meantime, views are divided over whether the setup created by the Prophet constituted nation building. This controversy is irrelevant to the main issue of whether Islam is a political system or not. Even if the record of the Prophet in Medina did indeed amount to founding—and ruling over—a state, such record does not constitute a part of the prophetic mission which excluded the enforcement of the Message. In this respect, it is untrue that the verses which exclude the enforcement powers have been abrogated by later Medinan verses.

In retrospect, while the Prophet did not found a state or establish any state-like structures or otherwise act as a statesman, yet, Prophet Muhammad did wield power and authority by far exceeding that of a tribal head, statesman, military leader, or political leader.[23] Some went to the extent of regarding the Prophet as a ruler by divine governance; and in that capacity he was immune from error.[24] In reality, while that unlimited power and authority wielded by Prophet Muhammad was divinely conferred upon him and readily accepted by his companions and his new allies in the Medina community, that power was not conferred for nation-building purposes.[25] That power was conferred upon the Prophet for the specific and sole divine purpose of securing the transmission and spreading of God's Message, which purpose cannot be compared in terms of importance and priority to that of mere statesmanship or a political function. Moreover, Prophet Muhammad did not exercise the divine powers conferred upon him under a continuing divine guidance.[26] He was basically, in the performance of his mission, acting on his own judgment,[27] in consultation with his companions, according to the verses on *shūra* (consultation). Only in specific instances was Prophet Muhammad divinely guided. However, even then, guidance came in the form of revelation and not actual divine governance, leaving flexibility for the Prophet to interpret the revelation and determine the means and methods for implementation. Consequently, the leadership of the *umma* of believers was a necessary tool to ensure that the communal environment did not distract the Prophet from performance of the divine mission.

The Caliphate

The Prophet died without designating a successor or specifying a mechanism for choosing one.[28] That behavior, action, or inaction—howsoever it is perceived—is indicative of the Prophet's status, the attributes of that status, and the Prophet's own perception of it.

What is certain is that Prophet Muhammad was a prophet and a messenger of God. The fact that he did not designate a successor indicates that Prophet Muhammad was clear about the fact that neither the function of prophet nor that of messenger were transferable, whether in his lifetime or following his death. Moreover, being of the *intuitu personae* type, the functions of prophet and messenger of God could not either devolve automatically by way of succession to any potential natural or designated heir.[29] This is consistent with two firm premises: (1) the functions of prophet and messenger of God are divine appointments that do not devolve to other humans without divine intervention; and (2) God's own assertion in the Qur'an that Prophet Muhammad is the last and final prophet and messenger decisively ends any potential discussion over the possible devolution of the function of prophet and messenger.

With respect to the claim that Prophet Muhammad founded and ruled the first Islamic state in Medina until his death, the fact that the Prophet died without designating a successor is indicative of his own perception of his role and defeats that claim. One might object, suggesting that the Prophet might perhaps have left the choice of successor to his people after him. This approach is an unlikely one because, if indeed the Prophet was a statesman and nation builder, then the first thing a nation builder would do is to design a mechanism for devolution of power, so as to ensure that the nation he builds can survive and strive following his disappearance from the scene.

This is not to say that Prophet Muhammad did not have the qualities and attributes of a leader and statesman.[30] He certainly had important qualities, those required to carry out the duties of prophet and messenger of God, including those required of a statesman and nation builder. Nevertheless, he devoted his qualities exclusively to the performance of his divine mission and to no other objective, not that of statesmanship nor that of nation building. Indeed, Prophet Muhammad did display and exercise his impeccable qualities in leading the *umma* of believers, as part of his mission which people erroneously perceived to be political in nature. However, being part of his divine mission, that leadership function is also not subject to transfer or devolution to, or acquisition by, any other human being.[31]

The Enlightened Caliphate

Upon the death of the Prophet, certain tribal leaders of Medina rushed to hold a meeting and select a successor to lead their community. The Prophet's companions who accompanied him on his hijra from Mecca were not invited to that meeting. In their mind, they had invited the Prophet to lead their community at the time of their intertribal feuds; and as these feuds had ended, they had no further need for an outsider to lead their community. However, before they had selected the successor leader, 'Umar and Abou Bakr, among the Companions, found out about that meeting and rushed to join it. There were arguments and counterarguments as to who should be the next leader. None of the arguments advanced were of a religious nature or drawn from, or by reference to, the Holy Qur'an or the Prophetic Tradition. Instead, the debate was of a tribal nature: the Companions claimed that the next leader should be from the Companions, that is, from *Quraysh* where the Prophet came from; while the *anṣār* of Medina claimed that the leader should be from their ranks, because they opened their doors to the Prophet and helped establish and build the roots of the strong *umma* he left behind. In the course of the heated debate, the *anṣār* of Medina suggested that there be two leaders, one from each side, while the Meccan Companions countered that the leader should be from their ranks, but conceding that the second in charge could be from the *anṣār* of Medina. Fights were even said to have erupted, causing injuries to some. In the end, the episode ended in a *fait accompli* designation of Abou Bakr as successor to Prophet Muhammad in the leadership of the community of Medina.[32] While Abou Bakr got the vetting *bay'a* or approval of a large number of notables among a majority of Meccan Companions and *anṣār* of Medina, he failed to obtain the approval of the lead notables of Medina, such as Sa'd Ibn 'Ubada. In addition, while the Prophet's cousin and prominent companion, 'Ali Ibn Abi Taleb, gave his nod of approval, later events indicated that he did so reluctantly, believing that his close family ties to the Prophet entitled him to some priority right of succession in the leadership of his community. Thus the seeds of the great discord among Muslims, which ended in the major schism within Islam into the Sunni and the Shi'a sects, were starting to take root.[33]

Abou Bakr, as first successor of Prophet Muhammad to the leadership of the community of Medina, took the title of caliph. The terms "caliph" and "caliphate," the latter being the political system headed by the caliph, mean successor and succession. The term caliph appears in the Holy Qur'an twice only, but not within the meaning of political successor. In the first instance, the term is used to describe the role of general trustee which God, in the exercise of His divine governance, assigned to Adam and to all of humankind through Adam, when He created him.[34] That trusteeship is not of the nature of delegating a function to be performed on behalf of God or for the purpose of fulfilling any divine purpose or objective.[35] Instead, it is a form of autonomous assignment, to be freely organized by the trustee, for the exercise of which humankind will be judged based on the results of each individual's performance. In the second instance, the term is used to describe the role of special trust assigned by God to King David for the specific purpose of setting forth and administering a system of justice.[36] So it is a divine mission to be fulfilled by David in person and no one else. Apart from these two instances, the Holy Qur'an does not address the functions of caliph, statesmanship, or nation building, or otherwise deal with or regulate any other activities relating to them. Strangely enough, some found in the mere use by the Holy Qur'an of the term *khalīfa* for trustee a divine indication that the position of caliph is a divinely mandated function, wherein the power of leadership is individual, thereby excluding collective leadership.[37]

On that basis, the functions assumed by Abou Bakr and the title that he adopted to perform them were not divinely assigned or provided for by God, in the Holy Qur'an or elsewhere. Since God had expressly declared in the Qur'an the final and permanent conclusion of all divinely assigned prophetic missions and activities, the functions assumed by Abou Bakr could only be secular functions, exercisable exclusively within the framework of the trusteeship attributed by God to humankind through Adam. If that is the case, then whose successor was Abou Bakr by holding the title of caliph? He could not possibly have been the successor of God because he was not appointed by God, and in any event God had announced the decision to discontinue further human appointments. Nor could he have been the successor of Prophet Muhammad as prophet and messenger because those functions are not transferable in any form nor under any circumstance.[38] That leaves only the role of Prophet Muhammad as de facto leader of the community of Medina.[39]

Therefore, Abou Bakr and the caliphs who succeeded him were successors of Prophet Muhammad as leaders of the community of Medina, but with a very important and major difference: while they held the basic functions to lead the community, they did not have the unlimited authority that God had attached to Prophet Muhammad's leadership, which is specific to the nontransferable divine mission entrusted to him.[40] Consequently, the caliph had to build the bases necessary to create and establish his own authority, that which signaled the transformation of that function into a secular political function, that of nation building, where the power being wielded is not divine power, nor is it divinely based, and accordingly could not be justified on religious grounds. However, because the first four caliphs were the closest and most faithful companions of the Prophet, who accompanied him and witnessed his career from beginning to end, they considered it to be their duty, and actively sought, to safeguard his achievements and follow in his footsteps with the spread of the Divine Message. Again, though its subject matter consisted of a divine message, their intervention in spreading religion was an entirely human endeavor and initiative which could be pursued by any person without being invested with political and military power, following Verse 16:125, *"Call to the way of your Lord with wisdom and fair counsel, and debate with them in the fairest manner."*[41] They were for that purpose called the Enlightened Caliphs.

This explains why, during his short tenure, Abou Bakr took upon himself the task of subduing the collective movements of apostasy which surfaced almost concurrently with the announcement of the death of the Prophet. This movement was perceived as the single most dangerous threat to the new faith. Abou Bakr was successful in eliminating that threat through the wars, known as the Ridda Wars, which he waged against the presumed apostates. Then he began the geographic expansion of Islam as a means to deal with the risks posed by the presence of two powerful, belligerent empires in the immediate vicinity of the Peninsula, namely the Persian Empire and the Roman Empire. Abou Bakr did not live to see the achievement of his expansionist endeavors. His successor 'Umar embarked upon pursuing the project of Abou Bakr and creating the state structure and institutions for the administration of the vast new Arabo-Islamic Empire.[42]

Unfortunately, the reality of the endeavor being undertaken as a nation-building project was not perceived in this manner at the time. In addition to the tasks of building institutions to administer the expanding empire, the Enlightened Caliphs perceived their role as twofold: (1) to maintain the solidarity of the community left behind by the Prophet; and (2) to persevere in the state-sponsored project of spreading the Message of God. To the members of the community, the role of the Enlightened Caliphs was perceived as a natural continuation of Prophet Muhammad's leadership. And to both the people and their leadership, that perception could be explained on both religious and sociopolitical grounds.

On religious grounds, as soon as the news of the Prophet's death emerged, Abou Bakr tried to pacify the agitated crowds, telling them that, if it was Muhammad whom they worshipped, Muhammad is dead, and if worship was truly and in its entirety to God, then God is alive and never dies. On sociopolitical grounds, Prophet Muhammad conveyed the Message in a tribal environment lacking a state structure. When he left, that tribal environment had not changed, except that certain tribal customs had been replaced by ethical rules and moral values derived from the Divine Message, in an attempt among believers to install faith as a primary bond which took priority over tribal ties.

As a corollary, and since there were no state structures or written laws, the natural tendency of the Enlightened Caliphs, in the early days following the death of Prophet Muhammad, was to emulate him, as life in the Arabian Peninsula was then still simple, without sophisticated customs, needs, or other requirements. For all practical purposes, the system negotiated by the Prophet in the form of the Charter of Medina, together with his personal behavior in implementing it, were perceived as being nearest to perfection. People were therefore safe if they did as the Prophet would have done in each instance which required a decision or judgment. It was sufficient to recollect or figure out what the Prophet had done or would have done in a similar instance, with the Qur'an and Prophetic Tradition serving as primary reference, followed by tribal customs that were not inconsistent with the new faith.[43] But this approach suffered a serious drawback. From a theological perspective, God did not intend to have the Prophet's role imitated because he did not produce any more prophets, a further proof that the role of the Prophet was not political (for it to be imitated). The fact is that the Prophet's behavior as leader of the community and legislator was nevertheless the subject of imitation by way of so-called religious duty. The perception of the new faith as an all-encompassing system, which included a political and legal system, was then emerging and starting to take root. This was the starting point of perceiving Islam as *dīn wa dawla*, or religion and state.

The simplicity that characterized the daily life of the community of Medina in the days of Abou Bakr gradually started to change as issues became increasingly complex during the tenure of the second Enlightened Caliph, 'Umar. By this time the armies of the caliph had stepped out of the Arabian Peninsula, crossing to the northeast into Mesopotamia and Persia, and to the northwest into the Levant of the Byzantine Empire, namely the lands bordering the eastern seashore of the Mediterranean Sea, otherwise known as *Bilād al-Shām*. The small, simple desert community of Medina had grown into a multiethnic, multireligious empire which included, in addition to the allies among the Arabian tribes who adopted Islam, the civilized and sophisticated populations which had advanced in the fields of Hellenistic and Persian sciences, literature, philosophy, and the arts. This vast new empire could no longer be led along the leadership pattern of the Medina community, and the second Enlightened Caliph, 'Umar, went about overseeing the organization of the state. However, he did not create a state structure from scratch. Neither he nor any of the Companions and followers had the know-how or experience in nation building for a nontribal, multiethnic, and multicultural society. He therefore elected to maintain in place most of the existing state structures and institutions as found in the conquered lands, while appointing a superstructure of Muslim Arab elements to head the system, ensure compliance with the faith, and, at the same time, learn the art of statesmanship. The system that 'Umar shaped was thus a combination of the existing structures as inherited, together with a modified version of the sociopolitical system of Medina, adapted to the new environment.

Because of their statures, personalities, and integrity, Caliphs Abou Bakr and 'Umar were able to continue the leadership of the community of believers as it was expanding, without any meaningful or threatening internal political dissentions and strife. However, that would no longer be the case following the death of 'Umar and the accession of the third and fourth Enlightened Caliphs, 'Uthman and Ali, respectively, in the midst of major dissentions and controversy among the Companions and tribal chiefs. It was the beginning of the great discord which saw the birth of the basic schism between Sunni Islam and Shi'i Islam, then between the mainstream ruling cast and the party of the *khawārij*, who adopted an extremist, puritanical interpretation of Islam and perceived all those who claimed to lead the community as heretics deserving capital punishment.[44]

While the strife between the two feuding sides essentially concerned the wielding of political power, their arguments and counterarguments in the dispute shared a common denominator: they were strictly of a religious nature. Each side was seeking to preserve religion, alleging that the antireligious behaviors and vagaries of the other side were endangering the continued relevance and purity of the Divine Message and the survival of Islam.

The Enlightened Caliphate as a political system, in which people seemingly have a say in the appointment of the ruler, came to an end. Mu'awiya, in a forceful move to end the confusion arising from the discord that had started in the days of 'Uthman and attained great heights in the days of 'Ali, proclaimed himself caliph and moved the seat of the caliphate from Medina to Damascus. There he founded the Omayyad Caliphate which was to be ruled by a dynasty descending from him.

The Omayyad and Subsequent Caliphates

The Omayyad Caliphate, which lasted close to ninety years (from 661 to 750 A.D.),[45] remained a so-called "Islamic" system of government only in name because Mu'awiya, its founder, retained the title of caliph, which was the title adopted by the first four caliphs who succeeded the Prophet.[46] However, that system was in actuality a unilateral, authoritarian system in which power devolved upon the death of each caliph to the eldest of his male children or, depending on family intrigues, to the most powerful next-of-kin.[47] Then power devolved to other dynasties, that is, from one ruling family to another, when the successor dynasty had the power to overthrow an outgoing dynasty, weakened by internal strife. That same pattern repeated itself when the Abbasid dynasty replaced the Omayyads to create the Abbasid Caliphate, with the added twist, rightly observed by John Esposito, that the caliphs started appropriating "the Persian-inspired title, Shadow of God on Earth" by further emphasizing the claim to rule by divine mandate and transforming their title into that of deputy of God.[48] The same pattern continued when several regional dynasties assumed control of various regions of the Abbasid Empire, and finally all that confusion ended with the advent of the Ottoman dynasty. The Ottoman sultans reunified a large segment of the empire into the powerful Ottoman Caliphate and ruled it for five centuries until the end of World War I in the first quarter of the twentieth century. That date signaled the official end of the caliphate, which remains today the synonym for the Muslim system of government.[49]

What all these dynasties and caliphates had in common was that, in spite of their true nature and structure as kingdoms comparable to any other kingdom of the Middle Ages, and except for a few specific instances, they maintained an Islamic facade, claiming to raise high the banner of Islam, spread its message, and rule by the Shari'a, following in the footsteps of Prophet Muhammad and abiding by his traditions.[50] Some caliphs even sometimes assumed a theocratic aura, claiming to rule by divine right.[51] In retrospect, this Islamic facade was added onto the state structures and political systems, commencing with the first succession following the death of the Prophet; initially, it was a natural continuation of the relatively simple lifestyles of Medina and Mecca. Then, as matters grew in complexity, the religious stamp and outlook had already taken sufficient root to become an inherent attribute of the state system.[52]

Also, it is important to note that, in the period immediately following the death of Prophet Muhammad, there were no clerics and *fuqahā'* to speak of because the Enlightened Caliphs themselves and their fellow companions of the Prophet were qualified to serve as natural spokespersons on religious matters. Indeed, most of them had memorized substantial parts of the Holy Qur'an and, most of all, had witnessed the tradition of the Prophet while in his company. In fact, companions who memorized the Qur'an were often sent to faraway places to teach the faith to newly converted Muslims. They were also known as *qurrā'*, that is, those who read the Qur'an. In their concern to continue the legacy of Prophet Muhammad, it was therefore easy for the caliphs to ensure compliance with the precepts of the new faith that he left them by testing issues and solutions against religious criteria as they arose, prior to implementation, all of which reinforced from the outset the perception of Islam as a political and legal system.

However, as the numbers of companions began to dwindle over time, some because of old age and others killed in wars, a new class of "learned" clerics who had studied the Qur'an and the Prophetic Tradition was rising through the ranks and replacing the Companions as authorities on religious matters, with the caveat that the Companions who died took with them their memory of prophetic traditions, till then oral. This rising group of *fuqahā'* had an important role to play, that of providing religious legitimacy and clearance for the actions of the rulers. In certain cases, the rulers genuinely sought and followed the guidance of the *fuqahā'*; and in most other cases, they abused their role and bought their legitimacy with favors and temporal power. The *fuqahā'* and clerics were thus developing into an informal clergy, and the joint venture between rulers and clergy grew into a quasi-institutionalized framework. Mohammed Charfi traces the start of this joint venture to Mu'awiya, the very first caliph of the Omayyad Dynasty that ended the rule of the Enlightened Caliphs.[53]

This was the background for the fear that innovative rules, extracted from a liberal interpretation of the Qur'anic text, might be inconsistent with the Revelation. This fear had encouraged the invention of rules and their attribution to the Prophet, which made it easier on rulers and ruled peoples alike to follow Prophetic Tradition, including knowingly forged traditions, than to trust one's own or another person's judgment in the interpretation of the Holy Qur'an. This had the further negative effect of artificially and unnecessarily expanding the scope of religious dogmas through the sacralization of human interpretations and of forged prophetic traditions: it was not to the benefit of the religious establishment and rulers to acknowledge the truth about the secular nature of the endeavor altogether and to legislate in the best interests of the people, while observing the universal basic values and ethical principles that the Divine Message reminded people of. The *fuqahā'* did not correct the misperception but instead reinforced it when they made themselves indispensable to the political caste to find religiously vetted solutions for them and to maintain religion as reference in every action or inaction by the rulers, thereby perpetuating the close association between rulers and clergy.[54]

Retrospective on the Charter of Medina System

While the contractual system negotiated by the Prophet with the Muslim and non-Muslim inhabitants of the Medina region did not amount to a state constitution, yet, that system survived the death of the Prophet and permeated the various caliphates that have ruled the Islamic nations ever since. That same system has even survived the last caliphate and permeated the nations that emerged following the liquidation of the Ottoman Empire, being the last in the series of caliphates.

What the Charter of Medina did was to recognize the multi-religious diversity of the community of Medina and record the need to secure a harmonious coexistence within that diversity, wherein each party promises the protection of God to the others (*dhimma*)[55] as long as they comply faithfully with the provisions of the Charter. Under that system, each party is free to retain its religion and worship in accordance with its rules. The rules derived from each religion govern the adherents to it, and disputes are settled under that party's jurisdiction and in accordance with its own mechanisms for settling disputes. Interparty disputes, however, are referred to the Prophet for arbitration.[56] With that in mind, one can understand that the system in question is not indicative of a state structure. On the contrary, it is indicative of a temporary fix, in the absence of state structures, wherein each side handles its problems under a framework of autonomy. In other words, it is a mosaic-type system that does not forge any form of integration among the members of the community. However, it was a convenient interim arrangement, for any period necessary to enable the Prophet to perform his divine mission.

Paradoxically, while the system was intended to be temporary it survived and became a permanent arrangement for the coexistence of Muslims, Christians, and Jews in the areas falling within the predominantly Muslim environment of the caliphate system. Under the Omayyad and Abbasid Caliphates, the system continued under the name of the *dhimmī* system, in which Christians and Jews lived under a special status and paid the *jizya* tax. Under the Ottoman Caliphate, the system was transposed into the so-called millet system. Then, following the emergence of the Arab nations from Ottoman rule in the first quarter of the twentieth century, each nation gave some form of autonomy to its various religious communities to adopt their own laws and organize their own courts to settle disputes on matters of family law and inheritance. Thus, the hastily devised system initially intended to secure a temporary peaceful coexistence—as opposed to full and permanent integration—among the Muslims coming from Mecca and the tribes of Medina composed of Jews, Muslims, and others, survived the completion of the Prophet's mission. To date it continues to plague pluralistic societies in the nations that emerged from the dissolution of the Ottoman Caliphate.[57]

CHAPTER 8
Islam and the Myth of a Divine Theory of State

Although Taha Hussein subscribes to the belief that the Prophet was continuously under a state of uninterrupted divine revelation, he rightly asserts that nowhere does the Qur'an set forth a divine theory of state. He also observes that the system of government that the Muslim Arabs devised, following the death of Prophet Muhammad and ensuing their geographic expansion, was a uniquely secular system, deeply inspired by the noble principles and values contained in the Holy Qur'an, but at the same time unlike any of the systems then prevailing in the occupied lands.[1] That religion was used, following the death of the Prophet to found a state and organize its structures, or that it was declared the law of the land under the caliphates or in nations with Muslim majorities, does not justify defining the caliphate, or any other such nation, as an Islamic state system.[2] The use of Islam to devise a political system was not a religious act nor did it fulfill any requirement of Islam. It was merely a convenient bond to extend power and strengthen the regime. In the words of Abdou Filali-Ansari, "A religion can be universal but a state cannot."[3]

While the transition from the Enlightened Caliphate into that of the Omayyad dynasty may have been perceived as a potential transition into secularism, in reality it signaled the beginning of the association between the religious establishment and the ruling families. Mohammed Charfi rightly observes that religion was breached in the process of selecting the first caliph to succeed the Prophet, that is, as of the very first day following the death of the Prophet. In that process, there were no issues derived from the Qur'an or the Prophetic Tradition. The only concern on each side was that the new chief be one selected from their ranks.[4]

This brings us to the core issue of whether a specific environment is necessary for the Muslim person to be a good Muslim, that is, to live his or her Islam. In other words, it is necessary to determine to what extent Muslims need a state apparatus that wields sufficient power to create an adequate so-called "Islamic" environment to enable them to live their faith and observe its tenets. Assuming there is no need to wield state power to create an "Islamic" environment, the next issue would be to find out if Islam provides for a theory of state which, if not mandatory, would be advisable for living Islam. Finally, since there are large numbers of Muslim peoples who live in nations in which they constitute the majority without, however, declaring these nations as Islamic, we will consider whether modern constitutional principles are compatible with Islam. However, before exploring if and how the Holy Qur'an deals with politics and state, it is useful first to consider in general terms the doctrinal perception of the Islamic state and its organization.

The Doctrinal Theory of the Islamic State

Abu-l-A'la al-Mawdudi argues, "'Obey God and His Prophet.' In this Qur'anic command lies the supreme innovation introduced by Islam into the social structure of Arabia: the establishment of a novel political authority possessing legislative power."[5] This statement is fairly representative of a general perception of Islam as an all-encompassing religion that extends its umbrella over the matters of state. Al-Mawdudi goes even further, asserting

> Islam and nationalism are diametrically opposed to each other... The ultimate goal of Islam is a world-state in which the chains of racial and national prejudices would be dismantled and all mankind incorporated in a cultural and political system, with equal rights and equal opportunities for all...[6]

The Islamic doctrine, as developed over time by the various schools of Islamic jurisprudence, has put together a comprehensive Islamic theory of state, commencing with the definition of the form of state, which includes the attributes of the head of state, the method of his nomination and appointment, his terms of reference, his general duties, and the instances in which he can be removed.[7] In this section, we will explore the basic elements of this doctrinal theory of state and consider to what extent, if any, such elements may be founded in the Holy Qur'an.

The imam, in Islamic jurisprudence, is the head of the state. He is the supreme leader of the so-called Islamic *umma*, that is, the geographic areas in which live a majority of Muslims. According to al-Mawardi, the imam is also a caliph, that is, "a successor to the prophethood role of the Prophet in the protection of religion and governing in the hereunder on earth."[8] That is why having an imam at all times is an absolute necessity. The imam must fulfill certain conditions to qualify for that position. He must be a free Muslim male descended from the tribe of *Quraysh* who is just and courageous, and free from any meaningful physical or intellectual disabilities.[9] In accordance with this doctrine, Muslims wherever they may be belong necessarily to one and the same *umma*, and the Islamic *umma* is thus necessarily one nation; it can have only one imam. The first imam to be duly and properly designated is the legitimate imam, and any others are therefore imposters. If, due to exceptional circumstances, there is more than one imam appointed, the doctrine—depending on those circumstances—allows for a certain legitimacy for their coexistence.[10]

The imam is appointed by a select group of people who are vested with the authority to speak for and make decisions on behalf of the *umma*. They are called *ahl al-ḥall wa-l-'aqd*, that is, those who hold the authority to bind and release. Therefore, according to the doctrine, most Muslims have no say in the selection of the imam. In fact, *ahl al-ḥall wa-l-'aqd* is a group which, in the words of Sa'deddine al-Taftazani, is made up of "the learned in religion, the leaders and the nobility."[11] That doctrine specifies stringent conditions for membership in that select group. First, the candidate must enjoy a high level of rectitude and generosity, in the sense that he must have all the important good qualities and none of the vices. Second, the candidate must be learned and erudite, mainly in the religious sciences and also in the science of identifying the best interests of the *umma* and running its affairs. He must be capable of exercising *ijtihād,* that is, extracting solutions from general principles set forth in the Qur'an and the Prophetic Tradition, and/or from solutions previously adopted in cases that may have something in common with issues at hand. Third, the candidate must have a sound mind and be wise.[12]

Note the wide discrepancy between the easy and relatively simple conditions of eligibility for the post of imam, and the stringent conditions for membership in the select group who hold the authority to bind and release. This clearly is a highly elitist system where authority, both over and on behalf of the citizens of the Muslim nation, is attributed to clergy and 'ulama', and then used by them to maintain their standing in the joint venture between ruling families and the religious establishment. The appointment of the imam by that elite group is done by way of *mubāya'a*, that is, a pledge of allegiance made by every member of the group separately. The doctrine goes on to specify that the imam who receives the pledge of allegiance is usually nominated by his predecessor at any time during his tenure, and the pledge may be secured during the lifetime of the nominating imam.[13]

The rules set forth in the doctrine for the running of state affairs provide for the *de facto* nonremovability of the ruler. These rules also state the duties of the subjects toward the imam, but mention no rights that they may claim against him. These duties are primarily to obey the imam, almost unquestionably; to pay their dues of zakat;[14] and to participate in any "holy war" that the imam may call on his able subjects to join.[15]

If the ruler fails to carry out his duties, in terms of observing the rules of Shari'a and doing what is in the best interests of his subjects, he may not be removed from office. The negative effects of *fitna*, or sowing discord, arising from removing a ruler and replacing him by far outweigh the negative effects of any nonobservance by the ruler of his duties of office. Based on this consideration, the doctrine has provided for only one instance in which a ruler may be removed from office, namely if he commits a serious disobedience to God. Under no other circumstances may the ruler be removed.[16] Otherwise, rebellion against the ruler is perceived as a means of sowing discord, for which serious divine penalties are in store.[17]

Finally, the most basic duties of the imam are to revive and preserve religion in accordance with its primary established foundations and the consensus of the early Muslims, and to ensure that the laws of God embedded in the Shari'a are fully implemented and complied with, by way of enforcing Shari'a and Prophetic Tradition.[18] For that purpose, the imam must cooperate with the *ahl al-ḥall wa-l-'aqd* in seeking and obtaining from them what the law is, namely their interpretations of the Qur'an and Prophetic Tradition on issues as they arise,[19] together with any necessary new legislation in such areas or cases on which the Qur'an and Prophetic Tradition are silent, or which have not been addressed by the relevant schools of thought. The imam must also wage jihad wars as and when he deems it, in his sole discretion, necessary or appropriate, such as to repel an aggression against the Muslim nation or against those who resist Islam after having been invited to convert, until they either embrace Islam or accept the inferior *dhimmī* status.[20] In pursuing his duties, the imam must in principle perform the duty of *shūra*, or consultation. However, the framework for the exercise of this duty, as set forth in the doctrine, ended up severely curtailing its scope, (1) by deciding that its scope does not extend to matters which, according to the imam, are clearly set out in the Qur'an, the Prophetic Tradition, or a learned solution over which a consensus exists; (2) by stating that consultation is only of *ahl al-ḥall wa-l-'aqd*, and not all the citizens, unless the consultation is about whether or not anyone is aware of any prophetic tradition addressing the issue under consideration, in which case anyone can be consulted; and (3) the outcome of the *shūra* consultation process is nonbinding.[21]

In support of the above, the doctrine cites the following scriptural foundations, among many other verses.[22]

With respect to the pledge of allegiance process for appointment of the imam, or for the confirmation of that appointment:[23]

Q48:10—*Indeed,* those who pledge allegiance *to you, [O Muhammad]—they are actually pledging allegiance to Allah. The hand of Allah is over their hands. So he who breaks his word only breaks it to the detriment of himself. And he who fulfills that which he has promised Allah—He will give him a great reward*;

Q48:18—*Certainly was Allah pleased with the believers when they pledged allegiance to you, [O Muhammad], under the tree, and He knew what was in their hearts, so He sent down tranquility upon them and rewarded them with an imminent conquest*;

Q60:12—*O Prophet, when the believing women come to you pledging to you that they will not associate anything with Allah, nor will they steal, nor will they commit unlawful sexual intercourse, nor will they kill their children, nor will they bring forth a slander they have invented between their arms and legs, nor will they disobey you in what is right— then accept their pledge and ask forgiveness for them of Allah. Indeed, Allah is Forgiving and Merciful;*[24]

With respect to the duty of obedience owed by the citizens of the Muslim nation to the imam and the elite group of the *ahl al-ḥall wa-l-'aqd*, that is, in support of the claim that the sovereignty of the nation is exercised by that select group of people:

Q4:59—*O ye who believe! Obey God, and obey the Apostle,* and those charged with authority among you. *If ye differ in anything among yourselves, refer it to God and His Apostle, if ye do believe in God and the Last Day: That is best, and most suitable for final determination;*

Q4:83—*When there comes to them some matter touching (Public) safety or fear, they divulge it. If they had only referred it to the Apostle, or* to those charged with authority among them, *the proper investigators would have Tested it from them (direct). Were it not for the Grace and Mercy of God unto you, all but a few of you would have fallen into the clutches of Satan;*[25]

With respect to the concept of *shūra*, or consultation, in running the business of state:

Q3:159—*So by mercy from Allah, [O Muhammad], you were lenient with them. And if you had been rude [in speech] and harsh in heart, they would have disbanded from about you. So pardon them and ask forgiveness for them* and consult them in the matter. *And when you have decided, then rely upon Allah.*

Indeed, Allah loves those who rely [upon Him];[26]

Q42:38—*Those who hearken to their Lord, and establish regular Prayer;* who (conduct) their affairs by mutual Consultation; *who spend out of what We bestow on them for Sustenance;*[27]

With respect to the duty of the imam to collect, and that of each citizen to pay, the ṣadaqāt, or alms:

Q9:103—*Take of their wealth a freewill offering, to purify them and to cleanse them thereby, and pray for them; thy prayers are a comfort for them; God is All-hearing, All-knowing;*[28]

With respect to the duty of the imam to personally perform or otherwise oversee performance of basic administrative duties of the state:

Q38:26—*O David! We did indeed make thee a vicegerent on earth: so judge thou between men in truth (and justice): Nor follow thou the lusts (of thy heart), for they will mislead thee from the Path of God: for those who wander astray from the Path of God, is a Penalty Grievous, for that they forget the Day of Account;*[29]

With respect to the claim that God reserves severe punishment for those who rebel and by that action sow discord among the community:

Q5:33—*Those who fight against Allah and His Messenger and run about trying to spread disorder on the earth, their punishment is no other than that they shall be killed, or be crucified, or their hands and legs be cut off from different sides, or they be kept away from the land (they live in). That is a humiliation for them in this world, and for them there is a great punishment in the Hereafter.*[30]

None of the features of the doctrine of the Islamic state are set forth in the

Qur'an, and the Qur'anic verses cited in support of certain features of the doctrine do not constitute valid support, as we shall demonstrate.[31] In this respect, the late Muhammad 'Abed al-Jabiri observes the absence in the Qur'an of any reference to a state. Yet, he notes that the Qur'an contains regulations that Muslims are required to observe, such as corporeal punishments for certain crimes, and that some of these regulations, such as the jihad and conquests, require somebody to be in charge of organizing their collective performance, be it a ruler, a caliph, a state, or merely a tribal chief.[32] In reality, the rules in question are of the nature of principles and ethical values that need to be legislated, and such legislation can only be secularly accomplished, as opposed to being enacted by a Muslim ruler or Muslim state, so as to prevent the rights of the non-Muslim members of the community from being ignored.

Is an Islamic Environment a Requirement of Islam?

Ashgar Ali Engineer argues "[i]n the Qur'an...there is no concept of state, nor of territorial nationalism. In fact religious scriptures are hardly supposed to deal with such questions. It nowhere states that it is obligatory for Muslims to set up a religious or a theocratic state."[33] Apart from the superfluous claims that an Islamic state is necessary to ensure the continuity of the Prophet's leadership of the community of believers,[34] the requirement for an Islamic public authority is presumably rendered necessary to implement and ensure the enforcement of the Shari'a laws that govern various aspects of social life. Abdou Filali-Ansari discusses this potential requirement in his treatise on whether or not Islam is compatible with secularism.[35]

It is also generally perceived that the Qur'an has brought a model of political society to deal with the severe problems faced by the early Muslim Empire arising from the transition out of tribal into settled and agrarian cultures.[36] While it is true that the Qur'an has created a new moral order, it did not create a model for political society. The severe problems to which reference is made are due to the insistence of the early Muslim rulers and 'ulama' to use or abuse religion to make it include a political order. They misunderstood the role of Prophet Muhammad, and they did not properly understand the purpose of his refusal to appoint a successor and to ever allow keeping records of his actions and sayings. Precisely, his intended message was clear—namely that he was not founding a state but spreading a message.

Clerics and *fuqahā'* have, in the course of justifying their claim about Islam being necessarily a faith and a system of government, advanced the idea that Muslims can live their faith and fulfill all the requirements set out in the Qur'an and the Prophetic Tradition as an *umma* only in a proper environment in which the believers can constitute an *umma*, enjoin the good and forbid the evil, and otherwise live collectively in accordance with the requirements of Shari'a.[37] A state made up substantially of Muslims, or in which Muslims constitute an overwhelming controlling majority, is therefore necessary to cultivate and preserve the Islamic identity, and to prevent nonbelievers and nonconforming believers[38] from endangering that Islamic identity.

The Concept of Umma: Is Islam an Identity?

In the early days of Islam, the term *umma* had no political connotation. It was intended to refer to that bond of faith that brought together, first, the followers of Prophet Mohammad, then also Jews and Christians who share the faith in the same God. It meant the community of believers who shared that faith in common. It was a social concept intended to transcend narrow and often fanatical tribal bonds, to create a more meaningful common faith and spiritual values which could provide a stronger and more lasting bond than that of blood relations. Justice, love, and peace, under the infinite bounty of a kind God would replace internecine wars among people of different tribes and often, as well, among people belonging to different substrata of the same tribe. The *umma* was intended to establish a new social order based on deep principles of cooperation, where the weak are supported by the strong, and where the forces of evil are replaced by faith in a common God.

However, the conviction that Muslims by themselves constitute an *umma*, which can survive only in the context of a state in which they maintain a controlling majority, started to form as early as the first

Enlightened Caliphate, following the death of Prophet Muhammad. Abou Bakr took up the title of successor of the prophet of God (*khalīfa* or caliph), purporting to extend the leadership of the community of Medina. In reality, all the steps that he took were toward the creation of a fully fledged state. In addition, the new state established Shari'a as its law, namely the principles and rules found in the Qur'an, as implemented and supplemented by Prophetic Tradition. That legal setup was found to be necessary because one of the important purposes of the Message brought about by Muhammad was to replace certain reprehensible tribal customs with a more humane, rational, and fair set of moral and ethical principles.

With the end of the Enlightened Caliphate and the beginning of the hereditary caliphate of the Omayyads, the developing clergy of *fuqahā'* and clerics started supplying the caliphs with the so-called Shari'a-based laws, as necessary to administer and maintain law and order in the ever-expanding new state, and at the same time provide religious legitimacy for the caliphs. The end and lasting result was a powerful state, governed by authoritarian caliphs under a religious legitimacy, which identified all actions with Islam and maintained an objective of ever-expanding that state. Expanding the state would presumably be achieved by way of spreading the Message of Islam further and bringing in more converts. Thus the expansion of the Islamic state was perceived as an expansion of Islam, which conferred upon the state the Islamic identity. As Islam was the identity of that state, and as Muslims identified with that state, Islam became also the identity of the Muslim majorities that lived in it. Islam as an identity became even stronger as the state expanded toward regions with non-Muslim majorities. State and Islam had become synonymous.[39]

In retrospect, the perception of Islam as a faith and as a state, then as an identity, evolved from the initial concept—developed by the early commentators, then taken up by later religious scholarship—that Muslims constitute an *umma*, a community with a common bond, that of the new faith.[40] Shaykh Sobhi al-Saleh describes the *umma* as a large global community in which all members share a common deep faith and constitute one universal community with its specific personality, markedly distinguished from other nations by a shared true desire to live together and strive collectively in carrying out the mission of spreading the Message of Islam and realizing justice among all humankind. In his definition of the *umma*, Shaykh Sobhi al-Saleh quotes Louis Gardet's definition of the *umma* by reference to a certain specific authenticity, characterized by a religion which specifies for each member, individually and collectively, the full and complete conditions and rules for life in all its spheres, without exception, namely the family, social, political, legal, economic, and spiritual spheres, without even forgetting paradise reserved for each believer in the hereafter. According to that theory, these unique characteristics are supposed to prevent the *umma* from division and disintegration.[41] In reality, that description of the *umma* is at best utopian, because, while Islam has provided universal guiding principles for peoples' lives in this life and the hereafter, it abstained from micro-regulation so as to leave for humankind their space of freedom; and the reality is that Muslims have through the ages split into multiple sects which, at times, did not live peacefully together. Abdelmajid Charfi attributes that sense of identity to the concept of *ijmā'*, or consensus, in the following terms: "It [meaning *ijmā'*] continues to play one of the most important roles in the conscience of the believers and incessantly fashions their vision of the past as well as that of the present as the primary basis of belonging to the Muslim community."[42] However, that perceived religious identity constitutes the seed of fanaticism.

The concept of *umma*, in that sense, was never contemplated in the Qur'an. Nowhere does the Qur'an use the term *umma* in the express or implied sense of an identitarian framework for Muslim peoples. The term *umma* appears forty-seven times in the Qur'an.[43] In twenty-three of the forty-seven times, the term *umma* is used as a reference to a group or community of people who have something in common, but may or may not necessarily share the same faith or creed.[44] That term is also used nineteen times as a reference to a group or community of people who do share a common faith,[45] in three of which only that shared common faith is specifically the Message of Islam.[46] Finally, in two instances, the term *umma* is used as a reference to a pluralistic community of people whose common denominator is the belief in one or the other of God's messages—

namely Jews, Christians, and Muslims.[47] While the term *umma*, in a few verses mentioned here, refers to the community of those who adhered to the Message brought by Prophet Muhammad, that term generally has been used as a generic name for a community of people who have something in common, that is, a bond different from the prevailing tribal bond, that bond being most often a common faith. On that basis, the modern usage of the term *umma* refers to the vast community of people who share a spiritual bond through their common faith, Islam.[48] In this respect, that definition can be taken a step further to observe that what the Qur'an intended to encompass under the aegis of the *umma* as a community of faith is Islam in its widest meaning, that which includes all divine messages brought by God's prophets and messengers, commencing with Abraham. In two separate series of verses,[49] in each of which God recounts a sequence of prophets and episodes relating to their peoples, the concluding verses are: *"Indeed this, your religion, is one religion, and I am your Lord, so worship Me"*[50] and *"And verily! this your religion (of Islamic Monotheism) is one religion, and I am your Lord, so keep your duty to Me,"*[51] respectively. In other words, all these people, across the ages, constitute one and the same *umma*.

In light of all the references mentioned above, it becomes clear that the Qur'an did not expressly or implicitly include a state or political organization in the meaning of the term *"umma."* Consequently, there is no implication whatsoever that a Muslim should, necessarily or even preferably, live with fellow Muslim brothers and sisters in a self-contained, exclusive community. On the contrary, if we look at the first community to be effectively called *umma*, we find that the *umma* is a pluralistic society which includes all believers, whether they are Muslims or non-Muslims; it even makes some room for nonbelievers.[52] This was indeed the community that Prophet Muhammad himself founded in Medina upon his arrival.

This community, as *umma*, and its charter, the Constitution of Medina,[53] which was signed among all parties to inaugurate that community, are indicative of this on several grounds: (1) the Charter describes the community as an *umma*, and at the same time does not create a state or any state structure, which clearly indicates that a state is not part of the requirements for Muslim life; (2) the Charter further specifically states that the *umma* then being founded is made up of Muslims and non-Muslims, thereby defining the *umma* primarily as a pluralistic community, as opposed to an exclusively or even predominantly Muslim community[54]; (3) the Charter does not attribute to the Muslims of Medina any privileged or otherwise special status, nor does it place Jews and other non-Muslim parties in any inferior status within the new *umma*, thereby implying that all its members are equal[55]; (4) the Charter does not provide that the Shari'a brought about by the Message of Islam should serve as the law of the land; instead it provides expressly that each group remains governed by the relevant laws of that group,[56] a further confirmation that the argument advanced about the need of an Islamic state to secure the application of Shari'a is not an Islamic requirement, that is, a requirement of the Qur'an or an established practice under Prophetic Tradition; and (5) the implementation of Shari'a among the Muslim members of the new *umma* was not deemed a mandatory requirement, because several clauses declare tribal customs to be applicable, such as tribal collective responsibility for crimes committed by their members.

The conclusion to be drawn from the provisions of the Qur'an and the Constitution of Medina is that the caliphate established following the death of Prophet Muhammad, commencing with the Enlightened Caliphate and followed by the monarchy-type hereditary caliphate, was not the result of a religious requirement. It was an entirely man-made system which need not carry any Islamic epithet, despite the fact that it may have implemented Shari'a as the law of the land, and from time to time contributed to the spread of the Message of Islam. Islam as a faith is far more important and relevant than as a national identity. Indeed, when a Muslim identifies the *umma* with the state and places them both under the umbrella of Islam, then the national identity gets confused with religious identity. Then if the nation is controlled by a majority belonging to a certain faith, namely to Islam in the case of the caliphate in its various iterations throughout the history of the Islamic Empire, then religion becomes the primary identity.

This is what Abdullahi An-Na'im advances as premise:

[T]he Muslim peoples of the world are entitled to exercise their legitimate collective right to self-determination in terms of an Islamic identity, including the application of Islamic law, if they wish to do so, provided that they do not violate the legitimate right of self-determination of individuals and groups both within and outside the Muslim communities.[57]

This is a dangerous premise in many respects: (1) it destroys the principles of democracy by allowing religious identities to compete with the national identity, (2) it destabilizes the democratically set up institutions of the state, (3) it creates a *de facto* federation of religious communities, and (4) to the extent that such right to self-determination would belong to every religious group living in a given state, and bearing in mind that the identities that are of a religious or sectarian nature are almost always exclusive, the nation suffers and can disintegrate.[58]

For his part, A. Soroush notes "one of the greatest theoretical plagues of the Islamic world…, that people are gradually coming to understand Islam as an identity rather than a truth." Soroush observes that truths can coexist and cooperate with each other, whereas identities fight each other, and he concludes that the Islam of identity is belligerent and leads to wars as opposed to the Islam of truth which leads to peace.[59] This explains that the defense by Tariq Ramadan of the concept of multiple identities[60] in one person is neither plausible nor practical. In fact, caution should be observed to avoid confusing identities with diversity, because an identity constitutes a strong link and bond, and a conflict of identities can be lethal.

Notable examples, from recent and less recent history, can be advanced to illustrate this point. One such example in recent history can be found in the political structure of Lebanon, in which nineteen religious communities barely coexist within a mosaical legal and political system. That system (which is to a certain extent derived from, and rooted in, the Constitution of Medina model though itself not a political system), recognizes the diversity of its citizenry but fails to invest that diversity into an integrated secular environment, where diversity is an element of enrichment as opposed to an element of division. As a result, nineteen sectarian identities overshadow the national identity. Another, less recent, example is found in the Ottoman Empire, which was also based on a sectarian system (the millet system), where various religious communities are governed by their individual legal and judicial institutions. That sectarian system gave birth to multiple religious and ethnic identities which overshadowed the national Ottoman identity and, among other reasons, led to the disintegration of that empire.

In what A. Sachedina describes as "religiously inspired and sustained nationalisms,"[61] such nationalisms become synonymous with fanaticism.[62] Indeed religion as an identity has been the root and common denominator among all extremist, religiously motivated, political and paramilitary movements.[63] In Islam, it started as early as the final days of the Enlightened Caliphate when the *khawārij* revolted and turned against the fourth Enlightened Caliph 'Ali: in their opinion, Caliph 'Ali compromised on religious principles in conducting the policies of state.[64] The same can be said of more recent religiously motivated political movements which thrive in various countries of the Muslim world, for whom the concept of *umma* as an overall and global umbrella has facilitated the spread of the idea of an Islam which transcends all cultures.[65]

In retrospect, the concept of Islam as an identity is in every respect un-Islamic. The Qur'an has affirmed that God has purposely placed people in pluralistic communities, made up of believers and nonbelievers; and they should strive to live and interact together.[66] The Qur'an goes further to specifically spell out that all believers, irrespective of the Divine Message through which they became believers, constitute an *umma* because of their commonality of belief in God. Therefore, all believers, in the widest sense of the term, can claim that shared common bond as part of their individual identities. If certain Muslims were now to decide to adopt Islam as primary identity and live within *ummas* made up of Muslim people only, then they are going against the will of God. The same applies to any people who may claim their respective religions as primary identities. Instead, there is no harm for national groupings who share certain characteristics in common, derived from Islam, to consider themselves as part of specific cultures whose common denominator is Islam, but which otherwise are identified by their ethnic and other cultural particularities.

From this same perspective, we should easily be in a position to dismiss claims that Islam provides for the concept of *imamate* as the institution vested with the leadership of the Muslim *umma*. The term imam is derived from the term *umma*; it designates the leader of the *umma*. The early iteration of the role of imam was a mere leadership in prayer at a time when the entire Muslim community was limited to the early converts who needed to bond together in the midst of the sea of pagans that surrounded them. The same went for the first Muslim batch of migrants who went to Ethiopia, then to the companions who accompanied the Prophet on his journey to Medina. However, following the arrival of the Prophet and his companions to Medina and the founding of the pluralistic community, the concept of Muslims-only *umma* came practically to an end. Since the *umma* is primarily pluralistic, and since there is no specific environment in which Muslims must live to preserve their faith, then the concept of *imamate* becomes a purely theoretical one because there are no nations made up exclusively of Muslim people which may benefit from the leadership of an imam.

The Command to Enjoin Good and Forbid Evil (*al-amr bi-l-ma'rūf wa-n-nahiy 'ani-l-munkar*)

This brings us to the next alleged requirement for Muslims to live in an Islamic state that they control. According to the doctrine under review, the Holy Qur'an requires Muslims to command *ma'rūf* (the good) and forbid *munkar* (the evil), and they can do so only in an enabling environment that they control.[67]

To start with, it is important to set out the meaning of the terms *ma'rūf* and *munkar*, wherever used in the command in question. The terms *ma'rūf* and *munkar* appeared in several Qur'anic verses outside the scope of that command, wherein the term *ma'rūf* has been used in three global senses, namely (1) reasonableness, and generally accepted custom;[68] (2) decency of behavior and speech;[69] and (3) performing good deeds.[70] The term *munkar* was used in the sense of rejection of the Message of God[71] and in the sense of evil.[72] However, when both terms are used together in the context of the overall command to enjoin good and forbid evil, the interpreters were more inclined toward a whole different meaning, where *ma'rūf* is the belief in the unicity of God and the prophethood of Prophet Muhammad, and *munkar* is the pagan belief in man-made deities, the rejection of the unicity of God, and disbelieving in the prophethood of Prophet Muhammad.[73] The command to enjoin good and forbid evil appears nine times in the Holy Qur'an.[74]

The two terms can encompass all potential meanings combined, namely with respect to *ma'rūf*, the basic belief in the unicity of God and his message, and the virtues of decency, reasonableness, and performing good deeds; and with respect to the term *munkar*, the negation of God and his message, and all that is evil, ugly, and unreasonable.

The command to enjoin good and forbid evil is thus substantially about the spreading of the message of God, including a call to observe ethical principles and moral values, because they serve to create a just and fair community and harmony among people. Bearing in mind that every rule and command set forth in the Divine Message has a moral foundation for the good of the people to whom the Message is addressed,[75] a duty to spread the Message will contribute to the establishment of a better, more harmonious, society. The Arabic language construction of the command *amr bi-l-ma'rūf* is also a qualifier of the manner in which the order should be fulfilled, that is, by way of equity, fairness, and kindness, as opposed to being imposed by force. Mohamed Talbi rightly reminds us of God's injunction, contained in Verse Q41:34: "*Good deeds and evil deeds are not equal. Requite evil with good, and he who is your enemy will become your dearest friend.*"[76]

The command to enjoin good and forbid evil has both collective and individual aspects. From an individual perspective, a person enjoins the good and forbids the evil within that person's own reasonable and legitimate means. By way of example, parents will raise their children in a proper environment where good and evil are continuously explained in such a manner as the performance of good and abstinence from evil become a second nature in the children as they grow up. Similarly, in their own particular social environments, people will enjoin good and forbid evil through their own behaviors, by giving the proper example, that is, primarily by living their own faith and respecting the faiths of others, then by doing good deeds themselves, acting reasonably and decently, and abstaining from any evil activities that hurt other people.

From a collective perspective, the command to enjoin good and forbid evil is performed when a government, meaning a secular government, enacts and enforces general laws that create a just order, secure freedom of faith for all people, and provide an environment of tolerance and acceptance in which each person may spread the message of his or her own faith in a rightful, respectful, and peaceful manner. The creation of a just order is accomplished, among other means, by way of fighting corruption.[77] That command is also performed from a collective perspective when Muslims are able to form civil societies which promote the Message of God, without any undue pressures. It has been pointed out that the right of the people to rebel against the ruler has traditionally been religiously founded on, and justified by application of, the command to enjoin good.[78] This command may possibly have been used to legitimize removal of a ruler in the sole event he commits a serious breach of religious duties. However, that command is good enough to serve as basis for the right of the constituency, exercisable according to laws and regulations of the secular state, in any serious circumstance in which a ruler fails to preserve the national interest, and not only in case of a religious breach on his part. In the wise and accurate words of Mohamed Talbi, the command to enjoin the good is in our days exercised by a Muslim person exclusively "by way of using his voter card."[79]

With respect to the religious component of the command to enjoin the good, that of the belief in the Message of God, only a secular environment secures freedom of faith for all. In fact, even in a single-denomination society where all people share the same faith, they may not have the freedom to deviate from the generally adopted interpretation of that faith for fear of finding themselves excluded from that society. Similarly, with respect to promoting good deeds and dissuading from evil, it is important to recall that these values and principles are part of *fiṭra*. They are innate to human nature from the time of creation of humankind, and as such they are not the exclusive addition of any new or earlier message, without forgetting the valuable contributions of the various messages to the importance of these values. Finally, and bearing in mind the rich variety of meanings included in the overall sense of enjoining good and forbidding evil, that command may be perceived as advice for the ruler to act with wisdom, patience, and flexibility in his or her dealings with people and in the decisions that he or she makes.

While this command is primarily about creating a good society by way of spreading the potential benefits and bounties deriving from the acceptance of God's Message, it does not legitimate any action toward the enforcement of the Message. Contrary to the views of many early commentators of the Qur'an,[80] the Qur'anic command to enjoin the good and forbid evil does not impose any duties on a Muslim person—whether individually or collectively—nor confer upon that person any license or right to control the behavior of others by sanctioning what they do in light of that person's perceptions of what is good or evil. Unfortunately, this is not an understanding which is unanimously shared among Muslim clerics; and extremists use that command to justify their zeal in taking matters into their own hands to enforce their radical interpretations of the Message of Islam on governments and on individuals, Muslims and non-Muslims alike.[81] Similarly, that command does not impose on, or otherwise confer upon, the government or a ruler any duties or obligations to enforce any part of the faith, including the observance of worship-related requirements (such as imposing prayers, the fast of Ramadan, or payment of zakat), dress codes, eating prohibitions, or other forms of personal behaviors of people, all of which are of the realm of God, as sole and ultimate judge. In fact, we may recall that Prophet Muhammad was not empowered to enforce any part of the faith on people. For that reason, the tradition imputed to Prophet Muhammad about the duty of each person to enforce the command to enjoin good and forbid evil, cannot be considered as true and authentic;[82] and if the Prophet had no such mandate, *a priori* the successors of the Prophet cannot claim to exercise on his behalf a mandate that he did not have in the first place.

This principle is solidly set forth in the same verses which provide for the command to enjoin good and forbid evil: "*They are those who, when We empower them in the land, perform the prayer, hand out alms, command the good and forbid evil. To God is the outcome of all matters*" and "*My son, perform the prayer, command to virtue and forbid evil, and* bear with patience whatever befalls you. *This is a course of action upright and prudent.*"[83] From these verses, it is clear that the command to enjoin good and forbid evil is one that can be performed only through wisdom, compassion, and rational discussion, without coercion of any kind, because ultimately God is observant and He reserves judgment. There exists another verse in the Qur'an which, sets forth the principle that no one is responsible for the evil done by others, which in turn confirms that no one has the religious duty to personally intervene and physically and forcefully enjoin the good and prevent the commitment of evil, as follows: "*O believers, take good care of your souls. A person who strays cannot harm you if you are guided aright. To God is your ultimate homecoming, all of you; and He shall inform you of what you used to do.*"[84] Commentators have stressed the individual empowerment of people to enforce the command by relating a controversy that arose as to whether the command to enjoin good and forbid evil was abrogated by this verse or the other way around, and conclude that the command remained in full force and effect.[85] However, not accepting the concept of abrogation of verses by others within the Qur'an, both verses are relevant, are in full force and effect, and have their own respective scopes of application. The contradiction disappears and the verses become fully harmonious when, consistent with basic freedoms and human rights, enforcement powers are excluded from the command to enjoin good and forbid evil.

The next issue that led to awkward views and positions is that of determining to whom the command, to enjoin good and forbid evil, applies and whether it is a duty of each individual Muslim or only of some people who fulfill the required qualifications to perform it. That issue came up because of the syntax of Verses Q3:104 ("*Let there be* among you a group *who call to virtue, who command the good and forbid vice*"), Q3:110 ("You are the best community ever brought forth among mankind, *commanding virtue and forbidding vice, and believing in God*"), and Q22:41 ("They are those who, when We empower them in the land, *perform the prayer, hand out alms, command the good and forbid evil. To God is the outcome of all matters*"),[86] in which God appears to address a specific audience rather than everyone. With respect to Verses Q3:104 and 110, most commentators believe that the group being addressed is that of the companions of the

Prophet who left Mecca with him on his hijra, the migration to Medina.[87] Indeed, this group was fleeing Mecca to a safer haven where they could freely worship and spread the Message, hence enjoin good and forbid evil. However, Muhammad 'Abed al-Jabiri considers that, according to the context of Verse Q3:110, the people being addressed are the *anṣār,* that is, the Muslims of Medina and not the companions from Mecca.[88]

Other commentators considered that the people being addressed are the elite group of *ahl al-ḥall wa-l-'aqd* which constitute the foundation of the doctrine of the Islamic state[89] that we discussed above; and to yet others, another elite, the 'ulama', or learned clerics who have memorized the Qur'an and studied Prophetic Tradition and other religious sciences.[90] Presumably, because of their scholarly learning, they are best placed to tell what is good and what is evil, so that they may be enjoined or, as the case may be, forbidden. However, such interpretation is not warranted, first, because the understanding of the Qur'an, as a message accessible to all is not the exclusive domain of an elite of scholars and clergy, and second, because the concepts of good and evil are not revealed primarily to those who study the science of religion or any other science; they are part of *fiṭra* which is innate in every human being and develops with all individuals as they grow up watching the example of parents who raise them.[91]

The people being referred to in the verses quoted above are simply those who, in every community, usually are civic minded, take initiative, and offer community service. The command to enjoin good and forbid evil is a duty—as opposed to a privilege—incumbent on all Muslims, each in accordance with his or her means.[92] This is what justifies the duty of each parent to raise children by way of enjoining good and forbidding evil. The same goes for teachers in schools, members of civil associations, and every individual within its immediate environment. This also explains why the command in question, on an individual level, does not include any enforcement power, so as not to create chaos in society and to preserve at all times the essential freedoms of people under the law.

Finally, the command to enjoin good and forbid evil is a duty which is equally incumbent upon male and female Muslims. That principle is expressly set forth in Verse Q9:71.

> *The Believers, men and women, are protectors one of another: they enjoin what*
> *is just, and forbid what is evil: they observe regular prayers, practice regular*
> *charity, and obey God and His Apostle. On them will God pour His mercy: for*
> *God is Exalted in power, Wise.*[93]

That equality among men and women in sharing the duty of enjoining the good and forbidding evil, as set forth in the Qur'an, is the strong evidence that control within the family is not the exclusive domain of men, and that in society women cannot be excluded from leadership functions based on religious grounds, including leadership of the nation.

Divine Governance and political governance have traditionally been conflated. This is an immediate outcome of not treating Islam as secular, the assumption being that every action in our lives is religion-bound and that political governance of humankind can stand in the way of the exercise by God of His sovereignty. However, in most cases, many scholars, rulers, and clergy have found the respective scopes of divine sovereignty and human political governance to be indistinguishable and have ruled that it is part of people's religious duty to enforce God's sovereignty based on their own or previously sacralized interpretations of the faith. More particularly, the trusteeship's main purpose, as mandated by the Qur'an, is in the words of Ahmad Moussalli "to fulfill the divine commandments, *including the application of Islamic law, the development of morality, and enjoining the good and forbidding evil.*"[94] The fulfillment of divine commandments and application of religious law have thus been construed as inherent parts of the trusteeship and of the command to enjoin good and forbid evil. In reality, divine justice should not be expected to be enforced by a nonexistent enforcement agency. Trusteeship, as a divinely bestowed attribution of power to humankind concurrently with creation, predates Islam and Islamic law. Thus, it could not have included that delegation; and, the command to enjoin good and forbid evil should not be perceived as a tool for replacement of the Final Day of Judgment or as an instrument of divine justice.

In light of this, a secular state is the only environment which conforms with the requirements of Islam,[95] because the command to enjoin good and forbid evil is a basic principle of people's sovereignty and secularism, in the sense that (1) the command in question can serve as a reasonable basis and foundation for that secular state, especially since it is derived from *fiṭra* where the sense of right and wrong is inherent in human nature; and (2) the overall guiding objective of democratic institutions is generally to promote good and prevent evil. From a Muslim's individual perspective, a secular state that enforces the freedom of faith is one in which a Muslim can, individually, enjoin good and forbid evil by being able to spread the Message without any fear of reprisals. From the collective perspective of Muslims, a secular state is usually a state where the laws of the land, as enacted by the legislative authority, would usually be consistent with the principles of Shari'a if they are founded on natural law and the general values of justice, fairness, and compassion. Similarly, the enforcement by the state of local laws, including such laws as may imply enjoining good and forbidding evil, is different in nature from the enforcement of God's commands set forth in the Qur'an. The enforcement of secular laws falls within the jurisdiction of humankind according to the prerogatives and powers that God conferred upon humans under the trusteeship, whereas God reserved enforcement and judgment of religious commands to Himself, exclusively.

Dār al-Islam and *Dār al-Ḥarb*

Following the determination that Islam does not require that Muslims live in an "Islamic state" and that, instead, a secular state is a more appropriate environment for them in which to freely live their faith and perform its requirements, it remains to determine whether or not the continued distinction between *dār al-Islam* (the abode or state of Islam) and *dār al-ḥarb* (the abode of war) remains relevant. Sachedina places that division of the world within other *fiqh*-related concepts that have nowadays become obsolete, being perpetuated by Western scholars.[96] Unfortunately, that construct is not as defunct as it should have been, and it is not only Western scholars who continue to brandish it. Instead, it is still very much alive in the Islamist day-to-day vocabulary.[97]

Under that distinction, *dār al-Islam* is expected to be a state exclusively for Muslims where any non-Muslims would be tolerated only if they fully submitted to Muslim rule, accepted a status in that state inferior to that of Muslims, and paid the *jizya* tribute to the Muslim state for as long as they live in it. By contrast, *dār al-ḥarb* is any nation which is controlled by non-Muslims. As such, it is considered a nation potentially at war with the nation of Islam, because the nation of Islam would sooner or later fight it in order to impose Islam upon its citizens.

Under prevailing Islamic scholarship on political theory, *dār al-Islam* consists of one comprehensive nation which includes all lands in which Muslims predominate and can exercise control. This concept is derived from the overriding presumptive principle that one and only one caliph can assume the general *wilāya* over Muslims, irrespective of ethnic, racial, or language differences among them, and wherever their lands may be located. A person who accepts the position of caliph when another duly appointed caliph is in place may even be the subject of capital punishment. The political theory has allowed for some exceptions dealing with situations that are a fait accompli, in which the legitimate caliph cannot reach or exercise control due to difficulties of communication, among other reasons. Exceptions have even been legitimized when the denial of the second caliph is likely to create disturbances among the nations that chose those caliphs. According to that theory, therefore, not only are Muslims expected to live in their own state, but that state must ideally be one state ruled by one caliph.[98]

The distinction between *dār al-ḥarb* and *dār al-Islam* is no longer necessary. In retrospect, it was never necessary in the first place because that division of the world is nowhere to be found in the Holy Qur'an; and because a Muslim's most appropriate environment is a secular state and not a so-called Islamic state. Accordingly, a Muslim person can live in any nation which allows that person to freely worship and fulfill other religious requirements—provided, always, that political submission by a Muslim person to a non-Muslim state or to a secular state headed by a non-Muslim ruler does not force that person to infringe on any Islamic injunctions or requirements. Furthermore, the concept of *dār al-ḥarb* (abode of war) is not consistent with Islam, either, because pluralism is inherent to Islam, and Muslim peoples are not naturally at war with non-Muslim people or nations, nor do they have any obligation to act belligerently vis-à-vis non-Muslims. In this respect, Khaled Abou El Fadl rightly observes that the many discussions promoting peace which are found in the Holy Qur'an "would not make sense if Muslims were in a permanent state of war with nonbelievers, and if nonbelievers were a permanent enemy and always a legitimate target."[99] On the contrary, Muslims are charged to recognize and accept peoples of other faiths as part of their religious Islamic belief.

Analysis of Potential Scriptural Foundations

We have seen that a Muslim person need not live among other Muslims, in a state controlled by Muslims, headed by solely one caliph. It is apparent that a secular state as an environment for Muslims to live in is superior to a purely (and often artificial) Islamic state or political environment. However, it is necessary to determine if there are in the Holy Qur'an principles and requirements which, when put together, would amount to a theory of state, that is, a set of basic rules and principles which should be realized in a state to render it appropriate for Muslims to live in.

What is certain is that Muslim scholars did develop what amounts to an Islamic theory of state. That theory is based on scholars' interpretation of certain provisions of the Holy Qur'an and Prophetic Tradition (problems of accuracy and authenticity notwithstanding), including in particular the practice of Prophet Muhammad in the Medinan period. In addition, this theory takes into account the practice of the rulers during the various caliphates who assumed power following the death of Prophet Muhammad, but with particular emphasis on the period of the first two Enlightened Caliphs, Abou Bakr and 'Umar. To determine if there truly exists a divine theory of state in Islam, it is essential to scrutinize the scriptures which constitute the basic and sole divine source of the Islamic faith.

The Doctrine of the Islamic State

If Islam encompasses a theory of state, then does one find in the Qur'anic verses terminology which indicates this, such as imam, caliph, caliphate, election, accountability, etc.? This is what we will try to answer, bearing in mind that if Islam does not recognize a religious authority in the first place, one would not, in the absence of such sanctioning authority, logically expect to encounter a so-called "Islamic" political authority, divinely mandated.[100]

The function of head of state, in Islamic scholarship, has been denominated as *al-imāma al-'uẓma*, or the sublime *imamate*, that is, the supreme leadership of the *umma*. On the other hand, that same scholarship declares the caliphate, more particularly the Enlightened Caliphate of the first four caliphs who succeeded the Prophet,[101] as the typical Islamic state. We will therefore identify the instances in which these terms have been used in the Qur'an and determine if indeed they referred to a form of government or state structure. We will also identify the instances in which the term *ḥukm* was used to determine the scope of that term. Regarding the other terms which refer to a political system, such as state, government, administration or others, none of them appear in the Qur'an.

First, we will start with the term *ḥukm* which has several meanings in the Arabic language, one of which is for organized government and ruling. By considering the uses, in the Holy Qur'an, of that term and its derivatives from the root *ḥkm*, it is possible to ascertain whether or not the Qur'an did eventually regulate the functions of government. Sixty-eight instances can be identified in which the term *ḥukm* or a derivative of it has been used, excluding the uses of the derivatives *ḥikma* which means wisdom, and *al-Ḥakīm* which constitutes an attribute of God. In the sixty-eight identified instances, the term has been used in a wide range of meanings, namely as a reference to the Qur'an,[102] God's final judgment,[103] divine sovereignty,[104] arbitration and litigation—whether in general[105] or arbitration by the Prophet[106]—, wisdom,[107] God's decision or decree (*qaḍā'*) in His wisdom,[108] or even as a reference to poor human judgment and behavior,[109] respectively. This leaves one instance, appearing in Verse Q4:58 and containing a general guiding principle to humankind in the performance of their trusteeship, under the watchful divine eye according to divine sovereignty, as follows:

Verily! Allâh commands that you should render back the trusts to those to whom they are due; and that when you judge between men, you judge with justice. Verily, how excellent is the teaching which He (Allâh) gives you! Truly, Allâh is Ever All-Hearer, All-Seer.[110]

This is a general principle of justice and trust that applies equally to rulers in performing their duties, and to individuals as well in their relations among each other. In this verse, the highlighted term is a version of the corresponding term in Arabic, derived from the term *ḥukm* and it is not about government or other forms of ruling over people. Thus it can be concluded that nowhere in the Holy Qur'an did the use of the term *ḥukm* or any of its derivatives ever constitute a reference to organized government.

Concerning the leadership of the state, the term imam is often used to refer to the supreme leader of the *umma*. The term imam, in the singular and the plural forms, appears twelve times in the Qur'an. It appears twice in the sense of record of deeds in connection with the Final Judgment[111]— that is, the records of all the good and evil deeds of each individual during his or her lifetime, based upon which he or she will be judged on the day of resurrection. On two other instances, the term imam is used in the related meaning of proof and evidence.[112] That term is also used in yet another related meaning, as an example or role model and guide.[113] The term imam has also been used in the sense of leader of people in five of the remaining six instances, three times in the sense of prophet leading by divine guidance,[114] and two times in the completely opposite, sarcastic sense, as a reference to the leaders of the evil disbelievers who strive against all divine guidance.[115] In one instance, the term is used as a reference to peoples in general to whom God attributes the earth and who take charge of their own destiny, that is, in the sense of trusteeship.[116] The common denominator in all three instances in which the term imam is a leader of people is the fact that the leaders in question lead people by divine guidance. For that purpose, they are appointed by God, that is, they neither seized power by force, nor came to power through inherited succession, nor were elected by fellow people. Therefore, in all three cases in question, the role of the imams was not a political role.

As for the form of state, called caliphate, and its supreme leader, called caliph, both terms are derived from the same root term, which means succession. The proponents of the all-encompassing concept of Islam as religion and state consider the caliph (*khalīfa*) as a successor of Prophet Muhammad in his leadership role of the first community organized in Medina, assumed to be the seed of a state. That root term for succession (namely *KhLF*) with all its derivatives, appears in the Holy Qur'an seventeen times. In five instances, the term is used in the context of the trusteeship that God granted to humankind over their lives on earth.[117] Then, in eleven instances, the term is used in the sense of succession by certain populations to control and exercise authority in replacement of other populations on the way to extinction.[118] This is the case of populations that God extinguished by way of punishment for collective sinning excesses or collective insistence on rejecting God and His messages. Only in one instance was the term used in the sense of governing on earth, but it was an instance specifically decided and implemented by God Himself. In that case, God announced that Prophet David had been ordained by God as king over his peoples.[119] Here too, then, the term *khalīfa* and its derivatives were never used in reference to any express or implied, divinely ordained, human political order or state structure, contrary to the claims made under the doctrine of the Islamic state.[120]

Based on the specific instances in which the terms imam and caliph, used in the Qur'an, specifically refer to a certain leadership of people, it is clear that such role was one attributed to certain prophets in the performance of a specific divine mission under divine guidance. In those instances, (1) the leader in question is exclusively selected by God and is never chosen or elected by other prophets or any other humans; (2) the mission is divinely assigned, and not otherwise left to the discretion of the designated person; and (3) the performance of the designated prophet is divinely guided. This is specifically confirmed in Verse Q2:124, in which Prophet Abraham, upon being informed by God that he will be designated to lead his people as imam, pleads with God for the designation to continue among his descendants. God responds that the role of imam does not devolve automatically by succession, because God does not select people who may be evildoers.[121] Therefore, God reserves the choice of imams to Himself and does not share it with anyone. Consequently, and bearing in mind that Prophet Muhammad was declared as the last and final prophet, God has not designated any human being for any mission whatsoever, including that of imam at any time following the death of Muhammad.

Another important consequence is that no divine mission of any kind ever devolved from one human being to another. Therefore, contrary to claims made under the doctrine of the Islamic state described above, (1) the Qur'an did not provide for anyone to perform the function of supreme imam for leadership of the *umma* following the death of Prophet Muhammad; (2) the caliphs who succeeded Prophet Muhammad did not inherit any of the Prophet's divine duties or functions; and (3) whatever role they played or functions they performed, they were purely secular political functions, organized and performed according to the trusteeship attributed by God to humankind, but necessarily under God's watchfulness and, in any event, without prejudice to Divine Governance.

Finally, and although we do not include Prophetic Tradition among the scriptural sources of the faith, yet Prophetic Tradition did not include any meaningful traditions of the Prophet indicating that he treated the state and government as necessary tools to maintain and implement the faith, or that he offered a theory of state or other instructions on statecraft.

THE HEAD OF STATE, OR THE IMAM

The claim that the imam must be an Arab male from the tribe of *Quraysh* has absolutely no foundation in Scripture. Such claim is even in direct contradiction with the provisions of the Holy Qur'an. If that is the case, then anything to the contrary imputed to Prophetic Tradition cannot be true or accurate because the provisions of the Holy Qur'an prevail over any other provisions wherever they appear.

First, that the imam must be a male person is contrary to the equality of sexes set forth in the Qur'an, and would violate the general spirit of the Qur'an, which contains no provision that expressly or implicitly provides that women cannot perform leadership roles in society.[122]

Second, that the imam must be an Arab from *Quraysh* is a totally baseless claim. There is not a single express provision to that effect in the Qur'an; nor is there any implicit reference therein, either. In reality, such a claim is in direct violation of an express provision of the Holy Qur'an[123] which declares (1) that all people are absolutely equal; (2) people are of diversified ethnic and language backgrounds; and (3) there is no preference, as far as God is concerned, based on ethnic or language background whatsoever, such preference among peoples being strictly biased toward those who are more pious than others. The doctrine cites countless traditions of the Prophet in which he has presumably confirmed that the imam must at all times be from *Quraysh*.[124] That statement cannot be true, first because the Prophet has not left behind any hint as to how to deal with his succession. In fact, such silence is consistent with the *intuitu personae* nature of the duties of Prophet and Messenger of God. It is not true, either, on grounds of being inconsistent with the provisions of the Qur'an.

The appointment process of the imam, by way of *bay'a* (a unilateral pledge of allegiance to a preselected nominee), as set forth in the doctrine, is not provided for anywhere in the Qur'an, contrary to the claims made in the doctrine and the verses to which the doctrine wrongly refers. The instances referring to pledges of allegiance given to the Prophet, stated in Verses Q48:10 and Q48:18, are totally unrelated to the appointment of the imam on three grounds: (1) the legitimacy of the Prophet derives from his selection by God and not from any allegiance pledged to him by the faithful; (2) the Prophet never was or acted as head of state or nation; and (3) the circumstances referred to in those verses relate to a peace pact that the Prophet concluded with the people of Mecca, in which his companions renewed their allegiance to him as a sign of support of his decision to conclude the peace. Also, the instance of allegiance referred to in Verse 60:12 does not relate to the appointment of an imam; instead, it is about a group of women who came to pledge their allegiance to, and confirm their acceptance of, the new faith brought about by the Prophet.

Nor does the Holy Qur'an provide for the specific duties of the imam specified in the doctrine that are of a strict religious nature, such as the duty to protect and revive religion, preserve the Message, impose the implementation of the faith, and establish Shari'a as law of the land.[125] As far as revival of the religion is concerned, it is thereby implied that Islam is under a continuous risk of disappearance and that its continued existence depends exclusively on the role of the imam. In other words, the survival of Islam is contingent on an Islamic state headed by a supreme imam.[126] This is a totally unwarranted element of the doctrine because it relies on the preposterous implication that God needs and relies on the imam for the survival of His religion. In reality, God has no need for anyone to keep His religion alive or to "revive" it. In Verse Q15:9, He confirms that *"We, Ourselves, have sent down the Dhikr (the Qur'ān), and We are there to protect it."*[127]

With respect to the preservation of the Message, here too we come across an unacceptable objective formulated by Muhammad Rashid Rida, that of maintaining religion "in accordance with its primary established foundations and the consensus of the early Muslims."[128] It is an unacceptable objective because it prohibits all forms of *ijtihād* outside the scope of official and exclusive *ijtihād* of the imam or sponsored or permitted by him.[129] This approach has led to Islam's being framed, within its early iteration, in defiance of the universal nature of Islam and in total violation of the basic right and duty of each Muslim to have his or her own understanding of Islam.

As for the duty of the imam as head of state, set forth in the doctrine of the Islamic state, to impose the observance of Islam by way of enforcing worship requirements and enacting Shari'a as law of the land,[130] that duty is nonexistent. It is in direct breach of the provisions of the Holy Qur'an which we elicited earlier and which preclude imposition of the faith.

Finally, we come to the duty of the imam, or head of state to consult his constituency on matters of state, as stated in the doctrine of the Islamic state, through the concept of *shūra*. This concept of *shūra* is perceived as the foundation of the highest Islamic political model and point of reference, namely the state that Prophet Muhammad has presumably founded and headed in Medina.[131] Despite that the scope of the duty of consultation has been severely curtailed by the doctrine, yet the concept of consultation, as set forth in the Qur'an, was never intended as a principle of state governance, but instead as a mechanism for the preservation of the Muslim community during the career of the Prophet, whose leadership of the community was thus a form of special-purpose theocracy, of a temporary nature. Indeed, in Verse Q3:159, the Prophet was being advised by God to be nice to his companions, as he had always been to them, so that they maintain their support to him in the performance of his divine mission, of which fighting wars had become an important element. In this context, and although their views are immaterial because God himself is guiding His Prophet on his mission, it is important to nurture the Companions' egos by consulting them and making them be part of the process.[132] This explains that the outcome of the consultation is not binding on the Prophet and that he may proceed, following the consultation process, with the implementation of his decision in spite of that outcome. The same goes with respect to Verse Q42:38. It is part of a series of verses which define the believers as those who submit to God (Verse Q42:36), avoid sins, forgive when angry (Q42:37), obey God, perform prayers, conduct their activity in mutual consultation, spend only from money legitimately earned (Verse Q42:38), and stand up in defense of their rights when aggressed or otherwise follow the path of forgiveness which God prefers (Verses Q42:39 to 43). Therefore, Verse 42:38 was not intended to serve as a principle of political governance, but instead as a general principle of good social behavior where interaction with other members of society through consultation is the preferred behavior.

Based on the above, the stubborn rejection of democracy by traditional-minded clergy and jurisprudents on grounds that *shūra* is its Islamic equivalent is totally unfounded, in more than one respect.[133] First, *shūra* is not a tool of state governance, while democracy is. Second, assuming it is a tool of state governance, *shūra* is at best a consultation process whose outcome is not binding on the ruler, whereas democracy is a participatory process where consultation is its principal element, and the outcome of that process in a democratic system is binding on the ruler. Third, and most importantly, unlike the case of democracy where the participation in the political process is intended to be open to everyone, the *shūra* process, as historically implemented by contrast to its divine intent, is discriminatory: it did not extend to all the citizens but to an elite from them which was initially made up of the Companions, then got restricted to the so-called *ahl al-ḥall wa-l-'aqd* among the jurisprudents and clerics.

To discredit democracy as a product of the West, the concept of *shūra* has often been advanced to intimidate reformists who advocate the adoption of institutions that have been successfully applied outside the Muslim world, despite the fact that such institutions may not be inconsistent with the principles of Islam. In this respect, Hamid Enayat points up the complexity of the task.

> What is blatantly missing from contemporary Muslim writings on democracy, in spite of all the claims to the contrary, is an adaptation of either the ethical and legal precepts of Islam, or the attitudes and institutions of traditional society, to democracy. This is obviously a much more complex and challenging task than the mere reformulation of democratic principles in Islamic idioms.[134]

The task in question is complex and challenging because of the confusion resulting from refusal to acknowledge the secular nature of Islam; and that confusion leads to the continued perception of Islam as a form of government. When Islam is perceived as a truly secular and humanistic value system, as opposed to a mere political and legal system, then instead of endeavoring to Islamize democracy or otherwise democratize *shūra* and the caliphate, the transcending values and principles of Islam can be applied to enrich any political system secularly conceived and agreed to by the relevant society, under the trusteeship of humankind, without regard to any discrimination based on religion, race, or social background.[135]

In the end, democracy, whether a product of the West or otherwise, is not inconsistent with Islam. On the contrary, as a secular form of social organization, it does offer the appropriate forum for the participation by each individual who so desires in the fulfillment of the duties and the exercise of rights under the trusteeship that God attributed to humankind. In particular, democracy is a forum for the building of consensus, or *ijmā'* as a source of law and a mechanism for the adaptation to progress.

In retrospect, while the Prophet did not build and lead a state, the caliphs who succeeded him did build one. Despite any claims to the contrary, the caliphs undertook that task in their capacity as politicians and not in any capacity of successor to the Prophet or as part of implementing or enforcing religion.

THE CONSTITUENCY OR THE *JAMĀʿA* OF MUSLIMS

According to the doctrine of the Islamic state, the constituency of the Islamic state, headed by the imam, is made up of the members of the *umma*—the nation—namely the believers (or the *Muslim jamāʿa*) who constitute the majority as well as people from other faiths who are in the minority. They have important duties, but practically no political rights. One would expect that if the imam has obligations, then the constituency would have the corresponding rights to expect the imam to perform these obligations. Religious scholars of various schools and affiliations have endeavored to list and define the scope of the constituency's rights against the ruler using the command to enjoin good and forbid evil.[136] Ahmad Moussalli presents these views with particular focus on the moral legitimacy of political power being based on free choice, the rule of law, and the respect of people's rights to freedom, equality, and justice.[137] While in appearance the concepts are forceful in terms of rights of the ruled, in reality the practice is disappointing because the system so conceived by the doctrine is based on the traditional concept of *shūra*, under which the consultation is nonbinding on the ruler, who remains almost omnipotent. It is an elitist system which is contrary to the spirit of Islam. It grants freedom of action to the joint venture of the elite, made up of the ruler and his family, associated nobility, scholars, and clergy, all using—and often abusing—religion. Among other abuses, they retain the right to decide on what is good and what is evil in the exercise of the command to enjoin good and forbid evil.

In particular, while in theory the constituency has powerful rights, in practice the doctrine decides otherwise, in more than one major respect. First, if the constituency does not get what it expects from the imam, that is, if the imam fails to perform his duties, the constituency is not entitled to redress the imam or in the main remove him from office. Second, the members of the constituency have no direct or indirect say in any matters of state nor in any of their presumed rights, because those rights have been hijacked by that elite group called *ahl al-ḥall wa-l-ʿaqd*. Third, none of the authors who tried to embellish the doctrine by hiding the actual practice has given any assurance about the non-Muslim minorities sharing equal rights. One cannot but observe that some of the authors, namely al-Mawardi and Ibn Taymiyyah, cited by Ahmad Moussalli in support of the so-called democratic outlook of the doctrine in terms of safeguarding the rights and votes of the constituency, are those who have camouflaged those rights into, and usurped them in favor of, *ahl al-ḥall wa-l-ʿaqd* and, through them, the ruler.

Yet there is no basis for such injustice in any of the Holy Qur'an's provisions. In addition, there cannot be any reasonable basis for such injustice in the Prophetic Tradition because the Prophet never behaved as a head of state nor claimed to set the foundations for an Islamic state. Not only is that aspect of the doctrine of the Islamic state not founded in Scripture, it is contrary to the human rights set forth in the Qur'an. A class of 'ulama' has provided support to the rulers in ordering that submission to the supreme imam is an act of faith, even if he is unjust and fails to carry out his duties, thereby denying the right to rebel except in extreme cases of departure from religion, such as turning into or behaving as an infidel (or *kufr*), which is determined by that same class of 'ulama'.[138]

With respect to the individual duties of the members of the constituency stated in the doctrine, the duty of obedience to the imam and to the elite group of *ahl al-ḥall wa-l-ʿaqd* is said to have been provided for in Verses Q4:59 and Q4:83: *"those with authority"* to whom these verses refer are presumed to be the imam and the members of the learned elite. Previously in Chapter 3, the context of verse Q4:59 was addressed in connection with the discussion of Prophetic Tradition as a potential source of Islam. In fact, that same verse had been advanced as basis for imitating everything that the Prophet may have presumably said, done, or not done in his lifetime— namely the duty to obey the Prophet. Now that same verse is advanced as the basis for the duty to obey the imam, in his capacity as successor of the Prophet, and the *ahl al-ḥall wa-l-ʿaqd*, in their capacity as the learned elite. Thus, if the believers must obey the Prophet, then they must obey, as well, his successors who have inherited his status and duties. However, the context of this verse is totally irrelevant to both the Prophetic Tradition and the duty to obey the ruler. The context of this verse is a specific one in which the Prophet, in preparation for a war, had designated someone to lead a group of fighters. When a notable among his companions who was expected to be part of that group refused to obey the leader so designated by the Prophet, the dispute was brought to the Prophet for settlement.[139] In Verse Q4:83, it is a context of war, in which people are enjoined to avoid falling into the traps of Satan by ignoring rumors and obtaining the truth about the situation directly from the Prophet or those with authority. Note the sequence in verse Q4:59: obey God, obey the Messenger, and obey those with authority, and in Q4:83: refer to the Apostle, or to those charged with authority.

Who are "those with authority"?[140] They are certainly not the learned elite or any other self-appointed few. Instead, they are the people to whom the Messenger has delegated authority. Did he have that power? Yes, God gave him that power in Verse Q4:64[141] to enable him to perform his duty, that of spreading the Message; and he used that authority to designate a leader for the group of fighters in connection with a defensive war against people who aimed to prevent him from performing his mission. This means that the effect of this verse does not extend beyond the lifetime of the Prophet, because the mission of the Messenger could not be inherited, and his authority could not be transmitted. The position, then, is as follows: (1) as far as the obedience to the Prophet is concerned, it ends with the end of the period of the exercise of his authority; and (2) as far as the rulers are concerned, there is no blind duty to obey them if they are not appointed by the Prophet, and then only while the Prophet was alive and maintained that authority; as for any other rulers, obedience or the lack thereof is a secular matter and depends on the agreed principles of the relevant political system. This explains how a verse descended in connection with temporal leadership, designed to secure the ability of the Prophet to go about the discharge of his Divine Mission, acquires an unintended meaning and scope when it is taken out of context to serve as a divine basis for blindly obeying the ruler.

With respect to the duty to pay zakat or alms to the ruler and the corresponding right of the latter to collect it from the constituency, that duty and right are entirely contrary to the freedom of faith and other express provisions of the Holy Qur'an. The zakat is a worship-related obligation of the believers that they perform under the watchfulness of God and for which they are rewarded or punished in the hereafter on the Final Day of Judgment. In the first place, any attempt to institutionalize the collection of the zakat is equivalent to enforcing the faith upon people, in violation of the divine injunction to the Prophet to limit his mission to spreading the Message and abstaining from acts of enforcement. Second, zakat was never intended to stand as a tax to fund state obligations. It was instead intended to serve as an act of worship that each believer dispenses among those whom he or she believes to be the most deserving. Therefore, the collection of zakat by the state would deny to the believer the freedom to select his beneficiaries, as his or her conscience dictates.[142] In fact, zakat, being a payment of alms for charitable purposes, is at times due, by way of priority, to relatives who are in need.[143]

If that is the case, what is the context and scope of the provisions of Verse Q9:103 used in support of the claim relating to the duty of the believers to pay zakat to the ruler and the corresponding right of the ruler to collect it? Verse Q9:103 provides as follows: *"Take of their wealth a freewill offering, to purify them and to cleanse them thereby, and pray for them; thy prayers are a comfort for them; God is All-hearing, All-knowing."* In reality, this verse was revealed in connection with certain people who repented and brought money to the Prophet—at their own initiative and without any coercion. They asked him to distribute these monies on their behalf to the needy in fulfillment of their divine worship-related duty to spend on charity. To their request, the Prophet responded that he was not for the time being allowed to do so. So this verse came down to tell him that there was nothing wrong if he took their money and applied it in the way the payers desired, and then prayed God on their behalf for God's forgiveness of their sins[144]—clearly not about collecting zakat as a government tax. This meaning becomes clear when Verse Q9:103 is construed in light of the preceding verse (Q9:102—*"And others have confessed their sins; they have mixed a righteous deed with another evil. It may be that God will turn toward them; God is All-forgiving, All-compassionate"*), which tells about those who need to seal their repentance by way of cleansing their souls with the payment of alms. That meaning is confirmed in the subsequent verse (Q9:104—*"Do they not know that God is He who accepts repentance from His servants, and takes the freewill offerings?"*) in which God reserves the power to accept the repentance if He is satisfied that it is genuine.[145] Simply put, this is another example of a Qur'anic text taken out of context to support something which is not otherwise permitted by, or provided for in, the Qur'an.

Regarding the duty imposed by the doctrine on the constituency to obey the ruler's call for jihad, the so-called sacred war, which he may at any time make in his sole discretion, the concept that jihad is about wars must be firmly rejected. The concept of jihad is discussed at length in Chapter 10, in which the limited and now rare instances of jihad which may involve the use of force and violence are examined. To refute the duty to obey a ruler's call for jihad, the same argument that was made to refute the collection of zakat as a religious duty of the head of state will serve. Indeed, like zakat, jihad is an individual worship-related requirement which is imposed on believers, and which believers perform in accordance with their own understanding of the faith, in their entire freedom of faith. While it is only normal for any head of state to call his citizens to arms when there is an aggression on the nation, that call and the corresponding duty of citizens to respond to that call are matters of secular law, adopted and enforced under the trusteeship of humankind subject to human sanctions.[146]

Finally, regarding the presumed severe punishment reserved for rebellion against a ruler and the ensuing discord among the community, as is presumably set forth in Verse Q5:33 previously cited, this verse does not purport to support the claim made in connection with rebellion. In fact, that verse is taken out of context, and, when placed in context, it will become clear that it was a limited-scope verse, revealed for a specific circumstance which was unrelated to statecraft and social law and order. That verse was revealed specifically to warn against those who fought the Prophet to obstruct his divine mission of spreading the Message of God.[147] This explains that such act is described as an act of war against God; it purports to prevent the fulfillment of God's will through the intermediation of the Prophet. The effect of that verse thus ended with the completion of the Prophet's mission.

The doctrine of the Islamic state, as described and analyzed here, is deficient in many respects and, to a great extent, fails to secure certain basic human rights for individuals living under the *imamate*, such as minority rights. Several of those areas are considered in detail in the relevant chapters on human rights. The doctrine of the Islamic state may have been advanced, progressive, and liberal in the days in which it was conceptualized, by comparison to human rights elsewhere in the Middle Ages. However, in today's terms and by application of the universal nature of Islam, that doctrine has, in various respects, become obsolete and even un-Islamic.

It is important to recall that modern-day Islamists, following the lead of 'ulama' and rulers, have—for obvious reasons—claimed that Islam is both religion and state, *dīn wa dawla*.[148] They have advanced, in support of such claim, the principles of *shūra* (consultation) and *ijmā'* (consensus) for the exercise of political rights in the administration of state affairs. Then they have legitimized the shelving of *shūra* and *ijmā'* and all the principles set forth in the Scriptures on the basis that obedience and submission (*ṭā'a*) to a ruler takes precedence over any other consideration, unless he commits a major religious sin. By doing so, they erected an artificially well-dressed facade of Islamic theory which in reality adversely affects Islam as a message and religion, and then dismissed the essence of *shūra* and all the progressive principles brought about by Islam.

With Respect to Governance in General

The misreading of the concepts and provisions of the Holy Qur'an discussed above have resulted in a certain confusion in the minds of Muslims. Esposito and Mogahed, interpreting the public polls conducted on a wide scale among Muslims around the world, observe, "[o]verall, Muslims want neither a theocracy nor a secular democracy and would opt for a third model in which religious principles and democratic values coexist."[149] In reality, there is no need for such a third model, because democracy is not inconsistent with religion, and secularism is not a precondition to democracy: religion and democracy are not likes, and their individual scopes are different.

Islam is not religion and state, and it does not sanction a political authority, whether entrusted with religious or any other authority. Yet, Islam is not neutral to state organization and practice. Indeed, the Holy Qur'an contains several general principles of good governance that are grounded in *fiṭra*, which have over the years invariably served to guide the behavior of people in general and continue in particular to constitute the basis of good political governance by humankind.

On that basis, the Qur'an contains valuable guiding principles from which any society stands to benefit if they are applied to found domestic legislation in the organization of the state. First, God sets forth the guiding principle of coexistence and mutual acceptance in a pluralistic, multiconfessional society based on freedom of faith (Verse Q5:48).[150] Another primary guiding principle is the command to enjoin good and forbid evil (set forth in Verses Q3:104 and 110, and Q22:41) and its corollary, the command to prevent the spread of corruption (set forth in Verses Q2:188 and Q7:85).[151] The Qur'an also insists on the principles of justice and fairness in dealings among people.[152] These principles, when combined with the principles of virtue and good conduct stated in the Shari'a and implied in the command to enjoin good and forbid evil, lead to the achievement of social peace.[153] The Qur'an even sets forth a social principle relevant to the administration of public finances, namely the collective duty of the community to attend to the poor and needy using monies from charitable payments and war spoils.[154] Finally, we also find in the Qur'an the numerous social, ethical, and moral principles with legal and economic implications which constitute valuable foundations for legal and economic orders, and for freedoms and human rights.[155]

While Islam itself is secular, it is perfectly conceivable that those who want to build an "Islamic state" may design an Islamic political system whose principles are based on the guiding principles of Shari'a, including a code of laws inspired from, and incorporating, these general principles. Such a system can be very modern and address countless current issues and problems.[156] But then it is a system which is "Islamic" only to the extent that it is inspired by the principles and rules set forth in the Holy Qur'an. It would be as Islamic as any other entirely different system which also incorporates the noble principles of Islam. Yet, neither system would be deemed to be the universal, divinely mandated Islamic state that God never mandated. Any such system would be a secular system, freely enacted by Muslim believers in accordance with their faith and according to the trusteeship of humankind installed by God.

CHAPTER 9
Islam and Shari'a

Comparative law encompasses the study of the major legal systems applied around the world, including the common law system adopted mostly in the Anglo-Saxon countries; the civil law system adopted in Europe, primarily derived from Roman law and the civil code of Napoleon; and the Islamic law which is in force in Saudi Arabia and serves as default reference in other nations with Muslim majorities.

Even though several nations with Muslim majorities have enacted legislation through action of their secular legislative bodies, they cannot be considered truly secular nations because (1) their legal systems are based on the assumption that their laws must at all times be Shari'a compliant; (2) their constitutions are based on the assumption that Islam, as a legal system, serves as source of law when the "secularly" enacted laws are silent on certain issues; and (3) entire sectors of the law are governed by Shari'a provisions which are adopted as law of the land, such as family law and certain aspects of criminal law.

Islam, like Judaism, has by now acquired a deeply rooted reputation as a legalistic religion.[1] Among the three Abrahamic faiths—Judaism, Christianity, and Islam—Judaism and Islam are categorized as the messages that brought divine law to organize the lives of their adherents. This is the basis of the claim that Islam regulates every aspect of daily life.[2] Thus, the Islamic law developed by the schools of jurisprudence is portrayed and presented as inherent in Islam, where good Muslims must apply the "laws of God." Islam is also advocated as an economic system, because the economic norms and principles for organizing the economic and financial relations among people can all be found in the Islamic Shari'a. In fact, it is commonly believed that, since Medina was the first Islamic nation founded by Prophet Muhammad, the Qur'an primarily legislated for it.[3]

We have previously shown that the Medina setup was not an arrangement characteristic of state organization. Nor was Shari'a meant to provide the legislative framework for that "state." Unfortunately, that conception of the Medina setup has oriented—perhaps disoriented—the entire perception of Shari'a. Instead of being a set of universal ethical and moral principles adequate to found a universal social order to replace limiting tribal customs, Shari'a became a mere narrow legal system aiming to help the Prophet rule Medina, and thereafter serve as a tool of divine governance.

First, it is essential to clarify the actual meaning and scope of Shari'a to determine the extent to which it may be considered a legal system. Then we should consider whether or not Shari'a constitutes a tool of divine governance and determine the extent to which Shari'a may or may not preclude Islam from being a secular way of life, as opposed to a political and legal system, religiously mandated. We should also explore the interpretation of the Qur'anic verses which contain either law provisions or provisions that may have a legal connotation. Finally, it is important to consider certain aspects of the law and certain economic issues that are generally perceived by Muslims and non-Muslims to be of the essence of Islam, including family law, criminal law, and Islamic banking, in the hope of illuminating modern-day efforts to reform "Islamic" Law.

Islamic Law, *Fiqh*, and Shari'a

Definitions and Syntax

Shari'a, *fiqh*, and Islamic law are often used interchangeably as three names for one and the same legal system, commonly known as Islamic law.[4] Very frequently even, Islam as a religion is altogether reduced to its divine legal component.[5]

To start with, we shall set aside *fiqh* which is the science of jurisprudence. That science was developed by the early learned specialists to extrapolate the detailed rules of the faith primarily from the provisions of the Holy Qur'an, the Prophetic Tradition, the traditions of the first four caliphs, and those of other close companions of the Prophet.[6] They included the rules of worship and other divinely prescribed injunctions and restrictions relating to day-to-day matters. Therefore, *fiqh* is a human science, and the compendia that the *fuqahā'* (scholars or learned clerics who practiced and applied the *fiqh*) have compiled, constitute in their entirety a human work product. Except for the Holy Qur'an, all sources that the *fuqahā'* used to develop that jurisprudence are entirely human, including the interpretations of the Qur'an. Thus, *fiqh* and *fiqh*-derived jurisprudence are neither divine nor otherwise sacred.

Based on the above, Islamic law is the work product of *fiqh* in the legal sector. It is a body of laws covering most, if not all, basic sectors of the law, including the modern-day equivalents of constitutional law, family law, criminal law, the law of contracts and commercial transactions, administrative law, and international law. That body of law is very elaborate because it evolved primarily as case law. It covers even hypothetical issues that the *fuqahā'* systematically considered by way of anticipation. It is only toward the latter period of the Ottoman Empire that a codification effort was conducted to bring out the various subjects of Islamic law in the form of codes, similar to European codes of law enacted around that same time period. That effort started with a semiofficial codification of civil law following the Hanafi school of jurisprudence,[7] which was commissioned by the Ottoman administration from a committee of jurists. The end product was officially called *Majallat al-Aḥkām al-'Adliyya*, and was commonly referred to as the *majalla* code (in 1876). Though the *majalla* code was never officially enacted as law, it soon became the de facto law of the land which tribunals implemented as a reference civil law under the Hanafi doctrine. Later the Ottoman legislative body enacted the family law code *qānūn ḥuqūq al-'ā'ila* governing domestic relations, again substantially following the Hanafi doctrine, but with certain provisions adopted from other schools, namely the Shafi'i and the Maliki schools of jurisprudence. From then onward, various Arab countries enacted laws in various sectors, expressed to be codifications of, or derived from, Islamic law which in turn are said to embody Shari'a.[8]

In the strict sense, Shari'a means a path or way offered by God leading to the basic truth.[9] Thus Shari'a is the divine scriptural foundation on which Islamic law, by way of *fiqh*, has been based and from which it has been derived. In this sense, Shari'a is the collection of verses which contain provisions with a legal connotation or which put in force moral values serving as basis for legal provisions. However, following the perception of Prophetic Tradition as a divinely revealed source alongside the Holy Qur'an, the *fuqahā'* extended the scope of Shari'a to include the traditions of the Prophet and his immediate companions that bear legal implication or contain moral principles which can serve as basis for legal provisions.[10] Some authors have also extended that definition to also encompass the interpretations of the Qur'an and Prophetic Tradition by way of *ijmā'* (general consensus) and *ijtihād* (rational thinking and argumentation).[11]

The proponents of Islamic law as a sacred compendium of rules and interpretations that accumulated over the years conveniently take advantage of the confusion between Shari'a, Islamic law, and *fiqh*[12] to avoid the task of distinguishing between the divine and the human, drawing upon divine guidance, and offering laws which serve the best interests of time and place.[13] The perception of Shari'a as a comprehensive and final detailed body of laws is unfortunately shared by many, and it places Muslims and Islam in a rationally untenable position, as follows: (1) God sent Prophet Muhammad to carry His Message as a blessing to all humanity (Verses Q7:52 and 203, Q16:89; Q21:107; and Q27:77) and, in His divine governance and as sole legislator, He sent Shari'a to humankind to organize their lives; (2) however, since God is the sole legislator and humans cannot legislate, and bearing in mind that God has declared Prophet Muhammad's mission as the last and final one, humans must survive by interpreting and reinterpreting the Shari'a until the Final Day; (3) but things get further complicated because common humans are not able by themselves to comprehend and enjoy God's blessing on them and must, for that purpose, rely on the work of human interpreters; therefore (4) the only option left is to be ruled and governed by, or in joint venture with, clergy, 'ulama', *fuqahā'*, howsoever called. Such thinking is clearly in direct contradiction, and is thus inconsistent, with the mandate that God gave each human being, by the mere fact of his or her creation, under the trusteeship.

For the purpose of this discussion, the meaning of Shari'a will be limited to the provisions of the Holy Qur'an as sole divine source of the universal Message. Without prejudice to the overwhelming practical importance of framing the exact scope of each term as and when used,[14] it should be reiterated that these definitions of *fiqh*, Islamic law, and Shari'a are for the sole purpose of presenting the materials of this chapter and avoiding confusion between divine and nondivine sources, mindful that these terms may have otherwise been used interchangeably in other works.[15] Indeed, that risk of confusion is real, as John Esposito points out: "As a result, over time the distinction between God's immutable law as found in revelation and many of the legal regulations which were the product of fallible human reasoning or local custom became blurred and forgotten."[16]

The Scope of Shari'a

Although verses are not clearly classified into chapters with corresponding headings, the contents of the Holy Qur'an can be classified into five broad categories of provisions: (1) verses that reveal the attributes of God and His eternal character; (2) verses which tell stories of ancient peoples and their prophets in general terms, without specific details of time or place, and are destined to serve as examples for the entire human race to which the message brought by Prophet Muhammad is addressed; (3) verses containing the principles and rules of worship and adoration of God; (4) verses that deal with basic commandments and principles of individual and social conduct; and (5) verses which articulate rules and principles dealing with everyday life and which eventually carry a legal connotation.

The first three categories are part of what the Qur'an calls the "occult" or the "unknown" (al-ghayb). The occult or unknown is about the whole truth that only God knows in its entirety and which he has chosen to reveal in part, leaving the rest to be revealed on the Final Day. The part of the truth being revealed, offers examples to help believers better understand God's Message and enable them to grasp the worship and adoration requirements of God and fulfill the basic obligations associated with the faith. None of these three categories contains rules of law, because they do not touch the daily lives of people or their relationships with each other.

By contrast, the two other categories of Qur'anic verses which deal with daily life are, despite the finality of the particular Qur'anic text, amenable to reinterpretation from time to time following the evolution of time and place. They are made up substantially of general principles of morality and civility in dealing among humans. The principles included in these two categories of verses afford a wide spectrum of implementation modalities, such as the principles of justice and equity, among many others. Alternatively, certain provisions may consist of specific detailed rules revealed to address specific circumstances or according to prevailing social customs, whose change over time can justify a modification in, or even the suspension of, their implementation.

The verses in the two categories which impact the day-to-day lives of people and their relationships with each other, whether containing general principles or detailed rules, represent a very small fraction of the entire Holy Qur'an. Out of over sixty-four hundred verses representing the entire Qur'an, the number of verses in the latter two categories do not exceed two hundred, or fewer than four percent.[17] In particular, in the field of contract law, there are very few commands, namely those mandating the overriding duty of justice, the prohibition of Riba, and the requirement for strict compliance with agreements. In matters of procedures, the Qur'an sets forth the standard for proof of debts and wills. In criminal law, five punishable crimes are provided for with their punishments—namely murder, theft, adultery, calumnious accusation of adultery, and brigandage. Finally, in family law, a number of rules relate to marriage, divorce, and inheritance. Contrary to the prevailing view that it blindly mandates application of punishments, the Holy Qur'an urges, first and foremost, compassion on the part of society so as to grant clemency and forgiveness to perpetrators.[18]

When the underlying principles and messages for each of these topics are considered, we find all the more reason not to view them as part of a legal system, but instead as part of a value system which entices people to forgive and refrain from reprehensible behavior.[19] While the principles set forth in these verses do not add up to a fully fledged legal system, they are enough to constitute a solid value system and to provide the moral foundations for any just and fair legal system. Together, these verses constitute the divine Shari'a that characterizes Islam. Viewed from that perspective, Shari'a is nowhere to be compared with, or otherwise confined to, the narrow framework of a code or series of codes containing legal provisions. It is instead a divinely charted multifaceted path which leads to salvation.[20] That is why the theory of relative application of Shari'a advanced by the late Muhammad 'Abed al-Jabiri,[21] according to which the ruler, in his wisdom, decides on how much of Shari'a to enforce in the context of the relevant society, is not applicable. In fact, the application and enforcement of Shari'a under any context requires the human legislation of laws which embody the principles and ethical values brought by Shari'a. It is only within such a framework that detailed rules can then be designed relative to the specific context. It is in this sense that the term Shari'a, and terms derived from the root word *shara'a*, have been used in the Holy Qur'an.

The Qur'an contains five verses in which a word derived from the root word *shara'a* has been used, four of which possess a meaning relevant to our subject.[22]

> Q5:48—*To you We revealed the Book with the Truth, confirming previous Scriptures and witnessing to their veracity. So judge between them as God revealed and do not follow their whims, to turn you away from the truth revealed to you. For every community We decreed* a law *and a way of life. Had God willed, He could have made you a single community—but in order to test you in what He revealed to you. So vie with one another in virtue. To God is your homecoming, all of you, and He will then acquaint you with that over which you differed.*[23]

In this verse, God places the Message revealed to Prophet Muhammad in the context of previously revealed messages and declares it to be a form of reiteration of those previous messages. God also announces that each such previous revelation constitutes a valid path to salvation. Thus, as used in this verse, the highlighted word *shur'a*, as a derivative term from the root *shara'a*, means a path, namely a reference to the straight path which leads to God. In other words, the terms *shur'a* and *shara'a* are not about the revelation of a legal system, even though the revealed path may contain rules, injunctions, and restrictions which may serve to strengthen the foundations of a legal system. They are rather about God's reiteration that all divine revelations, starting with the revelation to Abraham, are valid paths toward salvation.

> Q42:13—*He has* ordained *for you of religion what He enjoined upon Noah and that which We have revealed to you, [O Muhammad], and what We enjoined upon Abraham and Moses and Jesus—to establish the religion and not be divided therein. Difficult for those who associate others with Allah is that to which you invite them. Allah chooses for Himself whom He wills and guides to Himself whoever turns back [to Him].*[24]

In this context, the verb *shara'a* as used stands for "to ordain"; and what is ordained in this instance is the entire religion and not only its element which consist of legal rules.

> Q42:21—*Or have they other deities who have* ordained *for them a religion to which Allah has not consented? But if not for the decisive word, it would have been concluded between them. And indeed, the wrongdoers will have a painful punishment.*[25]

In this verse, it is the same verb being used in exactly the same meaning as in the immediately preceding instance.

> Q45:18—*Then We put thee on* the (right) Way of Religion*: so follow thou that (Way), and follow not the desires of those who know not.*[26]

In this verse, it is the term Shari'a which is used and not a word derived from the common root *shara'a*. However, that term is used in its pure meaning in Arabic as a structured path leading to a certain objective which, in the instance, is the way of religion that leads to God. It is worthwhile to note that this is a Meccan verse. This means that it was revealed prior to the revelation of most of the verses which contain injunctions, rules, and restrictions which might carry a legal connotation. Yet, that term carries a wide scope which extends to all aspects of the new faith, without limitation to the mere injunctions, rules, and restrictions with a legal connotation.

This brings us to the observation and conclusion that Shari'a transcends, and is thus substantially more important and relevant in our lives and religious understanding than, a mere legal system. While a legal system is a one-size-fits-all body of rules for all people to follow and comply with, Shari'a instead is a path made up of divine universal guiding principles which are suitable, at all times and in all places, to found and drive the progress of moral, social, legal, and economic systems.[27]

Shari'a and Islamic Law

Defined as a divine path consisting of universal guiding principles, Shari'a has consistently, and ever since the early days of Islam, served as the foundation for Islamic law, as developed by the *fuqahā'*, both clerics and scholars of the various schools of jurisprudence. However, the extreme flexibility that God afforded Muslims, through the structure of Shari'a as a tool of progress, was ignored and refashioned into a rigid system which sacralized the *fiqh* output built around Shari'a, endowing it with a divine aura called "Islamic law." While in the first few centuries of Islam, the early *fuqahā'* of Islam had already achieved a clear understanding of Shari'a as a divine path of guiding principles,[28] that sad state of affairs occurred toward the end of the fourth century following the hijra, when it was decided to crystallize the state of *fiqh* of that time by imposing a ban on *ijtihād*.

On such basis, the founders and members of the schools of jurisprudence developed their compendia of rules, regulations, and laws in a comprehensive manner so as to encompass the various facets of day-to-day life, including the rules applicable to worship requirements. They categorized the principles of Shari'a into (1) *'ibādāt*, which deal with worship requirements, and (2) *mu'āmalāt*, which regulate relations and transactions among people. These early Muslim scholars essentially designed jurisprudence to include their particular iterations of worship requirements and legal systems, inspired from Islamic values, but also inspired from other civilizations with which the Muslims interacted.

These differing systems, with their legal components, reflected the needs of their environments in terms of time and geographic location. This explains the fact that the schools of jurisprudence which developed in Arabia, namely the Hanbali and Maliki schools, reflected the simplicity of life in Arabia and the conservative nature of its inhabitants, while the Hanafi school, which developed in Baghdad, and to a lesser extent the Shafi'i school, which came out mainly in Cairo, reflected the more complex multicultural, multiethnic societies of Baghdad and Cairo.[29]

However, this activity spread to such a great extent and at such a pace that at times it became fuel for political and racial disputes within the wide Arab-Islamic Empire. Before long, it had become an easy way to create rules favoring one political cause over another, or one ethnic group over the other. The proliferation of legal compendia in the name of Islam led the scholars of the four main schools of jurisprudence to reach a consensus on the need to abstain from further *ijtihād* and impose an end to the process of *ijtihād*. Consequently, the renewal of doctrine came entirely to a halt and gave way to the work of exegetes who, despite the volume of their output, had to restrict the scope of their activity to interpreting and paraphrasing existing doctrinal theses. This development, which took place in the eleventh century, marked the beginning of the decline of Muslim peoples.

While the scholars of the four principal schools of jurisprudence never claimed that the *fiqh* that they had developed was divine, yet, as a result of the banning of *ijtihād*, Islamic jurisprudence gradually became sacralized, first, when the *fiqh* of *'ibādāt* came to be viewed as immutable because it deals exclusively with the relations of humanity with God; and second, when scholars observed the ban on *ijtihād* and abstained from progressing Islamic law other than under the most compelling circumstances, and then only under the cover of interpretation and reinterpretation of the same original *fiqh* compendia.[30] As a result, Shari'a became identified with the aggregate iterations of the schools of jurisprudence at the time that *ijtihād* was banned, and thereafter.

Strictly speaking, Shari'a—as a universal set of divine principles and a value system—contains detailed provisions only in the fields of family law and criminal law, which, to the unsuspecting layman, could resemble legal codes.[31] However, in all other sectors of the law, including the law of obligations and contracts and international law, the legal provisions are exclusively in the form of general principles covering core concepts without any detail. For example, in the category of the law of obligations and contracts we find the principles of justice and equity, the duty to honor one's own commitments under a contract, and advice regarding the need to authenticate certain contracts through witnessing requirements. In the category of certain special contracts, we find rules regarding honesty in trades involving buying and selling, the need to forbid usury in dealings, and generally the prevention of betting on trade-related uncertainties.

Does that mean that Shari'a is then primarily about family law and criminal law? The answer again is negative. It is true that detailed rules may be found in the Holy Qur'an about marriage and divorce and the distribution of estates in case of death and inheritance. It is also true that detailed rules, though to a lesser extent than in the case of family law, may be found relating to specific crimes in the field of criminal law, such as the rules about flogging adulterers. However, the real reason for this should be searched for elsewhere than in any purpose to establish a legal system, since such a purpose would have extended beyond just family and criminal law, mainly into laws governing contracts, obligations, business and trade, domestic and international relations, etc.

The true purpose of Shari'a, or divine law, can be found in one of the principal purposes of the Message of Islam—namely, to set forth a universal value system for interaction among humans and, in that context, to replace brutal and reprehensible tribal laws and customs founded on the tribal bond with new, wider-ranging principles of justice, equity, and compassion founded on the bond of Islam.[32] With that in mind, the specific rules prescribed become unimportant per se, to the extent that they serve to address the underlying purpose of the relevant rule, that is, the relevant higher principle that the Message is trying to convey.[33] For that reason, any alternative solution that achieves the same purpose and fulfills the higher principle in question could be welcome.

The Holy Qur'an sets forth, unequivocally, the true meaning and purpose of Shari'a in Verses Q4:26 to 28.

Allah wants to make clear to you [the lawful from the unlawful] and guide you to
the [good] practices of those before you and to accept your repentance. And Allah
is Knowing and Wise (26). Allah wants to accept your repentance, but those who
follow [their] passions want you to digress [into] a great deviation (27). And Allah
wants to lighten for you [your difficulties]; and mankind was created weak (28).[34]

These verses follow a long series of verses of a seemingly legal nature. However, God immediately dispels any potential confusion about the purpose of these verses and sets forth clearly that his concern is about our salvation, not about creating a legal system.

The Anatomy of Shari'a

Shari'a between Divine Governance and Secular Government

Based on attendant views of Shari'a, A. Filali-Ansari discusses three potential views of secularism and Islam: (1) Islam has no need for secularism; (2) Islam is hostile to secularism; and (3) Islam is compatible with—that is, is not hostile to— secularism.[35] From the first viewpoint, he cites the work of Hassan Hanafi and Muhammad 'Abed al-Jabiri. For Hanafi, Islam is neutral to secularism because Shari'a is first a legal system for the pursuit of the collective good, in light of the overall objectives of Islam, and because the class of clergy, including *fuqahā'* and muftis, is integrated within society and does not constitute a separate hierarchy which seeks to impose religious norms on society as a whole. For al-Jabiri secularism is not at issue because the separation of the temporal and religious realms occurred early in the history of Islam, under the rule of Mu'awiya, the first Omayad caliph.

From the second viewpoint, Islam is incompatible with secularism because Islam called for the creation of a religious community to be governed by the principles of the faith and the rules of conduct embodied in Shari'a. In other words, Shari'a serves as a constitution for such community. For that purpose, the state, whose ideal model can be found in the Enlightened Caliphate, is perceived as the instrument for the implementation of this constitution and the submission of society to its transcendent provisions, which no one can modify.

From the third viewpoint, a view which Filali-Ansari supports, Islam may be considered as fully compatible with secularism. Filali-Ansari calls for liberating Islam and its message from the countless doctrines developed over time and for preventing the contamination of religion by history. He cites for that purpose the supporting opinions of three prominent scholars, Mahmoud Taha, Fazlur Rahman, and 'Ali Abdel Raziq. In this light religion should not be perceived as a social discipline to be imposed by vigilant guardians of the faith who wield powers of state, but instead as a personal engagement, an act of faith, and a free will to submit to God. While each of these three scholars reaches this conclusion through a different path, Filali-Ansari concludes that Islam and secularism are not likes and cannot be compared to each other. Islam is a universal religion, whereas secularism is a mode of sociopolitical organization which attributes to religion a specific role in the lives of humans. But secularism should in no way be seen as an attempt to eliminate, or to act as a substitute for, religion. With this understanding in mind, Islam may be viewed as compatible with secularism.

But there is a fourth viewpoint, presented here in this work, which involves the recognition that Islam itself is secular. Unlike conservative clerics who believe that Shari'a, as a tool of divine governance, is the only law which humans are permitted to employ, even to the exclusion of humanly legislated laws,[36] Shari'a in reality is a product—rather than an exclusive tool—of divine governance. It consists of a set of universal divine principles and values that guide the way for humans, as trustees of God's creation, at all times and in all places.[37]

The view that Shari'a is the only acceptable law governing the lives of Muslims is supposedly founded on a number of Qur'anic verses which the advocates of this view advance to support their claims.[38] These are, in particular, the series of verses which exhort prophets and people to judge by what God has revealed to the prophets ending with Prophet Muhammad, and deem those who do not do so as disbelievers and wrongdoers.[39] But importantly, in the last verse in that series, Verse Q5:50, God confirms that His entire purpose was to abrogate and replace the tribal rules which prevailed in the *jāhiliyya* prior to the revelation of the Qur'an.[40]

Consequently, judging in accordance with "what God has revealed" (*al-ḥukm bima anzala-l-Lāh*) is not about judging in accordance with a legal system inspired or revealed by God. It is about judging and behaving in accordance with the principles of justice set forth as guidance in the Qur'an, as opposed to reprehensible tribal laws and traditions. Since God has given humankind moral values and principles sufficient to illuminate the way, it is incumbent upon people to enact fair and just secular legislation guided by such values and principles. Then secular legislation and divine values and principles may guide the path of judges in applying the law. For example, Verse Q16:125 (*"Call to the way of your Lord with wisdom and fair counsel, and debate with them in the fairest manner. Your Lord knows best who has strayed from His path; He knows best who are guided aright"*)[41] illustrates how the Qur'an sets forth principles of dialogue and respect for the views of others, and then secular laws provide the detailed rules which frame freedom of expression and discussion.

On the other hand, the view that Shari'a is the only acceptable law for Muslims is also founded on the concept that God is the sole legislator under divine governance, a view which associates and equates legislation with governance.[42] In reality, while divine governance is an ongoing blessing from God that will last forever, divine enactment of ethical principles and values has ended by divine declaration in Verse Q5:3 (*"Today, I have perfected your religion for you, and have completed My blessing upon you, and chosen Islam as Dīn [religion and a way of life] for you"*).[43] By declaring Prophet Muhammad as His last and final messenger, and his mission as the last and final prophetic mission, God announced His resolve to leave his creatures to exercise trusteeship to organize their lives and to legislate for themselves guided by the universal principles of Shari'a.

Therefore, while the Holy Qur'an as a whole contains a general framework for divine governance and justice, that framework is only suitable for God to use in pursuing His governance and administering His justice.[44] Humans cannot claim to use God's means to administer earthly justice. Instead, Shari'a is the framework that God has bestowed on humans, as His trustees, in order to organize their lives and strive to fulfill the purpose of God's creation. God will then, on the Last Day, judge people on their success in fulfilling that purpose. Therefore, Shari'a is a solid foundation for secular government. In this sense, Muslims not only are free but are called to legislate for their daily lives, guided by the principles set forth in—or derived from— Shari'a.[45] Following our understanding of the universal nature of the Message of Islam brought by Prophet Muhammad, and because the Message did not appear in a vacuum, when a certain rule is revealed in minute detail to deal with specific events during the lifetime of the Prophet, the guiding principles of Shari'a can be found in the underlying message to be derived from the relevant verse and the circumstances that called for its revelation.

The Structure of Shari'a

The verses which make up the Shari'a did not take the form of a list of do's and don'ts, like ordinary legislation. Instead we find numerous nuances in the Qur'anic verses which make up Shari'a.

A first category of verses contains rules and provisions which are in the form of straightforward injunctions to do, or abstain from doing, something specific, the violation of which constitutes a religious sin. This is the case in verses setting forth actions which are designated as haram, such as those which prohibit the consumption of certain foods (pork and dead animals' flesh, among others),[46] the prohibition of usury (*riba*),[47] or the prohibition to marry certain close relatives.[48] It is also the case in verses which prescribe basic worship requirements, mandate respect and obedience to parents, or require absolute honesty in commercial transactions, especially in terms of properly using the scale in sale transactions for measuring the quantities to be delivered against payments received.[49] The do's and don'ts included in this category must be done or abstained from, per se, for no stated reason. There is no flexibility for the person to act differently in light of specific circumstances, except in the specific cases of exemption expressly cited in the Qur'an. This is the case regarding the permission to consume prohibited foods either under duress or in circumstances where there is no alternative but to consume it to avoid starvation. This is also the case regarding permission to disobey parents in matters which involve disobedience to God. On the other hand, because of their specificity and the divine purpose, which is not announced in the verse, the list of matters divinely prohibited as haram, can neither be extended nor reduced under any circumstance.[50]

Another category of verses contains rules and provisions which are also in the form of injunctions to do, or to abstain from doing, something specific—often justified by a raison d'être—and whose breach may or may not constitute a religious breach.[51] This is the case generally with most verses in the Shari'a category which contain do's and don'ts, but whose interpretation and updating depend on their underlying message and purpose, and eventually also on their continued relevance. It is also even the case with verses which involve the worship of God and His unicity, where God frequently provides evidence and examples to convince people to believe. Also of this category are the verses which mandate that certain acts be witnessed by one, two, or more persons, such as the marriage act and a sale transaction.[52]

Bearing in mind that the purpose of requiring witnesses is to verify the occurrence of the transaction and the conditions upon which that transaction was concluded, it could be safely concluded that the requirement in question has nothing to do with the validity and legitimacy of the transaction itself but constitutes only a means to prove it and prove its terms so that disputes among the parties and their potential serious consequences may be avoided. In other words, if that same transaction could nowadays be authenticated by a notary public, or if the transaction and its terms could be established beyond reasonable doubt in another manner, the same purpose is achieved and the transaction would be valid and enforceable, despite the lack of the stipulated number and gender of witnesses.

The same can be said of corporeal punishment in most cases of criminal law instances. Indeed, the main purpose of punishing theft by amputation of the thief's hand is to prevent the thief from stealing again by depriving him of the tool of theft and informing others that the person in question is a thief so that they may beware of him or her. That same purpose could be achieved if the person in question was temporarily removed from society and placed in jail, and his name and act are made public through the criminal records.

A third category of verses contains rules and provisions in the form of strong advice to do or abstain from doing something. This is the case with verses which dissuade people from gambling or consuming alcoholic drinks which could make them drunk.[53] In the case of gambling and consuming alcohol, the prohibition is not phrased as a sacrilegious act (haram) like the prohibition of consuming pork. Instead, people are strongly enjoined to "avoid" gambling and alcohol because they constitute openings through which we can be unconsciously led to commit sins or hurt ourselves.[54]

In other words, the rules in question are for the sake of self-preservation. Indeed, unlike haram actions, actions under this category cease to be prohibited if the person is careful by consuming alcohol in moderation without getting drunk or gambling with minimal amounts which could have been spent on an otherwise nonobjectionable activity, yet without bringing any particular benefit. The injunctions in this category, because of their nature as injunctions for a stated purpose, can be reduced or extended to other actions which share the same underlying purpose.

A fourth category of verses contains rules and provisions in the form of mere tolerance, in the sense that they do not provide for a right or a prohibition, yet allow a certain practice or tradition to continue by way of tolerance until the times are appropriate to enact a prohibition. As previously discussed, Islam has sought to change many theretofore reprehensible tribal customs which had been either unfair or the cause of discord, violence, and bloodshed among tribes. It did not expect the change to occur overnight, but instead tolerated the continuation of the objectionable situation at times to address certain specifically impending conditions, but in any event so that the desired change could take place gradually over time.[55] This is the case of the temporary toleration of polygamy, slavery, and revenge, among other things.

With respect to polygamy, Muslims in general have unfortunately interpreted it as a divine right. It is traditionally accepted that Islamic law allows polygamy because it gives a man the right to marry up to four wives.[56] Countless arguments are advanced to praise the so-called "wisdom" of such a right, including on the grounds of greater sexual needs of men and as a means to prevent or otherwise minimize the instances of adultery on the part of men, among other arguments.[57] When presidents Atatürk and Bourguiba, of Turkey and Tunisia, abolished polygamy in the context of the modernization of family laws, voices rose against them, declaring their actions as contrary to God's law because presumably they infringed "sacred" rights that God had granted in the Qur'an.[58] However, when read without the prejudices arising from longtime doctrinal interpretations, it becomes clear that the Qur'an consecrated the freedom of marriage and that monogamy is the preferred solution of God. Polygamy was a solution simply tolerated for reasons of a social nature justified by the prevailing circumstances and which have become for a long time obsolete.[59] Verse Q4:3 of the Qur'an stipulates that men could marry up to four wives simultaneously, provided they can maintain a just and equal treatment among them.[60] Then Verse Q4:129, found in the same sura as Verse Q4:3, confirms that it is not possible for men to maintain justice and fairness among women.[61] In light of these seemingly contradictory stipulations, one wonders about the wisdom of allowing the right or freedom to marry up to four women, if such right or freedom is subject to an impossible condition. The answer is simple: polygamy, as provided for in Verse Q4:3 is neither a right nor a freedom. It is rather an exceptional situation that God tolerated for reasons stemming from the social circumstances in which the Qur'an was revealed,[62] and for other reasons also mentioned in the Qur'an.

For example, we note that the verses in question were revealed during the period of the wars fought by the Prophet, in which countless men lost their lives, leaving behind widows and orphans in need of support: absent a state organization, polygamy was one way to secure that support, and the institution of alms (zakat) was another.[63] This explains that Verse Q4:129, which confirms a man's inability to be fair and just among wives in a polygamous relationship, contains God's understanding of that temporary—and at times even necessary—situation, and provides advice about doing one's best not to give up trying as much as possible to be fair. On that basis, it becomes clear that, when Presidents Atatürk and Bourguiba abolished polygamy and declared monogamy as sole permissible standard, they did not infringe on Shari'a. Instead, they put an end to a situation which was merely tolerated, thereby fulfilling the true will of God expressed through the aforesaid impossible condition of justice and equity among spouses.

With respect to slavery, many non-Muslim orientalists and even a number of Muslim thinkers have deemed slavery a divinely sanctioned institution. They have derived that perception from various verses which set forth the standards of fairness and compassion for dealing with slaves,[64] bearing in mind that there are no verses in the Holy Qur'an which expressly condone or otherwise prohibit slavery. That said, and as is the case with polygamy, an unprejudiced reading of the Qur'anic verses involving slavery would overwhelmingly indicate that God's message to humanity is that slavery must end,[65] an objective to which the Holy Qur'an contains ample exhortation. However, it would be tolerated for the period required to end slavery in light of the prevailing social environment.

Even in the sphere of criminal law, the *lex talionis* (law of retaliation) appears to embody and legalize the institution of revenge which was deeply rooted in the tribal psyche and, to a certain extent, continues to characterize a number of Muslim communities. That external appearance and perception notwithstanding, the *lex talionis* institution can be attributed to tolerance, as evidenced by its framing within the concept of *ḥudūd* and the preferred *qiṣāṣ* option of replacing the corporeal punishment with monetary compensation. In this light, what Muslim and non-Muslim thinkers interpreted as a divine sanction of tribal revenge and corporeal punishment is nothing more than a temporary tolerance, pending the heeding of God's advice to shed it entirely.[66]

Ignaz Goldziher rightly observes the extent to which inherited ideas and values become part of social heritage and the difficulty in accepting new ideas and values that was faced when transiting from the pagan *jāhiliyya* into Islam. He concludes that "no true Arab could agree to renounce his inherited ideas of virtue."[67] It is under these circumstances that God, in His ultimate divine wisdom, allowed reprehensible tribal customs to continue by way of tolerance until they could be overcome by Muslims and eradicated from Muslim society. They were certainly not intended to be made part of Islam and of Shari'a, as the *fiqh* and its interpreters claim.

Finally, we come to the category of verses which contain rules and provisions which are subject to certain upper or lower limits, namely the *ḥudūd*. The Holy Qur'an prescribes what it calls *ḥudūd* to address various situations such as the penalty of amputation of the hand for a thief and the penalty of flogging for the adulterer. Also, from the rules applicable to inheritance, the Holy Qur'an prescribes for the male a share double that of the female in the allocation of shares in the estate. These rules have been and continue to be perceived as fixed, immutable divine prescriptions that are resistant to change, thereby ignoring their nature as *ḥudūd*, that is, as limits.

The dogmatic approach adopted by the vast majority of *fuqahā'* and jurisprudents of Islamic law relies on an interpretation of the term *ḥudūd* as a divine immutable rule or deterrent.[68] By extension, the divine aura of *ḥudūd* was also attributed to rules presumably laid down by Prophet Muhammad—that is, to Prophetic Tradition as well—such as the death sentence to punish those who commit apostasy, the stoning of an adulteress to death, and flogging for drinking alcohol. This explains why Islamic law could not keep up with evolution through the centuries from the time of the suspension of *ijtihād,* which hindered the capacity of the rule of law to adapt as conditions of time and place changed. This was an immediate consequence of the jurisprudents' understanding and using the term *ḥudūd* in the exclusive sense of punishment for criminal acts and as a fixed and rigid rule. By contrast, Cherif Bassiouni perceives the *ḥudūd* from the perspective of human rights as limitations and restrictions aimed at preventing "arbitrary and despotic limitations on human freedom." For example, when a criminal is punished, he or she is prevented from arbitrarily hurting the freedoms of others.[69]

In reality, in the Arabic language of the Qur'an, the term *ḥudūd* does not mean "law," "commandment," or "punishment." There are no provisions in the Qur'an which suggest such meaning of the term *ḥudūd*, including where used in the context of criminal offences or in connection with the inheritance of family estates. The term *ḥudūd* is the plural of *ḥadd* which simply means a "limit" or "margin," and such limits or margins can only be a reference to some maxima or minima.[70] This understanding is further corroborated by the provisions of the Qur'an itself, where: (1)

people are cautioned against "transgressing" the bounds framed within the *ḥudūd*; and transgression has only one meaning, that of stepping over, or under, certain stated limits, depending on whether such limits consist of minima or maxima (such as in Verses Q2:229 and Q65:1); and (2) in the instances where God is making a firm commandment, He does not use the term *ḥadd*. Instead He uses the term *amr*, or order, among other terms, such as in Verse Q65:5.

Any other interpretation of the term *ḥudūd*, such as the one adopted by the jurisprudents (i.e., as a fixed law or command), has no foundation in the Arabic language and, in any event, would be in direct contradiction with the express provisions of the Holy Qur'an. This interpretation is further confirmed by the fact that the term *ḥudūd* is used in the Qur'an more often in connection with family law than with criminal law.

On the other hand, God only and no one else may establish *ḥudūd*. Consequently, *ḥudūd* can only be found in the Holy Qur'an and nowhere else, such as in the Prophetic Tradition. This is expressly set forth in the Qur'an, in Verse Q4:14: "*But those who disobey God and His Apostle and transgress His limits will be admitted to a Fire, to abide therein: And they shall have a humiliating punishment.*"[71] It is very important to note the syntax in this verse. While it expressly mentions punishment of those who disobey God and the Prophet, when it comes to transgression of *ḥudūd* the reference is solely to the limits imposed by God because the Prophet is not empowered to impose *ḥudūd*. This is a confirmation that the *ḥudūd* are set by God only and no one else. A further clarification is needed: the concept of *ḥudūd* is not limited to criminal law and family law. It applies generally to most of God's commandments included in His Message. Indeed, in Verse Q9:97 He says: "*The Bedouins are more stubborn in unbelief and hypocrisy, and apter not to know the bounds of what God has sent down on His Messenger; and God is All-knowing, All-wise,*" where the term "bounds" is the rendition of the term *ḥudūd*.[72] This is a clear indication that God has framed His Message in the form of flexible guidelines, which in turn are framed in ranges within limits, as opposed to specified laws.[73]

This proper understanding of the term *ḥudūd* should fundamentally change our understanding of a substantial part of Shari'a. Instead of dealing with fixed and immutable rules, Shari'a becomes an open body of principles, flexible enough to adapt to change, as expected from a universal body of guiding principles valid for different times and places. Shari'a thus has the built-in power to evolve, adapt, and lead progress. On that basis, and in light of the true meaning of the term *ḥudūd*, the penalty of amputation of the hand should be understood as an upper limit for punishment of the crime of theft—to symbolically eliminate the tool of theft—and the share of a woman being one half that of the male in the allocation of a deceased person's estate is a minimum reserved share.

All other provisions in the Holy Qur'an are legally neutral, in the sense that they neither impose obligations nor set up prohibitions. Yet, many rules of law and a myriad of restrictions have been unduly imposed under Islamic law, for the simple reason that they appeared in the course of some story in the Qur'an. One needs to be careful not to attribute mandatory effect to expressions or statements, or simply to stories told or expressed in a narrative tone. An obligation must be phrased as one, and its underlying universal message must be detachable from its local social context.

Because traditional Islamic *fiqh* considers Islamic law as an embodiment of Shari'a, and deems Shari'a as a joint product of the Qur'an and Prophetic Tradition, Shari'a came to be confused with Islamic law. While the finality of the Qur'anic text, in itself, could not bring any serious harm to the evolution of Islamic law, the perceived immutability of the Prophetic Tradition and its binding nature had a far greater adverse impact. It resulted in Islamic law crystalizing in its early iterations of the first few centuries of Islam, preceding the closure of *ijtihād*. In fact, the Qur'an contains only general principles and relatively few detailed rules. Had it been treated as the sole source of Shari'a, the jurisprudence could have, despite the finality of its text, devised a theory for the evolution of the rule of law. Unfortunately, not only was Prophetic Tradition treated as divine revelation and elevated conceptually to the level of the Qur'an, but for all practical purposes, it became treated as a primary source of Islamic law, often to the exclusion of the Holy Qur'an itself.[74] A number of reasons led to that unfortunate situation.

First, the Qur'an, as a divine text revealed in the Arabic language, remained for a very long time inaccessible to the majority of believers,[75] that is, to the Arabic-speaking believers who did not have the opportunity to memorize it, until they could lay their hands on a hand-copied, and later a printed, edition of the Qur'an; and to non-Arabic-speaking believers, until the first translations started making their way to the non-Muslim world.[76] Second, believers often felt a certain fear arising from the Qur'an's being the sacred word of God. To alleviate that fear, they turned to books of exegesis and compilations of the Prophetic Tradition, in spite of the subjective nature of the former and the lack of authenticity of the latter. In addition, Prophetic Tradition covers a wider range of issues, in greater detail, than in the Qur'an, and it is generally perceived as the embodiment of the scriptural commands.

In light of this outline of the general categories of Qur'anic rules included in the Shari'a, it can safely be said that Shari'a is not a legal system. Similarly, while there is only one Shari'a that is divine, there can be several sets of Islamic laws covering the same subjects in different manners, all of which are human-made and compliant with Shari'a.[77] Except for very few verses dealing with domestic relations and certain specific criminal acts which are phrased in the form of *ḥudūd*, none of the Shari'a rules are phrased in straightforward legal language. God wanted Shari'a to be universal, like the rest of the Message of Islam of which it is a principal component. On that basis, any interpretation of Shari'a as a legal system in fact obstructs Islam's universality. The most important consequence of Shari'a being universal is that it can, in all times and places, serve as a strong and sound basis for the enactment and updating of legal systems adapted to their particular environments. Thus while Shari'a is immutable, following the immutability of its divine origin and nature, Islamic laws which are enacted by secular human legislation are not immutable and must be updated from time to time to address changing human needs.

In retrospect, the failure to perceive Shari'a as such is what ultimately explains that legal systems, wrongly called Islamic law, lag so much behind modern legal systems and impede the progress of Islamic societies. On this basis, it can be appreciated why secular legislation is the most appropriate tool to give effect to the noble principles of Shari'a whose universal nature can in every place and age lead progress.[78] In Verses Q4:17 and 18, we are told:

> *Verily, God's acceptance of repentance relates only to those who do evil out of ignorance and then repent before their time runs out: and it is they unto whom God will turn again in His mercy—for God is all-knowing, wise; (17) whereas repentance shall not be accepted from those who do evil deeds until their dying hour and then say, "Behold, I now repent"; nor from those who die as deniers of the truth: it is these for whom We have readied grievous suffering (18).*[79]

With such specific injunctions from God, humanity has no choice but to heed His advice and legislate for such crimes, in such a manner as to give full opportunity for perpetrators to repent. This is indication that Shari'a and its verses were intended to be not a legal system but a sacred body of guiding principles for all times, where reward and punishment must be commensurate with the requirements of each time.

A Retrospective of Certain Sectors of Shari'a

As certain sectors of Islamic law have been codified, they are practically considered to be an embodiment of Shari'a, possessing all the sanctity of divine law. This is the case with family law and contracts law. Other sectors which did not find their way into formal codes continue nevertheless to receive approval by the four major schools of *fiqh*. The provisions compiled by *fiqh* schools are often recognized to be as binding as those that are codified and implemented as such. This is the case with criminal law in certain countries which apply the corporeal punishments set forth in the *fiqh* books. These and other provisions have recently started being introduced into modern legislation, including the rules governing so-called "Islamic banking."

Here we will attempt to address a few of the issues which we believe are most typical of Islamic law in people's minds. The purpose is to demonstrate that these issues, in most instances, are more reflective of customs and traditions than of Shari'a and Islam.

Family Law

John Esposito and Dalia Mogahed rightly observe, "[f]amily law is viewed as the 'heart of the Shari'a' and the basis for a strong, Islamically oriented family structure and society."[80] That perception indeed exists and was reflected in the responses of a large cross-section of people around the world in connection with a widely conducted poll cited by Esposito and Mogahed. However, it is important to remember that family law is the sector *par excellence* through which the Qur'an sought to change and reverse tribal laws and prejudices.

Under family law, one mainly finds the subjects of domestic relations, namely the provisions applicable to marriage, divorce, and raising children; and inheritance of a deceased person's estate. With respect to domestic relations, Shari'a is stigmatized with the perception that Islam is the religion of polygamy, divorce at will through simple pronunciation thereof by the male, and other features arising from a chauvinism entitling males at their sole discretion and with total impunity to freely use, abuse, and dispose of their wives, daughters, and female slaves. With respect to the rules of inheritance applicable to allocation of a deceased person's estate, Islamic law is characterized by the prohibition of making wills in favor of an heir, the nonadmission of a non-Muslim person to inherit from a Muslim deceased person, the inability of the descendants of a person who died before the person whose estate is being distributed to receive the share that would have otherwise been allocated to their ascendant had he remained alive, etc.

In this section, we will deal with issues relating to the rules of inheritance and estate allocation. Issues of domestic relations will be discussed, together with a review of relevant Shari'a provisions and their implementation, in Chapter 14 which addresses gender equality in Islam within the overall context of human rights.

To start it is important to affirm that all issues of domestic relations and inheritance are of a purely secular nature. Indeed, in Islam, even the marriage contract itself and related customary ceremonials, howsoever celebrated, are entirely secular acts.[81] Unlike the marriage celebration in the Christian faith which is considered a sacrament requiring the intervention of a priest, marriage in Islam is an ordinary, secular contract. It is a private contract, like any other contract, which is concluded between two persons, a male and a female, who are of legal age. That contract is concluded with the mutual consent of the two parties, the bride and the groom. There are no specific ceremonial formulae to be pronounced by either party to conclude that contract. The contract of marriage, as a private contract between the bride and the groom, can include any terms and conditions that the two parties may wish to introduce to it, and such terms and conditions are binding on both parties, unless they are of a nature which is inconsistent with the essence of marriage.

As a secular contract, marriage does not require the intermediation, or any form of intervention, by a cleric or shaykh or other religious person. All that is required is that the contract be authenticated by the presence of a certain number of witnesses. Even that particular requirement has no religious bearing other than to confirm that the marriage has taken place and the terms upon which it was concluded. Accordingly, if a different method of authentication can produce at least the same level of certainty as that provided through a required number of witnesses, then the marriage contract concluded with that alternative method of authentication should be valid, as if it was witnessed in the manner set forth in the Shari'a. On that basis, when the Republics of Turkey and Tunisia secularized their legal systems, the local secular legislations that they enacted providing for an entirely secular form of marriage were not, by the mere fact of being secular, offensive to Shari'a. Thus, voices which from time to time oppose the secularization of family law in countries that maintain the requirement for religious celebration of marriage are often voices of the religious establishments who stand to lose influence over the day-to-day lives of Muslims.

With respect to the rules governing inheritance through the disposition of deceased peoples' estates, unlike what is affirmed by *fiqh* and the Islamic Shari'a courts in nations which apply Islamic law in whole or in part, there is no provision anywhere in the Shari'a which precludes transmission of wealth by inheritance to non-Muslim relatives and heirs. Traditionally, Muslim men married to non-Muslim women have sought to allocate to their wives, by way of a will, a share in their estates at least equivalent to the share that a Muslim wife would have received.

On the other hand, all the rules providing for specific allocations of shares in an estate among the various members of the immediate and extended families are expressly termed as *ḥudūd*. What that means is that, contrary to the now generally accepted interpretation consistently applied, this allocation is not intended to be a final allocation, universally and mandatorily applicable at all times and in all places. This is indicative of the divine purpose of getting into that specific level of detail. The divine purpose of getting into the detailed allocation mechanism is to operate a social change and modify reprehensible tribal customs and traditions that were unfair and discriminatory. Indeed, in the tribal system, inheritance went almost invariably to the male descendants and ascendants of the deceased person, and often it went to the eldest male descendant if there was one, to the exclusion of his younger brothers. This was the case because the eldest male descendant became the chief of the family and thus became the heir as well to the responsibilities and obligations toward the rest of the family. This explained that all the wealth went to the person who would assume the obligations and liabilities of the deceased person.

Furthermore, the tribal society of Arabia was essentially a male dominant society where no meaningful rights were recognized for the female population of the tribe. That female population was perceived as a source of risk because, if a female person were to be involved in any attack or other dispute, shame would befall on the entire tribe and could lead to bloodshed to cleanse that shame. This explains why very stringent restrictions were imposed on females of that society which prevented them from taking care of their own lives, in return for which the male population was made responsible for doing it on their behalf and for them.

With this background in mind[82] it is easier to understand why the Qur'an qualified these allocations as *ḥudūd*. Indeed, it wanted to set a minimum share that female heirs would receive despite any consideration to the contrary. However, because the Qur'an wanted a sure process that would lead to full recognition of female rights, it did not break entirely with the tribal customs and traditions that it sought to modify and abolish. Instead, it phased in the rules of fairness and justice so that, in time, achievement of the stated divine purpose could take place gradually. It is for that purpose that the male ascendants and descendants were made the residual heirs after securing the minimum share for the female heirs. Here too, if the secular legislator decided to raise the allocations above the stated minima so as to establish full gender equality, or to reallocate the shares as to include other heirs that are as deserving of a share in the inheritance, such action would be favorably perceived from the perspective of fulfillment of divine purpose.

Still on the subject of inheritance, substantially the share allocations in an inheritance are grouped in three verses following the method of case law with numeric fractional allocations.[83] For that purpose, the *fiqh* developed a mechanism for disposing of unallocated shares in cases where all the fractions allocated to existing heirs would, when added together, exceed or fall below one hundred percent of the estate. In the first instance, the case of excess, all allocations are reduced on a pro-rata basis (*al-'awal*) by the excess amount. In the other instance, that is, when the combined allocations fall below the entire estate, all allocations are increased on a pro-rata basis (*al-radd*) so as to make up the shortfall. This mechanism is not provided for in the Qur'an and has been developed by *fiqh* by applying best judgment. Yet, with time, that mechanism, together with all other mechanisms, rules, and principles developed by the jurisprudents of *fiqh* for estate allocation, were sacralized as they became part of Shari'a. As a result, the distinction between what is divinely revealed and what is humanly constructed became blurred.

From our vantage point now it can be seen that the *fuqahā'* of the early few centuries of Islam found it suitable and acceptable to devise these adaptations without any idea that these adaptations would one day be elevated to the rank of, and be made a part of, Shari'a. There is no reason why today's *fuqahā'* should not be able to do for our time and age the same as their predecessors so wisely did for their time. In this light, it should not be deemed un-Islamic if, as necessary and consistent with the divine social purpose of revelation in the field of domestic relations and inheritance, the principal divine messages underlying the specific allocations are extracted and used to design a comprehensive body of laws suitable for diverse times and places. This is the essence of the secular nature of Islam.

Another typical example of human interpretations wrongly finding their way into the scope of the immutable divine Shari'a is the ban on wills made in favor of heirs. In spite of the Qur'anic provisions which specifically favor and encourage people to organize the disposition and transmission of their estates prior to their death through writing wills, *fiqh* has found a way to ban, except for limited purposes, the validity of wills. According to the *fiqh*, a person may establish a will in which he or she may dispose of up to one-third of the estate, and then only to persons who otherwise would not be among the heirs. What that means is that no one may modify the legal allocation of shares in the estate among the heirs, but that the amount to be distributed among the heirs may be reduced by up to one-third if the deceased person had left a will in favor of a person who is not a listed heir. These rules, which are nowhere to be found in the Holy Qur'an, are said to be derived from Prophetic Tradition, namely the following statement of the Prophet: "No person may establish a will in favor of an heir."[84]

The Holy Qur'an expressly provides for the writing of wills. It even favors such practice and encourages every person to do it, almost in a mandatory tone, suggesting that the poor be included as beneficiaries.[85] Verse Q2:180 states: "*It is prescribed, when death approaches any of you, if he leave any goods that he make a* bequest to parents and next of kin*, according to reasonable usage; this is due from the God-fearing.*"[86] Then, immediately following, Verse Q2:181 confirms the importance and sanctity of the will and offers the following clarification: "*If anyone changes the bequest after hearing it, the guilt shall be on those who make the change. For God hears and knows (All things).*"[87] These two verses are unequivocal about the validity, and even the advisability, of making wills in favor of heirs, since the parents and the next of kin— namely the siblings and children—constitute the first line of entitlement among the heirs. This understanding is further confirmed in Verses Q4:11 and 12, which specify the allocations of shares in the estate, where each allocation is specifically indicated to be calculated from the assets remaining after payment of the outstanding debts of the deceased person and after giving effect to any will that he or she may have left.

In light of the unequivocal sanctity of wills evidenced in clear terms in the Holy Qur'an, it becomes unnecessary to accept the interpretations of the early-days exegetes who considered that Verses Q2:180 and 181 (which set forth the sanctity of wills) had been abrogated by the Prophet's tradition that wills may not be made out to heirs, and by Verses Q4:11 and 12, and Q4:176 (which set forth the allocation of shares in the estate among the heirs, thereby negating the relevance of a will). These arguments are not plausible. First, we have already established that divine words represented in the verses of the Holy Qur'an could not be abrogated by human action represented by Prophetic Tradition. Second, we have also established that there are no provisions in the Holy Qur'an that are not operative because they have been abrogated by other verses. Instead of risking the associative suggestion that the Prophet, a human being, can alter the word of God, it is more relevant and convincing to perceive the Prophet's prohibition of making wills in favor of heirs within the overall importance and role of Prophetic Tradition as a guiding example in *ijtihād* and jurisprudence based on the true purpose of Revelation, which can be found by extracting the underlying message from Qur'anic verses. In this case, the Prophet had a good reason to—and exercised wisdom when he did—decree the banning of wills in favor of heirs. By doing so, the Prophet was preventing males in a society which continued to be plagued by tribal customs from attempting to thwart the application of the newly enacted allocations of estates, in favor of reverting to the old allocations based on tribal male chauvinism. Therefore, that ban was only temporary, meant to prevent whatever actions could hinder the implementation of the newly established social order, until the new rules based on fairness, justice, and equity could gradually become part of the new way of life.

A major injustice in estate allocations was a result of another human interpretation of divine provisions. This is the interpretation of the term *walad*. Traditional Sunni Islam has consistently deemed that *walad* means the male descendant. On that basis, major injustices resulting from prevalent male chauvinism have been inflicted upon female descendants of deceased persons and their next of kin and have resulted in estates going to extended male relatives while depriving closer female descendants of their rights.[88] That is how, if a person dies leaving only female descendants, up to two-thirds of the estate only might go to the daughters and the balance to the nearest male kin. This unfair outcome is the result of an erroneous interpretation of the term *walad* appearing in the Qur'an as the male child. In fact, *walad* is a gender-neutral term which simply means a child, male or female. This interpretation is erroneous because a Qur'anic verse expressly indicates that *walad* is the generic term for a child who could be either a male or a female.[89] When the term *walad* is properly interpreted, these injustices would be substantially removed. However, it is worth mentioning that the Shi'i jurisprudence adopts the proper interpretation of the term *walad*, as a child without preassignment of gender, and that interpretation is the correct one. This explains why, in practice, often wealthy Sunni people with female-only descendants convert to Shi'sm solely to ensure that their daughters are not deprived of the part of their parents' wealth which would have otherwise gone to the male next of kin among the cousins or uncles.

Finally, we get to the last of the major flaws in the interpretation of the divine scripture which led to injustice, namely the deprivation of the descendants of a person who would have been among the heirs had he or she been alive at the time of death of the person whose estate is being disposed of. The most common and typical example is when an older person dies leaving children—say two—who are alive, as well as the family, namely the wife and children, of a third child who had died previously. Under modern legislation, the family of the previously deceased child receives one-third of the estate representing the share of their father had he remained alive when their grandfather died. However, in Islamic law, as currently practiced, the estate would be allocated among the two children then alive to the exclusion of the wife and children of the third child who had died previously. The injustice in this case lies in the fact that those who are most in need of support are the ones who are unjustly deprived of their fair share in the estate, while those who are presumably well established financially would receive their entire shares plus a pro-rata share of the share which should have been allocated to the family of third child. Here, too, this injustice is the direct result of a misinterpretation of the Holy Scripture.

This misinterpretation is the outcome of a literal reading, without any consideration of logic or fairness, of the first sentence of Verse Q4:11 *"Allah directs you concerning your* children*: for a male there is a share equal to that of two females."* In their reading, the jurisprudents simply assumed that the term "children" means children who are then alive, without any particular reason or other justification for that assumption. Then later on, as that injustice started unfolding,[90] jurisprudents of an extinct school of *fiqh* found a solution through an interpretation of Verse Q2:180,[91] cited above, whereby the deceased person, who has grandchildren whose parent had died before that person, is presumed to have made a will in favor of those grandchildren by the share which would otherwise have devolved to their parent. This solution was adopted by the Egyptian, Tunisian, and Syrian legislators when enacting their particular family law legislations.[92]

What the *fiqh* heritage brought us in centuries of compilations is a body of laws which no longer resemble the noble objectives of Shari'a and the principles set forth in the Holy Qur'an. In the words of Robert Bellah,

> Unfortunately, in accordance with the way Islamic law developed, it was the post-Quranic and not the Quranic provisions that became the effective precedents in Shari'a family law. While a family ideal of mutual respect and obligation between all family members continued to be enjoined as exemplary, in fact practices tending to undermine inner family equality and solidarity and elevate patriarchal arbitrariness were pronounced legitimate.[93]

Criminal Law

The *fiqh* jurisprudents have, with respect to criminal offences, classified the punishments into three categories: (1) *ḥudūd*, for the punishments prescribed for offenses which fall within the scope of divine public order; (2) *qiṣāṣ*, for punishments imposed in the interest of the victim, which can therefore be replaced by monetary compensation (or even be forgiven by the victim or his or her heirs); and (3) *ta'zīr*, for the penalties prescribed for misdemeanors which are not provided for in the Qur'an.[94]

In this section, we will address only the category of offences for which the capital punishment is prescribed according to the *lex talionis* (the Mosaic law of retaliation) and those for which *ḥudūd* are prescribed, because they stigmatize Shari'a with the perception that Islam is the religion *par excellence* of cruel, outdated corporeal punishments: capital punishment for murder, amputation of a limb for theft, flogging for adultery, and so on. That perception comes from two generally well-accepted and rarely challenged understandings, namely that *lex talionis* is an essential element of Islam, and that the corporeal punishments set forth in the Qur'an constitute sacred and immutable rules which remain eternally in effect.

In reality, these two *fiqh*-drawn perceptions should be challenged because they derive from human interpretations of the divine Scriptures, which miss the point. With respect to the *lex talionis*, it is true that this concept is unequivocally referred to in Verse Q5:45:

> *And We ordained for them therein a life for a life, an eye for an eye, a nose for a nose, an ear for an ear, a tooth for a tooth, and for wounds is legal retribution. But whoever gives [up his right as] charity, it is an expiation for him. And whoever does not judge by what Allah has revealed, then it is those who are the wrongdoers.*[95]

However, the interpreters overlooked the highlighted words "*for them*" appearing at the beginning of that verse which indicate to whom the *lex talionis* is ordained, namely the people mentioned in the immediately preceding Verse Q5:44:

> *Indeed, We sent down the Torah, in which was guidance and light. The prophets who submitted [to Allah] judged by it for the Jews, as did the rabbis and scholars by that with which they were entrusted of the Scripture of Allah, and they were witnesses thereto. So do not fear the people but fear Me, and do not exchange My verses for a small price. And whoever does not judge by what Allah has revealed then it is those who are the disbelievers.*[96]

As a result, when the provisions of Verse Q5:45 are placed in context, and are then read in conjunction with the provisions of Verse Q5:44, it becomes clear that the *lex talionis* was prescribed and ordained for the Jews (*Banu Isrā'īl*, the sons of Israel). That said, one might legitimately think that, since the Message revealed to Prophet Muhammad does not abrogate but reconfirms the previous divine revelations to God's prophets, including the revelations made to Moses in the Torah, the *lex talionis* would remain as binding in Islam as it is in Judaism. While the premise is certainly true, the corollary is not necessarily so. This brings us to the second misperception and misinterpretation of the divine Scriptures, namely with respect to the finality and immutability of the corporeal punishments set forth in the Holy Qur'an, in general.

As Muhammad Shahrour has noted in his groundbreaking study on Islam and the Holy Qur'an,[97] Shari'a in its divine law aspects is, unlike Mosaic Law, substantially characterized by *ḥudūd*, instead of the *lex talionis*. Shari'a thus provides people the flexibility to select their solutions in accordance with their needs and adapt them to their individual environments, while observing the limits set forth in the Shari'a.

Based on this premise and the premise that the Qur'an confirms the previous messages without abrogating them, we come to the following perception of Shari'a based on which the provisions of the Qur'an may be interpreted.

First, by reference to the *lex talionis* brought about by Mosaic law, a criminal offender should expect to be punished for the crime so perpetrated; and the perpetrator should think thoroughly before committing the crime, because the punishment can replicate the harm that he or she inflicts upon the victim.

Second, by reference to the concept of *ḥudūd* introduced by Islam, while the punishment of a crime should be commensurate with, and not exceed, the harm inflicted through the relevant criminal act, yet the actual punishment may be adjusted to take into consideration the circumstances of the perpetrator or those of the environment surrounding the perpetration of the crime.

Third, under both Mosaic law and Muhammedan law, the victim may be entitled to compensation, which he or she may renounce as an act of charity and pardon to the perpetrator.

Important conclusions may be drawn from this transition, over time, of the *lex talionis* into the legal conception of *ḥudūd*, that is, from a system where specific punishments are prescribed to a system where the punishment is stated in the form of a range within which flexibility is provided to select the appropriate level commensurate with the magnitude of the act and its circumstances.

From the perspective of judicial administration and maintenance of collective peace and harmony, the concept of basic justice is determined and confirmed, namely that of being responsible for one's own acts and paying for the sufferings of others resulting from one's actions. However, the punishment to be inflicted upon the criminal is not unlimited and at most can be similar to the harm that he or she inflicted on the victim. It is usually the case when the crime was premeditated. Yet, if the perpetrator did not premeditate his act or did not otherwise anticipate the extent of the harm so caused, these circumstances could be taken into consideration to reduce the punishment. Finally, whenever the punishment is ordained for the benefit of the victim—such as in the *qiṣāṣ* (retaliation) category of criminal acts—then the victim may, by way of a charitable act, waive it by pardoning that criminal act.

From the perspective of legislative science and evolution, the transition into the concept of *ḥudūd* brings out the most important rule and principle, one that has been and continues to be ignored. It is the principle that solutions of all kinds, including legal solutions, must adapt to changing times and places. In other words, the interpretation and implementation of Shari'a must, in adhering to its universal nature, evolve over time and space concurrently with social evolution.

When God revealed the concept of *ḥudūd* to His Prophet, Muhammad, He was not merely replacing one rule by another. He was sending a message to humanity that the rules that He reveals from time to time are universal, and for that purpose humanity must at all times make the best of them by consistently adapting them to changing times. That is why it is necessary to identify and extract the underlying general principle and message in each element of Shari'a, because only that general principle and message, as opposed to the immediate and external purport thereof, is adaptable to changing times. This dynamic is illustrated with two examples. The first, which deals with the crime of premeditated murder, exemplifies the adaptive implementation of the *lex talionis*. The second, which deals with the crime of theft, brings into focus the extent of the flexibility and the potentially unlimited array of options that the concept of *ḥudūd* brings in dealing with the criminal and the victim.

The crime of murder is dealt with in Verses Q2:178 and 179.

> *You who believe, fair retribution is prescribed for you in cases of murder: the free man for the free man, the slave for the slave, the female for the female. But if the culprit is pardoned by his aggrieved brother, this shall be adhered to fairly, and the culprit shall pay what is due in a good way. This is an alleviation from your Lord, and an act of mercy. If anyone then exceeds these limits, grievous suffering awaits him (178). Fair retribution saves life for you, people of understanding, so that you may guard yourselves against what is wrong (179).*[98]

Prior to the revelation, there was a tribal custom according to which, when a person from a certain tribe was killed or injured by another person from a different clan, the entire tribe would rise to take its revenge for its member and go out to chase, hunt down, and kill the murderer and any other person from his or her family and tribe that they could find. According to the lex talionis which came in a previous revelation, but was nevertheless kept partially in effect in the Muhammedan message, it is the murderer in person and no one else who must suffer the death penalty, irrespective of the gender or social condition of the murdered person. However, the Muhammedan message started by setting forth the principle that no person may be punished for the sins, crimes, or other faults of any other person.[99] Then Verse Q2:178 introduced the compensation as a potential substitute for revenge from the murderer whose level and amount are specified in light of local custom. For instance, if the victim was a free person, then the family of the deceased must be paid the relevant compensation amount corresponding to the customary price for blood money payable in connection with a free person. If the murdered person was a slave, then the blood money would be at the applicable rate payable in connection with the murder of a slave. On that basis, compensation thus appears as a means to preserve life, because it saves all the killing that may result from a vendetta by the family or clan of the victim to take their revenge. God is thus advising and encouraging humanity to seek compensation instead of retribution. Compensation could also be waived in whole or in part, depending on the will of the victim or his or her next of kin, but then we are in the domain of charity.[100]

As for the crime of theft, it is provided for in Qur'anic Verses Q5:38 and 39. While, indeed, the Holy Qur'an provides for the amputation of the hand of the thief, yet that punishment being a *hadd* (singular of *hudūd*) constitutes a maximum limit for the penalty. What that means is that the judge, who ultimately rules on the appropriate punishment, may exercise discretion in inflicting any lesser punishment, starting from nothing. The only limit though is that the punishment for theft may not exceed the amputation of the hand. For example, a theft may not be punished with amputation of two limbs, or by death. It can, however, be punished by a mere compensation commensurate with the value of the stolen objects. It can even be pardoned, as Caliph 'Umar did when he pardoned thieves who stole to feed their children in a year of famine and starvation. This interpretation is further supported by the provisions of Verse Q5:39. While Verse Q5:38 prescribes the *hadd* of amputation, Verse Q5:39 brings the following clarification: "*But whoever repents after his wrongdoing and reforms, indeed, Allah will turn to him in forgiveness. Indeed, Allah is Forgiving and Merciful.*"[101] God is thus advising to choose a penalty preferably below the prescribed limit so as to give a chance for the thief to repent.

Given this background, and since God has provided humanity with alternatives to tribal customs of revenge, and then has brought further options adapted to the time and place, God expects humanity to heed His example by continuing to advance the methods of Shari'a implementation in any manner, suitable for its time, which could provide a better administration of justice so as to ensure enhanced fairness, justice, and crime prevention.[102]

When God granted the victim's next of kin the rights of retaliation, His purpose was not to satisfy any vengeance feelings of that next of kin. Instead the purpose was only to prevent excessive revenge bloodshed arising from a collective tribal retaliatory punishment, and to replace it by a better option, namely to pacify the parties and encourage the victim's kin to pardon and accept a compensation. God did so mainly because there was no state apparatus to administer justice on behalf of the community. Going by the underlying purpose previously stated, the divine example that God provided us should constitute the basis for further advancements to be enacted by humanity universally, such as a state-organized administration of justice where the criminal gets his punishment and the victim and his or her next of kin get compensation. In particular, in the case of the crime of theft, the purpose of amputation of the hand of the thief is symbolically to eliminate the tool of theft and thus prevent the thief from stealing again.[103] That purpose could presumably be achieved if a state apparatus assumed the administration of justice and imprisoned and required of the thief some form of rehabilitation which would deter any potential future act of theft.

The same could be said of nearly all corporeal punishments divinely ordained. The most plausible conclusion is that, while justice, fairness, and peace—both individual and collective—are divine purposes, their implementation among people are secular endeavors that humanity must carry out, guided by the provisions of Shari'a and their express and underlying principles.

Islamic Banking

"Islamic banking" is a relatively recent institution which developed as a presumably legitimate opportunity to offer banking services on an interest-free basis, subject to certain do's and don't's set forth in the Holy Qur'an construed as prohibiting conventional banking activities. The divine do's and don'ts which have traditionally served to demonize conventional banking activities are those dealing with the prohibition of *riba*, or usury, namely Verses Q2:275 to 276, Q2:278 to 280, and Q30:37 to 39. To the prevailing jurisprudence, *riba* consists primarily of the remuneration paid for borrowed money over and above the principal amount. *Riba* was also extended to include the remuneration of idle funds.

A careful reading of the above verses reveals that the prohibition of *riba* came about in the context of setting forth the ideals for *ṣadaqāt*, that is, charitable acts, as opposed to loans in commercial transactions. In fact, *riba* is prohibited in connection with charity when lending aims to assist a needy person. In that case, seeking remuneration entails taking advantage of the hardship of that person. The charitable nature of the loan, as contemplated in the Holy Qur'an, is further confirmed in Verses Q2:245 and Q64:17. The subject of commercial loans was nowhere contemplated in these verses, or elsewhere in the Holy Qur'an.

Riba is not interest charged by commercial banks on loans in the ordinary course of business. If the remuneration on commercial loans was indeed prohibited, then so-called "Islamic banking," as nowadays practiced by Islamic banks, or as taught in courses on Islamic law, would be as reprehensible as conventional banking.

This prohibition should be understood in the geographic and historic context of the Revelation.[104] In the tribal environment of the Arabian Peninsula of the sixth century, tribesmen lived off trade, mainly between the peninsula and the Levant to the north, and between the peninsula and Yemen and Abyssinia to the south. Trading then was not financed by commercial loans. Traders and their partners used their own funds to conduct their businesses. Nevertheless, lending activities still existed, but they were confined mainly to noncommercial purposes. They were carried out by money lenders who lent money to people in severe need, taking maximum advantage of that need. In other words, people borrowed money only as a last resort, if they ran out of means to survive and feed their families and could not find someone to help them by way of charity. In their desperation people entered into expensive borrowing transactions which they could spend the rest of their lives laboring to pay off.

Loan transactions entered into between money lenders and people in need generally would share the following characteristics: (1) any such loan would be a consumption loan, the proceeds of which were used by the borrower to feed hungry dependents or repair a roof or pay another outstanding obligation; (2) as a consumption loan, it was a nonproductive loan; (3) the borrower of such loan, in dire need and out of desperation, was willing to accept any terms and pay any price to obtain the loan; and (4) the lender had every opportunity to take advantage of that situation and extract the best price before advancing the needed funds.

Based on this lending physiognomy and viewed in this context, *riba* becomes the exorbitant price extracted, under difficult, compelling circumstances, by unscrupulous money lenders from needy people.[105]

Several conditions must be met for a remuneration to constitute *riba*. The remuneration must be truly exorbitant so as to reach several folds the amount of the principal amount of the loan or the reasonable value of the relevant transaction. In Verse Q3:130, the Holy Qur'an describes *riba* in this way: "*O you who believe, do not exact usury, twofold and several fold. And fear God, so that you may prosper.*"[106]

The exorbitant price must have been specified by the party to the transaction advancing the funds or, in the case of a loan, by the lender exploiting the needful condition of his counterpart at the receiving end. This is what the Qur'an confirms in reference to the particular circumstance that Islam sought to prohibit, namely the practice of money lending of that time.[107]

The loan or other transaction under which funds are advanced to the person in need must consist of a charitable act, which implies that the recipient must be deserving of charity,[108] as set forth in Verses Q2:245 ("*Who is it that would loan Allah a goodly loan so He may multiply it for him many times over? And it is Allah who withholds and grants abundance, and to Him you will be returned*")[109] and Q64:17 ("*If you offer up to God a goodly loan, He will amply repay you for it, and will forgive you your sins: for God is ever responsive to gratitude, forbearing*").[110] Finally, the transaction, as far as the recipient of the funds is concerned, is nonproductive, such as in a consumption loan. This is what modern-day legal systems call "usury" and prohibit as such. In this light, *riba* is not limited to lending transactions. It extends to any transaction in which the remuneration paid to the person advancing funds is exorbitant and is obtained by way of extortion and exploitation, such as in a sale and purchase transaction, a leasing transaction, etc.

With this in mind, it becomes clear that *riba* is not about interest charged by banks and paid by borrowers on commercial loans, or interest paid by banks to their clients on deposited monies, or any other form of interest legally and legitimately charged and paid in the ordinary course of business.[111]

In historical perspective, Islamic banking as practiced nowadays, in reality, most often mirrors conventional banking. Transactions types have been tailor-made to achieve the same purpose of an ordinary loan transaction, while calling them something else, such as a sale and purchase transaction, or a leasing transaction by reference to Verse Q2:275.

One such common transaction, *murābaḥa*, is a purchase and sale agreement in which the purchase price is paid in installments, designed to cover the cost of the goods and the cost of money for the period of the installments. This transaction is an almost exact replica of a loan transaction, which carries substantially the same risks on each of the two sides of the transaction. It allows the so-called seller (who in reality is none other than a lender) to charge interest and exercise rights similar to those of a lender, and the purchaser (who in reality is none other than a borrower) to pay interest on the loan and assume obligations similar to those of a borrower.

The same can be said of a loan which takes the form of *ijāra*, or leasing transaction, where the item to be funded is leased, instead of being sold, to the borrower. Such type of transaction is often used by Islamic banks either as an alternative to a *murābaḥa* transaction or for asset refinancing where the bank buys the asset to be refinanced from the borrower and leases it back again. Here again the modalities are endless to replicate the terms of the conventional loan transaction that would have otherwise been entered into.

From a depositor's viewpoint and going by the criteria which characterize *riba*, it is hardly thinkable that a person who opens an account with a conventional bank and earns interest on deposits placed in that bank could be blamed for committing the sin of receiving *riba* on idle moneys. First, conventional banks never pay interest at exorbitant rates because their rates are based on, and are thus a function of, the cost of money on the financial markets. Second, the deposits that clients make into banks are productive because the banks use these funds in transactions that earn them a margin over the interest payable by them on deposits. Third and most importantly, the depositor could never be perceived as a lender to the bank trying to take advantage of the bank's need and inexperience.

Given all of the above, the claim that payment or receipt of interest on conventional loans or bank deposits constitutes per se the sin of *riba* can be refuted. The claim that conventional interest is different from the markup that Islamic banks receive under a *murābaḥa* transaction can also be rejected. Consequently, conventional banking is not *a priori* repulsive to Islam,[112] because if it were, Islamic banking as generally practiced to mirror transactions of conventional banking would be as reprehensible.[113] They are both founded on similar considerations and aim to achieve the same objectives, using different ways and transaction names. The fact is that what is prohibited is *riba* and not the lending transaction per se, because *riba* entails the pursuit of immoral results through immoral means.

Advocates of Islamic banking equate the return on funds which are not exposed to some risk of loss to the return on idle funds and consider it as *riba*. To illustrate, Shaykh Sobhi al-Saleh considers income earned from lending as a prohibited form of illicit enrichment, originating from an activity which promotes the existence of a class of lazy, unproductive people who sit idle, except for chasing after borrowers (sic).[114] This logic, which assumes that a loan is risk-free, derives from a lack of familiarity with the mechanics of lending transactions and the potential losses lenders often sustain in the ordinary course of business as a result of borrowers' defaults.

Similarly, and according to modern *fiqh*, bank deposits are deemed to be idle funds from the depositor's perspective, which render interest payable by the bank on deposits equivalent to *riba*. *Fiqh*, however, chose to ignore that the funds deposited in a bank account do not sit idle, because the bank acts as an intermediary by investing them in productive ventures from whose income the bank pays interest on the deposit. From that same perspective, the *muḍāraba* is another form of transaction that has been proposed for structuring deposits in Islamic banks. It is a form of transaction which substantially replicates quasi-equity investments, whereby a person entrusts funds to another, typically an active partner, under a silent partnership-type arrangement providing for a return based on revenue sharing.

This perception is based on the view that money has a social function and must be used productively for the benefit of society so as to contribute to its development. Therefore, money should not be left sitting idle. This social purpose of money is what explains that earnings from idle money are equated to *riba*. This is the perception of socialist-minded *fuqahā'* who advocate the repression of the personal interests of the individuals in favor of the interests of society, which are expected to take priority over any other interests. Such views have no foundation in the Scriptures, except through farfetched interpretations of verses taken out of context. Instead, they are founded on certain traditions attributed to Prophet Muhammad,[115] which are either fabricated like many prophetic traditions, as discussed earlier, or which were rendered in certain specific contexts which are no longer consistent with the twenty-first century. Essentially, there is nothing in the Holy Qur'an which requires or otherwise encourages a person to invest hard-earned funds in ventures in which that person has no knowledge or experience. Nor is there any requirement for risk-averse people to expose their earned assets to risk, or else renounce any opportunity to invest them productively on a relatively low-risk or risk-free basis. On the contrary, the Qur'an contains countless advice for people to spend wisely and avoid squandering their funds and avoid taking undue risks.[116] Any other interpretation would require the investor to take risks similar to those of gambling.

Most modern-day *fiqh* has failed so far to acknowledge and accept the evolution of the role of money from a mere instrument of exchange in a certain transaction into a commodity which itself may be the subject of transaction. As a commodity it has a cost, and interest payable on a loan, as well as the price or other form of remuneration payable under other transactions (such as a sale or leasing transaction) represent at least the cost of money, as a commodity. Similarly, modern-day *fiqh* has also failed to acknowledge the relevance and legitimacy of the fact that remuneration is typically commensurate with the extent of risk taken by the investor.

Unfortunately, modern-day thinkers continue to be blinded by old-time exegeses which generalize a prohibition, while they are fully aware of the specific purpose of that prohibition. For example and following the views of the thirteenth-century Ibn Taymiyyah, Shaykh Sobhi al-Saleh cites the reprehensible reasons for banning *riba*. But then he fails to draw the appropriate conclusions with respect to loan transactions in which those reasons are absent or other types of transactions in which those reasons are present.[117] In fact, modern-day transactions, and their motivations and functions in society and the economy, cannot be judged by reference to outdated social environments and practices.

When seen from the perspective of the true nature of each transaction, it becomes superfluous to treat conventional interest as *riba* or to strive to replicate the terms and objectives of conventional banking transactions through so-called Islamic instruments. Whether called *muḍāraba*, *murābaḥa*, leasing, purchase and sale, sale and lease-back, or any other name bearing the so-called seal of "legitimacy," all have the same religious value, as long as they pursue the same objectives.[118] It is best to view matters for what they truly are or represent and then render a judgment on their ethical and social value. On that basis, interest is *riba* if it is exorbitant and is extracted through exploitation of the dire need or inexperience of the borrower; and *riba* is *riba*, whether the underlying transaction is a loan, sale, lease, or any other transaction.

Based on the above, the following observation by Mahmoud A. El-Gamal acquires particular importance.

> By attempting to replicate the substance of contemporary financial practice using premodern contract forms, Islamic finance has arguably failed to serve the objectives of Islamic law (*maqāṣid al-Shari'a*): Wherever the substance of contemporary financial practice is in accordance with Islamic law, adherence to premodern contract forms (with or without modification) leads most often to avoidable efficiency losses, thus violating one of the main legal objectives that defined classical Islamic jurisprudence. Conversely, by focusing on Islamicity of contract forms rather than substance (in part to justify efficiency losses), Islamic finance has often failed to serve the economic purpose for which certain premodern contract structures were codified in classical jurisprudence.[119]

Economic Aspects of Shari'a

Jurisprudents have gone to great lengths to carve an economic system out of Shari'a, in terms of assigning divinely mandated social and economic functions to certain economic topics, such as personal ownership of assets, personal work and labor, emigration in pursuit of income for survival, earning a living, and spending of earned income.[120] This is how Islam is at times perceived as a comprehensive economic system that stands in between, but avoids the evils of, Marxism and capitalism.[121] In his efforts to portray the Shari'a as a comprehensive economic system, Shaykh Sobhi al-Saleh describes how Shari'a embodies elaborate principles which safeguard the rights of workers, namely the rights to take some rest, not to be abused, and to be remunerated adequately and promptly, among other such principles.[122] He also brings forward an elaborate theory about land acquisition by way of reviving and exploiting abandoned land. He further describes how that right to retain public land expires after three years if the holder fails to revive that land.[123] In this respect, he glorifies the action of certain caliphs which, in his opinion, opened the way to legitimize the nationalization of private properties for public purposes, including redistribution of wealth.[124] While such assumptions may or may not be valid objectives for good governance, they are nowhere to be found in the Holy Qur'an, and the author assimilates specific actions by rulers to religious dogma and makes them an integral part of Shari'a.

In reality, Shari'a cannot and should not be considered a comprehensive economic system in the same way as we consider it not to be a legal system. Yet, it embodies valuable moral and ethical principles about human rights and the function of wealth in individual prosperity and collective well-being, from which legislators may build secular economic systems that are suitable for diverse circumstances.[125]

It is from this perspective that the Holy Qur'an encourages the accumulation of wealth by legitimate means, yet enjoins the wealthy to set aside sufficient funds to assist those who are less fortunate and in need.[126] This is what the institution of zakat stands for. Indeed, the wealthy are enjoined, for their own sake, to avoid extravagance and squandering of wealth in spending, yet must pay zakat for the collective well-being. Thus, zakat appears as a levy on the fortunate for the common good. As such, it is mandatory, as opposed to mere charity, which is optional.[127] In other words, in the same spirit that wealth can be taxed under an ordinary system of law without such taxation being deemed as a restriction on human rights, Islam taxes wealth through the institution of the zakat.

Reforming Islamic Law

The *fiqh*-based iterations of Islamic law, which grew out of the minds of scholars from the major schools of jurisprudence of the early days, represented learned, progressive, and comprehensive efforts to build legal systems out of Shari'a. As such, they were successful in incorporating principles of Shari'a into legal systems for their time and place without any implication that such iterations could one day be construed as divine Islamic law and require specialists to converge periodically and endeavor to find loopholes to make meager, long overdue changes. But this is exactly what happened following the banning of *ijtihād* which resulted in the Islamic law, becoming "universal" and change-resistant. Over time, Islamic law gradually became an obstacle to progress.[128]

Recently voices have risen seeking change and proposing a fundamental overhaul of the Islamic legal system. Such voices were bold because they tried to expose the false sacralization of tradition and history. However, the overwhelming majority of reformers, including the boldest and most willing to advocate for reform, never doubted the existence of *the* Islamic law, that is, a unique, well-defined legal system, derived from—and embodying the Shari'a brought about by—Islam. This is the case with the reformers of the late nineteenth and early twentieth centuries, such as Imam Muhammad Abdu and Jamaluddin al-Afghani. It is also the case of more modern reformers, such as Abdullahi An-Na'im, who call for the modernization of Islamic law without challenging the concept of so-called Islamic law in the first place. By contrast however, and in addition to Muhammad Shahrour, Asaf Fyzee was among the few thinkers who called for removing the tag of legal system from Islam, asserting the individual nature of religion versus the public nature of law, which is enforced by the state.[129]

There is a basic difference between treating the provisions of Shari'a as a body of higher principles of morality and ethics versus as specific rules of law. In the latter instance, Shari'a becomes a unique code of law that needs lots of scrutiny to modify, whereas in the former case, multiple man-made secular codes can coexist which may be different one from the other, but whose common element is compliance with the general principles in question. If adopted, the secularist approach to legislating laws that are consistent with the principles of Shari'a should allow no limitations on the scope and horizons of reform. This should explain the difficulty in which modern thinkers who call for reform of Islamic law find themselves when they continue to perceive Islamic law as divine,[130] whether or not they demonize secularism. Fazlur Rahman, for example, asserts that because Islamic law is based on divine moral values, the entire structure of theology, morality, and law would collapse if the process of reinterpretation stops and as a result society stagnates or moves toward secularism.[131]

But any legislation which is enacted on the basis of these moral values is by definition man-made. In other words, man-made laws are secular in their essence. As such they may be changed, as necessary, reflecting changing needs. Thus the fear expressed by Fazlur Rahman is unjustified because the road of secularism, which is inherent in Islam, is the only available option for humanity to legislate for the progress and development of Muslim society, whether through reinterpretation or otherwise. Most importantly, there is no risk for the so-called structure of theology, morality, and law to collapse, because the universal nature of Islam is founded, in part, on the flexibility and adaptability of the principles of morality and the rules of law embodied into Shari'a.

It is ironic that *fiqh* may have, knowingly or inadvertently, contributed to the sacralization of human exegesis and jurisprudence. Yet, the same *fiqh* that strove to design general principles and mechanics for change and adaptation of Islamic law is living proof that Islam is secular and is not a legal system. In the end, and true to the divine purpose of human trusteeship, wisdom lies in continuous human review of best interests which lead to timely legislative changes as needed. Such changes should be made in a straightforward and direct way instead of using convoluted means that attribute those changes to God's governance.

In this respect, it is of interest to mention a certain attempt at designing a new modernist concept for Islamization which was initiated in 1981 by a group of Egyptian thinkers. That concept was translated on their behalf by Ahmad Kamal Abou al-Majd into a manifesto detailing the principles for the creation of a modern society from social, economic, and political perspectives.[132] While the proposed concept is not exactly a secular system, and while certain of its aspects may be challenged,[133] yet it constitutes a substantial qualitative leap forward toward a true universal perception of Islam as an engine of progress in several important respects. These comprise namely the realization that Islam is not a political system, nor a legal or economic system, but that it contains basic principles and rules of ethics and social justice capable of shaping any system that is relevant to a society, and able to deal with that society's own specific interests and lead its progress. Most importantly, the proposal advocates a primordial role for the mind, recognizes the legitimacy of a pluralistic society in which all citizens are equal regardless of their respective creeds, supports full recognition and enforcement of human rights, and encourages overcoming complexes about historic experience and imitation of the early Muslims so as to look substantially and exclusively at addressing the challenges of the times and the interests of the people, while keeping to Islamic values and principles.

In sum, the principles relating to governance in general, and to legal and economic relations among people in particular, are not part of any religiously mandated state or religiously sanctioned theory of state, nor of other religiously mandated legal and economic systems. These principles, together with other higher principles of ethics and morality, are included in the Qur'an by way of divine guidance to humankind in the exercise of the trusteeship and achievement of progress.[134]

Therefore, while there is not a single specific legal system called "Islamic law," there can be an infinite number of laws which can be deemed compatible with Shari'a. Authors, ancient and recent, have striven to establish the compatibility of Islam with all different types of government systems, and all economic and legal systems (communism, capitalism, socialism, etc.). So some found Islam socialist or communist, others sought to find it supportive of capitalism and free ownership of property. In reality, Islam is not a political system, not a legal system, not an economic system. It is a faith and a way of life based on higher principles and promoting freedom in every respect.

Chapter 10
Humanism and Individualism in Islam

"What my mother taught me, in drawing from the depths of the Islamic heritage, is the image of a man linked, to others, to nature and to life... I understood, thanks to her, that Islam was before anything a humanism."[1]
—Abdennour Bidar

Besides being a message conveying divine truths, Islam is a way of life consisting of a body of universal principles that serve to guide and enable the footsteps of willing and desiring humans in the path toward God. Contrary to many claims, Islam neither carries nor requires political and legal systems to explore that path, or to serve as a proper environment for striving toward the discovery of divine truths. Instead, it offers a Shari'a, a bundle of moral ethical principles and a value system which provide tools to guide humanity.

Unfortunately, many Muslims are confused about the proper scope of the idea that Islam is a set of universal principles, as opposed to a specified system of laws and preordained political structures. This confusion can be observed in the results of surveys of Muslim women around the world, reported and analyzed by John Esposito and Dalia Mogahed, according to which women are eager for freedom and self-confidence, but are shy about it and are not sure how much freedom they might claim without violating Shari'a rules and limits. This confusion betrays their unease with departing from old customs for fear of failing to comply with the perceived mandated way of life.[2] What was intended to be a humanistic and individualistic religion became codified over time into a rigid framework.[3]

As a value system and body of principles, Islam relies by necessity on an acknowledgment of the intimate nature of faith, freely expressed by each individual based on his or her own personal convictions. Divine transcendence can be felt only on an individual basis. Thus faith, as an individual discretionary choice, requires a free humanity that is entitled to the use of its critical mind so as to achieve conviction. Only then can humanity be held accountable on an individual basis, on each person's individual achievements and legacy and motivated by a person's free will and action. This explains why Islam is not a rigid, preordained social order organized as a political system and endowed with divine laws and rules, in that a collective organization and program are irrelevant to the intimate nature of faith.[4]

In this chapter, we will explore the extent to which Islam offers to the individual a way toward self-fulfillment based on the intrinsic value and worth of the human being, which will illustrate the scope of the humanistic nature of Islam. We will then explore the true meaning of jihad, as an expression of humanism, with a particular focus on the pacific nature of Islam, to dispel misunderstandings surrounding jihad as a sacred war or as a divine command to fight a sacred war.

The Scope of Humanism and Individualism in Islam

Definition

The religious and secular literatures include a wide range of definitions of the term "humanism," reflecting a range of religious, social, and political convictions. While the term relates to the worth of the individual human being as the ultimate maker of the individual's own well-being and destiny, it has been used and misused by thinkers from a wide spectrum of creeds to describe and justify those creeds. Thus we may read about religious humanism, Renaissance humanism, secular humanism, and others. In certain definitions, even atheism is cited as a prerequisite for humanism. For the purposes of this work, we will explore the humanistic aspects of Islam based on relevant scriptural evidence, as we attempt to articulate the framework set forth in the Qur'an for such humanism. We will also attempt to clarify the meaning of individualism in this context.

As a body of principles for a way of life, Islam is primarily concerned with the relationship between the individual and God, his or her Creator, in which are set forth, among other topics, guidelines for the worship of God, otherwise called in the Arabic language *'ibādāt*. Islam is also a framework for the establishment of harmonious relationships among the creatures of

God, including dealings with one another, which are called in the Arabic language *mu'āmalāt*. The first relationship, that of the individual and God, when successfully managed, culminates in the achievement of faith, or *al-īmān*. The latter, dealing with the relationship among individuals, is founded on acting in good faith and the performance of good deeds, or *al-'amal al-ṣāliḥ*. Both *al-īmān* and *al-'amal al-ṣāliḥ* constitute the two primary components of the Straight Path, or *al-ṣirāt al-mustaqīm*.

Considered from another perspective, Islam is concerned with *al-dunia*, or life on earth, as well as with *al-ākhira*, or the afterlife following the death of each individual. This is what is meant when Islam is referred to as a religion and way of daily life, or *dīn wa dunia*.[5] This perspective rejoins the previous one: the *'ibādāt* (guidelines for worship), as the primary tool for the management of the individual's relationship with God, is at the same time the guideline toward that individual's final achievement in *al-ākhira* (the afterlife); the *mu'āmalāt* (relationships among people) deal with the individual's performance in this life, or *al-dunia* which, in turn, provides the main record for conducting the Final Judgment process in the *al-ākhira*. In either case, humanism and individualism are of the essence of the Message of Islam.

From the perspective of *al-īmān*, or faith, the relation between the individual and the Creator is a direct, unmediated, relationship. Except for a few specified acts of worship which are performed based on general rules, everything else in that relationship is unscripted and entirely personal between each individual and God. To that purpose, a relationship is most sincere and genuine when it emanates from the individual's own understanding of the Message and convictions, following his or her own script deemed most conducive to successful communication with God. This explains several key aspects of the Qur'an: (1) God addresses each person individually in the direct form "*ya ayyuha-n-nās*" (O people), and not through clergy or other learned erudite; and (2) God judges each person individually based on that person's own convictions rather than on collective convictions formed by elders.

Islam is the *dīn al-fiṭra*, or religion of simplicity. *Fiṭra* also means simplicity of understanding, and this is the Islamic version of that concept.

Thus, *fiṭra* can be perceived as an innate predisposition leading to the knowledge of God. God already created us with the qualities we need for relating to Him. That is why His prophets, including Muhammad, came to us in succession so as, among other purposes, to act as reminders (*mudhakkir*)[6] and so their messages might serve as remembrances.[7]

From the perspective of *al-'amal al-ṣāliḥ,* the performance of good deeds in dealings among individuals, the Holy Qur'an does not provide any specific scripts. It does provide for general principles and moral values which serve to justify good actions and provide the incentive to perform them. Each of such relations among people is unique, because each individual is unique and relations are not divinely prescribed. By contrast, in many of the ancient references in the fields of *fiqh* and Prophetic Tradition a great number of relations are scripted and labeled as being Islamic or un-Islamic. Here too any prescribing assumes an imposition of specific interpretations on others, let alone usurping God's judging prerogatives so as to predetermine what His judgment will be. Alija Izetbegović makes an interesting connection between *īmān* (faith) and *al-'amal al- ṣāliḥ* (good deeds) when he observes that what characterizes Islam is the idea that faith must be coupled with action. For that purpose, *īmān* is implemented primarily by way of performance of the five daily prayers, and *al-'amal al-ṣāliḥ* is implemented primarily by way of imposition of the zakat (or the obligation to pay alms).[8]

Both relationship tracks, namely the track of the individual relationship with God and that of relations among individuals, are thus reliant and founded on humanism and individualism. In the first instance, the relationship with God is entirely free on the part of the individual, in the sense that each person is free to establish and maintain his or her own relationship with God through faith. God so decided in the Holy Qur'an, in Verse Q18:29: *"And say, 'The truth is from your Lord. Now, whoever so wills may believe and whoever so wills may deny.' Surely, We have prepared for the unjust a fire, whose tent will envelop them."*[9] This is also stated in Verses Q73:19 and Q76:29: *"VERILY, all this is an admonition: whoever, then, so wills, may unto his Sustainer find a way,"*[10] among many other verses.

One might question the genuineness of a freedom of faith that is coupled with a resounding threat against those who fail to believe. But for those who do not believe, the threat is irrelevant; and for those who believe, their choice is necessarily an individual, responsible choice.

Because freedom of faith is individually exercised, God has instituted, in unequivocal terms, the principle of individual accountability in Verse Q17:15: *"Whoever adopts the right path does so for his own benefit, and whoever goes astray does so to his own detriment, and no bearer of burden shall bear the burden of another, and it is not Our way to punish (anyone) unless We send a Messenger;"*[11] and also in Verse Q45:22: *"And Allah created the heavens and earth in truth and so that every soul may be recompensed for what it has earned, and they will not be wronged."*[12] Accordingly, on the Final Day there will be no collective judgments; no one will pay for the sins of others. If Islam did not recognize individualism and humanism, then God would have resorted to collective judgment. Yet, He decreed only individual judgments. In this respect, despite the fact that the Qur'an contains certain stories of collective punishments of peoples past, yet the principle of individual accountability was not breached because these same stories make it clear that people who were undeserving of punishment were saved.[13]

Concerning relations among individuals, God only asked for people to perform good deeds, without giving a definition or providing examples of what constitutes a good deed. He did, however, set forth in the Shari'a some guiding principles to be followed by humans in order to achieve good deeds, and those principles do not need to be learned or taught by specialists. They are innate in every individual's humanity, as part of *fitra*.[14] If people speak kindly to their brethren, deal justly with them, abstain from cheating, hurting, or doing anything that causes harm to them, and practice forgiveness, their actions are bound to be good deeds. In this sense, Islam gives to each individual the opportunity to fulfill his or her humanity to its maximum limits, without any restrictions.

Finally, until the Final Day, with faith and good deeds, humans will have the entire freedom which God gave them to fulfill themselves and apply their potential in the achievement of their aspirations that they may freely set for themselves, or in proceeding onto the straight path. In either case, God did not prescribe the behavior of people, but instead He granted them freedom of choice and action, and held them accountable for their actions and relations.

Human Dignity and the Essence of Islam

Human dignity, which constitutes the foundation and pillar upon which humanism is built, is of the essence of Islam. It is true that God created the human being from human clay and "despised" water,[15] as many exegetes have often repeated to demean humans, stress their subservience, and conclude about their worthlessness. Yet, God made sure to dispel such implications and conclusions by stressing the perfected proportions and beauty that he applied in His creation, as set forth in Verse Q40:64: "*Allah it is Who appointed for you the earth for a dwelling-place and the sky for a canopy, and fashioned you and perfected your shapes, and hath provided you with good things. Such is Allah, your Lord. Then blessed be Allah, the Lord of the Worlds!*"[16] and Verse Q64:3: "*He has created the heavens and the earth in just proportions, and has given you shape, and made your shapes beautiful: and to Him is the final Goal.*"[17]

He even breathed His own divine spirit into humans in order to emphasize the honors that His human creatures deserve, as witnessed in Verses Q38:71 to 74.

> *Behold, thy Lord said to the angels: "I am about to create man from clay (71): When I have fashioned him (in due proportion) and breathed into him of My spirit, fall ye down in obeisance unto him." (72) So the angels prostrated themselves, all of them together: (73) Not so Iblis: he was haughty, and became one of those who reject Faith (74).*[18]

Most important of all, He bestowed on humans, by preference to all other creatures, a mind to ponder and senses to enrich that mind, and He gave Adam a thorough education by teaching him the nature of things, as set forth in this series of verses.

> Q2:30 to 34—"*Behold, thy Lord said to the angels: 'I will create a vicegerent on earth'. They said: 'Wilt Thou place therein*

one who will make mischief therein and shed blood?—whilst
we do celebrate Thy praises and glorify Thy holy (name)?' He
said: 'I know what ye know not'. (30) And He taught Adam the
nature of all things; then He placed them before the angels,
and said: 'Tell me the nature of these if ye are right'. (31)
They said: 'Glory to Thee, of knowledge We have none, save
what Thou Hast taught us: In truth it is Thou Who art perfect
in knowledge and wisdom.' (32) He said: 'O Adam! Tell them
their natures'. When he had told them, God said: 'Did I not
tell you that I know the secrets of heaven and earth, and I
know what ye reveal and what ye conceal?' (33) And behold,
We said to the angels: 'Bow down to Adam' and they bowed
down. Not so Iblis: he refused and was haughty: He was of
those who reject Faith (34)." [19]

Q17:70—*"NOW, INDEED, We have conferred dignity on the*
children of Adam, and borne them over land and sea, and
provided for them sustenance out of the good things of life,
and favoured them far above most of Our creation." [20]

Q32:9—*"Then He gave him a proportioned shape, and breathed*
into him of His spirit. And He granted you the (power of)
hearing and the eyes and the hearts. Little you give thanks." [21]

To confirm the worth and honor that He bestowed on humanity, God
appointed humanity to be His trustee on earth, and ordered the angels
to prostrate to Adam in witness of such honor and achievement, all as
witnessed in Verse Q6:165: *"It is He who made you the vicegerents of the*
earth and raised some of you in ranks over others, so that He may test
you in what He has given you. Surely, your Lord is swift in punishing, and
surely He is Most-Forgiving, Very-Merciful." [22] This is also confirmed in
Verses Q15:26 to 31.

Indeed We created man from a ringing clay made of decayed mud (26). As for
the Jānn (the first Jinn), We had created him earlier from the fire of the scorching

wind (27). Recall when your Lord said to the angels, "I am going to create a human being from a ringing clay made of decayed mud (28). When I form him perfect, and blow in him of My spirit, then you must fall down before him in prostration (29)." So the angels prostrated themselves, all together, (30) except Iblīs (Satan). He refused to join those who prostrated (31).[23]

With this in mind, one can better assess the rebuttals of humanism's exaltation of the "purely human potential." They cite for that purpose Qur'anic verses about the vile evolution of humans from sperm which, presumably, is inconsistent with any dignity and with any potential for self-fulfillment beyond the bounds scripted by God for each individual.[24] Such a conclusion is unwarranted because, when these verses are put in their proper context, their meaning and intent are entirely different. These verses came in the context of responding to those who rejected the existence of, and allege the lack of need for, God. The message to them was that, if God had the power to control the beginnings of humanity by way of creation even from vile origins, would He not have at least similar powers to control the end. Such claims are generally made by atheists who reject God altogether and hence do not wish to believe, and have no interest in whether or not humanism is compatible with religion, or the nonexistent.

The same can be said of other claims made by Islamists that humanism is inconsistent with divine governance and with verses of the Holy Qur'an which seem to denigrate humanity and to deny humans their dignity.[25] Such objections forget that only God is perfect and that everything else is imperfect. Thus, though created with a nice image and endowed with the breath of God's spirit, yet humankind is imperfect because it is not divine. Nevertheless, and despite the misgivings of the angels and the attitude of Satan, these failings did not result in disqualifying humankind from the honor of receiving God's trust, and God was not dissuaded from naming humankind as His trustee.

Humanism does not imply an independence from God, because the respective realms of God and humanity are not in conflict one with the other. Considering the place of humanism and human dignity in Islam and following a personal experience with a religious group in college, French philosopher Abdennour Bidar notes that the level of misery and unhappiness mounts the more a person rejects the imperfections of humanity and seeks instead to draw closer to the perfection of God. He criticizes widespread teachings about the futility of this life and its imperfections, which may impel a striving to reject human imperfections in order to draw closer to divine perfection. Bidar, instead, recalls that God has created humans "in a most noble image"[26] after having breathed in them through Adam His own spirit, named them as trustees, and asked the angels to prostrate before Adam, after having taught him "the nature of all things,"[27] in recognition of the stature of humankind. Bidar adds that God Himself gave humanity, what amounts to a lesson in humanism: He emphasized the worth of this life and of human nature with all the capabilities that He gave it to navigate between sin and virtue by incarnating Himself into the person of Jesus Christ. Bidar's essential message is that humans should not try to reject their humanity when God has chosen for Himself to live humanity through incarnation.[28] While Bidar's perception of the worth and dignity of humankind is impeccable, one could question the steps by which he arrived at this perception, through an unwarranted interpretation of the trusteeship as a full and final legacy of divine governance from God to humankind, including the transfer of His divine attributes.[29]

For Bidar, trusteeship is an evolutionary process which commenced with the initial creation and will continue until humankind achieves a certain degree of perfection and creativity through the gift of divinity derived from God's spirit. When that degree of perfection and creativity has been achieved, God will then hand over the legacy, that of divine governance. That theory goes on to affirm that, at such time, there will presumably be no further need for God, and humanity would achieve immortality. To Abdennour Bidar, this explains why God has announced the end of the series of prophecies which commenced with Adam, passing through Noah, Moses, and Jesus, among others.

With that interpretation of the trusteeship concept, Abdennour Bidar was attempting to establish that the Self-Islam that he advocates could be an Islam without submission to God, that is, an Islam in which humans have their own worth and dignity and are not stigmatized by subservience to God, as the only purpose for their existence in this life. According to this theory, when evolution has been collectively completed toward perfection and immortality, subservience to God becomes irrelevant because then God will have withdrawn entirely, and the paradise described in the Holy Qur'an will not depend on a prior death, resurrection, and afterlife, but will exist in this life.[30] Bidar reaches this conclusion starting with the analysis of the terms *khalīfa* and *khilāfa*, which he understood as a reference to a succession (as opposed to a form of administration function in a second-in-line role), a true succession;[31] and that succession could not be other than a succession to God, following which God would no longer be.

In response to Bidar's theory, "self-Islam," is already achieved. It has been so ever since creation. Self-Islam does not need to await the completion of humankind's impossible evolution to perfection, immortality, and divinity because each individual is entitled, at any time in its discretion, to freely fashion his or her faith using the mind. The concept of *khilāfa* is not necessarily about the legacy and inheritance of the universe, similar to the succession which occurs upon someone's death or disappearance. The concept of inheritance is expressed in the Holy Qur'an using the root term *waratha* and its many derivatives, such as *irth* and *mīrāth*. These terms were used in the Holy Qur'an primarily in the sense of God being the sole and ultimate heir of everything, earth and skies,[32] and in the sense of people succeeding to others and inheriting their own spaces on this earth.[33] Thus, if God declares himself as the sole and ultimate heir of everything, it means that He has made clear the eternal nature of divine efficacy. Moreover, God has also announced in Verses Q55:26 and 27 that *"Every one who is on it (the earth) has to perish (26). And your Lord's Countenance will remain, full of majesty, full of honour (27),"*[34] thus leaving no chance either that anyone will ever become immortal before reaching the afterlife. Until then, and as God has confirmed it in Verse Q2:255.

> ...*There is no god but He, the Living, the All-Sustaining. Neither dozing overtakes Him nor sleep. To Him belongs all that is in the heavens and all that is on the earth. Who can intercede with Him without His permission? He knows what is before them and what is behind them; while they encompass nothing of His knowledge, except what He wills. His Kursiyy (Chair) extends to the Heavens*

and to the Earth, and it does not weary Him to look after them. He is the All-High, the Supreme.[35]

As a result, the concept of *khilāfa* must have a meaning which is different from inheritance, consistent with the provisions of the Holy Qur'an which provide that the appointment and empowerment of humankind as *khalīfa* are not awaiting any evolution process, the same having taken place already ever since the initial act of creation. The concept of trusteeship then, by reference to modern legal concepts, is like a freehold where the title remains with God[36] and all other attributes of ownership pass on to humankind. These attributes remain indefinitely with humankind, for as long as there are humans alive. Thereafter, the legacy reverts to God as the sole and ultimate heir of the earth and skies. This explains that humans have been declared equal and granted the freedom to build, manage, enjoy, and dispose among themselves all that God has entrusted to them. Under that concept, the freedom granted to humankind is almost absolute. It is to be exercised in this life, in full dignity and without any implied submission. At the same time that freedom is exercised under divine governance and subject to ultimate accountability—on the Day of Judgment—for the quality with which trusteeship has been exercised by each individual. Thus, divine governance is about God making His Compassion available to humankind, offering guidance to—and answering the prayers of—anyone who so desires and asks. What in the end appears in Bidar's concept of "succession" as a postponed, potential freedom from subservience contingent upon the evolution of humankind toward presumed succession to God, is in reality—given the more reasonable understanding of the terms *khilāfa* and *khalīfa*—a true empowerment and attribution of freedoms contemporaneous with the act of creation. All subsequent evolution thus becomes the direct result of individual and collective human effort in performing the duties, and exercising the powers, of trustees, using the mind and senses with which God endowed humankind. This structure constitutes the framework for Islamic humanism within which humans can strive toward, and eventually achieve, self-fulfillment.

Faith and Humanism

Belief in God and humanism are not incompatible. God blessed each person with freedom, choice, and power. People use this empowerment and, at times, seek God's help and guidance in finding the straight path. Notwithstanding that God is the sole sovereign over the entire universe that He created, yet, in His infinite compassion and wisdom, God has divided the universe into two realms under His Governance: the realm of humanity concerned with life on earth and the realm of God. In the realm of humanity, human beings remain free in return for accountability and the acceptance of God's Final Judgment. This is the essential basis of the humanistic vocation of Islam.

The compatibility of humanism with Islam has been challenged by several authors on grounds that humanism is irrelevant to, if not inconsistent with, Islam because it assumed that God has ruled on every issue affecting humanity. In any event, humanity has no conceivable role in the presence of divine governance, because the life of every individual is predestined to the minutest details, from the time each person is born until he or she dies. Previously in this study, the claim that every aspect of life has been predetermined was disproven. It was argued that it is divine governance that prepared a way for the emergence of a humanism embracing the fullest potential of each person, when God empowered humanity as His trustee with full freedom to act, guided by accountability. Thus, arguments derived from the respective realms of God and Caesar in universal governance become unnecessary because the realm of humanity is attributed by God under divine governance.

Unnecessary, too, is the claim that since everything belongs to God and nothing belongs to Caesar, our human world is imposed from above by a nonhuman force and is thus not conducive to the fulfillment of a humanist ideal.[37] This viewpoint falsely equates Caesar and God, as if they shared the rule of this human world, forgetting that God created Caesar. Therefore, to give Caesar his due does not imply that such due must be withdrawn from the prerogatives of divine sovereignty. Though God is Almighty by virtue of his Oneness, He has delegated most governance on earth to humankind, His trustee, as He called Adam when He created him.

The ground is certainly not level between God and humanity, when one is the creator and the other is the creation, and where one is Almighty and the other has only such powers as the Almighty has bestowed on it.

But the essential point is that humanism does not require, nor should it imply, a competition between God and humanity, or some independence of humanity from God. The answer is found in a simple question: Can a person act in freedom to fulfill his or her humanity to the fullest extent? The answer is "yes," because that freedom, as a gift received from God by His design and with His fullest blessing, has become inherent in human nature by way of *fiṭra*. As such it is not interfered with by God throughout the lifetime of each individual, unless that individual prays for God's interference, or unless that interference comes by way of divine compassion to take him or her out of harm's way.

It is in this sense that the reference to the overwhelming intervention of God, *Allah-u- ghālibun* (God is predominant), referred to in the Qur'anic Verse Q12:21,[38] in the context of the tale of Yusuf (Joseph), should be understood. Indeed, this verse and the inscription in mosques about God's predominance are cited to cast doubts over the compatibility of humanism with Islam.[39] However, when placed in its proper context, what this verse refers to is that, by saving Joseph, God prevailed over the intentions of evil; He saved the good. So *Allah-u- ghālibun* means that God prevails over the forces of evil and, at times, He may intervene to save those who deserve it from evildoers. According to the Holy Qur'an, God intervened to enable Muslims win the battle of Badr. He also intervened to save Joseph, to vindicate Moses, and to protect Mary, among other examples. God's interventions, as ultimate sovereign, should be perceived from the perspective of preventing the forces of evil from depriving humanity of its potential for self-fulfillment. Seen from this perspective, God's dominance appears as an added guarantee and safeguard of humanism.

Practical Manifestations of Humanism

Humanism as a philosophy reflects a belief in the predisposition of human beings and their ability, through science as a product of the human mind and reason, to solve their own problems. For that, humans possess the ability, based on scientific reasoning and on freedom of choice and action, to shape their own destiny. The fulfillment of human potential to achieve the happiness, freedom, and progress of humankind is grounded in human values derived from, among other sources, earthly experiences and human relations. The potential to attain the good life can be realized by consistent hard work and self-development, with due regard for the collective welfare, and through appreciation of the beauty and perfection in nature. In order to provide an opportunity for individuals to realize their potential as human beings individually, and to prosper collectively, it is necessary for people to avail themselves of freedom of expression and civil liberties in all aspects of life—economic, political, and cultural.[40]

In addition to the general divine delegation of authority and sovereignty to humankind by virtue of the trust that God placed in humanity, the Holy Qur'an contains countless illustrations of the humanistic nature of Islam. The Holy Qur'an has, throughout the Message, made numerous appeals for the use of the mind and reason, a tool that God expects people to use in order to improve the conditions of their lives, through scientific research and discovery. Because human beings have been endowed with mind and with the physical ability to conduct their lives, God decreed that they shall manage on their own and that they shall reap results that are commensurate with their work, without reliance on any supernatural powers to provide assistance. They might pray to God, who might help or otherwise provide inspiration, but it remains that they have to count primarily on themselves and on no one else.[41] As a further corollary of being endowed with mind and reason, and as a counterpart for accountability in this life and the hereafter, people possess free choice. This free choice is a prerequisite to their entitlement to fulfillment of their humanity in this life. This explains, in part, the repeated divine injunctions in the Qur'an to set slaves free, so that they too may gain an opportunity to experience self-fulfillment as human beings. In the Holy Qur'an, each individual is repeatedly encouraged to reach out to others by going beyond simply fulfilling one's own duties and obligations, or giving and claiming one's own rights. God often encourages people to bring out what is best in human nature, such as to forgive (*'afuw*);[42] to be generous in giving to those that are in need and deserve help (*ṣadaqāt*),[43] which God equated to a favor to Him and thus treats it as a loan upon Himself;[44] to perform good deeds in dealings with fellow humans (*al-'amal al-ṣāliḥ*); and to be virtuous in claiming from, and giving to, others (*iḥsān*).

Al-'amal al-ṣāliḥ (good deeds) is the single most important requirement that God has placed on His trustees in managing their lives and relations with each other in this life, in exactly the same way that He made *īmān* (faith) the single most important vehicle toward salvation in the relations of humankind with God. The Holy Qur'an goes a step further to consider *īmān* alone to be insufficient for salvation; *al-'amal al-ṣāliḥ* is the other indispensable requirement for that purpose. This explains the very large number of Qur'anic verses in which *īmān* and *al-'amal al-ṣāliḥ* are cited together,[45] in tandem, as vehicles toward salvation. Thus *al-'amal al-ṣāliḥ*, which is primarily destined to deserve God's reward, could—when coupled with *īmān*—earn the ultimate reward on the Day of Judgment, that of eternity in paradise,[46] after conversion of bad deeds into good ones.[47]

It does not matter which Abrahamic faith one follows to achieve the *īmān* side of the equation, and *al-'amal al-ṣāliḥ* is an entirely human quality which is not primarily faith-related.[48] Moreover, eternity in paradise, being the ultimate reward for those who combine *īmān* with *al-'amal al-ṣāliḥ*, is a further proof that what humans do for their lives on earth is essential to attaining paradise. However, what an individual does in dealing with others could be more important than what that person does for God, because God is satisfied with belief in Him and does not need anything to be done for Him. In any event, God confirms that people who perform good deeds do so for their own sake and not for the sake of God or anyone else.[49] The Holy Qur'an does not specify what constitutes an act of *al-'amal al-ṣāliḥ*. It does, however, specify that good deeds are not measured in absolute terms. Instead, they are measured in accordance with the abilities of each person.[50] The Qur'an also cites that *iṣlāḥ,* or reforming what is evil or sinful, counts as an act of *al-'amal al-ṣāliḥ*.[51] *Iḥsān* is also particularly included in the category of acts qualifying as an act of *al-'amal al-ṣāliḥ*.

Iḥsān is an act of good will performed by one person toward another involving the renunciation of a right. *Iḥsān* taps into the highest human virtues of compassion[52] toward parents, close relatives, and people in need,[53] such as the virtues of charity and generosity,[54] forgiveness,[55] patience,[56] and most importantly, the noble behavior of countering an evil act from another person with a good deed.[57] *Iḥsān* is the human quality that is most favored and rewarded by God,[58] because humanity shares that quality with God,[59] who is the most compassionate, a further evidence of the spirit that God breathed into humankind upon creation. For this purpose, all persons who act with *iḥsān* deserve the love of God[60] and His manifold rewards,[61] including the reward of eternal paradise.[62]

The point to be made here about humanism being of the essence of Islam is that *iḥsān* is not promoted solely for the purpose of satisfying God and earning His rewards. The main purpose for promoting *iḥsān* is to secure the self-satisfaction of the individual and, from there, to secure harmony among humans. Therefore, it is not another duty to God whose benefits trickle to humanity. *Iḥsān* is primarily an act benefiting the individual who performs it, as well as benefiting that individual's fellow humans. It is precisely for this reason that God equates the acts of *iḥsān* to favors to Him, and treats them as loans upon Himself.

Humanism and Individualism

Humanism and individualism are not synonymous. Humanism is about the inherent worth and freedom of the individual as a human being, as well as about the human capabilities to achieve self-fulfillment based exclusively on the innate qualities of each individual, without reliance on supernatural powers. Individualism, for its part, is not about egoism, that is, the unchecked freedom of the individual to behave with impunity, in an abusive manner, to achieve self-centered objectives without regard to others. The individualistic aspect of humanism is concerned with a focus on individual freedom of action toward self-fulfillment, and the fulfillment of individual success and a good life, the rational counterpart of which is primarily individual accountability based on individual reason. It is from this recognition of the obligatory link between reason and freedom as God-given attributes to humankind that Islam can be appreciated as a religion that values individualism and humanism. Abdolkarim Soroush observes that because emotionalism breeds devotees, it is essential to foster independence of the mind as a means to preserve the integrity of the individual personality and freedom.[63] Indeed, devotees do not necessarily worship with conviction but by way of *taqlīd* (or imitation), whereas reason breeds true believers.

From this perspective, the common good is what is good for each individual in the community, as opposed to a preset common good which is different from, or comes at the expense of, the individual good. The collectivity and its interests are not different from the individuals who form that collectivity and their individual interests; it is individuality that breeds diversity and plurality.[64] Some thinkers have alleged, or perhaps simply assumed, that under Islam the collective interest of the community prevails over individual interests, and that each individual should, for the general benefit of the community, suppress personal interests that are inconsistent with the interests of that community.[65] Qur'anic verses are even cited to that effect. These verses are either taken out of context or their meaning is unnecessarily widened to include what is not intended. The immediate concern is to determine what the collective interest is and who sets that collective interest. This has been a wide door through which some rulers and clergy have sought to control people claiming the right and power to set those collective interests.

Bearing in mind that reward and punishment in Islam are based on individual, as opposed to collective, accountability,[66] each person must as a precondition of that accountability have the opportunity to freely interpret and understand the Divine Message, to freely decide if and how he or she complies with it, and to freely determine what his or her own interests are and how to pursue them.[67] The only limitations in that case lie in the need to preserve the freedom of every other individual in the community, and then the duty to observe any potentially restrictive laws duly adopted by that community to regulate their lives in common and balance their individual interests. From that perspective, the entire community benefits when each individual has an equal opportunity for self-fulfillment and the collective good naturally benefits every individual.

By contrast, in a truly humanistic environment, the virtues of *iḥsān* and *al-'amal al-ṣāliḥ,* goodwill and good deeds, constitute solid bridges—first, among the particular interests within a given community, but also between those individual interests and the collective well-being of the community. For example, an individual must respect the rights of others and is fully entitled to demand respect for his or her rights. Subject to each individual in a community complying with that basic standard, social order is maintained. However, the level of harmony and the quality of fulfillment of individual interests rises when certain people, of their own volition and desire, perform good deeds which exceed the call of duty, or are willing to forgive or otherwise forego part of their individual interest in favor, and for the benefit, of people less fortunate, all of which in turn raises the level and standard of well-being of the entire community.

Individualism may thus be perceived as an integral part of humanism through which fulfillment of one's own legitimate interests leads to self-fulfillment and contributes to the welfare of the entire community. Following that same perception, jihad as an individual endeavor can be considered a typical expression of humanism.

Jihad as an Expression of Humanism

The Way of God

We have observed that *īmān* (faith) and *al-'amal al-ṣāliḥ* (the performance of good deeds) are the two primary components of *al-ṣirāt al-mustaqīm* (the straight path).[68] Jihad is the tool that leads people through that path in their endeavor to draw closer to God. In the words of Seyyed Hossein Nasr, "Jihad is therefore the inner battle to purify the soul of its imperfections, to empty the vessel of the soul of the pungent water of forgetfulness, negligence, and the tendency to evil and to prepare it for the reception of the Divine Elixir of Remembrance, Light and Knowledge."[69]

Getting closer to God is not about withdrawing from humanity to achieve godlike perfection. Instead, it is about striving toward complying with God's advice in achieving the standards which secure eternal salvation, through proper and pious faith, while at the same time living one's humanity to its fullest extent through, primarily though not exclusively, *al-*

'amal al-ṣāliḥ. The process of self-improvement which draws humankind closer toward God is a long but sure process. The journey toward divine truth proceeds along a certain path, *sabīl-il-lāh,* or the way of God.

Thus jihad is the endeavor that each Muslim is called upon to make in order to proceed along that way, as set forth in clear, express terms in the Holy Qur'an.[70] In Verse Q5:35, God confirms that jihad is the means that secures success in drawing nearer to God along His way: *"O you who believe, fear Allah and seek means of nearness to Him, and carry out Jihad in His way, so that you may succeed";*[71] and in Verse Q29:69, God guides those who strive onto His path: *"As for those who strive in Our way, We will certainly take them onto Our paths, and indeed Allah is with those who are good in deeds."*[72] Interestingly, Abdulaziz Sachedina even places jihad in the realm of *fiṭra.*[73]

Jihad: An Attribute of *Īmān* and an Act of Worship

Strictly speaking, the term jihad in Arabic consists of striving, that is, exerting a personal effort to achieve a certain purpose. In Islam, therefore, jihad is essentially a personal, human effort. It is about self-improvement, because the more an individual fulfills his or her own humanity, the better God's purpose in establishing human trusteeship is achieved. From that perspective, jihad is primarily an individual—not collective—endeavor, but it could also be practiced collectively among individually willing persons. Mohamed Talbi observes that, through the exemplary expression of humanism along the way to God through *īmān,* a true Muslim sets a good example and thereby spreads the Message.[74] As an individual human endeavor, jihad appears in the Holy Qur'an as an essential attribute of *īmān,* or faith.

> Verses Q61:10 to 12—*"O believers, shall I direct you to a commerce that shall deliver you from a painful chastisement? (10) You shall believe in God and His Messenger, and* struggle *in the way of God with your possessions and your selves. That is better for you, did you but know. (11) He will forgive you your sins and admit you into gardens underneath which rivers*

flow, and to dwelling-places goodly in Gardens of Eden; that
is the mighty triumph (12)."

Verse Q49:15—"*The believers are those who believe in God and*
His Messenger, then have not doubted, and have struggled
with their possessions and their selves in the way of God;
those -- they are the truthful ones."[75]

More particularly, jihad is also portrayed as an act of worship and is cited
in Verses Q22:77 and 78 among the most important of the acts of worship,
namely prayer and the payment of alms to the poor.

> *O you who have believed, bow and prostrate and worship your Lord and do*
> *good—that you may succeed [77]. And* strive *for Allah with the striving due to*
> *Him. He has chosen you and has not placed upon you in the religion any difficulty.*
> *[It is] the religion of your father, Abraham. Allah named you "Muslims" before*
> *[in former scriptures] and in this [revelation] that the Messenger may be a*
> *witness over you and you may be witnesses over the people. So establish prayer*
> *and give zakat and hold fast to Allah. He is your protector; and excellent is the*
> *protector, and excellent is the helper [78].*[76]

Forms of Jihad

Because jihad is primarily an individual endeavor, an attribute of faith, and
an act of worship whose sole and specific purpose is to navigate the path
of God in the endeavor to draw closer to Him, it becomes clear that jihad
is not about warfare, fighting, and violence,[77] despite all the literature and
propaganda to the contrary that Muslim and non-Muslim media and so-
called "learned" sources insist on claiming.[78]

Jihad can take two main forms, personal human endeavor and financial
endeavor. Jihad through personal human endeavor, or jihad *bi-n-nafs*,
consists of spiritual and physical endeavors. The spiritual endeavors are
those that each individual may make in order to learn, understand, meditate
on, and grasp the Divine Message. The spiritual process involves pondering
the underlying meaning of each part of the Message and its purpose. The
physical endeavors consist of the actions that the individual attempts in

order to implement the outcome of the spiritual endeavors, where each successful attempt constitutes a step forward in the path of God, and draws that individual closer to Him. Some of the most notable examples of physical endeavors are assisting others in understanding the Divine Message and its values and ethics, performing good deeds, and assisting others in their efforts to advance along the way of God. Thus, striving to be a good citizen and a useful member in the community is the essence of jihad.

Jihad may also take the form of jihad *bi-l-māl*, or financial endeavor, when a person contributes money toward the success of a collective effort or to assist someone else in his or her own personal endeavor. This would pertain to financial contributions made toward the creation and establishment of institutions which provide social services, help to raise the quality of life in the community, and increase awareness about performing good deeds.

The individual who strives to navigate the path of God and succeeds in drawing closer to Him is the one who draws the divine reward of his/her endeavor, through personal satisfaction and a promise of eternal life in paradise. As such, the individual who performs jihad does so for the sake of his or her own personal interest, and that of no one else, including God. Even as individual jihad benefits the entire community, yet the performance of jihad by each person aims to serve his or her own personal interest, that of living harmoniously with others and drawing personal satisfaction out of being useful to the entire community. God expressly declares that He has no need for anyone performing jihad for His sake, or for any divine cause, in Verse Q29:6 and 7: "*Whosoever* struggles, struggles *only to his own gain; surely* God is All-sufficient nor needs any being *(6). And those who believe, and do righteous deeds, We shall surely acquit them of their evil deeds, and shall recompense them the best of what they were doing (7).*"[79]

This brings us to the conclusion that, contrary to the prevailing perception among many Muslim[80] and non-Muslim thinkers, jihad is not about fighting wars for the sake of God or for the sake of anyone else.[81] Summarizing mainstream Islamic belief, John Esposito describes jihad, citing Verse Q4:95, as a struggle to establish the rule of God, namely a struggle or even a holy war against the forces of evil and unbelief that might call for the sacrifice of one's life.[82] But Verse 4:95 does not refer to waging "war (jihad) for God," and it nowhere states that anyone has been mandated to "establish God's rule" or to fight for that purpose. This is not what fighting in "*the way of God*" is about. Second, as supported by the Holy Qur'an, God has no need for anyone to fight for Him.[83] Because it is not for the sake of God or for any other divine purpose, jihad should not be confused with a sacred war. In fact, no war is sacred in Islam, even if it can be justified by any of the few grounds on which fighting may be permitted, or tolerated, in accordance with the provisions of the Holy Qur'an.[84]

While jihad is primarily about self-improvement and progression in the way of God, it can exceptionally take the form of fighting in only one circumstance, and that is when Muslims, individually or collectively, are persecuted and prevented by force from freely performing their acts of worship, and as a result their progression in the way of God is obstructed. In that case and as a last resort, jihad may take the form of fighting for the sole purpose of restoring free striving in the way of God, and then only until the obstruction has been removed. In such exceptional circumstances, jihad may take the form of personal and direct involvement in fighting (jihad *bi-n-nafs*) or making financial contributions toward funding the collective fighting effort (jihad *bi-l-māl*).

In retrospect, Islam is primarily a religion of love and compassion. The message of love and compassion is found all over the Holy Qur'an. While the message of justice is stressed throughout the text, through the concepts of *al-'adl, al- qist,* and *al- mīzān,* yet the message of compassion prevails.[85] Unfortunately, over the years, Muslims and their governments have stressed and given precedence to the message of justice, representing it by the sword. They have glorified the sword as a symbol of justice. However, that glorification of the sword was diverted into a glorification of violence, presumably by using the sword to restore justice. However, those who stressed the message of justice have totally ignored the fact that this same Message has placed compassion on a level higher than that of justice. This is the concept of *iḥsān* (goodwill). That concept was pejoratively and wrongly interpreted or practiced as a concept of mere charity, whereas it is a reference to benevolence and compassion, both of which are promoted as human values applicable to all persons and not only due to the underprivileged by the affluent.

The Pacific Nature of Islam: The Rejection of Violence

The subject of violence, fighting, and wars continues to be the one specific subject which is most misunderstood and misused in Islam. It is widely misused by fundamentalists of political Islam and political anti-Islam, that is, by Muslim and non-Muslim fundamentalists in the advancement of their agendas for wide-ranging purposes, including religious fanaticism.[86] Similarly it is widely misunderstood by many others, again Muslims and non-Muslims, who are not directly informed, but listen and fall prey to the scare tactics of fundamentalists on both sides.[87] In either case, claims and assertions about the violent nature of Islam have been allegedly based on scriptural references which are either taken out of context or outright misunderstood. They are also based on Prophetic Tradition, namely traditions abusively imputed to the Prophet and to his companions.

In this section, we will follow the course that we set to ourselves throughout this study, that of relying exclusively on the provisions of the Holy Qur'an for clarification. We will do so because of the unreliability of records of Prophetic Tradition which were compiled from generations of word-of-mouth transmission extending over two hundred to three hundred years. In this respect, the Prophetic Tradition, most unfortunately, contains countless instances of glorification of violence, unnecessarily and wrongly imputed to the Prophet of Islam, including graphic depictions of what Muslims ought to do with their enemies and so-called enemies of God. But the Qur'anic verses are clear and straightforward about the rejection of violence and the treatment of fighting as a course of last resort. This scriptural evidence should deny all credibility to any tradition to the contrary imputed to the Prophet, unless any such tradition was then politically motivated by aggressions against the Prophet and his companions aimed at preventing the performance of his mission.

Issues of peace and violence appear in over one hundred thrity verses of the Qur'an. Some of these verses were taken out of context, others were removed from the logical sequence of verses which deal with the subject, and yet others were simply misinterpreted. In fact, the Qur'anic verses dealing with fighting revolve around various concepts, each of which has received wide-ranging interpretations. For that purpose, it is imperative that key terms be closely reviewed to explain the proper definitions for them, by reference to their specific contexts, before clarifying the conditions for permitted fighting and elucidating the true meaning of verses which were misconstrued as license for indiscriminate violence and conquest.

Definitions and Syntax

Subject to relevant conditions, fighting or jihad is permitted *fī sabīl-il-lāh* (in the path of God), against the *kuffār* (unbelievers) and the *mushrikūn* (those who associate other deities with God), in order to repel an aggression, end a *fitna* (public discord), or until a situation prevails whereby *al-dīn kulluhu li-l-lāh (*the principles of God's religion prevail). The meanings that are attributed to these terms determine whether peace or violence is characteristic of Islam.

Fighting and jihad: In the post-Qur'anic literature, fighting and jihad have often been used almost interchangeably,[88] whereby jihad is the brand name of the sacred war,[89] and fighting is the generic name for the acts of violence that are carried out in waging sacred wars. Thus all fighting permitted under the Qur'an has indiscriminately been deemed as sacred.[90] This confusion comes from the fact that some verses use the form *fight*, while others use the form *perform jihad*. In reality, there should be no confusion, because while jihad is a personal human endeavor which, exceptionally only, might take the form of fighting, not all fighting qualifies as jihad.

Furthermore, whether or not it takes the form of jihad, fighting is never sacred. In fact, the Holy Qur'an describes all forms of fighting as hateful, being at times a necessary evil ordained for some lesser evil purpose, as in Verse Q2:216: *"Prescribed for you is fighting, though it be hateful to you. Yet it may happen that you will hate a thing which is better for you; and it may happen that you will love a thing which is worse for you; God knows, and you know not."*[91] As a result, there are instances of fighting which are religiously permitted or merely tolerated under certain conditions; and there are instances of fighting which are religiously mandated and which then might qualify as jihad.

Fī sabīl-il-lāh: To be religiously mandated, fighting must be carried out *fī sabīl-il-lāh*, among other conditions. *Fī sabīl-il-lāh* is another expression that has been misused or misunderstood. Fighting and violence were legitimized for purposes never contemplated, let alone approved, by the Holy Qur'an. Some of such purposes are even repulsive to, and inconsistent with, the Divine Message. Unfortunately, that term has been misconstrued by many—though often in good faith—to mean that fighting is religiously mandated "for the sake of God" or for the purpose of advancing God's cause or securing the prevalence of His word.[92] Several thinkers have advocated the duty to seek to secure the prevalence of God's sovereignty as a way of submission to His will and acceptance of His determination. Accordingly, Muslims should perform jihad in order to forcibly resist and remove all obstacles that may appear in the way of, or prevent, the prevalence of God's will and determination.[93]

There is a major difference between submitting to God's will and undertaking jihad to cause the prevalence of God's will and sovereignty. The former, namely consent and submission to the will of God, is a passive act, whereas the latter suggests an active intervention on the part of human-kind to change something of God's doing. This latter suggestion implies the fallacy that humankind should help to realize a change which is beyond the control of God, and that God needs human assistance in bringing about that change. This attitude is built on the irrational assumption that jihad is about supplementing the powers of God instead of what it is truly about, namely, improving ourselves and getting closer to God.

The expression *fī sabīl-il-lāh* simply means "in the way of God,"[94] that is, the path that helps us draw nearer to God. Strictly speaking, the term *sabīl* means road or way, although from a modern linguistic perspective, the construction of the expression as "for the sake of God" is possible. However, of the two potential constructions of the term *fī sabīl-il-lāh*, only the one indicating the way of and path toward God is plausible. As set forth in Verse Q29:6, God is not dependent on humanity, nor does He need anyone to do anything for His sake or to advance His cause. On the contrary, He is Almighty, and it is humanity that is dependent on Him. On more than one occasion, God declared that He is the one who intervened and helped Muslims win fights undertaken for legitimate purposes, yet for their own sake.[95] Thus there is a major difference between the obligation to follow "God's path" and the obligation to help "God's will." Whereas the former is an individual—religiously mandated—endeavor, the latter implies a collective enforcement duty at a time where God never mandated anyone, not even His prophet, to enforce His will.

The Holy Qur'an mentions several categories of people among potential targets of permitted, or otherwise mandated, use of violence. However, confusion can be found between these categories in the Muslim and non-Muslim literature on violence in Islam, including the works of the commentators of the early periods of Islam. It is important to clarify the exact meaning of each category so that the verses which set forth the conditions and circumstances under which violence may be exercised can be properly analyzed and understood.

Mu'minūn: The term *mu'minūn*[96] (believers) has been generally attributed to Muslims, that is, those who received the Message brought by Prophet Muhammad, believed in his mission as prophet and messenger of God, and accepted the Message. However, this unduly restricts the scope of the term "believers," because that term applies primarily to everyone who has believed in the basic faith brought about by the successive messengers of God who preceded Prophet Muhammad, namely the existence and unicity of God, the Final Day, the Final Judgment, etc. In the Holy Qur'an, the *mu'minūn* are defined by what they believe rather than by the denomination that they profess. It is not enough for a person to profess that he or she is Muslim, Christian, or Jewish. It is what that person believes and practices that counts toward being deemed a believer or not. This is expressly set forth in the Holy Qur'an in the verses that follow.

Verses Q8:2 to 4—*The true believers are those whose hearts are filled with awe at the mention of God, and whose faith grows stronger as they listen to His revelations. They are those who put their trust in their Lord (2), pray steadfastly, and give in alms from what We gave them (3). Such are the true believers. They will be exalted and forgiven by their Lord, and a generous provision shall be made for them (4).*[97]

Verses Q23:1 to 11—*Successful indeed are the believers (1) Who are humble in their prayers (2), And who shun vain conversation (3), And who are payers of the poor-due (4); And who guard their modesty (5)—Save from their wives or the (slaves) that their right hands possess, for then they are not blameworthy (6), But whoso craveth beyond that, such are transgressors (7)—And who are shepherds of their pledge and their covenant (8), And who pay heed to their prayers (9). These are the heirs (10) Who will inherit paradise. There they will abide (11).*[98]

Based on these definitions, the term *mu'minūn*, or believers, does not exclusively point to Muslims, in the narrow sense of the word; it includes Christians and Jews, as well. It may also include any other person outside these three faith categories who believes in one God and whose beliefs are consistent with the provisions of these verses quoted above.

People of the Book: By contrast, the term "People of the Book" refers to those who profess one of the faiths set forth in any of the Divine Messages brought about by God's messengers, up to and including Prophet Muhammad. The People of the Book are those who have received—and professed their adherence to a message contained in—a divine book, namely, the Torah, the New Testament, and the Qur'an. It does not matter whether or not they truly believe in the faith to which they profess to adhere. Accordingly, and from a general perspective, Jews, Christians, and Muslims are considered to be People of the Book. But in the context of the Holy Qur'an, the term is mainly used as a reference to the Christians, Jews, and Sabeans.

Munāfiqūn: This term refers primarily to those who hide their true faith and profess another faith without truly believing in it. Their public profession of faith and performance of acts of worship is motivated by self-interest, ranging from fear of reprisals to hidden plans to undermine the Message and harm the Prophet and his companions. While the term could reasonably apply to the untruthful profession of any faith, it has been used in the Qur'an exclusively in connection with people from Mecca who professed the Islamic faith but failed to join the community of believers in their hijra to Medina. It also applies to certain people of Medina who conspired against the Prophet and aided his enemies of Mecca. The *munāfiqūn*, then, are substantially *kuffār* or *kāfirūn* (unbelievers)[99] within their inner selves, who publicly profess Islam or such other faith so as to appear among the believers.

Kuffār: The *kuffār* (plural of *kāfir*) are the unbelievers who do not believe in all or some of the basic creeds of the faith as set forth in any one of the divine messages brought by God's messengers, such as the existence and unicity of God, the Final Day, and the Final Judgment. They can be pagans who believe in deities other than God, or they can be atheists. However, there are also People of the Book, namely Muslims, Christians, and Jews, who may qualify for the epithet of *kuffār* when they fail to believe in one or more of the fundamental creeds of the relevant faith to which they profess to adhere.[100]

Mushrikūn: This term refers to pagans of Mecca, Medina, and other locations who associated other deities with God. They are often referred to in Qur'anic translations and other literature on Islam as the "associators." They include those who believe not in God but in other exclusive or special deities. They also include those who may believe in God, yet recognize some role of intercession for their ancient deities.

Fitna: The term *fitna* derives from the verb *fatana,* which means swaying or perverting. However, used as a noun, it has several meanings ranging from trouble, commotion, and persecution to temptation and perversion. As used in the Holy Qur'an, *fitna* is the act of the *mushrikūn* of Mecca who strove, by way of temptation, mischief, and/or persecution and use of force, to sway their brethren of Mecca from their new faith, Islam, so that they might return to their previous pagan worship of idols.[101] *Fitna* is also used to describe the acts of some Jews and *Munāfiqūn* of Medina[102] who, like the *mushrikūn* of Mecca, strove as well to turn the Muslims away from their new faith. The *fitna* that the people of Mecca spread is considered by the Qur'an to be more evil than the infliction of death. The impact of *fitna* as so described is presumably because the *mushrikūn,* through persecution and use of force, inflicted harm and injury upon their family members who embraced Islam and drove them out of their homes, forcing them to leave Mecca on the hijra to Medina.[103] Some exegetes, such as al-Tabari, have equated *fitna* with *shirk*, or the association of deities with God. This interpretation is too restrictive and contradicts principles set forth in the Qur'an.

Al-dīn kulluhu li-l-lāh: The expression *al-dīn kulluhu li-l-lāh* has received an unfortunate, widely accepted interpretation, which is a primary reason that Islam has gained a reputation as a religion of violence. Literally, *al-dīn kulluhu li-l-lāh* means "so that religion will be entirely for God." This unfortunate interpretation went on to infer that this expression means that the religion of God should absolutely prevail.[104] Under such interpretation, fighting should continue until every associator became a Muslim, which some interpreted in the wider sense of submission to God, and others in the narrower sense of Islam which includes acknowledgment of Prophet Muhammad's prophethood and mission, and acceptance of the Message brought by him.

It is sufficient to state here that: (1) such an interpretation is in direct contradiction with the basic principles of Islam, set forth in various verses of the Holy Qur'an; (2) the correct meaning of the expression *al-dīn kulluhu li-l-lāh* is that the principles set forth in the Qur'an, which contains the "religion of God," should at all times prevail, namely, freedom of faith and worship for all, the only exception being the Holy Haram of Mecca, in which the worship of God only, and no other deity, may be performed because it is the most sacred shrine of Muslims and contains the Kaaba; and (3) even if that expression meant the establishment of submission to God, then Christians and Jews would still be compliant because, as People of the Book, they worship and submit to God.

Basic Misconception about Violence in Islam

Despite the many verses in the Holy Qur'an which advocate peace and which place restrictions on the use of violence, there persists a widely held and deeply rooted belief that Islam is a religion of violence. This idea appears in countless publications by orientalists and Muslim scholars. It is disseminated via satellite television programs of Muslim fundamentalist creeds, as well as radical Christian and Jewish media and political think tanks. It has also been echoed and reinforced over the last decade by media and political activists through their continual references to such sources.[105] This widely held, yet unfounded perception, is rooted in a most unfortunate misconstruction of Qur'anic provisions by a large majority of early and modern exegetes. They determined that the Qur'anic verses which strictly regulate and restrict the use of violence have been abrogated by *Sūrat al-Tawba* (Sura 9: the Repentance), which starts with a blanket authority to the effect that all truce and peace arrangements previously entered into with the *kuffār* and *mushrikūn* are terminated, some immediately and others after a certain time. They also treated all previous restrictions on fighting as having been lifted by virtue of several verses in that same sura which incite to violence without preconditions. A number of verses from other suras of the Holy Qur'an which glorify fighting till the end are further cited to reaffirm the abrogation of verses restricting the use of force and calling for peace. Furthermore, according to these same interpretations, the end of belligerence can happen only with the death or conversion of the enemy to Islam.

Because of the magnitude of its damaging effect, here we will focus solely on the misconstruction of *Sūrat al-Tawba*. The other misconceptions will be discussed in the following section, in connection with the discussion of Qur'anic verses which severely restrict the use of violence.

Sūrat al-Tawba

The misconstruction of *Sūrat al-Tawba* consists first in the fact that it was taken out of the context of its revelation. Then its external meaning was assigned a universal intent. The importance of keeping in mind that the Holy Qur'an did not appear in a vacuum can never be stressed enough.[106] Instead the Qur'an was revealed in a specific environment to spread a universal divine message, to change certain deeply rooted traditions and customs, and to demonstrate how a universal message could be adapted to widely ranging circumstances. With respect to its specific context of revelation, *Sūrat al-Tawba* is said to have been revealed last, or close to last, in the order of revelation of the Divine Message and less than one year prior to the victory of the Prophet in Mecca, which would be followed by his death.[107]

In that period, the Message brought by Prophet Muhammad was steadily gaining ground, and the Prophet's increasing influence among the tribes of the Arabian Peninsula was raising the concerns of the powerful leadership of Mecca and its highly influential anchor tribe, the *Quraysh*. They were observing suspiciously the flow of tribes gathering from all over the peninsula to declare their submission to God and their acceptance of His Message, as conveyed through Prophet Muhammad. For that purpose, they had been endeavoring to incite violence against Prophet Muhammad and his companions. At the same time, the leadership of the neighboring Byzantine Empire was also observing with concern the successes of the Prophet's mission and the expanding sphere of his influence, and attempting to impede his mission by fomenting trouble around him and keeping him busy fighting.

These pressures from all directions could have led to the failure of the Prophet's mission. It is within this environment that *Sūrat al-Tawba* came to empower the Prophet and provide him the widest freedom and flexibility to eliminate his detractors.

Therefore, *Sūrat al-Tawba* is a message dedicated to the impending critical situation with which Prophet Muhammad had to contend.

> *Here is a disavowal (proclaimed) by Allah and His Messenger against the Mushriks (polytheists) with whom you have a treaty (1). So, move in the land*

freely for four months, and be aware that you can never frustrate Allah, and that Allah is going to disgrace the disbelievers (2). And here is an announcement, from Allah and His Messenger, to the people on the day of the greater Hajj, that Allah is free from (any commitment to) the Mushriks, and so is His Messenger. Now, if you repent, it is good for you. And if you turn away, then be aware that you can never frustrate Allah. And give those who disbelieve the 'good' news of a painful punishment (3)... So, when the sacred months expire, kill the Mushriks wherever you find them, and catch them and besiege them and sit in ambush for them everywhere. Then, if they repent and establish Salāh and pay Zakāh, leave their way. Surely, Allah is most Forgiving, Very-Merciful (5).[108]

From that beginning, the tone is set: Prophet Muhammad and his companions are the exclusive addressees of *Sūrat al-Tawba*, and no one else. The first and third verses of that sura specifically refer to the various pacts entered into previously between the Muslims and the pagans of Mecca and those of other tribes. The most important one is the Hudaybiyya pact that had been entered into a few months earlier between the Prophet and the nobility of Mecca regarding the performance by him and his companions of the upcoming Muslim hajj. The timing, too, indicates specificity: it is the start of the sacred period during which the annual pilgrimage is performed, preceded and followed by the annual trading period during which caravans from all over the Arabian Peninsula and the neighboring areas converge into Mecca. Finally, and most importantly, the objective is specific: the Prophet needed peace in order to complete the fulfillment of his divine mission.

The limited and exceptional nature of the provisions of *Sūrat al-Tawba* is further determined by framing the exception within the confines of the *kuffār* and *mushrikūn* who had already committed to peace under a pact with the Muslims but did not keep their word. Therefore, they were people who had previously committed belligerent acts against the Prophet and Muslims, and who continued to display that belligerent attitude. In this respect, the first verse of *Sūrat al-Tawba* declared "the end of peace pacts that failed to maintain the peace." However, this was not an authorization to fight the *kuffār* and *mushrikūn,* who had never antagonized the Prophet and the Muslims and thus had no reason to enter into peace arrangements of any kind with them.

Because *Sūrat al-Tawba* was revealed to address a narrow and specific circumstance, it is important to avoid any rush to extend its impact beyond its immediate purpose, for the simple reason that its scope cannot be rationally and reasonably extended beyond that specific scope. Indeed, the first verse released the Muslims from then existing pacts with the pagans to the exclusion of any others. Any extension of the scope of that release beyond the immediate circumstances under which it was revealed would translate into a standing license for Muslims not to honor their commitments in the future, which would be inconsistent with the Qur'anic insistence on abiding by undertakings, covenants, and treaties. In the second verse, the four months' grace period reflects that the release came at the beginning of the sacred period, preceding and extending beyond the pilgrimage period. Thus it is not a general grace period which must precede each declaration of war. Finally, if this entire sura was intended to enable the Prophet to complete his mission, then it is an indication that the intent of that sura of exception must end when that mission ends. That mission ended with the death of Prophet Muhammad, and no one has inherited it nor has it passed to any other person, following God's clear determination that Muhammad would be His last and final Prophet and Messenger.

Since the circumstances under which those verses descended cannot be repeated, their effect ended with the cessation of those circumstances. Highlighting this fact, Muhammad 'Abed al-Jabiri[109] and Niazi Ezzeddine[110] have noted the absence from *Sūrat al-Tawba* of the usual opening verse, "*Bismillahi-r-Rahmāni-r-Rahīm*," ("In The Name of God the Compassionate, the Merciful"). They both consider the fact that this sura is the only one in the entire Holy Qur'an which does not start with that opening verse indicates that it is not to be given a wide scope, beyond the immediate circumstances of time and place.[111]

Other than *Sūrat al-Tawba*, *Sūrat al-Ahzāb* contains a number of verses about the Prophet and his companions fighting the *al-Khandaq* war. These verses contain some scolding to those who are afraid to fight and to the *munāfiqūn* who run away to avoid fighting.[112] We also find similar verses in other suras which were revealed in conjunction with the successive wars that the Prophet had to fight in order to safeguard his mission.[113] They all incite believers to fight in the way of God and promise a direct path to paradise for martyrs,[114] in such a way that, at times, one gets the impression that the Qur'an glorifies fighting.[115] That is not true, because these verses were circumstantial, in the sense that the authorized use of violence is limited strictly to fighting against those who (1) drove the Prophet and his companions out of their homes and out of Mecca; (2) committed violent aggression against them; (3) tried to prevent the Prophet from spreading his message; and (4) sought to stop the Companions and believers from practicing their new religion.

By their circumstantial nature these verses are no longer applicable or binding on anyone after the death of the Prophet, because the mission of the Prophet has not been passed on to anyone. Verse Q3:195 summarizes this.

> *So, their Lord answered their prayer: "I do not allow the labor of any worker from among you, male or female, to go to waste. You are similar to one another. So, those who emigrated, and were expelled from their homes, and were tortured in My way, and fought, and were killed, I shall certainly write off their evil deeds, and shall certainly admit them into gardens beneath which rivers flow, as a reward from Allah. It is Allah with Whom lies the beauty of the reward."*[116]

Despite the exceptional, restricted nature of these provisions, the authorization to use violence was not a blanket, discretionary one. God made sure from the outset to specify the circumstances justifying such authorization in Verse Q9:13: "*Would you not fight a* people who broke their oaths and conspired to expel the Messenger, *and it was* they who started (fighting) against you for the first time*? Do you fear them? But Allah has greater right that you fear Him, if you are believers.*"[117] This verse sums up in this way the reasons for which the order to fight the associators of Mecca came: first they broke their pacts with the believers; then, they forced the Prophet out of Mecca; and they followed their misdeeds by initiating aggression against Muslims in Badr and elsewhere. In this light, should this verse constitute a final and definitive divine verdict that all nonbelievers should be killed unless they declare Islam? Clearly not, because the stated purpose for this rule is that the nonbelievers in question are the Meccans who have broken several pacts and have displayed a determination to do away with Muslims and Islam. If the circumstances have changed, the rule can change by applying our understanding of the universal nature of Islam. Universal should not be construed to mean that an interpretation made fifteen centuries ago should continue in effect universally and forever. Universal means that it should constantly adapt and evolve over time.

Even though *Sūrat al-Tawba* proclaims a limited license to fight, it nevertheless contains words of caution against unnecessary violence or provides some justification for that temporarily authorized excessive violence. Indeed, immediately after the Prophet is released from all pacts, he is cautioned not to commence fighting against any groups who did not break their pacts and continue to abide by them (Verse Q9:4: *"Except those of the Mushriks with whom you have a treaty, and they were not deficient [in fulfilling the treaty] with you, and did not back up anyone against you. So fulfill the treaty with them up to their term. Surely, Allah loves the God-fearing."*)[118] In addition, the Qur'an provides an explanation for the exception relating to the license to continue fighting till the end, namely till conversion to Islam or death of the enemy. In this respect, the Qur'an explains that the pagans referred to in Verse Q9:1 cannot be trusted any longer because they have consistently broken their commitments under peace pacts, and they did so in particular every time they found themselves strong or the Muslims were in a difficult situation as to appear particularly vulnerable, as in Verse Q9:8: *"How [can there be a treaty] while, if they gain dominance over you, they do not observe concerning you any pact of kinship or covenant of protection? They satisfy you with their mouths, but their hearts refuse [compliance], and most of them are defiantly disobedient"*).[119] It is also noteworthy how *Sūrat al-Tawba* itself provided guidance over the fighting process to secure that it ended when the aggression and *fitna* ended.

With this in mind, *Sūrat al-Tawba* advises the Prophet and believers to fight, commencing with the belligerents who are closest to them. Verse Q9:123 provides: *"O you who have attained to faith! Fight against those deniers of the truth who are near you, and let them find you adamant; and know that God is with those who are conscious of Him."*[120] A number of exegetes have interpreted this verse as an order to organize systematic fighting against all non-Muslims without distinction, whether associators or People of the Book, starting with the closest and proceeding to those who are further away. In reality, this verse simply says that believers ought to fight those who are close to them, whose geographical proximity allows them to cause harm to believers by threatening their faith and preventing them from observing their religion. The interpretation used to bolster the order to fight all non-Muslims systematically starting with the closest is baseless because it is contrary to the principle of nonaggression and ultimately leads to the irrational conclusion that Muslims must fight universally until every individual becomes a Muslim. Al-Tabari even guesses who that closest side might be and concludes that it is the Byzantine Empire. Such determination by itself is irrational because the Byzantines were not *kuffār* but were believers as People of the Book. al-Tantawi further argues.

> Rather, God ordered believers to fight starting with the closest to their homelands because fighting was legitimized to secure the success of spreading the call to Islam which, in turn, was addressed first to the closest. It was therefore wise that they start fighting their immediate neighbors so as to prevent their mischief, and because it was not within the power of Muslims then to fight all unbelievers and to conquer all the nations at the same time. Starting with the closest was made a priority.[121]

This interpretation defies essential principles of Islam, namely the following: (1) spreading the call to Islam was the exclusive duty and privilege of Prophet Muhammad, and no one else. Those believers addressed in the verse in question are the Companions of the Prophet whom he called to arms while he was performing his mission; (2) the Prophet, in the performance of his mission was not empowered to spread the Message by force. He was to do so only by words of wisdom and good exhortation (Verse Q16:125); and (3) many of the neighbors of the early Muslims were Christians, Jews, and Sabeans, all of whom are declared by the Qur'an to be People of the Book, or believers by virtue of their adherence to prior revelations and messages of God.

Finally, most telling was the behavior of Prophet Muhammad in handling the situation arising from the declarations made in *Sūrat al-Tawba*.

In spite of the widest powers conferred to him to eradicate all *mushrikūn* and *kuffār,* who at one time or another displayed a belligerent attitude toward him and Muslims, the Prophet always seized every opportunity to use wisdom, restraint, and judgment so as to minimize the use of violence.[122]

These signs of caution, in an otherwise license of last resort, are there by way of reminder of what Islam is all about and of the restrictions on the use of violence. Didn't God forewarn believers against aggressing the unbelievers who did not aggress them because of their faith? Indeed, this is the essence of the message of Verses Q60:7 to 9.

> *Perhaps God will create affection between you and those among them with whom you were at enmity, for God is Omnipotent, and He is All-Forgiving, Compassionate to each (7); As for those who have not fought against you over religion, nor expelled you from your homes, God does not forbid you to treat them honorably and act with fairness toward them, for God loves those who act with fairness (8); God, however, forbids you to ally yourselves with those who fought against you over religion, expelled you from your homes or contributed to your expulsion. Whoso allies himself with them—these are the unjust (9).*[123]

This is the most explicit statement that there can be no divinely sanctioned aggression against anyone, including associators of Mecca. It states specifically that God prays that there be good relations and esteem between the believers and their brethren and families who remained behind and did not participate in fighting and driving them out of their homes. It also states that God does not sanction fighting those Meccans who continue to reject the Message if they do not fight against believers because of their religion. God goes even further as to encourage friendly contacts and engagements.[124]

Conditions for the Use of Violence

While God may have declared certain individuals among the People of the Book as *kuffār, mushrikūn,* or *munāfiqūn*, yet He has not given authority to anyone to make that determination in order to fight them. He did not grant such authority to humans, because only He is able to know what beliefs the inner souls of people truly carry. Therefore, God did not grant a license to fight or commit any act of violence against people for the sole reason that they are *kuffār*, *mushrikūn,* or otherwise. Nor did he grant a license for violence against any other people or for any other reason, except under certain very strict conditions. In fact, the Holy Qur'an specifies strict conditions for initiating, conducting, and ending acts of violence.

CONDITIONS FOR COMMENCING USE OF FORCE

The essential condition for the use of violence in Islam is a prior aggression by the party against whom violence is used. The use of force to repel an aggression, in general, is simply permitted without regard to the identity of the aggressor or to the purpose of the aggression. However, fighting becomes a religious obligation when the aggression is perpetrated by the *kuffār*, *mushrikūn*, or *munāfiqūn* against Muslims because of their religious beliefs. In such case, the purpose of the aggression is either to punish the holding of such beliefs, to prevent believers from freely worshiping and advancing along the way of God, or to create a *fitna* by forcing Muslims to revert to paganism or to abandon Islam. In other words, fighting is mandatory when it is *fī sabīl-il-lāh* (in the path of God).[125] However, in either case, the Holy Qur'an cautions against aggression as follows in Verse Q2:190: "*And fight in the way of God with those who fight against you*, but aggress not; God loves not the aggressors."[126] Therefore, according to this verse and others, the use of violence is permitted or mandated in the following circumstances, exclusively: (1) to repel an aggression,[127] whoever the aggressor may be; (2) to quell a *fitna*; (3) to remove any obstruction placed upon Muslims in the way of God; or (4) to end fighting among believers.

During the lifetime of Prophet Muhammad, the expression *fitna* also included a fourth circumstance for the use of violence, which did not survive the end of his divine mission upon his death. Prophet Muhammad's mission was to receive the revelation of, and spread, God's Message. The first Muslims, represented by the Prophet's companions of Mecca and Medina, were enjoined in the Holy Qur'an to obey the Prophet and help with his mission. When the *kuffār*, *mushrikūn*, or *munāfiqūn* committed acts of aggression against the Prophet to prevent him from performing his mission, they were for all practical purposes obstructing the way of God, hence the fighting against them to stop that aggression fully counted as fighting *fī sabīl-il-lāh*. It should be clear here that only fighting to repel the use of force by the Prophet's enemies to prevent him from performing his mission could qualify as fighting *fī sabīl-il-lāh*. Accordingly, any fighting to spread God's Message and impose its acceptance was expressly prohibited, as stated in Verses Q4:79 to 81:

> *Whatever good comes to you, it is from Allah and whatever evil visits you, it comes from your own selves. We have sent you to be a Messenger for the people. Allah is enough to be a witness (79). Whoever obeys the Messenger obeys Allah, and whoever turns away, then, We did not send you to stand guard over them (80). They say, "Obedience (we observe)." But when they go away from you, a group of them conspires at night contrary to what they say. Allah records what they conspire. So ignore them and put your trust in Allah. Allah is enough to trust in (81).*[128]

In other words, this verse is telling us: God sends messengers to be obeyed, and obedience to the Prophet is equivalent to obedience to God himself. Yet, God cautions against imposing that obedience and instructs the Prophet to leave alone those who do not obey, leaving it to God to have the final say on punishment. This is consistent with God's justice, under which every opportunity is given to each person to repent, until the last minute. In sum, first, fighting in order to impose God's Message is not an option; second, if the Prophet did not have that authority, no other individual till the end of time, including his faithful companions and successors, could lay claim to it.

Fighting for the sole reason that the other side is made up of *mushrikūn*, *kuffār*, *munāfiqūn*, or any other denomination other than Muslims is clearly not permitted. They must first begin the aggression, using violence, before Muslims are permitted or mandated to fight them back. Any form of aggression which is not coupled with the use of violence does not constitute sufficient ground for countering with violence. In fact, and primarily in order to minimize the risk of turning to violence, God advises in the Holy Qur'an that verbal or other forms of nonviolent aggression should be dealt with by staying away from the aggressors, as follows in Verse Q4:140:

> *And, indeed, He has enjoined upon you in this divine writ that whenever you hear people deny the truth of God's messages and mock at them, you shall avoid their*

*company until they begin to talk of other things—or else, verily, you will become
like them. Behold, together with those who deny the truth God will gather in hell
the hypocrites.*[129]

God further advises that, to the extent possible and in order to avoid
the risk of violence, Muslims should consider first turning away from
aggression by way of hijra;[130] or moving to another location which is more
welcoming. He had similar advice for the Prophet himself.[131]

For that purpose it is necessary to reject views which have legitimized
the so-called "offensive jihad" in certain circumstances, including the
fulfillment of the responsibility of humankind to achieve *"the success of
God's cause."*[132] To make that point, reference is often made to Qur'anic
Verses Q9:41, Q5:33, Q9:12, and Q9:29. In reality, evidence suggests
that: (1) God does not like aggressors under any circumstances as set
forth in Verse Q2:190; (2) God has not mandated upon Muslims to strive
for the success of His cause, but has only mandated the Prophet and his
companions to strive to spread God's Message without imposing it; and (3)
on that basis, the quoted verses are exclusively addressed to the Prophet
and his companions whose efforts to spread the Message were being
obstructed. Therefore, the universal nature of these provisions, which
survives the end of the Prophet's mission following his death, is limited to
the lessons learned from it and the underlying ethical values resulting from
such lessons, for instance that legitimate fighting is restricted to fighting
conducted to repel an aggression.

Furthermore, jihad by way of violence has also been legitimized by
modern and older scholarship as a tool of struggle against injustice and
for the restoration of divinely ordained justice set forth in the Shari'a,
such being part of the role of the Prophet or the imam.[133] Here too there is
no reference in the Holy Qur'an to any such role for either the Prophet or
the imam, nor is there anything in it which allows the attribution of that
role to him. Indeed, enforcement is not about forcing people to believe
but mainly about imposing the guidelines included in the Message. Thus,
if the Prophet had no such role, then the imam does not have it. In any
event, the Qur'an does not mention the existence of any successors to
the Prophet, whether as imams or otherwise, nor does it attribute any role

to them. Conscious that his mission is not transmissible to anyone, the Prophet consistently abstained from leaving any will or entrusting any of his companions to carry out any missions on his behalf that he himself did not initiate, let alone to be performed following his death.

Finally, it is important to note the principle that fighting against believers is not permitted under any circumstances, because true believers would neither create *fitna* among the believers nor obstruct the way of God. Indeed, in the Holy Qur'an, believers of all faiths are enjoined to submit their disputes to arbitration.[134] For that purpose, Muslims are not entitled to decide for themselves who is a believer or not a believer among those who profess to be believers, because that determination falls within the exclusive realm of God, as set forth in Verse Q4:94:

> *O you who believe, when you go out in the way of Allah, be careful, and do not say to the one who offers you the Salām (salutation), "You are not a believer" to seek stuff of the worldly life. So, with Allah there are spoils in abundance. In the same state you were before; then Allah favored you. So, be careful. Surely, Allah is All-Aware of what you do.*[135]

God did not grant that authority, first, because the identification and punishment of *kuffār* or associators falls exclusively within the jurisdiction of God; and second, each sinner is given an open-ended chance to repent until the time of death. Therefore, license to fight is granted only against those of the associators and the *kuffār* who initiate aggression. Prophet Muhammad, during his prophetic career, closely observed that principle, even with people whose insincerity was obvious.[136] However, to the extent that some of his companions and successors may have behaved differently with *munāfiqūn* when they went after them for apostasy, they did so exclusively on political grounds and not on religious grounds. This principle does not apply among Muslims only; it applies among all believers, including Muslims, Christians, and Jews. As People of the Book, Christians and Jews are expressly recognized as believers. On that and other bases, the wars waged to achieve the wide-scale conquests following the death of the Prophet do not qualify as jihad[137] nor were they wars sanctioned by the Holy Qur'an. Instead they were ordinary wars of expansion waged for political purposes,[138] among others.[139]

However, there are two instances in which violence may be used against believers. First, it is permitted for a believer to fight someone who claims to be a believer, in order to repel an act of aggression by that person. Second, it is also permitted to fight against believers when they fight against each other, and then only to the extent necessary to restore peace among them. In the first case, the fighting becomes legitimate because, by committing an act of aggression against another believer, the aggressor would have demonstrated not being a true believer. In the latter case, fighting is justified by the overriding objective of restoring the peace among believers, as set forth in the Qur'an in Verse Q49:9:

> *If two parties of believers fight one another, then make peace between them (fa-ṣliḥū baynahum) [by removing all causes of conflict]; then, if one party of believers transgresses against another, [selfishly violating their rights,] then fight the transgressors until they obey once more God's commandment. Then, when transgressors have submitted [their will once more to His], make peace between them with fairness and justice (bi-l-'adl), and act equitably (w-aqṣitū) [so that the rights of neither party are violated]. Lo! God loves the equitable.*[140]

Abdulaziz Sachedina stresses the importance of this verse in building peace on solid grounds of equity and justice, and rightly extends its effects beyond believers.

LIMITATIONS ON, AND TERMINATION OF, PERMITTED ACTS OF VIOLENCE

While Muslims are granted a license to conduct acts of violence under specified conditions, such license is not open-ended. Muslims must strictly observe the rules of reciprocity and proportionality, in the sense that the intensity of their response to the aggression should be just enough to put an end to the aggression, with means reasonably comparable to those used by the aggressors. They must exercise restraint. This is spelled out in the Holy Qur'an in Verse Q2:194, as follows: "*Fight during the sacred months if you are attacked: for a violation of sanctity is [subject to the law of] just retribution. Thus, if anyone commits aggression against you, attack him just as he has attacked you—but remain conscious of God, and know that God is with those who are conscious of Him.*"[141] In other words, the violence used to repel an aggression should not aim at the extermination of the aggressors. Instead, violence should be limited to achieve an end to that aggression. That is why, despite the need to prepare all the force required to fight back against the aggressors, God makes sure to specify in the Holy Qur'an that if the aggressors lean toward peace and offer signs to that effect, Muslims should seize that opportunity, agree to make peace with them, and put an end to the fighting. The importance of peace as an objective is stressed when God enjoins that it be given a chance, even when the aggressors offer peace in order to deceive, as set forth in Verses Q8:60 to 62:

> *Prepare against them whatever force you can, and the trained horses whereby you frighten Allah's enemy and your own enemy and others besides them whom you do not know. Allah knows them. Whatever thing you spend in the way of Allah, it will be paid to you in full, and you shall not be wronged (60). And if they tilt toward peace, you too should tilt toward it, and place your trust in Allah. Surely, He is the All-Hearing, the All-Knowing (61) If they intend to deceive you, then Allah is all-sufficient for you. He is the One who supported you with His help and with the believers (62).*[142]

In essence, then, the use of violence in Islam is no longer permitted when the aggression has ended. Primarily, aggression ends when fighting by the aggressors ceases as a result of peace having been agreed to among the fighting parties. However, when fighting is justified by the existence of— and need to quell—a *fitna*, aggression is deemed ended when the *fitna* has been effectively quelled. Similarly, when fighting has been initiated by Muslims *fī sabīl-il-lāh*, then the aggression is deemed ended and fighting must stop when the obstruction of the way of God has been removed and a situation whereby *al-dīn kulluhu li-l-lāh* is established. In the Holy Qur'an these principles are clearly spelled out.

> Verse Q2:193—*And fight them until persecution is no more, and religion is for Allah. But if they desist,* then let there be no hostility except against wrong-doers.[143]

> Verses Q8:38 to 40—*Tell those who disbelieve that if they cease (from persecution of believers) that which is past will be*

forgiven them; but if they return (thereto) then the example of the men of old hath already gone (before them, for a warning) (38). And fight them until persecution is no more, and religion is all for Allah [i.e. al-dīn kulluhu li-l-lāh]. *But if they cease, then lo! Allah is Seer of what they do (39). And if they turn away, then know that Allah is your Befriender—a Transcendent Patron, a Transcendent Helper!(40)*[144]

These Qur'anic verses dealing with violence, and other verses as well, have been grossly misinterpreted and misconstrued in more than one respect. In addition to the basic misconstruction of *Sūrat al-Tawba*, described previously, the most damaging misconstructions are the ones relating to the interpretations of the terms *fitna* and *al-dīn kulluhu li-l-lāh*, where *fitna* has been interpreted as *shirk*, or the sacrilege of associating other deities with God, and *al-dīn kulluhu li-l-lāh*[145] has been interpreted as the imposition of God's religion, by way of forcing every associator to submit to God. To illustrate the impact of such misinterpretations and misconstructions, let's rewrite the verses cited and replace the misconstrued terms, namely *al-dīn kulluhu li-l-lāh* and *fitna* with their own erroneous interpretations.

Verse Q2:193—*And fight them until [shirk] is no more, and [Islam prevails]. But if they [abandon shirk by adhering to Islam], then let there be no hostility except against wrong-doers.*

Verses Q8:38 to 40—*Tell those [Kuffār] that if they cease (from [shirk]) that which is past will be forgiven them; but if they return (thereto) then the example of the men of old hath already gone (before them, for a warning) (38). And fight them until [shirk] is no more, and [Islam as religion of Allah absolutely prevails]. But if they [abandon shirk and embrace Islam], then lo! Allah is Seer of what they do (39). And if they turn away, then know that Allah is your Befriender—a Transcendent Patron, a Transcendent Helper! (40).*

The construction of these verses as illustrated in these examples is not plausible simply because it defies logic and reason, and is inconsistent with other verses of the Holy Qur'an. In the first place, *fitna* cannot possibly just mean the sacrilege of association of other deities with God, because God described *fitna* as an aggression which outweighs murder against Muslims, in line with the injunction to fight only by way of reaction to an aggression. Therefore, if disbelievers and associators keep their beliefs to themselves and do not commit an act of aggression, then fighting them on the part of the Muslims becomes itself an aggression, where God has expressly rejected aggressors (Verse Q2:190).

On the other hand, Prophet Muhammad could not have understood this verse to grant a license, and convey an authority, to fight against people simply because of their faith, for the purpose of forcing them to embrace Islam, because his mandate was limited to conveying the Message without forcing anyone to accept it. Therefore, if the Prophet of Islam did not have the power to coerce people into embracing Islam in any manner, let alone by way of aggression, then certainly ordinary Muslims cannot lay claim to such power.[146]

Finally, the misconstruction of these verses is inconsistent with the express provisions which enjoin upon the Muslims to accept any offer to make peace in order to end the fighting (Q8:61, cited above). Similarly, the expression *al-dīn kulluhu li-l-lāh* could not mean that it is a divine injunction to eradicate all religions from the universe or even just from the Arabian Peninsula, as is attributed to a tradition of the Prophet. For the same reasons set forth in the preceding paragraph, the tradition in question attributed to the Prophet could not be true.

Therefore, the only logical and reasonable interpretation which remains is that violence must be ended when all aggression has stopped, *fitna* has been stopped, and the freedom of Muslims to worship and live their religion is no longer obstructed. This is what restoring a situation in which religion is all to God is all about, namely an environment in which the noble principles enjoined by God, such as justice, fairness, freedom of faith, *iḥsān*, and performance of good deeds, can be freely expected, observed, or performed.[147] We would add to these milestones, however, one which is specific to Prophet Muhammad and his companions, that is, the unimpaired freedom to fulfill the Prophet's mission in conveying the Message. These misconceptions, to which some may have adhered in good faith out of ignorance, or out of learning from other extremists, have led to the rise of extremist groups who have relied upon Qur'anic verses taken out of context to project the violence that they advocate as being divinely mandated.[148] Thus, in light of all the above, violence is permitted only to repel aggression or to quell a threat of perversion of one's religious belief, and it must be ended when the permission has served its purpose. That said, the Holy Qur'an not only regulates the use of violence but instead, and primarily, calls us to peace and praises the virtues of maintaining peace and of not using violence in the first place.

Finally, the most serious misconstruction of the Holy Qur'an's verses is the application of the concept of abrogation in order to set aside all the verses in which God has regulated the use of force.[149] Bearing in mind that (1) the verses which advocate peace, *iḥsān*, and, where strictly necessary, calculated violence in dealing with aggression, have been mainly revealed in the Meccan and early Medinan periods of the Prophet's career, and (2) whereas the verses which incite to violence and permit its use on a wider scale have been revealed mainly in the latter part of the Medinan period in the Prophet's career, many have concluded that the verses revealed during the Medinan period must prevail because the earlier verses were revealed when Muslims were still weak and battling for their own day-to-day survival. This is how support is provided for the claim that the Medinan verses have abrogated Meccan verses which are inconsistent with them.[150] Flowing from that same concept, Abdelmajid Charfi provides a critical discussion of the general view in Muslim jurisprudence of the golden age, as expressed by al-Sarakhsi, according to which offensive fighting is legitimized following the legitimization of unconditional fighting by the Prophet.[151]

These interpretations are untenable because they defy the basic principles of interpretation. They are also unacceptable because they run counter to all noble principles of Islam. There are no contradictions between the verses revealed in each of the particular periods in the

Prophet's mission. While the verses of the earlier period set forth the basic principles of peace and restraint when faced with aggression, those of the latter period represent the exceptions that God allowed the Prophet because he was being attacked; hence, *Sūrat al-Tawba* came by way of exception and for a limited, nonreplicable period and circumstances. This is in conformity with the basic, most elementary, principle of interpretation according to which provisions of an exceptional nature, or specific to a given circumstance, do not abrogate general, universally applicable principles. Furthermore, these interpretations are also unacceptable because they constitute an affront to the majesty and perfection of God. In fact, a prominent exegete of the Holy Qur'an, al-Qurtubi, had no problem confirming that Verse Q9:73 has superseded all prior verses which urge Muslims to seek peace, bestow pardon, and act with compassion with the enemy.[152] But it is inconceivable that God has now allegedly given blanket authority to fight the unbelievers without prior aggression on their part because in Verse Q2:190, which is claimed to have been abrogated as well, God did not say only that Muslims should not be aggressive, but also that He did not like aggressors. Following this logic, we would reach the irrational conclusion that God has changed His mind and now likes aggressors. Similarly, in Verse Q2:216, God has expressed how He perceives, and how He feels about, fighting and violence: He simply finds them hateful. Could He have changed overnight His perception of fighting and violence so as to glorify them? Certainly not, because in the Verses of *Sūrat al-Tawba* and other similar verses elsewhere, He has reluctantly, and for a limited purpose only, allowed the exceptions to take place.

Despite the exceptional nature of the provisions of *Sūrat al-Tawba* and its like cited here, even *Sūrat al-Tawba* contains restraints that the exegetes have often ignored. For example, a part only is extracted from Verse Q9:36 to evidence the general unrestricted lifting of restraints on fighting, as follows: "*Fight against the associators on a wide scale*";[153] however they omit the continuation of that verse, which stipulates: "*just as they fight against you on a wide scale.*" Therefore, it was not an unconditional license for the Muslims to commence aggression and fight because they got stronger. Instead, it was an authorization to respond, meaning that the permission to fight on a wide scale is justified by the wide-scale aggression initiated by unbelievers, but then only up to the same intensity of fighting initiated by the enemy. This was illustrated by the behavior of Prophet Muhammad following his glorious entry into Mecca when he pronounced his verdict reciting Verse 92 of *Sūrat Yusuf* (Q12:92): *"He said: Have no fear this day! May Allah forgive you, and He is the Most Merciful of those who show mercy."*[154]

The exceptional nature of fighting is reiterated in certain verses of *Sūrat* al-Hajj, which was revealed shortly before *Sūrat al-Tawba*, and they summarize the relevant circumstances eloquently.

> *God safeguards the believers; God loves not every treacherous renegade (38). Leave is granted to those who are being attacked, for they were wronged, and God is assuredly capable of sending them victory. They are those who were driven out of their homes without just cause, only because they said: "Our Lord is God" (39). Had God not caused people to restrain one another, destruction would have fallen upon monasteries, churches, oratories and places of prayer, where the name of God is often mentioned (40). God will assuredly uphold those who uphold Him. God is All-Powerful, Almighty. They are those who, when we empower them in the land, perform the prayer, hand out alms, command the good and forbid evil. To God is the outcome of all matters (41).*[155]

In other words: (1) God does not allow fighting or the use of force in order for people to defend Him against those who wronged Him; on the contrary, He is the one who defends the believers; (2) the authorization granted to believers to fight back is justified by the fact that the believers were driven out of their homes and towns unjustly, solely because they worship God, which means that God has not given a blanket authorization to show aggression against anyone, even nonbelievers, if they do not start the aggression; and (3) those to whom God grants a land where they can worship have no mandate there to impose the faith, their sole mandate being to exercise that worship and call for the ethics of the new faith without enforcing them, thereby creating the proper environment for freedom of faith, leaving God to act as the ultimate judge. On that basis, all verses appearing in the suras revealed in the latter Medinan period which appear to enjoin believers to fight without conditions[156] should be read in conjunction with the verses that set forth the preconditions for the use of violence, namely (1) a prior aggression (2) which uses force and (3) whose purpose is to deter people from proceeding on the path to God.

Returning to our views regarding abrogation, God did not abrogate earlier verses by later verses. He did not do so because any claim to the contrary constitutes an affront to His own Perfection and ultimate Compassion. It is not conceivable that God could have possibly enjoined believers to observe high moral principles of peaceful coexistence and nonaggression and then later on unleash them against their surroundings just because they got stronger: such is not the behavior of a Most Compassionate creator. Nor could God have made a mistake in enjoining peaceful behavior, then later changed His mind and corrected His previous course of action, because God is Perfect and does not make mistakes. Instead, in His ultimate Compassion and Justice, God has set forth the noble principles and has guided His Prophet and Messenger in their implementation, with the necessary flexibility to secure the implementation of his mission, that of spreading His Message.[157]

The Call to Peace is of the Essence of Islam

The basic ethics of Islam are built on humility. Muslims are encouraged to offer peace when faced with aggression: "*And the servants of (God) Most Gracious are those who walk on the earth in humility, and when the ignorant address them, they say, 'Peace!'*"[158] Therefore, although violence is permitted to repel aggression, yet peaceful means to avoid violence must be tried first. In support of this approach, we would recall that the Prophet and his companions were directed to leave Mecca altogether, precisely in order to avoid violence. Then violence was first allowed within limits, only when, despite the emigration to Medina, the Meccan pagans pursued the aggression against the Prophet and his companions.

In further support of this insistence on peace and serenity, the Holy Qur'an provides in Verses Q41:33 to 35.

> And who speaks better than he who calls men to the service of God, does what is right, and says: "I am a Muslim"? (33) Good deeds and evil deeds are not equal. Requite evil with good, and he who is your enemy will become your dearest

friend (34). But none will attain this attribute save those who patiently endure; none will attain it save those who are truly fortunate (35).[159]

In fact, these verses encourage Muslims to be patient and display an attitude of endurance, and God promises to reward those who display that attitude. More particularly, there is no justification for dropping that attitude for a belligerent attitude under any circumstance, other than unavoidable violence being used in the aggression. Even ridiculing of the religion and making fun of God's words in the Qur'an are no justification to commit violence.[160]

God warns against using violence to spread His Message. He affirms in no uncertain terms in Verses Q16:125 to 127 that spreading His words should be done only with the utmost wisdom, without any coercion, let alone the use of force.

Call to the way of your Lord with wisdom and fair counsel, and debate with them in the fairest manner. Your Lord knows best who has strayed from His path; He knows best who are guided aright (125). And if you punish, punish with the like of what you were punished; but if you bear with patience, then best it is for the patient (126). Bear with patience, for your patience comes solely from God. Sorrow not for them, nor be vexed by the guile they practise. God stands with the pious and with those who are virtuous (127).[161]

Therefore, there is room for *iḥsān* (goodwill) even under the most adverse circumstances. In addition to the advice given to the Muslims for dealing with *kuffār*, the Holy Qur'an also has offered advice for dealing with other believers, namely Christians and Jews, as in Verse Q29:46.

And do not argue with the followers of earlier revelation otherwise than in a most kindly manner—unless it be such of them as are bent on evil doing—and say: "We believe in that which has been bestowed from on high upon us, as well as that which has been bestowed upon you: for our God and your God is one and the same, and it is unto Him that We [all] surrender ourselves."[162]

In the end, Islam is a religion of peace, as its name states. All mandated acts of worship among the pillars of Islam are geared toward strengthening the meaning of peace: salat (or prayer) and *ṣawm* (or fast of Ramadan) are for the inner peace of mind; zakat (or alms giving) and hajj (or pilgrimage to Mecca) are for social peace, and jihad—the true jihad—is for religious peace. In this respect, Seyyed Hossein Nasr stresses the importance to always keep in mind Verse Q48:4[163] and concludes that "whether one speaks of sakīnah, or the Hebrew equivalent shekinah, or for that matter pacem or shanti, the reality emphasized by Islam remains that the source of peace is God Who is Himself Peace and without Whom there can be no peace on earth."[164]

Pacifism and tolerance are further evidence that Islam is secular. Not only is the other tolerated, the other is accepted and welcomed as friend and as family. Muslims and other believers among the People of the Book may live in peace with each other, befriend each other, and marry among each other. In this respect Islam is not only secular but inherently progressive, as well.

PART THREE
The Progressive Nature of Islam

Islam did not spread by the sword, as it is widely claimed. It is true that the Arabs, following the death of Prophet Muhammad, launched their armies in every direction to conquer neighboring lands, mainly inhabited by Sabeans, in the Persian Empire to the east and northeast of the Arabian Peninsula, and the Christians of the Levant, part of the Byzantine Empire, to the west and northwest. But contrary to popular perception, the masses of non-Muslims who adopted Islam did not convert because they were forced to do so.

Indeed, some of those who converted to Islam did so to avoid the inferior *dhimmī* status offered to them and the payment of the head tax, otherwise known as the *jizya*. Observing that there was no need for violence to spread Islam, Abdelmajid Charfi points out, "The wars initiated by the early Muslims against their neighbors … [were] motivated exclusively by profane purposes."[1] However, a great majority of converts found in Islam secularism, tolerance, and religious freedom. As John Esposito notes, some may have been oppressed by their priests or religious leaders and sought refuge in the compassionate environment of early Islam.

> Religiously, Islam proved a more tolerant religion, providing greater religious freedom for Jews and indigenous Christians. Most of the local Christian churches had been persecuted as schismatics and heretics by a "foreign" Christian orthodoxy. For these reasons, some Jewish and Christian communities had actually aided the invading Muslim armies.[2]

Commenting on the secular attitudes of the early Muslims who built and expanded the Muslim Empire, Abdelmajid Charfi rightly observes:

> [They] did not feel any urge to provide a religious justification for their life organization; for that purpose they enacted rules for administration, finance, land distribution… inspired by Byzantine and Sassanid systems, giving priority to the general public interest and requirements of the time, without the slightest worry that such systems ought to be Islamic or otherwise being aware that they might acquire a divine label.[3]

Recognition of Islam's secular attributes is essential to understanding Islam as a continuing source of empowerment and change. In a true and free Islamic environment, each Muslim is empowered through a direct relationship with God, in which each person worships and communicates with God without intermediaries, free of pressures from those claiming the authority to represent religion and religious knowledge.

Recognition of the secular nature of Islam is an essential condition for freeing Islam and its adherents from the limiting effects of history and tradition by rendering their desacralization possible.[4] It could allow modernity to overcome the dominant influence of the authenticity current, whose adherents, notes Derek Hopwood, "see change as the corruption of original cultural values, and as something which can be reversed by new beginnings. The present to them is but an interval between perfect origins and their re-establishment."[5] While fundamentalists who champion a dogma of purist authenticity in the hope of reestablishing the perfect origins may be few in number, their impact is significant as a result of the weight of religious tradition and the reverential fear of change. Chapter 11 explores the concept of progressivism and its scope in Islam.

The most important impact of the desacralization of Islamic religious history could be the lifting of all limitations on the free exercise of the human mind. Countless restrictions have been placed on the use of the mind ever since the religious establishment took over the privilege of interpreting the Holy Qur'an and deciding what the religion ordains and prohibits. Instead, it will be demonstrated in Chapter 12 that faith is not—and cannot be—inconsistent with rational questioning and argument, and that in a secular environment the power of the mind can and should at all times be the most powerful engine of progress and change.

Another aspect of the desacralization of Islamic religious history is the rejection of a monolithic perception of Islam and Muslims as an integrated whole, referred to as *dār al-Islam* (the abode of Islam), in which non-Muslims can only exist in an inferior status. Instead, Islam as a faith and way of life—as opposed to *dīn wa dawla* (religion and state)—not only mandates the tolerance of others but acknowledges and accepts them as equals. Humanism in secular Islam is the foundation for a pluralistic society—hence a progressive one in which each group accepts, interacts with, and learns from the others. In Chapter 13 we will examine the perception of non-Muslims—believers or otherwise—by Islam.

Desacralization of religious history could also help to eliminate restrictions imposed on the fundamental rights and freedoms of Muslims by clergy and *fuqahā'* in the name of Islam and that of God's sovereign will. Recognition of the secular nature of Islam can restore to humankind what God their creator granted them; namely, the power to manage their lives in this life, as His trustees, including the power to freely make choices and be responsible for such choices. This will be explored in Chapters 14 and 15 before reflecting on the subject of Human rights in Islam in Chapter 16.

To return to the sources of Islam is to return to an Islam which does not fear progress but assuredly engenders it. The fact that Islam is inherently secular constitutes the guarantee of its progressive nature.

CHAPTER 11
The Concept and Scope of Progressivism in Islam

A number of the regions inhabited by Muslim majorities face extraordinary challenges in terms of security, capacity building, and development. They suffer from low economic outputs, undeveloped legal systems, low rates of literacy and educational achievement, and a high number of authoritarian regimes. In the face of such challenges, Muslim clerics and thinkers claim that Islam contains solutions to all issues and problems, and much time is spent searching for ways to adapt and to advance that are in keeping with Islamic traditions. Others blame Islam for the failures of its adherents to keep up with progress.

However, the problem is not with Islam, but with the general understanding of Islam. Not only is Islam capable of adapting to progress, it is of itself an engine of change capable of setting directions for progress, instead of merely reacting to events and trying to adapt to them. To the challenge posed by Tariq Ramadan— "[i]t is indeed a haunting question at the end of this second millennium to know whether Islam and the Muslims will embark on the train of progress"[1]—one could respond that the Message of Islam embodies progress on an eternal basis. But it remains up to us as Muslims to determine how to progress and to commit to maintaining an open mind toward Islam so as to find inspiration from within it and follow its lead toward progress.

Progress and Progressivism

Progressivism, in reference to Islam, is a philosophy and outlook of reform in all sectors of modern life, with a special emphasis on the protection of human rights, including political rights. The use of the term "progressivism" in this context should be distinguished from its use in the West where it may have particular connotations as a left-of-center political concept.[2]

The stasis that can be observed in various Muslim societies is often deepened by a religious culture which breeds a fear of God by promoting strict adherence to inflexible, change-resistant beliefs. Innovation is blamed for raising the wrath of God. This explains countless restrictions placed on innovative interpretation of the Scripture and the replacement of the culture of *ijtihād* by the culture of *taqlīd*: the blind imitation of the Prophet, his companions and successors, and the 'ulama'. In reality, change is inherent in God's creation and is an essential part of the Divine Message. The Holy Qur'an provides for it.

Mohammad Shahrour offers a theological explanation of the phenomenon of change based on two divinely inspired guiding concepts: *ḥanīfism* (the changing nature of matter) and *al-ṣirāt al-mustaqīm* (the straight path). According to Shahrour, *ḥanīfism* is a form of dialectic consisting of the changing nature of everything that is outside the realm of God and His attributes. Thus, that changing nature is of the essence of the entire universe—the earth, the planets, the stars, humankind, animals, and everything else which has a material existence. By contrast, *al-ṣirāt al-mustaqīm* includes the external existence of God and His attributes, together with the rules of conduct that can lead humanity on the path of God to ensure salvation. Within that global divine realm, *ḥanīfism* and *al-ṣirāt al-mustaqīm* are immutable: the changing nature of material existence will never cease to change, and the nature of God and the path leading to Him can never change. Together they constitute the divine order.[3] On that basis, while the Divine Message contained in the provisions of the Holy Qur'an, including the Shari'a principles, cannot change, our understanding and implementation of it will necessarily change. Therefore, according to Shahrour, any attempt to resist change is contrary to the nature of God's creation and His will. A look into the Prophetic Tradition, the traditions of the Companions, and the teachings of the major schools of jurisprudence indicates—and provides an early example of—the necessity, desirability, and proper practice of change and evolution following the evolution of social mores and human needs through time and space.[4] Indeed, the Prophet, his companions and successors, and the jurisprudents of the major schools led progress through the principles of religion, making exceptions and adapting Qur'anic rules to cope with change, while the jurisprudents adapted Shari'a to the various locations into which Islam expanded. For example, among the Enlightened Caliphs who succeeded the Prophet, 'Umar Ibn al-Khattab made bold moves toward change and progress as he embarked on the task of building the state structures for Muslim Arabs' expanding empire. Similarly, the Hanafi and, to a lesser extent, the Shafi'i schools of jurisprudence that developed in Baghdad and Egypt, respectively, in the heart of the newly conquered areas of the Byzantine and Persian Empires, produced a distinctive model of progress, commensurate with the level of advancement of the people who inhabited those areas. Shari'a thus did not have any initial difficulty in adapting to the enlightened environment prevailing. From that time onward, it led progress into the long era of scientific, economic, and cultural advancement which led to the Renaissance.[5]

By contrast, the Hanbali and Maliki schools of jurisprudence, which developed in Medina, reflected that city's continuing conservative environment. This division is understandable, given the geographic location of each of the major schools. While the living environment in Medina and throughout the Arabian Peninsula was still fairly simple, having remained free of foreign cultural influences from the Middle East and Persia, that of Baghdad was far more advanced and diversified, bearing the fruits of interaction between the various cultures of the region. The problems of society in Baghdad, far more complicated than those of society in Medina, required the pioneering search for solutions not specifically dealt with in the Holy Qur'an and Prophetic Tradition.

The difference between now and then is clear. Now, Muslims in general have inherited Islam with all the accumulations of its history. Our understanding of Islam is therefore rigidly defined and leaves little room for cautious progress, not enough to cope with the challenges of modernity. However, the Muslims of the early period were free of these restrictions; hence they were fully able to benefit from Islam as a driver of change. Their religious knowledge of Islam was still candid and direct, untainted by the sacralized knowledge of others and, most importantly, unrestricted by the prohibition of *ijtihād* that was instated a few centuries later. They were not fanatics. They were open to other cultures and ready to interact with them, both giving and taking, as Roger Caratini observes.

> [T]en or eleven centuries ago, in Baghdad, one could do geometry like Euclid, philosophy like Plato or Aristotle, astronomy like Ptolemy and medicine like

Galen; in short, one could think like the pagan Greeks, while being deeply Muslim, and that is not so much because of the belief in one God and the Last Judgment, but because everyone lived according to the value system established by the Qur'an, which had nothing in common with Greek thought.[6]

The builders of the great Muslim Empire and culture were true progressivists, and Islam served them as an engine for leading progress.

Progressivism is not about simply coping with modernity. It is about actively and creatively fashioning modernity and progress. That is why it is not possible to subscribe to the view which advocates rethinking and reforming Islam in light of modernity, using the values inherent in modernity in order to set new foundations for Islam based on modern-day human rights.[7] Long before they were formulated and declared by "modernity," these human rights were recognized by Islam and declared to be inherent in human nature. Islam does not need to be rethought and reformed every time modernity advances. When it is perceived in this manner, Islam becomes irrelevant. Indeed, when Shabbir Akhtar observes Muslims' perception of Western modernity as the West's problem and questions how long Muslims can continue to think of modernity as someone else's problem,[8] the question that he asks implies a perception of modernity as a problem—rather than as a challenge toward progress—as well as a perception of progress defined exclusively by the West.

But progress is not achieved by striving toward a cautious reinterpretation of Islam in a quest to cope with modernity, where modernity is presumably construed as the achievements of the West.[9] Counter to that approach, progressivism is the courage to take the best from the others, reject the shortcomings of Muslim societies, and, most importantly, disengage from unexamined habits, and reject *taqlīd* (imitation). Such an approach is possible only with the full recognition of both the universal and secular nature of Islam.

Progressivism Inherent in the Universal Nature of Islam

Progressivism is inherent in the universal nature of Islam, and the Message of God is relevant to addressing changing needs and customs from one location to another and from one generation to the next. Islam is universal precisely because it is capable of leading change and, when necessary, adapting to it. What is universal—and thus embodies progressivism—in Islam is the Message as formulated by God in the Holy Qur'an, as opposed to how it was understood and implemented by humans, including the Prophet, the Companions, or any other person, no matter how learned that person might be. For that reason, views regarding the insufficiency of the Holy Qur'an, without the Prophetic Tradition for its interpretation and understanding, are not plausible.[10] What the Holy Qur'an is blamed for is precisely what makes it universal, and any view of Prophetic Tradition as a necessary complement to the Qur'an is an unwarranted use of that tradition to overshadow the universal nature of the Divine Message.

In addition, the assignment of such a role to Prophetic Tradition constitutes an abdication by humankind of the right, and a failure in the duty entrusted by God, to use the human mind. In any event, such views constitute a disavowal of divine justice and a denial of the completeness and perfection of God's Words. Any subjection of the universal nature of Islam and of God's Message to limiting human traditions and custom prevents progress.

This progressive understanding of the universal nature of Islam was not discovered by modernists but was voiced in the early nineteenth century by the Indian educator, politician, and reformer Sir Sayyid Ahmad Khan. In his book *Tafsīr*, Ahmad Khan warned, "Ḥadīth-based *tafsīr* tends to limit the meaning of the Qur'an to a particular historical situation, thus obscuring its universality."[11] These sound views caution against confusing the universal message with its time-and-place-bound human understanding, which can never be universal. This is perhaps the reason why Nurcolish Madjid, while agreeing with Muhammad Shahrour's views about the changing nature of everything besides God and His attributes, goes on to consider all values and general principles set forth in the Holy Qur'an, other than the value of *taqwa*, to be of a changing nature, and thus nonuniversal.[12] Belief in the changing nature of everything other than God and His attributes is not in contradiction with the belief that the values and principles set forth in the Holy Qur'an do not change, because as God's word they are divine. However, if the values do not change, their application can and should change with time and place.

To illustrate this, the Holy Qur'an created a revolution when, fifteen centuries ago, it overturned the tribal system of inheritance and replaced it with general principles for disposing of the estates of deceased persons more equitably among descendants and other relatives, after the prior settlement of debts and the respect of the deceased person's wishes expressed in a will. The main revolutionary message in that new system was not about the detailed allocations contained in specific verses of the Qur'an which the 'ulama' developed to fit the circumstances of their time into a comprehensive law on inheritance. Instead it was about change itself. The message was that the customary tribal system was too rigid and hindered social and economic progress. The principles brought about by the Holy Qur'an contained the necessary flexibility for constant adaptation to evolving needs.

Two things occurred to obfuscate the progressivism of the new principles which would obscure their universal nature. First, there was a total disregard of an important proviso in the Holy Qur'an which describes the proposed allocations of inheritance shares as *ḥudūd,* that is, limits in the sense that the Qur'anic share allocations are minimum reserved share allocations to people who could potentially have been deprived under the preexisting tribal system.[13] Second, a limited and temporary ban on wills imposed by the Prophet was taken out of context and deemed to abrogate the verse of the Qur'an which encourages people to organize their estates by way of wills. This misinterpretation gave the Prophet's action a divine scope and rendered the ban in question permanent.[14] In reality, what the Prophet did was to impose a temporary measure to prevent people from circumventing the new inheritance scheme by reverting to the tribal system being overturned.[15] The outcome was dramatic and rigid: the inheritance became restricted to the exact allocations set forth in the Qur'an without the proviso intended to provide flexibility for change and adaptation to changing needs. This explains why Muslim nations which apply the Islamic law system of inheritance still administer a most unfair and inequitable system of inheritance. Countless similar examples can be cited.

The Divine Message should, in each age and place, be read and understood with that time's needs, issues, and values in mind. It is insufficient every now and then to attempt to reinterpret the Islamic heritage in order to adapt it to modern conditions. Nor is it expedient to try to find middle solutions between the respective positions of traditionalists and modernists.[16] Yet, the issue is still addressed through advocacy pressuring Muslims in general to empower Islamic centers of learning to develop Islamic law. However, while centers of learning have a major role to play in providing guidance, they should not be considered substitutes for the individual freedom of thought of Muslims. It is the prerogative of people as trustees, through duly designated secular legislatures, to legislate for progress. On religious grounds, no Muslim person should abdicate his or her rights to interpret and understand. Islamic centers can develop their own philosophies and contribute their thoughts and solutions to duly organized legislatures. But they should not label them as the "Islamic" system and then expect acceptance and compliance by Muslims. The issue is the need to adopt an outlook and perception that is based on universalism.[17]

A reason that Muslim communities are constrained in leading progress lies in their remaining inflexibly custom-centered instead of advancing toward new, open-minded perspectives and approaches which transcend heritage and tradition while preserving and enriching them. Didn't the Prophet advise each person to read and understand the Qur'an as if it was revealed directly to him or her?[18] Mohamed Talbi illustrates this universality.

> It [the Qur'an] invites us…to an infinite revelation, a revelation that continues to unfold as our universe continues to unfold before us, and the context of our lives follows and changes…The Quran is guidance (*hudan*)…We follow the vector toward which it guides us, that is toward the future, that of our grandchildren, instead of towards our ancestors (the salaf).[19]

Sadly, rigid sacralization of history can unintentionally deter us from listening to God. When understood from its progressive perspective, Islam is not a dead religion of the past which is studied solely as part of history. It is one that addresses the concerns of our parents *and* ancestors, is capable of answering our own questions, and bears the seeds that address the aspirations of our children and grandchildren.

Progressivism Is Made Possible by the Secular Nature of Islam

Islam is not a political, legal, or economic system. Instead, it is a faith and an individually directed way of life. It is thus a body of principles designed to frame the rights of individuals and facilitate relations of people with each other in an atmosphere of freedom, peace, understanding, and mutual acceptance, all of which characterize that way of life. Contrary to prevailing perception, Islam is humankind-centered. God created this world and entrusted its development and management to humankind as His trustees. For that purpose, He endowed humankind with guidance, universal values, and principles which are adaptable to changing circumstances over time and space. Therefore, as human beings we have the right and power to organize our lives in our own ways and as fits our needs. While God is omnipotent and watches over us as His creatures, we should not rely on God or His angels to legislate for us and manage our lives, or to create development, happiness, and prosperity for us: progress is within our own power and reach.

Progressivism is inherent in Islam, and its secular nature constitutes the proper environment and precondition to lead and achieve progress on a continuous basis. There have been arguments about the extent of liberal ideology present in Islam. For those who include exegesis and customs in the fold of Islam, there is little room for liberalism and progressivism. Similarly, salafis and fundamentalists who, among other restrictions, stick to the letter of the text rather than to its message, make no room for reinterpretation over time; hence, their rejection of liberalism.

Modernity, in the context of Islam, is often discussed primarily by reference to Western liberalism and progress,[20] and as if the accession to modernity and life advancement depended on a reform of Islam. First, the discussion of liberalism and Islam need not to be undertaken in relation to Western—or any other—liberalism. Islam is liberal, inherently and autonomously, in the sense that it fosters a free mindset which rejects any restrictions on the use of the mind and is not resistant to change from entrenched customs, practices, and prevailing interpretations. Relative to traditional Islam (which sacralizes customs) and revivalist Islam (which sacralizes Prophetic Tradition and the early interpretations of the Scripture), true Islam simply means Islam without the added weight of those traditions, customs, accounts, or commentaries that limit people's progress and that freeze Islam in time and space. On the other hand, Islam is perfect and does not need to be reformed. What require change and reform are aspects of Muslim societies and culture so that Muslim peoples can advance, if they apply the universal principles and values of Islam. In this respect, Khaled Abou El Fadl raises an interesting and important dilemma.

> The temptation is enormous for Muslims to adopt a defensive posture, insisting that Islam is perfect and that the inherited doctrines and dogmas of the Islamic tradition do not in any way contribute to the plight of Muslims in the modern age. Understandable though this defensive posture might be, it is a position that has its costs...As sinful as fitna might be, I believe that what is at risk in the ongoing conflict between the moderates and puritans is nothing less than the very soul of Islam. Therefore, it is a greater act of sin for Muslims to indulge in a state of apathetic indifference.[21]

The insistence on renewing tradition, in spite of the short-term potential effects of such renewal, finds its justification in the fact that Islam does not aim only at unity and harmony among Muslims. As a universal religion, it aims at achieving harmony among all of humankind. There is no *fitna* when recognition of the root cause of the stated schism is intended to restore harmony among humankind as a whole, in testimony to the pluralistic nature of Islam.

To the extent that Islam is not a political system or a system of governance, people are collectively empowered to design and implement the most appropriate governance systems to address changing needs, continuously improve living conditions, and better understand the values granted by God.[22] Similarly, because of the empowerment of humankind as God's trustees, people were entitled to legislate and to enact laws best-suited to particular needs and objectives. When we confuse divine Sharia'a with man-made Islamic law and call it Sharia'a, we confine ourselves to a narrowly restrictive legal system which is then wrongly attributed to God.[23] A way to restore to people the freedom to self-legislate is to acknowledge the secular nature of Islam and to recognize that the divine Sharia'a is not, and was never intended to be, a legal system. Indeed divine Sharia'a transcends all systems and constitutes a point of reference for guiding and inspiring man-made legal systems in all times and ages. Thus, divine Sharia'a can be properly understood only when the chains of history embodied in man-made Islamic law are removed.[24]

This brings us back to an understanding of progressivism, namely the courage to disengage from rigid customs and practices, and to reject *taqlīd* (imitation). This view is rejected by a significant number of thinkers, who are not yet prepared to acknowledge the secular nature of Islam. Even for the most receptive scholars of Islam, such as Omid Safi, a progressive Muslim agenda must nevertheless remain *Islamic* "in the sense of deriving its inspiration from the heart of the Islamic tradition." Safi emphasizes, "[i]t cannot survive as a graft of Secular Humanism onto the tree of Islam, but emerge from within that very entity."[25] While it is helpful to consult tradition in seeking guiding examples of change and progressive thinking, such methodology and approach should not constitute a precondition. Being universal, Islam is for everyone and not just for Muslims. As such, it is for ordinary people, and only scholars can be held to such standard because they can access, understand, and evaluate tradition. On the other hand, tradition is essentially for Muslims, because it emanates from our beliefs, acts, and customs, and does not concern nonbelievers. There is also a compelling need to free Islam from its chains as an "identity."

A Muslim progressive agenda should not be perceived as "a graft of secular humanism onto the tree of Islam" because secularism is inherent in Islam. Secularism is the means by which Islam flourished and expanded, in the first centuries of its revelation, into a widely diversified culture and source of knowledge and enlightenment. It is the erosion of secularism that led to the weakening and downfall of that empire. Scholars often observe how moderate Islamists adapt and adopt into Islam modern principles of human rights, the rule of law, limitations on political power, and the like, as developed in the Enlightenment era.[26] In reality, the Enlightenment principles that are frequently referred to are the principles of secularism, most of which were already embodied in Islam long before the advent of the Enlightenment. Recognizing that Islam is secular is a way of acting to restore Islam as an engine of progress.

Khaled Abou El Fadl rightly points out the many challenges facing Muslim societies and the multiplicity of representations of Islam, which he attributes in part to the disintegration of historical institutions of Islamic learning which did not leave any credible formal bodies capable of speaking authoritatively for Islam. He observes that those who spoke for Islam often were educated in Western institutions according to Western scientific methods and thus became part of Western culture.[27]

However, in addition to the disintegration of institutions of Islamic learning, the actual challenges threatening many Muslim societies, and the proliferation of destructive misrepresentations of Islam, relate to continued resistance to secularization. Opposition to secularization by religious institutions has inhibited various forms of progress as being offensive to religion. If the secular nature of Islam were to be acknowledged, then the need for a class of religious authorities who solely speak for Islam could be reexamined. This may explain why the message of Islam did not provide an institutional framework for such authority, and it is what perhaps privileges Islam and makes it humanistic and individualistic. Mohamed Talbi rightly denies to anyone the power to speak *for* Islam, or to impose upon others the nature of the faith, commenting, "I do not subscribe to any trend which speaks in the name of Islam, establishing itself as an ultimate authority and authoritative source."[28] In the end, Islamic culture and Western culture are not alien to each other. Western culture, in its crucial Renaissance phase, was strongly influenced—if not initiated—by Islamic culture, and there should be no reason for Islamic culture not to benefit from the development and progress of Western culture.

CHAPTER 12
Islam and the Mind

Humayun Kabir reminds us that Islam at first appeared as a "liberal and democratic movement whose color- and race-blind message of equality and fraternity affected equally the intellectual and the underprivileged."[1] The Islam that Kabir speaks of is one that predates the constraints that would gradually overtake and delimit the exercise of reason and rational thought as instruments of faith. Matters dealt with conclusively by an express provision of the Qur'an, by Prophetic Tradition, or by *ijmā'* (consensus), would be withdrawn from the scope of permitted *ijtihād*. As such, they became unanswerable to rational consideration but instead had to be "accepted as is by way of absolute submission and abdication to God's governance and that of his prophet."[2] This notion, as advanced by Sh. Y. Qaradawy, echoes similar earlier positions called for by many of the early days' *fuqahā'*, such as a call by Imam al-Shafi'i which was tantamount to relinquishing one's mind and abdicating its use in deference to the so-called "learned ones," and then only within strict limits.[3] Here we can begin to see the construction of the first set of artificial impediments to the use of the mind, which included the following key assumptions: (1) despite the fact that God's Message is addressed to all people without discrimination, not every human being created by God and endowed with a mind may use it to consult, understand, and live by God's Message, but only those who have spent years scrutinizing the works of religious science; (2) assuming that after years of religious education a person could fulfill these conditions, he or she may apply rational thinking only within a sphere limited to subjects not otherwise dealt with in the Holy Qur'an and the Prophetic Tradition, as well as to those over which no *ijmā'* (consensus) had been expressed; and (3) the use of the mind beyond the limits of the permitted subjects constitutes a rebellion against divine governance.

For his part, Shaykh Muhammad Sa'id Ramadan al-Buti denies the legitimacy of efforts toward renewal of the *fiqh* process through *ijtihād*, which constitutes an affront to the early and later *fuqahā'* who developed that science, and an accusation of error against them. From that perspective, only a very narrow window of *ijtihād* is allowed in matters of detail not addressed previously, and then only if performed by an elite minority presumably qualified to do so using the same thought process devised by the elders.[4] As a result, al-Buti assigns humans to two possible categories, with no third alternative in-between, namely the *mujtahid*, or the elite few scholars who may use their mind to perform *ijtihād* within that preset narrow window, and the *muqallid*, or the massive majorities who fall into the category of imitators. Under such a structure, only the *mujtahid* have the power to say what can and cannot be done in daily matters from a religious perspective. The *muqallid* have no alternative but to imitate the *mujtahid* and to follow their guidance, with the extraordinary understanding that fatwas (opinions) issued by the *mujtahid* are binding on the *muqallid*. Al-Buti even goes so far as to require each person to follow his or her imam and, worst of all, strongly cautions against people freeing themselves from the imam by studying the sources of religion, which he considers to be foolish and hazardous.[5]

These and other impediments raised against the use of the mind, together with those who advocated and taught them, are the factors that would obstruct paths to progress. Yet, the Scriptures containing the Divine Message are clear about the right and duty of each Muslim to apply rational thinking using the powers of the mind.[6] The Holy Qur'an is not neutral over the use of the mind. Rather, it encourages rational thinking and consideration without limitation, including with regard to the essence of faith.

Impediments to the Use of the Mind

Three major impediments thwart or eliminate the use of the mind. First, it is often advocated in Islam that faith and reason are incompatible. Second, it is also claimed that the use of the mind is useless and at best incompatible with divine governance. These claims have directly resulted in the sacralization of tradition and *taqlīd* (imitation), the third major impediment to the use of the mind, to which people have generally succumbed out of fear of committing a *bid'a*, or innovation—the single most negative consequence of not following tradition.

Faith and Reason: Perception of Incompatibility

Īmān, or faith, is perceived as the antidote to reason, because faith resides in the heart and reason resides in the mind.[7] The argument goes as follows: (1) if a subject matter requiring faith was rationally demonstrable, then faith would be irrelevant since conviction exists; and (2) it is only when the human mind is unable to rationalize a certain premise that the matter becomes one of faith.

It is true that in the Holy Qur'an, as in the previous Scriptures revealed by God to His earlier prophets, there are certain matters in the faith which defy the ability of the human mind to scientifically demonstrate them, such as the existence and unicity of God, His creation, the survival of the human soul following the death of the human body, the Final Day and Judgment, the resurrection, and life after death. If people could see God, then there would be no need for faith: the heart need not be confused with abstraction if the mind can perceive ironclad proof. The Holy Qur'an has ruled this out, telling us: no one—not even the prophets—can see God or attain His knowledge. God reveals himself to humans from behind a veil, or through an angel or archangel. However, He can at any time provide revelations to any person.[8]

This may explain the early suspicions of, and general antagonism toward, philosophers and philosophical thought in general—Greek philosophy in particular.[9] Philosophy is blamed for sowing doubt and confusion in the minds of people, while God's messages contained in the Scriptures provide inner comfort, with assurances of paradise to the deserving.[10]

Greek philosophy predates both Christianity and Islam, among the monotheistic religions. In the early period of Islam, Greek philosophy was rediscovered and translated into Arabic. Abu Hamid al-Ghazali is frequently referred to as the reformer who, in the eleventh century, strove and successfully managed to refute the arguments of the philosophers.[11] However, in reality, al-Ghazali did not refute philosophy as a discipline or as an activity that is primarily the product of the mind. What he refuted were certain specific conclusions reached by Greek philosophers which were incompatible with the basic tenets of Islam. In other words, he did not consider the application of philosophic reasoning to religious matters to be incompatible with faith, nor did he advocate blind submission or abdication of one's own power to think, question, and critique.

Greek philosophy was not alone in eliciting objections. All forms of philosophy have been viewed suspiciously because philosophy is generally perceived as an external influence, foreign to Islam and to Islamic culture and traditions.[12] However, Islam cannot be adversely affected by foreign influence because it is universal and encompasses all other monotheistic faiths and, most importantly, embraces multiple races and ethnicities. 'Abbas Mahmoud al-'Aqqad attributes the cautious attitude toward philosophy to the role of religious authorities who strove to monopolize all matters relating to faith and metaphysics. For that purpose, he recalls the strong belligerence against—and persecution of—philosophers in Europe during the Middle Ages when the Church wielded substantial power. He further observes that, by comparison and during that same time period, the absence in Islam of a clergy that wielded official power was instrumental in allowing some important philosophy to survive, such as that of al-Farabi, Ibn Sina (Avicenna), Ibn Toufeyl, Ibn Rushd (Averroes), and others.[13]

Although, in the Holy Qur'an, matters that typically require faith are limited, God offered powerful circumstantial evidence through scriptural foundations for the sanctity of the mind. In the words of Shaykh Muhammad 'Abdu, "Islam, in this call to the belief (or *īmān*) in God and His unicity is founded on nothing less than the rational evidence."[14] God thus drew these matters of true faith closer to the minds of people and elevated them to the level of belief, though short of that of conviction. Hence, the faithful are called "believers," where belief lies between faith and conviction, but closer to the latter. By providing circumstantial evidence in connection with the most essential issues of faith, God was sending another message, namely that everything is subject to rational questioning and critique, without exception, because only then can *īmān* be genuine and whole.[15] Jamaluddin al-Afghani expresses this concept clearly.

> Islam is almost unique among religions in censuring belief without proof, rebuking those who follow suppositions, reproaching those who act randomly in the darkness of ignorance, and chiding them for their conduct. This religion demands that the pious seek proof [for their beliefs] in the sources of their religion.[16]

From another perspective, Talbi offers a convincing link between faith and reason, whereby faith, which he describes as intelligent freedom, constitutes the logical culmination of the reasoned reading of God's signs.[17] Shabbir Akhtar even advocates "a 'critical Koranic scholarship'—in the larger attempt to make it relevant to modern man," which in his opinion serves to preserve the Qur'an and ensure that it remains at all times relevant and alive. For that purpose he applies a rabbinical maxim which states: "It is better to profane the Torah than to forget it."[18] Moreover, as Moroccan nationalist leader 'Alal al-Fassi proposes:

> Īmān occurs only as a result of reflection, research and thinking, i.e., following the mental efforts that the individual exerts to reach the conviction about the existence of God and the relevance of having faith in same. Faith is therefore developed from the mind.[19]

This view coincides with that of prominent Shi'i cleric, 'Ali Shari'ati, who asserts that it is not acceptable to blindly follow the dogma set by the forefathers in matters relating to the creed which are accessible to the mind, because the faith of the imitator is then deficient.[20] This points out the humanistic nature of Islam in the sense that God did not want people to believe solely out of fear of potential punishment, but instead out of true and genuine love for God and inner comfort about His Compassion. This is exactly what is reflected in the Qur'anic Verse Q2:260.

> And when Abraham said, "My Lord show me how You give life to the dead." He said, "Why, do you not believe?" "Yes," he said, "but so that my heart may be reassured." Said He, "Take four birds, and twist them to you, then set a part of them on every hill, then summon them, and they will come to you in haste. And know that God is Mighty, Wise."[21]

Abraham's reaction to God's enquiry about his faith did not shock God. On the contrary, it satisfied God that Abraham was taking seriously the circumstantial evidence that He offered him.[22] In the same vein, the argument that takes place between Abraham and his people about the unicity of God and the potential role of their deities reflects the importance of the role of the mind in faith-related matters.

> His people argued with him. He said, "Do you argue with me about Allah while He

has already led me to the right path?... My Lord encompasses everything with His knowledge. Would you, then, take no lesson? (80) How can I fear that which you associate with Him, while you do not fear (the evil fate of) your having associated with Allah something for which He did not send down to you any authority? Now, which of the two parties has more right to be in peace? (Tell me) if you know (81). Those who have believed and have not mixed their faith with injustice are the ones who deserve peace, and it is they who are on the right path (82). "[23]

These and countless other examples from the Qur'an are further proof that unconditional belief without question is neither inherent in, nor a requirement of, Islam.[24] On the contrary, true *īmān* and salvation require belief. In other words, not only are faith and reason compatible, but faith in Islam requires the use of the mind.[25] In the words of Hisham Jait, "The Qur'an aims to prove the existence of the creator, as sole creator; this explains the rational formulation and the call to ponder and reflect."[26]

Based on the scriptural encouragement of rational enquiry, we find a confirmation that, beyond being merely tolerated, philosophy is primarily encouraged following the encouragement of pondering and rational consideration of God's evidences. For some, philosophy is perceived as an attempt by the philosopher to judge the word of God, which presumably defies the provisions of the Holy Qur'an, according to which God is the final judge.[27] This perception is difficult to justify because philosophy is not about judging the word of God. The philosopher instead analyzes, interprets, and reasons about the word of God. He does not take it on face value. He verifies the faith exactly as God encouraged him to do, because God wants true faith, that is, with true belief. The mind and reason are the tools that God gave humankind to devise philosophy, as a tool of progress toward ultimate truth. It is through the power of the mind and rational thinking that God gave humankind the means to use revelation as a starting point in order to seek divine truth. God did not reveal all truths—only some of them.[28] However, He provided humankind with the means which lead to the truth. Thus, while only a small part of the Truth was revealed, God did not say that humanity shall remain forever unable to increase its knowledge. On the contrary, these little truths are the threads to be used with the effort of the mind to increase knowledge and acquire more truths.

While philosophy and reason may not always explain all tenets of faith, none of the tenets of the faith contradicts either philosophy or reason. If any such tenet of faith contradicted reason, then that tenet would not be genuine. Shaykh Muhammad 'Abdu expresses this succinctly: "In case of contradiction between the mind and an action being imitated, one should adopt the solution to which the mind points."[29] In other words, while it might not be always possible to rationally explain all the tenets of the faith, it is hard to think of any tenets that are rationally impossible or difficult to accept. It is therefore necessary to determine what constitutes the basic tenets of the faith, because not everything found in the Scriptures is a tenet of faith. While stories in the Scriptures may not be rationally plausible at face value because they take an allegorical form, remaining neutral to such stories does not reduce the faith. Instead, the basic tenets which constitute the pillars of *īmān* cannot be rationally implausible, and for that reason the absence of conclusive rational proof is no reason to abandon faith, or to doubt it.

Shaykh Sobhi al-Saleh refers to the conflicting dualities within human nature, such as the struggle between religion and the mind, where human nature is saved from its confusion by God's guidance or *al-huda*.[30] But there is no conflict between the mind and religion which requires *al-huda* from God to settle, because God's guidance in the first place comes through the mind. Is it possible that God created humankind, gave people reason and mind, and charged us with stewardship of the world, only to receive the Revelation and not to use the mind for any other purpose?[31]

Two diametrically opposed responses toward modernity can be observed among some Muslim people: isolationism and imitation. The isolationist response blocks the mind from all innovation and development. Talbi identifies this reaction as starting around the time of the first defeats of the Mu'tazila movement by the *Ash'aris* in the eleventh century and the rise of the philosopher Ibn Rushd (known in the West as Averroes) in Cordoba, Spain, at the beginning of the twelfth century.[32] At the other extreme, all experiences from the past which constitute the Muslim cultural heritage are set aside in favor of a blind imitation of the early elders. In reality, both attitudes extrapolate from history a presumed impact of religion on political and military power because they blame the loss of the grandeur that Islam achieved in its early period on innovation and departure from tradition.

Of these two responses, isolationism has been proven to be more damaging because it advocates the absolute sufficiency of the teachings of the Qur'an and those of the Prophet, negating any benefit in learning from the others.[33] Such an attitude is in direct contradiction with the teachings of the Prophet, who said: "Seek knowledge even if you could only find it in China"; and "The pursuit of knowledge and science is preferable for God to the prayer, the fast, the hajj, or the jihad."[34] Surely, when he said so, the Prophet was not expecting to find Muslims in China for people to learn from. What he meant was that knowledge and science were worth every effort, including going a long way to find them, and that they should be acquired wherever they can be found. Similarly, the Prophet knew the value of knowledge and the mind when he placed them ahead of worship, because worship is meaningless without knowledge and proper use of the mind.

The credibility of these traditions of the Prophet is further enhanced by the Qur'anic verses which exhort people to seek knowledge.[35] Most importantly, when God created humankind, He ordered the angels to prostrate before Adam because He had endowed humankind with a mind, the tool of progress that humankind needs to perform the trusteeship of the world that God charged us with caretaking. The endowment of humankind with a mind enables each individual to choose to be either good or evil and be accountable for such choice.[36] Abdelmajid Charfi notes of this aspect of humanity and the challenge of rising up to the freedom of choice, "[i]t is into one's self, one's own intelligence and reason, and equally into nature that each individual must tap for the teachings through which to fulfill one's human condition...."[37] God has made people subject to temptation to wrongdoing, namely because humans have a free will with which to resist and remain immune to the pressures of temptation to lead them astray. God made people with a free will. This means that people are capable of distinguishing right from wrong and need not rely exclusively on religion to do so.[38]

This may explain the fact that the Divine Message did not reveal all truth, but rather enough truths that—when coupled with the power of the mind—would enable humankind to explore and discover more truths. On this basis, and bearing in mind that God has endowed the human mind with the ability to distinguish right from wrong and instructed humankind to use that mind, we should reject the claims of those whom Ann E. Mayer calls "ethical voluntarists," that "whatever God willed had to be accepted as just and believers were not entitled to use criteria based on the exercise of human reason to make independent judgments about what constituted justice."[39] To illustrate, a twentieth-century exegete, Shaykh Muhammad Mutwalli Sha'rawi has noted that, while people start life with free will, yet when they elect to believe, they willfully and irrevocably relinquish that freedom as they submit to the will of God.[40] Such a claim is implausible. First, divine governance is an integral aspect of God's attributes. Divine governance is not contingent on each individual's choice to believe or not to believe, and submission to God's governance is not an option that a person is deemed to have exercised upon becoming a believer. Second, while the human mind is capable of telling right from wrong and just from unjust, there is no sure way to determine what God has willed and when He did so. The occurrences in any person's life are not necessarily signs of God's will, and the calamities and afflictions experienced by people from time to time do not necessarily emanate from God's will. Unfortunately, the mainstream of Muslim peoples (including clerics and jurisconsults) still assign everything to God's will. This mainstream movement contends that any innovative use of the mind could lead to straying from revealed truths, and instead advocates deferring to the wisdom of God, which is reflected in the wisdom of clerics in the religious establishment.

Mohammad Iqbal encapsulates the reasonable and rational approach: "The only course open to us is to approach modern knowledge with a respectful but independent attitude and to appreciate the teachings of Islam in the light of that knowledge, even though we may be led to differ from those who have gone before us."[41] This approach is the one that is closest and most in conformity with *fitra*.[42] People seek knowledge and progress, and an inner alarm can sound when religious values and ethics have been transgressed. The alternative approach—that of digging into the Qur'an and religious tradition in an effort to chart a limited, trafficable road to achieve some progress—inevitably will be insufficient. This suspicion of, and enmity toward, the mind, which has accumulated over many centuries—since the defeat of rational thinking represented by philosophy and the Mu'tazila—also accounts for the erroneous understanding of the concept of divine governance and support for predestination in Islam.

Predestination and Free Will

Murad Hoffman describes predestination as a governance-related paradox, whereby either God is the cause of all acts, in which case humans are not responsible for their actions and cannot be subjected to God's punishment, or humans are the creators—and thus in control—of their own actions, in which case God ceases to be the creator of all things and sovereign over all acts.[43]

The concept of predestination by divine will continues to stand as a resilient impediment to progress by Muslim societies. Under this concept, God has already decided how many people will be born and die from the time of Adam's creation until the end of times. He has determined every move of every creature that He has created from the time of its conception until its last day. He has also preordained every occurrence, good or bad, that may involve every creature. All of this is written by God in the eternal Preserved Tablet, or *al-lawḥ al-maḥfūẓ*. Therefore, because God knows and controls everything, anything that happens to any divine creature and everything that any such creature does, is designed, construed, and authorized by God, hence is intended and predetermined by Him. This, as the concept goes, is a direct corollary of divine governance.

Under such heavy-handed divine control, it is useless for people to use their minds, because they have no choice in what they do or how they live. The mind is thus preprogrammed from the time of conception to operate concurrently with God Himself. Consequently, if humans have no choice, then they also have no will, be it free will or otherwise. Thus they have no incentive to use their minds, because that use has no chance of changing what God has already preordained. At best, then, the mind may be used primarily to pray ever harder, but hopelessly, for God to change His mind and modify what He may have preordained. This form of belief relieves the individual from any form of accountability, leaving no option other than to rely on God, dreading the worst and praying for the best. Since all that occurs is the direct expression and result of God's will, no one should be expected to get credit for any good deed, or to be held responsible for a bad one.

This fatalistic mood did not exist in the days of the Prophet, the Companions, and the first few successors who oversaw the establishment and initial territorial expansion of the Islamic Empire. It came about with the development of Islamic philosophical thought, following the rediscovery of Greek philosophy. Islamic philosophical thought was mainly a reenactment of Greek philosophy, with rational interpretation and demonstration of religious faith at the center of the debate. This is what the Mu'tazila philosophers of the second century of Islam tried to do, which earned them the wrath of the religious conservatives, to the extent that philosophy became a taboo subject and was even at times banned. In fact, the prevailing conservative view, represented by the *al-Ash'ariyya* doctrine, could be narrated in this way: God is the sole and unique deity of all people of all times and places (Allah *rabbu-l-'ālamīn*). Therefore, His Message is addressed to all of them and as such is eternal or at least for as long as there remains any *'ālamīn*. At the same time, the Holy Qur'an— being the Divine Message and word of God—is an integral aspect of God and is as eternal as God is, in the sense that it has existed and will continue to exist concurrently with God's existence.

Such a perception and view could not be accepted and digested by the rational minds of those imbued with Greek philosophy—namely, the Islamic philosophers of the Mu'tazila group. Indeed, it did not make sense to them that the Qur'an had existed eternally when its revelation was in part, and at times, interactive with—or reactive to—events as they were unfolding in Mecca and Medina, since the start of revelation. In that case it defied reason that God would allow confusion and doubt regarding the Qur'an's authenticity, accuracy, and completeness. Also, it was not plausible to perceive the Qur'an as having existed long before the occurrence of the events during which God was guiding the Prophet. Therefore, to the Mu'tazila, the Holy Qur'an was created over time by God for a universal purpose.

In response to the Mu'tazila position, the only way their opponents could insist on their view was to accept its most important consequence, predestination. Indeed, if God's word could not be rationally perceived extraneously to God, that is, if the Qur'an as God's word could only be inherent in God and had existed eternally, before any of the events cited in it had existed, then such events were known to God since then because He preordained them following His intention to do so. Then, most naturally, everything God's creatures do, enjoy, or endure is designed and preordained by God.

However, this view, advocated by the *Ash'aris*, was not sufficient to satisfy all religious conservative groups. In fact, a group, known as the *Mourji'a*, went the extra step of claiming that this controversy, being a matter of *ghayb* (the unknown), should no longer be subjected to arguments which led nowhere and, instead, people must accept the faith unquestioningly.[44] The final victory over the Mu'tazila in the thirteenth century A.D. led to a state of lethargy where mental activity is purposeless and unable to create change or achieve progress. There was no longer any incentive to reason, create, or innovate.

That mental—then physical—lethargy became legitimized by the referencing of verses which were distorted to promote reliance on God instead of reliance on one's own self by thinking, analyzing, and making sound decisions; and then by making the right effort to act on them. The Holy Qur'an enjoins believers to trust in God by application of the concept of *tawakkul*. This concept has been distorted into *ittikāl* (or blind reliance), meaning neglecting one's own duty of diligence and expecting change and progress without doing what is necessary to deserve them. Both terms, *tawakkul* and *ittikāl,* derive from the same root, *wakala*, which means mandate and trust, where the former implies a reasoned and mindful trust, and the latter implies a neglectful, abdicative reliance. The concept of *tawakkul* derives from God's attribute as *al-wakīl*, or the trustworthy, that is, the only one to be trusted. Abdelmajid Charfi attributes this state of affairs to a deliberate effort on the part of the rulers, past and recent, aided by the religious establishment, to spread such beliefs in order to keep the masses in a state of ignorance and obedience.

The doctrine of predestination is nothing other than an echo of the words uttered by Muawiya when he took over power: "If God had not judged me capable to shoulder this function, He would not have given it to me; and if God had hated our situation He would have changed it." This explains how despotism and exploitation were justified.[45]

The prevalence of the religious conservative views on predestination produced a prolific literature to justify predestination in reliance on scriptural sources, as well as on traditions of the Prophet, mostly fabricated, unrealistic, and, in any event, in contradiction with his more established traditions and with the Divine Message in the Holy Qur'an.

The presumed supporting evidence about predestination taken from the Holy Qur'an can be attributed to two categories of verses: (1) verses which are presumed to confirm that free will among humankind is purposeless, since humankind is subject to overriding divine will, and that the will to comply with God's prescriptions and rules, even when coupled with actual compliance, is no guarantee of salvation; and (2) verses which reveal that God has, ever since the time of creation, established a *kitāb* (or record) which presumably contains comprehensive preordained information about past, present, and future occurrences to all creatures of God, alive or inanimate, including mountains, seas, lands, rivers, trees, animals, insects, and human beings. The verses in both categories have either been misunderstood and misinterpreted, or simply taken out of context and distorted.

DIVINE GOVERNANCE VERSUS ARBITRARINESS

The first category of verses is comprised of those which state that God bestows His blessings and guides, or denies, His bounties and leads astray—at will in His sole discretion. These verses have been interpreted in such a way as to remove any incentive for people to reason and exercise free will, because God in His discretion presumably has already chosen who will receive the blessings and who would be led astray. The verses which apparently attribute that discretionary behavior to God are countless.[46] But a few select examples demonstrate the ease with which verses can be misinterpreted or distorted.

Two very important verses, Q18:23 and 24, have been advanced as containing irrefutable proof that people have no free will and that any action by anyone is subject to God's overriding will: *"Do not say of anything: 'I will do it tomorrow' (23), without adding 'If God wills.' When you forget, remember your Lord and say: 'May God guide me and bring me nearer to the Truth' (24)."*[47] It is important to recall that this verse has been grossly taken out of context (see Chapter 4) and is totally unrelated to the denial of free will by the overriding divine will. Instead, it is about a specific instance in which the Prophet had promised something which is within God's control. Hence God's message to him is about the need to abstain from promising things that are outside his control without properly reserving God's position, within whose control that promise lies.

Numerous verses in the Holy Qur'an presumably provide that God chooses who receives certain privileges and blessings to the exclusion of others. For example, Verse Q2:90 provides that God may bestow a blessing on whomever He wills from His believers, thereby implying an unfair preference.[48] In the context of this verse, God was responding to the behavior of some Jews who were upset that God had blessed with divine revelation someone who is not from the Sons of Israel or *Banu Isrā'īl*, namely Prophet Muhammad. Similarly, in Verse Q3:13, it is stated that, where two parties are fighting, God may grace any of the two parties with victory, again implying an unfair advantage. When placed in context, the unfairness disappears. In that particular case, the fighting was between one side fighting in the way of God (*fī sabīl-il-lāh*) and the other side unbelievers aggressing the former. In such a case, it is only normal to expect God to be on the side of those being aggressed and prevented from seeking God's path.

The Holy Qur'an also provides, in numerous instances, that God decides who will be guided by Him and who will be led astray. For example, in Verse Q2:272, God addresses Prophet Muhammad, stressing the fact that he was not sent to force anyone toward guidance, but that instead God will guide whomever He elects to guide. Despite the apparent discriminatory tone of the verse, God provides the assurance that in so doing he will not be unfair and no one will be unjustly treated.[49] Therefore, divine discretion is always framed within divine justice. Then, in Verse

Q2:269, it is provided that God bestows wisdom on whomever He chooses for that blessing without any further criteria for the selection process. Placed in context, this verse comes at the heel of a string of verses about the ethics of spending money, in which Satan is accused of pushing people toward unwise spending which may lead to poverty, compared to God's advice which leads to rewards and blessings. In such a context, it is fair that God should elect those who receive the blessing of wisdom among those who, in the first place, displayed receptivity to wisdom by not succumbing to temptation. The verse ends by reminding us that only those who apply their reason and mind may appreciate such action by God.[50]

In another example, Verse Q6:111[51] appears among a string of verses in which unbelievers place insurmountable demands on Muhammad to prove his case and convince them that his message is genuine. Among other things, they demand that he performs miracles, which are beyond his control. Thus, in that verse, God tells him that, no matter how many miracles he might offer them, they will not believe because only those whom God wills and chooses will believe. Clearly, such an approach may imply the futility of appealing to anyone's mind for guidance, since only those whom God selects would be so guided, which again appears as a gross unfairness. However, such an interpretation is a total misconstruction of the verse, because in this instance God was substantially offering consolation to His prophet about the futility of his effort with these people because they had already made up their minds and were strongly determined not to be swayed into believing Muhammad. Clearly, in such cases, only divine intervention could break that determination and coerce deniers into believing, which God has always refused to do, so as to preserve humankind's freedom of choice.

A similar example can be found in Verse Q10:100, where God asserts his discretion over who believes and who does not: "*It is not (possible) for anyone that he believes except with the will of Allah.*" However, the purpose of that assertion becomes clear when we read that verse in the context of the immediately preceding verse, Q10:99: "*Had your Lord willed, all those on earth would have believed altogether. Would you, then, compel people, so that they become believers?*"[52] In this example too,

God reiterates to His prophet that he should not force anyone to believe because, if that was indeed necessary, God would have done it. Instead, God has given everyone the chance to personally determine right from wrong, and the freedom to decide for him- or herself if he or she wants to believe. The person electing to believe will then be assisted and guided toward faith, while the rejecters will be left to go astray and suffer the appropriate consequences.

In all verses in which God announces that He guides and leads astray at will, two misconstructions need clarification. In the first place, God's guidance has been erroneously interpreted to mean that God is the one who chooses who becomes a believer and gets rewarded, despite the possibility that the person or persons chosen may be evil and reluctant to believe. A similar misinterpretation implies that God may lead someone astray who was otherwise a believer, and that person would get punished instead of being rewarded. In reality, when placed in context and read in conjunction with other provisions of the Qur'an, God's guidance is not about changing a person from a nonbeliever to a believer, nor is leading someone astray about turning a believer into a nonbeliever. Such an interpretation defies all provisions in which God declared that He does not commit an iota of injustice toward anyone. Instead, God's guidance is directed toward those who have already displayed basic belief and genuine intentions to progress along the straight path toward God. Those are the people whom God elects to guide. Similarly, people who have clearly shown no interest in believing and have even defied God's rules and advice will not receive God's guidance— He will leave them free to go astray. While God, as Almighty creator, could have turned every person around, He has instead opted to let every individual choose freely whether or not to believe. Therefore, what at first seems to be an unfair use of discretion in deciding who gets God's guidance and who does not, is actually an expression of exemplary divine justice where God applies His Almighty knowledge to identify those striving in His path and grants them His guidance. Ultimately, God guides the person who is willing to receive divine guidance, and denies that guidance and lets stray the person who has hopelessly declined all invitations to believe, rejected all evidence provided by God, and defied God's basic injunctions.[53]

This brings us to a very controversial verse that is often brandished as the irrefutable evidence about God's predestination overriding humankind's free will, namely Verse Q76:30, which—on its face—implies that no person can willfully plan an action unless that action meets God's corresponding preordained plan: *"But you cannot will it unless God wills [to show you that way]: for, behold, God is indeed all-knowing, wise."* However, when that verse is placed in context and read in conjunction with the preceding verse and the subsequent one, the text is as follows:

> *VERILY, all this is an admonition: whoever, then, so wills, may unto his Sustainer find a way (29). But you cannot will it unless God wills [to show you that way]: for, behold, God is indeed all-knowing, wise (30). He admits unto His grace everyone who wills [to be admitted]; but as for the evildoers—for them has He readied grievous suffering [in the life to come] (31).*[54]

Placed in context, Verse Q76:30 takes on a meaning totally unrelated to predestination, namely that any person may decide to seek his or her way onto the path of God (Verse 29), but that only God can guide him or her onto that path (Verse 30). Therefore, God must be willing to provide that guidance, which He would do if the person is genuine in his or her desire (Verse 31).

Finally, in the category of verses in which God, on the Final Day of Judgment, selects those who will receive His reward or punishment, the impression of divine arbitrariness is removed by the reminder that God has imposed upon Himself the obligation not to be unfair or unjust to anyone. Also, He has promised to be lenient with most sins and infractions of His will and advice, with the exception of one—not to associate anyone with God. Bearing in mind that God cannot be unjust or unfair, what may appear to humans as unfair would not be due to an injustice of God, but to the main difference between divine justice and human justice. In human justice, only committed acts are punishable; intentions are never punished if they do not translate into unlawful, punishable acts that are actually committed. Any human being may be full of hatred and evil intentions and spend an entire lifetime preparing to cause harm to someone or to a group of people. However, if that hatred and those evil intentions do not materialize into the commission of or the attempt to commit a damaging act, that person will never be tried and punished. But that same person, when faced with divine justice, is most likely to be punished for the evil intentions that remained with that person throughout his or her lifetime, if that person died before repenting.[55] What may not seem fair to us humans, as far as God's reward and punishment are concerned, would certainly be due to the fact that we have no means to tell who holds and who does not hold ill intentions inside his or her heart and soul, whereas God can; His knowledge is limitless. For example, in a reference to potential hypocrites, the Holy Qur'an states in Verse Q29:10:

> *Among men there are those who say, "We believe in Allah," but when they are persecuted in (the way of) Allah, they take the persecution of men, as equal to the punishment of Allah. And should any help come from your Lord, they will certainly say, "We were with you." Is it not that Allah knows well what lies in the hearts of the people of all the worlds?*[56]

Accordingly, humans do not have the means to always grasp and assess divine justice. Thus, to the extent that divine justice may rely on information not available to humans, humans are in no position to grasp and comprehend certain manifestations of divine justice.

Finally, once more, divine governance—though discretionary—is not about the exercise of abusive or arbitrary divine power. It is about the exercise of divine wisdom by the Creator in rewarding genuine belief and striving toward God's path, and punishing the blind refusal of faith without giving serious consideration to God's invitations to believe and encouragements to do so. In the end, God does not act arbitrarily. He observes—and listens to—the true intentions of people and offers His compassion whenever He senses the slightest display of good intentions.

PREDESTINATION AND DIVINE JUSTICE

In the second category of verses used to deny or minimize the relevance of using the mind, we find verses alluding to God's presumed preordainment of all things that may occur to any person. Most early Islam and modern-day commentators interpreted these verses as a reference to *al-kitāb al-mubīn* (the clear and comprehensive book) containing God's order of the universe and of all creatures in it—including humankind—that He created, for their entire duration. Thus, every activity in the day-to-day life of every individual, from the time of conception to the time of death, is presumably known to God in advance of its occurrence and recorded in the preserved tablet, or *al-lawḥ al-maḥfūẓ,* since the creation of the universe. Even before a person is born, God is said to have preordained that such person would be conceived and born, when the birth would occur and to which mother and father, how long that person will live and how death will occur, where and how that person will live, what that person will do for a living and who his or her friends will be, and in the end, whether that person will be rewarded or punished on the Day of Judgment.

The verses on which the theory of predestination is based are those in which appear the Arabic words derived from the root *kataba.* They refer to the figurative divine action of writing, whereby God has written what He had preordained in a book, or *kitāb,* a derivative of the root *kataba.* In fact, in almost every occurrence in which God is said to have written something, the exegetes adhering to the concept of predestination have rushed to declare that such ordinance was made in advance of its occurrence in the book of creation, *al-lawḥ al-maḥfūẓ* (the preserved tablet). Reviewing every instance in which the root word *kataba* or any of its derivatives is used in the Holy Qur'an shows that, depending on the context of each instance, the meaning changes. Eight different meanings for the terms *kitāb* and *kataba* may be identified.

The primary and most common usage of *kitāb* is as a generic term for the Holy Qur'an and each of the divine Scriptures revealed by God to the predecessors of Prophet Muhammad, prior to revelation. The term *kitāb* has been used in this way in the Qur'an approximately two hundred times: as a reference to the Holy Qur'an in the case of the opening of several suras, such as *"Alif, Lam, Ra. [This is] a Book whose verses are perfected and then presented in detail from [one who is] Wise and Acquainted"*;[57] and as a reference to the other Scriptures that preceded Prophet Muhammad's mission, in all verses in which Christians and Jews are referred to as *ahl al-kitāb* (People of the Book), by reference to their individual Scriptures.

Second, *kitāb* refers to a formal deed which people write to evidence the conclusion of a transaction, such as a deed of marriage.[58]

Third, the derivative term *kutiba* and some variations of it are used in the sense of issuance of divine ordinances in the way of rule making, such as the form *kutiba 'alaykum* (it has been ordained upon you that...), without, however, any implication of predestination. It is in this form that God ordained the prayer (salat)[59] and fasting of Ramadan obligations,[60] and the general pronouncements relating to fighting,[61] the writing of wills before death,[62] *qiṣāṣ* (punishments) and the *lex talionis* (law of retaliation), when certain crimes have been committed, among other rules and pronouncements.[63] In this group, we can also find the verses containing divine ordinances granting certain rights and legitimacies, such as certain women's rights,[64] the legitimization of marital relations during the month of Ramadan,[65] and other halal and haram related commands.[66]

Fourth, the term *kataba* and its derivatives refer to individual decisions of God which are made in the ordinary course of business with respect to one or more specific individuals, such as for rewarding specific good deeds.[67] The imploration of God to record us among those who bear witness to the truth does seek an individual decision by God.[68] The same goes for the imploration of God to ordain, for the person making that imploration, that he or she be acknowledged for a good deed in this life and the hereafter.[69]

Fifth, *kataba* is even used in the sense of a unilateral commitment by God in the form of *kataba 'ala Nafsihi* (He took it upon himself), such as the unilateral commitment to grant His compassion generously on the Final Day,[70] His commitment not to punish anyone who erred by mistake,[71] or His commitment to reward jihad in the way of God.[72]

Sixth, *kitāb* has been used to mean a record kept on each person, based on which God will render His Final Judgment. That record comprehensively keeps track of all of an individual's good and bad deeds during his or her lifetime.[73]

Seventh, and close to that same meaning, are instances where the *kitāb* has been used to convey a sense of God's infinite knowledge of all things which are privy to Him, that is, matters that are unknown to humankind, also referred to as *al-ghayb*.[74]

Eighth, and finally, we come to a category of meanings which may imply predestination in some sense.

QUR'ANIC VERSES WHICH APPEAR TO IMPLY PREDESTINATION

Next we will look more closely at those verses which include implications of predestination and attempt to elucidate their meanings.

Qur'anic Verse Q9:51 provides as follows: "*Say: 'Never can anything befall us save what God has decreed! He is our Lord Supreme; and in God let the believers place their trust!'*"[75] Al-Tabari and al-Razi present a very deterministic interpretation of this provision by referring all the way back to the *lawḥ al-maḥfūẓ*, in which whatever befalls any person has presumably been preordained by God from the time of first creation.[76] Verse Q9:51, which is often quoted by determinists, thus may when placed in context be understood as follows: When Prophet Muhammad was preparing for the battle of Tabouk, countless people reluctant to join the ranks of the warriors objected, the most common reason for their reluctance being fear of dying in war.[77] In an effort to entice them to join the ranks of fighters, God gave His prophet this series of verses, which ultimately promised them victory, assuring that what God has decided will happen. Victory has been ordained because war is being waged for a legitimate purpose and He will help them to win. This is the interpretation given by al-Tabarsi and Ibn 'Ashour.[78]

This verse sheds light on important issues. Many determinists have relied on this verse to justify lack of action and laxity. They believe that God has predetermined what will happen irrespective of any action that one may take. The context of this verse shows clearly that it has nothing to do with predestination. It is about putting an end to unfounded pretexts made by lax people to justify their inaction and refrain from going to war with the Prophet. In fact, the *kitāb* in question is not about God having preordained the time of death of each person, whether in war or otherwise. The *kitāb* in question is about what happens following the laws of nature that regulate the universe that God created. If, in the face of the use of force, people do not participate in defending themselves, no one else will do it for them, and they will be defeated and could lose their lives.

This verse also sheds light on the true meaning of *tawakkul* (trust in God), as opposed to laxity and reliance on God. The message here is that it does not help that people cite fears and risks to justify abstaining from doing what needs be done. Instead, people must perform their duties and place their trust in God. God will then handle fears and risks.

There are also the verses which apparently provide that God will destroy each village, town, or city when its preassigned term has come to an end, and where no such village, town, or city may last more or less than the preset term. Such provision is attributed to Verses Q15:4 and 5: *"And never have We destroyed any community [for its wrongdoing] unless a divine writ had [previously] been made known to it (4) [but remember that] no community can ever forestall [the end of] its term—and neither can they delay [it] (5)."*[79]

According to many scholars, including al-Tabari, al-Zamakhshari, and al-Razi, every community got assigned a predetermined term, by the end of which it would be destroyed. However, among most translators, Muhammad Asad is perhaps one of the few who correctly understood that a community is first forewarned and only after such warning is it destroyed. This is consistent with the provisions of Verse Q26:208 which state: *"We did not destroy any town unless it has had warners."*[80] An interpretation based on predestination would be unacceptable because it defies divine justice and God's attributes, and ignores the clarification that God provided in the Holy Qur'an itself that collective punishment occurs only following an unheeded warning. This explains the language in Verse Q15:5 according to which, once a community has been warned, God ordains a time frame for compliance.[81]

Verse Q17:58 on the same subject further confirms that interpretation: *"And [bear in mind:] there is no community which We will not destroy before the Day of Resurrection, or chastise [even earlier, if it proves sinful,] with suffering severe: all this is laid down in Our decree."*[82] In fact, everything that God created must end by the Final Day. It is a law of nature that God has set forth from the outset of creation that everything, other than God Himself, has a beginning and an end. However, there is nothing to prevent God from proceeding to destruction before the Final Day if the community in question has failed to repent following warning.

From this array of uses and meanings of the root term *kataba* and its main derivative, *kitāb,* one can conclude that events and occurrences derived from the laws of nature are the only true preordained realities. If the leaves on the trees fall each autumn, it is because under the laws of nature trees shed their leaves in the fall and get new ones in the spring. When people die at a certain age, that event is preordained in the sense that, following the laws of nature, no individual is eternal, and people have a certain life span, without being able to know in advance how and when each individual will die.

Verse Q3:145 is a typical enunciation of a law of nature which has been interpreted as evidence of predestination: "*It is not the choice of a person to die without the will of Allah, death being* a time-bound destiny. *Whoever seeks a reward in this world, We shall give him out of it, and whoever seeks a reward in the Hereafter, We shall give him out of it. We shall soon reward the grateful.*"[83] Interestingly, only the Qur'anic translation by Mufti Muhammad Taqi 'Uthmani, among the translations consulted, rendered the term *kitābann mu'ajjalann* as a time-bound destiny, instead of a preordained time. When one reads the Arabic text carefully, it simply declares the life span of human beings to be limited in order to reassert that no creature of any kind is eternal and that human beings, who are no different from other creatures, have a limited time span, without specifying that limit.

Even intervening calamitous events which precipitate the end of the life of a person before its reasonably expected span have been unduly attributed to God, following Verse Q57:22: "*NO CALAMITY can ever befall the earth, and neither your own selves, unless it be [laid down] in Our decree before We bring it into being: verily, all this is easy for God.*"[84] Here again, commentary has proliferated about the detail with which God has ordained every minute in the life of every creature before it was even conceived.[85] On that basis, people should neither be happy about whatever good befalls them or be upset about calamities, because all is decided by God beforehand.

However, that reading is not evident. What has been ordained or decreed by God, whether before or after creation, are the laws of nature. For example, if someone is caught in an earthquake and happens to be passing under falling debris from buildings, that person might die. In that case, it is not the particular death under a certain building at that moment in time that is preordained. What is preordained are the corresponding laws of nature according to which an earthquake causes those structures that are not strong and flexible enough, to break; and whoever happens to be passing under falling debris of that structure could die, under the laws of cause and effect. Similarly, the quality and duration of human life, as well as the yield of agricultural activity, have substantially improved and increased in the last two centuries. In these cases, what God has preordained is not the quality and duration of the life of every person and every plant for every place and every time. Instead, what God has preordained are the laws of nature and the ability of humankind to discover them and use them to consistently develop the science which contributes to the improvement of the quality of life and the quality of plants and agricultural production.

The same applies to every aspect of daily life and interaction of humankind with nature and the universe.[86] Thus, the laws of nature are said to be "preordained" because they either recur at reasonably predictable intervals under reasonably predictable circumstances, or because they contain relations of cause and effect which enable a person to expect or understand the resulting effect of a given cause. The same thing can be said about the actions of human beings who are endowed with minds to think and with free will and choice. While the choices that people make may not be predictable, the outcome of the choices that they make can often be determined by the laws of nature, which is the essence of the decision-making process.

Any other interpretation would be inconsistent with divine justice. In fact, God has set forth basic principles of ethics and morality for harmonious interaction among people within and across communities, with all the diversity that God has created. For that purpose, He warned against infringing these rules in order to prevent harm being caused by some to the others, and promised to reward compliance and to punish noncompliance. Thus a reward and punishment system can be built only upon freedom of choice and action[87] and is therefore incompatible with predestination. It is inconceivable that any individual could be made to suffer eternal punishment for having committed actions that he or she had no choice to avoid. Also, rewarding someone for good deeds done by that person while he or she never had any good intentions, but was forced by God to do them, would defy fairness. The basic elements of divine justice have been set forth in the Holy Qur'an, and they all rely on free will and free choice.

God has said that He does not commit a single iota of injustice: *"He does not wrong anyone by as much as the weight of a speck of dust: He doubles any good deed and gives a tremendous reward of His own."*[88] This stems from His overriding divine justice of not inflicting injustice upon people generally: *"These are the Signs of God: We rehearse them to thee in Truth: And God means no injustice to any of His creatures."*[89]

Good deeds are rewarded and, provided repentance did not occur before death,[90] bad deeds are punished on the Day of Judgment, based on the lifetime of each individual.[91] Divine justice is based on compassion, in the sense that first, and despite all the threats of punishment found in the Qur'an, God is likely to pardon every sin, short of associating other deities with Him, as set forth in Verses Q39:53—*"Say: 'O my people who have been prodigal against yourselves, do not despair of God's mercy; surely God forgives sins altogether; surely He is the All-forgiving, the All-compassionate"*;[92] and Q4:48: *"Surely, Allah does not forgive that a partner is ascribed to Him, and He forgives anything short of that for whomsoever He wills. Whoever ascribes a partner to Allah commits a terrible sin."*[93]

God's compassion is expressed in the assertion that good actions of believers are never wasted but are always acknowledged and rewarded, as expressed in Verse Q3:171: *"They receive good tidings of favor from Allah and bounty and [of the fact] that Allah does not allow the reward of believers to be lost."*[94] Most importantly, Verse Q6:160 provides that God's compassion is revealed through the fact that God's reward is so generous that He multiplies the rewards for good deeds, whereas the punishment would never exceed the harm done: *"Whoever comes [on the Day of Judgment] with a good deed will have ten times the like thereof [to his credit], and whoever comes with an evil deed will not be recompensed except the like thereof; and they will not be wronged."*[95]

Any consideration of divine justice is incomplete without a discussion of the extent of God's knowledge. According to the attributes of God, as rendered in the Qur'an, God is the *"All Knower"* in the sense that the scope of His knowledge is limitless. But is that knowledge limitless before or after events occur? Does God know of everything that takes place, every act performed or planned, before or after the fact? On first thought, one might say that the scope of His knowledge extends to events before and after they occur. But any assumption that God knows of things before their occurrence is a return to predestination. Such a view defies infinite divine compassion. If God knows that a bad occurrence is about to afflict a person, wouldn't God in His utmost mercy and compassion intervene to prevent it? In the end, if God knew of all things before they occurred, it means that they are preordained and preset, and He is the only one who could have preordained them, which brings us back to the conflict with unlimited divine justice. That is why the term *ghayb* refers to knowledge which is exclusively available to God and does not include any implication of a scope which predates the occurrences.[96] With this in mind, one can better appreciate the meaning of Verse Q6:59 which is often offered as proof of predestination.

> *And with Him are the keys of the unseen; none knows them except Him. And He knows what is on the land and in the sea. Not a leaf falls but that He knows it. And no grain is there within the darknesses of the earth and no moist or dry [thing] but that it is [written] in a clear record.*[97]

This verse is simply about God's infinite knowledge of all occurrences, including *ghayb* occurrences of which humankind are not aware, and the reference to the clear record, or *kitāb mubīn*, is a reference to the laws of nature. Yet, the fact that God is omniscient does not imply, and should not be construed as indicative of, predestination.[98] That said, and to avoid any potential confusion with the attribute of God as the Almighty, it should be clarified that, while God has the infinite power to predestine our actions and all occurrences affecting our lives to their minutest details, this does not mean that He effectively exercises that power to do so.[99] Yet, in His infinite compassion, God might intervene to direct certain occurrences, in answer to the prayers of believers.

Taqlīd, Bid'a, and the Sacralization of Tradition

The fear of using the mind has resulted in *taqlīd*, blind imitation of the early interpretations of the Holy Qur'an and Prophetic Tradition, as well as of the views, analyses, and commentaries of the Companions and early Muslim jurisconsults. As shown earlier in this study, the Holy Qur'an is the sole source of Islam. Centuries of imitation of the early interpretations and practices was made possible by a sacralization of Prophetic Tradition, of the traditions of the Companions of the Prophet, and of the exegeses and elaborations of the early religious scholars of the Qur'an and the jurisconsults of Islam.[100]

That sacred aura over all the practical and mental religious activity of the early days derives primarily from the prevailing deeply rooted tribal customs which venerate imitation of the fathers and forefathers. Ignatius Goldziher notes the tenacity of this attitude.

> The Arab liked to stress when speaking of his virtues that in practicing them he was striving to resemble his forefathers, he displayed in this practice an attitude, refusing to accept anything new which was not founded in transmitted custom, and opposing everything which threatened to abolish an existing custom.[101]

That attitude also derives from the sacred aura placed around the person of Prophet Muhammad[102] and everything he did, said, or implied—that is, Prophetic Tradition. The Prophet was, and continues to be, perceived as a supernatural human who is infallible. Given such a perception, it is natural to venerate the actions done and words uttered by the Prophet as a divine complement to the Qur'an and, as such, as a primary source of Islam. That aura surrounding the Prophet and his legacy should be kept in mind when contextualizing the impediments to the use of the mind considered here.

The sacralization of early Muslim traditions and their continued imitation are not in and of themselves impediments to the use of the mind.[103] But they constitute the immediate and long-lasting outcome of two related impediments, namely the concept of *bid'a* (innovation), and the abolition of the practice of *ijtihād* established in the fourth century after the hijra, following a consensus to that effect among the adherents of the four major schools of Islamic thought and jurisprudence. It is clearly destructive that certain modern-day thinkers continue until now to praise that action of putting a stop to *ijtihād* and, worst of all, continue to spread reverential fear of, and warn against, any less than cautious application of *ijtihād*. S. M. Zafar, among others, cites the fear of abusing *ijtihād,* and through it modifying the rules of Islam.[104] This view ignores the fact that *ijtihād* is a duty of every Muslim, and that the Qur'an was intended for, and addresses, all people, not just the Muslims, and certainly not just the so-called "learned" among them. Moreover, this illustrates why secularism is so necessary, because in a secular system progress can be achieved by enacting or amending a law instead of having to maneuver through religion to change rules that, in the first place, have no bearing on religion.

The concept of *bid'a* is founded on Prophetic Tradition according to which Prophet Muhammad said: "The most trusted discourse is found in the book of God, the best guidance comes from Muhammad, the most evil things consist of innovations, every innovation is a heresy, every heresy is equivalent to misguidance, and each misguidance ends up in hell fire."[105]

Based on this tradition of the Prophet, which places innovation prominently among the sins deserving eternal punishment, the minds of many Muslims have been paralyzed and terrorized by fear of hell.[106] Innovation was thus deemed an act of *shirk*, or association with God, because God has sent a complete message, and whoever adds to or removes from that message is putting himself or herself in the place of—or on a par with—God.

In order to assess the impact and intent of this tradition of the Prophet, the statement needs to be contextualized. Following the death of the Prophet, the Holy Qur'an remained inaccessible to ordinary mortals because it did not get written and compiled into one officially sponsored version until almost thirty years later. Until then it was partly written and held by the scribes of the Prophet, or memorized in fragments by the Prophet's companions. Even when the Holy Qur'an was compiled into a comprehensive version, it remained for several generations inaccessible to ordinary people because no copies of it were available for people to acquire. Their only access to the text of this new religion consisted in calling from memory what they or their immediate families, friends, and neighbors might have memorized of the Qur'an, recalling what the

Prophet may have done or said, listening to what people might recount about the Prophet and the Companions, and later on considering what the exegetes and *fuqahā'* may have said about certain parts of the Qur'an and Prophetic Tradition.

At the same time, Islam had appeared in a well-defined and established tribal environment. It aimed, among other things, to change outmoded customs of the times. So there was a fear that tribal customs, which Islam endeavored to abolish or change, might creep back into the new creed.

In this light it is easier to understand the concern to protect and shield the basics of the new religion from any heresies that might endanger the faith of those who had embraced Islam. Thus, the heresies of concern that the Prophet was referring to were those which might affect the absolute fundamentals of faith and worship: (1) with respect to the faith, the belief in the unicity of God and his angels, the prophecy of Muhammad, the Final Day, and the eternal afterlife; and (2) with respect to required worship, the salat (prayer), the fast of Ramadan, the payment of zakat, and the performance of the hajj pilgrimage at least once in a lifetime for those who could endure it and afford it.

These essentials were not to be modified in any manner or under any circumstances so as to prevent the pagan creeds of the Meccans from returning to the main place of worship in Mecca, or elsewhere. This is the actual extent of the scope of *bid'a* (innovation) that the Prophet meant to proscribe. Since both the Holy Qur'an and the Prophet encouraged people to think, the concept of *bid'a* was not intended to block the use of the mind by encouraging blind imitation of creeds and practices based, many times, on mere hearsay. Nor was it intended to prevent the modification of certain practices which were merely tolerated, as opposed to being prescribed. This interpretation is fully in line with the provisions of the Holy Qur'an and other traditions of the Prophet himself that will be discussed in connection with *ijtihād*, all of which encourage thinking, pondering, and questioning so as to achieve true belief.

The initial effect of that Prophetic Tradition relating to *bid'a* was relatively limited because it deterred exegesis only during the few decades following the Prophet's death.[107] Thereafter, came a period during which intellectual activity flourished and expanded into the fields of Qur'anic exegesis, *fiqh*, and philosophy, a period of intense activity that lasted until the enactment of the ban on further *ijtihād*. Ironically, what Prophet Muhammad sought to prevent when he enacted the rule about *bid'a*, namely preventing the return of the pagan rites and customs of the *jāhiliyya* through latter-day heresies, is precisely what was allowed to return through the extension of the scope of *bid'a* by the Prophet's successors and by early-day clergy.[108] It is particularly noteworthy that, subsequent to the closure of *ijtihād*, a period of decline and regression started around the mid-thirteenth century, during which the use of the mind was almost demonized under the pretext of preventing the occurrence of any potential *bid'a*.[109] During that period of decline and regression, there were no advances to speak of in the fields of Qur'anic exegesis[110] and legal science,[111] any output in such fields being strictly limited to exegeses of already existing commentaries and *fiqh* treatises.

That period even saw the reversal of the methodology of bold *ijtihād* initiated by the Prophet, Caliph 'Umar, and the Companions.[112] For example, the part of the Holy Qur'an revealed in Medina is more permissive than that of Mecca, namely with regard to certain rules which were bent by way of tolerance to attract and retain converts, such as the rules on *mu'allafa qulūbuhum*, where certain hypocrites were bribed to keep them in the faith to prevent mass reversals of their followers. Instead of treating these tolerances as an example of flexibility and adaptability to prevailing circumstances, the exegetes interpreted them as new rules abrogating and superseding rules previously set forth. The end result was that the Medinan tolerances permanently replaced the primary rules. Their exegesis became sacralized at the expense of the changes that Islam wanted to bring about. *Jāhiliyya* customs were perpetuated by early exegetes, which were later followed blindly through *taqlīd* and the refusal of *tajdīd* (renewal and progress), thereby granting legitimacy to the extension of the scope of the *bid'a* concept.

The concept of *bid'a*, or innovation, understood in its widest sense, remains alive today because of the continued oppressive control over religion by certain clergy, within and outside the official religious establishments, and by their political supporters.[113] A significant number of Muslims, out of fear of innovation and heresy, continue to allow their lives to be guided by centuries-old views and commentaries.

The concept of *bid'a* has acquired a new, totally unwarranted application represented by the rejection of progress attributed to the West: products of the minds of unbelievers are treated as heresies to be avoided. In retrospect, the Prophet's warning against *bid'a* had a very specific purpose when made, one that is no longer pressing in our day. To the extent that there should remain any relevance for it, it should remain, as it had been initially intended by the Prophet, limited strictly to the sphere of the basic faith and worship, to the exclusion of any other spheres of day-to-day life.

In addition, since copies of the Holy Qur'an are now widely available to every Muslim, it is important to refrain from making accusations of *bid'a* every time the mind is used to challenge transmitted dogma and interpretations, because the duty to use the mind is founded in the Holy Qur'an itself. We may recall the famous response of the fourth Enlightened Caliph, 'Ali Bin Abi Taleb, to the *khawārij* when they rejected the compromise agreed on with Mu'awiya on the basis that it is inconsistent with God's sole and exclusive governance: "The Qur'an, which exists in between the two covers of the Book, does not speak; instead it is men who speak."

Nasr Hamid Abizaid offers this comment:

> The minds of men and the level of their knowledge and understanding are the ones who set the intent of the text and phrase its meaning. This clearly denies the existence of any conflict between the mind and the Scripture; instead the conflict arises between the mind and the oppressive authority of the text...and it is the dwindling authority of the mind which is responsible for the backwardness that we suffer from.[114]

This is precisely what the reformers Jamaluddin al-Afghani and Muhammad 'Abdu meant when they called for the reform of Islamic teaching institutions so that curricula would focus more on the role of the mind in achieving progress and less on the views of predecessors and the need to imitate them.

Scriptural Foundations for the Use of the Mind

Examining the role of independent reason in the interpretation of religious claims, Shabbir Akhtar addresses what he considers a basic disquiet about finding one's way in light of two disparate commitments, namely the commitment to the primacy of faith and the commitment to the primacy of reason.[115] Not only is there no contradiction or paradox of any kind between faith and reason, God encourages faith through rational conviction, including questioning in order to achieve that conviction. In this respect and describing the approach adopted in the Holy Qur'an, Jacques Berque observes: "It is not an intuitive or simply passive call, but is instead a direct appeal to the rationality of mankind."[116]

Recalling his personal experience of reading the Qur'an for the first time after he learned the Arabic language, Maurice Bucaille observed that "as of the first few suras, I was stunned by the repeated invitations addressed to humankind to think and reflect, through the observation of natural phenomena, over God's Might."[117] All the evidence that God has offered in the Holy Qur'an in His call to the faith enables people who accept the faith to do so out of conviction and not out of fear or mere emulation of others.

That is why numerous verses start by describing the Qur'an as a message which is clear and enlightening: "*THESE ARE MESSAGES of the Qur'ān—a divine writ clear in itself and clearly showing the truth*" (Verse Q27:1) and "*O mankind, there has come to you a conclusive proof from your Lord, and We have sent down to you a clear light*" (Verse Q4:174);[118] expressed in lucid language that people can comprehend: "*Behold, We have bestowed it from on high as a discourse in the Arabic tongue, so that you might encompass it with your reason*" (Verse Q12:2);[119] and conveyed to people through a messenger who, himself, is clear and perceptive in conveying the Message and the warnings contained in it: "*How shall the message be (effectual) for them, seeing that an Apostle explaining things clearly has (already) come to them*" (Verse 44:13).[120]

As a result, God declares that He has made the Message accessible and easy to grasp: "*Hence, indeed, We made this Qur'an easy to bear in mind: who, then, is willing to take it to heart?*" (Verse 54:32)[121]

While a number of verses concerned with ethical principles and advice relating to daily life issues and relationships address believers, the core of the Holy Qur'an deals with basic tenets of the faith, and for that purpose it addresses humankind universally, namely God's creatures endowed with a mind. This explains that the Message in the Holy Qur'an is primarily addressed to six groups.

The first group is the *uli-l-albāb,*[122] or those who are endowed with reason and wisdom, but which most translators have rendered as those with understanding,[123] insight,[124] and wisdom.[125] *Uli-l-albāb* are thus defined as those who are selective after careful consideration,[126] *"who listen [closely] to all that is said, and follow the best of it: [for] it is they whom God has graced with His guidance, and it is they who are [truly] endowed with insight!"* (Verse Q39:18).[127] The addressees of the Message were also designated as *uli-l-abṣār,* or those with vision: *"It is God Who alternates the Night and the Day: verily in these things is an instructive example for those who have vision,"* (Verse Q24:44).[128]

The second group is the *qawmin ya'qilūn,* derived from the root *'aql,* or the brain, meaning those who are receptive with their minds and can reason, found in Verse Q2:242: *"In this way God makes clear unto you His messages, so that you might [learn to] use your reason."*[129]

The third group is the *qawmin yafqahūn,* those who, having gotten the Message into their minds, understand and grasp it, seen in Verse Q6:98: *"And He it is who has brought you [all] into being out of one living entity, and [has appointed for each of you] a time-limit [on earth] and a resting-place [after death]: clearly, indeed, have We spelled out these messages unto people who can grasp the truth!"*[130]

The fourth group is the *qawmin yatafakkarūn,* or those who not only understand and grasp the Message but reflect and ponder over it, evidenced from Verse Q16:44: *"(We sent them) with clear signs and scriptures. And We sent down the Reminder (the Qur'an) to you, so that you explain to the people what has been revealed for them, and so that they may ponder."*[131]

The fifth group is the *qawmin yatadhakkarūn,* or those who heed and remember the lessons, evidenced in Verse Q6:126: *"This is the path of thy*

Lord, a straight path. We have detailed Our revelations for a people who take heed."[132] More particularly, we can find in Verse Q3:7 a direct link between heeding the lessons and the use of the mind, as well as a solid link between knowledge and faith. In other words, God is telling us that we cannot heed the lessons without using the mind, and that the use of the mind is essential for acquiring faith, because knowledge leads to faith.

> *He is the One who has revealed to you the Book (the Qur'ān). Out of it there are verses that are Muhkamāt (of established meaning), which are the principal verses of the Book, and some others are Mutashābihāt (whose definite meanings are unknown). Now those who have perversity in their hearts go after such part of it as is mutashābih, seeking (to create) discord, and searching for its interpretation (that meets their desires), while no one knows its interpretation except Allah; and* those well-grounded in knowledge *say: "We* believe therein; *all is from our Lord." Only the men of understanding observe the advice.*[133]

The sixth and final group is the *qawmin yuwqinūn,* those who, following understanding and reflection on the Message, seek to achieve inner conviction and certainty as seen in Verse Q45:20: "*This [revelation, then,] is a means of insight for mankind, and a guidance and grace unto people who are endowed with inner certainty.*"[134] Inner certainty is the stage when, confident of inner conviction, faith is achieved and acts of worship are performed with total confidence, defined in Verse Q27:3: "*[a guidance and a glad tiding to the believers (2)] who are constant in prayer and spend in charity: for it is they, they who in their innermost are certain of the life to come!*"[135]

These six groups and their accompanying Qur'anic passages demonstrate that the Qur'anic Message sought to promote the faith primarily by appealing to the mind and to reason through the provision of circumstantial evidence which, in matters relating to the *ghayb,* or the unknown, provide an inner feeling of satisfaction versus conviction based on tangible proof.[136] Moreover, God is so certain about the mental capabilities of people that He often admonishes them about ignoring His signs. Thus we find countless verses expressing disappointment about people failing to reason,[137] understand and grasp,[138] reflect and ponder,[139] take heed of lessons,[140] or seek inner conviction and certainty.[141]

Since the addressees of the Holy Qur'an are humankind, a species which can think using the mind, God has, in His appeal to the mind included in the Message countless proofs and evidences in the form of signs and examples, or *āyas* and *amthāl*, materials for thinking and pondering. These materials are wide-ranging in their topics.[142] "*THUS, INDEED, have We propounded unto men all kinds of parables in this Qur'an, so that they might bethink themselves; [and We have revealed it].*" (Verse Q39:27)[143] In fact, in Verse Q3:7, God places the Qur'anic signs and examples in two major categories, those included in verses which are clear in their purport and meaning, and those included in verses which are allegorical.

Āyas Related to Ghayb

God's signs and examples address various topics. The first type includes those which consist of circumstantial evidence relating to basic elements of faith, together with everything else which falls in the *al-ghayb* category, whose knowledge is the exclusive domain of God.[144] They are not accessible to humankind nor can they be proven with tangible evidence.

> *NOW THEY [who deny the truth] are wont to ask, "Why has no miraculous sign ever been bestowed upon him from on high by his Sustainer?" Say, then: "God's alone is the knowledge of that which is beyond the reach of human perception. Wait, then, [until His will becomes manifest:] verily, I shall wait with you!" (Verse Q10:20)*[145]

This is the case of the signs and examples dealing with:

The essence, and certain attributes of, God, from Verse Q24:35:[146]
God is the Light of the heavens and the earth. The parable of His light is, as it were, that of a niche containing a lamp; the lamp is [enclosed] in glass, the glass [shining] like a radiant star: [a lamp] lit from a blessed tree—an olive-tree that is neither of the east nor of the west—the oil whereof [is so bright that it] would well-nigh give light [of itself] even though fire had not touched it: light upon light! God guides unto His light him that wills [to be guided]; and [to this end] God propounds parables unto men, since God [alone] has full knowledge of all things.

The essence of creation, life, and death, from Verse Q42:29:

And among His signs is the [very] creation of the heavens and the earth, and of all the living creatures which He has caused to multiply throughout them: and [since He has created them,] He has [also] the power to gather them [unto Himself] whenever He wills.[147]

Giving life to the dead, from Verse Q2:73:

We said: "Apply this [principle] to some of those [cases of unresolved murder]: in this way God saves lives from death and shows you His will, so that you might [learn to] use your reason."[148]

This life and the hereafter, from Verses Q10:23 and 24:

But when he delivereth them, behold! they transgress insolently through the earth in defiance of right! O mankind! your insolence is against your own souls—an enjoyment of the life of the present: in the end, to Us is your return, and We shall show you the truth of all that ye did (23). The likeness of the life of the present is as the rain which We send down from the skies: by its mingling arises the produce of the earth—which provides food for men and animals: (It grows) till the earth is clad with its golden ornaments and is decked out (in beauty): the people to whom it belongs think they have all powers of disposal over it: There reaches it Our command by night or by day, and We make it like a harvest clean-mown, as if it had not flourished only the day before! thus do We explain the Signs in detail for those who reflect (24).[149]

The Final Day, resurrection, Final Judgment, hell, and paradise, from Verses Q3:106 to 108:

On the Day when some faces will be (lit up with) white, and some faces will be (in the gloom of) black: To those whose faces will be black, (will be said): "Did ye reject Faith after accepting it? Taste then the penalty for rejecting Faith" (106). But those whose faces will be (lit with) white,—they will be in (the light of) God's mercy: therein to dwell (for ever) (107). These are the Signs of God: We rehearse them to thee in Truth: And God means no injustice to any of His creatures (108).[150]

Certain worship-related matters, as found in Verses Q3:96 and 97:
The first house set up for the people is surely the one in Makkah having blessings and guidance for all the worlds (96). In it there are clear signs: The Station of Ibrāhīm! Whoever enters it is secure. As a right of Allah, it is obligatory on the people to perform Hajj of the House—on everyone who has the ability to manage (his) way to it. If one disbelieves, then Allah is independent of all the worlds (97).[151]

The *al-ghayb* category of verses is also about those examples drawn from stories of previous prophets and messengers of God, as well as of ancient peoples who were chastised by God for mistreating His messengers or otherwise failing to heed His messages. This is the case of the lesson-laden *āyas* associated with Adam and Eve,[152] Noah,[153] Saleh and his people Thamud,[154] Lot,[155] Joseph,[156] Moses,[157] David and Goliath,[158] Solomon and Saba',[159] and Jesus and Mary,[160] among other tales,[161] including tales of miracles associated with some of them.[162]

Āyas Relating to Laws of Nature and Society

In the second category of *āyas* and *amthāl* are those signs and examples derived from the laws of nature and the laws of society, which belong in the categories of knowledge and social relations, and which are accessible to the mind of, and can be explored and further discovered or developed by, humankind. In this respect, it is important to point out that the *āyas* and *amthāl* included in the Qur'an do not constitute, nor should they be perceived as, comprehensive laws of science or rules of society. Instead, they constitute sufficient indication by the Creator to His trustees that

He has endowed them with the mind to discover and amplify the laws of nature and to develop the laws governing their particular communities in the most suitable form for their relevant times and places.[163] This confirms the earlier thesis in this work that the Holy Qur'an is not, nor does it claim to constitute, a comprehensive body of detailed rules for every facet of life, because in reality the Holy Qur'an and the Divine Message are more than mere political, legal, and economic systems.

LAWS OF NATURE

In this subcategory are found the verses dealing with the overall framework of God's creation of the universe, such as Verse Q2:164.

> *Behold! in the creation of the heavens and the earth; in the alternation of the night and the day; in the sailing of the ships through the ocean for the profit of mankind; in the rain which God Sends down from the skies, and the life which He gives therewith to an earth that is dead; in the beasts of all kinds that He scatters through the earth; in the change of the winds, and the clouds which they Trail like their slaves between the sky and the earth;—(Here) indeed are Signs for a people that are wise.*[164]

In this and other verses, one finds particular reference to various natural phenomena which draw attention to the infinite creative power of God.

Verses Q45:12 and 13—the seas over which boats can float and navigate:

> *IT IS GOD who has made the sea subservient [to His laws, so that it be of use] to you—so that ships might sail through it at His behest, and that you might seek to obtain [what you need] of His bounty, and that you might have cause to be grateful (12). And He has made subservient to you, [as a gift] from Himself, all that is in the heavens and on earth: in this, behold, there are messages indeed for people who think! (13).*[165]

Verse Q41:39—the rain that sustains life on earth:

> *And among His Signs in this: thou seest the earth barren and*

desolate; but when We send down rain to it, it is stirred to life and yields increase. Truly, He Who gives life to the (dead) earth can surely give life to (men) who are dead. For He has power over all things.[166]

Verse Q34:9—cosmic natural disasters:

See they not what is before them and behind them, of the sky and the earth? If We wished, We could cause the earth to swallow them up, or cause a piece of the sky to fall upon them. Verily in this is a Sign for every devotee that turns to God (in repentance).[167]

Verses Q40:67 to 69—the life cycle of humankind and other living creatures from conception and birth, through growth, aging, death, and resurrection:

It is He who created you of dust then of a sperm-drop, then of a blood-clot, then He delivers you as infants, then that you may come of age, then that you may be old men—though some of you there are who die before it—and that you may reach a stated term; haply you will understand (67). It is He who gives life, and makes to die; and when He decrees a thing, He but says to it "Be," and it is (68). Hast thou not regarded those who dispute concerning the signs of God, how they are turned about? (69).[168]

The *āyas* and *amthāl* of the Qur'an, which point to the laws of nature, go into some detail in order to stimulate the mind to explore the scope and purpose of such laws. In exercising the trust granted by God, humankind can then continue to advance social and scientific development. Thus, in connection with the creation of the skies, we are told about:

The sun and the moon, together with the alternation of the day and night, and their potential uses for the purpose of counting and computation of time and years, found in Verses Q10:5 and 6:

It is He who made the sun a radiance, and the moon a light, and determined it by stations, that you might know the number of the years and the reckoning. God created that not save with the truth, distinguishing the signs to a people who know (5). In the alternation of night and day, and what God has created in the heavens and the earth—surely there are signs for a god-fearing people (6).[169]

The stars which serve as guidance and navigation beacons on land and sea, found in Verse Q6:97:

It is He who has appointed for you the stars, that by them you might be guided in the shadows of land and sea. We have distinguished the signs for a people who know.[170]

The bountiful uses of rain and other water sources for life sustenance in general, and more particularly to grow food and raise cattle, found in Verse Q6:99:

It is He Who sendeth down rain from the skies: with it We produce vegetation of all kinds: from some We produce green (crops), out of which We produce grain, heaped up (at harvest); out of the date-palm and its sheaths (or spathes) (come) clusters of dates hanging low and near: and (then there are) gardens of grapes, and olives, and pomegranates, each similar (in kind) yet different (in variety): when they begin to bear fruit, feast your eyes with the fruit and the ripeness thereof. Behold! in these things there are signs for people who believe.[171]

Raising honey bees to produce honey and benefit from their healing quality, found in Verses Q16:68 and 69:

Your Lord revealed to the honeybee: "Make homes in the mountains, in the trees and in the structures they raise (68). Then, eat from all the fruits, and go along the pathways of your Lord made easy for you." From their bellies comes out a drink of various colors in which there is cure for people.

Surely, in that there is a sign for a people who ponder (69).[172]

The inherent sustenance and continuity of life among all living creatures—humans, animals, and plants—arising from their conception and creation, found in Verses Q26:7 and 8, and Verses Q30:20 and 21:

Have they not looked at the earth, how many of the noble pairs (of vegetation). We have caused to grow in it? (7) Surely, in this there is a sign, but most of them are not believers (8)[173] and *It is among His signs that He has created you from dust, then soon you are human beings scattered around (20). And it is among His signs that He has created for you wives from among yourselves, so that you may find tranquility in them, and He has created love and kindness between you. Surely in this there are signs for a people who reflect (21).*[174]

LAWS OF SOCIETY

In this subcategory are found the *āyas* and *amthāl* which deal with human relations ranging from matters related to the most intimate inner self of the individual to the wider spheres of the family, the community, and humanity as a whole. While there are several verses in the Holy Qur'an that deal with varying social issues, the focus here is only on those verses which construe the relevant messages as *āyas* and *amthāl* for further consideration and pondering. It is within this range that the following can be placed, namely:

People are invited to perform introspections, from Verses Q51:20 and 21.

AND ON EARTH there are signs [of God's existence, visible] to all who are endowed with inner certainty (20), just as [there are signs thereof] within your own selves: can you not, then, see? (21).[175]

People are reminded that life on earth is ephemeral and that the permanent life in the hereafter should be kept within sight, from

Verse Q10:24.

*The likeness of the life of the present is as the rain which We send
    down from the skies: by its mingling arises the produce of the
    earth—which provides food for men and animals: (It grows)
    till the earth is clad with its golden ornaments and is decked
    out (in beauty): the people to whom it belongs think they have
    all powers of disposal over it: There reaches it Our command
    by night or by day, and We make it like a harvest clean-mown,
    as if it had not flourished only the day before! thus do We
    explain the Signs in detail for those who reflect.*[176]

Charity in human relations is central to preparation for the life
hereafter, and charity is rewarded several-fold, from Verse Q2:261.

*The likeness of those who expend their wealth in the way of God
    is as the likeness of a grain of corn that sprouts seven ears, in
    every ear a hundred grains. So God multiplies unto whom He
    will; God is All-embracing, All-knowing.*[177]

The same applies to civility in human relations, where using
sincere instead of insincere language is valued, from Verses
Q14:24 to 26.

*Have you not seen how Allah has set forth a parable: A good word
    is like a good tree, having its root firm and its branches in
    the sky (24). It brings its fruits at all times with the will of its
    Lord. Allah sets forth the parables for the people, so that they
    may take lesson (25). And the parable of a bad word is like a
    bad tree, removed from the top of the soil, having no firm root
    (26).*[178]

In spite of the fact that eternal life in the hereafter is what counts
most in the end, yet life on earth ought to be harmonious among
people. Starting from the immediate family circle, rules of fairness
should be established between husband and wife, such as the
guarantee of women's rights in case of separation by divorce or

death, found in Verses Q2:241 and 242.

And the divorced women, too, shall have [a right to] maintenance
in a goodly manner: this is a duty for all who are conscious of
God (241). In this way God makes clear unto you His messages,
so that you might [learn to] use your reason (242). [179]

Within that family circle and the wider one of the social
environment, it is important to abstain from sin whose effects can
extend beyond one's own self; hence the general advice about the
need to distinguish right from wrong found in Verse Q13:17.

[Whenever] He sends down water from the sky, and [once-dry]
river-beds are running high according to their measure, the
stream carries scum on its surface; and, likewise, from that
[metal] which they smelt in the fire in order to make ornaments
or utensils, [there rises] scum. In this way does God set forth
the parable of truth and falsehood: for, as far as the scum is
concerned, it passes away as [does all] dross; but that which
is of benefit to man abides on earth. In this way does God set
forth the parables. [180]

Specific advice is provided on various topics, such as ones relating
to alcohol and gambling, found in Verse Q2:219.

They ask you about drinking and gambling. Say: "There is great
harm in both, although they have some benefit for men; but
their harm is far greater than their benefit." They ask you
what they should give in alms. Say: "What you can spare."
Thus God makes plain to you His revelations so that you may
reflect upon this world and the hereafter. [181]

Reaching beyond the immediate social environment, people are
reminded of the diversity among humankind based on race and
tongue, so that they may interact among each other in harmony,
found in Verse Q30:22.

Among His other signs are the creation of the heavens and the earth and the diversity of your tongues and colors. Surely there are signs in this for all mankind.[182]

Faith and Knowledge

The Holy Qur'an specifies the purpose of filling the Message with signs (*āyas*), as follows in Verse Q57:9: "*He is the One Who sends to His Servant Manifest Signs, that He may lead you from the depths of Darkness into the Light and verily God is to you most kind and Merciful.*"[183] Passage from the "depths of Darkness" into the "Light" takes place by exercising the faculty of reasoning, which leads to the accumulation of wisdom. The mind is therefore a necessary instrument in the formation of faith, because it is the locus where the knowledge provided by God, or acquired by humankind, is processed. Consequently, true faith is solidly grounded in wisdom. This explains that the main role of God's messengers is to provide teachings which lead primarily to wisdom, evidenced in Verse Q2:151: "*As also We have sent in your midst a messenger from among you, who recites to you Our verses, and purifies you, and* teaches you the Book and the wisdom, *and teaches you what you did not know.*"[184]

While the Holy Qur'an is not a book of science, its revelations propel the ascent of science. It condemns paganism, sorcery, and other similar processes. It sets forth the principle that God has calculated everything and written natural laws, thus assigning to the mind the mission of discovering these laws and building on them. That is the sanction of science.[185] Because the laws of nature are about knowledge accessible to the human mind, that knowledge can be developed and increased, as a necessary step toward the improvement of the human conditions of life. That is why, in the Holy Qur'an, God appeals to people to learn and to increase their knowledge.[186] Humankind was created by God with a mind to distinguish it, and was made trustee of the world, in charge of one's own welfare and prosperity.

Learning is gained by processing experience acquired from the countless *āyas* and *amthāl* contained in the Divine Message for reflection, but also primarily through two important sources: (1) from one's own inner self, through introspection and further reflection, evidenced in Verse Q12:108: "*Say [O Prophet]: This is my way: Resting upon conscious insight accessible to reason, I am calling [you all] unto God—I and they who follow me. And [say:] 'Limitless is God in His glory; and I am not one of those who ascribe divinity to aught beside Him!'* [187]; and (2) from the external world through one's own senses, primarily sight and hearing, through which information is acquired and then transmitted to the mind for processing into perceptions and solid knowledge. In fact, those who insist on keeping their sights and hearing blocked, remain in darkness, as seen in Verse Q6:39: *"And those who deny Our signs are deaf, and dumb, in darkness. He whom God wills, He sends astray, and whom He wills, He sets him on a straight path."* [188] Thus, beginning from creation, humans were endowed with their distinguishing feature, found in Verse Q32:9: *"Then He gave him a proportioned shape, and breathed into him of His spirit. And He granted you the (power of) hearing and the eyes and the hearts. Little you give thanks."* [189] With every birth thereafter, those same basic tools of learning have been granted, evidenced in Verse Q16:78: *"And God has brought you forth from your mothers' wombs knowing nothing—but He has endowed you with hearing, and sight, and minds, so that you might have cause to be grateful."* [190]

It is clear that God has glorified knowledge, and elevated those who are knowledgeable, because of their importance for harmonious living and progress in this life, but primarily also for the achievement of faith, as necessary for progress toward eternal life. For that purpose, and to foster awareness, God has multiplied the examples and signs in the Holy Qur'an to promote knowledge: *"We cite these examples for people, but no one understands them except the knowledgeable ones."* [191] Prophet Muhammad, as well, sought to promote knowledge. As a result, signs offered by God must fit within a knowledge-based system that the mind processes and from which it draws its conclusions. Thus these signs become part of the inner self of the person who acquires them, as evidenced in Verse Q29:49: *"Nay, here are Signs self-evident in the hearts of those endowed with knowledge: and none but the unjust reject Our Signs."* [192]

It is important to note, that the knowledge being promoted by God is not religious knowledge [193] but instead is scientific knowledge, in the widest sense of the word, including social science, all of which is essential for humankind to perform the divine mandate entrusted to it ever since creation. Considering the potential conflict between science and knowledge based on religious faith, Sadeq Jalal al-'Azm asks, "Can I in all honesty and sincerity continue to accept inherited beliefs without betraying the principle of intellectual integrity?" He concludes assertively that "religion as it reaches the core of our lives and affects our intellectual and psychological composition is inconsistent with science and scientific knowledge in form and substance, as well as in letter and spirit."[194] Clearly here, al-'Azm is referring to heritage as opposed to religion itself, because it is the heritage represented by the mainstream religious establishment that took a hostile attitude toward science. For his part, Fazlur Rahman reports the views of Sayyid Ahmad Khan on the issue, setting forth a clear perception of science in Islam.

> For him there is no doubt that the modern scientific spirit or the laws of nature must set criteria for judging the acceptability of a certain faith. So judged, Islam turns out to be, among the religions of the world, most in conformity with the laws of nature, and of all religious documents the Qur'an is the most rational. Since Muslims have grossly misunderstood and misinterpreted the Qur'anic world view in the past, and since the orthodox Muslim theology is no longer valid, a fresh theology must be created from the Qur'an in the light of modern experience.[195]

On this basis, the view that faith-based knowledge cannot be reconciled with scientific knowledge can be rejected. In fact, Sadeq Jalal al-'Azm cites Verses Q23:12 to 14[196] and asserts that the concept of continuous creation of everything, as set forth in that verse, is irreconcilable with the scientific rules of cell multiplication and modern science.[197] However, he ignores that the continuity of creation is explained by the fact that God created each species, then decreed its continuation through multiplication in accordance with the laws of nature that He ordained by way of *kitāb*.

In the end, if God's primary objective is to bring humankind from the depths of darkness into the Light, it is because God himself is the first and ultimate Light, as He describes Himself in Verses Q24:34 and 35 of the Holy Qur'an using examples accessible to the human mind.

AND, INDEED, from on high have We bestowed upon you messages clearly

*showing the truth, and [many] a lesson from [the stories of] those who have
passed away before you, and [many] an admonition to the God-conscious (34).
God is the Light of the heavens and the earth. The parable of His light is, as it
were, that of a niche containing a lamp; the lamp is [enclosed] in glass, the glass
[shining] like a radiant star: [a lamp] lit from a blessed tree—an olive-tree that
is neither of the east nor of the west—the oil whereof [is so bright that it] would
well-nigh give light [of itself] even though fire had not touched it: light upon
light! God guides unto His light him that wills [to be guided]; and [to this end]
God propounds parables unto men, since God [alone] has full knowledge of all
things (35).*[198]

Thus, an important divine purpose of promoting the pursuit of knowledge
and science is to enable the faithful to comprehend the Divine Message
through the exercise of *ijtihād*.

Ijtihād as Rational Tool of Progress

Ijtihād is the use of rational thinking and argumentation to create rules
or solutions for circumstances not specifically provided for in the Holy
Qur'an, extrapolating from its provisions as sole divine revelation. There
is no consensus over this definition, a reflection of the lack of consensus
over the sources of Shari'a. Indeed, unlike the Baghdad schools of
jurisprudence which relied heavily on the use of *ijtihād*, the principal
schools of jurisprudence of Medina, namely the Hanbali and the Maliki
schools, took the more religiously conservative approach of simply
rejecting *ijtihād* as a source of Shari'a. They were satisfied that the Qur'an
and Prophetic Tradition had left no instance unregulated or any issue
unresolved.

In the previous discussion of terminology associated with Shari'a,
Islamic law, and *fiqh*, it was shown that (1) Shari'a is the body of general
principles set forth in the Qur'an which guide the worship-related matters,
matters of halal and haram (what is permitted or prohibited), and social
relations among humankind; (2) Islamic law is the body of rules and norms
developed by the jurisconsults from the Shari'a principles using various
techniques; and (3) *fiqh* is the science which enables the development of
such a body of rules by learned jurisconsults. It was also noted that the
terms of Shari'a and Islamic law have been used interchangeably, with

the Shari'a being the prevailing term. In this section, Shari'a will be used in this wider sense to include the divine part found in the Holy Qur'an, together with its accretions deriving from Prophetic Tradition and *fiqh*.

Most traditionalist scholars believe that the purpose of *ijtihād* is to devise solutions for impending issues that do not have solutions in the other sources of Shari'a. This is the cautious and minimalist approach, because it assumes that everything else remains constant, in the sense that once a text has been interpreted or a solution has been derived, irrespective of when or where such action may have occurred, that interpretation and solution become an integral part of Shari'a which can no longer be the subject of further *ijtihād* except with utmost care and caution.

For example, after pointing to the importance of progressing Islamic law to cater to the best interests of the *umma*, Shaykh Muhammad Rashid Rida proposes that it is necessary before even any tradition or custom (no matter how outdated) can be modified by way of *ijtihād*, to refer the matter to a committee of learned people who have great mastery of the Arabic language and who are versed in religious science. That committee would then consider the matter and determine the advisability of the proposed change from their perspective. They alone are regarded as qualified to make such determination with respect to a mere tradition, that is, an ordinary product of the human mind turned sacred. In other words, Shaykh Muhammad Rashid Rida has thus—intentionally or not—legitimized the guardianship role of the religious establishment, while God, in the Holy Qur'an, never appointed or otherwise hinted at the need for, any guardian—including Prophet Muhammad—over people for any reason.[199] Following that same logic, even fatwas, or the opinions of jurisconsults or clerics on specific issues, have been given the same strength as religious dogma and rules have been established to determine when a fatwa might be modified, ignoring that in the first place the fatwa is only one among various vehicles for *ijtihād*, as opposed to being a tool of rule making.[200]

In reality, *ijtihād* must at all times be considered a principal and important tool of interpretation and reinterpretation of the divine text, with the aim of finding new understandings of it that benefit particular times and places.[201] The early *fiqh*, which continues to constitute the standard state of the art, cites *ijtihād* among the sources of Shariʻa (or more accurately Islamic law), but as a secondary source, ranking last after the two primary sources, namely the Holy Qur'an and Prophetic Tradition, and the other secondary source, *ijmā'* (or consensus). Unfortunately, because *ijtihād* ranks last behind the three other sources of Islamic law, its scope has traditionally been substantially narrower than that of the other three sources, a residual scope limited to the very few issues and areas for which solutions have not been identified through any other sources. This explains how impediments to the use of the mind managed to take root in Shariʻa-related traditions throughout Islam's history.

Starting from the premise that the Holy Qur'an is the sole source of Shariʻa, the scope of *ijtihād* is practically limitless and constitutes a primary engine of progress. It is thus the hallmark of the progressive and universal natures of Islam. One might question the necessity and relevance of *ijtihād* in the first place, in view of the position of this study that Islam is not a legal system and the Holy Qur'an is not a book of law. Surely, *ijtihād* remains an important tool of progress because Shariʻa remains a body of important rules and principles of (1) worship, in people's relations with God, and (2) ethics and morality, in people's relations among each other. Thus, our practice in worship and behavior with others must be Shariʻa-compliant. In light of this, *ijtihād* is the principal tool which allows us to understand and grasp the rules and principles of Shariʻa, interpret and reinterpret them as necessary in view of our best interests, and design and adopt legal systems—or simply solutions for impending issues—which are not offensive to any of the rules and principles of Shariʻa.

From this perspective, Muslims should not be deterred from *ijtihād* for fear of erring. Since the use of the mind is a human function, it is subject to error. Yet, God mandates us to use our minds, even at the expense of erring, and for that purpose He judges the intentions and not the results so as not to penalize a person who uses his or her mind in good faith. In fact, for humanity, the choice is between stagnation—as a result of relinquishing the use of the mind—and potentially falling into error when the mind is used. However, an error can be corrected. Getting out of stagnation can be a costly, difficult-to-surmount challenge. In the words of Muhammad Hamza,

> Whereas the conservative thought is premised on the need to protect against dissent in interpretation by treating it as *bid'a* and placing the dissenter on the path of sinful error, the new Islam does not fear difference nor consider it a threat to the Umma.[202]

That pursuit of *ijtihād* as a tool of progress should not be precluded by the pursuit of *ijmā'*.

Ijtihād and Ijmā'

Ijmā', or general consensus, has been cited as a factor limiting the scope of *ijtihād*. It is not permitted to devise new solutions or rules for situations that have already been resolved or regulated by *ijmā'*. *Ijmā'* is defined as a general consensus over a certain issue or rule. It is claimed that, when such consensus is achieved, the relevant rule or solution then becomes part of religious heritage, irrespective of the time in history when, or the geographic location in which, that consensus was achieved.

According to a tradition of Prophet Muhammad, he is said to have proclaimed, "[t]here can be no consensus on error or misguided behavior amongst my people." In other words, if there is a consensus among the people over a certain matter, their consensus cannot possibly result in wrongful decisions, because collective wisdom can only gather over right decisions. Ironically, there is no consensus among Muslim scholars and clerics as to whose consensus must be achieved to constitute an instance of *ijmā'*.[203] Assuming the authenticity of that tradition, Prophet Muhammad was clearly speaking of the people in his community, without discrimination, because he had in mind collective wisdom. However, this is not what the scholars and jurisconsults of Islam thought. Certain scholars thought that the consensus which constitutes the *ijmā'*, as a source of—or complement to— Shari'a, is the consensus of the four Enlightened Caliphs who first succeeded the Prophet, following his death. Others extended that circle to include the most prominent close companions of the Prophet, as well. Still, some more liberal thought settled on scholars and learned people of each time.[204]

Clearly, the view about *ijmā'* as consensus of the Enlightened Caliphs or the companions of the Prophet cannot be plausible because treating such consensus as source and integral part of Shari'a, excluded from scrutiny by the human mind, conveys sanctity to a human phenomenon by equating it to divine revelation. Such equation is sacrilegious because it associates the Enlightened Caliphs or the Prophet's companions, as human beings, with God. This is the essence of the sacralization of tradition, that of the Enlightened Caliphs and the Companions.[205]

On the other hand, in addition to being associative, the view that *ijmā'* is about the consensus of clerics and jurisconsults is also elitist and discriminatory. This latter view constitutes a slight improvement over the previous view in the sense that it provides for some continuation of the *ijmā'* process beyond the early days of Islam, which allows for some progress following changing times and places. However, it still provides a wide scope for sacralization of human heritage.

This leaves the approach to *ijmā'*, as initially conceived by Prophet Muhammad, namely the people of a community. This is the only rational and plausible approach, because it is the only one which incorporates the concept of collective wisdom. The *ijmā'* of the people thus represents the soul and pulse of the community at a time and place: hence the belief in the universal nature of Islam. As such, *ijmā'* is a tool of progressiveness.[206] In addition, it is the approach which does not associate human tradition with divine revelation.

This brings us to the true nature of *ijmā'*, as the product of collective wisdom at a relevant time and place, a wisdom which is innate in humankind by way of *fiṭra*. In other words, this is what constitutes, in plain language, the building of custom and traditions. Considered from this angle, *ijmā'* complements the effort to design a legal system derived from Shari'a. *Ijmā'* becomes a rich, beneficial, and meaningful source of law for particular times and places, and it can be modified at any time as necessary by legislative action or by newer emerging customs. This is comparable to law formation and change in our times. Customs are universally recognized as sources of law, next to legislation and judicial jurisprudence, but they can be reversed or modified at any time by newer legislation and customs.

Based on the above, *ijmā'* should not be seen as truly restrictive of *ijtihād*. All matters, including matters presumably settled by *ijmā'*, can legitimately be the subject of rational scrutiny by the human mind and are subject to change in light of general interests. Thus, any rule or solution achieved by way of *ijmāʿ* can be interpreted and reinterpreted. It can be changed by legislation. It can also be set aside by a court of law or by people contractually, all in light of the best interest of the parties and of the community. This is the essence of *ijtihād*, the outcome of which materializes in the form of new legislation, judicial decisions, or personal contracts.

Ijtihād and Prophetic Tradition

While Prophetic Tradition is not part of the divine Shariʿa, it nevertheless sets the standard for *ijtihād* in terms of understanding the provisions of the Holy Qur'an and solving problems not provided for in it. Prophetic Tradition may be seen as a guide to the provisions of the Qur'an. While nowhere in the Holy Qur'an is any indication found that God mandated the Prophet to explain or interpret the Qur'an, one does find provisions which, in addition to delivering the Message, expressly mandate the Prophet to teach us wisdom, as in Verse Q2:151.

> We have sent unto you an apostle from among yourselves to convey unto you Our messages, and to cause you to grow in purity, and to impart unto you revelation and wisdom, and to teach you that which you knew not.[207]

That wisdom concerns how to use one's mind to understand and be guided by the Qur'an. While the divinely revealed Shariʿa is binding and must be strictly complied with, Prophetic Tradition—in its widest scope, which includes the traditions of the Enlightened Caliphs—constitutes a body of examples and lessons in progressivism for their individual times, and they are worthy of emulation in our time. The traditions of the Prophet and those of his second immediate successor, 'Umar Ibn al-Khattab, have guided us in learning how to handle and make the best use of the Scriptures. In fact, the issue is whether the role of Prophetic Tradition should be construed as a source of—or a complement to— Shariʿa, or as a model and standard for *ijtihād*.

Daniel Brown discusses the efforts of nineteenth-century reformers Shah Wali Allah and Muhammad bin ʿAli al-Shawkani to advance religious thought in the face of crisis and change by proclaiming the scope of *ijtihād* to be virtually limitless.[208] Yet, despite their good will and endeavors, they were not successful and kept striving to catch up with modernity to no avail. While the concept of freeing the mind to practice *ijtihād* was the right approach, their starting point, of upholding the supremacy of Prophetic Tradition alongside the Holy Qur'an, was regrettable. Even more unfortunate is that, when he advocated an expansion of the scope of *ijtihād*, Shah Wali Allah, among others, advocated at the same time restricting its practice to one person who would act as reference, or to a category of learned people, all of which brings us to the recognition of an institutionalized clergy.[209]

Prophetic Tradition reports contradictory statements attributed to Prophet Muhammad about *ijtihād*. While in several statements he is reported to have warned against the use of the mind,[210] he is also reported to have said, "[i]f the judge who exercises *ijtihād* in making a decision reaches the correct solution, he receives a double reward, and if he fails to reach the right solution, he would still be entitled to one reward in any event."[211] This means that *ijtihād* is encouraged and is appreciated, irrespective of its outcome. In other words, it is better to try and to fail than to stagnate and not progress for fear of trying. *Ijtihād* is thus in essence an act of innovation which was specifically being encouraged by the Prophet. It is preferable to reject traditions which vilify the use of the mind as unauthentic, and to rely instead on the tradition quoted here as reference, for the simple reason that *ijtihād* is the main activity that Prophet Muhammad practiced during his prophetic career. However, assuming that the traditions which caution against the use of the mind were true and authentic, the Prophet would have done so for fear that his people might inadvertently incorporate into the Qur'an what is not in it. In this respect, again it is important to remember and keep in mind that for centuries following the death of the Prophet, the Qur'an was not accessible to all people, which made it necessary to ask "those who know." In this context, those who know are not the learned people who understand the Qur'an better than the ordinary person. Instead, they are those who know what the Qur'an says and can recite it for those who do not memorize it.

This might explain why the Prophet banned *bid'a*, or innovation, namely for fear that people might, out of ignorance, attribute to the Qur'an what was not in it. It is not plausible to attribute to the Prophet positions against the use of the mind generally, while people are urged to use the mind fully by countless provisions of the Qur'an.

Indeed, in addition to all the series of verses cited earlier in this chapter, a very important verse cautions against *taqlīd*, namely, blindly imitating customary heritage rather than using the mind, which leads to stagnation and prevents progress.

> *AND CONVEY unto them the story of Abraham (69) [how it was] when he asked*
> *his father and his people, "What is it that you worship?" (70) They answered:*
> *"We worship idols, and we remain ever devoted to them." (71) Said he: "Do*
> *[you really think that] they hear you when you invoke them, (72) or benefit you*
> *or do you harm?" (73) They exclaimed: "But we found our forefathers doing the*
> *same!" (74) Said [Abraham]: "Have you, then, ever considered what it is that*
> *you have been worshipping—(75) you and those ancient forebears of yours?"*
> *(76) "Now [as for me, I know that,] verily, these [false deities] are my enemies,*
> *[and that none is my helper] save the Sustainer of all the worlds" (77).*[212]

From this perspective, Prophetic Tradition should not, as suggested by traditionalists, serve as a limiting factor on the scope of *ijtihād*. Instead, Prophetic Tradition is witness to the practically limitless scope of *ijtihād*, whose only limits are the divine general principles and guiding rules of ethics and morality set forth in the Holy Qur'an.

Ijtihād and Divine Scripture

Apologists argue that Muslims are somehow *entitled* to a reasonable surface of *ijtihād* in order to adapt to changing times. However, *ijtihād* is portrayed at best as a right that needs to be used with great caution to avoid the trap that leads into sin. It may appear, at times, as a right or freedom on matters of basic faith, because it is up to each individual to think, reflect, analyze, and ponder the evidence provided by God to reach faith. Indeed, God offers countless proofs and examples of His unique existence, creation, and role, then invites people to reflect and ponder as necessary to achieve certainty and confidence in faith. However, in all other areas of the Message, *ijtihād* ceases to be an option and becomes nothing less than a formal duty over which humankind is accountable to God. It is a duty derived from the higher duty of each Muslim to seek knowledge through study, reflection, and education.[213]

That duty is contemporaneous with the time of creation, and constitutes a necessary corollary to the purpose of creation. When God created humankind, He decided from the outset that humans would be entrusted, as trustees, to organize their lives and administer His worldly creation. For that purpose, He gave humankind the tools, consisting substantially of the senses and the mind. In particular, He endowed them with free will so that they might, in their discretion, acquire and process the knowledge needed to enact laws to harmonize social relations and administer the divine trust.[214] God then sent His messages to humankind, culminating in the Holy Qur'an, in which people were, first, informed of that role. They were then provided with the tools to organize their lives harmoniously, consisting of certain truths pointing to the laws of nature and laws of society that God established in the form of *āyas* and examples, together with valuable guiding principles of behavior, morality, and ethics. Most importantly, God set for humankind principal objectives that they must strive to achieve, namely to establish the objectives of fairness and justice.

As a duty, people are accountable to God for their proper performance of the trust and the achievement of the entrusted legacy. In this respect, fairness and justice are about *al-'amal al-ṣāliḥ* (good deeds) and *iḥsān* (acts of good will), as necessary means that lead to *al-ṣirāt al-mustaqīm* (the straight path), which in turn leads toward the path of God. Together, they justify and exemplify the institution of jihad. This explains that the Divine Scripture urges humankind to strive toward learning and increasing their knowledge, and applying that knowledge toward the fulfillment of the duty of *ijtihād*. This further explains the nature of *ijtihād* as a divine duty, for the performance of which each individual will be held accountable by God on the Day of Judgment.

Because it is a duty, the scope of *ijtihād* in terms of subjects that may be dealt with by humankind using mind and reason is limitless. Therefore, in addition to matters which are not dealt with either in Prophetic

Tradition or *ijmā'*, matters that have been dealt with or resolved in the Divine Scripture, that is, the Holy Qur'an, are wide open for *ijtihād*. The only limit consists in not transgressing the bounds set forth in the basic principles of higher morality and ethics provided for in the Holy Qur'an, whether stated expressly in the form of rules, or *ḥudūd*, or merely implied in the underlying message of the provisions. This is precisely what the Holy Qur'an has encouraged humankind to do: handle the provisions of the Qur'an in a wise manner by pondering and reflecting, but also by not implementing blindly and without regards to the objectives of the Message, the interests of the community, and the general public order.

Recalling the numerous appeals to rationality in the Holy Qur'an, Abdou Filali-Ansari rightly observes that religious commands are almost systematically justified by reference to higher principles and by their appeal to reason, all of which confers sanctity to the Qur'anic provisions containing these higher principles.[215] Filali-Ansari's assertion is of the essence of the Divine Scripture, namely that (1) there is an underlying message in each scripture addressed to humankind which may differ from its immediate external message which, most of the time, is addressed to the audience of the time and place of revelation; and (2) each underlying message consists of a basic universal principle of morality accessible to reason.[216] Most importantly, however, even the scope of these principles of morality may change with time and place. For example, Verse Q16:90 states: "*Lo! Allah enjoineth justice and kindness, and giving to kinsfolk, and forbiddeth lewdness and abomination and wickedness. He exhorteth you in order that ye may take heed.*"[217] In this example, justice and the doing of good deeds are not references to absolute justice and perfect behavior. Since absolute justice and perfect behavior are of the realm of the divine, then everything else is necessarily relative. On that basis, the particular scopes of justice and good behavior that humankind are enjoined by God to observe are relative values which change when circumstances change.

To the extent that the Divine Message contains the guiding principles for performing the duties of trust and the objectives to be achieved by humankind in the context of relations among people, such principles must be interpreted and understood by every individual. Therefore, *ijtihād* must be applied to every verse and aspect of the Holy Qur'an to carry out the interpretation and enable understanding. That is the starting point in the preparation for—and fulfillment of—the trust mandate.

In this respect, it is helpful to recall that the principles of interpretation consist of identifying the underlying message in each provision of the Qur'an, by interpreting it (1) in the context of, and bearing in mind, all other provisions in the Holy Qur'an which deal directly or indirectly with the subject matter; (2) in light of the geographic and social contexts of the time of revelation; (3) in light of the context and circumstances of revelation, including *asbāb an-nuzūl,* or the events that lead to the revelation; (4) and in light of the context and circumstances of the time and place of the interpreter; and—at all times—(5) with careful attention, so as not to extract meanings and perceptions which are inconsistent with other provisions of the Holy Qur'an.

Since each provision of the Holy Qur'an is subject to an initial scrutiny by way of *ijtihād* in order to understand its meaning and identify the initial immediate message and its purpose, a reinterpretation of each such provision is necessary every time that changes in circumstances occur or that provisions need to be understood in a geographic location or an environment which is different from that in which the initial interpretation occurred. The *fiqh*, or science of jurisprudence, has developed the general principle that rules change with changing times and geographic locations. In other words, the interpretations must change so as to take into full consideration the context and circumstances of the interpreter.[218]

This statement is fully in line with the universal nature of Islam because it assures that the interpretation and understanding of each provision is continuously updated so as to address circumstances of time and place. But more importantly, it assures continuous progress of the communities in question in pursuing the immutable, never changing objectives of Shari'a, namely, the pursuit of fairness, justice, and compassion, and progression on the path of God along *al-ṣirāt al-mustaqīm* .

That the rules must change following changing times, places, and circumstances has been the subject of a consensus (*ijmā'*) among the jurisconsults from the early days of Islam. Such *ijmā'* was not difficult to gather because it made sense. Rules founded on certain justifications, intentions, or customs would cease to be appropriate when such criteria changed or ceased to exist.[219]

In addition to instances of changes in circumstance, the interpretation of each verse of the Qur'an must change every time the understanding of that verse ceases to fulfill the objectives of the Divine Message. In certain cases, the application of the relevant verse may, and at times must, be set aside altogether in order to make certain that the objectives of the Divine Message prevail. Such actions may be taken as a temporary measure or on a permanent basis. This is precisely what Prophet Muhammad and 'Umar Ibn al-Khattab did during their careers as messenger of God and caliph respectively, in pursuing their duties. Recall the example cited earlier about Prophet Muhammad having decreed that it is prohibited to allocate any part of one's estate by way of a will to benefit any person who is naturally among the heirs. What jurisconsults considered as an abrogation of the Qur'anic text which asks people before dying to write wills to their closest kin, was simply a decision by the Prophet to set aside the application of the verse, without cancelling it. The intent was not to obstruct the Message's objective of changing tribal inheritance rules which deprive females from inheriting in the presence of male siblings, or other male relatives in the family. Since an important objective of the Divine Message is to restore fairness and justice toward women, the Prophet was right in viewing the will as a potential way for people to resist the change of tribal rules for devolution of estates. Recalling also the Prophet's tradition relating to the prohibition of innovation, or *bid'a,* indeed, he was not opposing *ijtihād.* He was cautioning against adding to, subtracting from, or otherwise modifying any provisions of the Holy Qur'an as a result of a person not being fully aware of all its provisions. After all, Prophet Muhammad is credited with leading the call for *ijtihād* by example.

Similarly, the Enlightened Caliph 'Umar took the lead in practicing *ijtihād* in its widest scope, including setting aside Qur'anic provisions every time that a primary objective of the Divine Message would be set back. Soon after he became caliph, he refused to allocate any part of the zakat funds to people known as *mu'allafa qulūbuhum*, despite express provisions of the Qur'an to the contrary.

> *Alms are for the poor and the needy, and those employed to administer the (funds); for those whose hearts have been (recently) reconciled (to Truth); for those in bondage and in debt; in the cause of Allah; and for the wayfarer: (thus is it) ordained by Allah and Allah is full of knowledge and wisdom.* (Verse Q9:60)[220]

In this text, the category of the *mu'allafa qulūbuhum* is rendered in the English version quoted here as *"those whose hearts have been (recently) reconciled (to Truth)."* In reality, they are people who are prominent and important in their own communities to whom Prophet Muhammad chose to pay monies out of the zakat funds in order to prevent their defection from Islam, which could trigger mass defections by their followers. Caliph 'Umar reasoned that this provision was necessary in the early days of Islam when Islam had not yet taken hold and converts were still being harassed in the hope of getting them to abandon Islam. However, by the time 'Umar became caliph, Islam had taken very strong hold and expanded into the neighboring empires. Accordingly, there was no longer any justification to continue bribing people to prevent their defection. Thus, he set aside a practice described by the Qur'an as being *"ordained by Allah"* in His *"knowledge and wisdom."*[221]

The implementation of certain Qur'anic verses may need to be set aside whenever there is an emergency or other necessity which justifies a temporary or permanent exception. It is what modern law calls *force majeure*, and it is *ijtihād* that leads to the identification of such circumstances and to charting the appropriate course of action in each case. For example, while pork meat is prohibited as haram, yet its consumption becomes legitimate on an exceptional basis if a Muslim finds nothing to eat but pork and possibly other spoiled harmful foods, and the choice then is between eating the prohibited or facing starvation or disease.[222] For that purpose, the Islamic *fiqh* has developed the principle of *al-ḍarūrāt tubīḥu-l mahẓūrāt*, meaning that necessities legitimize actions that are otherwise prohibited, and which found its way into *Majallat al-Aḥkām al-'Adliyya*, as Article 21.[223] Similarly, in a year of famine, Caliph 'Umar waived the penalty of amputating the hands of people who resorted to theft to stay alive and feed their children. On the other hand, the Qur'an has assimilated hardship instances to necessity where transgression of Qur'anic rules may be allowed if, in the particular instance, their application would create undue hardship.[224] However, while the exceptions made relate to specific instances, the overriding purpose of these exceptions would legitimize for the general public interest further exceptions with respect to any other similar instances of undue hardship or necessity.

Ijtihād is the principal tool of legislation, that is, enacting new rules, laws, and solutions with respect to all issues and matters of day-to-day life, whether provided for in the Holy Qur'an or not. In fact, matters provided for in the Holy Qur'an have generally been regulated by way of general principles of morality and ethics, leaving the details to the human trustees to design and implement as necessary from time to time. For example, the Holy Qur'an mandates that people must honor their agreements in general terms without much further detail. It is then our duty to enact the implementing rules as needed to encompass the customary contracts that prevail in our time and place, and to address our interests and facilitate relations among contracting parties and minimize disputes. In fact, if God has given us rules and principles in the Holy Qur'an, and if Prophet Muhammad has adopted a certain approach in resolving issues as they occur, this is primarily because these principles and rules have an underlying purpose. On that basis, there arose a technique called *qiyās*, or syllogism, whereby solutions are extrapolated from Qur'anic provisions by application of the principles of cause and effect.[225] Verse Q5:90 enjoins to people to abstain from consuming alcoholic drinks; then Verse Q5:91 spells out the reason for that injunction, namely that it affects the proper functioning of the mind.[226] On that basis, by way of extrapolation using *qiyās*, one could say that all substances that adversely affect the proper functioning of the mind, such as drugs, ought to be avoided.

Some provisions in the Holy Qur'an deal with specific matters but not in a mandatory form. In that case, people decide, in their best interest, to legislate for these matters by adopting solutions from the Qur'an or by devising their own, provided always that the general principles of fairness and justice are not adversely affected. Other matters are dealt with in the Qur'an in the form of *ḥudūd*; in that case, *ijtihād* is necessary to devise the most appropriate rules while keeping within the limitations and ranges included in the relevant *ḥudūd*. This is the case of most of the provisions dealing with criminal penalties and distribution of estates upon death, among other sectors. The flexibility left by God to His trustees to legislate through *ijtihād* has been intentionally given a wide scope so as to offer humankind the utmost freedom to satisfy people's best interests at the relevant time and place. It explains that certain schools of thought have, though with varying degrees of freedom and flexibility, provided for a way to deal with best interests through the concepts of *istiḥsān* in the Hanafi School, *al-maṣāliḥ al-mursala* in the Maliki School, and *al-istidlāl* or *istiṣḥāb al-ḥāl*, which roughly correspond to the modern-day legal concepts of exceptional circumstances, public order, force majeure, and presumption, respectively.[227] Unfortunately, these concepts never got the opportunity to achieve their purpose of putting an end to *taqlīd* (imitation) because of the undue, ever mounting restrictions on the scope of *ijtihād*.[228]

Thus we come to the realization that *ijtihād* is the single most important factor, after faith, in adapting our daily lives to the higher principles of morality and ethics brought about by the Divine Message, and achieving progress in knowledge, freedom, and justice. To be effective and achieve its potential, *ijtihād* requires freedom in every respect, namely free will and freedom of expression.[229] Freedom in the scope of *ijtihād* should go beyond the *fiqh*-imposed limitations relating to Prophetic Tradition, *ijmā'*, and even the works and fatwas of the jurisconsults of the different schools of thought, so as to encompass almost every provision of the Divine Message. In this respect, the nature of the relevant scriptural provision is necessary to assess one's freedom in how far *ijtihād* may or should be applied. In other words, it is important to clarify whether a scriptural provision sets forth a right, a freedom, an obligation or duty, a mere tolerance, or a circumstantial or basic rule, on a temporary or permanent basis. In fact, the trust created by God in favor of humankind is not a one-time process. It is an ongoing one. So is the duty and right to apply *ijtihād*.

Those rights and duties belong to every Muslim and are not a privilege limited to learned people, howsoever called. What Prophet Muhammad and Caliph 'Umar did was to act as role models and teach the requisite freedom in applying *ijtihād*. What they really did was to grasp the underlying Divine Message when, in certain verses, God permitted exemptions or alternative solutions under special circumstances. This is the case when, in Verse Q4:43, God permitted the ablutions for prayer to be carried out with a handful of sand in the absence of water. In that instance, God was not just making a one-time exception. Instead, He was giving an example of flexibility and offering a rational mechanism to develop and adapt religious commands and norms to match relevant circumstances in any other similar or comparable instances, using the mind.

Neither Prophet Muhammad nor Caliph 'Umar claimed any powers beyond those that are accessible to any other practicing Muslim to interpret, implement, or set aside the principles stated in the Divine Message, free from any of the restrictions and complexes introduced by *fiqh* following the ban on *ijtihād*.[230] While there was an early consensus over the relevance of the noble principle that rules must change following a change of circumstances or when they cease to fulfill the objectives of the Divine Message, the implementation in practice fell substantially short of the objectives of that principle.

Indeed, too many restrictions and limitations were placed on *ijtihād*. This study cannot agree with the views of Muhammad Arkoun, who blamed secularism for the discrediting of religion. Instead, religion and science complement each other and, in any event, secularism is not another theology or even theory that is a substitute for religion or competes with it. Islam is fully prepared to face the challenge of secularism and its modernity-related corollaries, because Islam is secular.[231]

This study also rejects the views of Shaykh Sobhi al-Saleh and other modern-day traditionalists who most of the time require, and occasionally simply expect, that any rule, decision, or solution arrived at through *ijtihād* must find support in a verse of the Qur'an, a tradition of the Prophet, or a tradition of the Companions, and other early learned good Muslims.[232] Such requirements, which entail the sacralization of human jurisprudence, can result only in obstructing progress. In reality, it should be sufficient that the rule, decision, or solution arrived at through *ijtihād* be consistent with any underlying message of the Qur'an, or otherwise contributes to advancing the moral objectives of the Divine Message and the best interest of the community. This should serve to remove any reverential fear of considering, pondering, and even questioning any provision of the Holy Scripture as a means of strengthening our faith and seeking progress.

At another extreme, Muhammad Hamza posits the self as a primary source of knowledge.

> [R]eligion is no longer the provider of explanations about things, the universe and the world; instead, it has itself become the object of explanation like any other phenomenon which is subjected to analysis…The human self now is the source of knowledge that can generate proofs, and that self can deconstruct and reconstruct and generate significances and frame positions.[233]

However while humanity is indeed qualified to analyze, question, and interpret the Scripture, yet a religious text is not like just any other phenomenon that can be deconstructed and reconstructed in the process of its analysis and interpretation because, while natural phenomena are discoverable through the laws of nature which are part of the Divine Creation, texts dealing with the *ghayb*-related phenomena remain inaccessible to the human mind.

In the endeavor to free Muslim thought from the evils of imitation of sacralized traditions, it is necessary to caution against blaming current problems on the early thinkers.[234] Indeed, a lot can be learned from them. By thinking freely, as they did, one would in reality be emulating them instead of merely imitating them. In the case of imitation, one copies solutions and falls into *taqlīd*, whereas in the case of emulation, one follows their example by copying their process of thinking to devise new rules that are better adapted to the needs of our time, which is the essence of *ijtihād*. Most importantly, when the early thinkers used their minds freely in interpreting the Divine Scripture and developing the science of *fiqh,* they never claimed that their output was divine, nor did they ever anticipate that the outcome of their endeavors would over time become sacralized and immutable.

Reflecting its true power and scope, *ijtihād* may be redefined as the rational process of interpretation of Shari'a and the creation of laws, rules, and principles which are Shari'a-compliant, with the objective of achieving, and securing continuous progress toward justice and fairness in the best interest of the community. When constraints on the use of the mind are lifted, as Mohamed Talbi points out, free thought can reemerge, and Islam can find in its own midst the freethinkers that it needs.[235] As Anthony H. Jones and Abdullah Saeed, quoting the views of Nurcolish Madjid, clearly assert, "[t]he challenge facing Muslims in the modern world is to recover the rational dimension of Islam that has, over the centuries, become overlaid with habit and custom."[236]

CHAPTER 13
Islam and 'Others'

There is an all too common perception that Islam only accepts and is comfortable with non-Muslims in an environment over which Muslims exercise dominant control and where those so-called 'others' submit to Muslims, accept an inferior status, and pay the head tax.[1] To the extent that there is nostalgia among revivalists for days long past, for which some revivalists pray and which they strive to reinstate, this perception conveys an inaccurate, destructive picture of Islam.[2] In reality, Islam is quite the opposite.

Islam is progressive. It has room for others as equals, as a true plurality. That pluralism in Islam is deeply rooted in freedom of faith, which is of the essence of the Message of Islam. However, apart from—and in addition to—freedom of faith, Islam is a new iteration of the Abrahamic faith which translated into successive revelations ending with the Message revealed to Prophet Muhammad, following the primary revelations to Moses and Jesus, the Christ. Therefore, the basic faith elements among all these revelations are substantially the same, the differences having possibly been taken out of context or misconstrued. In this respect, Mark Cohen observes, "[i]n polytheistic societies, the gods and their respective peoples tolerate one another's existence. Polytheism breeds what the modern world would call 'religious pluralism.' By contrast, monotheism is inherently exclusive."[3] In this statement, Mr. Cohen may perhaps be referring to the exclusive nature of the identitarian perception of monotheism. However, when Islam is rightly considered away from the temptations of treating it as an exclusive identity, its pluralistic vocation can then be found and appreciated.

Pluralism in Islam

Underscoring that Islam is "Western ... as well as African, Arab, and Asian," Tariq Ramadan points out, "Islam is one and unique from the perspective of the founding religious principles, yet it integrates a diversity of interpretations and a plurality of cultures. Its universality derives from this capacity to integrate the diversity within its founding unicity."[4]

The revelation of the Qur'an commenced in the pluralistic environment of Mecca, whose society comprised pagans who worshiped multiple deities, Jews, Christians, *ḥanīfs* who were neither Jews nor Christians but yet believed in one deity and an afterlife, and materialists who did not worship anything and believed in the finality of this life. The descending revelation did not purport to modify that society by any means other than the means of "wisdom and beautiful preaching" (Verse Q16:125) because each person could, after hearing the new Message, elect to retain whatever faith, or lack thereof, that person held.[5] It is only when Prophet Muhammad was forced out of Mecca and then harassed with his companions in Medina that "wisdom and beautiful preaching" became supplemented by defensive, potentially violent, means.

Islam not only accommodates diversity in its midst, it is essentially pluralistic. Pluralism is of the essence of Islam.[6] What distinguishes diversity from pluralism is that, in a diverse society, people merely coexist with, and tolerate, each other without necessarily being equal or interacting together, whereas, in a pluralistic society, people accept—and interact with—each other, as equals.[7] Therefore, a practicing Muslim is expected to accept and fully interact with others.

Sachedina points to two positions in the history of Islam which conjoined with other factors to obscure the pluralistic nature of Islam, namely: (1) Islam, being the youngest of the Abrahamic faiths, came into a pluralistic religious environment which it acknowledged but never rejected; and (2) the early Muslim community confronted the major task of securing an identity for its members within that monotheistic pluralistic environment.[8] With respect to the first position, the prevailing religions, as derived from the principal Abrahamic faith (Judaism and Christianity), should not have been simply acknowledged and then evaluated critically, because Islam mandates fully believing in them as a condition necessary for being a good Muslim. With respect to the second position, moving to make of Islam an identity was and continues to be a serious error because identities are exclusive, whereas Islam is inclusive and open minded.

Pluralism is a fact of life which characterizes human society. In refuting that there exists a so-called universal aspiration of a political mission by

Islam, as a religion, to create a worldwide community under the Shariʻa, Sachedina affirms, instead, the existence of a conception of universal moral order which is innate to human nature.[9] Thus, pluralism is innate and deeply rooted in every individual within that society as part of the human *fiṭra*, which is shared by humankind—believers and nonbelievers alike.[10] That human society is perceived by Mohamed Talbi as a truly pluralistic society where each person is entitled to the right to be different, yet accepts and fully interacts with others through discussion of differences. Because it is the duty of each Muslim to accept, as opposed to merely tolerate, the other, Talbi goes further to assert that it is the duty of each Muslim to abstain from indifference toward non-Muslims by communicating with others about what he or she thinks, considering that indifference is tantamount to a selfish comfort which leads to the erosion of dialogue and death of society.[11] In support of this view, Talbi quotes Verse Q2:143, which states: *"And thus have We willed you to be a community of the middle way, so that [with your lives] you might bear witness to the truth before all mankind, and that the Apostle might bear witness to it before you."*[12]

The Holy Qurʼan does not advocate the concept of one exclusivist religious *umma*,[13] characterized by one political system and one legal system, and stigmatized by an exclusive identity. Instead, humankind is characterized by diversity, and the *umma* is necessarily pluralistic, made up of believers in the various divine messages, as well as of nonbelievers, as Verse Q5:48 demonstrates.

> To you We revealed the Book with the Truth, confirming previous Scriptures and witnessing to their veracity. So judge between them as God revealed and do not follow their whims to turn you away from the truth revealed to you. For every community We decreed a law and a way of life. Had God willed, He could have made you a single community—but in order to test you in what He revealed to you. So vie with one another in virtue. To God is your homecoming, all of you, and He will then acquaint you with that over which you differed.[14]

This is further evidence of the multidimensional aspect of the universality of Islam in the sense that, in addition to Islam being for all times and all places, it is also for all faiths. Islam is wide enough to encompass under its umbrella all revelations of God that preceded Muhammad's mission, and enjoins acceptance and interaction among them. Better yet, the Divine Message included in the Qur'an does not limit society to the various iterations of Islam; it also encompasses nonbelievers.[15]

Islam has an open and universal multidimensional aspect which rejects perception of it as an exclusive identity.[16] That pluralism is solidly founded in the Divine Scripture and is of the essence of Islam. Restrictions, exclusions, or limitations, if any, are not part of Islam irrespective of their potential source, whether traditions or jurisprudence, which are of human origin.

The Scriptural Foundation of Pluralism

Pluralism was, in the first place, at the heart of God's design when He created humankind.[17] Commencing with Verse Q5:48 cited earlier, God made it clear that the purpose of the plurality that he created, coupled with the plurality of paths leading to salvation, is to "*vie with one another in virtue*," that is, to motivate people to interact with each other and seek excellence in competing to perform good deeds. In commenting on this statement and a similar one appearing in Verse Q2:148, Isa J. Boullata rightly observes that the competition enjoined by these verses is

> not against one another, but rather in a concerted effort to do good works…Each community is thus commanded to go forward in its good efforts, undertaken in conjunction with the others and in harmony with them. It seems abundantly clear that there is here a manifest Qur'anic principle of interfaith relations, based on harmonious religious pluralism.[18]

On the other hand, citing the creation of Adam and Eve by God, and the episode of their expulsion from the Garden of Eden following the choice that they freely made to eat from the forbidden tree after having been warned against it, Mohamed Talbi rightly observes that humankind chose freedom, and plurality—with all its risks—as the price of freedom.[19] In other words, freedom of choice breeds plurality, in line with God's own design.

God's design is evidenced in Verses Q10:19 and Q30:22, respectively.

> *There was a time when mankind were but one community. Then they disagreed among themselves: and but for a Word from your Lord, long since decreed, their differences would have been firmly resolved (Q10:19); and Among His other*

signs are the creation of the heavens and the earth and the diversity of your
tongues and colors. Surely there are signs in this for all mankind (Q30:22).[20]

The decree referred to in Verse Q10:19 is precisely the reference to, and confirmation of, God's design. Thus, plurality did not just occur as an outcome of hazard. It occurred in accordance with God's considered will, as set forth in Verse Q11:118: *"And had thy Sustainer so willed, He could surely have made all mankind one single community: but [He willed it otherwise, and so] they continue to hold divergent views."*[21] This design by God, essentially based on freedom of choice granted to humankind, carries two important consequences: (1) because, humans can freely choose their faith, that is, what they believe in and how they act to fulfill that faith, God will guide those who choose to believe and follow the straight path, as stated in Verse Q42:8: *"And if Allah willed, He could have made them [of] one religion, but He admits whom He wills into His mercy. And the wrongdoers have not any protector or helper"*;[22] and (2) most importantly, freedom of choice calls for accountability for the choices that people make; thus in Verse Q16:93, God specifies that He will ultimately render His judgment over the choices made by humankind: *"For, had God so willed, He could surely have made you all one single community; however, He lets go astray him that wills [to go astray], and guides aright him that wills [to be guided]; and you will surely be called to account for all that you ever did!"*[23]

Talbi characterizes plurality for a practicing Muslim by courteous interaction with peoples from other faiths and ideologies, without forgetting submission to God.[24] Submission to God means letting God exercise His prerogative of judgment and not do it on His behalf. Indeed, God is the sole enforcer, and He has not mandated anyone to do it on his behalf, not even His own Messenger, all as set forth in Verse Q39:46: *"Say: O God! Creator of the heavens and the earth! Knower of all that is hidden and open! it is Thou that wilt judge between Thy Servants in those matters about which they have differed."*[25] On that basis, it becomes totally futile to claim, as some did, that the Qur'anic Message aims to promote a reversion to the original state of unity of humankind referred to in Verse Q2:213 through the concept of the Muslim *umma,* all of which is directly counter to God's design for diversity and pluralism.[26] In fact, while by way of *fiṭra* humankind share the belief in an ultimate one and only creator and mover, this does not necessarily imply the unicity of the path leading to God and, for that reason, the diversity of paths which converge into God's design for pluralism should not be negated. Therefore, it is not necessary, natural, or realistic that people should all once again return to a state of a single community for them to believe in—and worship—the same God. This can be, and has been, achieved through pluralism, as God willed it.

Moreover, the plural society so created by God includes not only believers. It encompasses believers and nonbelievers alike, as indicated in Verse Q64:2: *"It is He Who created you: one of you an unbeliever, another a believer; and God sees full well what you do."*[27] That, too, follows God's design, as witnessed by His warnings to His Prophet against forcing a change toward a uniform society of believers only, in the following verses: Verses Q10:40 and 41: (*"And there are among them such as will in time come to believe in this [divine writ], just as there are among them such as will never believe in it; and thy Sustainer is fully aware as to who are the spreaders of corruption (40). And [so, O Prophet,] if they give thee the lie, say: 'To me [shall be accounted] my doings, and to you, your doings: you are not accountable for what I am doing, and I am not accountable for whatever you do (41);'"*[28], and Verse Q10:99: *"Had your Lord willed, all those on earth would have believed altogether.* Would you, then, compel people, so that they become believers."*[29] Citing belief in the coexistence of good and evil as set forth in Qur'anic Verse Q21:35, Muhammad Shahrour concludes that the idea that one day everyone on earth will become a believer should be abandoned.[30]

The plurality mandated by the Holy Qur'an is based on equality on earth among all people, including nonbelievers. Contrary to the views[31] which deny the possibility for Muslims to live with non-Muslims in an environment of equality, believers and nonbelievers are, in this life, equal, and the latter cannot be harassed or forced into believing. Each and every individual, irrespective of his or her faith, should have an unobstructed opportunity, throughout their entire lifetime, to make choices freely, including the choice to believe or not to believe, while God retains the exclusive, undivided, power to evaluate each individual's faith and performance on the Day of Judgment, as set forth in Verse Q22:17: *"Those who believe (in the Qur'an), those who follow the Jewish (scriptures), and the Sabians, Christians, Magians, and Polytheists—God will judge between them on the Day of Judgment: for God is witness of all things."*[32] The golden rule, however, for judging performance allocates the weight exclusively to the extent of each person's piety and righteousness, thereby excluding any preferences among adherents to one or the other of the divine revelations.[33] This is very eloquently wrapped up in Verse Q49:13, in which God addresses all of humankind, and not just the believers among them: *"O mankind, We created you male and female, and made you into nations and tribes that you may come to know one another. The noblest among you in God's sight are the most pious."*[34]

Noteworthy in this respect is the fact that the purpose of plurality on earth is for people to learn to interact with each other as equals (*"that you may come to know one another"*). On that basis, Islam did not come for people to melt into one identity or otherwise to dominate one another. On the contrary, Islam stressed diversity and safeguarded the particularities of the various components of society.[35] Thus Islam did not come to replace or eliminate diversity. On the contrary, while it retains diversity, it enjoins people to preserve their diversity through ta'āruf (knowing and interacting with one another).

While people from diverse backgrounds are expected to accept and interact with each other through ta'āruf, this must occur in the "Muslim" plural society under the sanctity of the right to differ, without any regard as to whether Muslims constitute the majority or are in the minority. In fact, M. A. al-Jabiri cites Qur'anic Verses Q3:103 to 105 and observes that Islam strongly condemns fanaticism and radicalism because religious dissent leads to *fitna* (discord) and conflict. Instead, it urges moderation as a means to secure the spirit of solidarity within society while safeguarding the right to differ (Verse Q16:125).[36] These observations of al-Jabiri aptly address the concerns of Mohammed Charfi about religion's potential tendency toward "expansion, and through it, toward domination and coercion," after recalling Rousseau's observation that, in the days of multiple cults and deities which predated religious monotheism, there were no wars of religion.[37] Indeed, Omid Safi rightly observes that religious differences are in reality cause for celebration.[38] This should explain the necessary link between the divinely ordained pluralism and universality of Islam, the former being a necessary condition for the latter.

Going one step further, in a true pluralistic society, Muslims and non-Muslims, irrespective of who is in the majority or in the minority, should have exactly the same rights, and those rights are entitlements founded in the same divine origin and are not bestowed by those in the majority.

None of the verses cited here can be claimed to have superseded or abrogated, or to have been superseded or abrogated by, any other verse or verses of the Holy Qur'an. In fact, the verses reviewed in this section belong both to the later Meccan period and to the later Medinan period. In this respect, Mahmoud Ayoub rightly observes that dietary and marriage restrictions which constituted social barriers among the various religious communities were lifted by a Qur'anic sura late in Prophet Muhammad's time in Medina,[39] referring rightly to Verses Q5:5 and Q29:46. Thus any negation of plurality and of the equal status of all people in Islam constitutes a direct affront to God's considered decision to create diversity; and that is a pluralistic environment where, among other considerations, not everyone is expected to adhere to the final Message, and where God, instead, reserves the exclusive power to judge people by what they do and what their inner selves believe and hide.[40]

To illustrate, the first iteration of that pluralism was affirmed through the first society that was established in Medina shortly after the hijra (the migration of Prophet Muhammad and his companions from Mecca to Medina). The Medina society, as organized following the Prophet's hijra, was a truly pluralistic society, a model of interaction and mutual acceptance, as opposed to a model of mere coexistence, whose constitutive rules were spelled out in the Charter of Medina, entered into among the various components of that society.[41] Under that charter, the society of Medina included Muslims and Jews. That society, in terms of its constitutional organization, was truly pluralistic[42] in the sense that Muslims and Jews were equal.[43] It was neither a Muslim society nor a Jewish society. Yet, it was a society for all its component parts (including nonbelievers), and with which Muslims and Jews alike could identify and consider as their own.

Islam and the People of the Book

Notwithstanding that Islam encompasses all previous divine revelations since Prophet Abraham, yet there exists a certain monolithic perception of Islam according to which the Message brought by Prophet Muhammad superseded all previous messages.[44] According to that perception, Islam is the only religion acceptable to God, and for that purpose all verses encouraging peaceful preaching to—and coexistence with—non-Muslims, including the People of the Book, have been abrogated. Accordingly, and following some extremist views, the Message of Islam must be spread universally and, where possible, be imposed by the sword indiscriminately among pagans and, to a certain extent, among the People of the Book as well.[45] The apparently intolerant provisions in the Holy Qur'an, whether against the nonbelievers or the People of the Book among Jews and Christians, were specifically directed against the pagans and the People of the Book of Mecca and Medina, and their individual surroundings, because they had expressed enmity against the Prophet and moved to obstruct the performance of his mission.

This explains that the monolithic perception of Islam presumably relies on verses of the Holy Qur'an, which have been misunderstood. Unfortunately, this approach has created xenophobia among adherents to radical Islam, which in turn unleashed a reverse xenophobia, more commonly known as Islamophobia, especially among Europeans whose countries have received an influx of Muslims from various countries.[46] In reality, this monolithic perception of Islam arises from the fact that these verses have been taken out of context and grossly misinterpreted.

> Q48:28: *It is He Who has sent His Apostle with Guidance and the Religion of Truth, to proclaim it over all religion: and enough is God for a Witness.*[47]

This verse has been misinterpreted to mean that the message brought by Prophet Muhammad was the only divine message of truth, intended—as such—to prevail over and supersede all other religions, including previous messages of God.[48] Instead, when placed in context, this verse in reality refers to the success of Muhammad's mission among the idolaters, and the victory of God's Message over "pagan religions"—not the previously revealed Abrahamic Faiths.[49] This is also what Muhammad Asad refers to as "the false religions" in his translation of the meanings of the Holy Qur'an.[50] Indeed, this verse came immediately following the major victory by the army of the Prophet over the Meccan army of *Quraysh* in the Hudaybiyya battle and the peace pact then entered into to provide for a peaceful takeover of Mecca by the Prophet and his companions, at the time of the next hajj season.

Thus the context of the verse clearly shows that it does not purport to reach and discredit the various revelations and messages of God predating Prophet Muhammad's mission but was mainly concerned with asserting the prevalence of the religion of God over paganism. This interpretation finds its confirmation in the next Verse 29 of the same sura (Q48:29) whereby reward is promised to the companions of the Prophet who display their true faith and seek God's favors by performing the prayers, as well as to their counterparts who are referred to in the Torah and the Gospel.[51]

> Q9:5—*So, when the sacred months expire, kill the Mushriks wherever you find them, and catch them and besiege them and sit in ambush for them everywhere. Then, if they repent and establish Salāh and pay Zakāh, leave their way. Surely, Allah is most Forgiving, Very-Merciful.*[52]

> Q9:29—*Fight those People of the Book who do not believe in Allah, nor in the Last Day, and do not take as unlawful what Allah and His Messenger have declared as unlawful, and do not profess the Faith of Truth; (fight them) until they pay jizyah with their own hands while they are subdued.*[53]

Sayyid Qutb, a prominent leader and theologist of the Muslim Brotherhood of the mid-twentieth century, describes the above provisions Q9:5 and 29 as representing the final and conclusive position of Islam toward nonbelievers and People of the Book, whom he equates to nonbelievers. According to him, these provisions of *Sūrat al-Tawba* supersede all previous verses of the Qur'an which call for recognition and acceptance of plurality.[54] As discussed in Chapter 10, the provisions of *Sūrat al-Tawba*, which clear the way for fighting and subduing all non-Muslims among pagans, Christians, and Jews, are scope-specific, and are no longer in effect ever since they served their purpose of guiding the footsteps of Prophet Muhammad in the performance of his divine mission. These provisions do not extend to the relationship among Muslims, Christians, Jews, or pagans of any other time or location because the Prophet's Mission has been accomplished and, in any event, no one has inherited any part of that Mission. The view that Verse Q9:29 is the conclusive position of Islam against plurality is not plausible because it implies that God may have previously made the wrong revelations and sent the wrong messages.

Even then, the license to fight the non-Muslims of Mecca and Medina was not an open-ended one until they are exterminated. Fighting had to end when the purpose stated in Verse Q2:193 was achieved.

Q2:193—*And fight them until persecution is no more, and religion is for Allah. But if they desist, then let there be no hostility except against wrong-doers.*[55]

With respect to Verse Q2:193, the concept of *fitna* to which this verse refers, namely the practice by pagans of harassment and persecution of believers to divert them from, and cause them to renounce, Islam has been discussed. This verse, therefore, is about the specific practice of the idolaters of Mecca at the time of the Prophet and should not be construed as preventing peaceful coexistence and interaction among believers of various denominations, and between believers and nonbelievers.

Q3:19—*Truly, the (recognized) religion in the sight of Allah is*

Islam . Those who have been given the Book did not differ (among themselves) until after the knowledge had come to them, (and all this) due to envy against each other. Whoever denies the verses of Allah, then, Allah is swift at reckoning.[56]

Q3:85—*If anyone desires a religion other than Islam (submission to God), never will it be accepted of him; and in the Hereafter He will be in the ranks of those who have lost (All spiritual good).*[57]

In reading Verses Q3:19 and 85, both early and later exegetes have focused on their external sense. As a result they have advanced an exclusivist perception of Islam, treating these verses as evidence that God accepts, and approves of, only Islam—in the narrow sense of the Message brought by Muhammad—as true religion, to the exclusion of any other religion;[58] hence the claim that the Message brought by Prophet Muhammad has superseded all previous divine revelations, including the revelations to Moses and Jesus.[59] However, a closer look at these verses in proper context reveals the exact opposite, namely, that God not only tolerates diversity but mandates and demands plurality. Their context clearly reveals that the reference to Islam, as being the sole religion acceptable to God, is a reference to Islam in the widest sense of the term, namely to the Abrahamic faiths in general which are characterized by trust in God, being the true meaning of the term *Islam* in the Arabic language.[60] In addition, and most importantly, that interpretation is confirmed in the Holy Qur'an itself in Verse Q3:84, which immediately precedes Verse Q3:85, quoted above.

We believe in God, and in what has been revealed to us and what was revealed to Abraham, Isma'il, Isaac, Jacob, and the Tribes, and in (the Books) given to Moses, Jesus, and the prophets, from their Lord: We make no distinction between one and another among them, and to God do we bow our will (in Islam).[61]

Indeed, according to this verse, the duty of a Muslim believer is not only to acknowledge the Messages revealed to all the prophets who preceded Muhammad but to believe in the substance of these revelations. In addition, by specifying that He does not differentiate between any of them, God is further cautioning believers against underestimating these revelations which preceded the revelations to Prophet Muhammad, and the carriers of the Messages who brought them. That understanding is confirmed in Verse Q3:85 in which God renders His verdict about Islam, in its wide sense, as the only religion acceptable to Him. Thus Islam is not only the religion contained in Prophet Muhammad's message. Islam encompasses the divine revelations to all the Prophets who preceded Muhammad. Perceived from this universal perspective, Islam becomes the religion whose fundamental components are those that are common in all such revelations, namely: trust in God the Creator, the belief in the unicity of God and the Last Day, and the performance of good deeds,[62] as evidenced by the terms of Verse Q2:62.

> *Surely, those who believed in Allah, and those who are Jews, and Christians, and Sabians—whosoever believes in Allah and in the Last Day, and does good deeds—all such people will have their reward with their Lord, and there will be no reason for them to fear, nor shall they grieve.*[63]

In light of the above, the monolithic perception of Islam as described, including its claim of abrogation of verses enjoining peaceful preaching of Islam and kindly argument with the People of the Book, is tantamount to a rejection of God's creation and design.[64] This is unacceptable primarily on rational grounds. First, Muslims are as much people of the Book as Christians and Jews are. Second, believing in what God has revealed and fighting are two entirely separate issues, because the fighting is in response to an aggression, whereas the belief has to do with the basic truths that God has revealed and reconfirmed repeatedly through subsequent revelations.[65] What is particularly relevant to note here is that the toleration and acceptance of the other that God instituted from the outset was not a temporary measure decided by God; and since it was not a temporary measure, there was no reason to believe or expect that He could potentially change His mind. Instead, God was squarely telling us that what He revealed to us is a reconfirmation of previous revelations. Therefore, He could not have changed His mind on that count because if that was the case, everything that He revealed to Prophet Muhammad—that is, in the Qur'an—would then be negated and fall apart.[66]

Now, bearing in mind that the purpose of plurality in God's design set forth in Verse 49:13 is for people to know each other in an environment of equality, as opposed to dominating each other, the subordinate status of the People of the Book during the successive caliphates was not founded on Divine Scriptures, but was instead entirely politically motivated.

The *Dhimmī* Status

Unfortunately, the pluralistic and egalitarian society in Medina did not last past the death of Prophet Muhammad. In fact, following the death of the Prophet, his immediate successors proceeded to create state structures, while successfully going about the expansion of that state by conquest. These conquests brought diverse populations into that new state: Christians and Jews of the Levant; Sabeans, Magians, and Manicheans from Persia; Hindus from India; and other religious and ethnic groups enriched the diverse demographic pool of the new empire. The expanding society remained for a few centuries pluralistic in the sense that this ethnic and religious mix lived harmoniously together. Their mutual acceptance and interaction ignited a boom of progress and led to the development of one of the greatest civilizations in history.

However, that new society lost its egalitarian ethos which had prevailed during the days of the Prophet when the conquerors emerging from the Arabian Peninsula imposed on all non-Muslims, other than pagans, the so-called *dhimmī* status.[67] In this respect, it is important to add a historical note. In describing here the predominantly inferior status attributed to the People of the Book throughout the Muslim Empire, that value judgment is made from a strictly religious perspective and exclusively by reference to the Holy Qur'an, which preaches a pluralistic society where all people are equal irrespective of their creeds, such creeds being accounted for exclusively on the Day of Judgment.[68] However, value judgment from a historic perspective is different, because it is made by reference to what other societies practiced at a certain time in history. Thus, from that historic perspective, the *dhimmī* status was instead, for its time in history and by comparison to the treatment of non-Christians in Christian Europe, perceived as a relatively close-to-egalitarian status because non-Muslims enjoyed most of the rights of Muslims in terms of freedom of movement and expression, freedom to undertake any business activity, and equality before the law.[69]

The *dhimmī* status, as developed by the *fiqh* science based on the practice of the early successors of Prophet Muhammad who built the Muslim Empire, was a contractual arrangement whereby the Jews, Christians, Zoroastrians, and adherents of other religions which provide for a monotheistic perception of divine governance, were recognized as citizens of the Muslim Empire, but with rights that were inferior to those of their Muslim compatriots.[70] Under that status,[71] *dhimmīs* were generally considered as free members of the state, but without the right to serve in the imperial army. Their protection, as citizens, had to be ensured by the state. In return, they were required to pay a head tax called *jizya*. *Dhimmīs* were generally entitled to work in any profession of their choice. They could even assume political and administrative functions within the Muslim state, as witnessed by the many of them who assumed higher office wielding substantial power. *Dhimmīs* were also entitled to freely worship in accordance with their own faiths. However, although not contemplated in the initial practice of the Prophet,[72] *dhimmīs* were subjected to certain restrictions whose nature, magnitude, and scale of enforcement differed from time to time, and from one location to another.[73] These restrictions included the duty to wear distinctive clothing, the prohibition of riding horses and camels, and restrictions on building and rebuilding houses of worship.[74]

Attempts have been made to rationalize the *dhimmī* status so as to find equality of treatment among Muslims and People of the Book who are subjected to the *dhimmī* status. The reasoning is as follows: (1) a Muslim person pays zakat, a tax which demonstrates one's loyalty to the state, whereas the *dhimmī* person pays *jizya*, another form of head tax; (2) to the extent that the amount payable on account of *jizya* exceeds that of the zakat, the excess represents the fair counterpart for exemption from the duty of jihad, being the equivalent of military service; and (3) *dhimmīs* are entitled to the same standard of justice and to all other rights of citizenship enjoyed by Muslims.[75] This reasoning, in every respect, mixes the divine with the man-made and deviates substantially from the essence of the Message. In fact, as indicated earlier, Zakat was never meant to be treated as a tax to be collected by the state, even if the state were to spend it as required by the Holy Qur'an. Instead, zakat is of the nature of alms payable directly by each Muslim to the poor and to other categories of people entitled to receive it. It is part of the freedom of faith, in the sense that each person is free to pay it or not, exactly as each person is free to pray and fast or not to, subject to accountability to God on the Final Day, all of which no one is empowered to enforce. Similarly, jihad was never intended to be construed as military service. Instead it is a Muslim's highest form of achievement in his or her endeavors on the path toward God which, under specific and exceptional circumstances only, could take the form of military action. Finally, unlike the rights of Muslims which are considered natural entitlements, the rights of *dhimmī* are attributed rights, such rights being defined and framed in the document which grants that status to them on a case-by-case basis.

Throughout the Muslim Empire, and through its several iterations across the various ruling dynasties,[76] the People of the Book enjoyed a form of legal and judicial autonomy, in the sense that, within each religious community, relations among its adherents were governed, and disputes were settled, by the laws and jurisdictions that were specific to that community. However, relations among adherents of two different religious communities were governed, and disputes were settled, by Shari'a laws and courts. In other words, Muslims and non-Muslims among the People of the Book lived side by side as in a mosaic, where non-Muslims among the People of the Book enjoyed some legal and judicial autonomy, but under the rule of the Muslims. That is why Islamic law and courts constituted the common law and common law court system of the Empire. They served to govern relations and settle disputes among Muslims, and between Muslims and adherents to the respective non-Muslim faiths.

Although the *dhimmī* status remained in effect for many long centuries following the death of Prophet Muhammad, that status was at no time truly founded on the provisions of the Holy Qur'an.[77] Instead, it was based on just one verse of the Qur'an which was misconstrued, namely Verse Q9:29.

> *Fight those People of the Book who do not believe in Allah, nor in the Last Day, and do not take as unlawful what Allah and His Messenger have declared as unlawful, and do not profess the Faith of Truth; (fight them) until they pay jizyah with their own hands while they are subdued.*[78]

As discussed earlier and despite various interpretations to the contrary,[79] this verse does not purport to constitute a position of Islam toward Christianity and Judaism, as faiths. It represents a position against a specific category of People of the Book, at a specific time, in a specific place. The People of the Book targeted in this verse are those who lived in Medina and other locations of the Arabian Peninsula during the mission of Prophet Muhammad, and who, besides having possibly held beliefs that were blasphemous to their individual religions, were primarily belligerent against the Prophet. Therefore, it is not even a position against all the People of the Book in that specific place and time, but only against those who had displayed their enmity against the Prophet and initiated violent action against him aiming at disrupting the performance of his mission. In other words, this verse is directed against people who resemble very much the Muslim hypocrites and the associators of Mecca.

Because the overall atmosphere was one of belligerence, it was normal that the victor would levy a ransom against those who were defeated, hence the *jizya* contemplated in Verse Q9:29. In other words, what the Prophet was ordered to impose upon the People of the Book referred to in that verse is in the nature of war reparations that the defeated party traditionally pays to the victorious party. This explains the fact that, long before Verse Q9:29 was revealed, the Prophet actually imposed the *jizya* on the defeated parties in some but not all cases. That compensation is traditionally paid once or, at times, over a number of years, depending on the terms of peace as dictated to the defeated party by the victorious party. It was not intended to constitute a permanently recurring payment in return for protection and other rights under a permanently inferior status based on faith.

Similarly, the fact that Verse Q9:29 contemplates the payment of *jizya* "*with their own hands while they are subdued*" has been wrongly interpreted as a description of a divinely mandated, humiliating, inferior political and social status within a so-called Islamic state. It was a mere reference to the humiliation that a defeated party naturally suffers when paying war reparations under an imposed peace achieved on terms dictated by the victorious party.[80]

It is indicative to note that Prophet Muhammad did not impose the *jizya* on Jews and other non-Muslims in the Charter of Medina. It is true that the relevant verse then had not yet been revealed. However, since the Prophet was substantially acting under divine guidance when performing his mission, if *jizya* was an essential part of living as a non-Muslim under Muslim rule, then God would have revealed to him the need to levy the *jizya* independently from circumstances of war in which the Muslims are the victorious party.[81] Any interpretation to the contrary, whether in connection with the nature of the *jizya* or the permanently inferior status represented by the *dhimmī* status, would defy the essence of Islam as a wide-ranging umbrella which encompasses all divinely revealed faiths since Prophet Abraham. It would also defy the pluralism which is of the essence of Islam, as well as the principles of equality and the freedom of faith that are inherent in it.

Finally, it is worth noting that the *dhimmī* status was extended to peoples who believe in deities other than God of the Abrahamic monotheisms, such as to Mazdeans, Zoroastrians, Hindus, and Chinese.

Other Cultures

Describing his own experience, Abdennour Bidar expresses the natural integration of Islam within any culture: "I am a 'French Muslim'…who is nourished at the centre of my being by the Testimony of faith and the Qur'an, but also by French culture which, through its thinkers, its authors, its artists has given my Muslim spirituality a color that is particularly special."[82]

The issue of the relations of Islam with other cultures has been brought to the forefront concurrently with the wave of globalization, as reflected in the recent interest by non-Muslims in Islam and the opening of the debate over Islam outside the Islamic communities. Abdou Filali-Ansari discusses this theme in reference to the views of Samuel Huntington, Bernard Lewis, and Ibrahim Hanafi that Western culture and Islamic culture are essentially irreconcilable.[83] Yet, Mohamed Talbi rightly points out that Western civilization is a synthesis of the three Abrahamic cultures, namely the Judaic, Christian, and Islamic cultures, to which he refers as the Judeo-Islamo-Christian civilization.[84]

Unfortunately, over the years, the Arabo-Islamic culture has been framed by some into religious boxes in such a manner that other foreign cultures are often viewed by religious conservatives as being suspicious and are thus submitted to "blood" tests to determine their compatibility with—and even suitability for—Islam. It is again the archaic Abode of Islam versus the Abode of War (*dār al-Islam* and *dār al-ḥarb*) mentality, urging rejection of everything coming from outside the Abode of Islam. In the words of Abdel-Wahab M. Elmessiri,

> Instead of providing a universal Islamic frame of reference for Muslims (and non-Muslims too) in a complex modern age, the issue became how to "Islamize" certain aspects of Western modernity…And this inevitably meant the eventual atrophy of those aspects of the Islamic worldview that have no equivalent within the modern Western worldview. Ironically, those aspects constitute the very essence and source of supreme contribution of the Islamic worldview to the universal civilization.[85]

The monolithic perception of Arabo-Islamic culture ignores the Prophetic Tradition according to which the Prophet is reported to have promoted the duty to seek knowledge, then spread it. Clearly, the Prophet was urging people to closely interact with other cultures because of the mutual benefits in terms of education that such interaction brings. He did not limit the interactive learning to people from the same culture. In this respect, Khaled Abou El Fadl calls for a constructive engagement with modernity, as he rightly points out the risks of what he calls "Westoxification" in dismissing everything that is influenced by the West.[86]

That view is not specific to the Islamist perception of Western culture; it is more generally indicative of a monolithic perception of any culture which is foreign to Arabo-Islamic culture. The views of Elmessiri would remain as valid if we removed from them the term "Western" every time that it appears in the text. In reality, adopting elements from Western, or any other, culture, should not be construed as an exercise in imitation of the West, or in the adoption of substantive solutions designed or retained by the West; it is not about copying another culture. Instead, it is about an emulation process, consisting in the adoption by people from the Arabo-Islamic culture of some of the tools of modernity that the West may have developed, so that more tools of their own and, most importantly, more relevant solutions may be developed.[87] Abdolkarim Soroush takes up this theme and criticizes the general xenophobic tendency to reject everything which is alien. In particular, he criticizes the frequent attempts to trace the roots of Western sciences to Muslims in order to justify their embracing Western science and technology nowadays.[88]

From the perspective of the West, prior to its renaissance the West interacted with Arabo-Islamic culture, without finding any complex about taking full benefit from it and making the best out of it. The West learned from it, adopted it, adapted it, and then developed it.[89] This is what cultural interaction is all about. And from a Muslim perspective, while all that knowledge did not necessarily originate from Muslim peoples, Islam's openness toward pluralism provided the forum and environment for science and knowledge which originated elsewhere to be adopted and adapted so as to make it possible to develop further, to flourish, and to spread.[90] That interaction and tolerance which accompanied the start of Islam, together with the greater benefits that were gained from them, are a testimony to the pluralism inherent in Islam. It is an approach similar to that advanced by Muhammad Iqbal for the progress of Muslims.[91]

This approach is the one closest to, and most in conformity with, *fiṭra*. We seek modern knowledge and progress, and an inner alarm will sound when religion is transgressed. Calls for revivalism should not aim at reviving and retrieving early Islamic traditions and solutions, but instead aim at reviving that early Islamic environment of pluralistic openness and interaction. Abdolkarim Soroush rightly observes that our Islamic tradition and culture should not be perceived as the goal but as the point of departure.[92] Speaking of the apologetic orientation among Muslims in defending Islam against what they perceive as an onslaught of orientalism, Westernization, and modernity, Khaled Abou El Fadl notes the failure by apologists to engage Islamic tradition as "a dynamic and viable living tradition."[93] Indeed, the main challenge does not lie in defending Islam against the West, but in realizing Islam within Muslim communities. However, if that is done with the same sense of hesitation and reluctance as is implied from the reservations that Islamic countries put forward when they adhered to international conventions on universal human rights,[94] then antagonists would be handsomely vindicated.

Recalling the diverse pluralism of Muslim society as it expanded after the death of the Prophet, Ahmet Karamustafa praises the global and universal nature of Islam, suggesting, "The emphasis on Islam's globality enables us to acknowledge and cherish its transcultural, transethnic, transracial, transnational, in short, its truly humanistic dimensions."[95] Examining further the universal and global vocation of Islam, Humayun Kabir recalls the Qur'anic verse in which Prophet Muhammad is told that God has sent countless prophets and messengers to all the peoples on earth, and that he was only told about some of them. Kabir poses that the Holy Qur'an may in fact have referred to envoys to the Indian and Chinese peoples.[96]

In reality, there is no clash of religions, nor is there a clash of Islam and Western culture. The clash is *within* particular Muslim societies themselves: those societies which are dominated by the influence of clergy who believe and teach that Qur'an and Islam have regulated—and should regulate—everything, including science, as opposed to the belief that Islam is open-minded and progressive, its main impetus lying in its having released the powers of the mind and science. The clash also is between certain Western societies imbued with Islamophobia and those religious conservatives trying hard to export distorted, appropriated traditions which they label as Islam.

In addition to religious diversity, the pluralism inherent in Islam is not restricted to the diverse groups, including Muslims, that may be found within the same community or, speaking in modern terms, within the same nation, as nations and other groupings are the outcome of coincidences in history. Pluralism is universal because God so decided, namely that His creation would form a pluralistic global society in which the diverse groups would interact together, by adopting and adapting, in their endeavors to achieve the best performance of the duties of divine trust.[97] From that perspective, one can appreciate the importance of not losing sight of the secular nature of Islam which honors and guarantees respect for pluralism within a predominantly Muslim society. For that reason, it is essential to reject any Islamist views which advocate a specific religious political system, based on claims that Islam joins this life and the hereafter in an ideal and undivided unity.[98] Having examined and challenged the perception of Islam as a political and legal system in previous chapters, it should simply be reemphasized here that such views are based on the false assumption that Islam and Islamic societies are monolithic, homogeneous communities where the religion of the ruler and that of the majority of society must prevail without making room for the rights of other groups, no matter how minor such groups may be. In any event, the only link that exists between this life and the other life is the fact that, ever since God put them in charge of their lives, humans are free to behave with the certainty that God will make His judgment for the hereafter on the basis of how that freedom was used.

Islam is not only about diversity of faiths and cultures. There is also substantial diversity within Islam itself. This is the humanistic aspect of Islam, in which each person is afforded the privilege to understand and establish a direct and unique relationship with God; and that understanding may be different from the common understanding or that of another person.[99] On that basis, an important observation can be made: freedom of faith is the backbone of the diversity and pluralism which characterize Islam.[100]

Islam, Judaism, and Christianity

The Holy Qur'an addresses Judaism and Christianity from several perspectives. They are, first, discussed as divine revelations of the same truth, which is embodied in the message that Prophet Muhammad sought to convey. However, because of the historical implications of the rise of

Islam in a mostly pagan environment in which there existed a visible and solid presence of Christianity and Judaism,[101] it is unsurprising that there would be frictions between the adherents to the new faith, and Christians and Jews with whom they interacted.[102]

The essence of these three religions is the same:[103] what unites them is divine, and what separates them is man-made. To better appreciate this reality, it is helpful to review the general commonality among the various iterations of the Abrahamic faith, as revealed to Prophet Muhammad.[104] On that basis we can then consider the relations of Muslims, Jews, and Christians as they evolved during the days of the Prophet and following his death.

Islam and the Abrahamic Faith

Alija Izetbegović clarifies the historical frame necessary to review Islam's relation to the Abrahamic faith.

> Islam has two histories: a history which precedes the emergence of Muhammad (peace be upon Him) and a history subsequent to that emergence. That subsequent history is the history of Islam in its narrow sense, and it cannot be properly understood if the researcher was not sufficiently aware of the preceding history of Islam, namely the periods of Judaism and Christianity, respectively.[105]

Foundationally, Judaism and Christianity are understood as divine revelations which, together with Islam, constitute the Abrahamic faith. Islam, Judaism, and Christianity are thus iterations of the same Abrahamic faith.[106] This is rendered in the Holy Qur'an from different perspectives.

The Holy Qur'an advances the clear statement that the foundation of Islam, as embodied in Prophet Muhammad's message, consists of a new iteration of the faiths previously revealed by God through His various prophets and messengers over time, but adapted to the relevant time and place. That is why Prophet Muhammad is informed that the Message that he carries is a confirmation of the messages previously revealed and conveyed, as set forth in Verses Q3:3 and 4.

> *Step by step has He bestowed upon thee from on high this divine writ, setting forth the truth which confirms whatever there still remains [of earlier revelations]: for it is He who has bestowed from on high the Torah and the Gospel (3) aforetime,*

as a guidance unto mankind, and it is He who has bestowed [upon man] the
standard by which to discern the true from the false. Behold, as for those who
are bent on denying God's messages—grievous suffering awaits them: for God is
almighty, an avenger of evil (4).[107]

The immediate corollary of this statement is that, since the core of
what has been revealed to Prophet Muhammad is not substantially different
from what was revealed to his predecessors, including Moses and Jesus,[108]
it is not enough for Muslims to merely tolerate, accept, and interact with
Christians and Jews as a submission to God's design for a pluralistic
society, nor is it enough to solely believe in the Message conveyed by
Prophet Muhammad. Instead, Muslims must also believe in those previous
revelations in the same manner that they believe in the Message addressed
to them, through Prophet Muhammad. That instruction is embodied in
Verses Q2:2 to 5.

This Book is not to be doubted. It is a guide for the righteous (2), who believe in
the unseen and are steadfast in prayer; who give in alms from what we gave them
(3), who believe in what has been revealed to you and what was revealed before
you, and have absolute faith in the life to come (4). These are rightly guided by
their Lord; these shall surely triumph (5).[109]

That is why, we are told by the Qur'an, Prophet Muhammad and the
believers who followed him have believed in those previous revelations,
because they were brought by reliable prophets and messengers among
whom the believers should not discriminate, as provided in Verse Q2:285.

The Messenger has believed in what was revealed to him from his Lord, and [so
have] the believers. All of them have believed in Allah and His angels and His
books and His messengers, [saying], "We make no distinction between any of His
messengers." And they say, "We hear and we obey. [We seek] Your forgiveness,
our Lord, and to You is the [final] destination."[110]

To the extent that the Message brought by Prophet Muhammad and
embodied in the Holy Qur'an was indeed a new iteration of the same faith,
one might be justified to wonder whether or not it was necessary to send
that new message. The answer is set forth in a string of verses, Q6:154 to
157, which specifically address this consideration.

Then We gave Mūsā the Book, perfect for the one who does good, and explaining every thing in detail, and a guidance and mercy, so that they may believe in meeting their Lord (154). And this (Qur'an) is a blessed Book We have sent down. So follow it and fear Allah, so that you may be favored with mercy (155). (Had We not sent this book,) you would (have an excuse to) say, 'The Book was sent down only upon two groups before us, (i.e., the Jews and the Christians) and we were unaware of what they read' (156). Or you would say, 'If the Book had been sent down to us, we would have been more adhering to the right path than they are.' Now there has come to you a clear sign from your Lord, and a guidance and mercy... (157).[111]*

Thus while Verse Q6:154 sets forth the sufficiency of the two previous revelations in any event, Verse Q6:157 justifies the further iteration by way of ascertaining that the Arabs receive a revelation, in their own language and addressing their own context and environment. This is consistent with God's practice of sending his prophets and messengers widely to reach the maximum numbers of people. This is why, in Verses Q4:163 to 165, He ascertains that the prophets and peoples referred to in the tales of the Qur'an are just a few among many of whom God did not tell his Prophet.

We have revealed to you, as We revealed to Noah and the prophets after him. We revealed to Abraham, Ishmael, Isaac, the Tribes; to Jesus, Job and Jonah, Aaron and Salomon; and We revealed the Psalms to David (163): prophets whose stories We narrated to you already and prophets whose stories We have not narrated to you—And God spoke to Moses in plain speech—(164) prophets, bringers of glad tidings as well as warners, lest mankind have any argument with God after their coming. God is Almighty, All-Wise.[112]

Contrary to the prevailing perception of a monolithic Islam which draws on Islam being the final iteration of the Abrahamic faith to claim that it has abrogated and superseded all previous revelations and messages, adherence to—and compliance with—the faith contained in each of the previous revelations is by itself sufficient for the adherent to please God and gain salvation.[113] This is what Verses Q5:44 and 46 to 48 assert, namely that (1) the Torah, as revealed to Moses, contains guidance and light by which rabbis and prophets may judge for the Jews; (2) He also gave the Gospel to Jesus, confirming the Torah and containing guidance and light for the Christians in rendering their judgments, among other things; (3) He revealed the Qur'an to Prophet Muhammad that he and his people might be guided; and (4) He concluded with the evident fact that each revelation is a sufficient faith for its adherents.

> *For every community We decreed a law and a way of life. Had God willed, He could have made you a single community—but in order to test you in what He revealed to you. So vie with one another in virtue. To God is your homecoming, all of you, and He will then acquaint you with that over which you differed.*[114]

Then came the crystal-clear terms of Verse Q2:62 which reiterated the sufficiency of each such faith with particular reference to salvation.

> *Those who believe (in the Qur'an), and those who follow the Jewish (scriptures), and the Christians and the Sabians—any who believe in God and the Last Day, and work righteousness, shall have their reward with their Lord; on them shall be no fear, nor shall they grieve.*[115]

The reason for that diversity in valid paths resides in the commonality of the basic faith, namely the belief in God and the Last Day and in the performance of good deeds. Indeed, this verse comes following a series of verses about the Jews in which God encourages them to believe in the Message of Muhammad and reminds them of all the good things He gave them throughout their history.

In order to avoid any potential implication that Muhammad's Message is the only acceptable path, and that their failure to accept it could lead to their damnation and retribution, God reiterates His assurances to them and to all those who believe in the unicity of God and the finality of this life, and who perform good deeds. On this subject, Issa J. Boullata rightly observes, "[w]hen the Qur'an elsewhere does mention specific religious communities whose faith centers on the one and only God, it recognizes the existence of good people within each community and announces that they deserve divine reward." Boullata goes on to conclude that such a theme "strengthens the principle of religious pluralism, as it implicitly rejects all notions of exclusivism and election in Islam. In other words, the Qur'an does not favor one religious community over another."[116]

This conclusion is further confirmed in Verses Q2:111 and 112, on the occasion of some bickering which occurred among Jews, Christians, and

Muslims in Medina over the question of who among the adherents of the three faiths may, or may not, reach paradise.

And they say: "None shall enter Paradise unless he be a Jew or a Christian." Those are their (vain) desires. Say: "Produce your proof if ye are truthful" (111). Nay,-whoever submits His whole self to God and is a doer of good,—He will get his reward with his Lord; on such shall be no fear, nor shall they grieve (112).[117]

Ultimately, in terms of *īmān*, or basic faith, the requirements for deserving God's mercy and reward are simple and do not include the detailed creeds in which the Abrahamic traditions may differ,[118] as confirmed in Verses Q8:2 to 4.

The true believers are those whose hearts are filled with awe at the mention of God, and whose faith grows stronger as they listen to His revelations. They are those who put their trust in their Lord (2), pray steadfastly, and give in alms from what We gave them (3). Such are the true believers. They will be exalted and forgiven by their Lord, and a generous provision shall be made for them.[119]

In Verse Q46:13 matters are made yet simpler, because what matters most is the firmness of belief in the unicity of God, and everything else becomes a detail: *"Surely, those who say, 'Our Lord is Allah' and then stay firm, they will have no fear, nor shall they grieve."*[120] This explains the sanctity that the Qur'an attaches to the places of worship of all divine faiths.[121] This further explains the divine warnings against rendering God's revelations as mutually exclusive,[122] thereby prompting adherents of all iterations of the Abrahamic faith to uphold Islam in its most generic sense, which encompasses all these iterations.[123] Indicative in this respect are the reflections of Ignaz Goldziher.

I truly entered in those weeks into the spirit of Islam to such an extent that ultimately I became inwardly convinced that I myself was a Muslim and judiciously discovered that this was the only religion which, even in its doctrinal and official formulation, can satisfy philosophical minds. My ideal was to elevate Judaism to a similar rational level.

In response, Hamid Dabash comments:

One can easily see that much of Goldziher's love and admiration for Islam is in fact an intellectual extension of his devotion to his own faith, to Judaism…If at the mature age of forty, Goldziher says that since his early youth two mottos from the Hebrew Bible and from the Qur'an have been the guiding principles of his life, then his lifetime scholarly devotion to Islam and his unflinching commitment to Judaism were integral to each other and part and parcel of the same character.[124]

Goldziher was able to live his Judaism, but he readily accepted Islam because he did not find it in contradiction with his original faith. Simply put, this means that he saw no contradiction between Judaism and Islam.

For this reason, all the prophets and messengers who have preceded Prophet Muhammad, commencing with Abraham, were Muslims in the sense that they submitted to God by adopting the basic tenets that are common to each of the faiths that He revealed.[125] Verse Q3:67 provides that *"Abraham was neither a Jew nor a Christian, but he was one inclining toward truth, a Muslim [submitting to Allah]. And he was not of the polytheists."*[126] For that purpose, each of such prophets and messengers had similar missions, namely to receive the Revelation and convey the Message; and from that perspective they were all equal, as set forth in the following set of verses, Q2:131 to 133 and 135 to 136.

When his Lord said to him "Submit," he said "I have submitted [in Islam] to the Lord of the worlds" (131). And Abraham instructed his sons [to do the same] and [so did] Jacob, [saying], "O my sons, indeed Allah has chosen for you this religion, so do not die except while you are Muslims" (132). Or were you witnesses when death approached Jacob, when he said to his sons, "What will you worship after me?" They said, "We will worship your God and the God of your fathers, Abraham and Ishmael and Isaac—one God. And we are Muslims [in submission] to Him" (133). They say, "Be Jews or Christians [so] you will be guided." Say, "Rather, [we follow] the religion of Abraham, inclining toward truth, and he was not of the polytheists" (135). Say, [O believers], "We have believed in Allah and what has been revealed to us and what has been revealed to Abraham and Ishmael and Isaac and Jacob and the Descendants and what was given to Moses and Jesus and what was given to the prophets from their Lord. We make no distinction between any of them, and we are Muslims [in submission] to Him" (136).[127]

This is the scope of Islam, and it explains why the Abrahamic faith, with its major iterations as brought about by Moses, Jesus, and Muhammad, has been given the global generic name of Islam.

While God has declared all His prophets and messengers as equal, without any preference, there are certain verses which, if taken out of context, might imply certain preferences. There are two verses in the Qur'an in which such implication may transpire, namely, Verse Q2:253: "*And those Messengers, some We have preferred above others; some there are to whom God spoke, and some He raised in rank. And We gave Jesus son of Mary the clear signs, and confirmed him with the Holy Spirit*";[128] and Verse Q17:55: "*And thy Lord knows very well all who are in the heavens and the earth; and We have preferred some Prophets over others; and We gave to David Psalms.*" [129]

Most of the early exegetes[130] have gone to great lengths in interpreting these verses to attribute to God discriminatory preferences among prophets and messengers, and such interpretations were echoed by modern-day thinkers.[131] These views disregard the series of verses above in which God stresses their equal status. The term used for presumed divine preference is the verb *faḍḍalna,* which comes from the root word *faḍl,* which means a favor. If in the verses quoted above we replace "preferred" with "favored," the intent becomes clearer and the apparent inconsistency disappears. Most translators have employed terms of preference or excellence of one over the others, or even one exceeding the others.[132] Yet, two translators have conveyed the proper intent of the verse by using the terms of favor and bestowal of certain human gifts.[133] In fact, while God treats and considers all His prophets and messengers as equal, yet—and without prejudice to that equality—He favored each of them with certain special gifts, as necessary to enable each of them to best perform his mission. That is why He favored David with the Psalms, Jesus with the miracles, Moses with talking directly to him,[134] Muhammad with being sent as compassion to all humankind, etc. The ranks are not of the prophets and messengers over each other. Instead, they are ranks in this life, as necessary for the proper fulfillment of the mission entrusted to each prophet or messenger, such as David and Salomon being made kings, and Muhammad being granted the nocturnal visit described in *Sūrat al-Isrā'*.

While Islam, as one iteration among other iterations of the Abrahamic faith, enjoins tolerance, acceptance, and interaction among adherents of that global faith through its respective iterations, that injunction was not reflected in the actual relations of Muslims, Jews, and Christians of the Prophet's era.

Muslim, Jewish, and Christian Relations of the Early Period

If indeed Muslims are enjoined to accept and interact with Jews and Christians because of commonality of faith, then one could legitimately question the wisdom of the early wars waged against the Jews and Christians, and the expulsion of the Jews from Medina by the Prophet and his companions.[135] In this respect, let's start by observing that Jewish rabbis are often accused in the Qur'an of forging segments of the Torah in order to cover up certain realities and spread alternative heresies.[136] Similarly, both Jews and Christians are often admonished for not accepting the prophecy and mission of Muhammad; hence their rejection of God's Message embodied in the Holy Qur'an.[137] However, none of these accusations went to Jews and Christians in general as adherents of their particular Abrahamic revelations. These accusations were targeting the Jews and Christians of the Arabian environment within and around the Prophet's own environment.

With respect to the Jewish tribes of Medina, the start of relations was concomitant with the Prophet's hijra from Mecca to Medina—namely, with the enactment of the Charter of Medina. However, these relations started to deteriorate early on, especially following the early successes of the Muslims in their wars against the Meccans—after the battle of *Badr*—and other surrounding tribes of idolaters. The Jews were being accused of sowing the seeds of discord among the Muslims of Medina, and between them and the companions of the Prophet from Mecca, in repeated efforts to sway them from their faith.[138] These relations further deteriorated following the bloody battles of *Uhud* and *al-Khandaq* in which the Jews were perceived as, and accused of, aiding and abetting the idolaters of Mecca who were keen on defeating the Prophet and his mission altogether.[139] With this background in mind, the wars against the Jews which resulted in their expulsion from Medina were not motivated by intolerance against, or lack of acceptance of, Judaism on the part of the Muslim component of the community. In the words of John Esposito, "The motivation for such actions was political rather than racial or theological."[140]

The Holy Qur'an contains countless verses which confirm that Islam has no issues with Judaism in general, but that problems are limited to specific people or groups of people and their behaviors.[141] Instead, such wars and the resulting expulsions were politically motivated, with the Jews being blamed for breaking the covenants undertaken by them from time to time, commencing with the Charter of Medina.[142] Notwithstanding political belligerence, the books of traditions about the society of Medina during the days of the Prophet abound with accounts about the good relations, social interactions, and business dealings among Jews and Muslim immigrants coming from Mecca on the one hand and the Muslim *ansār* of Medina on the other.[143] In an environment lacking any state structure for administration of justice, expulsion from Medina was then considered the sole means to put an end to aggressive actions by Jewish tribes. That state of circumstantial belligerence between Jews and Muslims of Medina is further confirmed when we observe that Jews in general enjoyed a harmonious, prosperous life in Islamdom, as compared to their life in Christendom, and that is at a time when state structures had come into existence with the development and expansion of the Muslim Empire.[144]

Regarding the relations of the Prophet with Christians prior to the Revelation, he had an early acquaintance with their faith from his stops at their monasteries on trading trips to Damascus, as well as through his close relationship with the priest Waraqa Ibn Nawfal, who was the cousin of his first wife Khadija. Following the Revelation, an early encounter occurred shortly after his migration to Medina when he received a delegation from Najran that came to discuss matters of basic faith.[145] In that encounter, the main bone of contention was about the Christian concept of the Trinity and the divinity of Jesus Christ, versus the Islamic concept of Christ as an entirely human prophet and messenger of God and the puritanical conception of the unicity of God. Muslims insisted that, based on Qur'anic revelation, beliefs relating to the divinity of Christ and the Trinity were nowhere to be found in the Gospel and the Bible, such being innovations that had found their way into Christian Scriptures and were inconsistent with divine revelations.[146] Here, too, Qur'anic verses are countless about fighting not being occasioned by theological and faith-related differences, in the sense that the Holy Qur'an reserves a very special status for Jesus and his mother, wherein Jesus as prophet and messenger together with the Virgin Mary are thoroughly dignified.[147]

From the revelations of the later Medinan period, we come to the observation that the Qur'an made a clear distinction between the integrated conception of Islam, Judaism, and Christianity under the global unifying umbrella of the Abrahamic faith, on one hand, and the troubled relations among the adherents of the various iterations of that faith, namely Muslims, Jews, and Christians. Unfortunately, that distinction is seldom made. To illustrate, Shabbir Akhtar mentions a deadlock in relations among Muslims, Christians, and Jews, and observes that it is difficult to break it given God's silence following the end of Prophet Muhammad's mission.[148] Yet, in reality the silence of God is fully justified because God has condemned that rivalry and given His verdict by declaring all three paths as equal and legitimate paths to the truth and salvation. God went even further and confirmed that it was His intention that people be diverse and not share exactly the same path, even if they share the same creed.

While it is true that the polemical dialogue among these three branches of the faith was under way ever since Prophet Muhammad moved to Medina and continued almost through the end of his mission,[149] yet, the deterioration of relations and the ensuing violence was not attributable to any theological differences, but was essentially political in nature.[150] This is can be gleaned from several Qur'anic verses in which God appears to be guiding His Prophet toward a peaceful approach by reminding him consistently that not all Jews and Christians are alike, in the sense that many of them are peaceful, honest, and pious, while others are corrupt.[151]

That same peaceful approach is also stressed as the Prophet is guided to use dialogue and logical argument with his detractors among the adherents of the other Abrahamic faiths while leaving final judgment to God.[152] It is specifically spelled out that fighting must be avoided, or at least kept as a last resort, should the other side insist on a course of enmity. For that purpose, the Prophet is enjoined to remind those detractors that Muslims, Christians, and Jews, alike, worship the same God[153] and stand together on the same side against idolaters.[154]

It is in this same context of a hostile environment in Medina that we would place Qur'anic Verses Q3:118, Q4:140, and Q5:51 and 57 which caution against befriending the People of the Book. In fact, considering each of these verses separately, one immediately finds that the people targeted have taken belligerent action by expressing their enmity toward the Muslims, either by creating an environment which could foster separation among believers (Verse Q3:28), displaying hatred (Verse Q3:118), conspiring with the enemy (Verse Q5:51), ridiculing Muslims and their faith (Verse Q5:57), or simply badmouthing them (Verses 4:140 and Q6:68). In fact, in addition to the direct enmity of Jews toward Muslims in the context of the Medinan society of the time of the Prophet, there was a fear that Muslims who had fled from the defeat of the battle of Uhud, and others who were reluctant to join the war effort alongside the Prophet, would find refuge among the Jews and thus eventually turn against their fellow believers. This explains the cautions against befriending Jews which appear in several verses revealed around the same period. Note, however, that in none of these verses are the Muslims enjoined or authorized to use violence against Jews among the People of the Book. As long as the latter have not initiated the use of violence, Muslims should only abstain from befriending them and staying in their company.[155] This belligerence among Muslims and Jews did not survive the particular circumstance in which it came about in the Medinan context, as Mark Cohen observed with respect to subsequent periods: "The relatively relaxed ambience of interfaith relations in the Islamic marketplace created trust, which in turn encouraged partnerships for profit between members of the Jewish minority and their friends among the Muslim majority."[156]

These verses have been, and continue to be, gravely misinterpreted and misconstrued by exegetes who consider that living in an equal environment with non-Muslims is recognition of a relation of loyalty based on other than faith. They claim that Christians and Jews cannot and should not be trusted by Muslims, citing among other reasons that they do not believe in the entire Qur'an and the mission of Prophet Muhammad. Such interpretation is in direct contradiction to the pluralistic environment that Islam has sought to create. It is in direct contradiction with the verses which specifically enjoin Muslims to befriend all those who do not use violence against them, whatever their faith or lack thereof may be, such as in Verses Q60:8 and 9.

> *As for those who have not fought against you over religion, nor expelled you from your homes, God does not forbid you to treat them honorably and act with fairness toward them, for God loves those who act with fairness (8); God, however, forbids you to ally yourselves with those who fought against you over religion, expelled you from your homes or contributed to your expulsion. Whoso allies himself with them -these are the unjust (9).*[157]

Moreover, in Verse Q5:5 which appears in the same sura as Verse Q5:51 previously cited, Muslims are specifically told that they can eat the food of, and marry from among, the People of the Book.

> *This day, good things have been made lawful for you. The food of the people of the Book is lawful for you, and your food is lawful for them, and good women from among believers, and good women from among those who were given the Book before you, provided you give them their dowers, binding yourself in marriage, neither going for lust, nor having paramours. Whoever rejects Faith, his effort will go to waste and, in the Hereafter, he will be among the losers.*[158]

Clearly, one would not eat with, or otherwise marry, people that cannot be befriended in the first place.

With the above in mind, it is now possible to address the concern of Abdennour Bidar when he states that his fellow Muslims perceive him at times as a "diluted Muslim" because he refuses to acknowledge certain verses of the Qur'an which are discriminatory or hostile toward Jews and other so-called infidels.[159] His concern is addressed by recognizing the historiological character of these verses as opposed to a legislative purport, in the sense that they do not address a permanent universal position vis-à-vis their religion but address instead the behavior of peoples at a specific time in history, in a specific geographic location.

This brings us to the issue of the ban on non-Muslims from entering

Mecca and Medina. It is presumably based on a Qur'anic verse and a tradition of Prophet Muhammad. The verse is Q9:28, which provides as follows: "*O ye who believe! Truly the Pagans are unclean; so let them not, after this year of theirs, approach the Sacred Mosque. And if ye fear poverty, soon will God enrich you, if He wills, out of His bounty, for God is All-knowing, All-wise.*"[160] The Prophetic Tradition is one according to which Prophet Muhammad is presumed to have said, "There can be no coexistence between two religions in the Arabian Peninsula."[161] The cited verse and tradition are not sufficient to serve as valid foundation for the said ban. With respect to the cited verse, it does not constitute a valid basis for banning all non-Muslims from the entire areas of the cities of Mecca and Medina. The ban targets the pagans exclusively and does not extend to the People of the Book or to any other non-Muslims who believe in God as the one and only deity. In addition, the scope of that verse is specifically limited to the city of Mecca, and then only to the compound in that city which contains the Holy Mosque and the Kaaba.

More particularly, that ban was revealed in conjunction with the first hajj mission entrusted by Prophet Muhammad to his companion and future successor, Abou Bakr, and by way of dedicating that sacred shrine to the worship of God to the exclusion of any other deities.[162] This explains the reference in the verse to the compensation that God will confer upon the Muslims of Mecca for the loss of business that might ensue from that ban.[163]

As far as the Prophet's tradition, cited above, is concerned, there is serious doubt over its authenticity because it is inconsistent with the provisions of the Qur'an, and pluralism is of the essence of Islam. As stated previously, Islam, Christianity, and Judaism are not three different religions. As three iterations of the same Abrahamic faith, they constitute one and the same religion. This should refute statements which attribute the ban to the Prophet and describe it as religious apartheid.[164] In reality, Prophet Muhammad banned pagans from the Holy Shrine of Mecca only because it was previously a destination for multi-deity pagan worship; and the expulsion of Jews from Medina was exclusively politically motivated. On that matter, it is instructive that Prophet Muhammad allowed the

Christians of Najran, who visited him in Medina, to pray in his own mosque despite all the theological differences that they had and which were related in *Sūrat al-'Umran* (Q3).

Despite the clarity of Verse Q9:28 with respect to the limited scope of the ban—namely to pagans and to the holy shrine of Mecca—the ban was first extended to cover all mosques, wherever located. Then it was further extended by the Omayyad Caliph 'Umar Bin Abdul Aziz to all non-Muslims, without distinction, that is, to include the People of the Book. Finally, the exclusion of the People of the Book from the entire areas of the cities of Mecca and Medina came about much later, centuries after the death of the Prophet, without being founded on any scriptural bases. In this respect, and despite the claim by Muhammad Hussein Haykal to the contrary,[165] the Christians of Najran whom the Prophet had previously welcomed into his own mosque were displaced from the Peninsula by Enlightened Caliph 'Umar Ibn al-Khattab on purely political grounds unrelated to the presumed ban of non-Muslims therefrom. In fact, his move did not affect any Jews or other Christians that were not removed with those of Najran.

In the end, contrary to the views expressed by exegetes and "clergymen" that Christians and Jews are in essence idolaters for failing to acknowledge and accept the prophecy of Prophet Muhammad and his message embodied in the Holy Qur'an, in truth, it is sufficient for them to believe in their own Scriptures and carry out their attendant duties in order to earn salvation on the Day of Judgment. It is the duty of Muslims to acknowledge and accept the Scriptures revealed to the prophets of God who preceded Prophet Muhammad as an integral part of their Muslim faith. In this respect, Verses Q57:28 and 29 provide as follows:

> *O ye that believe! Fear God, and believe in His Apostle, and He will bestow on you a double portion of His Mercy: He will provide for you a Light by which ye shall walk (straight in your path), and He will forgive you (your past): for God is Oft—Forgiving, Most Merciful (28). That the People of the Book may know that they have no power whatever over the Grace of God, that (His) Grace is (entirely) in His Hand, to bestow it on whomsoever He Wills. For God is the Lord of Grace abounding (29).*[166]

This means that (1) those Christians and Jews who comply with their own faiths are deemed to be believers, as set forth in the verses previously cited; (2) if, in addition, they believe in the Message of Muhammad as well, then Verse 28 assures them that their reward will be doubled in recompense for that additional belief; (3) Verse 29 explains that God is free to give a better reward for the higher standard of belief.

Thus, it is essential to dispel the views often advanced by scholars which place Islamic perception of Christianity and Judaism within a phase-based mode of behavior whereby (1) in the early days of the Revelation when the Muslims were still weak, Christianity and Judaism were looked upon with kindness; then (2) as Islam gained in strength, the divide separating Muslims from Christians and Jews grew wider; and (3) when Islam reached its apogee and Muslims became strong, there was no longer a need to extend tolerance to non-Muslims, including the People of the Book.[167] These phases are not as clear or evident as that theory may imply. The confusion dissipates when a distinction is made between Christianity and Judaism as religions in terms of faith and the actual relations between the Muslims and the adherents of those religions.

While the perception by Muslims of Christianity and Judaism as religions may not change, yet, relations with the faithful of those religions can change, deteriorating for the worse or evolving for the better. Always keeping in mind the universal nature of Islam, each person, in each generation, is entitled to read and understand the Holy Qur'an as if it were revealed to him or her. In our day we must read and understand the Holy Qur'an in light of our own standard of rationality, education, and understanding. This would enable us to welcome the call by Sachedina when he asks Muslim thinkers to "prod believers to go beyond the normative community to foster a cross-cultural discourse in which the Islamic tradition—together with Christianity and Judaism—provides a credible voice of guidance, not governance."[168]

Chapter 14
The Right to Equality

Islam imposes no limitations on the expression and interpretation of internationally recognized human rights, as set forth in the Universal Declaration of Human Rights, including all international declarations, treaties, and conventions. The scope of this discussion of Islam and human rights will continue to focus on religious texts and their doctrinal interpretation. It will not extend to the varying degrees of implementation of human rights by individual countries and institutions. Unfortunately, universal human rights are often glorified rhetorically, while rights are ignored or routinely violated, most often in the blind pursuit of political interests and objectives.

As set forth in the Holy Qur'an, the right to equality among all people—Muslim and non-Muslim—is absolute, despite the numerous discriminatory practices that are often observed on more than one level. Abdelmajid Charfi points out the extent to which religion was corrupted and rendered subservient to practices unrelated to religion for no reason other than to legitimize such practices. Charfi observes how wars of conquest resulted in the creation of social classes based on unprecedented scales of riches, whereby commanders and tribal heads accumulated slaves, land, gold, houses, and ornaments, among other treasures, all of which directly violates the ethics of Islam. These socioeconomic discrepancies among the newly created classes resulted in social relations characterized by obedience, loyalty, and submission of the weaker to the more powerful, undermining the relations that Islam sought to establish based on social justice and equality. Charfi further calls attention to the extent to which this reality influenced the directions of *fiqh*, theology, and ethics, and was sanctioned by Muslim clerics and learned people of that time.[1]

Any recognition of the right to equality begins with the elimination of all forms of discrimination among people, irrespective of any differences and discrepancies based on race, gender, religion, nationality, or social or economic background.

The Principle of Nondiscrimination

Muhammad 'Abed al-Jabiri observes, "Islam guarantees two types of human rights: general rights...human rights in the absolute sense, and special rights...such as the rights of people who are vulnerable, women's rights, and the rights of non-Muslims."[2] However, it is preferable not to categorize special rights as human rights because they start from a premise of inequality, which translates into a relationship of subordination. Indeed, the stated special rights of women, non-Muslims, and minorities, among other categories, are not set forth in the Qur'an as human rights per se. Instead, they are of a temporary nature, intended to redress a wrong and change old customs. What count are general rights, and these must be available to all—males, females, minorities, Muslims, non-Muslims, everyone without exception.

The message of equality among all people was conveyed by God through the episode of creation, whereby all human beings of all times, irrespective of gender, race, color, background, belief, or faith, share the same process of creation. All people were created from clay, received God's spirit, and were appointed by God as trustees. Thus, no one has been excluded from this process. The principle of equality among all people, which is derived from the first act of human creation, was further confirmed by various Qur'anic verses with respect to all humans created subsequent to the initial creation.

> Q6:98—And He it is who has brought you [all] into being out of one living entity, and [has appointed for each of you] a time-limit [on earth] and a resting-place [after death]: clearly, indeed, have We spelled out these messages unto people who can grasp the truth![3]

> Q49:13—O mankind, We created you male and female, and made you into nations and tribes that you may come to know one another. The noblest among you in God's sight are the most pious.[4]

In these verses, it is clear that the equality is absolute, without discrimination on any account, whether of gender, creed, origin, color, or social extraction. This is confirmed with the affirmation that piety and consciousness of God are the only criteria by which people can be distinguished. Indeed, even prophets—including Prophet Muhammad—are equal with all other people and thus do not hold a privileged rank above other people, as set forth in Verse Q18:110: *"Say: 'I am but a man like yourselves, (but) the inspiration has come to me, that your God is one God.'"*[5]

Equality is not only established at creation or birth. People remain equal throughout their lifetimes, that is, until death and in the hereafter when they appear before God on the Day of Judgment, as expressed in Verse Q31:28: *"[For Him,] the creation of you all and the resurrection of you all is but like [the creation and resurrection of] a single soul."*[6] Thus, this verse sets forth the comprehensive nature of the principle of equality of all people at all times without discrimination on any count whatsoever. On that same basis of strict equality, the rewards and punishments on the Final Day will be allocated commensurately with the performance of each individual in this life. Then the *darajāt,* or degrees of distinction,[7] will be allocated by God accordingly.[8]

However, this equality is, strictly speaking, in the eyes of God and may not correspond with people's perceptions of each other. God has created people as equals. They will be equally subject to the laws of nature. Everyone, without exception, has a limited lifetime and dies, and they will all together resurrect and face judgment based on the same criteria. However, each individual, in his or her lifetime, exercises his or her faculties and enjoys free choice. Each individual will react differently to temptations, opportunities, and other occurrences. Depending on the choices that people make at every moment of their lives—the manner in which people act and react in their daily lives, how much education each person may seek and achieve, their level of activity and endeavors—some will be happier than others, some will be rich, others will be poor, some will live longer than others, and so on, all of which may appear to run counter to the equality that God fashioned as an attribute of humanity.[9] Verse Q4:95 states:

> *Those of the believers who sit still, other than those who have a (disabling) hurt, are not on an equality with those who strive in the way of Allah with their wealth and lives. Allah hath conferred on those who strive with their wealth and lives a rank above the sedentary. Unto each Allah hath promised good, but He hath bestowed on those who strive a great reward above the sedentary.*[10]

Here, it is clearly spelled out that those who sit back and do nothing, or do little, cannot expect to realize the same achievement as those who strive and work hard for a purpose. In other words, reward is commensurate with the extent of effort exerted, as spelled out in Verses Q53:38 to 40: *"That no soul burdened shall bear the burden of another (38); That man shall gain only what he endeavors (39); That his endeavour shall be noted (40)."*[11]

Several Qur'anic verses have been interpreted as attributing the inequality to divine governance and some divine wisdom, presumably based on the following verses:

Q6:165—It is He who made you the vicegerents of the earth and raised some of you in ranks over others, so that He may test you in what He has given you. Surely, your Lord is swift in punishing, and surely He is Most-Forgiving, Very-Merciful.[12]

Q16:71—God has bestowed His gifts of sustenance more freely on some of you than on others: those more favoured are not going to throw back their gifts to those whom their right hands possess, so as to be equal in that respect.[13]

When read in conjunction with the verses previously cited, it becomes clear that the intent of these latter verses, far from confirming any form of God's arbitrary election to favor people over others for no reason, is instead to enjoin those who were blessed with success and bounties to behave responsibly and give back to their communities a share of their wealth to be shared with those who were less fortunate. Any interpretation to the contrary would run counter to the principle of divine accountability. Thus, the Holy Qur'an is telling us: (1) the differences in reward are a confirmation of the principle of equality, that of the equal reward for equal hard work; and (2) even when a person has reaped the reward of his or her achievement, he or she must nevertheless act responsibly and share with lesser achievers. That divine wisdom of rewarding hard work also explains discrepancies in bounties based on faith and knowledge expressed in Verse Q58:11 (*"God will elevate to high ranks those who have faith and knowledge among you"*)[14] based on the general principle set forth in Verse Q49:13.

Despite the generality of the scope of the principle of equality set forth in the Holy Qur'an and its sufficiency to rule out all forms of discrimination on all counts, the Qur'an did expand on certain corollaries of the principle of equality, namely on account of gender, creed, family ties, social descendance or wealth, and race or color.

Nondiscrimination Based on Gender

Gender equality is the most important corollary of the principle of equality. The Holy Qur'an is explicit in asserting gender equality in every respect, without exceptions. Despite all the literature and propaganda to the contrary regarding the unfortunate condition of women, there are no exceptions to gender equality in the Qur'an.[15] The principle is set forth in general terms in the following verses:

> Q4:1—*People, be mindful of your Lord, who created you from a single soul, and from it [from the same essence] created its mate, and from the pair of them spread countless men and women far and wide.*[16]

> Q7:189—*IT IS HE who has created you [all] out of one living entity, and out of it brought into being its mate, so that man might incline [with love] toward woman. And so, when he has embraced her, she conceives [what at first is] a light burden, and continues to bear it. Then, when she grows heavy [with child], they both call unto God, their Sustainer, "If Thou indeed grant us a sound [child], we shall most certainly be among the grateful!"*[17]

> Q39:6—*He has created you [all] out of one living entity, and out of it fashioned its mate; and he has bestowed upon you four kinds of cattle of either sex; [and] He creates you in your mothers' wombs, one act of creation after another, in threefold depths of darkness.*[18]

Note that according to Verse Q4:1, it is not stated which gender came from the other or takes priority over the other. They both came from the same entity, and neither gender is superior or inferior to the other. They are equal: the trust (or *khilāfa*) granted by God was attributed to humankind as a whole, men and women equally.[19] Further, it should be noted that, in spite of widely prevailing myths, the Holy Qur'an does not adopt the biblical concept that Eve was created from the rib of Adam and that both Adam and Eve were thrown out of paradise because of Eve's fault. Thus, according to the Qur'anic Message, there was at no time any implication of a starting status for women inferior to that of men. In fact the temptation has been provoked by Satan and not by Eve, and God's pardon to Adam has erased any potential initial sin.[20]

Nondiscrimination Based on Creed

Examining aspects of democracy and equality in Greek thought and in Islam, Hamid Enayat observes:

> [T]he limitations placed by the Sharī'ah on the rights of non-Muslims are not permanent and unremovable, because non-Muslims always have the option to convert to Islam, and thereby overcome their political incapacity.[21]

This view arises from an insistence on perceiving Islam as another doctrine of state. In reality, if we reset the framework of divine governance and human government, then these issues will dissipate, because all people are equal before God. Discrimination between Muslims and non-Muslims, like any other discrimination, is man-made as evidenced in the *fiqh*-generated translations of Shari'a.

Contrary to what the early exegetes and the books of *fiqh* may say, the Holy Qur'an does not—directly or indirectly, expressly or implicitly— condone any form of discrimination based on creed. While issues relating to freedom of faith and nondiscrimination based on creed may not always have been distinguishable one from the other, as witnessed by the sad examples of world history, it can be observed that in actual Islamic history freedom of faith and nondiscrimination based on creed are two separate issues. In fact, while each individual is free to select the faith that he or she believes in, that choice determines the civil and political status by which that individual may be governed.

In Chapter 13, on Pluralism, the *dhimmī* status was discussed. Under this status, non-Muslims among the People of the Book retained their right to hold on to their non-Muslim faith, but submitted to a status which fell short of full citizenship in the Muslim state, at a time when the Holy Qur'an did not provide for such discrimination. There are also other areas, besides the political one, in which Islamic law has revealed discrimination based on creed, namely in the fields of inheritance and marriage. That said, besides the fact that freedom of faith is expressly asserted in the Holy Qur'an, there is absolutely nothing in the Holy Qur'an that permits any discrimination in this life based on creed.

With respect to the principles applicable to inheritance, early Islamic jurisprudence established the principle that non-Muslims cannot inherit from a Muslim, based on a tradition imputed to Prophet Muhammad,[22] and that principle continues to be in force in most countries which enforce Islamic law in the area of inheritance.[23] In reality, the Holy Qur'an does not provide for the exclusion of inheritance between Muslims and non-Muslims, whether they belong to the category of the People of the Book or that of nonbelievers. Bearing in mind that Prophetic Tradition is the Prophet's own *ijtihād* for his time and environment and that, as such, it cannot supplement or otherwise complement the Qur'an because the latter is perfect, should modern legislation decide to abolish that inheritance barrier among Muslims and non-Muslims, such action would not be inconsistent with the Holy Qur'an.

With respect to marriage, Islam prohibits the marriage between Muslims and idolaters for obvious reasons, as is the case with Judaism and Christianity. However, as a secular religion which respects freedom of choice and rejects any coercive enforcement of religious precepts in this life, Islam reserves judgment until the Final Day, upon which time judgment is rendered on the overall performance of each individual during his or her entire lifetime. For this reason, there should be no obstacle for a secular legislation to establish the equal right of each person to marry any other person of his or her choice without discrimination on the basis of creed, leaving to each person the absolute freedom and choice to comply or not with the religious precepts that he or she believes in.

This observation is important with respect to countries which still apply religious laws, including Islamic law, in matters relating to family law. For example, Lebanon is such a country in which there coexist eighteen religious communities whose faithful are governed by the laws, and are subject to the jurisdiction of the courts, of their own religious communities. All attempts made in the last seventy years to enact a national secular law for civil marriage have failed miserably, strongly opposed by the various religious establishments. In a country mired in divisions on confessional grounds, reaction against civil marriage turned out to be the one subject behind which most such religious establishments, Christian and Muslim, have consistently and successfully rallied. In reality, and without prejudice to positions on the subject taken by non-Muslim religious communities over which no view is expressed here, the enactment of civil legislation for family law, including civil marriage, is not repulsive to Islam for various reasons. In the first place, marriage under the Qur'an is a secular event which requires only the presence of a few witnesses to confirm the consent of the bride and groom. No religious personnel need be present to celebrate the marriage, despite traditions which have consistently provided for the involvement of such personnel. Yet, in addition to the mandatory celebration of the civil marriage in accordance with secular legislation, there is nothing to prevent a Muslim couple from electing to celebrate the marriage in the traditional manner with the involvement of the religious establishment.

On the other hand, even though the institution of a secular civil marriage would normally allow the wedding of believers and nonbelievers, each Muslim individual has free choice and remains free in deciding to whom he or she may be wedded, subject to accountability before God on the Final Day. However, in this respect, the wedding of a believer to a nonbeliever is among the actions which are prohibited "for a reason," as opposed to haram, matters which are prohibited in the absolute sense irrespective of any particular reason. The reason for the prohibition of marriage of a believer with a nonbeliever is to preserve the faith of the believer from possible adverse influences of the nonbeliever. From such perspective, if the believer can manage to maintain his or her faith, then there should be no reason for him or her to suffer any divine wrath.[24]

Still with respect to marriage, another situation involves discrimination based on both gender and creed at the same time: the right of a Muslim man to marry a woman among the People of the Book (a Christian or Jewish woman), while that right is not recognized to a Muslim woman (a Muslim woman is not allowed to marry a non-Muslim man) under the penalty of apostasy. Islamic law bases that right with its restriction to males only on Qur'anic Verse Q5:5:

> This day, good things have been made lawful for you. The food of the people of the Book is lawful for you, and your food is lawful for them, and good women from among believers, and good women from among those who were given the Book before you, provided you give them their dowers, binding yourself in marriage, neither going for lust, nor having paramours.[25]

While the text of this verse does not expressly enjoin that discrimination and thus does not offer any meaning to justify it, the reason advanced by the jurisprudence relies on the fact that since the man is the head of the family, the non-Muslim wife does not constitute a threat to his Islamic faith; whereas a non-Muslim husband would certainly constitute a serious threat to the creed of the Muslim wife.[26] On the same basis, we find some views which go a step further to prohibit even the marriage of a Muslim man to a woman among the People of the Book when that man lives in a minority status in a country with a predominantly non-Muslim population based on the following principal arguments: Permission for a Muslim man to marry a non-Muslim woman was initially designed for—and should thus be limited to—those who live in a Muslim nation within the so-called abode of Islam or *dār al-Islam*, a society dominated by the male component of the population and where the People of the Book are *dhimmīs* who pay the *jizya* tax by way of submission. By contrast, living conditions in nations where Muslims are in the minority, that is, within the abode of war or *dar al-ḥarb*, are such that the People of the Book do not occupy an inferior position to Muslims and therefore their emancipated women would constitute a threat to the faith of the Muslim man, hence the prohibition to marry, despite the provisions of Verse Q5:5.[27] Such views can be perceived as another application of the concept of *sadd al-dharā'i'* where rights are suppressed just by way of precaution. However, Hassan al-Turabi for his part is adamant that, under Qur'anic Verse Q5:5, cited above, there is no gender-related discrimination whatsoever, and thus every Muslim man and Muslim woman is entitled to marry a woman or a man among the People of the Book.[28]

Nondiscrimination Based on Nationality

Early Islamic jurisprudence established an impediment to inheritance based on the difference of abode. Thus a person who belonged to the *dār al-ḥarb* (the abode of war) could not inherit from another person who belonged to the *dār al-Islam* (the abode of Islam).[29] It has been already pointed out that, under *fiqh* (Islamic jurisprudence), the world was divided into the territories which were ruled by the Muslim Caliphate and made up the abode of Islam, while all other territories which were not under the control of Muslims constituted the abode of war, on the assumption that the territories of the latter abode constituted potential for future conquests by the Muslim Caliphate. That said, this impediment to inheritance devised by Islamic jurisprudence no longer exists, first, because ever since the end of the Ottoman Caliphate, the distinction between the abode of Islam and the abode of war has no longer been relevant, having been replaced by the concept of nationalities. Second, all countries that emerged from the Ottoman Caliphate but that nevertheless kept in effect the Islamic law on inheritance have specifically provided that the difference in citizenship between the deceased person and the heirs does not constitute an impediment to inheritance.

Nondiscrimination Based on Family Ties, Social Descendance, or Wealth

The Holy Qur'an has also expressly cautioned against discrimination among people on the basis of family ties (nepotism), social descendance, or wealth, in the sense that no favorable treatment should be given to a family member, a person descending from some nobility, or a rich person to the detriment of an unrelated person, a person of common lineage, or a poor person, respectively. This injunction is stated in Verse Q4:135.

O you who believe, be upholders of justice - witnesses for Allah, even though against (the interest of) your selves or the parents, and the kinsmen. One may be rich or poor, Allah is better caretaker of both. So do not follow desires, lest you should swerve. If you twist or avoid (the evidence), then, Allah is all-aware of what you do.[30]

In addition, Prophet Muhammad is credited, through his traditions, with having focused on nondiscrimination based on family ties and social descendance, as follows:

"You are all children of Adam, and Adam was created from clay; people should refrain from bragging about their forefathers";[31]

"O people, your predecessors have erred when they refrained from punishing the thief who came from a noble descent, while inflicting full punishment upon the thief who came from weaker ranks. I swear by the Truth that if Fatima, daughter of Muhammad had committed theft, Muhammad would have cut off her hand";[32] and

"We repudiate anyone who fights motivated by tribalism as well as the one who dies before having renounced tribalism."[33]

Nondiscrimination Based on Color or Race

While the Holy Qur'an has established the principle of absolute equality among people, reserving the extent of piety as the only cause for potential discrimination, it did not specifically list all areas for nondiscrimination, including nondiscrimination based on color or race. However, it was the Prophet Muhammad who was said to have specifically advised against such discrimination, in the following traditions:

"I am the brother of every pious person even if he were an Abyssinian slave, and I am innocent of every mischievous person, even if descending from the Qurayshi nobility";[34] and

"There is no preference for an Arab over a non-Arab, nor for a white person over a black person except on the basis of piety."[35]

Gender Equality

It should be clear that the Holy Qur'an has expressly laid out the principle of nondiscrimination based on gender, declaring the equality of men and women in all respects.[36] But, in reality, in spite of the absolute nature of the principle set forth in the Holy Qur'an, the practice has—and continues to—put that principle to shame.[37] In this respect, Qasim Amin rightly attributes the oppression of women to social traditions and customs which have been so absorbed by Islam that gender oppression came to be wrongly perceived as inherent in Islam.[38] Such practice is mainly rooted in pre-Islamic tribal customs.[39] It is also rooted in certain traditions which are most often wrongly attributed to Prophet Muhammad. Finally, that practice wrongly has found scriptural support in certain verses of the Holy Qur'an which were taken out of context and misconstrued.

Apologists[40] defend the perception of women in Islam using quotes attributed to the Prophet. Similarly, Islam bashers dig from the same sources of quotes attributed to the Prophet to find the exact opposite and report ugly stories about women. For example, the books of Prophetic Tradition which are considered by *fiqh* experts to be most reliable contain quite opposing sayings attributed to the Prophet. On the one hand, Prophet Muhammad, in praising women, is quoted as saying:

"Women are indeed the sisters of men";[41]

"The best person among you is the one who treats best his family; and I am the best among you in treating my family. Whoever honors women is a noble person and whoever insults them is a mean person";[42]

"Paradise lies under the feet of mothers."[43]

On the other hand, Prophet Muhammad is claimed to have said the exact opposite, wrongly attributing to him the following traditions:[44]

"If I were to order anyone to prostrate to another, I would order women to prostrate to their husbands";[45]

"There is no affliction more detrimental to men than women";[46]

"In Paradise, I observed that it was mostly populated by the poor; then in Hell, I found women making up the bulk of its population."[47]

While Prophet Muhammad is the most likely author of the quotations praising women given his exemplary morals and ethics, he could not have made the statements which denigrate women because they are inconsistent with the provisions of the Holy Qur'an. While the Prophet would not have made contradictory statements or ones which contradict the Holy Qur'an, the true reference should, at all times, be to the Holy Qur'an which—alone and to the exclusion of any other reference—is of divine origin.

The unfortunate outcome was the portrayal of a woman as an inferior, unstable creature, incapable of making sound judgment, and to be ashamed of.[48] For that purpose, jurisprudents sought to place a woman under the lifetime custody of a certain male lineage, commencing with the father, then moving to the husband. Should a woman remain unmarried or be widowed, she would return to the custody of her father, then brothers, uncles, cousins, and so on in that order of priority.[49]

Women, under Islamic *fiqh*, have suffered in almost every respect of their lives: first, as a female gender in general; second, in their role within the family (except as mothers); and third, in public life.

Women as a Gender

The Holy Qur'an is unequivocal in its assertion of gender equality which, ever since creation, is an innate attribute of human creation. From a gender perspective, the Qur'an is also explicit about not making any discrimination between men and women in all duties and obligations, as well as in punishment and reward. However, certain early exegetes have made the case for an alleged inferior nature of women in comparison to men's by reference to a few misconstrued provisions of the Holy Qur'an.[50] In reality, what these verses refer to are reprehensible tribal beliefs and customs according to which idols bearing female names are worshiped. In fact, the deities represented by the idols in the Meccan sanctuary were all given female names and, commencing with the Revelation, the belligerent pagans of Mecca treated their deities as daughters of God: hence these Qur'anic provisions which rejected God's paternity of any females; hence the misconstruction of these verses as an underestimation of women.

Other beliefs and customs deem women to be a dishonor to the family, hence the practice of burying newborn girls alive. It was a major objective of Islam to reverse such tribal customs and traditions, and to replace them with the human values of freedom, equality, and justice for the spreading of which God sent Prophet Muhammad.[51] In particular, God evokes the reprehensible evil nature of that specific tribal custom in Verses Q16:58 and 59, as follows:

> *When one of them is given the good news of a female child, his face becomes gloomy and he is choked with grief (58). He hides himself from people because of the (self-presumed) bad news given to him (and wonders): Shall he keep it despite the disgrace (he will face in the society), or put it away into the dust? In fact, evil is what they decide (59).*[52]

Similarly, proponents of the inferiority of women have advanced a short passage from another verse of the Holy Qur'an (Q3:36) which allegedly dismisses the equality of men and women in a rather sarcastic way: *"the male is not like the female."*[53] Unfortunately, it is erroneous and mischievous interpretations such as these that are achieved and spread when words are taken out of context which in reality have a completely opposite construction and meaning. Verse Q3:36 in full, reads as follows:

> *But when she had given birth to the child, she said: "O my Sustainer! Behold, I have given birth to a female"—the while God had been fully aware of what she would give birth to, and [fully aware] that no male child [she might have hoped for] could ever have been like this female—"and I have named her Mary. And, verily, I seek Thy protection for her and her offspring against Satan, the accursed."*[54]

Read in context, the passage in question is part of a statement which came in connection with the birth of the Virgin Mary. Her mother (the wife of Imran) was apologizing to God, who had blessed her with a child in response to her prayers, for having borne and delivered a female, in accordance with the prevailing beliefs about the inferiority of women and their exclusion from service in the houses of worship.[55] To these apologies, God responded that He knew very well what that outstanding female—Mary's mother—was carrying and bringing to life, and that no male could match that particular female then coming into being. In fact she was going in turn to bear and deliver God's word, prophet, and messenger, Jesus.[56] This is precisely what the quoted passage—the male not being like the female—was about; namely, that no male could claim to rival that female—the Virgin Mary—in honor and dignity. In witness of this interpretation, Verse Q3:37 confirms God's approval.

> *And so her Sustainer accepted her with goodly acceptance, and caused her to grow up in goodly growth, and placed her in the care of Zachariah. Whenever Zachariah visited her in the sanctuary, he found her provided with food. He would ask: "O Mary, whence came this unto thee?" She would answer: "It is from God; behold, God grants sustenance unto whom He wills, beyond all reckoning."*[57]

In further witness of God having created men and women as equals, He specifically and invariably attributed the various duties and obligations to both of them without any discrimination. Men and women are equally subject to the same duties: both must equally perform the prayers, pay zakat, fast during the month of Ramadan, and perform the hajj. While most of these duties have been phrased in gender-neutral language, prayers and zakat have been specifically addressed to both men and women.[58] Because men and women are equally subject to the same duties and obligations, they submit to the same standard of accountability in the hereafter on the Day of Judgment and share the same rewards and punishments for their respective acts; and in this respect, that equality is expressed in gender-specific language.

> Q16:97—*Whoever does good, male or female, while having faith, We shall make him live a decent life, and We shall recompense them with their wages, in accordance with the best of their deeds.*[59]

> Q33:35—*For Muslim men and women—for believing men and women, for devout men and women, for true men and women, for men and women who are patient and constant, for men and women who humble themselves, for men and women who give in Charity, for men and women who fast (and deny*

themselves), for men and women who guard their chastity,
and for men and women who engage much in God's praise—
for them has God prepared forgiveness and great reward.[60]

Q48:5 and 6—*[And] that He may admit the believing men and*
the believing women to gardens beneath which rivers flow to
abide therein eternally and remove from them their misdeeds—
and ever is that, in the sight of Allah, a great attainment—(5)
And [that] He may punish the hypocrite men and hypocrite
women, and the polytheist men and polytheist women—those
who assume about Allah an assumption of evil nature (6).[61]

By the same token, not only are men and women equally accountable
for their actions, but the rewards and punishments for their acts are also
equal; men are not punished more severely than women and vice versa.
That principle, namely that hurting women is punished as severely as
hurting men, is set forth in Verse Q33:58: *"As for those who hurt believing*
men and believing women without their having done anything (wrong),
they shall bear the burden of slander and a manifest sin."[62] Similarly to
equal divine rewards and punishments in the hereafter, men and women are
also subject to equal rewards and punishments in this life. It is on this basis
that God has decreed the same *ḥudūd,* or maximum penalties, for criminal
acts whether committed by men or women, such as the amputation of the
hand against the crime of theft,[63] one hundred lashes for adultery,[64] fair
retribution for homicide,[65] and so on. Even the monetary compensation
payable in lieu of—or in addition to—corporeal punishment should be
the same, irrespective of whether a man or a woman committed, or is the
victim of, the punishable crime according to Verse Q4:92,[66] even though,
in practice, there were diverging opinions under which the prevailing view
has ordered for the murdered man a higher compensation, namely double
that for a murdered woman.[67]

Finally, despite assertions to the contrary,[68] the Holy Qur'an did
not assign any specific social functions to the male and female genders,
respectively.[69] However, a large number of jurisconsults, clerics, and

apologist writers have attributed to men, because of their so-called stronger build and wiser judgment, the duty to work, earn a living, and provide for the family.[70] Instead, because of what is said to be their weaker build and lesser intellectual capabilities, women are assigned the functions of homemaking, child bearing and rearing, and watching over the comfort and well-being of husbands and children. Consider Verse Q4:32.

> *Hence, do not covet the bounties which God has bestowed more abundantly on some of you than on others. Men shall have a benefit from what they earn, and women shall have a benefit from what they earn. Ask, therefore, God [to give you] out of His bounty: behold, God has indeed full knowledge of everything.*[71]

We find the following explanation of this verse in one of the often referred to commentaries: "for men the reward of what they achieve in terms of jihad among other things, and for women the reward of their dedication in the obedience to their husbands and guarding their chastity."[72] These views are not limited to exegetes of the early Islam periods. They are still held by clerics and scholars today.[73]

Furthermore, because of these presumed inferior physical and intellectual capabilities, women are often perceived as vulnerable to the traps of men, who in essence are presumed to be wicked and always on the lookout to trap women and abuse them. That is why among ultraconservative families, every effort is made to minimize any potential contact between men and women by confining women to the home and if they need to leave home ensuring that they get out anonymously wearing attire which prevents others from recognizing them.

Contrary to all prejudices that we find in *fiqh* books and other works by clerics and 'ulama's, the Holy Qur'an did not mandate any specific functions to men or women or discuss them beyond noting the biological fact that it is women who carry children until they are born, or the observation that under the prevailing customs men work and provide for their families. On the contrary, God sanctioned and blessed women who went out with men on the migration to Medina and then participated with—and shared the same destiny of—men in hardship and fighting, expressed in Verse Q3:194 and 195.

"Our Lord, give us what You have promised us through Your messengers, and do not put us to disgrace on the Day of Judgment. Surely you do not go back on Your promise." (194) So, their Lord answered their prayer: "I do not allow the labour of any worker from among you, male or female, to go to waste. You are similar to one another. So, those who emigrated, and were expelled from their homes, and were tortured in My way, and fought, and were killed, I shall certainly write off their evil deeds, and shall certainly admit them into gardens beneath which rivers flow, as a reward from Allah" (195).[74]

Women in the Family

In the family, women are primarily perceived by *fiqh* as a necessary social and financial burden on their closest male kin, namely and in general order of priority,[75] the fathers, full or paternal brothers, paternal uncles, paternal cousins, and so on[76] who are legally entitled to act as their guardians and obliged to provide for their financial needs.[77] In particular, women are initially and primarily daughters, then subsequently and eventually wives and mothers. In each such iteration, except as mothers, women have been, and very often nowadays continue to be, demeaned through the wrongful attribution to them of an inferior status, in which they are discriminated against in terms of freedom of decision and action, and in terms of the financial rights to which they are entitled. That treatment of women, which is presumably founded in Islamic law and practice, is wrongful because it is in reality contrary to Islam and the divine Shari'a.

As Daughters

As daughters women are subject to the usual statutory guardianship authority of a parent or other relative, or to judicial guardianship designated by the judge, in the absence of a qualified statutory guardian. In this capacity, and until they reach the full legal age, females are not different from males. However, past the age of majority at which minors are legally emancipated and except under the Shi'i Ja'fari school of jurisprudence, women do not accede to full emancipation like their male siblings. In fact, according to the four major Sunni schools of jurisprudence and except with respect to financial matters,[78] women remain under the authority of their legal guardians until they are married, at which time that guardianship transfers to the husband. This means that the guardian is entitled to maintain his authority over a woman by way of controlling her movements, in and out of the home, controlling who she may or may not visit, whether she can work or not, how she should dress, etc. This constitutes the first aspect in which the rights of males and females are not equal. While guardianship over male children ends when they reach the legal age, guardianship over female children is not time-bound and may continue indefinitely, if they do not get married.

The immediate corollary of this unfortunate extension of guardianship over females is that guardians can, in most jurisdictions, exercise the power to approve or disapprove the marriage of a woman even though she has reached and passed the age of majority. In fact, the authorities would not process a wedding formality if the guardian is not present to conclude it on behalf of the bride under his guardianship. However, apologists often advance the fact that the power to marry the woman under guardianship is not absolute, because the guardian must first obtain the approval of the bride before concluding her marriage.[79] They fail to see that the issue is not only about marrying the bride against her will but about her inability to act freely and directly, without the intervention and intermediation of the guardian. Of the four Sunni schools of jurisprudence, only the Hanafi school allows a woman who has reached the age of majority to marry the person of her choice without the prior consent of her guardian, provided that the judge is satisfied that the groom comes from a similar family and financial standing, and is willing to pay the dowry in at least the amount deemed customary for a woman of similar standing.[80]

Note, however, that contrary to the prevailing position of the Sunni schools of jurisprudence in Islamic law, the Ja'fari school of jurisprudence, which is followed by the twelver Shi'a communities, stands out in asserting that male and female children equally accede to full emancipation upon reaching the legal age of majority.[81] In this respect, the Ja'fari school of jurisprudence is fully in line with the provisions of the Holy Qur'an with respect to nondiscrimination between males and females on issues of guardianship of females having reached the age of majority. In fact, there is nothing in the Qur'an to allow or justify the continued subjection of females to guardianship authority beyond that age.

As Wives

Contrary to the provisions of the Holy Qur'an which established the equality of men and women without exception, wives have in real life been—and continue to be—discriminated against and attributed a status which is inferior to that of their husbands, in terms of restrictions to their freedoms, as well as the attribution to them of lesser rights than to their husbands.[82]

The restrictions to the freedoms of women came in the form of automatic transfer of the father's authority deriving from the statutory guardianship (*al-wilāya 'ala-n-nafs*) to the husband immediately upon concluding the marriage celebration, in the form of *al-qawwāma*, presumably on the strength of Verse Q4:34 which, according to one of similar translations, provides that

> *Men are the protectors and maintainers of women, because God has given the one more (strength) than the other, and because they support them from their means. Therefore the righteous women are devoutly obedient, and guard in (the husband's) absence what God would have them guard. As to those women on whose part ye fear disloyalty and ill-conduct, admonish them (first), (Next), refuse to share their beds, (And last) beat them (lightly); but if they return to obedience, seek not against them Means (of annoyance): For God is Most High, great (above you all).*[83]

On the basis of these provisions, Islamic jurisprudence has decided that the guardianship exercised by husbands over their wives consists of the primary obligation of the wife to obey her husband, and the resulting powers of the latter to discipline his wife and control whether or not she may leave the home, and who she may or may not frequent. Khalil 'Abdul-Karim traces these traditions to the pre-Islamic Arab culture in which the husband was called the *ba'l* of his wife, a name traditionally attributed to male Phoenician divinities. 'Abdul-Karim refers to that origin to explain the perception of the husband's status and role as a god to whom utter respect and full obedience are due by his innumerable wives and slaves.[84]

He even considers that Islam has adopted and condoned these traditions and cites to that effect the verses of the Qur'an discussed in this section.

While there are grounds to agree with 'Abdul-Karim on the origin of these traditions, there are no such grounds to validate his view that Islam adopted and condoned such traditions. Their continued recognition is exclusively an abuse of temporary tolerance, as witnessed by the entire picture that comes out when all verses are put in context and are considered in light of one another.

Although there is consensus that guardianship does not extend to the financial assets of the married woman, from a factual perspective, husbands could control what women did with their assets by restricting their freedoms of leaving the home or contacting counterparts to manage their assets, using the powers of guardianship over their persons. Ann E. Mayer expresses this concern when she raises the unresolved issue of how to reconcile all the rights that the Qur'an has provided for women in terms of managing their own assets and conducting business with all the restrictions imposed in the Shari'a law in terms of men controlling their lives and restricting their movements.[85] The answer to that important question is that the restrictions imputed to Shari'a are in reality restrictions imposed by man-made *fiqh,* which may have had historic bases but certainly have no religious basis. Accordingly, such restrictions can and should certainly be removed because they have no divine content and are prejudicial to modern Muslim societies. In reality, the cited Verse Q4:34 is perhaps the verse of the Holy Qur'an which has received the widest range of divergent interpretations.

To start with, the men and women referred to in the verse in question were taken for granted by most exegetes to be husbands and wives, setting the stage for the framing of the relationship of subordination between men and women in the family.[86] By contrast, Ibn 'Ashour and Shahrour perceive the reference to men and women (as opposed to husbands and wives) as a statement of fact, in the context of a general gender allocation of roles, based on actual observation: men under the prevailing circumstances had a better access to the means of providing for the needs of women. Shahrour goes on to state that the role played in assuming the duty of providing for others is derived from access to the required means, including the money necessary to cover the expenses. For that purpose, they conclude that such duty to provide is not a permanent attribution of that function to men, but could be assumed—together with the control that comes with it—by women if they had those means.

In describing the role of men toward women, the term in Arabic used in the Qur'an is *qawwāmūn,* which typically means that they are "determined in providing support."[87] However, the early jurisprudents whose views later prevailed have understood that role, otherwise known as *al-qawwāma,* to mean guardianship or curatorship in the modern legal sense of the term, namely the guardianship of a minor with all the powers that are associated with it. For example, most of the recognized early exegetes of the Holy Qur'an (such as al-Tabari, al-Razi, al-Qurtubi and Ibn Kathir) as well as modern-day ones (such as al-Sha'rawi and al-Tantawi) have gone fully for the legal sense of guardianship to include all the powers that a father legally holds over his minor children. By contrast, Ibn 'Ashour and Shahrour do not see it as a universal and permanent statutory and legal entitlement, that is, an attribute of manhood, to control women. Instead, they perceive it as a de facto role deriving from the fact that men, in the desert tribal environment which prevailed during the period of the Revelation, were the ones who had the physical strength and the financial means required to provide for women.[88] Therefore, if times changed and women were to have equal access to the means of sustenance, they could act as providers to men and have their say. From that perspective, men and women are equal.

However, Mohamed Talbi refuses in the first place any implication of male superiority in the meaning of the term *al-qawwāma.* To him, that term is a mere reference to a legal obligation to provide for the needs of the family.[89] That divergence in the interpretation of the term *qawwāmūn* is reflected in the divergent manners in which the several translators of the Holy Qur'an into English have rendered this term in the English language: Abdullah Yusuf 'Ali (from whose translation we quoted this verse above), Muhammad A. S. Abdel Haleem, and Laleh Bakhtiar have opted for the concept of providing protection and maintenance using such terms as take good care and act as supporters of wives, respectively. Somehow close to that concept, is the rendition as caretakers by Mufti Muhammad Taqi 'Uthmani. For their part, Nessim Joseph Dawood and Tarif Khalidi went for straightforward authority and legal responsibility of men over women, respectively. Marmaduke Pickthall, Muhammad Asad, and Ibrahim Walk described men as being in charge of women.

Verse Q4:34, which deals with the relationship of men and women gives two reasons for the role given to men, namely (1) the fact that they spend from their wealth in providing for the needs of women, and (2) the existence of certain discrepancies in the allocation by God of bounties among men and women. The exegetes have described these discrepancies as gender-related preferences granted by God to men over women as an attribute of manhood, such as physical strength, wisdom, intelligence, education, etc., all of which contribute to a better ability on the part of men to earn a living and manage their lives and those of their wives. Among the translators of the Holy Qur'an into English, Dawood chose the "superiority" of men over women, whereas Pickthall and Mufti 'Uthmani referred to men who excel over women. In reality, here too there is no question of innate gender superiority. Simply put, in the desert tribal environment prevailing at the time of Revelation, men had a better opportunity than women to receive the bounties of God, and the verse in question was merely referring to that factual situation. In fact, if it was indeed a reference to a superiority which is innate in manhood, there would have been no need to explain the reasons for the stated role of men toward women.

A fourth area of diverging interpretation can be found in the manner in which the term *qānitāt*, which describes the attitude of good women toward their men, is rendered. Strictly speaking, this term is derived from the term *qunūt* which means devotion to God. Thus, women who are *qānitāt* are devout in their worship of God and are obedient to God. Unfortunately, that term was almost unanimously rendered by the translators of the Holy Qur'an as a reference to women who are obedient to God *and to their husbands* (such being equivalent to the association of husbands with God). As a result, the good woman becomes one who is obedient to her husband, thereby equating obedience to the husband to devotion to God. Only

Asad, Abdel Haleem, and Bakhtiar did not fall into the trap of extending obedience to husbands.

Now we come to the advice given to men on handling what Verse Q4:34 calls the *nushūz* of women. *Nushūz* is typically a form of belligerent attitude on the part of a woman with some reluctance and lack of interest on her part toward her husband. However, most exegetes treated the term as a direct reference to disobedience, considering that any disobedience to the husband, irrespective of cause, was repulsive to God.

Finally, we come to the ultimate punishment deserved by a woman who displays a *nushūz* attitude, namely what has been understood as the recourse to beating rebellious women. Here too, we face divergent interpretations. The term used for that punishment is *uḍrubūhunna* derived from the root term *ḍaraba*. The great majority of translators and commentators, from both early and modern days, understood that term to refer to beating. Thus the commentators went to great lengths in order to define the extent of permitted beating. In contrast, Laleh Bakhtiar, author of one of the most recent translations of the Holy Qur'an, rendered that term as "going away from them."[90]

However, it is Muhammad Shahrour who offers the most compelling interpretation of the term.[91] Shahrour explains that in the Arabic language the root-term *ḍaraba* can have several meanings besides beating. He rightly points to the fact that, in Arabic, different terms totally unrelated to the root term *ḍaraba* are used, depending on which part of the body is targeted by the beating or hitting. For that purpose, he is of the opinion that the term *uḍrubūhunna* as used in the context of Verse Q4:34 means to stand firm for one's position to disapprove and categorically reject the belligerent attitude of the woman. This is so because the subsequent Verse Q4:35 offers a solution to the firm rejection by the husband of his spouse's belligerence, from which may result a potential to end the marital relation between the couple, by suggesting a family-conducted arbitration process.

> *And if you have reason to fear that a breach might occur between a [married] couple, appoint an arbiter from among his people and an arbiter from among her people; if they both want to set things aright, God may bring about their reconciliation.*[92]

In light of the above, the prevailing, gravely erroneous understanding of this Verse Q4:34 continues to follow the views of the majority of early and contemporary exegetes, as translated by Nessim Joseph Dawood.

Men have authority over women because God has made the one superior to the other, and because they spend their wealth to maintain them. Good women are obedient. They guard their unseen parts because God has guarded them. As for those from whom you fear disobedience, admonish them, forsake them in beds apart, and beat them. Then if they obey you, take no further action against them.[93]

By contrast, this verse when based on the actual meanings of the terms described could be translated in this way.

Men stand out firmly to perform their duty of providing support and care for women because of the circumstances under which God has blessed them with the means to perform this duty and their ability to meet the spending requirements therefor. The virtuous women are obedient to—and devout in their worship of—God, and are faithful in guarding the intimacy that God has ordained to be guarded. To the extent that you might experience a belligerent and reluctant behavior by women toward you, exhort them to redress their attitude, refrain from sharing their beds, and eventually stand out firmly with your position. If they yield to your concern, do not seek any further action against them.

It may be concluded that Verse Q4:34 did not purport to subject women to the comprehensive guardianship of men over their persons, including the power of discipline.[94] Thus, it did not reverse or break from the equality of men and women, including the equality of husbands and wives, as seen elsewhere in the Holy Qur'an. As evidence that these provisions are not of a statutory nature, the Ottoman family law,[95] while maintaining the obligation of the wife to obey her husband, abolished the power of the husband to discipline his wife and replaced it by the principle that the personal relations between husband and wife must be governed by kindness and compassion.[96] This requirement follows the Qur'anic precepts that the relationship of wives and husbands should be based on love and compassion, relying on the honorable and kind treatment, which appears in Verses Q4:19 and Q30:21, respectively.

The concept of *qawwāma*, understood as a continuing guardianship of husbands over their wives has had the unfortunate consequence of serving to increase the might of men over women and widen the discrimination gap between them, in a manner never intended by the divine text. It is from this perspective that it is necessary to view the institution of polygamy, the lesser rights of inheritance by women, and the discretionary and exclusive right of husbands to unilaterally repudiate their wives, all under Islamic law and practice. Indeed, contrary to prevailing accepted rules and practice, Islam—as laid out in the revealed text which established the essential equality between men and women in every respect—did not condone polygamy, unilateral repudiation of wives by men, or discrimination between male and female heirs in the allocation and distribution of estates.

Regarding polygamy, it should be noted that a large segment of Muslim clerics continue to strongly advocate and praise the wisdom of polygamy as a right of each male Muslim person. Ahmad Moussalli describes the views of a salafi cleric on the issue of men's right to marry more than one wife based on ecological, biological, and social reasons.

> First, there are more women than men; second, it protects women from exploitation by men; third, if some women cannot bear children, they are not inhumanely divorced; fourth, if some women become permanently ill, their husbands marry others without divorcing them. He believes that such a scheme is more dignified for women who might suffer from biological defects or ecological imbalance.[97]

Such a position is untenable because, following that same reasoning, we would have to concede similar rights for women to dispose of multiple men where it is the man who suffers from these defects and imbalances, or is responsible for not being able to bear children, or should the number of men exceed that of women. Instead, recall that Islam, in its endeavor to modify reprehensible tribal, pre-Islamic customs, and to provide the best circumstances for their elimination,[98] took the cautious approach of tolerating (as opposed to condoning as an inherent right) the continuation of polygamy while raising the bar of conditions therefore and enjoining the adoption of monogamy.[99] This same pattern appears in connection with the institution of repudiation.[100]

The Holy Qur'an does not contain anywhere in its verses an express stipulation that the marriage relationship may be terminated by the unilateral declaration of either one of the couple, at will and in its discretion, or that men are exclusively entitled to exercise that power. Instead, that power was developed by *fiqh* and introduced by the jurisprudents as a basic right of men, and as an attribute of manhood. In this instance, the jurisprudence relied on the implied recognition of repudiation found in verses which purported to regulate its exercise. In reality, the institution of repudiation had, for a long time before Islam, been in existence in the tribal environment of Arabia, in which women were perceived as personal chattel that could be readily bought and sold, or hired and fired as wives. Actually, death and repudiation were the sole occasions under which marriages ended. This explains that we find in the Holy Qur'an verses which caution against certain actions that could complicate the unfortunate consequences of divorces by way of repudiation, which are so easily pronounced by husbands.

One such consequence is the disruption of family life arising from a hasty pronunciation of the repudiation. It also explains why the Holy Qur'an sets forth in Verse Q2:228 a mechanism for undoing that repudiation within a certain time frame thereafter. Yet, at the other extreme, the Holy Qur'an further sets forth in Verses Q2:229 and 230 a mechanism to prevent repeated frivolous repudiations of the same marriage relationship. Another consequence of repudiation is the uncertainty of the filiation of offspring to a woman who remarries shortly after the dissolution of the previous marriage. That is why Verse Q2:228 requires that a repudiated woman who is at an age in which she may still procreate should, before remarrying, observe a certain waiting period, so as to determine whether or not she is pregnant by the previous husband, and thereby avoid any potential confusion as to who might be the father of a child who is born to that woman subsequent to the repudiation.

Another consequence of the dissolution of the marriage is the loss by the repudiated woman of financial support previously provided by the repudiating husband. Again, the Holy Qur'an requires husbands who exercise the power of repudiation to do the necessary as to not abandon their ex-wives in need. In particular, Verses Q65:4 to 7 deal with the post-repudiation financial needs of a divorcée who is pregnant. Along the same lines, Verses Q2:230 to 232, Q2:236 and 240, Q4:19, Q33:49, and Q65:1 to 3 enjoin husbands to deal with their divorcées with kindness and compassion, and not to be abusive in restricting their post-repudiation freedom. Finally, Verses Q4:19 to 21 even caution men against abusing polygamy by marrying another person and keeping the first one captive against her will by refusing to set her free by way of repudiation.

These countless verses aiming at attenuating the excesses that may come out of the unlimited powers of male spouses have one principal purpose, that of creating an awareness of the reprehensible nature of repudiation. One might legitimately ask, why should the power of repudiation remain confined in male spouses to the exclusion of women?

First, the issue of repudiation by male spouses is dealt with as a *de facto* power predating the start of Revelation without acknowledging it as a right. On the contrary, Verse Q2:227[101] implies that it is something that God would merely tolerate under the prevailing circumstances, subject to the conditions and warnings set forth in the subsequent verses and others elsewhere.

Second, noting that such unilateral action might be taken lightly, conditions were placed to rationalize its use and protect the interests of women.

Third, while the context implies that repudiation is exercised by men following the prevailing tribal practice, it is nowhere expressly stated that only men can exercise repudiation. On the contrary, the verse immediately following Verse Q2:227 expressly enacts the equality of rights between men and women in a marriage relationship, from which it may be inferred that women too may exercise that right.[102]

Finally, while the separation by the couple is the solution of choice when a couple cease to be able to live together, God offers his preferred alternative for separation, namely first through the mutual negotiated consent of the couple,[103] then through a family-sponsored arbitration, in which all the circumstances surrounding the separation are considered and the rights of the parties are addressed so that the proposed separation may occur in an orderly manner, and with the least damage on either side.[104]

In this light, unilateral repudiation should not be construed as a basic freedom of man, an attribute of manhood. Instead, it is a mere tolerance of a primarily reprehensible but specific custom which prevailed at the time of Revelation, one that God has maintained in effect while engaging believers to examine its use pending its phasing out, through a two-part message: (1) marriage is a solemn union sponsored by God[105] that people should strive to maintain and shield from abusive and frivolous separations; and (2) human dignity and freedom require that such a union, despite its importance, need not remain inalienable if its continuity becomes untenable. In this and other respects, God has even elevated the proper and fair, nonabusive treatment of women, to the level of an act of piety.[106]

This brings us to discrimination against women in the field of inheritance based on two main issues derived from actual practice wrongly imputed to Islam, namely: (1) the fact that females are generally[107] attributed one-half of the corresponding share of males, that is, one-half of the share attributed to their husbands or brothers; and (2) the fact that one or more female children with no male siblings do not inherit the entire estate of the deceased father or mother as the case would be if there were male siblings. They inherit an allocated share, and the balance of the estate goes to the nearest male relative belonging to the category of 'aṣabas, male descendance. The discrimination that women continue to suffer in matters of inheritance is not only wrongly imputed to Islam, but it is primarily anti-Islamic.

When Islam appeared, it sought to create a social revolution by ending pre-Islamic tribal perceptions of women. In the inheritance system, aside from the fact that women were not allocated any share in an estate, they were themselves a subject of inheritance, that is, women left behind by a deceased person could be inherited by his heirs. That practice was expressly reversed in Verse Q4:19. Then, having been recognized as a full human being, as opposed to a chattel that could be inherited, women were recognized as the equals of men and were given the right to share in the inheritance of their fathers, mothers, siblings, and other family members, as well. In order to stress that entitlement, women were allocated a guaranteed minimum share, a benefit not shared by their male siblings.

Unfortunately, it is that concept of minimum share that early and modern exegetes and *fiqh* failed to note and appreciate its full implications.

Muhammad Shahrour[108] recognized that very important concept which revolutionized the inheritance mechanism in Islam long before any other civilizations even began giving rights to women. The breakthrough in the Qur'anic approach lies in the fact that, first, it recognized, in principle, women as the equals of men in terms of entitlement to receive a share of the estate of a common parent or other relative. Then, using the concept of *ḥudūd*, or limits, it secured a minimum share of which a woman cannot be deprived under any circumstances. Finally, it left the woman's share flexible so it could be increased above the minimum level should the prevailing system—which places on men the financial burden of supporting women—change.

Thus, the revolution brought about by Islam consisted of (1) establishing the principle of equality of males and females; (2) reversing the practice of depriving women of their rights, including the share in inheritance; and (3) offering a universal system which, then, provided basic fairness in balancing the rights and obligations of men with the rights and entitlements of women, but had the capacity, through the concept of *ḥudūd*, to constantly adapt and update that balance. Therefore, if a modern legislator in a predominantly Muslim country were to enact a secular inheritance law in which men and women inherit equally, as the late President Ataturk of Turkey did, he would be fulfilling the purpose of Islam—not breaching its provisions.

Considering the other instance of discrimination, that of withdrawing part of the estate in favor of more distant male—and occasionally other female—relatives where the deceased has left female children only, it constitutes a typical misconstrual of Qur'anic provisions and reliance on traditions of the Prophet, often unsubstantiated or misunderstood. In this case, paradoxically, the jurisprudence has continued the *jāhiliyya* principle of inheritance in the male lineage, treating the reserved shares set forth in the Qur'an, primarily to female kin, as exceptions which merely take priority, like debt or an allocation by will, within permitted limits. Accordingly, the males in the *'aṣaba* category are the common-law heirs by order of proximity to the deceased person. As such, they get all that remains after the allocations to those with priority claims.

The Sunni schools of jurisprudence have relied in reaching this conclusion on a tradition according to which the Prophet is alleged to have said, "[g]ive out the reserved allocations to their designees, and attribute the balance to the closest male kin."[109] By contrast, the Shi'a Twelver school of jurisprudence rightly rejected this approach, considering that tradition to be unreliable and also inconsistent with other provisions of the Qur'an. Those other provisions are verses which establish the principle of gender equality, in particular by specific reference to Verse Q33:6 which provides that the closest kin have a better claim than that of more distant kin.[110] On that basis, the Shi'a Twelver school of jurisprudence has reached the fair conclusion that the daughter of the deceased person inherits the balance of the estate by way of priority over more distant male kin.[111]

Thus, in all these examples cited above, the divine text has been wrongly construed as a legal system and the relevant rule of law taken out of context. The relevant context instead would have made clear that what the divine text really intended was to warn against, and encourage the alleviation of, the damaging consequences of polygamy, repudiation at will, and the inhuman perception of women in the Arabian society preceding the advent of Islam. The Holy Qur'an did not condone these practices and, in fact, on the contrary found them to be reprehensible. But the Qur'an tolerated them to move forward as a way of disengaging from them and then shedding them entirely.

This leads us to the conclusion that if today's secular legislators were to enact a law to adopt the monogamous system of marriage, ban unilateral repudiation, and institute judicial divorce instead, such enactment would not be in violation of Shari'a. On the contrary, it would be fully consistent with the spirit of Shari'a and a step forward in the fulfillment of its purposes. Indeed, Islam has granted women very important rights of which they continue to be deprived by ongoing practice based on Islamic law developed by *fiqh*. Islam grants to a Muslim woman the power to stipulate any conditions in the marriage contract which, in her opinion, can restore her to a status equal with her husband, and such conditions are, depending on the jurisdiction, generally enforced by the courts.

For example, a Muslim woman can seek and obtain a right similar to her husband's to repudiate him at any time at her discretion. She can also stipulate a condition of monogamy which, if broken by the husband, would result in dissolution of the marriage with financial consequences.[112] She can also stipulate the restoration of any other of her personal freedoms of action, the right to work outside the home, choose her friends, etc. However, all these rights have more gloss than true impact in a number of traditional communities where many women may not even be aware of the existence of such rights, let alone being able to prevent their guardians from choosing their mates and setting the terms of marriage on their behalf. It is in this context that one may appreciate Kecia Ali's criticism of feminist voices which glorify the right of women to stipulate conditions in the marriage contract.[113]

What is the solution? The solution is in the secular nature of Islam. It is necessary to enact new laws which supersede the laws attributing the imbalanced guardianship-based control powers of husbands over their wives. Failing to adopt such an approach, the rights of women derived from stipulations in the marriage contract remain limited to the sophisticated few women who are aware of these conditions—and who then find the courage, or can afford, to insist on them. Most importantly, without new legislation, an unmarried woman has no recourse to regain her rights and freedom from the father, brother, or other male guardian who exercises authority over her. For that purpose, and because family law is so closely associated with the human rights of the family members, it should no longer be kept subject to interpretations of clergy, 'ulama', or fuqahā'. Instead, human rights should be the subject of secular legislation, enforced by the secular courts, so as to guarantee the protection of these rights and their free exercise.

As Mothers

In contrast with the oppressive conditions women face in their roles as daughters and wives, as mothers women are relatively venerated and treated with deep respect. However, that veneration and respect has not led to the mother's entitlement to custody of her children in case of separation of the couple, except for a short period while the children are very young. The Prophetic Tradition is filled with anecdotal stories about the veneration that the Prophet had for mothers in general. Stories abound about his advice to his followers to respect and give mothers their due whether they are Muslims or non-Muslims,[114] believers or nonbelievers, such as—without limitation—waiving the duty to join a jihad war in order to stay by the side of the mother,[115] and the duty to obey mothers at any age. According to one tradition, in response to a man enquiring about the person most deserving of one's companionship, Prophet Muhammad responded, "'your mother'; 'then whom' asked the man; 'then your mother'; 'then whom'; 'then your mother'; and 'then whom'; 'then your father.'"[116] Prophet Muhammad is even reported to have proclaimed, "Paradise lies under the feet of mothers."[117] These traditions are consistent with the provisions of the Holy Qur'an which enjoin the respect for, and devotion to, parents as in Verse Q17:23 and 24.

> *Thy Lord hath decreed that ye worship none but Him, and that ye be kind to parents. Whether one or both of them attain old age in thy life, say not to them a word of contempt, nor repel them, but address them in terms of honour (23). And, out of kindness, lower to them the wing of humility, and say: "My Lord! bestow on them thy Mercy even as they cherished me in childhood" (24).*[118]

In particular, respect and gratitude to mothers is stated in Verse Q31:14.

> *And [God says:] "We have enjoined upon man goodness toward his parents: his mother bore him by bearing strain upon strain, and his utter dependence on her lasted two years: [hence, O man,] be grateful toward Me and toward thy parents, and remember that] with Me is all journeys' end."*[119]

In witness to the above, the Holy Qur'an recognizes the role of women as mothers through the stories of famous women such as Maryam (the Virgin Mary), her mother, and the mother of Moses. The Holy Qur'an also recognizes the role of women as leaders in public life in the story of the Queen of Saba'.

Women in Public Life

Despite the fact that the Holy Qur'an does not place any restrictions on women in public life, women's opportunities for effective involvement in public life have been severely restricted and very often denied by authority of male guardians over women in either of their capacities as daughters or wives. In doing so they have relied on grounds prepared for them over time by *fiqh* which were wrongly imputed to Islam and enforced by the overwhelming influence of the religious establishment. One could say that those grounds for the oppression of women were developed over time because in the early period of Islam numerous women held public functions and succeeded in performing their duties.[120]

In this respect, Leila Ahmed examines the role of women in public life during the days of Prophet Muhammad, in particular within his immediate surroundings.[121] She draws on the fact that during that time women were more active in public life and played an important role in collective worship and in warfare, assisting the armies of the Prophet. She attributes the restrictions and abuse against women that found their way into Islam to the influence of the Persians and Christians of the conquered lands around Arabia and to the then flourishing slave trade. She also attributes such regress in women's condition to collusion among the political and religious authorities.[122]

In fact, the religious establishment has, over the ages, created an environment of reverential fear in male guardians which compelled them to oppress women, mainly out of conformity with what they were brought up to believe are religious precepts mandating such oppression.[123] This is how Abul A'la al-Mawdudi unfairly extends the scope of guardianship to restricting women's freedom of movement, claiming, "God has prohibited the unrestricted intermingling of the sexes and has prescribed purdah (female seclusion), recognized man's guardianship of woman…"[124]

As will be demonstrated, Islam provides that women are fully entitled to complete and unrestricted involvement in public life, including assuming public and leadership functions. They are entitled to join the marketplace alongside men and to perform any work of their choice, without exception or restriction of any kind on account of what they may or may not wear for that purpose, or on account of the nonpermissibility of mixing with men in society or in the marketplace.

LEADERSHIP FUNCTIONS

"A people who entrust a woman to be their leader will never prosper."[125] This tradition is imputed to Prophet Muhammad. He is reported to have made the remark when he learned that Khosrow, the King of Persia, had been succeeded by his daughter after his death. That tradition is reported in the compendia of Prophetic Tradition which are generally recognized as "trustworthy." But this should not mean that this tradition is authentic, or—assuming its accuracy—that it has any normative force and effect. Despite the unreliability of Prophetic Tradition, Fatima Mernissi, examining women's rights, nevertheless goes to great lengths to trace the origins and veracity of that tradition in order to discredit the companion, Abou Bakra, who reported it, in the hope of setting that tradition aside. [126]

As previously shown, Islam did not predestine women and men to perform specific duties to the exclusion of others. Nowhere in the Holy Qur'an are women assigned the role of managing the home, attending to the service of their husbands, and raising the children, as is often claimed.[127] Nor does the Qur'an predestine men to leadership functions or otherwise provide for the exclusive endowment of men with physical power, wisdom, and good sense so that they may monopolize the right and duty to work and earn a living, provide support for the family, and exercise control and authority over women. On the contrary, the Qur'an provides as follows in Verse Q9:71.

> The Believers, men and women, are protectors one of another: they enjoin what is just, and forbid what is evil: they observe regular prayers, practise regular charity, and obey God and His Apostle. On them will God pour His mercy: for God is Exalted in power, Wise.[128]

Therefore, if God says that men and women can protect each other, enjoin the good, and forbid the evil, it means that they both have leadership potential with the necessary qualities and wisdom. While people among genders or within the same gender may have varying capacities, such discrepancies are not innate or otherwise inherent in one gender or the other. For that purpose, the distinction made by *fiqh* between ordinary leadership functions on one hand, and the leadership of the prayers and the leadership of the nation (commonly known as *imāma al-kubra*) on the other in order to declare the latter as being irrevocably closed to women, is totally unwarranted and unsubstantiated.[129] There is no basis for any requirement that women remain at home and abstain from public life. On that basis, and despite any *fiqh*-based opinions to the contrary, women may assume any public or leadership function, including the leadership of the nation and the leadership of prayer.

IN THE WORKPLACE

Nasr Hamid Abizaid describes a debate which took place in Egypt about unemployment.[130] In that debate, some participants observed that an increasing number of female candidates were taking jobs away from men. At the same time, they stressed the natural predisposition of women toward domestic work, advocating that they be required to stay home and do what they were created to do and what, in their opinion, befits their role in this life. That debate found strong support within the religious milieu.[131] In reality, to the extent that women may hold leadership functions, every woman is entitled to work, like any male counterpart, in any capacity that she wishes—not in any job or capacity which is deemed suitable to her condition as a woman and to abilities viewed as innate to women.[132] Each woman is solely empowered to decide for herself what she is capable of doing. Therefore, women are entitled to seek and to obtain the type of education that they need[133] in order to access, and succeed in, the workplace. There is no reason that the Prophet's tradition, "[s]eek to acquire education even if from China; the pursuit of education is a duty of each Muslim,"[134] should, in relation to women, continue to be misconstrued by limiting its scope to the study of religion and women's religious duties.[135]

Another reason advanced to restrict women's involvement in public life, in the workplace in particular, is the presumed risk of women mixing with men and potentially finding themselves in the "sinful" situation of being alone with a man who is not her husband or some other male guardian. Here, too, the Holy Qur'an does not prescribe the prohibition of women mixing with men, or even the advisability of preventing such mixing. Instead it is *fiqh*, supported by the religious establishment, which advanced the prohibition of women mixing with men for fear of adultery being committed. Such views are tantamount to assuming that adultery will occur every time that women and men mix with each other in public life.

"ISLAMIC CLOTHING"

In part due to unwarranted claims regarding the risk of adultery,[136] women have been enjoined to "seek protection" by wearing so-called Islamic clothing. This is based on the unsubstantiated assumption that Islam mandates a special form of clothing to be worn by women.[137] In reality, that injunction was developed by *fiqh* and continues to be asserted and promoted by the religious establishment. Thus, it is a man-made injunction which is primarily founded on the concept of *sadd al-dharā'i'* or banning by way of precaution anything which could result in a perceived religious sin. Such banning may include restrictions on rights and freedoms. Nasr Hamid Abizaid likens imposing the veil on women to civilian death, to a form of "female extermination inside the dark cloak hermetically closed." He adds, "it is tantamount to a burial operation over ground by way of preempting suspicions following the rule of 'warding off evil takes precedence over bringing benefits.'"[138]

The requirement of special clothing is also presumably founded on the following set of verses.

Q7:26—*O CHILDREN of Adam! Indeed, We have bestowed upon you from on high [the knowledge of making] garments to cover your nakedness, and as a thing of beauty: but the garment of God-consciousness is the best of all. Herein lies a message from God, so that man might take it to heart.*[139]

Q24:30 and 31—*Tell the believing men that they must lower their gazes and guard their private parts; it is more decent for them. Surely Allah is All-Aware of what they do (30). And tell the believing women that they must lower their gazes and guard their private parts, and must not expose their adornment, except that which appears thereof, and must wrap their bosoms with their shawls, and must not expose their adornment,* *except to their husbands or their fathers or the fathers of their husbands, or to their sons or the sons of their husbands, or to their brothers or the sons of their brothers or the sons of their sisters, or to their women, or to those owned by their right hands, or male attendants having no (sexual) urge, or to the children who are not yet conscious of the shames of women. And let them not stamp their feet in a way that the adornment they conceal is known. And repent to Allah O believers, all of you, so that you may achieve success (31);*[140] and*

Q33:59—*Prophet, tell your wives, your daughters, and women believers to make their outer garments hang low over them so as to be recognized and not be insulted: God is most forgiving, most merciful.*[141]

These three verses are some of the most widely misunderstood verses of the entire Holy Qur'an. Over the centuries and continuing to this day, women have been abused in the name of religion through reliance on these verses.[142] To start with, Verse Q7:26 is not about any particular dress code. The message in that verse is that people, men and women alike, must cover their private parts by way of decency. That verse follows upon the verses which describe the destitution of Adam and Eve and their exile from heaven into earth following the episode of eating from the forbidden tree, in violation of God's warning. This verse is intended to address the nakedness in which Adam and Eve found themselves following their act. Al-Tabari explains that Verse Q7:26 aimed to put an end to a widespread practice, which prevailed among pagans during the pre-Revelation period, of performing worship naked inside the holy place of Mecca.[143]

As to Verses Q24:30 and 31, they have been abused to set the stage for the onslaught on women's most basic personal liberties, such as their freedom of movement and expression. It is claimed that these verses specify who, among the people from the other gender, may look at the face of a woman and thus be physically in her presence. Then, Verse Q33:59 has been abused to require that women be covered entirely whenever they leave home, or when in company of people of the other gender, making it impossible for them, except in limited ways, to participate in public life (including joining the workplace), let alone attain their potential.

Regarding Verses Q24:30 and 31, the problem is with the interpretation of several of its provisions. In the first place, Verse 30 and the beginning of Verse 31 contain a general rule applicable to men and women, equally and to the same extent. It basically tells people to lower their gaze, that is, not to embarrass someone of the other gender by gazing over her or him. It also tells them to guard their private parts or to wear something that covers them. The purpose of that injunction is expressly stated, namely to promote decency and to protect individual boundaries of self-respect.[144] Therefore, averting the gaze and avoiding embarrassing staring is first a matter of simple decency.

While the concept of decency is universal, what constitutes decency is a matter of local custom which varies from one time and place to another. A second aspect of the issue of decency concerns what may create embarrassment in gender relations, in particular, the extent to which the gaze of a person in the presence of someone of the other gender may overstep that person's sense of privacy.

This is further clarified in Verse Q24:31. In fact, Verse 31 further suggests what the implications of the rule set forth in it and in Verse 30 may be on the female gender, namely that: (1) women should not let appear any of their adornments except that which is naturally apparent and cannot be dissimulated; and (2) adornments may be exposed only to the male persons who fall into one of the categories specifically listed in the verse.

The unfortunate interpretation that has gained such force was that the adornments referred to in Verse 31 consist of the face and hands of a woman, to the exclusion of any other parts of the body—including her hair—and any other ornaments that she might wear such as makeup, rings, bracelets, or necklaces which adorn the face and the hands or the clothes being worn.[145] This interpretation ignores the first part of Verse 31 which allows the exposing of adornments that "are apparent" without any restriction and to any person of the other gender. There is no indication whatsoever which allows the interpreters to decide that the adornments in question that "are apparent" are limited to the face and the hands to the exclusion of any other adornment or part of the body.

Then, in the next part of Verse 31, more details are provided by listing the persons to whom adornments may be exposed—close male family members and other people who would not have a sexual urge toward the female, such as older males and very young children. Therefore, when read in conjunction with Verse 30, what this verse is telling the woman is that she should dress and behave in a decent manner and to avoid exposing any part of her body, as well as adornments relating to them, which could provoke sexual instincts in the other gender. Accordingly, the adornments which "are apparent" that a woman may expose are determined in each time and place by the customs prevailing in that setting.

Confirming this, the style utilized in the verse in question is very telling: "*Qul li-Nisā'i-l-mu'minīn*," the Prophet is told ("tell the women of the believers"). In this form of address, the Prophet is commanded to warn the women of his time only and not women of all times. Otherwise, God would have addressed women directly as he addressed people directly. Anything passed on in the form of "tell" being addressed to the Prophet is primarily for the specific time only. Moreover, Zakaria Ouzon rightly observes that these two verses must be read in conjunction with Verses 27 to 29 of the same Sura 24 (*al-Nour*) which immediately precedes them. In that light, the injunctions set forth in Verses 30 and 31 appear to be strictly linked to the ethics of entering the houses of people in accordance with prevailing customs and, as such, are not intended to apply to all women of all times and places.[146]

With respect to Verse Q33:59, a careful reading indicates that this verse does not establish a standard for "Islamic" clothing for all times, as many religious conservatives claim. It certainly does not require that a woman should be entirely covered whenever she leaves home at any time of the day or night.[147] Instead, it addresses exclusively the Prophet, the women in his family, and other believing women of his time. It is not addressed to any women who lived after the time of the Prophet, in a social environment different from that of the Prophet's time. In fact, when read contextually it becomes evident that this verse addresses a specific circumstance under which women were often aggressed and abused at night when they left their homes to use the equivalent of toilets. Indeed, according to customs of the pre-Islam *jāhiliyya* period[148] which were then still in effect, women wore the veil as an indication that they were free women, thereby distinguishing themselves from slave women. Verse 31 advised that women should wear that veil at night if they went out so that male predators would recognize them as free women and abstain from any abusive actions against them. Thus, it was just practical advice inspired by the customs of the time whose specific purpose was to prevent women from being "insulted," as expressly set forth in the verse in question.[149] That advice was not intended to serve as a permanent rule for all times.

Over time the suggested clothing for that instance has become irrelevant since there are no longer, for the most part, slaves of either gender. The underlying message was simply for women to be diligent when they go out in order to avoid being targeted for abuse by people on the street. It was not intended to constitute a dress code for the "Islamic" way, for all times. But most importantly, it was never intended as a means to discriminate against women by attributing to them a condition inferior to that of men. Such discrimination would constitute an affront to human dignity that God bestowed on all women and men equally since creation, as it would also be inconsistent with the trust that God granted to humankind without any gender-based discrimination.[150]

Finally, and as a corollary of the equality of men and women in all capacities in which women may find themselves, it should be clear that any woman should be free to go into and out of her home as she pleases, to carry out her activities in public life. Verse Q33:33,[151] which is often used to promote the concept that women must stay home and keep to their "Islamic" clothing, does not apply to all women but is restricted to the wives of the Prophet. It comes following a series of verses relevant only to the Prophet, which end with the assertion that the women in the Prophet's family are not like—or subject to the same rules that apply to—any other women.

These findings are further testimony to the universal nature of the provisions of the Holy Qur'an, whereby rules must evolve continuously so as to adapt to changing times and places. It is important, in order to avoid stagnation and regression in society and to ensure progress, to prevent the universalization of desacralized interpretations of the Holy Qur'an, however—and by whomever—they are rendered.

The essential idea here is twofold: (1) men and women, alike, are free to wear what they feel comfortable wearing, provided that what they wear complies with standards of decency in their individual environments and provided that women may continue to wear the veil or any other form of clothing as a condition of their freedom of expression, in exactly the same way as those women who elect to wear lighter and more modern clothing; and (2) there will always be discrepancies in what does or does not constitute decent apparel, as a result of which men or women may wear what may not appear to others as entirely decent. In such case, and unless the attire that a person chooses to wear is punishable by domestic law, no one is entitled to prevent them from so doing because God did not give the power of enforcement to anyone (including his prophet) and reserves judgment to the Final Day. Until then, what may not be compliant with religion may not be redressed.

As a Witness

Verse Q2:282 is consistently cited in support of the claim that Islam discriminates against women by considering a woman's witness in law as worth half that of a man, in the sense that in the absence of one male witness, the alternative is to seek the testimony of two female witnesses.[152] The issue of testimony has been cited in several verses of the Holy Qur'an, namely in Verses Q4:6 (witnessing of returning assets to orphans upon attaining the age of majority), Q4:15, Q5:106 to 108 (witnessing a will), Q24:2 and 4 (witnessing of adultery), and Q65:2 (witnessing certain acts in connection with repudiation), without specifying the gender of the required witnesses. However, Verse Q2:282 is the only one in the entire Holy Qur'an which specifically requires that the witnesses must be males or females on a two-for-one basis.

It is unfortunate that the equation of one male for two female witnesses stipulated in Verse Q2:282 has been construed as the common law or general basis for dealing with the issue of witnesses in Islamic law. In fact, even when the Qur'anic requirement for witnesses is gender-neutral, we find that most exegetes of these verses have assumed that the witness requirement is always a reference to witnessing by males, and at times alternatively by females using the equation cited above.[153] Similarly, several of the translators of the Qur'an fell for that same trap.[154] In reality, there is nothing in the Holy Qur'an to justify such a conclusion. On the contrary, the fact that the Holy Qur'an uses gender-neutral language in phrasing the requirement for witnesses in all verses, other than Verse Q2:282, should—when coupled with all the provisions regarding equality of the sexes—indicate that the equation in Verse Q2:282 is the exception to the rule of nondiscrimination. In fact, the equation set forth in Verse Q2:282 is specific to commercial contracts to the exclusion of any other area of the law. Therefore, the requirement stated in Verse Q2:282 does not extend to the judiciary, that is, to testimony in all cases brought before a judge for resolution. Nor does it apply to any contractual arrangements among people, other than commercial contracts. Certain jurisprudents, however, have determined that the testimony of women is altogether unacceptable in criminal matters,[155] despite the fact that there are no provisions in the Holy Qur'an to justify such exclusion.

It would appear that even the case referred to in Verse Q2:282 is circumstantial, without any permanent bearing. In fact, that verse explains the rationale for that equation, a rationale derived from the circumstances of the time. The reason given in that verse for the equation is that women can forget, presumably because in the days of the Revelation women were not expected to be found in the marketplace. Thus, the presence of another woman as witness reduces the impact of forgetfulness. Clearly, what this verse tells us is that women were not involved in commercial matters. So they could not be relied upon to remember details of individual transactions with which they were not directly familiar. Simply by having given the reason, God is telling us that this equation has no basis in any presumed inferiority of women or lesser intellectual abilities among them.

This equation becomes irrelevant as circumstances change and women gain experience in the marketplace alongside men. It follows that in our time there is no reason why any authority should not be able to legislate rules for testimony without that temporary discrimination. As for the *fiqh*-derived nuances about restricting the scope of women's testimony in criminal matters, they are acceptable as a product of *ijtihād* for their particular time. This does not imply a religiously mandated law or a restriction of the power of a political authority to adopt rules of testimony that it finds suitable for a particular time and place.[156]

In light of the above, it can be concluded that Islam forcefully establishes the equality of women and men, and that it does not impose, recognize, or condone restrictions of any kind on the capabilities of women and their freedom to participate in family or public life as they please, at their discretion, with the same rights as men. This is not to deny the fact that the history of Muslim societies, like that of all civilizations, has continued to be marked by the imposition of restrictions on women and other members of society. But, it should be kept clear that such restrictions have been, are, and will always remain a product of social interaction. As such, they are not mandated by Islam.[157]

Along these lines, Raja Ben Salama rejects as cynical those statements about Islam having elevated women in dignity which are often repeated by Islamists who advocate for continued restrictions on the human rights of women on the grounds of their need for protection.[158] Indeed, Islam in the Holy Qur'an did bestow honor and dignity upon women. It carried a powerful message recognizing the role of women and their empowerment.[159] Unfortunately, it is the impact of male dominance on Muslim society which has humiliated women in the name of religion.

Recalling all verses on which traditionalists rely in order to perpetuate notions of the inferior status of women and their reduced rights, Tariq Ramadan rightly observes that the provisions of the Holy Qur'an setting forth women's rights, which in appearance fall below par with the rights of men, are in reality fair when placed in context and considered globally by comparison to the aggregate rights and duties of men. He concludes that, since men are no longer held accountable to their duties and obligations toward women, and since women are becoming more educated and emancipated, it is no longer fair to continue implementing a system of rights that has become obsolete as a result of the radical change in the values system. For that purpose he calls on *fiqh* to initiate a radical revision and reform of women's rights toward better gender equality.[160] While it is important to support that call for reform, we call for that support to come within the framework of the secular legislation of the state, as opposed to *fiqh*-driven solutions.

Social and Economic Equality

Social and economic equality are important elements of the human rights system that Islam sought to establish through the Divine Message. That message came to reverse the prevailing social, economic, and cultural tribal system based on gender and social inequalities. For that purpose it sought to establish social harmony through social and economic justice, the right to work, and the protection of property.

Social and Economic Justice

Despite their equality in principle, in reality people differ. They live in varied geographic locations and climates. They strive to survive and flourish in diverse social and economic environments. Their levels of material comfort and happiness differ widely. For that reason, Islam sought to promote social and economic justice primarily through the institution of zakat and through a body of general principles of conduct.

Having observed that (1) there are poor and wealthy people, (2) people are not always responsible for their state of poverty and wealth, and (3) such outcome is not the result of some divine predestination, God sought to alleviate the hardships of poverty by declaring a right for the disadvantaged in the wealth of those who are better off.

> Q30:38—*Hence, give his due to the near of kin, as well as to the needy and the wayfarer; this is best for all who seek God's countenance: for it is they, they that shall attain to a happy state!*[161]

> Q51:19—*And in their wealth and possessions (was remembered) the right of the (needy,) him who asked, and him who (for some reason) was prevented (from asking).*[162]

> Q70:24 and 25—*And those in whose wealth is a recognised right*
> *(24) For the (needy) who asks and him who is prevented (for*
> *some reason from asking) (25).*[163]

That is why God imposed on each Muslim person the duty to pay a fair share of his or her wealth to certain categories of people specifically listed in the Holy Qur'an, most all of whom[164] share a common characteristic—that of need. The allocation of monies to the poor has been provided in several places in the Holy Qur'an. Verse Q8:41 lists people in need to whom may be distributed God's share in the war booty.

> *AND KNOW that whatever booty you acquire [in war], one-fifth thereof belongs*
> *to God and the Apostle, and the near of kin, and the orphans, and the needy,*
> *and the wayfarer. [This you must observe] if you believe in God and in what*
> *We bestowed from on high upon Our servant on the day when the true was*
> *distinguished from the false—the day when the two hosts met in battle. And God*
> *has the power to will anything.*[165]

Verse Q9:60 sets forth the list of people among whom the alms, in general, are distributable.

> *Alms are for the poor and the needy, and those employed to administer the*
> *(funds); for those whose hearts have been (recently) reconciled (to Truth); for*
> *those in bondage and in debt; in the cause of Allah; and for the wayfarer: (thus*
> *is it) ordained by Allah and Allah is full of knowledge and wisdom.*[166]

Because of the importance of economic and social justice for the maintenance of social peace, God has elevated the giving of alms above the level of prayer and placed it at or immediately following faith itself, as expressed in Verse Q2:177.

> *Righteousness is not that you turn your faces toward the east or the west, but*
> *[true] righteousness is [in] one who believes in Allah , the Last Day, the angels,*
> *the Book, and the prophets and gives wealth, in spite of love for it, to relatives,*
> *orphans, the needy, the traveler, those who ask [for help], and for freeing slaves;*
> *[and who] establishes prayer and gives zakah; [those who] fulfill their promise*
> *when they promise; and [those who] are patient in poverty and hardship and*
> *during battle. Those are the ones who have been true, and it is those who are the*
> *righteous.*[167]

Further, God has enjoined in Verse Q2:264 that the giving of alms be consistently performed with humility and without repeated reminders by the donor of his or her generosity.

> *O ye who believe! cancel not your charity by reminders of your generosity or by injury—like those who spend their substance to be seen of men, but believe neither in God nor in the Last Day. They are in parable like a hard, barren rock, on which is a little soil: on it falls heavy rain, which leaves it (Just) a bare stone. They will be able to do nothing with aught they have earned. And God guided not those who reject faith.*[168]

Finally, He has promised the givers of alms His reward in the other life, including the full waiver of major sins.[169]

The Right to Work

While God has enjoined the giving of alms as one way toward social justice, the latter also rests on the equal right of each individual to work. The right to work constitutes a cornerstone in installing social justice.[170] Economic equality aims at securing the opportunity for all, through the right to work, to secure a level of income that is sufficient to meet their basic financial needs. It is for that purpose that the Holy Qur'an, together with Prophetic Tradition, exhorts people to seek knowledge and guides them in that direction.

The freedom and duty to work are, like other rights and freedoms, innate in human nature and derived from the purpose of creation. In fact, God designated humankind as His trustee to labor toward the development of this earth, exhorting them to strive in every direction to work, stopping only to perform Friday prayers, as expressed in Verses Q62:9 and 10.

> *Believers! When the call to prayer is made on the day of congregation, hurry toward the reminder of God and leave off your trading—that is better for you, if only you knew (9) then when the prayer has ended, disperse in the land and seek out God's bounty. Remember God often so that you may prosper (10).*[171]

Being innate in human nature, the Holy Qur'an addresses the right and duty to work in exhortative language, which alludes in Verse Q9:105 to its importance on the Day of Judgment.

> *Say: "Strive, and God shall see your striving, as also His Messenger and the believers. You shall be returned to the Knower of the Invisible and the Visible, and He will inform you of what you used to do."*[172]

And in so working, people need to strive to perform good deeds, that is, their work should be useful to them, to their families, and to their community, as set forth in Verses Q99:7 and 8: *"So, whoever does any good act (even) to the weight of a particle will see it. And whoever does evil (even) to the weight of a particle will see it."*[173]

Similarly, Prophetic Tradition includes ample evidence of the Prophet exhorting people to work and be productive. He is reported to have said, "The best means of earning is a blessed trade and work done by a person in his own hands."[174] He elevates work to the level of worship by pointing out that it is not sufficient to be a believer: "God, the Almighty, loves a believer who has a profession."[175] Prophetic Tradition also reports that God has called on people when they work to strive to achieve a job well done: "God, the Almighty, likes when a person does something to perfect his work."[176] And, since work is primarily a means to earn a living, the Prophet sought to enjoin people not to delay payment of workers' wages: "Pay the worker's wages before his sweat dries."[177] In this respect, the Prophet rightly concludes that earning one's living is inherent in, and an attribute of, human dignity: "It is preferable for a person to take a rope and use it to carry a bunch of wood on his back and sell them, instead of begging people for money, whether they give it to him or not."[178]

Consistent with the Message being a body of higher values and principles, as opposed to a legal compendium or a charter of rights and obligations, and as in other rights and freedoms, the Holy Qur'an has framed the virtue of work, then left the details to be lived out by humankind as best befits their circumstances. This explains the evolution that took place over time in setting forth a framework for the freedom to work: the freedom to choose one's career, job security, prevention of abuse, and exploitation of workers, etc. It also explains the role of domestic laws and international treaties and conventions to secure continued progress toward achieving economic and social justice. As long as domestic and international laws continue to improve the conditions and secure the rights of workers, there is no need to debate their compliance with Islamic Shari'a and principles, for they would certainly be welcome steps toward the realization of the social justice ordained by God.

The Safeguard of Personal Property

In return for the duty of the wealthy to assist the needy, the wealthy are entitled to freely accumulate and dispose of wealth, and for that purpose any property owner is guaranteed the right to freely hold and use that property in every legitimate way.[179] The Holy Qur'an therefore cautions against any infringement on properties, whether by force or cheating, after having equated the sanctity of property to that of the physical integrity of the person in Verse Q4:29:

> *Believers, do not consume your wealth among yourselves in vanity, but rather trade with it by mutual consent. Do not kill yourselves. God is merciful to you, but he that does that through wickedness and injustice shall be burned in fire. That is easy enough for God.*[180]

In addition, in Verse Q11:85 God enjoins that dealings with property should be on a fair basis so as not to deprive a property owner of the full value of that property.

> *Hence, O my people, [always] give full measure and weight, with equity, and do not deprive people of what is rightfully theirs, and do not act wickedly on earth by spreading corruption.*[181]

As a corollary, we find countless verses which establish freedom of contract and enjoin the faithful performance of contracts, because contracts are a means of legitimate creation of wealth. The failure to faithfully perform a contract adversely affects property and wealth.[182]

Because the ultimate aim of the Revelation is to promote social and economic justice, humans are cautioned against illegitimately seeking to increase their wealth. Among other things, people are cautioned against abusing wealth and property in order to seek power and spread corruption. People are continuously reminded of the social function of wealth, as in Verse 18:46: "*Property and progeny are the ornament of this present life, but those things that abide, virtuous deeds, are better in reward with your*

Lord, and better in prospect";[183] and in Verse Q64:15—"*Your wealth and your children are only a temptation, whereas Allah! with Him is an immense reward.*"[184] Having cautioned against the potential for abuse of wealth and other earthly temptations, the Holy Qur'an makes sure to specify that it is perfectly legitimate to enjoy these worldly things provided that people keep in mind the beauty of the goals resting with God, including putting wealth to good use for that purpose, as expressed in Verse Q3:14.

> *ALLURING unto man is the enjoyment of worldly desires through women, and children, and heaped-up treasures of gold and silver, and horses of high mark, and cattle, and lands. All this may be enjoyed in the life of this world—but the most beauteous of all goals is with God.*[185]

Here too, God has laid out the main principles: (1) the accumulation and preservation of wealth is a legitimate concern; (2) people need to avoid the temptation to abuse the power that comes with wealth; and (3) people must remain at all times aware of, and faithful to, the social function of wealth and the rights of the needy. Setting aside unnecessary concerns about compliance of domestic and international legislation with Shari'a, God has left it to the wisdom and good sense of His designated trustees to legislate the detailed rules that ensure the protection of wealth and secure the fulfillment of its social function in spreading economic justice.

CHAPTER 15
The Right to Freedom

The immediate corollary of the right to equality is the right to freedom. If all people are equal among each other, they are all equally free. Freedom is therefore a necessary attribute of human creation without which humans would be unable to fulfill their role as trustees, assigned to them by God. Freedom is thus inherent in the human dignity with which God endowed humankind when He ordered the angels to prostrate for Adam. The right to freedom is also a necessary condition of divine accountability, since God has endowed humans with a mind to enable them to distinguish right from wrong and make free choices, including those choices needed to resist wrongdoing. Since every individual is included and shares in the role of trustee, the right to freedom belongs to every individual.

Within this framework, the right to freedom includes all the basic freedoms that are recognized internationally. These are discussed in this chapter, with particular focus on freedom of faith and the misconstruction of Islam's position on slavery. Also examined are issues of justice, human dignity, and corporeal punishment, as derived from the right to freedom.

Islam and the Basic Freedoms

The Right to Life
Since human life is an aspect of God's creation, for which He ordered the angels to prostrate, the right to life is central to Islam. The Holy Qur'an sets forth this principle in forceful terms in Verse Q5:32 which declares each life to be worth the life of the entirety of humankind.

> *For this reason, We decreed for the children of Isrā'īl that whoever kills a person not in retaliation for a person killed, nor (as a punishment) for spreading disorder on the earth, is as if he has killed the whole of humankind, and whoever saves the life of a person is as if he has saved the life of the whole of humankind.*[1]

Because human life is sacred and valuable, the Holy Qur'an sought to dispel the impression that fathers and guardians own the lives of children under their guardianship by cautioning them against disposing of those lives. Thus, people were warned by the Holy Qur'an against killing their children under any circumstances, including poverty.

> Q6:151—*Say: Come, let me convey unto you what God has [really] forbidden to you: "Do not ascribe divinity, in any way, to aught beside Him; and [do not offend against but, rather,] do good unto your parents; and do not kill your children for fear of poverty—[for] it is We who shall provide sustenance for you as well as for them; and do not commit any shameful deeds, be they open or secret; and do not take any human being's life—[the life] which God has declared to be sacred—otherwise than in [the pursuit of] justice: this has He enjoined upon you so that you might use your reason."*[2]

> Q17:31—*Hence, do not kill your children for fear of poverty: it is We who shall provide sustenance for them as well as for you. Verily, killing them is a great* sin.[3]

Through these same verses about the value of the lives of small children, Islam sought also to put an end to the prevailing tribal practice of killing female newborns by burying them alive for fear of shame thought to be brought to a family by female progeny. In this respect, Verses Q81:8 and 9 admonish parents who bury their female newborn alive and ask what she might tell God, on the Day of Judgment, is the reason of her slaying: "*When the female (infant), buried alive, is questioned (8)—For what crime she was killed (9).*"[4] Hence, parents who commit such an atrocious crime certainly have gone astray and are accountable for their actions, as stated in Verse Q6:140.

> *Lost, indeed, are they who, in their weak-minded ignorance, slay their children and declare as forbidden that which God has provided for them as sustenance, falsely ascribing [such prohibitions] to God: they have gone astray and have not found the right path.*[5]

Finally, as the right to life is inherent in God's creation, a person is not even justified in taking his or her own life under any circumstance, as set forth in Verse Q4:29: *"Believers, do not consume your wealth among yourselves in vanity, but rather trade with it by mutual consent. Do not kill yourselves. God is merciful to you."*[6]

In light of these express provisions safeguarding the sanctity of human life, at any age and including one's own life, one might ask several questions about the potential scope of that sanctity. In light of Verses Q4:92 and 93 which deal with the sanction applicable to the slaying of believers, is sanctity reserved to the lives of believers only? Then, if human life is essentially sacred, what is the reason for making exceptions in Verses Q5:33 and Q17:33 in which killing is deemed to be just? Most importantly, what is the justification for all the verses in the Qur'an, namely the suras of the Cow and the Repentance, which exhort believers to kill nonbelievers and certain People of the Book. These questions are valid and immediate, and believers and nonbelievers alike are entitled to a convincing answer.

Again, the provisions of the Holy Qur'an must be read in context to be fully understood and for their intent to be appreciated because (1) the Holy Qur'an did not appear in a vacuum; (2) it was revealed at intervals and successively so as to guide the footsteps of the Prophet in the performance of his mission; and (3) the Holy Qur'an is not a code of law or a charter with sequential rules providing detailed regulations of the various aspects of life, but consists in general principles universally valid, the implementation of which is left to humankind to determine to meet their needs, in each time and place.

From this perspective, when looking at the verses dealing with the sanctity of life, one discovers the general principles that (1) life is sacred, and each life—whether a believer or nonbeliever—is sacred and worth that of the entirety of humanity; and (2) that sanctity is inherent in humanity by virtue of the creation and thus predates who is or is not a believer.[7] From that principle, the universal nature of the Revelation requires that exceptions be made as necessary in the best interest of the community, and that some of those exceptions may be universal, while other exceptions may be specific to a particular time in history.

With this in mind, the instances referred to in Verses Q4:92 and 93 relate to specific events that occured during the time of the Prophet and do not lay general principles for all times. Similarly, the exceptions regarding tolerance of the taking of life in cases required by justice is legitimized by the need to deter and prevent recurrence of homicides and to compensate the victims' families. However, the specific reference to retribution according to the law of retaliation is not in itself of a permanent nature but is a reflection of the prevailing circumstances of the time. In the absence of a state structure and institutions to administer justice, the right of the victim's heirs to make the necessary decisions relating to retribution is intended to replace the vengeance vendetta that used to follow the perpetration of each crime and that at times led to bloody wars within or between tribes. This is confirmed by the exhortation of victims' heirs to opt for compensation or, preferably, to consider pardon.[8]

With respect to the series of verses which appear to incite the killing of nonbelievers and People of the Book, and as indicated earlier, these are specific to the time of the Prophet and were intended to deal with those who fought the Prophet to prevent him from fulfilling his divine mission or to prevent the faithful from worshipping and practicing their new faith in the path of God. This explains the permission to fight by way of jihad, but only to repel aggression while seeking peace at every moment.

This right to life, then, as an attribute of creation and inherent in human nature, has important corollaries that can be examined in connection with the justice mechanisms for the protection of life and human dignity.

The Right to Privacy

The right to privacy derives directly from the right to life to the extent that privacy, as a necessary condition for personal freedom, is an important form of protection of life. In fact, as every individual is safe (prima facie) at home, the Holy Qur'an has declared the sanctity of homes in plain language in Verses Q24:27 and 28.

> *O you who have believed, do not enter houses other than your own houses until you ascertain welcome and greet their inhabitants. That is best for you; perhaps you will be reminded (27). And if you do not find anyone therein, do not enter them until permission has been given you. And if it is said to you, Go back, then go back; it is purer for you. And Allah is Knowing of what you do (28).*[9]

In addition to the privacy of one's home, Prophetic Tradition has reported about Prophet Muhammad having enjoined people to preserve the privacy of conversations with others: "What occurs during meetings must be kept confidential."[10] This right to privacy, consistent with the universal nature of the Holy Qur'an's injunctions, was further amplified and protected over time through the safeguards necessitated by the rules applying to the due process of law.

Freedom of Expression and Association

Consistent with the fact that Islam is not a political or legal system, the Holy Qur'an did not specifically address the freedom of expression and association. These freedoms are necessary corollaries of the role of the mind that God endowed humankind with and of the freedom of faith which serves as the basis of accountability on the Day of Judgment. However, it is important to note here that the institution of salat *al-jamā'a* (daily collective prayer), and in particular weekly Friday prayer, constitutes the primary forum for association and free speech. In fact, the institution of collective prayer is not about worship and prayer as much as it is a forum for social interaction and discussion of what is best for the society of believers. This explains that, over the history of Muslim societies, where the rulers may have been successful in muzzling freedom of speech, social movements were often born in mosques which embodied the realization of the basic freedoms of association and expression, because rulers could not—under any circumstances—prevent people from gathering to conduct prayers. This also explains the longtime partnership between rulers and religious establishments throughout the history of Muslim societies because of the influence that prayer leaders may have over what gets said or done within the walls of mosques, when rulers have placed restrictions on basic freedoms.[11]

Prophet Muhammad is reported to have equated free expression against oppression to an act of jihad because oppression could deprive people from proceeding on the path to God. Thus Prophetic Tradition reports the following tradition of the Prophet: "The best of jihad consists in expressing what is right in the face of an unjust ruler."[12] From this perspective, some authors have founded freedom of expression and association in *al-amr bi-l-ma'rūf wa-n- nahiy 'ani-l-munkar,* the divine injunction of the good and prohibition of evil.[13]

Based on the above, any measures adopted into domestic law or international charters and conventions which promote freedom of expression and association cannot be inconsistent with Islam. Only unjustified restrictions to these rights would be.

Freedom of Action: Islam and Slavery

Expressing his unease with the Holy Qur'an's treatment of the principle of equality, Farid Esack asserts, "[i]t is doubtful that we might truly consider the Qur'an as a reference to justify the contemporary conceptions of social equality and human rights." Citing that Verse Q4:1 "affirms the unicity of the source of our creation—one soul—and implies that all people are as a result equal," Esack adds, "[t]he reality is that the Qur'an contains also a number of injunctions detailing the different ways for treatment of slaves and free persons."[14]

Despite claims such as this one, Islam in fact considers slavery to be entirely repulsive to human rights and dignity. Consequently, and again contrary to claims made by Muslim and non-Muslim thinkers,[15] Islam does not condone slavery. The fact that the Holy Qur'an addresses certain aspects of slavery is not by itself an indication that it condones it. The reality is quite the opposite. The Holy Qur'an, consistent with its objectives of reversing prevailing tribal and other customs which are offensive to human dignity, has aggressively sought to eradicate slavery.

It is true that there is no conclusive ruling in the Holy Qur'an which provides for the prohibition of slavery or for its immediate abolition.[16] However, bearing in mind once more that the Holy Qur'an is not a code of law, its provisions dealing with slavery, when considered together, conclusively lead us toward a divine determination to end slavery.[17]

To start with, the Holy Qur'an did not in any of its verses set forth the principle that free persons could be enslaved. Nor did it specify under which circumstances free persons may be enslaved. Instead, it was *fiqh* jurisprudents who developed the chapter on slavery and defined the framework within which enslavement could be imposed on free people, thereby wrongly spreading the belief that Islam condones slavery.

Yet, even though it did not specifically condone the enslavement of others, Islam did implicitly acknowledge, by way of tolerance, slavery already existing. However, very early on after the start of Revelation—as early as the first Meccan period of Qur'anic Revelation—Islam exhorted Muslims to end slavery by treating the freeing of slaves as an integral part of the difficult path to virtue, alongside feeding the needy among orphans and the poor, in Verses Q90:12 to 17.

> *And what can make you know what is [breaking through] the difficult pass? (12) It is the freeing of a slave (13) Or feeding on a day of severe hunger (14) An orphan of near relationship (15) Or a needy person in misery (16) And then being among those who believed and advised one another to patience and advised one another to compassion (17).*[18]

This attitude toward slaves derives from the fundamental constant that all people were created equal. For that purpose, the Holy Qur'an mandates that slaves be treated well, as well as one treats one's own parents, as expressed in Verse Q4:36.

> *Worship Allah, and do not associate with Him anything, and be good to parents and to kinsmen and orphans and the needy and the close neighbor and the distant neighbor and the companion at your side and the wayfarer and to those (slaves who are) owned by you. Surely, Allah does not like those who are arrogant, proud.*[19]

The Holy Qur'an also mandates that the freeing of slaves be facilitated by anyone who holds slaves and by the wealthy who can use their money to help free slaves.[20] Based on these basic premises, and consistent with the divine determination that the most noble people in the sight of God are the most righteous,[21] the Holy Qur'an, in Verse Q4:25, goes on to assert that a slave who is a believer is preferred to a nonbeliever freeperson.

> *If one cannot afford to marry the free Muslim women, then (he may marry) the one you people own of your Muslim girls. Allah knows best about your faith. You are similar to each other. So, marry them with the permission of their masters, and give them their dues, as recognized, they being bound in marriage, not going for lust, nor having paramours. So, once they have been bound in marriage, then, if they*

commit a shameful act, they shall be liable to half of the punishment prescribed for
the free women. That is for those of you who apprehend to indulge in sin. But that
you be patient is better for you. Allah is Most-Forgiving, Very-Merciful.[22]

Furthermore, Verse Q2:177 places the freeing of slaves among the divinely
validated purposes for spending alms and other charity monies (zakat and
ṣadaqāt). That objective is even placed ahead of the duty of worship.

Righteousness is not that you turn your faces toward the east or the west, but
[true] righteousness is [in] one who believes in Allah, the Last Day, the angels,
the Book, and the prophets and gives wealth, in spite of love for it, to relatives,
orphans, the needy, the traveler, those who ask [for help], and for freeing slaves;
[and who] establishes prayer and gives zakah; [those who] fulfill their promise
when they promise; and [those who] are patient in poverty and hardship and
during battle. Those are the ones who have been true, and it is those who are the
righteous.[23]

Because the Holy Qur'an considers the freeing of slaves as a first concern,
it creates an environment for better opportunities to secure that slaves
be freed. For example, the tolerated limit of four wives in the case of
polygamy is lifted when the wives are slaves of the person marrying them,
with the following implications: (1) children born to a slave married to a
free person are free people, unlike the situation whereby a slave woman
is married to a slave man; and (2) a slave woman who is wedded to her
owner becomes a free person upon his death, unless she is freed earlier,
which would normally be the case.[24]

People are encouraged to free slaves, such being deemed by the
Holy Qur'an a means to evidence repentance following the perpetration
of certain acts, such as in case of *dhihār*, a form of divorce pronounced
frivolously.[25] Better yet, the eradication of slavery is so important that,
for the purpose of repentance, a person seeking to repent must search
for—and purchase—a slave to free if that person does not have slaves of
his or her own. Only if the repenting person cannot find a slave to free,
after diligent search, may he or she apply the alternative of fasting for the
required number of days.[26]

In retrospect, it becomes clear that, from its inception, Islam did not
condone slavery and the rights of free people over the lives of their slaves

other than by way of temporary tolerance mandated by the prevailing customs of the time, and then only pending its gradual eradication. This position of Islam on slavery, consisting substantially of an exhortation to end it, is consistent with the human dignity that God bestowed on humankind at the time of creation by breathing His own spirit into them. Accordingly, it is inconceivable that God may have allowed that any of His human creatures bearing His own spirit be owned and demeaned by others.[27]

Freedom of Faith

Citing a tradition of the Prophet which describes the Qur'an as the "Banquet of God," Mohamed Talbi compares Islam to God's tent into which every person is invited so as to join the banquet, and where the decision to accept the invitation is absolutely free.[28]Talbi uses this example to illustrate freedom of faith, namely the freedom of each individual to determine what he or she believes in. Freedom of faith then is made up of three main components, namely, the freedom to believe or not to believe, the freedom to differ with other believers, and the freedom to change one's faith at will, all of which are founded in the provisions of the Holy Qur'an.

The Freedom to Believe or not to Believe

Each person is free to believe or not to believe in God and in the Message that He revealed to Prophet Muhammad. This principle has been set forth and reiterated in the Holy Qur'an repeatedly throughout Prophet Muhammad's mission, that is, both during the Meccan period and thereafter in Medina. To start with, freedom of faith is a direct corollary of freedom of choice, which was discussed at length in Chapter 12. This is set forth in Verses Q76:2 and 3

> Verily, it is We who have created man out of a drop of sperm intermingled, so that We might try him [in his later life]: and therefore We made him a being endowed with hearing and sight (2). Verily, We have shown him the way: [and it rests with him to prove himself] either grateful or ungrateful (3).[29]

This means that each person, having been given the tools for using the mind, is free to make choices concerning every aspect of life, including the choice to accept the faith or reject it, with the usual accountability for such choice. For that purpose, each person is expected to make his or her own choice, and no one is entitled to make that choice for any other person. Freedom of faith also includes the freedom to live one's religion, but to the extent that the exercise of that freedom does not infringe on the rights of others to live their own religions. This is the essence of pluralism in Islam.[30] Also included in freedom of faith is the freedom to perform acts of worship or not to perform them, irrespective of whether the person is a believer or not.[31] Accordingly, any attempt—whether by individuals, state agents, or para-state actors—at coercing people to perform the prayer, to fast during the month of Ramadan, or to pay zakat constitutes a breach of the freedom of faith.

Freedom of choice in accepting or rejecting the faith is set forth in Verse Q2:256.

> *THERE SHALL BE no coercion in matters of faith. Distinct has now become the right way from [the way of] error: hence, he who rejects the powers of evil and believes in God has indeed taken hold of a support most unfailing, which shall never give way: for God is all-hearing, all-knowing.* [32]

This verse was revealed in connection with the evacuation of a belligerent Jewish tribe from Medina. Certain Arab families had tried to coerce their children, who had adopted Judaism, into converting to Islam in order to prevent their evacuation with those being expelled. That verse came to enjoin that those who had previously converted to Judaism must have the freedom to remain Jews, revert to paganism, or convert to Islam, according to their choice. Despite the circumstances of revelation of that verse, it illustrates the principle of freedom of choice, with all of its consequences.[33] This should serve to disprove statements made by those who refuse to acknowledge the Qur'anic call for freedom of faith and tolerance, such as the following comment by Dominique Urvoy on this verse: "The famous exclamation: 'no coercion in matters of faith'…never meant 'tolerance.' The verse itself does nothing more than to refer to the right of non-Muslims to convert to Islam without preventing them from doing so."[34]

While this verse may have been revealed to address a particular circumstance, it is in line with the more general principle set forth in *Sūrat al-Kafirun*, particularly Verse Q109:6 as follows: *"For you is your faith, and for me, my faith."*[35] The entire *Sūrat al-Kafirun* which contains that verse was revealed to put an end to an episode whereby the unbelievers of Mecca who consistently rejected Prophet Muhammad's efforts to rally to Islam, nevertheless kept trying to offer him a mutual accommodation which reconciled their respective faiths around a middle ground. The Prophet would in no way entertain any accommodation which kept any deities besides God; hence the final position set forth in *Sūrat al-Kafirun*. This verse thus sets forth the basic principle of freedom of faith, according to which, absent belligerence on the side of non-Muslims, the norm is for continued peaceful coexistence and interaction among the adherents of the relevant faiths, as expected in a typically pluralistic society in keeping with the essence of Islam.[36]

Because faith is a matter of freedom of choice, Prophet Muhammad was guided by revelation as to the manner in which he should fulfill his mission of preaching and inviting his audience to the new faith. That method is provided for in Verse Q16:125, which sets forth the principle that preaching cannot take the form of coercion and rude language: *"Call to the way of your Lord with wisdom and fair counsel, and debate with them in the fairest manner. Your Lord knows best who has strayed from His path; He knows best who are guided aright."*[37]

It is true that Prophet Muhammad, later in his career, did receive the authorization—and perhaps the order—to fight in the performance of his mission, all of which may not quite be consistent with the *"wisdom," "beautiful preaching,"* and *"the fairest manner"* mandated in Verse Q16:125. Yet, fighting was not intended to be an alternative method to conveying the Message and preaching that are set forth in that verse. Instead, it was only intended as a last resort to repel aggression and to remove any obstacle hindering Prophet Muhammad in the performance of his mission. Confirming the peaceful method for preaching and conveying the Message, God started by formulating the role of His messengers, including Prophet Muhammad, in Verse Q6:48, in the following terms: *"We send the apostles only to give good news and to warn: so those who believe and mend (their lives)—upon them shall be no fear, nor shall they grieve."*[38] That description of the role of the Prophet was first clarified in Verse Q42:48: "*We have not sent you [Prophet] to be their guardian; your only duty is to deliver the message.*"[39] Then, in Verses Q88:21 and 22, that role was further clarified to specifically exclude any enforcement role: "*So [Prophet] warn them: your only task is to give warning (21), you are not there to control them (22).*"[40] Then, in Verse 10:99, He cautioned his Prophet, in clear, straightforward language, against any act of coercion of people into believing: "*Had your Lord willed, all those on earth would have believed altogether. Would you, then, compel people, so that they become believers,*"[41] thereby confirming that, under the freedom of faith, no one may be compelled to believe or otherwise make any confession of faith.

Verse Q88:22 which limits the role of the Prophet to conveying the Message and to preaching—to the exclusion of the power of enforcement—was claimed by several exegetes to have been abrogated by the verses of *Sūrat al-Tawba* which authorized the Prophet to fight to end the belligerency of his enemies.[42] But the abrogation theory should be rejected for the many reasons previously discussed, especially when a text has been revealed under specific circumstances requiring that exception, but without adversely affecting the integrity of the principle. In addition, in this instance, assuming that Verse Q88:22 was indeed abrogated, the consequence would be blasphemous to God, namely in light of Verses Q88:25 and 26 which constitute the justification for Verse Q88:22. Indeed, if Verse Q88:22 did not include among the duties of the Prophet that of coercing people into believing, it is because that power is the exclusive right of God, in the sense that Verses Q88:25 and 26 state that: "*It is to Us they will return (25), and then it is for Us to call them to account (26).*"[43] Therefore, admitting the abrogation of Verse Q88:22 is tantamount to the blasphemous assumption that God has associated the Prophet in His powers to judge people or, at best, He has relinquished that power and conferred it to the Prophet.

In fact, God did not leave anything for humans to interpret as to this conclusion and understanding. He did confirm it in Verse Q2:272, in which He clearly placed the power to guide people and dispose of their faiths outside the realm of the Prophet.

Not upon you, [O Muhammad], is [responsibility for] their guidance, but
Allah guides whom He wills. And whatever good you [believers] spend is for
yourselves, and you do not spend except seeking the countenance of Allah. And
whatever you spend of good - it will be fully repaid to you, and you will not be
wronged.[44]

In this verse, God is telling all of us that guiding people to believe is His
sole prerogative, which He does not share with, nor delegate to, anyone,
including His Messengers. In other words, any attempt at forcing people
to believe, or to adopt a certain creed, constitutes an act of association with
God.

The immediate corollary of the stated limitation on the role of the
Prophet to preserve freedom of faith is that no one is allowed to investigate
the faith of others, as evidenced by the practice of the Prophet of refusing
to accuse the hypocrites of unbelief or apostasy, and preventing any of his
companions from making any such accusations.[45] Thus, if the Prophet did
not have such a power, then no one else can claim it—not a companion, nor a
caliph, or any member of the religious establishment,[46] then, now, or at any
time.[47] The reason is clear: only God can judge the true beliefs of people,
on the Day of Judgment.[48] This is expressly set forth in Verse Q42:15 as
God, addressing His Prophet, instructs him to inform his detractors that
each side is free to retain its beliefs and that God will ultimately bring
everyone together for accountability on the Day of Judgment.

So, (O prophet,) toward that (faith) invite (people), and be steadfast as you are
commanded, and do not follow their desires, and say, "I believe in whatever
book Allah has sent down. And I have been ordered to do justice among you.
Allah is our Lord and your Lord. For us are our deeds, and for you, your deeds.
There is no argumentation between us and you. Allah will bring us together, and
to Him is the final return."[49]

In the words of Abdulaziz Sachedina, freedom of faith "removes the God-
human relationship from human jurisdiction."[50] On this matter, Shaykh
Yusuf Qaradawy advocates for the freedom of any person to adopt and
believe in the opinions of hardliners among scholars without being
accused of religious extremism.[51] While in principle such position is fair
on grounds of freedom of faith, it ceases to be so when hardliners holding

such beliefs exert pressure—with or without threats of the wrath of God—on their audience to get them to rally to their opinions, or if they attempt to impose such opinions or lobby government to enforce them.[52]

Finally, freedom of faith is an instrument of the divine trusteeship established by God to sustain a pluralistic society in which people of varying faiths, and of no faith, can live in harmony and interact as equals, leaving matters of faith to God's judgment. In other words, faith-related matters are of the exclusive realm of God, where freedom of faith is not relevant. It is only relevant in this life that people are able to interact freely and prepare for the other life. In fact, Muslims are instructed in Verse Q4:140 to live in harmony with anyone of any faith in a normal pluralistic environment, but merely to stay away from people who might ridicule or denigrate their religion, as long as any such people do not aggress them or attempt to sway them from their faith.

> *And, indeed, He has enjoined upon you in this divine writ that whenever you hear people deny the truth of God's messages and mock at them, you shall avoid their company until they begin to talk of other things—or else, verily, you will become like them. Behold, together with those who deny the truth God will gather in hell the hypocrites.*[53]

Whereas no human being may be judged, rewarded, or punished in this life by another human being for the nature and quality of his or her faith, accountability remains entire in the hereafter. This also is set forth expressly in these verses in the Qur'an.

> Q10:108 and 109—*Say, "O people, the truth has come to you from your Lord. So, whoever accepts guidance accepts it to his own benefit, and whoever goes astray does so to his own detriment. And I am not responsible for you" (108). Follow what is being revealed to you, and be patient until Allah gives His judgment, and He is the best of all judges;*[54] and

> Q18:29—*And say, "The truth is from your Lord. Now, whoever so wills may believe and whoever so wills may deny." Surely, We have prepared for the unjust a fire, whose tent will envelop*

them. And if they will beg for help, they shall be helped with
water like oily dregs that will scald the faces. Vile is the drink,
and evil is the Fire as a resting-place.[55]

This examination of the freedom to believe or not to believe, leads us to the following understandings. First, a nonbeliever is free to believe or not to believe. He or she can continue to live in harmony with the believers in society sharing equal rights, with the option to believe at any time until the time of death. Second, a believer who adheres to any of the Abrahamic faiths previously revealed by God, namely Christianity or Judaism, is free to accept or reject Islam, as brought and spread by Prophet Muhammad, which means that remaining a Christian or a Jew, after hearing the Message of Prophet Muhammad, does not place the person who so remains in any category of disbeliever. Third, any person who has accepted Prophet Muhammad's prophecy and message, whether a believer in any of the previously revealed faiths or a nonbeliever, is free to differ in his or her faith with other believers or even adhere to any of the previously revealed divine faiths or return to paganism, in either case subject to God's exclusive jurisdiction over final accountability.

The Freedom to Differ with Other Believers

Islam appeared in the form of a divinely phrased message. It was revealed by God to His messenger Prophet Muhammad with the clear mandate to deliver that message to its addressees as received, unaltered. Even explanations were offered by God directly, by way of revelation and in the form of Qur'anic verses, when people solicited such explanations from the Prophet. The verses are those which start with the words *"yas'alūnaka"* (they ask you) and *"yastaftūnaka"* (they seek your opinion). This tells us that the Prophet was not expected to explain or add to the Divine Message. Similarly, the mission did not include any enforcement powers, for an important reason. Since enforcement implies an official understanding—that of the enforcer—to which every believer must adhere, denying that power is a clear indication that God does not favor imposing on believers any specific script for the faith, which explains that He reserves the exclusive power to judge the faith of every individual. This also explains why Islam did not contemplate a role for anyone—clergy, 'ulama', jurisconsult, or other—to determine the script to be followed by believers in formulating their faith.

Despite these facts, state-recognized religious establishments and individual 'ulama' have consistently taken positions regarding what may or may not be differed on. Shaykh Yusuf Qaradawy devotes an entire book to this subject, in which he presents in detail the levels of difference that are most common in the faith, ranging from advisable differences to those which are considered sinful. However, because of intolerance of differences among extremists and a tendency for aggression against those who express opinions which depart from what they consider to be the general "orthodoxy," Shaykh Qaradawy takes the wise measure of cautioning against declaring anyone who professes the basic creed of Islam (that there is no god but Allah and that Muhammad is the Messenger of God) as *kāfir*, or infidel, for fear of being considered an apostate. In support of this categorization, especially the sinful differences, Qaradawy cites a number of Qur'anic verses, including Q3:100 to 107, and Q49:11 and12. In this respect it should be clear that Shaykh Qaradawy's views are not extremist, but are representative of mainstream religious establishments. He presents his views covering this entire subject in a book entitled *Al-Sahwa al-Islamiyya bayna-l-Ikhtilaf al-Mashru' wa al-Tafarruq al-Madhmum* (The Islamic Awakening: Between Legitimate Disagreement and Hated Dispersion).

The provisions of the Holy Qur'an cited here are not about preventing differences of opinion among believers. Rather they are about preventing adversity and antagonism among believers, which may lead to adversity and strife. Therefore, these verses should have been cited in support of the freedom to differ, in the sense that people should be free to differ in their views, including on matters of faith, and that such differences ought to be respected. It is also in this context that we place the tradition of the Prophet cited by Qaradawy, namely: "I swear by the One who holds my life, you won't access paradise until you believe, and you won't believe until you love each other. Shall I tell you something which if you do it you'll love each other? Then spread peace among your selves."[56]Indeed, differences of opinion among believers should not preclude them from loving each other or be allowed to disrupt the peace among them.

The freedom to differ is almost absolute and comprehensive: each individual is absolutely free to formulate his or her faith in the manner most suitable for belief; each person is also free to translate his or her faith into acts of worship, regardless of what the general orthodoxy prescribes. That freedom has no limits except the limits necessary to allow others to exercise their own freedoms and to prevent any nuisances from affecting them. So that, in the end, only God judges the intentions of believers and nonbelievers, and renders His judgment.

The Freedom to Change Faiths: Apostasy

Mark Cohen contends that "asserting its superiority, Islam simply prohibits conversion to any religion other than itself."[57] Mr. Cohen is not alone in holding that misperception. He shares it with most other Muslim and non-Muslim scholars who fail to draw a line between Islam as divine revelation and Islam as history, including traditions.[58] Contrary to the prevailing *fiqh* interpretation of the Shari'a, freedom of faith also includes the absolute freedom to renounce one's faith after having accepted Islam, through Prophet Muhammad's prophecy and message.[59] This is about the freedom to convert to Christianity or Judaism, return to paganism, or adopt atheism. The abandonment of Islam is called *al-ridda,* or apostasy. Under *fiqh,* apostasy is a crime punishable by the death penalty. *Fiqh* has also extended the reach of apostasy and its harsh punishment beyond the strict rejection of Islam. It now can extend to certain actions and interpretations stretching beyond the traditional "orthodoxy" which are deemed by traditionalists as implicit rejection of Islam.[60] While the prevailing literature on Islamic law and *fiqh* attributes that finding to Shari'a, namely to certain verses of the Holy Qur'an and more specifically to Prophetic Tradition, this conclusion is an exclusively *fiqh*-generated conclusion based on an interpretation of the Shari'a, as opposed to being specifically provided for in it.

Islamic jurisprudence (*fiqh*) has principally based apostasy, as a crime punishable by the death penalty, on two traditions of the Prophet according to which Prophet Muhammad has presumably declared: (1) "Slay whoever changes his religion";[61] and (2) "The blood of a Muslim who confesses that there is no god but Allah and that I am the messenger of Allah, cannot be shed except in three cases: a life for a life; a married person who commits illegal sexual intercourse; and the one who turns renegade from Islam (apostate) and leaves the community of Muslims."[62]

Although the caliphs who succeeded the Prophet may have, rightly or wrongly, pronounced the death sentence against apostates, this first tradition imputed to Prophet Muhammad has generally been deemed as questionable because, besides being inconsistent with the Holy Qur'an's provisions on freedom of faith, it is not part of the body of traditions generally confirmed as solid and subject to consensus. Regarding the second tradition cited here, assuming its authenticity, it is clear from its context that the punishment is not about a change of faith. Rather, it is about deterring defections from the *umma* of Muslims which result in non-Muslims tainting the purity of the *umma* and causing *fitna*. In retrospect, such a punishment is entirely a construct and should not exist in reality because at no time in the history of Islamic nations has there ever existed a true so-called nation of Muslims, exclusively. At the height of the Muslim Empires, there were more non-Muslim than Muslim peoples in such empires. Furthermore, the Prophet's *sīra* (biography) has not reported a single instance in which Prophet Muhammad pronounced that sentence against any apostate.[63] Finally, a prominent jurisprudent of the Shari'a, Ibn Hazm al-Andalusi, observes, "[t]he execution of an apostate constitutes a sin because the Prophet had proscribed it, and had also denied 'Umar and Khalid Ibn al-Walid his authorization to enforce it."[64]

With respect to the Holy Scripture, *fiqh* bases its treatment of apostasy as a punishable crime on several verses of the Holy Qur'an which could only constitute such basis when taken out of context, such as in Verse Q2:217.

> *They ask you about the Sacred Month, that is, about fighting in it. Say, "Fighting in it is something grave, but it is much more grave, in the sight of Allah, to prevent (people) from the path of Allah, to disbelieve in Him, and in al-Masjid-ul-Harām, and to expel its people from there, and Fitnah (to create disorder) is more grave than killing." They will go on fighting you until they turn you away*

from your faith if they could, while whoever of you turns away from his faith and dies an infidel, such people are those whose deeds will go to waste in this world and in the Hereafter, and they are people of the Fire. They shall be there forever.[65]

In this verse people are cautioned against *fitna* arising from the attempts by the idolaters to sway them from their faith, because if they do succumb they will be punished on the Day of Judgment. Bearing in mind that *fitna* is a reference to the harassment and persecution perpetrated by the idolaters of *Quraysh* against believers in pressuring them to reject their faith, God describes *fitna* as being worse than killing. Thus, the outcome of *fitna* is equated to death. Similarly, because entry into the faith and rejection of it when they reach a certain scale could turn into *fitna*, apostasy was equated to spiritual death, hence the conclusion by the *fiqh* that apostasy might as well be punished by the death penalty.

That said, Muhammad 'Abed al-Jabiri rightly observes that in fact this verse does not sanction apostasy in this life, nor does it provide for any punishment for it, consistent with freedom of faith. In fact, it expressly stipulates that this sanction is of the exclusive realm of God.[66] It does add, however, that this punishment by God is reserved to the person who "dies as an idolater," that is, the one who lives following the apostasy and then dies—as opposed to being executed—which means that God first reserves the judgment to Himself, and then in His infinite compassion He would expect the apostate to repent and reintegrate the faith up until the last minute of his or her life, thereby excluding any punishment in this life which denies the apostate the option and opportunity to repent and be saved.

> Q3:85 and 86—*If anyone desires a religion other than Islam (submission to God), never will it be accepted of him; and in the Hereafter he will be in the ranks of those who have lost (All spiritual good) (85). How shall God Guide those who reject Faith after they accepted it and bore witness that the Apostle was true and that Clear Signs had come unto them? but God guides not a people unjust (86);*[67]

> Q3:90 and 91—*But those who reject Faith after they accepted it, and then go on adding to their defiance of Faith—never will their repentance be accepted; for they are those who have (of set purpose) gone astray (90). As to those who reject Faith, and die rejecting—never would be accepted from any such as much gold as the earth contains, though they should offer it for ransom. For such is (in store) a penalty grievous, and they will find no helpers (91).*[68]

These verses can only be considered and understood when read in conjunction with each other and in light of the entire series of verses from Q3:83 to Q3:91. It was previously shown that Verse Q3:85 was not inconsistent with the essential pluralism in Islam and that, by reference to Verse Q3:84, the apostasy mentioned in Verse Q3:85 was not about changing faith within the overall Islamic faiths of the Abrahamic monotheisms. This series deals mainly with reverting from an Abrahamic faith into idolatry. While the general context of these verses relates to people from Medina within the immediate surroundings of the Prophet, the exegetes were not unanimous as to their exact context, namely whether the reversion to idolatry was committed by Muslim companions or by individuals belonging to the People of the Book.[69] In our opinion, whether or not the apostates were Muslims or Jews among the People of the Book is irrelevant to the overall principle embodied in these verses, because the issue is of an entirely different nature, namely that of allocating jurisdiction over apostasy in terms of clarifying who can make that judgment and enforce it, and when that judgment can be made and enforced. The global picture can be grasped by looking at Verses Q3:84 to 91 as one series.

> *Say: "We believe in God, and in what has been revealed to us and what was revealed to Abraham, Isma'il, Isaac, Jacob, and the Tribes, and in (the Books) given to Moses, Jesus, and the prophets, from their Lord: We make no distinction between one and another among them, and to God do we bow our will (in Islam)" (84). If anyone desires a religion other than Islam (submission to God), never will it be accepted of him; and in the Hereafter He will be in the ranks of*

those who have lost (All spiritual good) (85). How shall God Guide those who reject Faith after they accepted it and bore witness that the Apostle was true and that Clear Signs had come unto them? but God guides not a people unjust (86). Of such the reward is that on them (rests) the curse of God, of His angels, and of all mankind (87); In that will they dwell; nor will their penalty be lightened, nor respite be (their lot) (88); Except for those that repent (Even) after that, and make amends; for verily God is Oft-Forgiving, Most Merciful (89). But those who reject Faith after they accepted it, and then go on adding to their defiance of Faith,—never will their repentance be accepted; for they are those who have (of set purpose) gone astray (90). As to those who reject Faith, and die rejecting,— never would be accepted from any such as much gold as the earth contains, though they should offer it for ransom. For such is (in store) a penalty grievous, and they will find no helpers (91).[70]

The salient principles governing apostasy that can be derived from these verses are the following: (1) Islam is the generic term for the religion revolving around the unicity of God as evidenced by the Abrahamic faiths from Abraham to Muhammad (Verse 84); (2) the rejection of Islam, understood as the religion of divine unicity constitutes a terminal sin which, consistent with the principles set forth in Verses Q4:48 and 116,[71] cannot be forgiven (Verses 3:85 and 88); (3) the apostate cannot, before the Day of Judgment, be punished for that capital sin of renouncing Islam by rejecting the unicity of God because, in His infinite compassion and mercy, God encourages apostates to repent, for which He leaves that opportunity open to them until the last minute of their lives (Verse 3:89); (4) unless they have repented from the specific sin of apostasy, the repentance of apostates who have persisted in defying the faith until the time of their death will not be accepted with respect to any other sins,[72] because the repentance for such other sins is futile; the sin of apostasy is sufficient by itself to doom the apostate on the Day of Judgment (Verse 3:90); and (5)   to avoid doubt, the operative time for condemnation of the apostate for eternal punishment is the time of death; that condemnation becomes a reality if the apostate dies before repenting (Verse 3:91).

Q5:54—*O you who have attained to faith! If you ever abandon your faith, God will in time bring forth [in your stead] people*

whom He loves and who love Him—humble toward the
believers, proud toward all who deny the truth: [people] who
strive hard in God's cause, and do not fear to be censured by
anyone who might censure them: such is God's favor, which He
grants unto whom He wills. And God is infinite, all-knowing.[73]

While the verses discussed above clearly state that the punishment of apostasy rests with God and no one else, Verse Q5:54 appears to hint at a potential terrestrial punishment in this life. Indeed, addressing the believers, it warns them against apostasy lest God cause their extermination and replace them with believers. Unfortunately, this is how several exegetes of the first few centuries of Islam understood the meaning of that verse.[74] They went even further, placing that verse in the context of the mass movement of apostasy that followed the death of Prophet Muhammad and which Caliph Abou Bakr undertook to fight and redress. Such interpretation fails several tests. It is inconsistent with God's retaining the power to punish apostasy and His declaration that punishment be postponed until after death of the apostate, with ample opportunity in the meantime to repent and be forgiven. Also, revelation of the Qur'an was completed prior to Prophet Muhammad's death and could not have referred to Caliph Abou Bakr's action against mass apostasy which followed the death of the Prophet.[75]Finally, the claim that God has used Caliph Abou Bakr and his army to punish the apostates in this life defies divine justice which upholds the principle of individual accountability versus collective punishment. In fact, in all instances of collective punishment that appeared in the *ghayb*-related tales of the Holy Qur'an—namely the punishments of the peoples of Aad, Thamud, Noah, Lot, and others—God made sure to reassure humankind of His divine justice by telling about all those whom He singled out and saved because they did not participate in the particular collective sins then being punished. The expectation of some defections from the faith occurring following the death of the Prophet was in fact contemplated in Verse Q3:144 in which such defections were declared as neutral to God but calamitous to those who defect, without any implication that they deserve the death penalty in this life.

Muhammad is no more than an apostle: many Were the apostles that passed away before him. If he died or were slain, will ye then Turn back on your heels? If any did turn back on his heels, not the least harm will he do to God; but God (on the other hand) will swiftly reward those who (serve Him) with gratitude.[76]

Therefore, Verse Q5:54 must have an interpretation which is different from what the exegetes have advanced, that is, which is not inconsistent with divine justice and compassion. In this respect, Ibn 'Ashour places the substance of this verse in the context of the principle that God and His religion are not affected by, nor do they suffer from the actions of, those who reject the faith.[77] That religion, being the religion of the truth, will always find honest and faithful believers to uphold it.[78]In other words, idolaters—whether they adopted Islam then rejected it or they never adopted Islam—cannot adversely affect Islam which will always have more believers than unbelievers.

Verse Q16:106—*As for anyone who denies God after having once attained to faith—and this, to be sure, does not apply to one who does it under duress, the while his heart remains true to his faith, but [only to] him who willingly opens up his heart to a denial of the truth: upon all such [falls] God's condemnation, and tremendous suffering awaits them.*[79]

In this verse God reminds people that the sin of apostasy is not punishable merely for having uttered words of apostasy, whether under duress or otherwise. What counts is what a person holds inside his or her heart, which cannot be known to anyone other than God. Therefore, since God is the only one who knows what the hearts of people hold to the exclusion of any human or other creation of God, then God reserves the exclusive power to judge people and punish apostates. In this respect, we recall the sad episode of the judgment rendered by an Egyptian court declaring a prominent author, Nasr Hamid Abizaid, an apostate by merely interpreting his published opinions on various religious issues as being tantamount to apostasy. His interpretations relating to such issues deviated from the general conservative orthodoxy.[80] That judgment was rendered on the basis of *fiqh*-derived opinions which treat any position on any religious issue which deviates from generally accepted interpretations as being tantamount to apostasy, even if the person in question had expressly declared his or her continued faith in Islam, let alone having formally rejected it. Unfortunately, *fiqh* assimilates apostasy to a crime of high treason against the *umma*, similar to high treason against one's country. This is yet another example of the serious risk arising from treating the *umma* as a state and Islam as an identity. Mohamed Talbi observes that freedom of faith is inherent in freedom of choice which belongs to each individual and is not the consequence of belonging to a religious community,[81] as some modern-day radical thinkers who do not differentiate between religion and state would claim.

For that purpose, recent scholars such as Muhammad Rashid Rida, Syed Qutb, Sultanhussein Tabandeh, Ismail al-Faruki, Muhammad Said El-Awa, Aboul A'la al-Mawdudi, and Shaykh Yusuf Qaradawy, among others, have "safely" opted for assigning apostasy that political dimension rather than taking the more difficult route of embracing freedom of faith.[82] They have tried to justify the death penalty for apostasy on grounds of protection of the higher interest of the state from the risk of subversion by the apostate. If that is the case, that punishment—in reality—should not be classified under the sin of apostasy. Instead it could be classified under the penalties for subversive actions, whatever the perpetrator's religious association. In other words, subversive action against the state is a secular crime and not a religious one, and its punishment should not be looked for in the Qur'an or Prophetic Tradition.

For all these reasons, contemporary scholars such as Shaykh Mahmud Shaltut, Shaykh Muhammad Sayyid Tantawi, Sobhi Mahmassani, Mohamed Talbi, Shabbir Akhtar, Jamal al-Banna, and al-Sadiq al-Nayhoum have challenged the construction of apostasy as a religious temporal crime deserving a temporal punishment, deeming it exclusively a religious act that only God can consider on the Day of Judgment.[83]Furthermore, Mohamed Charfi points to a regrettable *fiqh* position on apostasy based on so-called *ijmā' sukūti,* or implied consensus, arising from nonobjection to the political repression of apostasy by the Prophet's successors following his death.[84]

Thus, it becomes evident that freedom of faith, including the freedom of apostasy, is logically inherent in God's design and creation, including the corollary of divine justice and God's exclusive jurisdiction over judging the faith of his creatures. In fact, as indicated earlier, it was God's own design, when He created humankind, to create them in diversity and give them the freedom to choose, as His trustees, what they believe in and how they live that faith. From time to time, He sent messengers with truths and guidance, and reserved the exclusive right to render final judgment on their performance. Divine justice, for that purpose, would rely on an evaluation of human performance over an entire lifetime, particularly on the final evolution of each individual toward true faith. This means that each individual has a chance, until the last minute of life, to attain to faith, as expressed in Verse Q18:58: *"Your Lord is the Most Forgiving, the Lord of Mercy. If He seizes them for what they did, He may cause the punishment to befall them sooner, but there is an appointed time for them, from which they can never find a place of refuge."*[85] Therefore, because God is primarily most pardoning and forgiving, leaving the wrath of punishment to a last resort, any advance penalty administered in this life against an apostate by ruler, clergy, or any person or authority would constitute an obstruction of divine justice and an assault on divine prerogatives (the sin of *shirk*, or association with God), first because it denies the victim the opportunity and right to repentance and salvation, and most importantly, because the power to judge a person on faith-related matters is the exclusive domain of God. Whoever inflicts the death penalty on an apostate is obstructing the exercise of divine justice.

Bearing in mind that Prophet Muhammad is not reported in Prophetic Tradition to have condemned any apostate to death or to any other corporeal punishment, should we assume that Caliph Abou Bakr, who waged the Wars of Ridda to quell mass movements of apostasy in many areas of the Arabian Peninsula following the death of the Prophet, has betrayed the legacy of the Prophet and acted beyond the scope of his authority, in contempt of the provisions of the Holy Qur'an? The answer is "no."[86]

First, in spite of the lack of scriptural foundation for the death penalty for apostasy, the history of the Muslim Arab peoples reports that the early

Muslim caliphs who succeeded Prophet Muhammad generally applied the death penalty to apostates and that *fiqh* has treated, and continues to treat, capital punishment as a legitimate punishment for such crime. While unfounded and unjustifiable from the religious perspective, capital punishment for the crime of apostasy may have been justified from the secular perspective by the circumstances of the early days of Islam, namely the fear that the apostasy of a person or group of persons would trigger a larger movement of apostasy. However, the situation became entirely different and apostasy took a completely different turn when it exploded as one mass movement followed by another, first threatening the existing Islamic social order that the Prophet had left behind, and then—most importantly—threatening as well the emergence of the "Islamic" state that Caliph Abou Bakr had set forth to create, organize, and expand following the Prophet's death. Therefore, the mass apostasy movement was primarily perceived as a movement with potentially grave consequences for the survival of the "Islamic" state and, to a certain extent, the continuity of Prophet Muhammad's message altogether. From that perspective, the action taken by Caliph Abou Bakr should be viewed and analyzed as a secular political action—as opposed to a religious act—aimed at preserving or restoring public order.[87] From that perspective only, that is, exclusively on secular political grounds, repression of the mass movement of apostasy by Caliph Abou Bakr could be legitimized. However, it should never have been given a religious character or placed under a religious umbrella.[88]

But this conclusion is limited strictly to the period in history relating to the Wars of Ridda. It should not be generalized to legitimize, as Muhammad 'Abed al-Jabiri seems to suggest, the repression of apostasy under the rubric of public order instead of that of the freedom of faith.[89]Thus, while the punishment of collective apostasy was initially intended as an exception to the fundamental principle of freedom of faith, as enshrined in the Holy Qur'an, unfortunately the later *fiqh* jurisprudence legally authenticated this exception by construing—then eternalizing— apostasy as a terrestrial crime punishable by the death penalty.

In retrospect, arguments favoring the death penalty for apostasy drawn from the need to preserve the purity of the faith are unconvincing and fail the tests of rationality. In fact, recalling the stories of the hypocrites of Medina in the days of the Prophet, it was argued that

> no one should ever again consider adopting the Islamic faith without having first matured his or her decision following serious consideration in light of reason and science so that such conversion may be final and permanent..., it is also justified by our determination that access to Islam be reserved exclusively to those who firmly believe therein.[90]

Besides the unrestricted freedom of faith, such arguments would have been thinkable if conversion to Islam could be achieved only by preparing for and successfully passing the relevant test. In other words, that argument might have been considered if every newborn could adopt Islam only once he or she reached a certain age and then successfully passed a test of firm belief, assuming there was one. Such an approach cannot apply to Muslims by birth because they are not converts to be held to a standard of final and permanent choice. By the time they are of age to make a choice, it is too late for them, because any change on their part would be treated as apostasy and expose them to the death penalty.

It is important to recall that the purpose of restoring an environment in which *al-dīn kulluhu lillāh* (religion is all to God) is not about creating a monolithic society, as it has been presented in order to justify indiscriminate action against non-Muslims. Instead, it is about securing that the social environment remains at all times one in which the noble principles enjoined by God— justice, fairness, freedom of faith, *iḥsān*, and the performance of good deeds—can be freely expected, observed, or performed. In particular, and contrary to prevailing *fiqh*, adopting Christianity or Judaism after having converted to Islam does not constitute apostasy.

All aspects of the right to freedom discussed in this chapter are of the essence of human dignity that God has bestowed on humankind on creation, and it is in that same spirit that the Holy Qur'an provides for principles of justice aimed at preserving that human dignity.

Justice, Human Dignity, and Corporeal Punishment

The rights to equality and freedom require for their protection an overall right to justice. Without justice, it is not possible to prevent discrimination and enforce the right to equality; similarly, without justice, all other freedoms can be suppressed.[91] From that perspective, every individual needs justice to protect his or her freedoms against any restrictions attempted on them by anyone, whether by a public authority on presumed considerations of security or public order, or by other individuals pretending to exercise their rights. It is the justice system which defines the bounds of freedom for all concerned.

The Right to Justice

The right to justice is the means to ensure that all persons are protected equally under the law and equally enjoy the essential freedoms that are inherent in human nature, without discrimination of any kind. That right is set forth as a principle in Verse Q4:58: "*Verily! Allâh commands that you should render back the trusts to those to whom they are due; and that when you judge between men, you judge with justice. Verily, how excellent is the teaching which He (Allâh) gives you! Truly, Allâh is Ever All-Hearer, All-Seer.*"[92]

Because of the importance of the right to justice, people are enjoined not to withhold their testimony, but rather to act as witness and provide information that they may be aware of to help any seeker of justice prove his or her claim.[93] The right to justice acquires particular importance when it comes to safeguarding the inviolability of the person. In this respect, it rests on three important premises, namely (1) the principle of legality of the criminal penalties which adversely affect the freedom or, as the case may be, the physical integrity of the person; (2) the presumption of innocence; and (3) the principle of nonretroactivity of the law.

Because the Holy Qur'an is not a code of law, it does not provide for these principles in plain language from a legal perspective. Instead, the principle that no penalty may be administered for certain actions unless it is provided for in the law is addressed in connection with divine justice (Verse Q17:15), according to which God would not punish people unless He has sent them a messenger to inform and warn them: "*Whoever adopts the right path does so for his own benefit, and whoever goes astray does so to his own detriment, and no bearer of burden shall bear the burden of another, and it is not Our way to punish (anyone) unless We send a Messenger.*"[94]

Similarly, the principle of nonretroactivity of the law is also addressed from the perspective of divine justice in the sense that whatever God has decreed in the Qur'an specifically excludes preexisting conditions, using the formula *"excluding currently existing cases."*[95]

The principle of presumption of innocence was addressed by preaching the moral virtue of avoiding suspicion and hasty judgments against people, as set forth in several verses:

> Verse Q10:36— *For most of them follow nothing but conjecture: [and,] behold, conjecture can never be a substitute for truth. Verily, God has full knowledge of all that they do;*[96]

> Verse Q49:6—*O YOU who have attained to faith! If any iniquitous person comes to you with a [slanderous] tale, use your discernment, lest you hurt people unwittingly and afterwards be filled with remorse for what you have done*[97]; and

> Verse Q49:12—*O you who believe, abstain from many of the suspicions. Some suspicions are sins. And do not be curious (to find out faults of others), and do not backbite one another. Does one of you like that he eats the flesh of his dead brother? You would abhor it.*[98]

It is unfortunate that, despite the principle of legality, the early and later jurisprudents of the *fiqh* have developed into what they call Islamic criminal law a discretionary power of the judge to inflict *ta'zīr*, penalties of his or her choice for crimes which are not provided for in the Scriptures. The Islamist perspective boasts the superiority of the practice of *ta'zīr* over the principle of legality of the crime and punishment, because in countries which strictly adhere to that principle "numerous delinquents could escape justice despite the prejudice that they might inflict on society by their acts under the pretext that the law does not provide for the type of act committed," according to a paper submitted by the Saudi Arabian government's delegation to a colloquium on human rights.[99] Such an argument is unconvincing because a person who causes prejudice to another is bound to repair the damage under civil law, but without necessarily being physically or criminally punished. More seriously, this argument attributes a widespread discretionary power to the judge, ignoring the dignity and human rights of individuals who might wrongly be punished for acts committed in good faith and not otherwise labeled as crimes.

Finally, these three principles carry the necessary corollary that no one may be punished for the acts of others, thereby excluding the unfair practice of collective punishment. Because of its importance, the principle that states *"no bearer of burden shall bear the burden of another"* appears in the Holy Qur'an five times.[100]

Human Dignity and Corporeal Punishment

Islam is often criticized by non-Muslims for allegedly condoning corporeal punishment for a number of criminal acts. Muslim apologists go to great lengths to apologize for defending corporeal punishment, arguing that it deters crime.[101] For that purpose they cite statistics to demonstrate that Muslim countries which apply the corporeal punishments "prescribed" by the Holy Qur'an have lower crime rates than so-called civilized countries which ban corporeal punishment. In reality, both sides have missed the point. Non-Muslims reach this conclusion because they read the Qur'an without the logical historical or social background, or they observe the laws and practices of countries with Muslim majorities who have tailored their laws on so-called Shari'a law. Others consider corporeal punishment as necessary for the protection of human rights in particular.[102] They also focus exclusively on the solutions set forth in the Qur'an for the immediate audience at the time of the Revelation, to which they attribute a universal vocation without regard to the underlying universal message. As a result they fail to grasp the greater universal purport of these verses in the context in which they were revealed.

The principal corporeal punishments provided for in the Holy Qur'an relate to the crimes of homicide and other bodily injury,[103] theft,[104] adultery,[105] accusations of adultery of married women,[106] and the spreading of disorder and corruption on earth[107] (the equivalent of terrorism in today's terms). These punishments range from flogging, to amputation of hands, to execution. On their own initiative, the jurisprudents of *fiqh* have added additional instances of corporeal punishment which are not provided for in the Qur'an, namely executing an apostate, jailing a debtor in default, flogging a person caught drinking alcohol, and stoning an adulterer to death.[108]

In review, the important facts are the following: (1) the corporeal punishments provided for in the Holy Qur'an are prescribed as *ḥudūd,* that is, limits or maximum penalties not to be exceeded, as opposed to mandatory punishments; (2) the Revelation came in a tribal environment which lacked state institutions for the administration of justice; and (3) the purpose of the Revelation was primarily to reverse cruel and reprehensible tribal customs in force at that time.

With respect to adultery, when all of the verses dealing with the subject are collected and compared, the resulting viewpoint is that adultery, to be punishable, must be witnessed by four people. Thus it is practically impossible to prove it, unless it is an act performed in public, in which case it becomes an issue of pornography. In this respect, sadly enough, Abdelmajid Charfi rightly observes that, while the Holy Qur'an raises the bar for administering corporeal punishment for the crime of adultery by imposing almost impossible conditions, the secular laws of certain nations with Muslim majorities fail to maintain these conditions, thereby lowering the bar on these antiquated punishments.[109] That said, adultery when proven, is punished with one hundred lashes and not by stoning to death.[110] In this respect, it is useful to recall the relevant verses of the Holy Qur'an. Verse Q4:15 states: "*As for your women who commit adultery, call four among you to witness against them. If they so witness, confine them to their homes until death overtakes them or else God provides another way for them.*"[111] There is no mention of stoning to death in public, but instead a home confinement until death, and then that measure is only temporary, until "God provides another way," meaning another measure. That measure comes in Verse Q24:2:

> *The woman and the man guilty of adultery or fornication—flog each of them*
> *with a hundred stripes: Let not compassion move you in their case, in a matter*
> *prescribed by God, if ye believe in God and the Last Day: and let a party of the*
> *Believers witness their punishment.*[112]

As a result of the Revelation of Verse Q24:2, the upper limit of the punishment for adultery is one hundred lashes administered in public. It should be noted that Verse Q24:2 did not abrogate Verse Q4:15; it came to complement its provisions. Thus, both verses remain in full force and effect. Unfortunately, the proponents of the penalty of stoning to death advance the argument that the penalty in Verse Q24:2 has been abrogated and superseded by the practice of the Prophet, that is, by Prophetic Tradition.[113] But as discussed earlier in Chapter 3, a divine ruling cannot be reversed by human action.

Basically, the corporeal punishments appearing in the Holy Qur'an are not of the essence of Islam. What is of the essence of Islam is that the acts for which these punishments are prescribed—namely homicide, theft, adultery, accusation of adultery, and spreading corruption—are all reprehensible acts and should be prevented. These corporeal punishments were deemed a reasonable deterrent at the time of the Revelation, absent state structures to handle the protection of society, the deterrence being then achieved through the administration of punishment in public.

At the same time, these corporeal punishments were found to save lives, had the relevant punishable acts been left to retribution under tribal customs such as revenge vendettas, which take the lives of many more, or the fate that a woman would face if she were punished under tribal laws. In other words, the dignity of the perpetrators was sacrificed to protect the personal integrity and dignity of potential victims. However, if that same result could be achieved differently while safeguarding as well the dignity of the perpetrators, such solutions would not be inconsistent with Islam. On the contrary, they would be in line with the spirit of Islam.

From this perspective, any country that enacts secular legislation which excludes all forms of corporeal punishment while preventing the perpetration of punishable acts would be fully consistent with, and in fulfillment of, Islam and its objectives. In any event, corporeal punishments in the Qur'an are set forth in the form of *ḥudūd*, that is, as limits not to be exceeded, without any lower limits, an indication that they can be set aside entirely if the objective of preventing the crime from being committed can be achieved differently.

This examination of the rights to equality and freedom as expressed through verses of the Qur'an shows that Islam planted seeds of humanism and promoted an awareness of human dignity and human rights. Although it did not frame them into an integrated comprehensive theory of human rights, Islam has nevertheless recognized a wide spectrum of such rights, sufficient to develop a comprehensive theory, as the human rights conventions of the last few decades have done. While some Muslim countries have yet to unconditionally adopt and implement these rights, it is important to remember that human rights in Islam predate their equivalent in the West by several centuries. Unequivocally, Islam recognizes human rights as innate. For in essence, these rights are inherent in human creation.

CHAPTER 16
Reflections on Human Rights in Islam

A dangerous tendency that is current among both Muslims and non-Muslims, argue John Esposito and Dalia Mogahed, is the readiness to approach women's rights in the Muslim world as, "a struggle between Islam and Western egalitarian values."[1] This tendency, which extends to the entire range of human rights, is an extension of the misperception that human rights are the exclusive product of Western culture and values. Thus, striving to establish human rights in an Islamic environment is necessarily a struggle against Islam.

This ingrained perception of struggle between the West and Islam is even attributed by its claimants to major differences in philosophical values, as opposed to mere differences in perception. In fact, in the West human rights are mainly based on humanism and individualism. By contrast, in classical Islamic thought, human rights are often perceived as duties related to the social functions of particular rights. Human rights are thus based on—and justified by—the general interest of society.[2] Malek Chebel portrays any demand for freedom by a Muslim as a challenge and an act of disobedience to the ruler, and through him to the community.[3] Such assumptions need to change. Islam is humanistic and individualistic, and human rights are true rights and not duties dressed up as rights.

The fact that Shari'a contains general principles for social interaction should not lead us to deny Islam's humanistic and individualistic vocation. Islam's exclusive vocation to influence social norms is often insisted on in order to control individuals in the name of religion.[4] The sole purpose of invoking the so-called overriding social function of Islam is to deter Muslims from their freedom to fulfill themselves. As a result, human initiative gets buried and people are burdened with duties. They become embarrassed to acknowledge their rights, let alone dare to use them.

But human rights in Islam are real. They are *fiṭra*-based, and the only corresponding duty of the individual to society is the general one of not impeding others in exercising those same rights to the fullest extent. Communal solidarity, inherent in Islam, is not incompatible with the recognition and protection of human rights, and there is no order of priority between them. On the contrary, they complement each other, because it is communal solidarity that secures recognition of, and respect for, the rights of the individuals who make up the community.

In the early days of Islam, which were characterized by the absence of government structures, communal solidarity under the tribal system served as a mechanism for the group's survival. Unfortunately, that tribal concept of communal solidarity survived as a tradition rather than as an aspect of religious freedom. Human rights as individual rights are not *derived from* society but instead are *protected by* society. They derive from God by way of *fiṭra*, irrespective of whether the person is a believer or not.

Mohammad 'Abed al-Jabiri observes, "The concepts of right and duty are interrelated in the Arabic language and the Arab Islamic culture, where the right of a person is the quid pro quo for its duties."[5] This is true with respect to rights and duties considered in the context of social relations among people. However, from a universal perspective, human rights are legally of the nature of freedoms whose only counterpart is respect for the similar freedoms of others.[6] What distinguishes a freedom from a right is that a freedom is not contingent upon the performance of any duty toward any person. Freedoms exist by the mere fact of having been born a human being. They are natural rights or, in the Islamic lexicon, *fiṭra* based. They are not created by legislation. They are essentially acknowledged and declared.

Despite the widely accepted perception to the contrary—particularly in the West—human rights are of the essence of Islam. In this instance we are talking about rights, freedoms, and liberties that are attributed to every individual. They are a corollary to the human dignity that God bestowed upon each individual. Human rights thus derive from the humanism which is inherent in Islam. Ebrahim Yazdi, a leader of the Freedom Movement of Iran, rightly observes that belief in the unicity of God embodied in the *shahāda* demands "renunciation of the sovereignty claims" of any one person over another. Yazdi affirms, "It is [God's] design and command that man must be his own master and be free to govern himself. Man must not permit anyone to manipulate his will and life. Man must not tolerate despotism and dictatorship."[7]

As a result, human rights are not tools of divine governance and sovereignty. Although they are bestowed by God in the first place, their exercise by each individual is totally free, accountability for which takes place in the hereafter. Unfortunately, the religious establishment and *fiqh* failed to recognize the separate natures of divine governance and human governance, and maintained a close quid pro quo relationship between human rights and presumed rights of God under divine governance. That failure is at the root of the perceived conflicts between internationally recognized human rights, and restrictions imposed on them wrongly attributed to Islam.

Divine Sovereignty and Human Rights

The Universal Islamic Declaration of Human Rights states, "By the terms of our primeval covenant with God our duties and obligations have priority over our rights."[8] Human rights in Islamic *fiqh* are put forward as a quid pro quo for the rights of God, namely the duties that humankind owes to God under divine sovereignty. Instead, it should be established that human rights are bestowed by God on humankind as an essential attribute of humanity without counterpart, because what distinguishes humans from the rest of God's creation is the mind, upon which human dignity rests.

Rights of God versus Rights of Man

The perception that human rights are the quid pro quo for the rights of God is founded on the assumption that God, through some presumed covenant entered into with humankind at the time of creation, has granted to humanity human rights packaged among the attributes of divine trust, in return for their commitment to recognize God as creator and sole deity, and to respect God's rights.[9] This is a theory that was popular among early exegetes and that continues to influence modern-day Islamic thinkers.

Mohammad 'Abed al-Jabiri located the origins of the concept of human rights in the philosophical and literary movement in Europe, in the classical age, according to which human rights predated civilization. First, al-Jabiri cited the views of John Locke which assert that the universal nature of human rights is rooted in the natural rights—freedom and equality—which are inherent in humankind as of the early state of nature, before any collective authority existed and placed limitations on those rights. Then al-Jabiri noted the social contract of Jean-Jacques Rousseau by which human rights in their initial natural iteration were translated into civil rights founded on the general will and limited, as necessary, to ensure the fulfillment of the collective interests and general good. Finally al-Jabiri drew a parallel with a comparable theory about the origins of human rights in Islam, where human rights are the quid pro quo for the rights of God under that covenant between God and humankind. In fact, to the extent that—under that covenant—humans have presumably renounced all rights to worship any deity other than God, they have freed themselves from all authority other than that of God, and thus become free and equal under God's sovereignty. On that basis of freedom and equality, and the remaining human rights deriving from them, God granted humankind His trust over his earthly creation.[10] Verses Q7:172 and Q33:7 to 8 are cited in support of this theory.

> Q7:172—*AND WHENEVER thy Sustainer brings forth their offspring from the loins of the children of Adam, He [thus] calls upon them to bear witness about themselves: "Am I not your Sustainer?"— to which they answer: "Yea, indeed, we do bear witness thereto!" [Of this We remind you,] lest you say on the Day of Resurrection, "Verily, we were unaware of this."*

> Q33:7 and 8—*AND LO! We did accept a solemn pledge from all the prophets— from thee, [O Muhammad,] as well as from Noah, and Abraham, and Moses, and Jesus the son of Mary: for We accepted a most weighty, solemn pledge from [all of] them (7), so that [at the end of time] He might ask those men of truth as to [what response] their truthfulness [had received on earth]. And grievous suffering has He readied for all who deny the truth!*[11]

A number of compelling reasons disprove this theory. In the first place, God does not need any rights because He is sovereign, in His capacity as the Almighty. Accordingly, all people submit to Him, irrespective of whether they accept, and believe in, Him or not. They do so because that is how God created all things, in His Almighty capacity. For that purpose, the concept of divine rights appears superfluous because rights are usually claimed, with varying degrees of success, against the relevant obligors, whereas God the Almighty does not claim anything from anyone. In other words, God's sovereignty is limitless, and for that reason God has no need for rights because He wields power.

Second, in their relations with God, humans have no rights that they can claim from God, because the concept of a right is part of a bilateral or multilateral relationship where, for each right and right-holder, there exist an obligation and an obligor; and God does not owe any obligations to anyone. Instead, humans enjoy freedoms that God Has bestowed upon them under the scope of the trusteeship that He conferred. In this light, it should become clear that human rights are not rights of humans toward God but are rights of people among each other, within human society.

Third, a covenant is an agreement among equals, where a quid pro quo relationship exists between the parties to the covenant, that is, whereby the undertakings of one party constitute the justification for the undertakings of the other party to that covenant. In this case, there can be no true covenant between God and humankind because, under limitless divine governance, no one can claim to be the equal of God. On that basis, Verses Q7:172 and Q33:7 and 8 could only have been given a far-reaching scope. In fact, in Verses Q33:7 and 8, the reference is to a unilateral commitment to God by His prophets rather than to a covenant which is a mutual commitment. Then in Verse Q7:172, what appears as God having, at the time of the creation of Adam, summoned all of humankind as potential descendants of Adam in order to seek and obtain their renunciation to worship any deity other than God is simply inconsistent with God's attributes and designs. If indeed humankind had given the commitment in question, then they would, ad infinitum eternam, be believers, without any further need for God to periodically send His prophets and messengers to convey messages or to preach His attributes, namely His unicity, compassion, and justice, among others.

More importantly, if that commitment was indeed given, then all human beings for the rest of time would be believers and there would be no unbelievers, thereby erasing the need for any accountability and judgment on the Final Day. That is why, and unlike other early exegetes of the Qur'an who adhered to the theory of the covenant, al-Zamakhshari observed the unreasonableness of that interpretation and construction. He offered instead an interpretation according to which the summoning of Adam's descendants at the time of his creation was a figure of speech.[12] It was an allegoric reference to the endowment of every individual human being with a mind which, with a certain amount of effort, should be capable of attaining the truth, without any implication that every person will necessarily attain that truth, accept it, and become a believer. This is precisely why God cautioned against coercion in spreading the Message, so as to preserve each person's freedom of faith and belief. With that in mind, God nevertheless granted the trust to humankind, together with all the rights and freedoms that they might need in their endeavor, and called them to accountability for their actions on the Final Day.

Given all of the above, human rights are not—nor could they be— the quid pro quo for any covenants with God. As such, human rights are not contingent upon any specific duties to God. This perception of human rights, separately and independently from any so-called rights of God, is strongly anchored in the secular nature of human rights, a concept eloquently articulated by Khaled Abou El Fadl.

> The commitment to human rights does not signify a lack of commitment to God or a lack of willingness to obey God, but is instead a necessary part of celebrating human diversity, honoring God's vicegerents, achieving mercy, and pursuing the ultimate goal of justice... In the second half of the last century, a considerable number of Muslims have made the unfounded assumption that Islamic law is concerned primarily with duties, not rights, and that the Islamic conception of rights is collectivist, not individualist.[13]

Human rights thus are inherent in human nature by the mere act of creation. As such, they are innate and are part of *fiṭra*.

Every individual in humankind enjoys human rights, irrespective of the extent of one's faith or lack of it.[14] In this respect, Ahmad Moussalli observes, "[w]hile these human rights are fixed in principle, their material existence is changeable from one context to another and from one time to another."[15] Instead, only the scope of human rights may change over time and across geographic regions, because the existence of those rights is inherent in human nature, which does not change. The fact that certain rights were not enforced in history is no indication that they did not exist. They simply lacked recognition.

Human Rights as an Attribute of Humanity: The Role of the Human Mind and the Right to Seek Knowledge

The fact that human rights are innate, regardless of which faith—if any—each person holds, reflects the purpose and social function of those rights. They are destined to preserve the dignity of humankind, where each individual carries the spirit of God and is expected to participate in performing the duties entrusted by God to humankind. Abdulaziz Sachedina even considers human dignity to be the primary purpose of the Revelation.[16] As an attribute of humanity, human rights are not restricted to believers. They belong to all human beings by the mere fact of their humanity, and such rights have existed concurrently with creation before any prophet or divine message was ever sent to humankind.[17]

This explains why God has endowed each individual with a mind and reasoning capability. The role of the mind in Islam acquires particular importance because Islam is essentially secular, in the sense that Muslims must rely exclusively on the mind to understand religion without any intermediation by a church, or the like. From that perspective, the call for secularization launched by the philosophers of the Classical Age in Europe was not then a call for the rejection of religion. Similarly, the repeated calls by contemporary Muslim intellectuals for the secularization of all activities other than worship-related activities—such as legislation, administration of justice, and education—are also not calls for the rejection of religion. Instead, they constitute calls for reliance on the mind in defining the scope of human rights, among other things, and preventing any imposition by the church and other religious establishments, both Christian and Muslim, of their own respective interpretations, as unsolicited meddling on their part in state affairs and private lives.[18]

The Holy Qur'an describes the process in sequence of creation and disposition: First, God breathed His spirit into humankind upon creation and endowed it with the tools of the mind.[19] Then He designed the trusteeship and granted the trust to humankind.[20] Finally, He made everything on earth and in the heavens readily accessible and available to humankind, so that they may ponder and behave righteously in the performance of trusteeship,[21] under the watchfulness of God and subject to accountability to Him.

As a result, after empowering humankind with the mind, humans were made aware of the great dignity that God bestowed on them, commensurate with the tasks that He entrusted to them, as follows: (1) although humans were created from clay, their first dignification came in the form God's divine spirit being made an integral part of humankind's essence;[22] (2) this resulted in humankind's being created in the best image (Verses Q40:64, Q64:3, and Q95:4);[23] (3) then, to honor what He created, God ordered all angels to prostrate to this human creation (Verses Q38:71 and 72);[24] and (4) finally, in addition to the subjection of the earth to humankind, God's assurance came with the assertion that He spread them across the earth and made available to them all that is good and delicious, and preferred them over all His other creatures (Verse Q17:70). In a note to his translation of this latter Verse Q17:70, Muhammad Asad explains that the nature of the preference that God bestowed upon the descendence of Adam lies in the gift of the mind, which distinguishes them.[25]

Since people will be accountable for their choices and actions in fulfillment of their role as trustees, each person has a responsibility to use the mind efficiently and continuously to develop it through learning. Only then can humankind continue to cope with the responsibilities of trusteeship. For that purpose, not only is learning the human right of each individual. It is, before all, a duty.

God started by teaching Adam the nature of things so as to give him the knowledge necessary to convince the angels of humankind's worthiness of dignity and veneration, expressed in Verses Q2:31 to 34.

> *And He taught Adam the nature of all things; then He placed them before the angels, and said: "Tell me the nature of these if ye are right" (31). They said: "Glory to Thee, of knowledge We have none, save what Thou Hast taught us: In truth it is Thou Who art perfect in knowledge and wisdom" (32). He said: "O Adam! Tell them their natures." When he had told them, God said: "Did I not tell you that I know the secrets of heaven and earth, and I know what ye reveal and what ye conceal?"(33) And behold, We said to the angels: "Bow down to Adam" and they bowed down. Not so Iblis: he refused and was haughty: He was of those who reject Faith (34).*[26]

Following the giving of knowledge to Adam, the value of knowledge has been consistently exalted throughout the Holy Qur'an,[27] to the extent of comparing it to adherence to the faith.[28] Prophet Muhammad is even reported to have said that seeking knowledge is equivalent to an act of worship in the sense that it is more important than performing such acts of worship as prayer, fasting, and jihad.[29] This explains that, following his victory at the battle of Badr, Prophet Muhammad is reported to have determined to seek a ransom in kind from each prisoner, in the form of obligation to educate ten Muslim illiterates.[30] The compendia of Prophetic Tradition are filled with sayings and traditions of Prophet Muhammad in which he encourages Muslims to learn and increase their knowledge. In this respect, Humayun Kabir observes that, while prior to Islam most religions had reserved education to the select few, Islam made knowledge mandatory on a universal scale and accessible to all.[31]

If human dignity constitutes the foundation of human rights and is a product of the *fiṭra*, it becomes necessary to determine if the concept of international human rights is different from the concept of them in Islam.

International Human Rights and Islam

It is often advanced in Western scholarship, and in political propaganda, that Islam is incompatible with universal human rights, as adopted by the "civilized" nations, because it embodies major inequalities based on gender and religion, as well as restrictions on freedoms of all types. Unfortunately, these views are generally founded on (1) Qur'anic verses that are mostly distorted, misconstrued, misunderstood, or simply taken out of context; and (2) traditional *fiqh*-generated Islamic law—wrongly termed Shari'a. They are also founded on traditions which are most often wrongly imputed to Prophet Muhammad or that do not constitute part of the universal principles of Islam. Sadly enough, these views are frequently based on, and supported by, statements of current Muslim rulers, scholars, clerics, or political demagogues. But while it is one thing when Western propaganda misperceives Islam or attributes to Islam what is otherwise attributable to the behavior of Muslim peoples and nations, it is less excusable when such views are held and spread by Muslim institutions and scholars.

First it should be made clear that it is unfair and inappropriate, whether on the part of Muslim apologists or their detractors, to compare the detailed principles governing universal human rights—as declared in legal instruments enacted in the twentieth and twenty-first centuries—with Qur'anic verses selected randomly from the Holy Qur'an to determine if Islam and universally recognized human rights are compatible with one another.[32] While international and domestic legal instruments are part of one or more legal and political systems, Islam and the Holy Qur'an are neither a political nor a legal system, and there is no ground of logical comparison between twentieth-century human rights standards and Islamic civilization recalled through fourteen hundred years of Islamic history.[33]

Regardless of the fact that generally accepted human rights enacted by international and domestic legal instruments are described as universal, they remain reflective of the culture prevailing at a specific point in time, in a specific geographic region, including the aspirations toward a universal recognition of such rights. This explains that international institutions and committees were created to promote human rights and widen their scope of acceptance, monitor compliance with them, and prepare for enactment of further instruments improving on the definition and implementation of specific rights.

On the other hand, Islam is universal, revealed for all places and all times, and addressed to all people, without discrimination between believers and nonbelievers. This explains that, despite certain specific rules contained in it that were revealed for a specific purpose and time, the Holy Qur'an embodies a set of general innate guiding principles, readily accepted by people as part of *fiṭra*, which were entrusted by God to humankind, as trustees, to legislate the detailed implementation in each place and time, in accordance with their individual needs.

Looking back, the early Muslims were successful in translating the guiding principles of Islam into a comprehensive legal system, commonly known as Islamic law or wrongly, also, as Shari'a law.[34] That system, as a precursor of modern-day universal human rights, surpassed all other systems at the time recognizing basic freedoms, equality, and justice. All of this helped to win the hearts of people in the lands into which Islam expanded and, in turn, to provide a fertile environment for the rise of Muslim civilization. It is when Muslims failed to periodically update that translation that Muslim civilization fell into a downward spiral. Worse yet, modern-day Muslims went so far as to deny themselves even the right to translate the noble guiding principles of Islam into domestic and international legislation, under the misguided claim that Shari'a law is divine, thus comprehensive and perfect. In this manner, they ignored that the Shari'a that they referred to was not the divine Shari'a as revealed in the Holy Qur'an, but instead the man-made Shari'a law that the early schools of jurisprudence developed after incorporating the Prophetic Tradition, the traditions of the Prophet's companions, and the *ijmā'* (consensus) of the clerics and jurisprudents. Thus, the Shari'a law with which universal human rights are nowadays compared is nothing other than the iteration of the translation of the Qur'anic principles on human rights, made twelve centuries ago. Hence their inability to lead progress in accordance with today's needs, as opposed to the circumstances of days long past.

This should explain the approach here to the subject of human rights in Islam. It is not a commentary on a legal text. Instead, the aim is to describe general principles, place them in context, analyze their scope, then form an opinion as to the extent of their ability, at any given time or in any geographic region, to be translated into domestic laws capable of addressing the ever-changing needs of people in terms of the recognition and protection of human rights.

Reflections on Muslim Handling of Human Rights

Unfortunately, a number of Arab and Muslim countries have a dismal track record on human rights, both in terms of domestic legislation and practice. In defense of that record, political and security considerations are cited, but regrettably too, Islamic Shari'a considerations are advanced. This is not to imply that Arab and Muslim countries are alone in underperformance on human rights. "Western-civilized" (sic) countries share in underperforming on human rights, as well, especially when they lecture the world about human rights and then apply double standards at home and abroad, or support regimes which violate human rights or deny the freedoms of expression and faith to immigrants. However, the difference between the two sides is that on the West's side, it is the practice that lacks and falls short of the adopted legal requirements, whereas on the side of the concerned Arab and Muslim countries, it is primarily the domestic legislation on human rights that is lacking and, as a result, so is the practice.

Thus, the Arab and Muslim nations in question have a distorted perception of human rights following a general misperception of Islamic Shari'a. That perception has led to an exaggerated emphasis on community rights at the expense of human rights, a confusion in the application of domestic law, and a consistent usurpation of people's rights, alleging imperatives of Islamic Shari'a.

Muslim Nations' Perception of Universal Human Rights

While adhering to international conventions and declarations on human rights, a large number of Muslim nations have generally been reluctant to declare their attachment to, and demonstrate their compliance with, such conventions and declarations.[35] They have generally recorded their reservations pertaining to these conventions and declarations, alleging religious considerations derived from the inconsistency of the general formulation of a substantial number of human rights[36] with Islamic Shari'a. For that purpose, they have generally made their adherence subject to the provisions of Shari'a. This is with respect to the various declarations enacted subsequent to the Universal Declaration of Human Rights adopted and proclaimed by the General Assembly resolution 217 A (III) of 10

December 1948 (the Universal Declaration). In witness of that perception of the Universal Declaration, and despite their adherence to it as of 1948, Muslim nations that are members of the Organization of the Islamic Conference have adopted their own declaration of human rights in Islam, otherwise known as the Cairo Declaration of 1990,[37] which implicitly supersedes the Universal Declaration, as far as they are concerned.

The adoption and ratification by Muslim nations of the Cairo Declaration did not result in any improvement in their track record on human rights. While the widespread weakness of due process of law can be blamed for such a state of affairs, the main blame rests with the fact that Islamic Shari'a, according to which all provisions of the Cairo Declaration are to be construed and implemented, is a fluid concept, subject to the most subjective interpretations.

To start with, the Cairo Declaration does not contain a definition of Shari'a. Thus the entire provisions of the declaration are made subject to a law which is not defined. Even the Charter, as the founding document of the Organization of the Islamic Conference, does not contain a definition of Shari'a, nor does the convention on the creation of the Islamic Court of Justice, which is supposed to render judgments in light of Shari'a, provide a definition. As a result, the standard by which the Cairo Declaration is to be implemented must be found in outside sources.

Without prejudice to our understanding of Shari'a as being strictly the body of principles and values embodied in the Holy Qur'an based on which Islamic law was developed by *fiqh*, the common consensus is that Islamic Shari'a consists of "the totality of ordinances derived from the Qur'an and the Sunnah and any other laws that are deduced from these two sources by methods considered valid in Islamic Jurisprudence," as stated in the explanatory note to the Universal Islamic Declaration of Human Rights of September 19, 1981.[38] Thus, according to this definition, Shari'a is a body of laws which is not written anywhere in a unified code that can be reliably consulted when needed. Instead, it is the work of the jurisprudents of *fiqh* who did a great job, in the first three centuries of Islam, in designing a legal system out of the true divine Shari'a, the Prophetic Tradition (with all the issues about its reliability), and the works of other jurisprudents.

There are at least five recognized schools of jurisprudence, both Sunni and Shi'i, whose scholars have endeavored to design legal systems, but whose end results diverge on countless important issues, reflecting the different environments in which each school of jurisprudence arose. Divergences can even be found within the same school of jurisprudence, among its various scholars. Most unfortunate yet is the fact that the state of the law as devised by *fiqh* still reflects the eleventh century when it was decided to put an end to all *ijtihād* activity by jurists. Therefore, what is proposed in the Cairo Declaration is the application of an eight-hundred-year-old legal system to resolve issues of human rights in the twenty-first century. Even with that, we are not sure which school of jurisprudence it is supposed to implement, nor, assuming we knew which one, which jurist's opinion in that school should be followed.

It seems that, certain nations are wrongly hiding behind Islamic Shari'a in order to reject what they call international legislation and Western thought on human rights. Instead, the reality is that, without any direct or indirect implication that Western thought needs necessarily to be emulated, Islam and the divine Shari'a are progressive and can support any schemes for the protection of human rights. All human rights, as framed and articulated by the international conventions, are fully consistent with Islam because nothing in any such international conventions is repulsive to any provision of the Holy Qur'an and any of the higher principles and virtues set forth in it.

Usurpation of Rights and Freedoms Alleging Islamic Imperatives

Besides confusion about the construction and interpretation of the Shari'a, another important consideration that has led to human rights not being given the prominence that they deserve is the mistaken perception that community rights prevail over individual rights. Thus, individual rights are usurped in favor—and for the benefit—of collective rights. This premise should be rejected. While social considerations may justify certain restrictions on the scope of human rights, it should also be clear that the overall interests and welfare of the community do not prevail over the interests of the individuals in that community. Instead, the purpose of any potential restrictions on human rights is ideally to secure the unimpaired enjoyment of freedoms and exercise of rights by each and every other individual in that community. Moreover, the primary interest of the community is to create an environment in which all people can live in dignity, enjoy their freedoms, and exercise their basic rights. This is an immediate corollary of the fact that humanism is of the essence of Islam.

More important, however, is the usurpation of individual freedoms and rights on account of the principle of so-called *sadd al-dharā'i'*, a principle according to which, if a certain action can possibly result in a reprehensible outcome, that action may be banned by way of precaution no matter how remote that outcome may be. It is on that basis that many activities have been prohibited. In fact, most forms of poetry, painting, sculpture, and music have been banned in highly conservative circles on grounds that they constitute potential inlets through which harmful distractions may interfere to mislead the faithful from the worship of God.[39]

Such attitudes lack any basis in fact and function to sedate people just to prevent their minds from potentially being led astray. As far as painting and sculpture are concerned, the further explanation is offered that the painter or sculptor, when they produce an artwork, may experience euphoria for having "created" something, thereby associating themselves to God.[40] Despite the fact that nowhere are such arts prohibited in the Qur'an, it remains that God has not deprived humankind of the power of creation, meaning artistic, literary, and scientific creation using the mind that He endowed humankind with. Doesn't God imply that others can create within their limited sphere when He describes Himself as the best of the Creators, as in Verse Q23:14.

> *Then We turned the sperm-drop into a clot, then We turned the clot into a fetus-lump, then We turned the fetus-lump into bones, then We clothed the bones with flesh; thereafter We developed it into another creature. So, glorious is Allah, the Best of the creators.*[41]

It is on that basis of precaution that women's freedoms have been restricted over time, whether for their access to the workplace, or mixing with men—other than those who fall in the category of *muḥram* (a person whom a woman cannot marry due to proximity of kin relations), among other restrictions. It is presumably because a woman could—when seen by a man—be the subject of desire on his part, leading to possible attack and rape, that she should by way of precaution and in order to prevent such an opportunity from occurring, show as little of herself as possible or simply hide entirely behind her dark cloak or even stay home and not go out.

We cite this particular example because it exemplifies everything which is unreasonable about this theory and its ramifications. In other words, upholding the man-made *fiqh* concept of *sadd al-dharā'i'* is tantamount to legislating for everybody on the basis of the meanest standard of behavior. In fact, in this application, this theory shows contempt for God's creation and ignores the dignity of humankind by: (1) assuming that humankind, and men in particular, are beasts exclusively controlled by their instincts with no consideration for the role of the mind;[42] (2) treating women as *fitna*, that is, as potential causes of temptation and perversion by reference to men, and arbitrarily resolving that it is women instead of men who should hide themselves; and (3) as a result, depriving the economies of Muslim nations of nearly one-half of their productive capacity.

In reality, the theory of *sadd al-dharā'i'* was initially devised by *fiqh* for an entirely different purpose, in the field of commercial transactions, that of preventing people from resorting to legal fictions in order to legitimize a prohibited transaction. Thus, if one resorts to a legitimate transaction in order to achieve the purpose of a prohibited outcome, then that legitimate transaction would not be allowed to produce effects; it would be deemed as null and void.[43] This theory was never intended to be abused in order to deprive people of their human rights and basic freedoms. In retrospect, God kept Satan—the idea of darkness, evil, wrongdoing—active in witness to the freedom of humankind and acknowledgment of the role of the mind, and to help people continuously renew and strengthen their faith. *Sadd al-dharā'i'*, accordingly, will not destroy wrongdoing but will destroy the humanity of those who blindly practice this principle.

From the above, one can conceptualize the strong link between freedom and reason, and the mutual dependence of one on the other. God has blessed the creatures of humankind by blessing them with the mind so that they may act with reason. God gave humankind a tool with which to use the mind and apply reason, and that tool is freedom. As Abdolkarim Soroush points out, "We are impassioned about freedom and consider it the *sine qua non* of humanity because reason and freedom are inextricably intertwined. The absence of one would vitiate the existence of the other. Freedom belongs to the rational human beings."[44] Soroush then alludes to the destructive effects of the concept of *sadd al-dharā'i'*, noting, "[s]ome well wishers of humanity...may make the mistake of resenting freedom because it may allow the forces of darkness and corruption to surround righteousness." Soroush concludes, "This group must realize that denouncing freedom is itself an evil worse than any they might wish to fight. No one who is blessed with foresight and wisdom would rely on evil in order to establish the reign of the good."[45]

The move toward modernity in the field of human rights should not be perceived, as Ann Mayer argues, as a confrontation with Islam but instead as a confrontation with traditionalism. Actually, it is Muslims who should be confronting and rooting out rigid destructive traditions and habits which are construed and claimed as an application of Islam, when in reality such practices run counter to Islam's essence.[46]

Although human rights are innate in human nature and predate religions, they are a secular concept because they are concerned exclusively with relations among humankind in this life. This observation is consistent with the secular nature of Islam according to which God has given to us as human beings our place on this earth and made us trustees. Commenting on Ann Mayer's charge of a lack of comprehensive human rights scheme in Islam, Ahmad Moussalli observes that it would have been sufficient for her to look beyond the provisions of the Holy Qur'an into Prophetic Tradition, the early experience of Muslims, to develop a scheme of rights.[47]

But it is not necessary to develop a comprehensive scheme of rights which is specifically Islamic. It is sufficient that Islamic interpretations encourage and promote—let alone merely not object to—the widest forms of human rights that humans may adopt. Moussalli further criticizes Ann Mayer for considering human rights as universally valid based on the belief in "the normative character of the human rights principles set forth in international law and in their universality." But there is no fault in Ann

Mayer's approach on this point. Islam has a similar perception, too, through the concept of *fiṭra*. Indeed, *fiṭra* is a solid foundation for human rights because it moves the issue from the sphere of religious interpretation to that of secular legislation. What modern thinkers designed as "universal" rights, namely that they are inherent in humanity, God made inherent in his human creation.

As a concept inherent in *fiṭra*, human rights cannot be incompatible with the religions of God. It is futile to attempt to justify every right and its scope against the stipulations of religion. That is why the concept of human rights did not progress as long as thinkers either attacked religion on human rights grounds or attacked human rights on religious grounds. In fact, there are no areas of incompatibility whatsoever between Islam and universally adopted and declared human rights. There is no issue even to perceive them as a modern iteration of the universal principles of Islam.[48] Elucidating the nature of human rights, Mahdi Bazergan underlines their sanctity.

> God bestows both freedom and guidance concerning the consequences of actions. His mercy is infinite and His vengeance great. Thus freedom exists; so do responsibility and restraint. The choice is ours.[49]

CONCLUSION
Recovering the Message:
Reforming Our Perception of God

Calls for the reform of Islam can often be heard from modernist Muslim thinkers. For quite different reasons, similar calls can be heard from non-Muslim thinkers and politicians around the world—especially the Western world. In reality, Islam does not need to be reformed. The Word of God, embodied in the Holy Qur'an, is perfect. It is perfect because it is divine, it is universal, it is secular, and it is progressive. Instead, it is our understanding of Islam that needs reform. What needs to be reformed is our understanding of where Islam can be found. It is necessary to distinguish the human from the divine, because only the divine is perfect. Not only is it perfect, first and foremost it is beautiful.

Khaled Abou El Fadl suggests that this should be our locus: "the search for beauty in Islam—what is beautiful in Islam, about Islam, and in the lives of those who adhere to the Islamic faith." In making this search, he encourages us, it is essential to "take full account of the ugliness that often plagues Muslim realities, and it is through the process of engaging those unseemly realities that the search for beauty takes place."[1]

Only the Holy Qur'an, which contains the verbatim Message of God as revealed to His Prophet Muhammad, is divine. Everything else that comprises the sources of Islam alongside the Holy Qur'an is human. Some of that is beautiful, and some of it is not. Put differently, reform is not about changing, or "updating," Islam. Instead, it is about liberating Islam and Muslims from the "sacralization" of customs, habits, and texts that humans have throughout their history woven around the Holy Qur'an, as the sole divine text. Without diminishing their historical and jurisprudential importance and value, these elements remain in the end human, despite the fact that their subject matter may relate to God. That is why it is essential to desacralize tradition in order to restore to Islam its universal nature and its progressive orientation and impulse. It is this needed step which will enable Muslims to regain the freedom of choice and dignity that God has bestowed on each individual. This may allow relations among humans, as well as those between humans and God, to become more direct, genuine, and honest, and allow humanity a clearer perception of God. In fact, a distorted and blurry understanding of Islam leads to an equally distorted and blurry perception of God. The reform of our understanding of Islam may pave the way to reforming our perception of God.

Love versus Fear of God

Religions are not only about the worship and glorification of God, the Creator. They are first and foremost about the welfare of God's creation. Religious worship and glorification are ways to express gratitude to God for his blessings and creation.[2] Unfortunately, in Islam the accumulated religious literature from the past to now—made up of customs, exegeses, and jurisprudence—has often been used to restrict humankind's relations with God to a fear-based framework of subservience.[3] God is depicted as an Almighty power, watching over people and ready at all times to unleash His wrath at the slightest mistake.[4] This perception of God, inspired by the works of early commentators, gained in credibility and importance, as customs, exegeses, and *fiqh* became sacralized, supplanting the Holy Qur'an as the primary reference for understanding Islam. Muslims were thus being molded into a cast of mind whereby the Word of God had to be handled with care to avoid the Creator's wrath. This explains many of today's attitudes of ultraconservatism, and in reference to *sadd al-dharā'i'* (precaution), among other concepts. In fact, restrictions on freedoms, subservience, and obedience to God, through His presumed representatives among rulers and clergy, are depicted as a small price to pay to prevent God's wrath, following the adage "better be safe than sorry."

In reality, such an attitude and perception of God is what is most inconsistent with the revealed Word of God, the Holy Qur'an. As such, the Holy Qur'an does not call for the fear of, or subservience to, God. Instead, it calls for the love, adoration, and worship of God. It calls for humility and gratitude toward God. Seyyed Hossein Nasr observes that "one of God's Names is *al-Wadūd*, Love, and in the Qur'an there are numerous references to Love, or *ḥubb*"; and he cites several verses from the Holy Qur'an to that effect.[5]

The misperception of God and relations with God starts with serious misconstructions of several basic provisions of the Holy Qur'an, commencing with the verse epitomizing the purpose of creation, Verse Q51:56: "*And [tell them that] I have not created the invisible beings and men to any end other than that they may [know and] worship Me.*"[6] The term in Arabic used in this verse for "worship me" is *ya'budooni,* from the root terms *'abada* and *'abd.* These root terms have several meanings, ranging from service and slavery to idolization, adoration, and worship, and it is unfortunate that commentators have so greatly emphasized meanings associated with the former.

The evidence is overwhelming and unequivocal that, wherever that term was used in the Holy Qur'an to describe the relationship of humankind with God, the reference is to the adoration and worship of God.[7] The plural of *'abd* can either be *'ibād* for worshippers and adorators, or *'abīd* for servants and slaves. In the Holy Qur'an people are consistently referred to as *'ibād,*[8] a clear indication of the considered relationship of love and adoration for God from humankind.[9] Similarly, the difference becomes clearer when we find that such relationship is defined in the Holy Qur'an as *'ibāda,* or worship and adoration, and not as *'ubūdiyya,* or slavery and subservience.[10] Further, Verse Q21:26 expressly clarifies that the term is being used not to humiliate but to dignify humankind: "*They said that the Merciful has begotten a child, say instead they are* honored worshippers."[11] This is consistent with the essential freedom and dignity that underlie God's design in creation, namely to entrust humans with the custody and stewardship of earth and grant them the freedom to fulfill their duties with accountability.

From this perspective, subservience and lack of freedom are inconsistent with accountability for divine justice, without which the Final Judgment becomes irrelevant.[12] Instead of God having created us as slaves for no reason other than to serve him, as claimed by exegetes,[13] He created us to adore and worship him, that is, exclusively to love Him. That difference between the two meanings is decisive and changes entirely the perception of the relation between humanity and God from one of humiliation to one of dignity, consistent with the fact that God has breathed His own spirit into humankind, appointed us as trustees, and ordered the angels to prostrate to humanity, represented by Adam.[14]

The commentators of the early days, followed by many of the *fuqahā'*, clergy, and translators of today, focused on and perpetuated this relationship of humiliation in the service of God.[15] That concept of service and attending to the needs of God is a pagan concept which existed in the *jāhiliyya* society, as it did in other pagan polytheistic societies (such as in the old Egyptian, Roman, and Greek cultures). Nevertheless, it found its way into the understanding of Islam. In the *jāhiliyya* the deities did not exist outside the mind of their suitors. They needed the food, drink, and other paraphernalia to justify and maintain their existence. However, in the context of the unique God, His Message as embodied in the Holy Qur'an is clear about Him. Being the Almighty and perfect, God does not need the services of anyone. Had He been in need, He would have made everyone His slave. Instead, He elected to create humankind to love and adore Him, and for that purpose He endowed them with His spirit. In the end, being in need is an imperfection; and it is inconsistent with the perfection of God. This is what the Holy Qur'an asserts repeatedly, such as in Verses Q51:57 and 58: *"No Sustenance do I require of them, nor do I require that they should feed Me (57). For God is He Who gives (all) Sustenance—Lord of Power—Steadfast (for ever) (58)."*[16] The essence of this is set forth in Verse Q22:64: *"Unto Him belongs all that is in the heavens and all that is on earth; and, verily, God—He alone—is self-sufficient, the One to whom all praise is due."*[17]

Similarly, despite all the calls that we find in the Holy Qur'an to perform prayers in a timely manner, to fast during the month of Ramadan, and perform hajj, God has no immediate need for such rituals. Instead, when we perform them, we do so for our own sake, because we are the ones who need God, and not the other way around. We pray to God to heal our wounds, relieve our hunger, prevent or recover from illness, and to ask for forgiveness when we sin. But, most importantly, we pray to keep from doing wrong: *"Recite, [O Muhammad], what has been revealed to you of the Book and establish prayer. Indeed, prayer prohibits immorality and wrongdoing, and the remembrance of Allah is greater. And Allah knows that which you* do. "[18] We pray to God and thank God as a way to restore the warmth to our hearts and to help us overcome or cope with adversity (*"O YOU who have attained to faith! Seek aid in steadfast patience and prayer: for, behold, God is with those who are patient in adversity."*)[19] Thus we do not pray by way of favor to God but by way of helping ourselves. We fast during the month of Ramadan to heal biological discomforts and because it makes us feel what those who are less fortunate feel. We are then induced to fulfill our duties and obligations to our individual communities. Therefore, God calls on us to perform these duties toward Him as if He needed them, but for the sole purpose of making us more aware of our duties to our fellow humans and to enable us to remember His blessings and bounties. That is why the Holy Qur'an declares that whoever attains the faith, or otherwise performs good deeds, does so for his or her own sake, that is, his or her own good and welfare, all of which earns the rewards of God.[20]

Another misperception of God lies in the prohibition of making, keeping, or displaying pictures or statues of people and animals. Abdelmajid Charfi explains that such prohibition may have been justified in the early days of Islam for fear that idolatry could revive through such pictures and statues, but such prohibition can no longer be justified.[21] To the extent that today's continued attachment to—and imitation of—the past reflects a fear of making a mistake, such attitude totally ignores that divine justice judges primarily our intentions, and that a mistake made in good faith is not punishable.

However, the misconstruction of Qur'anic terminology that has most greatly fostered a perception of fear and terror over that of love of God concerns the concept of *taqwa,* which the Holy Qur'an countlessly calls for. Whereas a derivative verb of that term may mean to beware, the term *taqwa* is essentially about piety and devoutness, and the verb derived from it is about being pious and devout, despite the fact that, at times, it may mean to beware. Again, certain commentators and translators have interpreted that term within a framework of fear and terror of God in an unjustified manner.[22] In the first place, even when *taqwa* may have been understood to mean piety, yet its derivative verb was taken to refer to fear.[23] On the other hand, *taqwa* as a term for piety and devoutness means an internal feeling sustained by love and attachment to God, whereby faith and rectitude become a matter of individual conviction instead of one inspired by awe and fear without true conviction. Asma Barlas writes eloquently of *taqwa* as denoting "the essence of moral personality by orienting us toward God" and defines it as "our willingness to embrace virtue and refrain from evil by exercising our reason, intellect, and knowledge."[24]

A careful reading of the relevant verses of the Qur'an indicates that the term *taqwa* is not used in any context of fear or fear-related circumstances. A typical example can be found in Verse Q58:9 where the term appears side by side with the concept of righteousness (*al-birr*), thereby evidencing that piety is what matches and complements righteousness, and not fear. Verse Q2:177 defines *taqwa* clearly.

> *Righteousness is not that you turn your faces toward the east or the west, but [true] righteousness is [in] one who believes in Allah, the Last Day, the angels, the Book, and the prophets and gives wealth, in spite of love for it, to relatives, orphans, the needy, the traveler, those who ask [for help], and for freeing slaves; [and who] establishes prayer and gives zakah;[those who] fulfill their promise when they promise; and [those who] are patient in poverty and hardship and during battle. Those are the ones who have been true, and it is those who are the righteous.*[25]

God did not call for faith and rectitude out of fear of punishment. He called for faith and rectitude out of conviction so that all actions of people are motivated by a natural penchant for good.

While the primary focus of the Message is one of love and piety, fear-inducing language is nevertheless present in the Holy Qur'an, and that language is encountered in two diametrically opposed circumstances. At one end, it is language intended to warn against God's wrath those who exhibited a rebellious attitude against the Prophet and his companions, and went about fighting them and obstructing their path toward God. However, in most such instances, such language was not intended to spread fear but to convince the perpetrators to refrain from such actions against the Prophet and believers.

Where that language is geared toward the faithful, it is intended to appeal to their humility, and an inner fear mixed with love and gratitude, that is, a form of reverential fear of the type that one might naturally experience toward an elderly loved one to whom one looks up, such as parents, teachers, or other persons who had an important influence in one's life. This feeling is often expressed in the Holy Qur'an by the terms *khushū*[26] and *khishiya* among many other terms, all most often misinterpreted to mean fear and terror of God instead of the reverential fear imbued with piety and love.[27]

The culture of fear unfairly promoted by the interpreters of the Holy Qur'an, and aided by some clergy and others, has resulted in a call to ban most graphic arts (other than calligraphy) and abstain from most music and singing, among other pleasures of life, out of fear of enjoying, or otherwise indulging in, the pleasures of life.[28] For that purpose emphasis is first placed on the verses which highlight the ephemeral nature and futility of this life by comparison to the permanent nature of the other life following the Final Judgment. Then, emphasis is also placed on those verses which contain graphic depictions of the terrors of hell. Finally, and in order not to leave any free time without terror and fear, the traditions attributed to the Prophet and *fiqh* have bridged the gap between the two lives with the so-called fright of the grave (or '*adhāb al-qabr*), according to which the dead experience a torture in their grave while awaiting the Final Day. In reality, and contrary to what we read and hear, the Qur'anic Message in this and in every respect is a balanced one.

Besides the fact that there are no references in the Holy Qur'an which depict or otherwise even discuss '*adhāb al-qabr* or the torture of the grave, the language of the Qur'an encourages people to take full advantage of what life offers in terms of material pleasures of all kinds,[29] provided that one's duties and obligations toward others who are less fortunate are not forgotten and that the role of God in our lives and our welfare is well kept in mind. Stressing the importance of beauty in God's creation, Farid Esack cites His light over the heavens and the earth as expressed in Verse Q24:35.[30] And in Verse 7:32, God warns against any attempts to add to the list of prohibited things so as to obstruct the reasonable enjoyment of the pleasures of life.

> Say: "Who is there to forbid the beauty which God has brought forth for His creatures, and the good things from among the means of sustenance?" Say:

"They are [lawful] in the life of this world unto all who have attained to faith—to be theirs alone on Resurrection Day." Thus clearly do We spell out these messages unto people of [innate] knowledge![31]

In addition, while encouraging people to prepare at all times for the other life, God consistently reminds people not to do so at the expense of their right to enjoy the pleasures of this life. He sums this up in Verse Q28:77: *"But seek, through that which Allah has given you, the home of the Hereafter; and [yet], do not forget your share of the world. And do good as Allah has done good to you."*[32]

The language of the Qur'an is also a balanced language in the sense that, aside from the verses which depict the terrors of hell, there are also countless verses in the Holy Qur'an which depict the joys of Heaven and paradise. In fact, the verses depicting paradise by far exceed those depicting hell, thereby reflecting God's design for His justice to be based on wisdom and reason as opposed to fear, a divine justice which is inspired by infinite compassion.

Divine Justice: Compassion versus Vengeance

The culture of fear generated by the perception of an angry God at all times ready to inflict punishment has also generated a further impression that God is moved by a spirit of vengeance toward anyone who might even take more time than necessary to adhere to the faith, since His vengeance can occur, in His divine sovereignty, at any time, in this lifetime or in the hereafter.[33] In addition, God is allegedly depicted as unpredictable because He keeps repeating that, in His infinite power, He punishes at will anyone as He pleases. Therefore, even the person who adheres to the faith has no guarantee whatsoever of a reward and could still end up standing in line awaiting punishment.

Here, too, as in the case of the fear culture, this perception of a vengeful, unpredictable God does not stand up to scrutiny. First and foremost, God does not rush to punishment whenever a sin or a bad deed is committed. He gives ample time for people to assess and recognize what they did and, eventually, regret their acts and redress their behavior. In this respect, God observes that, if He practiced on-the-spot punishment, no one would be left on earth.[34] Therefore, the opportunity for repentance is an open-ended one, lasting through the final moments of a person's life.[35] It is specifically stated in the Holy Qur'an, by way of general principle, that repentance erases every sin.[36] Then, in almost every verse which warns against certain specific acts or sins, we find the firm promise of forgiveness for those who repent.[37]

It is even expressly stated that on the Day of Judgment, and despite the fact that nothing escapes the watchful eye of God and that He records every action and thought—good, bad, or neutral—of every person, God does not necessarily and automatically hand His judgment down based on a simple balancing of account, by counting the good deeds against the bad ones. While it is certain that a person with more good than bad to his or her credit will be rewarded, the reverse is not necessarily true. In other words, it is not evident that the person who has more bad than good in his or her account will receive the permanent punishment, because, in God's justice, compassion occupies a major space. In His infinite compassion, God has revealed that He forgives almost all sins, leaving very limited instances only outside the scope of His forgiveness.[38] God confirms that He even acts on partial repentance to wipe out all other sins, namely in the absence of individual repentance of each one. In confirmation, God observes that the only sin that He does not forgive outside a clear act of repentance is the sin of association of other deities or things with God.[39]

When discussing divine justice, it is important to keep in mind that God cannot and does not expect perfection from any person for the latter to avoid God's wrath, because perfection is an attribute of God that no one else shares with God. Therefore, divine justice does not set a benchmark derived from a state of perfection of humankind, because otherwise it would cease to be just. Consequently, and contrary to any claims of elitism in setting high, difficult-to-attain standards under divine justice, a person does not need to lead a saint's life in order to claim salvation. In this respect, Seyyed Hossein Nasr rightly observes that "God's Mercy, Compassion, Forgiveness, and Love are mentioned more times in the Qur'an than are His Justice and Retribution."[40]

In the end, God constantly reminds us in the Holy Qur'an of His compassion. Every single sura (chapter) of the Holy Qur'an, except one, begins with the assurance that it speaks *"In the Name of God, the Merciful, the Compassionate."*[41] We are reminded of all the good things that God bestows upon His creatures.[42] We are also reminded not to despair of God's forgiveness no matter what we do: *"Say: 'O my people who have been prodigal against yourselves, do not despair of God's mercy; surely God forgives sins altogether; surely He is the All-forgiving, the All-compassionate"*[43] In fact God has committed Himself to dispense compassion and mercy upon humankind,[44] based on which He makes Himself available to answer the prayers of people,[45] and that is the main purpose of the mission of Prophet Muhammad, as expressed in Verse Q21:107: *"We have not sent thee, save as a mercy unto all beings."*[46] These divine assurances to humankind about God's compassion and mercy, despite the commission of punishable deeds, are intended to exhort humankind to show compassion to fellow humans. Among non-Muslim writers, W. M. Watt is among the few who understood God's Message of mercy and compassion embodied in the Holy Qur'an. He points to the relevant provisions of the Holy Qur'an and concludes that "they are incompatible with the view that the Quran attempted to bring men to accept Islam by describing the terrors of the coming judgment. In such passages there is rather an appeal to men to respond to God's bounty."[47]

Islam versus Istislām

Islam is not about surrender to God's will.[48] Surrender to God's will is not the corollary to the decision of an individual to adhere to the faith and submit to God. No one can reject surrender to God. Given that God's sovereignty is infinite, it extends to all people; and all submit and surrender to God's will, whether they are believers or not. Moreover, because surrender to God relates to God's inherent attributes, Islam is not either about *istislām* (surrender) or an abdication by humankind of their rights and duties to what is wrongly perceived as God's predestination. Whereas God is sovereign and Almighty, yet He did not deprive His creatures of power and wisdom. On the contrary, He endowed humankind with mind, power, and wisdom, and gave them rights and duties to manage their affairs and lives under His watchful, compassionate eye.

Therefore, Islam is about an acceptance of faith in God and in his Will, acting in accordance with his advice and commands. God, in His infinite perfection, does not need anything from humankind other than their adoration and love, in return for which He offers mercy and compassion. Moreover, as the Almighty, God dispenses His blessings upon people, and He makes Himself available to listen and respond to peoples' prayers. He invites people to trust in Him and seek His help.

The call by God to trust in Him and in his compassion is referred to in the Arabic language as *tawakkul*,[49] a term derived from the root term *wakala* which means, among other references, to delegate. But this call to place our trust in God became experienced in reality over time as a state of helplessness and lethargy based on an utmost reliance on God, a state which is expressed in Arabic by the term *ittikāl*, yet another derivative of the root term *wakala*. While the call in the Holy Qur'an for *tawakkul* is a call for placing one's trust in God when seeking His compassionate help after the diligent performance of duties, *ittikāl* is an attitude which takes the form of helpless reliance on God on the part of the seeker.

The culture of *ittikāl* is often nurtured by statements asserting that everything in humankind's life, down to its minutest details, should be regulated by Islam, because in the end this is the primary role of religion. In this respect, it is often observed that since Islam, as a religion, came to improve the lives of humans, it is imperative for it to be able to provide solutions and address all situations which Muslims and our communities face.[50] That culture of *ittikāl* is not appropriate because it is not religion that must respond to developments and solve humankind's problems as they arise. That task is incumbent upon us, if we accept that religion gave us the means, the mind, and the freedom to act. Religion gave us the principles and the ethics, leaving it to us to enact the rules, the laws, and the processes, and to adapt or change them from time to time to foster development. Amir Shakib Arslan articulates this clearly.

> The Quintessence of Islamic teaching is that man should make proper use of his intellect which God has given him as a guiding light to help him think for himself, and that, having done everything in his power, he should resign himself to the Will of God, for the happy fructification of his labor.[51]

The misconstruing of Islam with *istislām* and of *tawakkul* with *ittikāl* has had the damaging effect of subjecting people to rulers and clergy—as translators of the will of God—and to wider global forces, which in turn has fed a state of helplessness among sectors of Muslim societies, impeding progress.[52] Mahmoud Ayoub cites a series of traditions of the Prophet presumably told by Abu Hurayra, and known as *aḥādīth al-shafāʿa*, or the traditions of intercession. According to Ayoub:

> It will be Muhammad who will intercede on behalf not only of the Muslims but the entire world. In a long and dramatic tradition related on the authority of Abu Hurayra we are told that on the day of Resurrection, people will be made to stand for seventy years. They will weep tears, and when their tears run out they will weep blood until the blood shall stop their mouths, and still they will not be judged. Then Muhammad will go and prostrate himself before God and intercede for people, not that they may be given paradise but at least that they must be heard—they must be judged—and hence the judgment begins.[53]

Looking back at such an alleged belief, we realize how the fabrication, intended perhaps to glorify the Prophet, ends up helping to convey a distorted image of God, entirely inconsistent with the essence of God. First, the culture of *shafāʿa* (or intercession) was developed as a means to dominate people by promoting ignorance and helplessness, consistent with the attitude of laying the blame on others in the face of accountability for one's own acts. Second, the culture of *shafāʿa* is an insult to God and to the Prophet, and may entail the sin of *shirk*. Is Prophet Muhammad supposed to tell God what to do? Is God that ugly, unfair, and cruel to call for the Final Day of Judgment, then turn his back on people for seventy years until someone comes to plead with him to render justice? It is the making and perpetuation of such stories and culture that are responsible for a state of helplessness among Muslims. This negative and damaging image of God, His Prophet, and Muslims must be undone. The first step toward that goal is to desacralize Prophetic Tradition, weed out the fabricated elements from it,[54] and restore its meaning and value as a guiding light for progress through *ijtihād*. *Tawakkul* and *Islam* are calls to make the best use of one's mind, while *ittikāl* and *istislām* call for relinquishing the mind and abdicating the will to use it.

Another damaging result of the *istislām* and *ittikāl* mentality is the preference by Muslims for the afterlife, whose pleasures and rewards are real, as opposed to the rewards and pleasures of this life, which are delusory. The pleasures of this life are even said to distort the mind of the believer into trading eternal life for this life and neglecting to prepare for eternity. This attitude has contributed to the evolution of the martyr mentality among some extremists, according to which the sooner this life ends the closer within reach the afterlife becomes. Such a perception, coupled with unfounded interpretations of certain verses of the Holy Qur'an which address the subject of martyrdom (*al-shahāda*),[55] may also have encouraged some to fight, or to recruit fighters, for religiously supported causes, in their quest for a quick transition into the other world through achieving martyrdom. In this respect, it is interesting to note the extent to which the concept of martyrdom has been extended to anyone who dies for any cause which may be linked directly or indirectly to religion. While martyrdom is strictly limited to those who die in fighting those who attempt to restrict one's ability to proceed on the path to God, that is, in defense of one's right to strive toward God,[56] the scope of martyrdom has been extended to include what people consider as fighting for the cause of defending religion, God, and the Prophet. Recruiters have often resorted to works of *fiqh* and justified their acts through Prophetic Tradition, mystifying martyrdom to recruit fighters for all sorts of causes.[57] These are unfortunately typical examples of how religion is abused with fabricated traditions imputed to the Prophet, which hide the beautiful in Islam and portray an ugly image of it.

The Beautiful Names of God

In light of this reformation of our perception of God in which we attempt to shed light on His true image, consider a viewpoint such as the following by Shabbir Akhtar: "Muslims do not see God as their father or, equivalently, themselves as the children of God. Men are servants of a just Master; they cannot in orthodox Islam, typically attain any greater degree of intimacy with their creator."[58] Such a statement ignores the description of the creation by God, according to which God has imported His own spirit into humanity through Adam. It also ignores the fact that God created humankind to adore Him and love Him, both of which constitute the essence of the parent-child relationship, as opposed to a master-slave relationship. What may be true, though, is that, Muslims are impeded in recognizing the beautiful image of God expressly set forth in the Holy Qur'an, as a result of religious education. On the one hand, many people refuse to understand God, His actions and commands, believing that our value system is different from His. We are told that the moral rules and values ordained for the human world are inadequate to coherently understand divine actions.[59] In our opinion, there is no difference between our morality and that of God, because in the Holy Qur'an God appeals to us and to our minds on more than one occasion to ponder His action. God may have reasons to have acted in one way or another that are not always evident to us. But then He often tells us those reasons, and if He does not do so, this should not invalidate our value system or otherwise mean that our system is irrelevant to God, because He ordered it. Surely, He is above it because He is Perfect; yet He does not disown it.

The code of ethics that we are talking about was created by God contemporaneously with the creation of humankind, that is, as part of *fitra*, long before He decided to start sending messengers with divine messages. On the other hand, what is even more limiting is the belief that Muslims may not attain intimacy with the Creator, at a time when God has made Himself accessible to human knowledge through His ninety-nine attributes, referred to as the Beautiful Names of God. Set forth in the Holy Qur'an, they provide insight into the essence of God, stressing the attributes of compassion and mercy which are echoed in the opening of each sura, and the attributes of justice, generosity, and kindness.[60]

Reforming our understanding of Islam and our perception of God is crucial on multiple levels. In the first place, it reflects into our perception of our own selves, in the sense that it can enable each Muslim to achieve inner peace and regain self-confidence, as so eloquently expressed by Malek Chebel: "It is clear that the guilt-inducing morality that we received in childhood is a veritable wall over our conscience that prevents us from being ourselves."[61] In other words, the glorification of God and

His attributes should not translate into contempt for us and humankind, because God's glory is manifested in His creation. On the other hand, the reformation of our understanding of Islam and our perception of God can also lead to the reformation of our own image as Muslims and that of Islam as a whole. As Mohamed Arkoun suggests, "Islam, in these discussions, is assumed to be a specific, essential, unchangeable system of thought, beliefs, and non-beliefs, one which is superior or inferior (according to Muslims or non-Muslims) to the Western (or Christian) system. It is time to stop this irrelevant confrontation between two dogmatic attitudes."[62] Only when our own understanding of Islam has been reformed can we intelligibly interact with, as opposed to entering into a contest against, other cultures.

Recovering the Message

Returning to our initial question, what happened to the Message of God, especially after the divide arose between what God revealed and people received, and what people made of it? Most basically, the Message was usurped by an elite which claimed succession to a mission that had ended long ago with the death of the Messenger, Prophet Muhammad, with the complicity of a religious establishment that was never intended to be.

In his valuable work on prophetic traditions, Daniel Brown asks, "Who speaks for God?" In light of the complexity of the interpretative process, he reviews the spectrum of modern controversies over sunna and *ijmā'*, including the views of those who suggest that it is the learned of the religious establishment who should guard that process, which is then vetted and guaranteed by *ijmā'* or consensus of the learned.[63]

In response to Brown's question of who speaks for God, no one has authority to speak *for* God. Instead, each person is entitled to, and can, speak *with* God. For that reason, the interpretative process need not be conclusive at any point in time, so as to preserve the universal nature of Islam and the humanism inherent in it. Further, to the extent that *ijmā'* may be indicative of some cultural specificities of any society at the relevant time, that *ijmā'* is certainly not that of the 'ulama'. The *ijmā'* that Prophet Muhammad mentioned in certain of his traditions, in the sense of a time-

and place-specific custom-building process as opposed to a normative process, is that of the *umma* as a whole.

Religion is not a science. It is a tool that God has proposed to all people to make them better and to make their world a better place. Because it is a tool meant for all to use, and because the Message is to all people and not solely to an elite, the Message is simple and the tool is an easy one to use. It does not require the study of a science to understand the Message and grasp the tools. Islam is not elitist.

From this perspective, recognizing the universal, secular, and progressive nature of Islam acquires all its importance. This is pivotal, particularly so that Islam may cease to be treated as a mere identity. Instead, Islam should be left to unleash its full potential, both as a religion which promotes and values the direct, unmediated relationship of humankind with God and as a complex, wide-ranging culture open to the others, and which avoids the divisive, defensive pitfalls of identity.[64]

Through secularism, Muslim nations and societies can regain their own paths to progress, consistent with Islam's universal nature. Rules can change without worrying about changing the rules of religion; and changes in political, legal, economic, and social systems need no longer fall under the impossible heading of reforming religion. Moreover, to the extent that the secular nature of Islam is recognized, acknowledged, and implemented, the interpretation of the faith can be democratized. That democratization can be realized by limiting the involvement of religious establishments in government and the law, desacralizing and desanctifying edicts made to address issues no matter how learned the issuer may be, restoring to God His exclusive role of judge and ceasing to usurp that role from Him. God then may be thought of not as a legislator but as a creator, a guide, and a watchful, compassionate, and loving Lord and patron.

The fullest recognition of the universal, secular, and progressive nature of Islam can be made possible only through education: teaching Muslims that we are not the slaves of God, and that our existence is not justified by the need to serve or to protect and defend God. Islamic education needs to focus on teaching our children about their freedoms and their equality with others, as well as teaching them the principles of morality and ethics that characterize the Message. Most importantly, there is a critical need to teach them about—and imbue them with—dignity and self-confidence.

Supported by such education, as Muslims we will then be in a position to end our submission to religious establishments and rulers as an expression of submission to God; to end the quest to subdue 'others' who do not share the faith; to accept pluralism, based on equality and freedom, founded on the trust in—and love of—God. Only then can one turn to God in full confidence to acknowledge His bounties and offer Him genuine praise and thanks through prayer and worship. When religious education has been reformed, then will it be possible to cease seeking to "reform" Islam, as modern-day revivalists call for.[65] Only then will it be possible to realize that it is our understanding of Islam that has been deficient all along; to realize that Islam, as a divine message, has been—and continuously remains—perfect.

Notes

Preface

1. Makarian, *Le Choc Jésus Mahomet*, 56.
2. See Abou El Fadl, "The Ugly Modern and the Modern Ugly," in *Progressive Muslims*, ed. Safi, 34. Abou El Fadl considers this approach to be apologetic. This view appears valid when the sole purpose of such an effort is to condemn, or distance oneself from, specific behaviors. But when viewing Islam and Islamic societies historically and globally, it is critical to distinguish between religion and its adherents.
3. See Arkoun, *Ayna Huwa al-Fikr al-Islami al-Mu'asir*, 109*ff.* Here Arkoun discusses this intellectual methodology.
4. See Noor, "What is the Victory of Islam? Towards a Different Understanding of the Ummah and Political Success in the Contemporary World," in *Progressive Muslims*, ed. Safi, 320*ff.* By way of example, French writer Marie de Solemne concedes: "Let's be frank, for most of us, Westerners, Islam never captivated us as much as from the time it scares us and imperils our moral, economic, and social equilibrium" (Chebel, *Islam et Libre Arbitre*, 13). For a brief but comprehensive overview of the perception of Islam in the West, see Andrea Lueg, "The Perception of Islam in Western Debate," in *The Next Threat*, eds. Hippler and Lueg, 7–31.
5. Prophet Muhammad's legacy and role will be constantly cited throughout this work. For that purpose, the phrase 'Peace be upon Him' will always remain in mind without the need to repeat it each time the Prophet is cited or mentioned.
6. See Hafez, *La Pensée Religieuse en Islam Contemporain*; Filali-Ansari, *Réformer l'Islam?*; Benzine, *Les Nouveaux Penseurs de l'Islam*; Taji-Farouki, *Modern Muslim Intellectuals and the Qur'an*; Enayat, *Modern Islamic Political Thought*; Hamza, *Islam al-Mujaddidin*. These works contain overviews of the courageous ideas advocated by modernists.

Introduction: Myths and Changing Realities

1. See Taha, chap. 5 in *The Second Message of Islam*. Taha attributes universality to the verses revealed in Mecca, thereby excluding the substantive Medinan verses as being circumstantial and having been revealed to address specific events in guiding the footsteps of the Prophet. This view considers only the external meaning and intent of the relevant verses and ignores their universally valid, underlying intended message.

2. See A. Charfi, *L'Islam entre le Message et l'Histoire,* 32*ff.* Charfi provides a description of the environment in the Hijaz and of the predominant role of the *Quraysh* at the start of the Revelation.

3. See Hussain, "Muslims, Pluralism and Interfaith Dialogue," in *Progressive Muslims,* ed. Safi, 252*ff.* Hussain observes that the immediate audience of the Qur'an was familiar with other religions. He offers some examples drawn from actual verses in the Qur'an which assume that the first immediate recipients of the Message were already familiar with the stories of Abraham and his sons, Jesus, Gabriel, Michael, Joseph, and Benjamin, among others from the Old and New Testaments of the Holy Bible.

4. See 'Abdul-Karim, *Quraysh Min al-Qabila ila al-Dawla al-Markaziyya.* 'Abdul-Karim describes the environment in and around Mecca as a context within which the Revelation must be placed and understood.

5. See Wahidi al-Nisaburi, *Asbab An-Nuzul.* This work describes the circumstances surrounding the revelation of certain verses of the Qur'an.

6. Moosa, "The Debts and Burdens of Critical Islam," in *Progressive Muslims,* ed. Safi, 115.

7. Walk, trans., www.altafsir.com. Qaradawi, *Al-Tatarruf al-'Ilmani,* 23. Qaradawi explains this verse as follows: "Shari'a…regulated the rights and obligations within the family, organized all matters pertaining to social exchanges and transactions between people, handled the affairs relating to the administration, the finances…and all matters relating to the rights of the shepherd and the herd, as well as international relations between the Islamic Umma and other nations."

8. Ibid., 44. Qaradawi makes the case against secularism, arguing that it confers upon people, by way of usurpation, powers of legislation which otherwise belong exclusively to God.

9. See M. Charfi, *Islam et Liberté,* 11. Here, Charfi brings attention to the wide divide existing between reality and what is taught in traditional Qur'anic schools.

10. See Zaman, *The Ulama in Contemporary Islam.* This book includes a comprehensive discussion of the role of the religious establishment represented by the "ulama" (religious scholars) through the institution of the *madrasa* (Qur'anic school), generally in Muslim countries but primarily in South Asia.

11. M. Charfi, *Islam et Liberté,* 21.

12. Rahman, introduction to *Islam and Modernity*; A. Charfi, *L'Islam entre le Message et l'Histoire,* pt. 2; M. Charfi, introduction to *Islam et Liberté.* See these works for a general description of what happened since the Revelation that lead to distortion.

13. Fluehr-Lobban, *Against Islamic Extremism,* 55.

14. See A. Charfi, *L'Islam entre le Message et l'Histoire*, 121. Charfi offers a good explanation of how the sacralization of tradition came to be.

15. Sachedina, *The Islamic Roots of Democratic Pluralism*, 13.

16. See Wadud, *Qur'an and Woman*, xi. Wadud illustrates the limitations arising from the *taqlid* (imitation) approach. She explains, "Before new ideas can be accepted, their legitimacy within Islam must be clearly established. Establishing legitimacy is most often achieved by drawing an analogy between the new idea and the preserved tradition as exemplified in cultural practices, [Shari'a] law or text." This insistence on establishing legitimacy outside of the divine source is an obstacle to progress, because that legitimacy is an obsolete legitimacy that has served its purpose at the relevant time. In that sense, legitimacy is not absolute, but rather relative. Legitimacy is a changing concept. As a result, *taqlid* has unnecessarily extended legitimacies beyond their reasonable time frames.

17. Sachedina, *The Islamic Roots of Democratic Pluralism*, 11.

18. See An-Na'im, *Toward an Islamic Reformation,* 2. An-Na'im observes, "The negative constitutional and human rights consequences of Shari'a appear to be entrenched by the assumed religious authority and inviolability of Shari'a. I believe that it is imperative to challenge and modify this assumption if we are to achieve significant improvements in the public policy and practice of Muslim countries. Yet, unless such challenges and modifications have religious legitimacy, they are unlikely to change Muslim attitudes and practice."

19. Akhtar, *A Faith for All Seasons,* 244n75.

20. See Karamustafa, "A Civilizational Project in Progress," in *Progressive Muslims*, ed. Safi, 100–101.

21. Watt and Bell, *Introduction to the Qur'an*, 50; De Prémare, *Aux Origines du Coran*, 57; Caratini, *Le Génie de l'Islamisme*, 204; Nöldeke, *History of the Qur'an*, 443.

22. D. Brown, *Rethinking Tradition in Modern Islamic Thought*, 1.

Part One: The Universal Nature of Islam

1. Barlas, *Believing Women in Islam*, 35.

2. See Muzaffar, "Universalism in Islam," in *Liberal Islam,* ed. Kurzman, 155*ff.*

3. See Qur'an 3:67, 6:163, 10:84, 10:90, 22:78.

CHAPTER 1: ISLAM DID NOT APPEAR IN A VACCUUM

1. The term *Jāhiliyya* appears four times in the Qur'an (3:154, 5:50, 33:33, 48:26). These four verses all refer to the pre-Revelation period when the revealed Truth about the unicity of God was still unknown, without any implication that *Jāhiliyya* was a period of total lawlessness, ignorance, or lack of culture.

For a vivid description of the social and political environment preceding the Revelation and career of Prophet Muhammad, see 'Abdul-Karim, *Quraysh, Minal-Qabila ila al-Dawla al-Markaziyya*. For an overview of the overall environment in and around the Arabian Peninsula during the start of the Revelation, see A. Amin, *Fajr al-Islam*, pt. 1; Shalabi, *Mawsu'at at-Tarikh al-Islami*, 1:81–180; Haykal, *Hayat Muhammad*, 83*ff.*; Hodgson, chap. 1 in *The Venture of Islam*, vol. 1; De Prémare, *Les Fondations de l'Islam*, 3; Lapidus, *A History of Islamic Societies*, 3–20; Caratini, *Le Génie de l'Islamisme*, 1:57.

2. See Hitti, *The History of Syria, Lebanon and Palestine,* 1:416*ff.*; Hitti, *History of the Arabs*, pt. 1; Hourani, *A History of the Arab Peoples*, 7–12. These works contain accounts of the environment in that region on the eve of the advent of Islam.

3. See A. Charfi, *L'Islam entre le message et l'histoire*, 30.

4. Arkoun, *Al-Fikr al-Islami*, 143*ff.*; 'Abdul-Karim, *Al-Judhur al-Tarikhiyya li-l-Shari'a al-Islamiyya*. See these works for a discussion of pre-Islamic customs (including Christian and Jewish customs) that found their way into the Qur'an.

5. See Lings, *Muhammad, His Life Based on the Earliest Sources,* 6–7; Haykal, *Hayat Muhammad,* 112. The Banu Hashim clan was charged with providing food and drink to the pilgrims. The 'Abd al-Dar clan held the keys to the Kaaba and provided other services, including holding the Mecca Assembly on their premises.

6. See Jait, *Fi al-Sira al-Nabawiyya*, 2:100*ff.* These pages provide a more ample discussion of the pre-Islamic hajj institution.

7. 'Abdul-Karim, *Al-Judhur al-Tarikhiyya li-l-Shari'a al-Islamiyya*, 21–29.

8. De Prémare, *Les Fondations de l'Islam*, 188*ff.*

9. 'Abdul-Karim, *Al-Sahaba wa-l-Mujtama'*, 197–217.

10. See 'Abdul-Karim, *Al-Judhur al-Tarikhiyya li-l-Shari'a al-Islamiyya*. This work contains a comprehensive roundup of pre-Islamic customs that found their way into Islam, especially with respect to civic life and dealings among people, including rules and regulations.

11. See Toshihiko, chap. 4 in *God and Man in the Qur'an*; Esposito, *Islam*, 3–5. Toshihiko's *God and Man* contains a comprehensive discussion of the different concepts of Allah among the pluralistic, pre-Islamic society of monotheists, Hanifs, and pagans. Esposito's *Islam* contains a description of the interaction with the monotheisms in and around the Arabian Peninsula.

12. See Qur'an 53:19, 53:20: "*Have you then considered Al-Lât, and Al-'Uzza* [19]; *And Manât, the other third?* [20]" (Muhsin, trans., http://www.quranexplorer.com/Quran/Default.aspx); Qur'an Q71:23: "*And they have said: 'You shall not leave your gods, nor shall you leave Wadd, nor Suwâ', nor Yaghûth, nor Ya'ûq,*

nor Nasr" (Muhsin, trans., http://www.quranexplorer.com/Quran/Default. aspx); Watt and Bell, *Introduction to the Qur'an*, 8.

13. See Andrae, *Les Origines de l'Islam et le Christianisme*, pt. 1. Andrae provides an overview of Christian implantation in the Arabian Peninsula around the start of the Revelation.

14. Ibid., 46*ff.*

15. M. Hussein, *Penser le Coran*, 35.

16. Toshihiko, *God and Man in the Qur'an*, 172.

17. See A. Amin, *Fajr al-Islam*, 201–202; Jait, *Fi al-Sira al-Nabawiyya*, 2:169; Abizaid, *Mafhum al-Nass*, 26–28. Amin's *Fajr al-Islam* and Jait's *Fi al-Sira* make reference to Jewish, Christian and Sabean traditions and myths that have influenced the interpretation of the Qur'an. Abizaid's *Mafhum* makes the case that the divine origin of the Qur'an is not inconsistent with analyzing the text in light of its cultural environment.

18. See 'Abdul-Karim, *Fatrat al-Takwin fi Hayat al-Sadik al-Amin;* Bar-Zeev, chap. 2 in *Une Lecture Juive du Coran*. 'Abdul-Karim's *Fatrat al-Takwin* includes an overview of Prophet Muhammad's interaction with monks and priests of the Christian faith. Bar-Zeev's *Une Lecture* discusses how Western authors who deny the divinity of the Qur'an claim that the Qur'an was authored or inspired (in part or in whole) by the works and teachings of Waraqa Ibn Nawfal and those Levantine monks.

19. Saeed, "Apostasy and Related Concepts," in *Freedom of Religion, Apostasy and Islam*, eds. Abdullah Saeed and Hassan Saeed, 35.

20. See Esack, *Le Coran: Mode d'Emploi*, 65. Esack offers an account of the environment around the time of the Revelation that includes a particularly descriptive passage from Kenneth Cragg's *Readings in the Qur'an*. See also Rahman, *Islam and Modernity*, 5.

21. Ayoub, *A Muslim View of Christianity*, 17. Ayoub cites Qur'an 45:24 as illustration.

22. See Jeffery, *The Foreign Vocabulary of the Qur'an*, 1–41. Jefferey describes how the Arabic language of the Qur'an was influenced by the other languages spoken in the areas surrounding the Arabian Peninsula during the period of the Revelation.

23. M. Charfi, *L'Islam et Liberté*, 94–95.

24. Ibid. 98; Qur'an 25, 32, 35, 36, 41, 26:29.

25. This depiction appears thirty-seven times in the Qur'an, including: 2:25, 3:15, 9:72, 15:45, 18:31, 22:23, 29:58, 44:52, 51:15, 85:11.

26. The implications on interpretation and universality are discussed in Chapter 4 of this book.

27. Filali-Ansari, *L'Islam est-il Hostile à la Laïcité*, 127. While this observation is valid, things changed rapidly when entire tribes converted to Islam, thereby restoring the weight of tribal rules. Hence Medinan verses addressed that fact through solutions based on temporary tolerance and exceptions.

28. See Esack, *Le Coran: Mode d'Emploi*, 82.

29. See Wahidi al-Nisaburi, *Asbab An-Nuzul*. This book cites the circumstances of revelation of each verse of the Qur'an for which specific circumstances could be identified. It does not claim to capture the circumstances of each and every verse. There are many verses, especially in the Meccan period of the Revelation, which were not revealed to address a specific issue or situation. Other verses—Meccan or Medinan—may have been revealed to address a specific occasion, yet the relevant circumstances were not remembered.

30. Akhtar, *A Faith for All Seasons*, 75.

31. H. Amin, *Dalil al-Muslim al-Hazin*, 12. See also 'Ashmawi, *Usul al-Shari'a*, 106*ff.*

32. Qur'an 4:43.

33. See Jait, *Fi al-Sira al-Nabawiyya*, 2:47*ff.* Jait's *Fi al-Sira* contains a more ample discussion of the pre-Islamic institutions of *ghazuw* and *tha'r*.

34. A. Charfi, *L'Islam entre le Message et l'Histoire*, 44–47.

CHAPTER 2: THE HOLY QUR'AN AS THE ESSENTIAL SOURCE OF ISLAM

1. In Arabic, *caliph* means successor, while *caliphate* refers to the state administration that was established following the death of the Prophet, whose chief is the *caliph*. While the term *caliph* initially referred to the successor of the Prophet, it later acquired a more generic meaning: the head of the state established by the Arabian Muslims who first received the Message. However, the *caliph* was never meant to receive divine revelation, because the Qur'an explicitly provides that Prophet Muhammad was the last and final prophet to receive universal revelation. Therefore, the *caliph* simply succeeded the Prophet as a spiritual and temporal leader of the newly formed community of the faithful who accepted the new Message. The first four *caliphs* were among the closest and most faithful companions of Prophet Muhammad who, following his death, laid the foundations of the Islamic state and fulfilled the Prophet's legacy to reinforce the new faith. For this reason, the first four *caliphs* were known as the Enlightened Caliphs (*al-khulafā' al-rāshidūn*). Abou Bakr Al-Siddiq, during his very short term, successfully subdued all movements of collective apostasy (wars of *Ridda*) which appeared following the Prophet's death and threatened the new faith. He also started the geographic expansion

of Islam and tackled military threats posed by the two neighboring empires: the Persian Empire and the Roman Empire. This task was continued by his successor 'Umar Ibn Al-Khattab who, in addition, created the state institutions for the government and administration of the expanding Arab-Islamic Empire. For more details on this period, see Rabbath, *La Conquête Arabe Sous les Quatre Premiers Caliphes*, vol. 1; Caratini, *Le Génie de l'Islamisme*, 373*ff.*; T. Hussein, *Al-Shaykhan*.

2.   In this work, the four Enlightened Caliphs will be referred to by their widely known first names: Abou Bakr, 'Umar, 'Uthman, and 'Ali.

3.   Plural of the term *faqīh*, which means the jurisprudent or scholar who analyzed and interpreted the divine text and Prophetic Tradition, and extracted from them the dogmas and rules for day-to-day life.

4.   See H. Amin, *Dalil al-Muslim al-Hazin*, 12–13.

5.   See Jait, *Fi al-Sira al Nabawiyya*, 2:22; A. Amin, *Fajr al-Islam,* 195. In *Fi al-Sira*—a biography of Prophet Muhammad—Jait asserts that the Prophet personally oversaw the recordation of the Qur'anic verses. He also inconclusively suggests that the Prophet may have had a role in deciding the order in which the verses of the Qur'an ought to be compiled. However, in *Fajr al-Islam,* Amin claims that the Prophet died without having initiated the compilation of the Qur'an.

6.   They were probably kept by the respective scribes who recorded them as uttered by the Prophet upon revelation.

7.   We call it a communal tie, as opposed to a religious tie, because the *umma*, created by Prophet Muhammad and based on the new Divine Message, is not made up exclusively of adherents to the new faith, but includes Christians and Jews as People of the Book. For more information on this topic, see Chapter 7 of this book.

8.   See Rabbath, *La Conquête Arabe Sous les Quatre Premiers Califes*, 1:43; Haykal, chap. 5–10 in *Al-Siddiq Abou Bakr*; Shalabi, *Mawsu'at al-Tarikh al-Islami*, 1:576–583; 'Ashmawi, *Al-Khilafa al-Islamiyya*, 180–186. These works contain further details about the wars of the *Ridda* (or apostasy). 'Ashmawi's *Al-Khilafa* contains a particularly interesting evaluation of the wars.

9.   See Haykal, *Al-Siddiq Abou Bakr*, 281–302; Haykal, *Hayat Muhammad*, 43ff.; Nöldeke, *History of the Qur'an*, 246ff.; Muir, introduction to, chap. 1 in *The Life of Muhammad from Original Sources*; Caratini, *Le Génie de L'Islamisme*, 208*ff.*; Jait, *Fi al-Sira al-Nabawiyya*, 2:22–24. These works contain further details on the initial process of compiling the Qur'an. In *Fi al-Sira*, Jait asserts that Prophet Muhammad had, prior to his death, reviewed the recorded segments of the Qur'an for accuracy and completeness, and decided the order

in which the verses of the Qur'an are compiled. He also refutes claims made by some orientalists that the Qur'an was still being drafted during the Abbasid Caliphate (De Prémare) or that there may have been discrepancies between the 'Uthmān official version of the Qur'an and those of certain Companions (De Prémare and Nöldeke).

10.   See Esack, *Le Coran: Mode d'Emploi, 119ff.;* Shalabi, *Mawsu'at,* 1:617; Jabiri, *Madkhal ila-l- Qur'an al-Karim,* 1:211–222; Nöldeke, *History of the Qur'an,* 2:233*ff.* These works provide accounts of the compilation process of the Qur'an. Esack's description is particularly thorough.

11.   Goldziher, *Madhahib al-Tafsir al-Islami,* 16*ff.* Goldziher discusses the compilations of 'Abdullah Ibn Mas'ud and Ubayy Ibn Ka'b. For potential discrepancies, see 'Abdessalam, *Tasa'ulat Islamiyya,* 14; Sfar, chap. 1 in *In Search of the Original Koran.*

12.   Arkoun, *Al-Fikr al-Islami,* 85*ff.*

13.   See Sfar, *In Search of the Original Koran.* Sfar is one such exception, having devoted the entirety of *Original Koran* to refuting the divine origin thereof and challenging its completeness and accuracy.

14.   T. Hussein, *Al-Fitna al-Kubra,* 1:376–378; Bucaille, *La Bible, le Coran et la Science,* 129*ff.* While the authenticity of certain passages of the Qur'an has sometimes been challenged, only minor segments of the Qur'an could have been involved. Thus, the fundamental rules of the faith and the codes of conduct contained within the Qur'an have never been called into question. Certain researchers have endeavored to establish the authenticity of the entirety of the Qur'anic text, at times using mathematical and other arguments (Ezzeddine, *Inthar min al-Sama',* 313*ff.*). Some orientalists, however, strived to discredit the concept of the authenticity, accuracy, and completeness of the Qur'an embodied in the *Al-Mus'haf al-'Uthmani* (De Prémare, *Aux Origines du Coran*).

15.   See Talbi, "Le Fait Cranique: Nature et Approches," in *Réflexions sur le Coran,* eds. Talbi and Bucaille, 32–41. Talbi offers an overview of how orientalists handled the origins of the Qur'an.

16.   Sfar, *In Search of the Original Koran,* 19.

17.   Nöldeke, chap. 1 in *History of the Qur'an.* See also Watt and Bell, chap. 2 in *Introduction to the Qur'an;* Sfar, chap. 1, 4 in *In Search of the Original Koran.*

18.   Muir, introduction to, chap. 3 in *The Life of Muhammad from Original Sources,* xxviii; De Prémare, *Les Fondations de l'Islam,* 278.

19.   Esack, *Le Coran: Mode d'Emploi,* 24–25, 136–137. For claims about the human origins of the Qur'an, see De Prémare, *Aux Origines du Coran,* 114–115; Sfar, *In Search of the Original Koran,* 75–77, 98; Andrae, *Les Origines de l'Islam et le Christianisme,* pt. 2.

20. See De Prémare, *Les Foundations de l'Islam,* 39. De Prémare cites a quotation from Théophile d'Édesse claiming that Prophet Muhammad discovered the concept of the one and only God as a young man, on his trading trips from Yathrib (the historic name of Medina) to Palestine. In reality, prior to the Revelation, Prophet Muhammad conducted his trading trips out of Mecca. He moved to Medina on the hijra some thirteen years after the start of Revelation when all trading activities were discontinued so he could focus exclusively on the Divine Mission. (The Levant is the region represented by the countries surrounding the Eastern Mediterranean.)

21. See 'Abdul-Karim, chap. 4 in *Fatrat al-Takwin fi Hayat al-Sadiq al-Amin*; Bar-Zeev, *Une Lecture Juive du Coran.* 'Abdul-Karim's *Fatrat al-Takwin* describes the potential role of Waraqa in preparing the Prophet for prophethood. Bar-Zeev's *Une Lecture* portrays the Qur'an as having been entirely pieced together from various Jewish sources. For more information on the latter subject, see De Prémare, *Aux Origines*, 125–127; Nöldeke, chap. 1 in *History of the Qur'an.*

22. Muir, *The Life of Muhammad from Original Sources*, xxviii.

23. De Prémare, *Aux Origines du Coran*, 30–32; Sfar, chap. 2 in *In Search of the Original Koran.*

24. See Suyuti, "Method of Revelation," in *Al-Itqan fi 'Ulum al-Qur'an,* ed. Suyuti; A. Charfi, *L'Islam entre l'Histoire et le Message,* 41; Watt and Bell, *Introduction to the Qur'an;* Sfar, *In Search of the Original Koran,* 19.

25. See Akhtar, *The Quran and the Secular Mind,* 126–131. Here Akhtar refutes the views of Kenneth Cragg.

26. De Prémare, chap. 2 in *Aux Origines du Coran*; Sfar, *In Search of the Original Koran*, 40–48.

27. Qur'an 20:114, 29:50, 75:16–19, 87:6–7.

28. See Jabiri, *Madkhal ila-l-Qur'an al-Karim,* 1:92. Jabiri supports the belief that Muhammad's message as a divine text was revealed to him verbatim. However, he does not believe that the alleged illiteracy of the Prophet is evidence that the Qur'an has divine origins.

29. Ibid., 181–190.

30. See De Prémare, *Les Fondations de l'Islam*, 355n17. De Prémare cites Islamic sources of the classical period who had discussed issues of accuracy and completeness with regard to the Qur'an.

31. De Prémare, *Aux Origines du Coran*, 65, 128–130.

32. Yusuf Ali, trans., http://www.altafsir.com; Qur'an 10:2, 15:14–15, 17:47, 25:8, 34:43, 38:4, 46:7–9, 51:52, 74:24.

33. Asad, trans., http://www.altafsir.com. See also Qur'an 37:36.

34. 'Uthmani, trans., http://www.altafsir.com. See also Qur'an 37:36, 51:52, 52:29.

35. 'Uthmani, trans., http://www.altafsir.com. See also Qur'an 6:25, 25:5–6, 68:15.

36. Yusuf Ali, trans., http://www.altafsir.com. See also Qur'an 25:5–6, 44:13–14, 46:7–9, 74:25.

37. Bahira is one of the Christian monks that Prophet Mohammad met in the monasteries along the trading route to the Levant. Bahira is said to have detected the signs of Mohammad's prophethood the first time he met him as a young adolescent accompanying his uncle on the journey.

38. Asad, trans., http://www.altafsir.com. See also Qur'an 6:50, 7:184, 10:15, 10:37, 23:70, 32:2–3, 34:46, 36:69, 46:8–9, 56:77–80, 69:40–43, 76:23, 85:21–22.

39. See Haykal, *Hayat Muhammad*, 175*ff*. Here Haykal provides a detailed account of that instance. See also Azem's *Dhihniyyat al-Tahrim*, a book entirely devoted to the episode of the satanic verses in conjunction with the condemnation by Ayatollah Khomeini of Salman Rusdhie's novel, *The Satanic Verses*.

40. Dawood, trans., *The Koran*, 238. The circumstances of this verse can be found in Wahidi's *Asbab an-Nuzul*, and the exegeses, Tabari, *Jami' al-Bayan fi Tafsir al-Qur'an*; Zamakhshari, *Tafsir al-Kashshaf*; Tabarsi, *Tafsir Majma' al-Bayan fi Tafsir al-Qur'an*; Qurtubi, *Al-Jami' li Ahkam al-Qur'an*; Ibn Kathir, *Tafsir al-Qur'an al-Karim*; Razi, *Mafatih al-Ghayb, al-Tafsir al-Kabir*.

41. Akhtar, *The Qur'an and the Secular Mind*, 123.

42. See Jabiri, *Madkhal ila-l-Qur'an al-Karim*, 222; A. Charfi, *La Pensée Islamique*, 40. These pages provide a detailed discussion of the areas of potential manipulation of some text of the Qur'an.

43. See Jabiri, *Madkhal ila-l-Qur'an al-Karim, 77ff.*; Shahrour, *Al-Kitab wa-l-Qur'an,* 139. These works discuss whether or not Prophet Muhammad was illiterate.

44. 'Uthmani, trans., http://www.altafsir.com; Qur'an 7:158.

45. Shawwaf, *Tahafut al-Qira'at al-Mu'asira*, 179–189.

46. Shahrour, *Al-Kitab wa-l-Qur'an*, 187–188; Jabiri, *Madkhal ila-l-Qur'an al-Karim*, 185.

47. L. Brown, *God'ed?*, 51*ff*.

48. De Prémare, *Aux Origines du Coran*, 116; Sfar, chap. 4 in *In Search of the Original Koran*.

49. Asad, trans., http://www.altafsir.com.

50. Yusuf Ali, trans., http://www.altafsir.com. See also Qur'an 19:97, 20:113, 26:195, 39:28, 41:3, 42:7, 43:3, 44:58.

51. Asad, trans., http://www.altafsir.com. See also Qur'an 16:103, 41:44.

52. Arberry, trans., http://www.altafsir.com.

53. Muhsin, trans., http://www.quranexplorer.com/Quran/Default.aspx. The translation error on which De Prémare may have relied derives from the Arabic term *tartil* (traditionally referring to a form of Qur'anic chanting) which was used in the highlighted segment of this verse. However, the root of the term in Arabic clearly refers to a string of items which follow each other in a gradual manner. For an analysis of the term *tartil* and its use in the Qur'an, see Shahrour, *Al-Kitab wa-l-Qur'an*, 196–198.

54. L. Brown, *God'ed?*, 127–131.

55. See Jabiri, *Madkhal ila-l-Qur'an al-Karim*, 211*ff*. Jabiri's *Madkhal* discusses this issue at length. For an orientalist's view on this subject, see Nöldeke, chap. 5, 6 in *History of the Qur'an*, pt. 2.

56. Rusafi, *Kitab al-Shakhsiyya al-Muhammadiyya*, 744.

57. See Qur'an 16:98–100. These verses offer good examples of instances in which the Prophet is warned against Satan tampering with the revealed verses (similar to the instance of the satanic verses).

58. See Qaradawi, *Al-'Aql wal-'Ilm fi-l- Qur'an al-Karim*, 289–292. Qaradawi attributes the *i'jāz* of the Qur'an to the fact that it describes facts that were only discovered centuries later. (In Arabic, *i'jāz* refers to inimitable super human qualities.)

59. See Akhtar, chap. 5 in *The Qur'an and the Secular Mind*. This entire chapter is devoted to the subject of the inimitability of the Qur'an from linguistic and artistic perspectives, among others.

60. See Talbi, "Le fait Coranique: Nature et Approches," in *Réflexions sur le Coran*, eds. Talbi and Bucaille, 55*ff*. This work contains an overview of the literature on the concept of scientific *i'jāz* and the excessive efforts of some to explain every scientific development that occurs throughout the Qur'an.

61. See Talbi, *Universalité du Coran*, 41. Prophet Muhammad is reported to have recommended that the Qur'an be read by each person as if it had been directly revealed to him or her.

62. Shahrour, *Al-Kitab*, 58–60, 185–191. See also Jabiri, *Madkhal ila-l-Qur'an al-Karim*, 181–189.

63. Medina is the former town of Yathrib, inhabited by the two feuding tribes of Aws and Khazraj (who early on converted to Islam) and by the Jewish tribes of Banu Qaynuqah, Banu al-Nadir and Banu Qurayza. Medina became known as the City of the Prophet, Medina being the Arabic word for city. The full name of Medina is Al-Madina al-Munawwara, meaning the city illuminated by the light of the Prophet and the Divine Message.

64. The term *ansār* refers to the Muslims of Medina who provided encouragement and support to the Prophet during his divine mission.

65. See Caratini, *Le Génie de L'Islamisme*, 113, 230*ff.*; Jait, chap. 6 in *Fi al-Sira al-Nabawiyya*, vol. 2; Nöldeke, *History of the Qur'an*, 53*ff.* These works contain information on the chronology of the Qur'an. In addition, Jabiri's *Fahm al-Qur'an al-Hakim* provides an exegesis of the Qur'an, with commentaries on its major themes, following the chronology of the Revelation.

66. Most verses from which the jurisprudents of the faith derived the rules of the *Shari'a* (upon which they built Islamic Law) were revealed in Medina when the Prophet was organizing the *umma*, including verses dealing with fighting, about which much is now being written and discussed by Muslims and anti-Muslims, alike.

67. Wahidi, *Asbab An-Nuzul.*

68. Ahmad Amin, *Fajr al-Islam*, 283*ff.*; Shalabi, *Mawsu'at*, 3:182–187.

69. During the Muslim month of Ramadan, *Laylatul Qadr* begins the night of the twenty-seventh, and continues through the day of the twenty-eighth.

70. Esack, *Le Coran: Mode d'Emploi* , 56.

71. 'Abdessalam, *Tasa'ulat Islamiyya*, 265*ff.*

72. See Qumni, *Al-Ustura wa al-Turath*, 251–276. The *fiqh* identifies three subcategories of abrogation of a verse by another verse: verses that were removed from the Qur'an but are still in force and effect; verses that continue to appear in the Qur'an but are no longer in effect; and verses that no longer appear in the Qur'an and are no longer in effect.

73. Khalidi, trans., *The Qur'an*, 457. "*Perhaps God will create affection between you and those among them with whom you were at enmity, for God is omnipotent, and He is All-Forgiving, Compassionate to each (7); As for those who have not fought against you over religion, nor expelled you from your homes, God does not forbid you to treat them honorably and act with fairness toward them, for God loves those who act with fairness (8); God, however, forbids you to ally yourselves with those who fought against you over religion, expelled you from your homes or contributed to your expulsion. Whoso allies himself with them—these are the unjust (9).*"

74. See Qurtubi, *Al-Jami' li Ahkam al-Qur'an*; Suyuti and Mahalli, *Tafsir al-Jalalayn*; Qutb, *Fi Zilal al-Qur'an*. These works contain exegeses of Qur'anicVerse 60:8 (Qurtubi, Suyuti, and Mahalli being among the early commentators, and Qutb being among the contemporary ones), which refer to the various verses appearing in Surat *Al-Tawba*. See also, Tabari, *Jami' al-Bayan fi Tafsir al-Qur'an*; Tantawi, *Al-Wasit fi Tafsir al-Qur'an*. Tabari (an early commentator) and Tantawi (a contemporary commentator) reject the

abrogation of Verse 60:8. For more on this topic, see the discussion of fighting and jihad in Chapter 10 of this book.

75. See Watt and Bell, *Introduction to the Qur'an*, 127; Qur'an 3:96–98, 3:41, 7:35, 7:106, 7:107, 7:132, 7:133, 10:92, 10:101, 11:103, 12:7, 12:35, 12:105, 14:5, 15:81, 17:1, 17:12, 19:10, 19:21, 20:22, 20:23, 20:54, 20:56, 21:5, 21:42, 21:91, 23:30, 23:45, 23:50, 25:37, 26:154, 26:196, 26:197, 27:12, 27:13, 27:93, 29:43, 29:44, 29:50, 30:20–25, 30:28, 34:9, 36:33, 36:37–41, 37:14–15, 40:81, 41:37, 41:39, 41:53, 42:29, 42:32–35, 43:46–48, 45:3, 54:2, 54:13–15, 57:9, 62:2, 79:20. Watt and Bell confirm the meaning of the term *āya* as a sign, except for one or two instances where it may allude to a verse. The term *āya* unequivocally refers to 'proof' or 'a sign' in the verses cited above.

76. See Toshihiko, chap. 6 in *God and Man in the Qur'an*. Toshihiko's *God and Man* provides an overview of the meaning of *āyas*.

77. See Qur'an 2:73, 2:118, 2:164, 2:219, 2:242, 2:266, 3:19, 6:65, 6:97–99; 6:105, 6:126, 7:32, 10:1, 10:5–7, 10:24, 10:67, 13:2–4, 15:75, 15:77, 16:11–13, 16:65–69, 18:17, 20:128, 26:7–8, 27:86, 29:24, 29:35, 30:20–24, 30:28, 30:46, 32:24, 32:26, 39:42, 39:52, 41:3, 41:53, 45:4–5, 45:13, 51:20–21, 51:37, 57:17. These verses illustrate the correlation between *āyas* and the use of the mind.

78. Qur'an 2:99, 2:242, 10:1, 10:15, 11:1, 15:1, 19:73, 24:1, 26:2, 28:2, 28:49, 28:50, 28:87, 39:29, 45:5, 45:8, 45:25, 46:7. See also Esack, *Le Coran: Mode d'Emploi*, 90–91.

79. See De Prémare, *Aux Origines du Coran*, 129–130. De Prémare uses this term in the French language to imply that because God does not recite, the Prophet may have had a role in the composition of the Qur'an.

80. Bakhtiar and Abdel Haleem are among the few translators who found it more rational—and rightly so—to use the terms 'recount' and 'relate,' instead of 'recite.'

81. Qur'an 2:106. We have looked at several English translations of this verse. The term *āya* is differently rendered in the various English translations as: 'verse' by Dawood, 'Uthmani, Arberry, and Khalidi; 'message' by Asad; 'revelation' by Pickthall, Yusuf Ali and Abdel Haleem; and 'verse' *and* 'revelation' by Muhsin. Only Bakhtiar's version renders the term as 'sign.' It is also worth mentioning that Yusuf Ali's translation may reveal a completely different understanding of the verse in question, namely that God does not modify His Revelation: "*None of Our revelations do We abrogate or cause to be forgotten, But we substitute something better or similar: knowest thou not that Allah hath power over all things?*"

82. Yusuf Ali, trans., http://www.altafsir.com.

83. See Yusuf Ali, trans., http://www.altafsir.com. Note 2140 accompanies the translations of Qur'an 16:101, 16:102. Yusuf Ali observes, "The doctrine of progressive revelation from age to age and time to time does not mean that Allah's fundamental Law changes. It is not fair to charge a prophet of Allah with forgery because the Message as revealed to him is in a different form from that revealed before, when the core of the Truth is the same, for it comes from Allah."

84. Ibid.

85. See Wahidi, *Asbab An-Nuzul*; Zuḥaylī, *Al-Mawsū'ah al-Qur'āniyyah al-Muyassarah*, 339; Kathir, *Tafsir al-Qur'an al-Karim*; Suyuti and Mahalli, *Tafsir al-Jalalayn*; Tabari, *Jami' al-Bayan fi Tafsir al-Qur'an*; Qurtubi, *Al-Jami' li Ahkam al-Qur'an*.

86. See Ezzeddine, *Din al-Sultan*, 636*ff*. Ezzeddine distinguishes between abrogated verses and verses that are "caused to be forgotten" (Verse 2:106), where the former verses are removed entirely from the Qur'an and the latter remain therein but become ineffective. However, Qur'anic verses do not become obsolete under any circumstance. We prefer the approach according to which every word of the Qur'an is and remains indefinitely a live message and in full force and effect, leaving humankind to make the necessary corrections as needed using the faculties that God endowed each person with.

87. Esack, *Le Coran: Mode d'Emploi*, 184.

88. There is a kind of consensus that Shari'a is a legal system which—though not phrased in the form of articles—can readily be converted into codes and articles. This topic is discussed in Chapter 9 of this book. See also M. Charfi, *Islam et Liberté*, 149. Here Charfi describes Mahmud Taha's view on the matter, and in particular his rejection of the abrogation of certain Meccan verses by Medinan verses.

89. Esack, *Le Coran: Mode d'Emploi*, 179; A. Amin, *Fajr Al-Islam*, 231; 'Ashmawi, *Hisad al-'Aql*, 59, 83–85.

90. See Ezzeddine, *Inthar Min al-Sama'*, 437–449. Ezzedine distinguishes between two types of verses. First, the verses containing the Truth which are for that reason permanent and eternal, and not subject to any abrogation, and second, the verses containing the Message—namely the rules of worship and personal conduct. According to Ezzedine, this second type of verse is subject to abrogation because presumably God has followed a gradual approach in imposing changes. Thus, the stricter verses abrogate the more lenient ones.

91. See Jabiri, *Al-Din wa al-Dawla*. Jabiri uses the concept of 'gradualism' in legislation to propose his theory of relativity in the application of Shari'a. For more information on this subject, see Chapter 9 of this book.

92. Dawood, trans., *The Koran*, 32.

93. Ibid., 64.
94. Ibid., 89.
95. Ibid., 26.
96. Ibid., 79.
97. The text of this Qur'anic verse is almost identical to Qur'anic Verse 2:173.
98. See Shahrour, *Tajfif Manabi' al-Irhab*, 38–39. Shahrour strongly rejects the concept of abrogation of God's verses.
99. De Prémare, *Aux Origines du Coran*, 120–124.
100. This consensus is not absolute among earlier commentators or contemporary scholars.
101. See Caratini, *Le Génie de l'Islamisme*, 111. Caratini observes that 86 of the 114 *sūrats* were revealed in Mecca.
102. Taha, *Al-Risala al-Thaniya min al-Islam*, 5–6. Taha's views on this matter are understandable because it is inconceivable that a substantial number of verses and *sūrats* revealed in Mecca were abrogated in Medina. It is also inconceivable that God would have placed the Prophet in harm's way for the sake of verses that he would abrogate soon thereafter.
103. Ibn Qayyim Al-Jawziyya, *Muftah Dar al-Sa'ada*, 126n2, 127n2.
104. See Qumni, *Al-Ustura wa al-Turath*, 249*ff*. Qumni's *Al-Ustura* illustrates the potential uncertainties and contradictions arising from the several categories and instances of abrogation that were retained by *fiqh*.

CHAPTER 3: THE NATURE AND ROLE OF PROPHETIC TRADITION

1. Mahmassani, *Falsafat al-Tashrī fi al-Islām*, 71; Fawzi, *Tadwin al-Sunna*, 30.
2. See Hammami, *Islam al-Fuqaha'*, 55–63. These pages contain a brief overview of the evolution of Prophetic Tradition as a primary source.
3. Esposito and Mogahed, *Who Speaks for Islam*, 10–11.
4. Lings, *Muhammad*, 25, 26; D. Brown, *Rethinking Tradition in Modern Islamic Thought*, 60; M. Hussein, *Al-Sira*, 205. Haykal, *Hayat Muhammad*, 127–129. Here Haykal cites but refutes this episode. For further discussion of this episode, see Rusafi, *Kitab al-Shakhsiyya al-Muhammadiyya*, 101*ff*.
5. Lings, *Muhammad*, 29–30; Haykal, *Hayat Muhammad*, 131. For similar stories picked from the traditional *sīra* books, see Esack, *Le Coran Mode d'Emploi*, 169; Caratini, *Le Genie de l'Islamisme*, 104–105; M. Hussein, *Al-Sira*, 201*ff*.
6. Hoffman, *Al-Islam ka-Badil*, 45.
7. See Watt and Bell, *Introduction to the Qur'an*, 34; Talbi, *L'Universalité du Coran*, 10–12; Jait, *Fi al-Sira al-Nabawiyya*, 1:44; Rusafi, *Al-Shakhsiyya al-Muhammadiyya*, 166–172.

8. See Jait, *Fi al-Sira al-Nabawiyya*, 1:71. With respect to the sacralization of Prophet Muhammad, Jait observes, "The status of Prophet Muhammad in Islamic civilization rose to the extent that Muslims invented miracles for him notwithstanding that the Qur'an keeps denying any such miracles and stressing on his human nature."

9. Haykal, *Hayat Muhammad*, 197–199.

10. See B. Lewis, *Islam*, 1:xviii.

11. Shafi'i, *Al-Risala*, 84–86, nos. 279–285; Hourani, *A History of the Arab Peoples*, 67–68; Esack, *Le Coran: Mode d'Emploi*, 165; A. Charfi, *La Pensée Islamique: Rupture et Fidélité*, 75.

12. See A. H. al-Ghazali, *Al-Mustasfa fi 'Ilm al-Usul*, 99–103; Ibn Hazm al-Andalusi, *Al-Ihkam Li Usul Al-Ahkam*, vol. 1, no. 93; D. Brown, *Rethinking Tradition in Modern Islamic Thought*, 51–52.

13. Shawwaf, *Tahafut "al-Qira'at al-Mu'asira,"* 201; Zamakhshari, *Tafsir al-Kashshaf*; Jaza'iri, *Aysar Al-Tafasir*. With regard to the works of Zamakhshari and Jaza'iri, see the exegeses of Qur'anic Verses 53:3, 53:4.

14. T. Hussein, *Al-Fitna al-Kubra*, 1:228; Hoffman, *Al-Islam ka-Badeel*, 44.

15. John (Gospel) 1.

16. See Mahmassani, *Falsafat Al-Tashrī Fi Al-Islām*, 65. This is the prevailing view in the Maliki, Hanafi, and Ẓāhiri schools of jurisprudence. While Shafi'i has rejected in principle the cross-abrogation between the Qur'an and Prophetic Tradition, he reached a solution confirming de facto abrogation of Qur'anic verses by Prophetic Tradition.

17. See Wahidi al-Nisaburi, *Asbab An-Nuzul*. This text is the main reference book on the circumstances of revelation of Qur'anic Verses. Wahidi (d.1075) recorded these circumstances of revelation from orally transmitted records from the time of revelation. He lived in the fifth century of the Hijra calendar, four hundred years after the death of Prophet Muhammad.

18. See D. Brown, *Rethinking Tradition in Modern Islamic Thought*, 61ff.

19. See Qaradawi, *Kaifa Nata'amalu ma'al-Sunna al-Nabawiyya*, 7, 25–26. Qaradawi's views on the divine origin of Prophetic Tradition are shared by A. H. al-Ghazali, Shafi'i, and Ibn Hazm Al-Andalusi.

20. See Mutwalli, *Mabadi' Nizam al-Hukm*, 71–77. Both the early and contemporary books of *fiqh* are filled with nuances regarding the scope of the Prophet's infallibility and the related scope and binding effect of Prophetic Tradition. However, such nuances are so thin that the end result is acquiescence to the widest possible scope of infallibility for the Prophet and his Prophetic Tradition.

21. D. Brown, *Rethinking Tradition in Modern Islamic Thought*, 62.

22. Ahmad Amin, *Fajr Al-Islam*, 233.

23. See Monneret, *Les Grands Thêmes du Coran*, 150–151; Qur'an 6:50, 10:20, 11:12, 17:59, 20:133, 25:7–9, 29:51, 29:52; A. Charfi, *La Pensée Islamique*, 52–61. Monneret cites the Qur'anic verses listed here as evidence for the human nature of Muhammad, based on the fact that he does not perform miracles. Charfi's *La Pensée* provides additional information on the subject.

24. 'Uthmani, trans., http://www.altafsir.com. See also Qur'an 7:35; 9:128.

25. Khalidi, trans., *The Qur'an*, 49.

26. Dawood, trans., *The Koran*, 49.

27. Khalidi, trans., *The Qur'an*, 103.

28. Ibid., 136.

29. 'Uthmani, trans., http://www.altafsir.com.

30. Khalidi, trans., *The Qur'an*, 229.

31. Yusuf Ali, trans., http://www.altafsir.com. See also Qur'an Q41:6.

32. Dawood, trans., *The Koran*, 328.

33. Ibid., 392. Other translators (including Pickthall, Yusuf Ali, 'Uthmani, Khalidi, Bakhtiar) have used the terms 'unlettered' or 'illiterates' to render the Arabic term *Ummiyyūn*, in the sense that Muhammad was an illiterate, as was the community from which he was selected. Arberry interpreted *Ummiyyūn* to mean 'common people' while Abdel Haleem interpreted it to mean 'people who had no Scripture.' However, Dawood's term, 'Gentiles,' remains the best translation as it reflects the commonality of Muhammad's background as opposed to a chosen people-type background.

34. Haykal, *Al-Siddiq Abou Bakr*, 49.

35. Monneret, *Les Grands Thêmes du Coran*, 150.

36. 'Uthmani, trans., http://www.altafsir.com.

37. See M. Hussein, *Penser le Coran*, 125*ff.* Hussein's *Penser* describes the divine guidance of the Prophet's footsteps and refers to occasional corrections of the Prophet's actions.

38. Dawood, trans., *The Koran*, 371.

39. 'Uthmani, trans., http://www.altafsir.com.

40. D. Brown, *Rethinking Tradition in Modern Islamic Thought*, 62.

41. Watt and Bell, *Introduction to the Qur'an*, 23.

42. An example can be found in *Sūrat 'Abasa* (He Frowned), in which Muhammad is blamed for having acted less than gently with a blind person who came to him seeking assistance. Qur'anic Verses 18:23 and 18:24 offer another example: *"Do not say of anything: 'I will do it tomorrow', without adding 'If God wills'. When you forget, remember your Lord and say: 'May God guide me and bring me nearer to the Truth'"* (Dawood, trans., *The Koran*,

207). When Prophet Muhammad promised to provide divine answers to his audience's questions regarding the story of the people of the cave, revelation stopped for fifteen days. After that, the above verses were received in which God made clear to the Prophet that as a human being with no divine qualities, he was not in a position to make divine promises. Tabari's exegesis, *Jami' al-Bayan fi Tafsir al-Qur'an*, further explains the circumstances of the revelation of *Surat 'Abasa*, as well as Verses 18:23 and 18:24. In another example, when the rich of Quraysh asked to meet with Muhammad alone without his companions who did not descend from rich and noble tribes, God commanded him (in Verse 18:28) to prefer the company of the believers, whether they were rich or poor, noble or ordinary, and not be lured by the company of the rich and prominent: *"And keep yourself (O Muhammad SAW) patiently with those who call on their Lord (i.e., your companions who remember their Lord with glorification, praising in prayers, and other righteous deeds) morning and afternoon, seeking His Face, and let not your eyes overlook them, desiring the pomp and glitter of the life of the world; and obey not him whose heart We have made heedless of Our Remembrance, and who follows his own lusts and whose affair (deeds) has been lost"* (Muhsin, trans., http://www.quranexplorer. com/Quran/Default.aspx). For more examples, see Muhammad, *Mushkilat al-Hadith*, 146*ff.*

43. The scholarship on Prophetic Tradition refers to a category of traditions called *Hadith Qudsi*, which consisted of Prophet Muhammad's verbatim repetition of divine statements.

44. See Esack, *Le Coran Mode d'Emploi*, 173. Esack discusses the perception that Prophetic Tradition confirms the essence of the Qur'an and that the religious life of Muhammad constitutes an interpretation of the Qur'anic message. Such perceptions are widespread among the older (Shafi'i, Ibn Hazm) and newer (Qaradawi) *fiqh* literature.

45. D. Brown, *Rethinking Tradition in Modern Islamic Thought*, 61.

46. Ibid., 50.

47. Jait, *Fi al-Sira al-Nabawiyya*, 1:12.

48. Zurayqi, *Al-Islam fi-l-Madina*, 7.

49. See Qur'an 21:5, 37:36, 52:30, 69:41.

50. See Qur'an 52:29, 69:42.

51. See Qur'an 15:6, 25:8, 26:27, 26:185, 34:43, 37:36, 44:14, 51:39, 52:29, 54:9, 68:2, 68:51, 81:22.

52. See Qur'an 6:25, 8:31, 16:24, 23:83, 25:5, 26:196, 26:197, 27:68, 46:17, 68:15, 83:13, 87:18, 87:19.

53. Watt and Bell, *Introduction to the Qur'an*, 28.

54. See Qur'an, 2:213; 6:48; 16:35; 16:36; 18:56. Verse 40:78 asserts that God has sent numerous prophets and messengers to other populations. However, their names do not appear in the Qur'an.
55. See Qur'an 10:47, 16:36, 16:84, 16:89, 35:24, 40:78.
56. See Qur'an 17:15, 26:208, 26:209, 36:70.
57. See Qur'an 17:106, 27:92.
58. See Qur'an 5:92, 16:35, 16:82, 24:54, 29:18, 64:12.
59. See Qur'an 2:143, 4:40, 4:41, 16: 89, 22:78, 33:45, 48:8, 48:28, 73:15.
60. See Qur'an 2:119, 2:213, 6:48, 6:92, 7:184, 7:188, 10:2, 11:2, 11:12, 13:7, 15:89, 17:105, 18:56, 22:49, 25:56, 26:115, 26:214, 28:46, 29:50, 32:3, 33:45, 34:28, 34:46, 35:23, 35:24, 38:4, 38:70, 41:4, 48:8, 51:50–51, 53:56, 67:26, 74:36. Note also that all three components of the prophetic mission are included in Verses 33:45 and 48:8.
61. Qur'anic verses that discuss Muhammad's mission 'to warn' (revealed in the latter part of the Meccan period and in the Medinan period), came within the context of events which raised the need to remind people of the warnings that Prophet Muhammad was entrusted to deliver.
62. See Qur'an 70, *Sūrat Al-Muddaththir*.
63. Urvoy, *Les Penseurs Libres dans l'Islam Classique*, 24.
64. See Qur'an 5:19, 22:49. These verses were revealed in the later Medinan period.
65. See Qur'an 2:255, 10:3, 19:87, 20:109, 34:23, 43:86, 53:26, 66:8. These verses deal with the topic of intercession.
66. Akhtar, *A Faith for All Seasons*, 200.
67. See Qur'an 2:143, 22:78.
68. Abdel Haleem, trans., *The Qur'an*, 54.
69. Ibid., 132.
70. See Qur'an 4:33, 4:79, 5:117, 6:19, 10.29, 13:43, 17:96, 22:17, 34:47, 41:53, 48:28, 58:6, 85:9.
71. Khalidi, trans., *The Qur'an*, 98.
72. Fluehr-Lobban, *Against Islamic Extremism*, 63; Rahman, *Major Themes of the Qur'an*, 31–32.
73. Qur'an 4:64: "*All the messengers We sent were meant to be obeyed, by God's leave. If only [the hypocrites] had come to you [Prophet] when they wronged themselves, and begged God's forgiveness, and the Messenger had asked forgiveness for them, they would have found that God accepts repentance and is most merciful*" (Abdel Haleem, trans., *The Qur'an* 56–57). While this verse is specific to Prophet Muhammad, there are countless others in which God exhorts the believers to pray to Him on behalf of the self, friends or family,

with the expectation that He would hear them and be benevolent in fulfilling their wishes. See also Qur'an 47:19.

74. See Qur'an 6:94, 7:53, 10:18, 26:100, 30:13, 74:48, 86:10.

75. Qur'an 2:48, 2:123, 2:254, 6:51, 6:70, 32:4, 39:42–44.

76. Dawood, trans., *The Koran*, 325. See also Qur'an 18:26.

77. Qur'an 16:111, 18:26, 39:43, 40:18–20, 82:19.

78. Khalidi, trans., *The Qur'an*, 469.

79. Zuḥaylī, *Al-Mawsūʿah al-Qur'āniyyah al-Muyassarah*, 562.

80. Yusuf Ali, trans., http://www.altafsir.com.

81. See Khalidi, trans., *The Qur'an*, 72; Bakhtiar, trans., *The Sublime Qur'an*, 103; Arberry, trans., http://www.altafsir.com. These three translators all interpreted this term to mean 'intercession.' The same term was rendered as 'mediates' by Dawood , 'speaks for' by Abdel Haleem, 'makes a (good) (bad) recommendation' by 'Uthmani, 'interveneth' by Pickthall, and 'rallies to' by Asad.

82. See Qur'an 2:255, 10:3, 19:87, 20:109, 21:28, 34:23, 43:86, 53:26.

83. See Andrae, *Les Origines de l'Islam et le Christianisme*, 79. While Andrae notes the absence of intercession, he makes an exception for angels because of their exemplary existence and life based on the prima facie sense of the verse without further considering the context in which that exception is made.

84. 'Uthmani, trans., http://www.altafsir.com.

85. Ayoub, *A Muslim View of Christianity*, 10–11. See also Qur'an 16:89.

86. Qur'an 6:70, 50:45, 51:55, 52:29, 80:11, 87:9 87:10.

87. Qur'an 21:107, trans. Arberry, http://www.altafsir.com.

88. Qur'an 10:108, 27:91, 27:92, 39:41.

89. Qur'an 33:45, 33:46: "*Prophet, We have sent you forth as a witness, a bearer of good tidings, and a warner (45); one who shall call men to God by His leave and guide them like a shining light (46)*" (Dawood, trans., *The Koran*, 297).

90. Khalidi, trans., *The Qur'an*, 310–311.

91. See Esack, *Le Coran: Mode d'Emploi*, 115.

92. Sachedina, *The Islamic Roots of Democratic Pluralism*, 96.

93. 'Uthmani, trans., http://www.altafsir.com. See also Qur'an 35:8, 39:41, 42:6, 51:54, 80:7.

94. 'Uthmani, trans., http://www.altafsir.com. See also Qur'an 2:119, 2:272, 3:19, 3:20, 4:80, 6:104, 11:86, 24:54, 42:48, 50:45.

95. Walk, trans., http://www.altafsir.com.

96. Khalidi, trans., *The Qur'an*, 221. See also Qur'an 17:54, 50:45, 53:29, 53:30.

97. Qur'an 3:128, 3:129: "*You have nothing to do with the matter, whether He forgives or torments them, for they are wicked (128). To God belongs what is in the heavens and what is on earth. He forgives whomsoever He wills and He*

torments whomsoever He wills. God is All-Forgiving, Compassionate to each (129)" (Khalidi, trans., The Qur'an, 54).

98. See Qur'an 4:80, 6:66, 6:104, 6:107, 10:108, 11:12, 11:86, 17:54, 39:41, 42:6.

99. Dawood, trans., *The Koran*, 179.

100. Abdel Haleem, trans., *The Qur'an*, 419.

101. Indeed *Sūrat Al-Hajj*, which was revealed around the time of the Prophet's final pilgrimage, contains verses (22:67–69) along the same spirit and line. See also Qur'an 5:92, 5:99 revealed toward the end of the Prophet's life.

102. Dawood, trans., *The Koran*, 297.

103. Qur'an 10:99, 10:100: "*Had your Lord willed, all those on earth would have believed altogether. Would you, then, compel people, so that they become believers (99)? It is not (possible) for anyone that he believes except with the will of Allah (100)*" ('Uthmani, trans., http://www.altafsir.com).

104. See M. Charfi, *Islam et Liberté*, 164–165. Here Charfi discusses and refutes the purported role of the Prophet as an enforcer.

105. Ibid., 163–165.

106. The term *umma* (the community) is not a synonym for the Islamic State. For more information on this topic, see Chapter 8 in this book.

107. Abdel Haleem, trans., *The Qur'an*, 57.

108. While belief in the one God is what bonds the *umma*, the pluralistic nature of Islam (based on freedom of faith) dictates that the *umma* should also welcome nonbelievers into their midst, as long as the nonbelievers are willing to live peacefully with the believers.

109. Khalidi, trans., *The Qur'an*, 89–90.

110. Qur'an 4:65: "*By your Lord they will not be true believers until they let you decide between them in all matters of dispute, and find no resistance in their souls to your decisions, accepting them totally*" (Abdel Haleem, trans., *The Qur'an*, 57).

111. Khalidi, trans., *The Qur'an*, 88.

112. Ayoub, *A Muslim View of Christianity*, 10–11.

113. Coulson, *A History of Islamic Thought*, 58.

114. 'Uthmani, trans., http://www.altafsir.com; Qur'an 4:136, 7:158, 24:62.

115. Dawood, trans., *The Koran*, 371.

116. A. H. al-Ghazali, *Al-Mustasfa*, 102.

117. Ibn Hazm, *Al-Ihkam Fi Usul Al-Ahkam*, pt. 1, no. 93. See also Qaradawi, *Kaifa Nata'amalu ma' al-Sunna al-Nabawiyya*, 35.

118. 'Uthmani, trans., http://www.altafsir.com.

119. See Fawzi, *Tadwin al-Sunna*, 29–36. These pages provide a brief description of the views relating to the scope of the Prophet's deeds and words which constitute universally binding Prophetic Tradition.

120. 'Uthmani, trans., http://www.altafsir.com.

121. *Tafsir al Kashshaf.*

122. *Anwar al-Tanzil wa Asrar al-Ta'wil.*

123. Mafatih al-Ghayb, *al-Tafsir al-Kabir.*

124. *Al-Wasit fi Tafsir al-Qur'an al-Karim.*

125. 'Uthmani, trans., http://www.altafsir.com.

126. See Shahrour, "Islam and the 1995 Beijing World Conference on Women," in *Liberal Islam*, ed. Kurzman, 141.

127. Asad, trans., http://www.altafsir.com. See also Qur'an 5:87, 6:140, 6:150, 7:32, 10:59, 66:1.

128. Qaradawi, *Al-Halal wa-l-Haram,* 75–76, 81, 90–91. Qaradawi offers an extended list of prohibitions, many of which are attributed to Prophetic Tradition.

129. Shafi'i, *Al-Risala*, 32–33nn96–103, 78–79nn252–259; Coulson, *A History of Islamic Law*, 56.

130. 'Uthmani, trans., http://www.altafsir.com. See also Qur'an 2:151, 2:231, 4:113, 62:2.

131. *Jami' Al-Bayan fi Tafsir al-Qur'an.*

132. *Tafsir al-Kashshaf.*

133. *Al-Jami' li-Ahkam al-Qur'an.*

134. *Tafsir al-Qur'an.*

135. Among the *fiqh* scholars, Shafi'i is the leading jurisprudent in advancing the view that the term *hikma* refers to Prophetic Tradition. Because the *hikma*, according to the Qur'an, is divine, Shafi'i was able to assert that Prophetic Tradition is as divine as the Qur'an.

136. *Khawatir Muhammad Mutawalli Sha'rawi.*

137. *Al-Wasit fi Tafsir al-Qur'an al-Karim.*

138. See Muhsin, trans., http://www.quranexplorer.com/Quran/Default.aspx. *"Indeed Allâh conferred a great favour on the believers when He sent among them a Messenger (Muhammad SAW) from among themselves, reciting unto them His Verses (the Qur'ân), and purifying them (from sins by their following him), and instructing them (in) the Book (the Qur'ân) and Al¬Hikmah [the wisdom and the Sunna of the Prophet SAW (i.e., his legal ways, statements, acts of worship)], while before that they had been in manifest error."*

139. 'Uthmani, trans., http://www.altafsir.com.

140. Ibid.

141. See Qur'an 17:39. Zamakhshari and Razi, among others, assert that the term *hikma* refers to important ethical duties (including the Ten Commandments). This is also the view of Shahrour (Shahrour, *Al-Kitab wa-l-Qur'an*, 67).

However, the *ḥikma* could not have referred to Prophetic Tradition because in Qur'anic Verses 31:12, 38:20 and 43:63, there are references to the *ḥikma* having been revealed to Prophets Luqman, David and Moses.

142. 'Uthmani, trans., http://www.altafsir.com.

143. *Al-Tahrir wa al-Tanwir* (commentary on Qur'an 3:164); Qaradawi, *Al-'Aql wa-l-'Ilm fi-l-Qur'an al-Karim*, 196–199.

144. Arberry, trans., http://www.altafsir.com.

145. 'Uthmani, trans., http://www.altafsir.com. See also Qur'an 16:64.

146. *Khawatir Muhammad Mutawalli Sha'rawi*. See also Esack, *Le Coran: Mode d'Emploi*, 189.

147. Coulson, *A History of Islamic Law*, 57; Qaradawi, *Kaifa Nata'amalu ma'al-Sunna al-Nabawiyya*, 65.

148. *Al-Tahrir wa al-Tanwir*.

149. 'Uthmani, trans., http://www.altafsir.com.

150. See M. Hussein, *Penser le Coran*, 30–31. Hussein suggests that the tradition of Qur'anic exegesis was actually initiated by the Prophet when he began answering the questions of his companions regarding the meaning of Qur'anic provisions (a practice which was then continued by the Companions).

151. See Qur'an 2:189, 2:215, 2:217, 2:219–222, 4:176, 5:4, 7:187, 8:1, 17:85, 18:83, 20:105, 79:42. In these verses, God's answers cover a wide range of topics, such as: the Final Day and Final Judgment, prohibited foods and actions, the sacred months, the spoils of war, the essence of the soul, and the mountains.

152. See D. Brown, *Rethinking Tradition in Modern Islamic Thought*, 76. Mawdudi's views are cited here.

153. Shafi'i, *Al-Risala*, 79–85, nos. 258–281; Coulson, *A History of Islamic Law*, 56.

154. This agreement is known as the 'Charter of Medina.' Many historians viewed this charter as the constitution of the first Islamic state.

155. Haykal, *Hayat Muhammad*, 233*ff.*

156. See Haykal, chap. 13, 15, 18–24 in *Hayat Muhammad*; Lings, sec. 42, 43, 51, 52, 66–68, 75 in *Muhammad*; Muir, chap. 12, 14, 19–22 in *The Life of Muhammad from Original Sources*. These works contain detailed accounts of the victory of the Muslims at Badr and the several military encounters that followed (including certain defeats, such as the one at Uhud), all of which culminated in the victorious reentry into Mecca.

157. See Haykal, chap. 14, 16, 18 in *Hayat Muhammad*; Lings, sec. 39, 46, 55, 57, 61, 63 in *Muhammad*; Muir, chap. 13, 15, 17 in *The Life of Muhammad from Original Sources*. These works provide a detailed account of the Prophet's

relationship with the Jews of Medina. See also Qur'an Q24:47–50. These verses define 'hypocrites' as those who declare their belief in Prophet Muhammad's message, then fail to confirm that declaration with the appropriate behavior (namely compliance with the Message and obedience to the Prophet).

158. See Shahrour, *Al-Kitab wa-l-Qur'an*, 549–554. Shahrour made a distinction between the respective implications of these two variations. In one instance (the command to "obey God and the Prophet"), he considered obedience to the Prophet as an adjunct to obedience to God. In the second instance (the command to "obey God and obey the Prophet"), he considered it an attribution of powers to the Prophet so that he may be obeyed with respect to what he commands as if they were divine commands. However, in either case the context does not allow attribution to the Prophet of any rule making prerogatives which survive him. Besides, while the distinction between the respective scopes of Muhammad's roles as prophet and as messenger could theoretically be considered, yet the classification of his respective acts in any of these two categories is not as evident.

159. See Qur'an 4:59–62, 4:64, 8:1, 8:20, 8:45, 8:46, 24:51–54, 33:70, 33:71, 48:17.

160. The contexts of the following Qur'anic verses do not imply any presumed rule making role of the Prophet: 3:31 and 3:32 (basic tenets of God's unicity), 3:132 (prohibition of *riba*), 4:13 and 4:14 (the need to comply with the rules applicable to inheritance), 4:69 and 4:70 (reward for believers who obeyed God and the Prophet), 5:92 (the duty to avoid the risks of alcohol and gambling), 9:71 (hypocrites who do not follow the lead of the Prophet), 24:55 and 24:56 (prayer and *zakat* obligations), 33:64–66 (nonbelievers regretting not having obeyed the commands of God), 58:12 and 58:13 (the ethics of being in the presence of the Prophet).

161. See Qur'an 4:41, 4:42, 4:115, 8:13 8:14, 33:36, 47:32 47:33, 72:20–23.

162. Wahidi, *Asbab An-Nuzul*. Qur'an 8:27: "*O you who believe, do not betray the trust of Allah and the Messenger—and do not betray your mutual trusts, while you know*" ('Uthmani, trans., http://www.altafsir.com). Under another potential scenario for that verse, a person from the Prophet's community may have sent secrets about the Prophet to Abu Sufian, leader of the Meccan polytheists seeking to fight the Prophet (Tabarsi, *Jami' al-Bayan fi Tafsir al-Qur'an*).

163. 'Uthmani, trans., http://www.altafsir.com.

164. See a similar instance in Qur'an 24:63: "*Make not the calling of the Messenger among yourselves like your calling one of another. God knows those of you who slip away surreptitiously; so let those who go against His command beware,*

lest a trial befall them, or there befall them a painful chastisement" ('Uthmani, trans., http://www.altafsir.com). Placed in its proper context, where hypocrites sneaked out from meetings with the Prophet when they did not like what he was saying, this verse is merely about the ethics of not leaving a meeting with the Prophet without his permission. It had nothing to do with compliance with any presumed rule making privileges of the Prophet, as Al Zamakhshari, Ibn Kathir and others seemed to imply.

165. Qur'an 59:7 (Arberry, trans., http://www.altafsir.com). Shawwaf, *Tahafut "al-Qira'at* al-*Mu'asira,"* 201; Qaradawi, *Kaifa Nata'amal ma' al-Sunna al-Nabawiyya*, 35.

166. Classical commentators (Ibn Jureij, Mawardi, and Zamakhshari) and modern-day commentators (Tantawi Sha'rawi, Sayyid Qutb, and Ibn 'Ashour) have read this verse segment out of context and thus identified it as a basic scriptural foundation for the primary role assigned to Prophetic Tradition as the source of Islam. In particular, Sayyid Qutb designed a theory of divine command to comply with everything that the Prophet said, did, and abstained from doing, which constitutes a universal basis of any human legislation, at all times. However, many other early commentators interpreted this verse in its proper context as it relates to distribution of war spoils (Ibn Kathir, Al-Mahalli and Al-Suyuti, Al-Tabari and Al-Razi). Most translators understood and translated this verse in its proper context.

167. Arberry, trans., http://www.altafsir.com.

168. Uthmani, trans., http://www.altafsir.com.

169. See Qur'an 60:4, 60:6. This is another similar instance, in which people are enjoined to follow the good model of Prophet Abraham and his companions in dealing with nonbelievers, and where Abraham had absolutely no rule-making powers.

170. Abdel Haleem, trans., *The Qur'an*, 56.

171. See Watt, *Introduction to the Qur'an*, 29. Here Watt provides commentary on Qur'anic Verses 4:59 and 4:64 (which discuss 'obedience to the Prophet'). Watt equates obedience to the Prophet to obedience to the Message that he carries, thereby negating any obedience to the prophet independent from the Message.

172. 'Uthmani, trans., http://www.altafsir.com.

173. This hadith is reported by Al-Razi in *Tafsir Mafatih al-Ghayb, al-Tafsir al-Kabir.* Then, in Qur'anic Verses 7:157 and 3:31, God encourages people to follow the Prophet's commands relating to prohibited and permitted things (as well as his *amr bi-l-ma'ruf*). The people's obedience regarding the Prophet's command is deemed an expression of love towards God. However, in these

verses, the reference is not to the Prophet's own commands, but to the divine commands that are included in the Message and are conveyed through the Prophet.

174. Zamakhshari (*Tafsir al-Kashshaf*), and Al-Razi (*Tafsir Mafatih al-Ghayb, al-Tafsir al-Kabir*).

175. Ibn Kathir,*Tafsir al-Qur'an al-Karim* (commentary on Qur'an 4:80)..

176. See Esack, *Le Coran: Mode d'Emploi*, 170. Esack discusses an argument, often advanced, that because the Prophet was infallible when conveying the Message, he necessarily remained infallible when explaining the Message. This argument does not hold up for three major reasons. First, Muhammad was an ordinary person; second, Muhammad's infallibility was strictly limited to conveying the Message, and even then, only on a de facto basis; and third, Muhammad's mission did not include explaining or enforcing the Message.

177. See Jamal, *Al-Islam al-Sunni*, 49–69. Jamal's *Al-Islam* provides a general perspective on the issues surrounding Prophetic Tradition.

178. What is true for the Holy Qur'an in terms of accuracy is not necessarily true for Prophetic Tradition, even though Muslims generally perceive Prophetic Tradition as being a true account of the Prophet's words and deeds. In addition to the differences of source and circumstances of recordation, there are other differences between the two primary sources. First, there are major gaps in the respective times of recordation of the Qur'an and Prophetic Tradition; and second, while there is a reasonable consensus regarding the accuracy and completeness of the Holy Qur'an, there is no such consensus regarding the completeness and accuracy of Prophetic Tradition.

179. 717–720 A.D.

180. See Ahmad Amin, *Fajr al-Islam*, 210*ff.*; Bucaille, *La Bible, Le Coran et La Science*, 126; Hamza, *Islam al-Mujaddidin*, 96–97.

181. A. Charfi, *L'Islam entre le Message et l'Histoire*, 177.

182. See Ezzeddine, *Din al-Sultan*, 83*ff.* Ezzeddine discusses the reasons for fabrication of prophetic traditions.

183. See T. Hussein, *Al-Fitna al-Kubra*, 4:228*ff.* It is the case of traditions made up to support the claim that the caliphate must remain in the Quraysh tribe in Mecca and thereby prevent its passage into the hands of other tribes in Medina or of other non-Arab peoples who converted to Islam.

184. Ahmad Amin, *Fajr al-Islam*, 212–213; D. Brown, *Rethinking Tradition in Modern Islamic Thought*, 96–98.

185. See Ezzeddine, chap. 13, 14 in *Din al-Sultan*. These two chapters provide specific examples of traditions which resemble provisions from the Torah and the Gospels.

186. Abu Abdullah Muhammad Ibn Ismail Al-Bukhari, *Sahih Al-Bukhari*; Abul Hussain Muslim al-Nisaburi, *Sahih Muslim*. These are the two compendia that are most widely relied upon by Muslim scholars, each containing over seven thousand traditions.

187. See D. Brown, *Rethinking Tradition in Modern Islamic Thought*, 85. Brown expresses the views of 'Abd al-Mun'im Saleh al-'Izzi, in defense of Abu Hurayrah, a companion of the Prophet and one of the most prolific transmitters of hadith. The Arabic term, *'adāla*, means probity and integrity.

188. Hamza, *Islam al-Mujaddidin*, 101–105.

189. At the other end of the spectrum, for a person to be deemed a companion of the Prophet, he must have closely befriended the Prophet for a sufficiently long and uninterrupted period of time (such as two to three years) and possibly participated in battles. Some also reserved that title for those Meccans who accompanied the Prophet on the hijra to Medina and the *Anṣār* of Medina, thereby excluding all new converts following battles. For an overview of the various views regarding who qualifies for the title of *ṣaḥāba* (companion of Prophet Muhammad), see Fawzi, *Tadwin al-Sunna*, 201–241; 'Abdul-Karim, chap. 1 in *Shadw al-Rababa*, vol. 1; Muhammad, *The Controversy over Prophetic Tradition*, 109; Shawwaf, *Tahafut "al-Qira'at al-Mu'asira,"* 258.

190. Mernissi, "A Feminist Interpretation of Women's Rights in Islam," in *Liberal Islam*, ed. Kurzman, 125; Jamal, *Al-Islam al-Sunni*, 58; H. Amin, *Dalil al-Muslim al-Hazin*, 63.

191. See M. Charfi, *L'Islam entre le Message et l'Histoire*, 140. Charfi cites Sheikh Mahmud Abu Rayya in order to assert that Abu Hurayra's companionship to the Prophet did not exceed three months. Charfi goes on to discuss Abu Hurayra's corrupt reputation during the reign of the first Ummayyad Caliph, Mu'awiya.

192. See Fawzi, *Tadwin al-Sunna*, 206–208. Fawzi provides other examples of reported companions who were too young to have accompanied the Prophet, let alone conveyed his traditions.

193. Ouzon, *Jinayat al-Bukhari*, 20–25; Foda, *Al-Haqiqa al-Gha'iba*, 58–62; Fawzi, *Tadwin al-Sunna*, 210-214. These and other similar stories are included in these references.

194. See H. Amin, *Dalil al-Muslim al-Hazin*, 31*ff.* Amin describes the various storytelling approaches that were adopted in the three most widely recognized biographies of Prophet Muhammad (written by Al-Waqidi, Al-Tabari, and Ibn Hisham, respectively). Amin asserts that certain authors decided to embellish, while other authors presumably stuck to the facts. However, for all practical purposes, that discussion is irrelevant to the essence of the religion as long as we accept that the Prophet is a human being. It is also fair to doubt stories

of the early traditionalists because their accounts were based exclusively on oral accounts passed from one generation to the next. No biographer of the Prophet ever actually knew him. In fact, the earliest biography was written by Ibn Is'haq, who died one hundred and thirty-six years after the death of the Prophet.

195. Caratini, *Le Génie de L'Islamisme*, 94–154; Jait, *Fi al-Sira al-Nabawiyya*, 2:212–213.

196. A. Charfi, *L'Islam entre le Message et l'histoire*, 22–23.

197. A. Amin, *Fajr al-Islam*, 208*ff.*; Ezzeddine, *Din al-Sultan*, 67; Mahmassani, *Falsafat al-Tashrī' Fi al-Islām*, 71*ff.* These references report the text of the tradition in question as follows: "do not write anything which is imputed to me; whoever may have so written anything other than the Qur'an should immediately erase it; however, you may discuss verbally any matter without limitation" (cited by Mahmassani). Proponents of the binding force of Prophetic Tradition cite another tradition in which the Prophet approved the course of action of one of his appointees in the conduct of public affairs—that of emulating the Prophet in the absence of a ruling from the scriptures. This instance does not support any claim about the binding force of tradition, nor does it cast doubt on the prohibition by the Prophet to record his traditions, because the episode is taking place during the lifetime of the Prophet and in a context similar to the one in which the Prophet lived. There is no implication here that the tradition would have universal effect beyond the Prophet's time and context.

198. See Rabbath, *Mahomet Prophète Arabe et Fondateur d'État*; A. Amin, *Fajr al-Islam*, 209. These works contain a detailed history of this period.

199. Ezzeddine, *Indhar min al-Sama'*, 94; *Din al-Sultan*, 591–592.

200. A. Amin, *Fajr al-Islam*, 221.

201. D. Brown, *Rethinking Tradition in Modern Islamic Thought*, 58–59.

202. Ibid., 49. Brown cites claims made by Sayyid Hussein Nasr and Abul A'la al-Mawdudi that the Qur'an cannot be understood without the guiding Prophetic Tradition.

203. See Esack, *Le Coran: Mode d'Emploi*, 184. Esack cites the possibility of abrogation of Prophetic Tradition by verses of the Qur'an. However, God and the Prophet are not equal. When necessary, God corrects the acts of the Prophet but does not abrogate them, because the traditions of the Prophet are not canons.

204. 'Uthmani, trans., http://www.altafsir.com. This verse came in connection with presumed manipulations of divine revelation by the Jews. Yet, the divine prohibition against imputing to God the deeds and words of humans is

universal and was vivid in the minds of the Prophet, his companions, and his successors.

205. 'Uthmani, trans., http://www.altafsir.com.

206. Watt and Bell, *Introduction to the Qur'an*, 86. In Qur'anic Verse 2:106—which is used to support the claim that verses of the Qur'an abrogate other verses rather than divine signs—the divine speech is entirely in the first person and leaves no room for anyone to abrogate other than God.

207. 'Uthmani, trans., http://www.altafsir.com.

208. These are the views of A. H. al-Ghazali, among other early *fuqahā'* and commentators. For further discussions on this matter, see Esack, *Le Coran: Mode d'Emploi*, 173. For a discussion of related contemporary controversies between the schools of Ahli Hadith and Ahli Qur'an, among others, see D. Brown, *Rethinking Tradition in Modern Islamic Thought*, 50ff.

209. A. H. al-Ghazali, *Al-Mustasfa*, 99. This conclusion is reiterated in Ibn Hazm, *Al-Ihkam fi Usul al-Ahkam*; Qaradawi, *Kaifa Nata'amal Ma' al-Sunna al-Nabawiyya*. This conclusion also coincides with the views of the leader of the Maliki school of jurisprudence, and indirectly with those of Shafi'i, who while rejecting in principle the cross-abrogation between Qur'an and Prophetic Tradition, reaches a substantially similar conclusion.

210. D. Brown, *Rethinking Tradition in Modern Islamic Thought*, 73.

211. Among the most important of these compilations are *Sahih Muslim*, *Sahih Al-Bukhari*, *Musnad Ahmad Ibn Hanbal*, *Malik's Al-Muwatta'*, *Sunan Abi Daoud*, *Sunan Ibn Maja*, *Sunan al-Tirmidhi*, and *Sunan Al-Nassa'i*.

212. This category includes proverb-like sayings about moral values and social behavior, among other things.

213. This category includes traditions about the often glorified sex life of the Prophet, as well as bizarre stories about djinns, devils, etc.

214. 'Abdul-Karim, *Shadw al-Rababa*, 3:132.

215. See H. Amin, *Dalil al-Muslim al-Hazin*, 73. Amin lists Ibn Khaldoun, Ibn 'Abd al-Barr, and Al-Nawawi as being among those who insisted on these additional substantive criteria for acceptance of any tradition imputed to the Prophet.

216. Yusuf Ali, trans., http://www.altafsir.com.

217. *Sahih al-Bukhari*, vol. 2 no. 2596; *Sunan Al-Tirmidhi*, vol. 3, no. 2203; *Sunan Abi Daoud*, vol. 2, no. 2881; and Al-Suyuti, *Al-Jami'i al-Saghir*, vol. 2, no. 1758. The consensus over the prohibition of making wills for the benefit of heirs in Islamic law, which has been incorporated into all legislations based on Islamic law, is not entirely based on the cited prophetic tradition. Other schools of law, such as Al-Shafi'i school, based it on the abrogation of the Verse Q2:180 by another later Qur'anic provision, that of Verse Q4:11 which

contains provisions relating to the allocation of the deceased person's estate among his/her heirs, including the parents and nearest of kin mentioned in Verse Q2:180. The argument went that since God has now provided a mandatory preset share to the parents and the close kin (Verse Q4:11), the so-called "command" to bequeath assets to them (in Verse Q2:180) becomes superfluous. This argument does not stand when, legally, the two cited verses are not inconsistent and deal with different legal institutions. In addition, the provisions of Verse Q4:11 expressly state that the rules of distribution set out therein apply only to the assets remaining after implementation of wills, without scope limitations of any kind.

218. He is Malik Ibn Anas al-Asbahi, founder and leader of the Maliki school of thought (also known as the Madhhab).

219. Mernissi, "A Feminist Interpretation of Women's Rights in Islam," in *Liberal Islam*, ed. Kurzman, 119.

220. Ouzon, *Jinayat al-Bukhari*.

221. 'Abdul-Karim, *Shadw al-Rababa*, 3:342–344. The views on the binding force of Prophetic Tradition (and its extension to the traditions of the Companions) remain unsubstantiated.

222. See Goldziher, *Muslim Studies*. Goldhizer devotes an entire chapter to the analysis of Islam's endeavor to abolish—among other tribal customs—tribal allegiance and pride, and to replace it with religious allegiance and pride.

223. While the Message is divine and perfect, Prophet Muhammad was an ordinary human being. Thus, the Prophet's exemplification of the Message would have been subject to normal and expected human failures (some of which God has brought attention to in the Qur'an).

224. D. Brown, *Rethinking Tradition in Modern Islamic Thought*, 68.

225. *Sahih Muslim*, vol. 4, no. 2362; *Al-Jami' al-Saghir*, vol. 2, no. 2570.

226. Ahmad Amin, *Fajr al-Islam*, 232.

227. See Qur'an 5:3: "*This day I have perfected your religion for you and completed My favor to you. I have approved Islam to be your faith*" (Dawood, trans., *The Koran*, 79). This verse is believed to have been revealed following the conquest of Mecca and the Prophet's performance of the final *hajj*. The Prophet died shortly thereafter.

228. It is the confinement of Islam's universal nature to the culture of the early days of Islam that explains why progress in a number of Muslim communities may be stifled. See also the views of Syed Ahmad Khan and Mohammad 'Abdu (summarized on page 64 of Daniel Brown's *Rethinking Tradition in Modern Islamic Thought*), both of whom see the merits of the Prophet's example, but do not attribute to it any binding effect (except for worship related matters). Of these two authors, Muhammad 'Abdu also accepted traditions dealing with

paradise, hell, and the final judgment (see *Risalat al-Tawhid* [*The Theology of Unity*], "Believing the Tradition of Prophet Muhammad" Peace be upon him), 158–159).

229. 'Abdul-Karim, *Shadw al-Rababa*, 1:66.

230. Cited by Mahmassani, *Falsafat al-Tashrī Fi al-Islām*, 71*ff.*

231. See D. Brown, *Rethinking Tradition in Modern Islamic Though*, 67. Here Brown summarizes the similar views held by the Ahl-i-Qur'an group.

232. Abizaid, *Al-Tafkir fi Zaman al-Takfir*, 167.

233. A. Charfi, *L'Islam entre le Message et l'Histoire*, 90–91; D. Brown, *Rethinking Tradition*, 35. Brown's *Rethinking Tradition* contains the views of Syed Ahmad Khan, who dismissed Prophetic Tradition on the grounds that it was unreliable, yet accepted its authority on matters of religion.

234. Shahrour, *Al-Kitab wal-Qur'an*, 549.

235. See Hoffman and Charfi, *Mustaqbal al-Islam fi-l-Gharb wa al-Sharq*, 60–61; Saeed, "Fazlur Rahman: A Framework for Interpreting the Ethico Legal Content of the Qur'an," in *Modern Muslim Intellectuals and the Qur'an*, ed. Taji-Farouki, 44. See also A. Charfi's contribution in Hoffman and Charfi's *Mustaqbal al-Islam*.

236. See A. Amin, *Fajr al-Islam*, 240*ff.* Individual traditions were categorized, depending on their respective subject matters, as binding or nonbinding. It is also in this respect that Prophetic Tradition was considered as a primary source of Islam, but for some, lower in priority to the Qur'an, and for others, equal to it. However, all this becomes irrelevant when Prophetic Tradition is perceived as a methodology as opposed to a set of substantive rules or solutions.

237. See H. Amin, *Dalil al-Muslim al-Hazin*, 74. Amin extends the historical value to made-up traditions because they inform of the political and/or religious circumstances then prevailing which encouraged forgers or politicians to make up—or commission the creation of—prophetic traditions. This is also the case of the modernists of the Indian subcontinent known as the ahl-i-Qur'an, for whom the Qur'an is the only source of faith to the exclusion of Prophetic Tradition. For a discussion on the schools of thought in the subcontinent, see D. Brown's *Rethinking Tradition in Modern Islamic Thought*, 38–39.

238. See M. Charfi, *Islam et Liberté*, 110. "The problem does not lie in their binding force."

239. D. Brown, *Rethinking Tradition in Modern Islamic Thought*, 13.

CHAPTER 4: THE SCOPE OF THE UNIVERSAL NATURE OF ISLAM: ISSUES OF INTERPRETATION

1. Talbi, "Le Fait Coranique: Nature et Approches," in *Reflexions sur le Coran*, eds. Talbi and Bucaille, 68, 71. Talbi explains universality as a continuing

revival of the Revelation—the Divine invitation to ponder the signs being an invitation to observe the universe's continuous revelation.

2. De Prémare, *Aux Origines du Coran*, 101ff.; Nöldeke, *Tarikh al-Qur'an*, 342ff.

3. See D. Brown, *Rethinking Tradition in Modern Islamic Thought*, 74. Brown cites Muhammad Rashid Rida, a pioneer of the era of enlightenment (which stretched from the late nineteenth to the early twentieth century), who wrote (in *al-Manar* 9:926), "It is self-evident to us, and none contests it, that our Prophet Muhammad was sent to all people—those of his own era, both Arabs and others, and those who came after him, until the day of Resurrection." In reality, Rida most likely had in mind that it is the Message that the Prophet carried that was sent to all people of all times and not the Prophet himself, because he died. The nuance between the two is tremendous and explains why the Qur'an is universal and Prophetic Tradition is not.

4. See Fluehr-Lobban, *Against Islamic Extremism*, 6; Lewis, *Cultures in Conflict*, 10. Lewis considers Islam to be universal, noting how it spread among peoples of various geographic regions and races. He contrasts Islam with Christianity, which he perceives to be substantially European. However, Islam is universal primarily because of its content and outlook, rather than its capacity to expand geographically and culturally. Furthermore, Christianity is primarily Middle Eastern in origin and is universal in the sense that it has spread widely across regions and races, thereby transcending its initial audience.

5. In Arabic, *rabbu-l-'ālamīn* as opposed to *rabbu-l-Mu'minīn*. This and other expressions—in which all the beings are addressed—appear countless times in the Qur'an, including Verses 1:2, 2:131, 5:28, 6:45, 6:71, 6:162, 7:54, 7:61, 7:67, 7:104, 7:121, 10:10 10:37, 25:1, 26:16, 26:23, 26:47, 26:77, 26:98, 26:109, 26:127, 26:145, 26:164, 26:180, 26:192; 27:8 27:44, 28:30, 29:10, 32:2, 37:87, 37:182, 39:75, 40:64, 40:65, 40:66, 41:9, 43:46, 45:36, 56:80, 59:16, 68:52, 69:43, 81:29, 83:6.

6. Qur'an, 21:25: "*And [this despite the fact that even] before thy time We never sent any apostle without having revealed to him that there is no deity save Me, [and that,] therefore, you shall worship Me [alone]!*" (Asad, trans., http://www.altafsir.com). Qur'an, 30:47: "*We had indeed sent before you messengers to their people. So they came to them with clear proofs. Then We took vengeance upon those who were guilty; and it was due on Us to help the believers*" ('Uthmani, trans., http://www.altafsir.com). Qur'an 40:78: "*We had sent messengers before you. Among them there are those whose history We have narrated to you, and of them there are those whose history We did not narrate to you. And it is not up to a messenger that he could come up with a sign without permission from Allah. So, when the command of Allah will*

come, matters will stand decided justly, and on that occasion all adherents of falsehood will turn into losers" ('Uthmani, trans., http://www.altafsir.com). Qur'an 57:25: *"We have indeed sent Our messengers with clear proofs, and sent down with them the Book and the Balance, so that people may uphold equity. And We sent down iron in which there is strong power, and benefits for the people; and (We did it) so that Allah knows the one who helps Him and His messengers without seeing (Him)"* ('Uthmani, trans., http://www.altafsir.com).

7.   Arberry, trans., http://www.altafsir.com.

8.   Ibid.

9.   Ibid.

10.   'Uthmani, trans., http://www.altafsir.com.

11.   Ibid.

12.   See Khalayfi, *Al-Islam al-'Arabi*, 10–17. Khalayfi also addresses the controversy of whether Islam is essentially universal or essentially Arab.

13.   See Talbi, "Le Fait Coranique: Nature et Approches," in *Réflexions sur le Coran*, eds. Talbi and Bucaille, 18*ff.*; Akhtar, *The Quran and the Secular Mind*, 160–169. Talbi places the Qur'an in the social and intellectual context of its environment.

14.   Akhtar, *A Faith for All Seasons*, 50.

15.   Saleh, *Al-Islam wa-l-Mujtama' Al-'Asri*, 165–175.

16.   M. Hussein, *Penser le Coran*, 21–22.

17.   Asad, trans., http://www.altafsir.com. Asad has captured the true meaning of the remaining part of this verse, namely that God helps guide those who want to be rightly guided and lets those who chose not to believe go astray. Most other translators went for predestination—in other words, the idea that God picks at his own discretion who will be guided and who will be led astray. This latter understanding linked to predestination contradicts divine justice.

18.   Dawood, trans., *The Koran*, 11.

19.   Yusuf Ali, trans., http://www.altafsir.com.

20.   Walk, trans., http://www.altafsir.com.

21.   Sawma, *The Qur'an Misinterpreted, Mistranslated, and Misread: The Aramaïc Language of the Qur'an*; Luxenberg, *The Syro-Aramaïc Language of the Koran*.

22.   Qur'an 12:2: *"We have sent it down as an Arabic Qur'an, in order that ye may learn wisdom."* (Yusuf Ali, trans., http://www.altafsir.com.) See also Qur'an 13:37; 20:113, 26:195, 39:28, 41:3, 42:7, 43:3, 46:12.

23.   Qur'an 16:103: *"We know indeed that they say, 'It is a man that teaches him'. The tongue of him they wickedly point to is notably foreign, while this is Arabic, pure and clear."* (Yusuf Ali, trans., http://www.altafsir.com.).

24. See Jeffery, *Foreign Vocabulary of the Qur'an*. Jeffery establishes a dictionary of foreign words used in the Qur'an and provides suggested meanings for them, depending on the source of each word. It is true that the surroundings, from the linguistic perspective, cannot be ignored for the proper understanding of the Qur'an. However, caution should be exercised in order to avoid searching for meanings of Qur'anic terms in the original languages from which these terms derive. Instead, because the Qur'an tells us that it is written in clear Arabic language, the meaning of such terms is the one prevailing among the Arabs who accepted and used them. Thus, the interpreter of the Qur'an should, instead of searching for the etymology of foreign words, focus on the sense in which the relevant words were understood and used by the Arabs after they entered the Arabic language.

25. Talbi, *Plaidoyer pour un Islam Moderne*, 55.

26. Khalidi, trans., *The Qur'an*, 424.

27. See Makarian, chap. 4 in *Le Choc Jésus Mahomet*. Makarian cites the works of Luxenberg and De Prémare.

28. Chebel, *Islam et libre Arbitre*, 250.

29. Qur'an 5:3: "*You are forbidden carrion, blood, and the flesh of swine; also any flesh dedicated to any other than God. You are forbidden the flesh of strangled animals and of those beaten or gored to death; of those killed by a fall or mangled by beasts of prey (unless you make it clean by making the death stroke yourselves); also of animals sacrificed to idols. You are forbidden to settle disputes by consulting the Arrows. That is a pernicious practice. The unbelievers have this day abandoned all hope of vanquishing your religion. Have no fear of them: fear Me. This day I have perfected your religion for you and completed My favour to you. I have chosen Islam to be your faith. He that is constrained by hunger to eat of what is forbidden, not intending to commit sin, will find God forgiving and merciful*" (Dawood, trans., The Koran, 79). Note that in this verse, the message relating to the 'perfection of religion' comes at the end of the series of prohibited foods, most of which were already made known to the Hebrews in their own scriptures, thereby including all food-related prohibitions and law-related rules as part of one and the same package, applicable to all humankind.

30. See Qur'an 33:40: "*Muhammad is not a father of any of your men, but he is a messenger of Allah and the last of the prophets*" ('Uthmani, trans., http://www. altafsir.com). 'Uthmani is among the very few translators who represented Prophet Muhammad as the last and final prophet. Most other translators have depicted him in their translations as the 'Seal' of the prophets—a figurative term referencing the seal that closes a document.

31. Akhtar, *A Faith for all Seasons*, 64–65.

32. D. Brown, *Rethinking Tradition in Modern Islamic Thought*, 48.

33. There are several doctrines (including certain Shi'a doctrines) that believe the Qur'an carries two meanings: an outward meaning (*al-ẓāhir*), and a secret inward meaning (*al-bātin*), the latter being accessible only to, and transmitted exclusively among, the Imams commencing with Prophet Muhammad as first holder and revealer of that meaning. Discussion of these doctrines goes beyond the scope of this work. For further details on this matter, see A. Amin, *Fajr al-Islam*, 266*ff.*

34. From a different perspective, the rise of Arab nationalism was initially rejected as un-Islamic on the grounds that it restricts the universality of the Islamic bond. For an overview of the polemic that arose in the Middle East with respect to Arab nationalism from the Islamic perspective, see Enayat, *Modern Islamic Political Thought*, 111–125. For a critique of the elitist perception of Islam as an expression of Arab national identity, see 'Ashmawi, *Al-Islam al-Siyasi*, 149*ff.*

35. Saleh, *Al-Islam Wa-l-Mujtama' Al-'Asri*, 169.

36. Rida, "Al-Khilafa aw al-Imama al-'Uzma," in *Al-Dawla wa-l-Khilafa Fi-l-Khitab al-'Arabi*, ed. Kawtharani, 97, 110–111.

37. Bidar, *Self-Islam*, 44–45.

38. Qur'an 49:13.

39. Qur'an 29:43; 'Uthmani, trans., http://www.altafsir.com. See also 'Ashmawi, *Usul al-Shari'a*, 24–26. 'Ashmawi makes some interesting observations regarding this issue.

40. See Al-Hafiz al-'Iraqi, *Takhrij Ahadith al-Ihya'*, vol.1, no. 2; Al-Suyuti, *Al-Jami' al-Saghir*, vol.5, no. 7838. The English version used herein is a general substantive rendition of the meaning of the Arabic text by the author.

41. H. Amin, *Dalil al-Muslim al-Hazin*, 164–165.

42. See A. Charfi, *La Pensée Islamique: Rupture et Fidélité*, 44–45. Charfi adds to these requirements the need for the consensus of the learned scholars in the time of the interpreter. Such a requirement reduces the accessibility of the Qur'an with regard to ordinary people and contributes to the sacralization of human thought and rigidification of Qur'anic understanding. While a certain level of knowledge may lead to a better grasp of Qur'anic concepts, it should not serve as a deterrent to the ordinary person.

43. Esack, *Le Coran: Mode d'Emploi*, 47.

44. Qur'an 62:2; Dawood, trans., *The Koran*, 392. See also Qur'an 3:138, 16:44.

45. Qur'an 7:52; 'Uthmani, trans., http://www.altafsir.com. See also Qur'an 17:106, 30:58, 39:27, 41:3, 54:17, 54:22, 54:32, 54:40.

46. Qur'an 43:2; Yusuf Ali, trans., http://www.altafsir.com.

47. Qur'an 44:58; 'Uthmani, trans., http://www.altafsir.com. See also Qur'an 12:1, 12:2, 14:4, 22:16, 27:1, 27:2, 39:28, 45:20.

48. Talbi, *Plaidoyer pour un Islam Moderne*, 55–56; Nabulsi, *As'ilat al-Hamqa fi al-Siyasa wa-l-Islam al-Siyasi*, 168–171. Nabulsi's text refers to commentary by Jamal Al-Banna, who advocates setting aside all exegeses of the Qur'an so that each person has the opportunity to understand the Qur'an in his or her own light.

49. See Qur'an 13:16: "*Say, 'Is it that a blind person and a sighted one are equal, or that all sorts of the darkness and the light are alike?'*" and Qur'an 39:9: "*Say: "Are those equal, those who know and those who do not know? It is those who are endued with understanding that receive admonition. It is only the people of understanding who are receptive of the advice*" (Yusuf Ali, trans., http://www.altafsir.com). See also Qur'an 6:50, 65:11.

50. 'Uthmani, trans., http://www.altafsir.com. Note 'Uthmani's scholarly approach in translating this verse, where a controversial term in Arabic is placed within parentheses next to the translated term so as to indicate the lack of consensus on the correct meaning.

51. See Tabari, *Jami' al-Bayan fi Tafsir al-Qur'an*; Qurtubi, *Al-Jami' Li Ahkam al-Qur'an*. Both authors cite a number of companions of the Prophet who made the claim that the *mutashābihāt* verses are among those that have been abrogated by *muḥkamāt* verses.

52. Tabari, *Jami' al-Bayan fi Tafsir al-Qur'an*; Ibn 'Ashour, *Al-Tahrir wa al-Tanwir*.

53. Among the classical exegetes, Ibn Kathir, Zamakhshari, Razi, and Sha'rawi opted for the ambiguous sense of *mutashābihāt* verses. For modern authors who did the same, see A. Amin, *Fajr al Islam*, 197; Jabiri, *Fahm al-Qur'an al-Hakim*, 3:136.

54. 'Uthmani, trans., http://www.altafsir.com.

55. Tabari, *Jami' al-Bayan fi Tafsir al-Qur'an*. The English text is the author's rendition of the original in Arabic.

56. See Jabiri, *Fahm al-Qur'an al-Hakim*, 3:165*ff.*; Shahrour, *Al-Kitab wa-l-Qur'an*, 35*ff.* These works provide a thorough and considered discussion (with examples) of the categorization of Qur'anic verses into *muḥkamāt* and *mutashābihāt*.

57. Zamakhshari, Allousy, and Tabarsi are among the exegetes who included the learned with God, as having access to the interpretation of *mutashābihāt* verses. Jalalayn, Ibn Kathir, Razi, Tabari, Sha'rawi, Tantawi, and Wahidi are among the exegetes who restricted interpretation of *mutashābihāt* verses to God only.

58. See Tabari, *Jami' al-Bayan fi Tafsir al-Qur'an*; Razi, *Mafatih al-Ghayb al-Tafsir al-Kabir*. These authors also cited other stories attributing the context of this verse to arguments with Jews. Qurtubi believes it applies to all those who had beliefs different from those of the Muslims and argued those beliefs by drawing support from the verses of the Qur'an.

59. See Filali-Ansari, *L'Islam est-il Hostile à la Laïcité*, 25, 26; Sachedina, *The Islamic Roots of Democratic Pluralism*, 6. These works discuss the topic of Islam as a civilization.

60. See Hamza, *Islam al-Mujaddidin*, 48*ff.* Hamza provides an overview of modernist thinkers who assert that Islam resides in the Qur'an only.

61. Moosa, "The Debts and Burdens of Critical Islam," in *Progressive Muslims*, ed. Safi, 114–115.

62. Unlike Islam, in non-Protestant Christianity the Church is an institution which claims divine statutory powers and authority with which the faith and its practice are regularly updated. For that purpose, the Church monitors progress of history and civilization and incorporates them from time to time into the general faith and practice, and reissues them officially to be binding on all adherents. Thus, if the Message is the engine of progress in Islam, it is the Church and evolving civilization that are the engines of progress in Christianity.

63. See Rahman, *Islam and Modernity*, 21. Rahman quotes the position of Shatibi.

64. A. Charfi, *L'Islam entre le Message et l'Histoire*, 141.

65. Suyuti, *Al-Jami' al-Saghir*, vol. 2, no. 1604.

66. Soroush, *Reason, Freedom and Democracy in Islam*, 21; Chebel, *Islam et Libre Arbitre*, 233.

67. Abizaid, *Al-Tafkir fi Zaman al-Takfir*, 37; 'Abdul-Karim, *Shadw al-Rababa*, 1:19.

68. Cooper, "The Limits of the Sacred: The Epistemology of 'Abd al-Karim Soroush," in *Islam and Modernity*, eds. Cooper, Nettler, and Mahmoud, 46; Engineer, "Rational Approach to Islam," in *Islam in Transition*, eds. Donohue and Esposito, 136.

69. Esack, *Le Coran: Mode d'Emploi*, 44.

70. D. Brown, *Rethinking Tradition in Modern Islamic Thought*, 101ff.

71. Rahman, chap. 1, 2 in *Islamic Methodology in History*.

72. See 'Ashmawi, *Usul al-Shari'a*, 73.

73. Arkoun, "Rethinking Islam Today," in *Liberal Islam*, ed. Kurzman, 214. The 'unthinkables' referred to by Arkoun should not exist. Everything should be thinkable, including the verses of the Qur'an that God consistently invites us to think about and ponder.

74. A. Charfi, *L'Islam entre le Message et l'Histoire*, 72.

75. Shahrour, "Islam and the 1995 Beijing World Conference on Women," in *Liberal Islam*, ed. Kurzman, 141; Soroush, *Reason, Freedom and Democracy in Islam*, 31.

76. Talbi, *Plaidoyer pour un Islam Moderne*, 48.

77. Muhammad Tawfiq Sidqi, "Islam is exclusively the Qur'an," *Journal al-Manar*, no. 9: 515–525. Sidqi is among the pioneers of the Arab Enlightenment movement of the late nineteenth and early twentieth centuries, and the Journal al-Manar was published by one of the leaders of that movement, Sheikh Muhammad Rashid Rida.

78. See Akhtar, *A Faith for All Seasons*, 75. Here Akhtar raises a similar question.

79. See H. Amin, *Dalil al-Muslim al-Hazin*, 12–13. Amin demonstrates how the Qur'an used the circumstances of the time to illustrate the Message and secure its acceptance, and thereafter transcended them with its universal scope.

80. Qur'an 62:2; Dawood, trans., *The Koran*, 392.

81. See Watt and Bell, *Introduction to the Qur'an*, 4. Watt and Bell cite examples of terminology used in the Qur'an typical of the relevant time's customs and way of life.

82. M. Charfi, *Islam et Liberté*, 144. See also 'Ashmawi, *Al-Islam al-Siyasi*, 51. 'Ashmawi observes that this view is not shared by the majority of traditional *fiqh* who unjustifiably consider that the universality of Islam lies in the conspicuous meaning of each verse, regardless of the specificity of its context.

83. Qur'an, 2:187; 'Uthmani, trans. http://www.altafsir.com.

84. See Nabulsi, *As'ilat al-Hamqa fi al-Siyasa wa-l-Islam al-Siyasi*, 169–170. Nabulsi negates any universality of the Qur'an merely because circumstances have changed since revelation and the external meanings of many verses are no longer relevant. He thus reaches the unfounded conclusion that verses that are no longer relevant should simply be set aside and ignored, provided they can be revived in the future if the circumstances allow it (in light of public interest).

85. Ouzon, *Laffaqa al-Muslimun Idh-Qalu*, 37–38.

86. See A. Charfi, *L'Islam entre l'histoire et le Message*, 186.

87. See Talbi, *Universalité du Coran*, 41.

88. See Sachedina, *The Islamic Roots of Democratic Pluralism*, 16. Sachedina suggests that Muslims should not feel inadequate regarding their reading and understanding of the Divine Message in the absence of the Prophet. In his lifetime, the Prophet did not systematically explain the Message (as this was not part of his prophetic mission). Instead, through his personal human *ijtihād*, he implemented the Message to the best of his abilities in a manner that befitted his time and place.

89. See Qur'an 2:189, 2:215, 2:217, 2:219, 2:220, 2:222, 4:127, 4:176, 5:4, 7:187, 8:1, 17:85, 18:83, 20:105, 79:42. In these verses, God responds to specific questions addressed to the Prophet by his companions for which the Prophet had no answers.

90. A. Charfi, *L'Islam entre le Message et L'Histoire*, 139.

91. Talbi, *Universalité du Coran*, 42.

92. See D. Brown, *Rethinking Tradition in Modern Islamic Thought*, 119. Here Brown cites works by Qaradawi and M. al-Ghazali.

93. Ibid.

94. Rahman, *Major Themes of the Qur'an*, 15.

95. See Qur'an 66:9: "*O Prophet, carry out Jihād (struggle) against the disbelievers and the hypocrites, and be harsh with them. Their final abode is Jahannam (Hell), and it is an evil end*" ('Uthmani, trans., http://www.altafsir. com).

96. Qur'an 5:32: "*For this reason, We decreed for the children of Isrā'īl that whoever kills a person not in retaliation for a person killed, nor (as a punishment) for spreading disorder on the earth, is as if he has killed the whole of humankind, and whoever saves the life of a person is as if he has saved the life of the whole of humankind*" ('Uthmani, trans., http://www.altafsir.com). See also Rahman, *Islam and Modernity*, 144.

97. See A. Amin, *Fajr Al-Islam*, 201. Amin brings attention to the fact that the *jāhiliyya* poetry, and the traditions of the Arabs in the period immediately preceding—and contemporaneous with—the rise of Islam could, together with all the events that accompanied the mission of the Prophet, contribute to a better understanding of the Message, namely its immediate purport and its underlying message.

98. M. Hussein, *Penser le Coran*, 19.

99. Arberry, trans., http://www.altafsir.com.

100. Dawood, trans., *The Koran*, 207.

101. Tabari, *Jami' al-Bayan fi Tafsir al-Qur'an*.

102. Khalidi, trans., *The Qur'an*, 24.

103. Ibn Kathir, *Tafsir al-Qur'an al-Karim*; Suyuti and Mahalli, *Tafsir Al-Jalalayn*; Tabari, *Jami'i al-Bayan fi Tafseer al-Qur'an*; Zamakhshari, *Tafsir Al-Kashshaf*.

104. See Razi, *Mafatih al-Ghayb, al-Tafsir al-Kabir*. This work contains an overview of the various views and nuances surrounding the abrogation of Qur'anic Verse 2:180.

105. See Qur'an 4:11.

106. Suyuti and Mahalli, *Tafsir Al-Jalalayn*; Qurtubi, *Al-Jami' Li Ahkam al-Qur'an*.

107. *Sunan Abi Daoud*, vol. 2, no. 2870.

108. See A. Charfi, *L'Islam entre le message et L'Histoire*, 90–91. Charfi compares the flexibility of the conduct of the Prophet to the rigidity of the views of the *fuqahā'*.

109. See Jabiri, *Fahm al-Qur'an al-Hakim*, 3:213n10. This note contains material on pre-Islamic customs relating to the devolution of the estate.

110. Filali-Ansari, *L'Islam est-il Hostile à la Laïcité*, 129.

111. See Taha, *The Second Message of Islam*.

112. It is important to avoid confusing the terms 'universality' and 'binding effect.' Many verses dealing with a variety of subjects are not binding, yet they are universal. Indeed, the Qur'an brings countless stories of other peoples and accounts involving prevailing customs of the time, all of which are not binding, yet remain universal because the underlying message that they present is relevant for all times.

113. See 'Ashmawi, *Usul al-Shari'a*, 98–99.

114. Qur'an 6:79: "*I have, indeed, turned my face straight towards the One who* created ('faṭara') *the heavens and the earth, and I am not one of those who associate partners with Allah*" ('Uthmani, trans., http://www.altafsir.com).

115. Talbi, *Plaidoyer pour un Islam Moderne*, 77. Talbi even equates *fiṭra* with human nature on page 87. See also Ayoub, *A Muslim View of Christianity*, 13.

116. Abdel Haleem, trans., *The Qur'an*, 258–259. The highlighted phrase in the quoted verse is the translator's rendition of the term *fiṭra*.

117. Sachedina, *The Islamic Roots of Democratic Pluralism*, 14.

118. See Khan, "Lecture on Islam," in *Islam in Transition*, eds. Donohue and Esposito, 36. Khan asserts: "The only criterion for the truth of the religions which are present before us is whether the religion [in question] is in correspondence with the natural disposition of man, or with nature. If yes, then it is true, and such correspondence is a clear sign that this religion has been sent by that person which has created man."

119. Akhtar, *A Faith for All Seasons*, 65; Jabiri, *Al-Dimuqratiyya wa Huquq al-Insan*, 157–158.

120. See 'Ashmawy in *Against Islamic Extremism*, ed. Fluehr-Lobban, 34*ff*. Here 'Ashmawy discusses the development of the ancient Egyptian religion and monotheism. He explains, "Gods were created by the Great God who was proclaimed to be one. The other gods were only names of the various attributes of the One God."

121. See Watt and Bell, *Introduction to the Qur'an*, 9. Watt and Bell cite a number of verses containing that depiction, including Qur'an 6:136, 6:137, 23:84–89, 23:91, 29:61, 29:63, 29:65, 39:38, 39:39, 43:8–15.

122. See Akhtar, *A Faith for All Seasons*, 114–120. Akhtar comments on how the principles of morality are innate in humankind, having been in existence

before the prophets. In support of this claim, he cites Quranic Verse 75:2: "*But nay! I call to witness the accusing voice of man's own conscience!*" (Asad, trans., http://www.altafsir.com).

123. Sachedina, *The Role of Islam in the Public Square*, 7.
124. Sachedina, *The Islamic Roots of Democratic Pluralism*, 34–35.
125. Abou El Fadl, "The Ugly Modern and the Modern Ugly," in *Progressive Muslims*, ed. Safi, 41.
126. Akhtar, *The Quran and the Secular Mind*, 106*ff.* Akhtar discusses the controversy surrounding whether religion is necessary (or relevant) to morally guide people in their social role.
127. Sachedina, *The Islamic Roots of Democratic Pluralism*, 82–83.

Part Two: The Secular Nature of Islam

1. Christmann, "Islamic Scholar and Religious Leader: Shaikh Muhammad Sa'id Ramadan al-Buti," in *Islam and Modernity*, eds. Cooper, Nettler, and Mahmoud, 66–67.
2. The term *fatwa* is used not in the pejorative sense of an edict, condemning people for their behaviors or opinions which do not correspond to those of the issuer, but as a reference to a legal opinion expressing the views of its issuer regarding a Shari'a-related matter.
3. In each environment, this class of clerics rises and operates in its own typical framework. In Egypt, this role is performed by the professors of the Al-Az'har University, a reputed institution of Islamic education; in Saudi Arabia, it is performed in part by the religious police, a government institution called the *Al-Amr Bil Ma'rūf wan-Nahiy 'anil-Munkar*; and in most other Islamic countries, it is performed by a grand mufti assisted by individual muftis for each geographic region of the relevant country.
4. Qaradawi, *Al-Tatarruf al-'Ilmani*, 96.
5. Filali-Ansari, *L'Islam Est-il Hostile à la Laïcité?*
6. Akhtar, *A Faith for All Seasons*, 17.
7. The term 'individualistic' should not be confused with 'egoistic.' See Chapter 10 of this book.
8. A. Charfi, *La Pensée Islamique*, 112.

CHAPTER 5: DEFINING SECUARLISM

1. See Soroush, introduction to *Reason, Freedom, and Democracy in Islam*, xvi–xix. This includes critical commentary from Mahmoud Sadri and Ahmad Sadri that describes a particularly antireligious perception of secularism among the founders of the sociology of religion—namely Max Weber, Emile Durkheim (in his early career), and Georg Simmel—who see secularism as a process that

should lead to the elimination of religion not only from the state but from the consciences and minds of people.

2. See Akhtar, chap. 3 in *The Quran and the Secular Mind*. This chapter includes a discussion of the perception associating secularism with atheism.

3. See Barvani, Falco, and Ramadan, *Faut-il Avoir Peur des Religions*. This text explores a range of perspectives on secularism.

4. Rahman, *Islam and Modernity*, 15; M. Charfi, *L'Islam et Liberté*, 193.

5. Qaradawi, *Al-Tatarruf al-'Ilmani*, 9–14. These pages contain an epistemology of the term *'ilmāniyya* (secularity). Qaradawi concludes that *'ilmāniyya* is antireligious and rejects the hereafter.

6. Akhtar, *The Quran and the Secular Mind*, 36.

7. Jabiri, *Ad-Din wa-d-Dawla*, 108.

8. See Barnavi, Falco, and Ramadan, *Faut-il Avoir Peur des Religions*, 71. For some in the Muslim Arab nations, 'secularism' is a taboo term associated with Western colonialism, local dictatorships, and belligerence against Islam. Many prefer to speak of a 'civilian system' instead.

9. Abdel-Wahab Elmessiri, "Toward a New Islamic Discourse," *Nawaat* (blog), accessed November 18, 2013, http://nawaat.org/portail/2006/01/23/towards-a-new-islamic-discourse/.

10. Akhtar, *The Quran and the Secular Mind*, 40.

11. Mark 12:17; Luke 20:25.

12. See 'Azm, *Naqd al-Fikr Al-Dini*. This text provides an atheist's view of secularism.

13. Soroush, *Reason, Freedom and Democracy in Islam*, 60.

14. An-Na'im, *Islam and the Secular State*, 2–5.

15. Filali-Ansari, *L'Islam est-il Hostile à la Laïcité*, 20.

16. Under freedom of expression, it is safer to criticize a secular authority and seek to change it rather than to criticize the state religion and seek to strike it down. Abou El Fadl, in *The Great Theft*, 20–21, discusses certain concerns over separation of church and state.

17. Although Islam does not recognize a formal church structure, the term 'church' is used as a generic term to refer to the Islamic religious establishment which wields power within its constituency.

18. Qaradawi, *Al-Tatarruf al-'Ilmani*, 15.

19. Soroush, *Reason, Freedom and Democracy in Islam*, 56–57.

20. See Filali-Ansari, *l'Islam est-il Hostile à la Laïcité*, 23. Reflecting on the potential interaction of the state with religion, Filali-Ansari observes, "religion governs the spiritual from the individual's perspective, it defines the foundations of ethics and constitutes the source of individual convictions…reason would

then handle the organization of society." This statement separates the spiritual from day-to-day life, when no separation is necessary—or advisable. By excluding religion in favor of reason from the organization of society, Filali-Ansari implies that reason and religion are potentially incompatible. For more on this topic, see Chapter 12 of this book.

21. An-Na'im, *Islam and the Secular State*, 4.

22. The general principles of secular governance are not inconsistent with Islamic principles, because Islam is secular.

23. Qaradawi, *Al-Tatarruf al-'Ilmani*, 17.

24. Mark 12:17; Luke 20:25.

CHAPTER 6: DIVINE GOVERNANCE AND HUMAN GOVERNMENT

1. Esposito, *Islam*, 4.

2. Zakaria, *Al-Haqiqa wa-l-Wahm fi-l-Haraka al-Islamiyya al-Mu'asira*, 11–20.

3. Qaradawi, *Al-Tatarruf al-'Ilmani*, 15*ff.*; Akhtar, *A Faith for All Seasons*, 194; Ayoub, *A Muslim View of Christianity*, 33.

4. Akhtar, *A Faith for All Seasons*, 137.

5. Abdel Haleem, trans., *The Qur'an*, 57.

6. 'Uthmani, trans., http://www.altafsir.com.

7. Ibid.

8. Ibid.

9. Ibid.

10. Ibid.

11. Walk, trans., http://www.altafsir.com.

12. Abdel Haleem, trans., *The Qur'an*, 56–57.

13. See Ghanem, *Allah wa-l-Jama'a*, 42–43. Ghanem observes that the term *ḥukm*—which is widely used in the Qur'an—was not used a single time in the sense of political rule, but was used instead in the sense of wisdom or arbitration.

14. The term 'exclusive' is intentionally used to indicate that while divine governance is absolute and comprehensive, God, in his infinite sovereignty, has empowered humankind through the concept of trusteeship.

15. Qaradawi, *Al-Tatarruf al-'Ilmani*, 20ff.

16. See Qur'an 6:62, 12:12; 12:40, 12:67, 28:70, 28:78, 60:10. In these verses, the term *ḥukm* is used to reference a divine decision or final judgment.

17. Wahidi, *Asbab an-Nuzul*. See also 'Ashmawi, *Al-Islam al-Siyasi*, 36–37. 'Ashmawi cites the conflict between 'Ali and the Khawarij, wherein 'Ali accepted the arbitration of his conflict with the future Caliph Mu'awiya, presumably in defiance of divine Islamic governance.

18. Qurtubi, *Al-Jami' li Ahkam al-Qur'an*.

19. Qur'an 24:47: "*But the hypocrites say, We have believed in Allah and in the Messenger, and we obey; then a party of them turns away after that. And those are not believers*" (Walk, trans., http://www.altafsir.com).

20. Ibn Kathir, *Tafsir al Qur'an*. This text interprets 'Umar's quote to encompass a requirement of obedience to the immediate successors of the Prophet (as leaders of the community of believers), and then to the caliphs and Imams.

21. Walk, trans., http://www.altafsir.com: "*And thus We have revealed to you an Arabic Qur'an that you may warn the Mother of Cities [Makkah] and those around it and warn of the Day of Assembly, about which there is no doubt. A party will be in Paradise and a party in the Blaze (7). And if Allah willed, He could have made them [of] one religion, but He admits whom He wills into His mercy. And the wrongdoers have not any protector or helper (8). Or have they taken protectors [or allies] besides him? But Allah - He is the Protector, and He gives life to the dead, and He is over all things competent (9).*" See also Mahally and Suyuti, Tafsir Al-Jalalayn.

22. 'Uthmani, trans., http://www.altafsir.com.

23. Asad, trans., http://www.altafsir.com.

24. 'Uthmani, trans., http://www.altafsir.com.

25. Yusuf Ali, trans., http://www.altafsir.com.

26. Asad, trans., http://www.altafsir.com.

27. 'Uthmani, trans., http://www.altafsir.com.

28. Ibid.

29. The Qur'an uses the term *khalīfa* to define humankind's role as trustee of the world. *Khalīfa* typically means successor. However, that meaning is not plausible because it implies 'replacement' which is inconsistent with the context. There is no consensus among the translators of the Qur'an regarding the meaning of the term *khalīfa*. Some of the translations offered include: 'viceroy' (Pickthall, Arberry, and the Royal Aal al Bayt institute), 'vicegerent' (Bakhtiar and Yusuf Ali), 'deputy' (Khalidi, 'Uthmani and Dawood), 'successor' (Abdel Haleem), 'successive authority' (Walk), and 'person who will inherit' (Asad). For his part, Muhsin chose the more neutral phrase, "place generation after generation on earth." In this book, the term 'trustee' is used because all other terms imply the idea of mandate, where one party acts for and on behalf of another. Such a role for humankind is not conceivable because God never acts through humans, and humans cannot perform divine duties.

30. Qur'an 2:29–33: "*It is He Who hath created for you all things that are on earth; Moreover His design comprehended the heavens, for He gave order and perfection to the seven firmaments; and of all things He hath perfect knowledge (29). Behold, thy Lord said to the angels: "I will create a vicegerent*

on earth." They said: "Wilt Thou place therein one who will make mischief therein and shed blood? - whilst we do celebrate Thy praises and glorify Thy holy (name)?" He said: "I know what ye know not. (30)." And He taught Adam the nature of all things; then He placed them before the angels, and said: "Tell me the nature of these if ye are right (31)." They said: "Glory to Thee, of knowledge We have none, save what Thou Hast taught us: In truth it is Thou Who art perfect in knowledge and wisdom (32)." He said: "O Adam! Tell them their natures." When he had told them, God said: "Did I not tell you that I know the secrets of heaven and earth, and I know what ye reveal and what ye conceal?" (33)" (Yusuf Ali, trans., http://www.altafsir.com).

31. 'Uthmani, trans., http://www.altafsir.com.
32. See Qur'an 10:14, 10:73.
33. See Esposito and Voll, *Islam and Democracy*, 26. Here, Esposito and Voll cite Mawdudi, "The real position and place of man, according to Islam, is that of the representative of God on this earth, His vicegerent; that is to say…he is required to exercise Divine authority in this world within the limits prescribed by God."
34. 'Uthmani, trans., http://www.altafsir.com.
35. Qur'an 8:53 ('Uthmani, trans., http://www.altafsir.com). See also Qur'an 13:11.
36. Lewis, *Islam*, 1:xviii.
37. See Abou El Fadl, *Islam and the Challenge of Democracy*, 25–27. Abou El Fadl discusses the allocation of rights among rights of God and rights of humans from an interesting perspective, the rights of God being those over which God retained the exclusive power of reward and punishment. This explains why it is objectionable to claim such power on earth under any pretext, including *al-amr bil ma'rūf wan-nahiy 'ani-l-munkar* (enjoining good and forbidding evil).
38. Yusuf Ali, trans., http://www.altafsir.com.
39. Qur'an 40:60: *"And your Lord says, 'Call upon Me; I will respond to you.' Indeed, those who disdain My worship will enter Hell [rendered] contemptible"* (Walk, trans., http://www.altafsir.com).
40. Qur'an 71:11–12: *"And He will cause the heavens to rain upon you in abundance, (11) and will help you with riches and sons, and will cause gardens to grow for you, and cause rivers to flow for you (12)"* ('Uthmani, trans., http://www.altafsir.com); Qur'an 17:20: *"Of the bounties of thy Lord We bestow freely on all - These as well as those: The bounties of thy Lord are not closed (to anyone)"* (Yusuf Ali, trans., http://www.altafsir.com).
41. Ghannoushi, "Participation in Non-Islamic Government," in *Liberal Islam*, ed. Kurzman, 90.

42. See Khan, "The Primacy of Political Philosophy," in *Islam and the Challenge of Democracy*, ed. Abou El Fadl, 65. Here, Khan discusses human sovereignty with regard to the concept of trusteeship and the inherent right of the individual to speak for religion.

43. Qaradawi, *Al-Tatarruf al-'Ilmani*, 24.

44. Ayoub, *A Muslim View of Christianity*, 33.

45. Qur'an 3:154

46. Esposito, *The Islamic Threat*, 32. Esposito describes the role of Muslim jurists in codifying the details of day-to-day life.

47. Arkoun, "Rethinking Islam," in *Liberal Islam*, ed. Kurzman, 207–208.

48. Akhtar, *A Faith for All Seasons*, 194.

49. Qaradawi, *Al-Tatarruf al-'Ilmani*, 20ff.

50. See Mahmassani, *Falsafat al-Tashrī Fi al-Islām*, 83–91. The schools of *fiqh* have derived their simile codes for all facets of life using syllogism (*qiyās*) and *ijtihād* based on the best interests of the community: preference (*al-istiḥsān*), public order (*al-masāliḥ al-mursalah*), deduction by logical processes (*istidlāl*), and deduction by presumption of continuity (*istiṣ'ḥāb al-ḥāl*).

51. Akhtar, *A Faith for All Seasons*, 9.

52. Ibid.

53. Qaradawi, *Al-Tatarruf al-'Ilmani*, 27ff.

54. See Qaradawi, *Al-Tatarruf al-'Ilmani*, 28–33. Qaradawi states, as a further argument against secularism, that it is improper for Muslims to live in a secular environment where Islam does not lead but is merely tolerated.

55. Yusuf Ali, trans., http://www.altafsir.com.

56. 'Uthmani, trans., http://www.altafsir.com.

57. See Qaradawi, *Al-Tatarruf al-'Ilmani*, 16. Qaradawi cites Qur'anic Verses 45:18 and 28:50 to support his claim that Islam has regulated all facets of life. These verses, when read in proper context, do not support that claim.

58. Tabari, *Jami' Al-Bayan fi Tafsir al-Qur'an*; Qurtubi, *Al-Jami' li Ahkam al-Qur'an*; Ibn Kathir, *Tafsir al-Qur'an al-Karim.* This interpretation is based on an explanation by Mujahid, a companion of the Prophet.

59. Razi, *Mafatih al-Ghayb al-Tafsir al-Kabir*; Ṭantawi, *Al-Wasit fi Tafsir al-Qur'an Al-Karim*; Ibn 'Ashour, *Al-Tahrir Wa al-Tanwir.*

60. Razi, Mafatih *Al-Ghayb al-Tafsir al-Kabir*; Qurtubi, *Al-Jami' li Ahkam al-Qur'an*;

61. Zamakhshari, Kashshaf, and Ibn 'Ashour, *Al-Tahrir Wa al-Tanwir.* This interpretation, based on predetermination, does not fit the context of the subsequent sentence of that same verse, because if every action was indeed predestined, there would be no justification to stand for judgment on the Final Day.

62. Tabari, *Jami' Al-Bayan fi Tafsir al-Qur'an*; Ibn Kathir, *Tafsir al-Qur'an al Karim*; Tantawi, *Al-Wasit fi Tafsir al-Qur'an al-Karim.*

63. H. Amin, *Daleel al-Muslim al-Hazin*, 125*ff.*

64. Shari'ati, *Ma'rifat al-Islam,* 56*ff.*

65. A. Charfi, *L'Islam entre le Message et l'Histoire,* 10*ff.* Charfi observes that this class of clergy is, to various degrees, incapable of renewing its approach to religion using modern-day knowledge because through their education they have become prisoners of outdated perceptions.

66. Babès, *Loi d'Allah Loi des Hommes,* 7.

67. See Barnavi, *Les Religions Meurtrières,* 69–70. A similar joint venture appears to have been conducted between the founder and first prime minister of the state of Israel, David Ben Gourion, and the orthodox wing of European Judaism at the time of the founding of the state.

68. See Fluehr-Lobban, *Against Islamic Extremism*, 68. Fluehr-Lobban cites 'Ashmawy, who highlights the correlation between religion and politics, which explains that joint venture.

69. Abou El Fadl, *Islam and the Challenge of Democracy*, 14–16.

70. See Qassem, *Azamat al-Khilafa wa Atharuha*, 266. It is further believed, though not sufficiently proven, that the banning of *ijtihād* was formalized when the next-to-last Abbasid Caliph, Al-Muntasir Bi-l-lah, formally decreed that all new religious interpretation and jurisprudence must follow the prevailing four major Sunni schools of thought.

71. The term *iftā'* refers to the act of issuing *fatwas*, or legal opinions.

72. See Veinstein, "Les Ottomans: Fonctionnarisation des Clercs, Cléricalisation de l'État," in *Histoires des Hommes de Dieu*, eds., Iogna-Prat and Veinstein, 179–202. This work offers a global description of the institutionalization of the religious establishment's role as a state function in the Ottoman Empire.

73. See A. Amin, *Zu'ama' al-Islah Fi-l- 'Asr al-Hadith*, 59*ff.*, 280*ff.*; Hourani, chap. 5, 6, 9 in *Arabic Thought in the Liberal Age; Hafez,* chap. 3, 4 in *La Pensée Religieuse en Islam Contemporain.* These works provide information on the lives and legacies of Muhammad 'Abdu, Jamaluddin Al-Afghani, and Muhammad Rashid Rida.

74. M. Charfi, *L'Islam et Liberté*, 40–41.

75. See Shahrour, *Al-Kitab wa-l-Qur'an*, 203–209. Here, Shahrour presents his views on the interpretation and understanding of the Qur'an.

76. See Qur'an 41:3 (Walk, trans., http://www.altafsir.com). See also Qur'an 19:97, 43:2, 43:3, 44:58.

77. See Esack, *Le Coran, Mode d'Emploi*, 43*ff.* Esack discusses the fear of accessing the Qur'an without the help of 'learned' intermediaries

78. See Abizaid, *Al-Tafkir fi Zaman al-Takfir*, 244. Abizaid attributes to the Qur'an a dual nature (divine and human), based on his observations about its origin and language. Such views are reminiscent of the debate over the nature of Christ that led to a major schism within Christianity.

79. Qur'an 7:131, 7:187, 8:34, 10:55, 12:40, 12:68, 16:38, 16:75, 16:101, 21:24, 27:61, 28:13, 28:57, 30:6, 30:30, 31:25, 34:28, 34:36, 39:29, 39:49, 40:57, 44:39, 45:26, 52:47.

80. Qur'an 9:11, 27:52.

81. Qur'an 3:7, 4:162.

82. Qur'an, 3:18, 16:27, 17:107, 22:54, 28:80, 29:43, 34:6, 47:16, 58:11.

83. Saleh, *Islam and Modernity*, 154–155.

84. Qur'an 6:104, 17:54.

85. Qur'an 11:123, 14:12, 64:13.

86. Walk, trans., http://www.altafsir.com.

87. Royal Aal al-Bayt Institute, trans., http://www.altafsir.com. In all translations that we have consulted, the term 'servants' does not render the true meaning of the Arabic term, *'ibādi*, which means 'worshippers'. See Chapter 10 of this book.

88. The leadership role of women is discussed in Chapter 14 of this book.

89. A. Amin, *Fajr al-Islam*, 92; 'Abdul-Karim, *Shadw al-Rababa*, 3:281–284.

90. See Talbi, *Plaidoyer pour un Islam Moderne*, 64. Talbi explains that this statement was made in the context of a colloquium held in Tunis on the theme of monotheisms.

91. Abdel Haleem, trans., *The Qur'an*, 162.

92. Qur'an 5:3: "*Today, I have perfected your religion for you, and have completed My blessing upon you, and chosen Islam as Dīn (religion and a way of life) for you.*" ('Uthmani, trans., http://www.altafsir.com).

93. See A. Charfi, *L'Islam entre le Message et l'Histoire*, 89–90. Charfi observes that Muslims who blindly follow clerics, heads of sects, and schools of Islamic thought make the mistake of accepting lords other than God, an action denounced in Qur'anic Verse 3:64.

94. Qaradawi, *Al-Tatarruf al-'Ilmani*, 47.

95. See Abizaid, *Al-Tafkir fi Zaman al-Takfir*, 24. Abizaid accuses Muslim clerics of boasting the freedom of Islam from priesthood, then behaving like priests.

96. Abou El Fadl, "The Ugly Modern and the Modern Ugly," in *Progressive Muslims*, ed. Safi, 46. See also Taji-Farouki, *Modern Muslim Intellectuals and the Qur'an*, 14. Taji-Farouki voices the concern that, "increasingly today those without formal training in the Islamic disciplines claim direct interpretive rights over the Islamic texts as equals with the ulama, and in direct competition with them. Any possibility of uniformity or continuity of interpretation, or

of a controlled diversity of readings, has been lost." However, exercising one's right to read and understand the Message addressed directly to him or her does not imply competing with anyone. It is also perhaps that pursuit of uniformity which secured the continuity and even perpetuation of millennium-old interpretations, customs and traditions which stood in the way of progress.

97. M. Charfi, *Islam et Liberté*, 159–160. See also A. Charfi, *L'Islam entre Le Message et l'Histoire*, 166nn146–147. A. Charfi refers to a quotation from the philosopher Kindi (extracted from Rasa'il al-Kindi al-Falsafiyya) in which he accuses clerics who wrongly used their positions to obtain power and personal gain of being without religion. He thus equates such practice to trading in religion where the trader disposes of the traded item (meaning religion) and looses it.

98. Abou El Fadl, "The Ugly Modern and the Modern Ugly," in *Progressive Muslims*, ed. Safi, 48.

99. See Foda, *Hatta la Yakun Kalaman fi-l-Hawa'*, 5–16. Foda criticizes imams who use the mosque as a forum to air their political views. Traditionally, the mosque is a place of worship, not a place for worshippers to discuss or challenge the views that the imam may express.

100. See Arkoun, *Al-Fikr al-Islami*, 67*ff*. These pages provide an overview of Kemalist Turkey's experiment in secularization.

101. Qaradawi, *Al-Tatarruf al-'Ilmani*, 106.

102. Ibid., 149–150.

103. Ibid., 154*ff*.

104. Ibid., 159.

CHAPTER 7: THE EVOLUTION OF THE ISLAMIC STATE

1. See M. Charfi, *Islam et Liberté*, 11. Here, Charfi highlights the problematic divide existing between reality and what schools are teaching.

2. 'Ashmawi, *Hisad al-'Aql*, 49–50, 55–60.

3. M. Charfi, *Islam et Liberté*, 162. See also the discussion of the theological and philosophical controversies among Sunnis, Shi'as, Ash'aris, and Mu'tazila over the respective roles of rulers and clergy and their conflicting potential claims to religious power, in Watt and Bell, *Introduction to the Qur'an*, 170*ff*.

4. Nettler, "Mohamed Talbi's Ideas on Islam and Politics: A Conception of Islam for the Modern World," in *Islam and Modernity*, ed. Cooper, Nettler and Mahmoud, 48–151. From a historian's perspective, Talbi asserts that although there is no scriptural foundation for an Islamic state, any system which respects people as individuals is necessarily 'Islamic.' He also observes that no true Islamic government has ever existed.

5.   Qaradawi, *Al-Tatarruf al-'Ilmani*, 22; Fluehr-Lobban, *Against Islamic Extremism*, 69; Hoffman, *Al-Islam ka-Badil*, 143; Moussalli, *The Islamic Quest for Democracy*, 30. On the perception of the community of Medina as a state and of the Prophet as a statesman, see Esposito, *The Islamic Threat*, 27–28.

6.   Caratini, *Le Génie de l'Islamisme*, 133. See also Akhtar, *The Quran and the Secular Mind*, 154. Akhtar discusses the fact that the Qur'an is sometimes perceived as a book of nation building.

7.   Ghazali, *Al-Mahawir al-Khamsa Li-l-Qur'an al-Karim*, 10.

8.   'Abdul-Karim, *Shadw al-Rababa*, 1:181.

9.   'Ashmawi, *Hisad al-'Aql*, 57.

10.   Shalabi, *Mawsu'at at-Tarikh al-Islami*, 1:558; Rida, "Al-Khilafa aw al-Imama al-'Uzma," in *Al-Dawla wa-l- Khilafa fi-l- Khitab al-'Arabi*, ed. Kawtharani; Qaradawi, chap. 3 in *Ma' A'immat al-Tajdeed*, pt. 2; 'Ashmawi, *Usul al-Shari'a*, 120. 'Ashmawi asserts that the Qur'an did not contain a single verse about a political system or system of government, nor did the Prophetic Tradition contain any traditions to this effect. For a comprehensive discussion of this subject, see Shamiyyeh, *Al-Islam: Hal Yukaddim li-l-'Alam Nazariyya Li-l-Hukm*.

11.   See 'Amara, *Al-Islam wa Usul al-Hukm*; Filali-Ansari, *L'Islam est-il Hostile à la Laïcité*, 28. Details surrounding the episode of 'Ali 'Abdel Raziq can be found in 'Amara.

12.   'Abdel Raziq, *Al-Islam wa Usul al-Hukm*, 77*ff.* See also 'Ashmawi, *Al-Khilafa al-Islamiyya,* 152–155. For a discussion of 'Abdel Raziq's views, see Filali-Ansari, *L'Islam est-il Hostile à la Laïcité*, 65–69; A. Charfi, *L'Islam entre le Message et L'Histoire*, 85.

13.   Rahman, *Islam and Modernity*, 13*ff.*; Hodgson, chap. 3 in *The Venture of Islam*, vol. 1; Jait, *Al-Fitna*, 29.

14.   Zurayqi, chap. 1 in *Al-Islam fi-l-Madina*. This chapter describes the social fabric in Medina immediately preceeding the hijra of the Prophet.

15.   See Haykal, *Hayat Muhammad*, 239. Here, Haykal provides the full text of the Charter of Medina, in Arabic. English translations may be found in various publications and on websites, including www.constitution.org/cons/medina/macharter.htm.

16.   Haykal, *Hayat Muhammad*, 238–241.

17.   Bulaç, "The Medina Document," in *Liberal Islam*, ed. Kurzman, 175. Article 23 of the Charter provides that disputes "must be referred to God and to Muhammad."

18.   See Wellhausen, *The Arab Kingdom and its Fall*, 7. While acknowledging that the Medina setup fell short of a state structure, and despite the presence of

pagans among the other adherents to the monotheistic faiths in that community, Wellhausen perceived the setup as a structure based on religion, tied by the bond of Islam.

19. 'Ashmawi, *Al-Khilafa al-Islamiyya*, 146.

20. M. Charfi, *Islam et Liberté*, 169.

21. A. Charfi, *L'Islam entre le Message et l'Histoire*, 88–89. See also Qur'an 4:59, 4:65, 4:105, 5:42, 5:43, 5:48–49, 38:22, 38:26, 60:10; 'Ashmawi, *Al-Khilafa al-Islamiyya,* 150. 'Ashmawi observes that the Arabic term *ḥukm*, which now has various meanings (including government, justice administration, and arbitration), did not extend to the concept of government when the Charter of Medina was written.

22. Hodgson, *The Venture of Islam*, 1:187; Jait, *Al-Fitna*, 31–36.

23. See Mutwalli, *Mabadi' Nizam al-Hukm fi-l-Islam*, 443ff. These pages provide an overview of the controversy regarding whether or not Islam is both religion and state, and the role of Prophet Muhammad as a nation builder.

24. See 'Ashmawi, *Usul al-Shari'a*, 174. 'Ashmawi advances the thesis that with Prophet Muhammad ruling over the community of Medina by divine governance, God was drawing (for humanity) the line between divine governance and human government. 'Ashmawi further asserts that nowhere in the Qur'an is there any reference to any form of human government for the period following the mission of the Prophet. In reality, the Qur'an did not address any forms of government even for the period of the Prophet, and the divine guidance that he received in Medina was strictly limited to the performance of his prophetic mission.

25. See D. Brown, *Rethinking Tradition in Modern Islamic Thought*, 69–70. Brown cites the views of Muhammad Aslam Jaipuri and Ghulam Ahmad Parwez who, as adherents to the doctrine of sufficiency of the Qur'an, assert that Prophet Muhammad led the community of Medina as a political ruler rather than as a Prophet. However, they also assert that the function of government is limited to enforcing God's law, ignoring the fact that the Qur'an expressly denied the Prophet any enforcement powers .

26. See 'Ashmawi, *Usul al-Shari'a*, 179. In support of his views on the uninterrupted divine guidance of the Prophet, 'Ashmawi cites Qur'anic Verse 8:67, in which God corrected the Prophet's behavior and decision with respect to prisoners of war at Badr. In reality, this verse is proof of the opposite, for had the Prophet been guided by divine revelation, no divine intervention would have been necessary to redress his decision.

27. A. Amin, *Fajr al-Islam*, 233–234.

28. M. Charfi, *Islam et Liberté*, 169.

29. Filali-Ansari, *L'Islam est-il Hostile à la Laïcité?*, 69.

30. Sachedina, *The Islamic Roots of Democratic Pluralism*, 78.

31. Lewis, *Islam*, 1:1. Here, Lewis discusses the necessity of an Islamic state.

32. See Jait, *Al-Fitna*, 38*ff*.; Haykal, *Hayat Muhammad*, 509–511; Madelung, *The Succession to Muhammad*, 28*ff*. These works describe the episodes surrounding the succession of Prophet Muhammad.

33. See T. Hussein, *Al-Fitna al-Kubra*, 1:152*ff*.; A. Amin, *Fajr al-Islam*, 266*ff*.; Shalabi, *Mawsu'at at-Tarikh al-Islami*, 1:573*ff*.; Madelung, chap. 4 in *The Succession to Muhammad*; Jait, *Al-Fitna*, 141*ff*. These texts provide information on the caliphal successions following the death of the Prophet which led to the Great Discord.

34. Qur'an 2:30: "*Behold, thy Lord said to the angels: 'I will create a vicegerent on earth'*" (Yusuf Ali, trans., http://www.altafsir.com). The term 'vicegerent' is a rendition of the term *khalifa*.

35. See the opposite views expressed in the Saudi delegation's presentation to the Colloquium organized in Geneva on October 30, 1974, on the subject of the Conception of Mankind in Islam and the Human Aspirations for Peace (*Colloques de Riyad, de Paris, du Vatican, de Genève et de Strasbourg sur le Dogme Musulman et les Droits de l'Homme en Islam*, 156): "Islam considers that God has entrusted to Mankind the task of implementing God's designs on earth; hence the dignity attributed to Mankind." In fact, God does not need mankind to achieve his purposes; instead, it is mankind that needs God's guidance.

36. Qur'an 38:26: "*O David! We did indeed make thee a vicegerent on earth: so judge thou between men in truth (and justice): Nor follow thou the lusts (of thy heart), for they will mislead thee from the Path of God: for those who wander astray from the Path of God, is a Penalty Grievous, for that they forget the Day of Account*" (Yusuf Ali, trans., http://www.altafsir.com).

37. Hoffman, *Al-Islam ka-Badil*, 140.

38. See Abou El Fadl, *Islam and the Challenge of Democracy*, 10. Abou El Fadl asks the pertinent questions on this issue.

39. See Qur'an 6:57: "*The Decision belongs to none but Allah. He relates the Truth and He is the best of all judges,*" ('Uthmani, trans., http://www.altafsir.com); Qur'an 12:40: "*Sovereignty belongs to none but Allah*" (Ibid.); Qaradawi, *Al-Tatarruf al-'Ilmani*, 22. Qaradawi concludes (based on Qur'anic Verses 6:57 and 12:40) that the Prophet and his successors cumulate religious leadership and statesmanship—described as "the rule of religion and governance of the matters of life on behalf of the Prophet of God." This concept is not plausible because if the Prophet himself did not have the mission to establish the rule of religion, how could his successors inherit a role that the principal did not have in the first place?

40. See 'Ashmawi, *Usul al-Shari'a*, 191–192. That was not always clear to the caliphs who, at times, behaved as if they had inherited the powers and attributes of the Prophet.

41. Khalidi, trans., *The Qur'an*, 221.

42. Rabbath, *La Conquête Arabe Sous Les Quatre Premiers Califes*, vol. 1; Caratini, *Le Génie de L'Islamisme*, 373*ff.*; T. Hussein, chap. 8–14 in *Al-Shaykhan*, vol. 2. These works provide further details on this period.

43. Filali-Ansari, *L'Islam est-il Hostile à la Laïcité?*, 35–36.

44. See A. Amin, *Fajr al-Islam*, 256*ff.*; Rabbath, *La Conquête Arabe sous les Quatre Califes*, 2:755*ff.* The *Khawarij*, more commonly known as *Kharijites* (a name derived from the Arabic root term *kharaja* which means to exit, leave, or turn against) are a group who turned against the fourth Enlightened Caliph, 'Ali, to signal their opposition to the arbitration agreed to by him to end an ongoing war against Mu'awiya (who was then the governor of Damascus and rebel leader). John Esposito (*Islam: The Straight Path*, 41–48) gives the following learned identification of the *Khawarij*: "They represent the earliest example of radical dissent in Islam and were the first, in a series of movements, to offer a different concept of the nature of the community and its leadership." Esposito then offers an overview of the divisions that occurred within the Islamic community during the period of the Caliphate, including the emergence of Shi'ism. See also A. Saeed, "The Historical context of the Debate on Apostasy and the Roots of Intolerance," in *Freedom of Religion, Apostasy and Islam*, eds., Abdullah Saeed and Hassan Saeed, 23*ff.*; Gardet, *Les hommes de l'Islam*, 209*ff.*

45. Excluding the period of Omayyad rule in Spain for eight centuries.

46. See Foda, *Al-Haqiqa al-Gha'iba*, 89. Foda observes that the Omayyad Caliphate succeeded in running the affairs of state because they knew how to separate religion from state.

47. See A. Amin, *Duha al-Islam*, 1:28. In this work, Amin observes: "In all truth, the Omayyad rule was nowhere near being an Islamic egalitarian system where Arab and non-Arab people are treated equally…the rule was an Arabian rule, where the rulers served the interests of the Arabs at the expense of the non-Arabs, and where the jahiliyya spirit prevailed over that of Islam, and where right and wrong differed depending on the person involved." See also, Hibri, "Legal reform: Reviewing Human Rights in the Muslim World," *Harvard International Review* (June 22, 1998).

48. Esposito, *Islam: The Straight Path*, 51.

49. The dissolution of the caliphate by Atatürk was perceived by some as a destitution, or dissolution, of Islam. For example, the Muslim Brotherhood preaches the need to recreate the caliphate so that Islam might be reborn.

50. See Filali-Ansari, *L'Islam est-il Hostile à la Laïcité*, 39–40. Filali-Ansari comments on the transformation of the nature of the caliphate upon Mu'awiya's accession to power—wondering if it was this accession that signaled the start of secularization. However, the relationship that developed between ruler and clergy under official attribute of the caliph as commander of the faithful, reaffirmed the nonsecular nature of the newly established system of government.

51. See A. Charfi, *La Pensée Islamique: Rupture et Fidélité*, 115; Jait, *Al-Fitna*, 135, 141*ff.*; Muir, *The Caliphate*, 240; A. Amin, *Fajr al-Islam*, 266*ff.*; 'Ashmawi, *Al-Khilafa al-Islamiyya*, 273; 'Ashmawi, *Al-Islam al-Siyasi*, 96–99. The concept of rule by divine right was already present in the period of the Enlightened Caliphs. 'Uthman is reported to have resisted his removal, claiming that he could not be removed by human mortals when he had been divinely designated. Furthermore, the supporters of 'Ali considered the function of caliph to be a divine one that only divinely designated people could fill. Abbasid Caliphs also claimed the divine right to rule.

52. See M. Chebel, *Islam et Libre Arbitre*, 158. Chebel observes that the political doctrines never dissociated between the worldly and divine attributes of the caliphs.

53. M. Charfi, *L'Islam et Liberté*, 179.

54. A. Charfi, *L'Islam entre le Message et l'Histoire*, 170; Sachedina, *The Islamic Roots of Democratic Pluralism*, 54.

55. Not to be confused with the *Dhimmī* regime (implemented during the various stages of the caliphate), under which non-Muslims pay *jizya* tax in order to receive the protection of the state.

56. Moussalli, *The Islamic Quest for Democracy, Pluralism and Human Rights*, 30–31.

57. This is the system currently enforced in Lebanon where each of the nineteen recognized religious communities of various denominations is given the right to enact its own laws and establish its own courts in the family law sector. This system, which continues to plague Lebanon, was central to the civil wars that took place during the last two centuries. For an overview of the implementation of this system in other Arab countries, see Mahmassani, *Al-Awda' al-Tashri'iyya fi-d-Dual al-'Arabiyya*.

CHAPTER 8: ISLAM AND THE MYTH OF A DIVINE THEORY OF STATE

1. See T. Hussein, *Al-Fitna al-Kubra*, 1:217–244. Hussein discusses the salient features of the system adopted by the Arab Muslims, compared with the so-called divinely mandated theory of state.

2.   Abizaid, *Al-Tafkir fi Zaman al-Takfir*, 35–36.

3.   Filali-Ansari, *L'Islam est-il Hostile à la Laïcité*, 67.

4.   M. Charfi, *l'Islam et Liberté*, 172.

5.   Coulson, *A History of Islamic Law*, 9.

6.   Mawdudi, "Nationalism and India," in *Islam in Transition*, eds. Donohue and Esposito, 74. Such claims are inconsistent with God's design to create diverse peoples who interact with each other and are equal, irrespective of whether or not they share the same faith. Islam and nationalism are not synonymous.

7.   See Mawardi, *Al-Ahkam al Sultaniyya*; Ibn Taymiyya, *Al-Siyasa al-Shar'iyya*; Rida, "Al-Khilafa aw al-Imama al-'Uzma," in *Al-Dawla wa-l- Khilafa fi-l-Khitab al-'Arabi*, ed. Kawtharani; Enayat, *Modern Islamic Political Thought*, 67–83. Enayat's *Political Thought* provides a summary of Rida's views on the Islamic state.

8.   Rida, "Al-Khilafa aw al-Imama al-'Uzma," in *Al-Dawla wa-l-Khilafa fi-l-Khitab al-'Arabi*, ed. Kawtharani, 53. Rida relies heavily on Mawardi's classic work, *Al-Ahkam al-Sultaniyya*, which constitutes the basic reference on Islamic doctrine of state. He also relies on Taftazani's classic work, *Sharh al-Maqasid*.

9.   Ibid., 59.

10.   Ibid., 81–88. These pages provide further details on this specific issue which falls outside the scope of this study.

11.   Ibid., 54–55.

12.   Ibid., 58–59; Mutwalli, *Mabadi' Nizam al-Hukm fi-l-Islam*, 598.

13.   Rida, "Al-Khilafa aw al-Imama al-'Uzma," in *Al -Dawla wa-l- Khilafa fi-l-Khitab al-'Arabi*, ed. Kawtharani, 64–65; Mutwalli, *Mabadi' Nizam al-Hukm fi-l-Islam*, 600*ff*. These two sources provide further details on the process of the *mubaya'a*.

14.   'Ashmawi, *Usul al-Shari'a*, 103*ff*.

15.   Rida, "Al-Khilafa aw al-Imama al-'Uzma," in *Al -Dawla wa-l- Khilafa fi-l-Khitab al-'Arabi*, ed. Kawtharani, 65–66.

16.   Ibid., 65; Sachedina, *The Islamic Roots of Democratic Pluralism*, 121–122.

17.   Sachedina, *The Role of Islam in the Public Square*, 16.

18.   Rida, "Al-Khilafa aw al-Imama al-'Uzma," in *Al -Dawla wa-l- Khilafa fi-l-Khitab al-'Arabi*, ed. Kawtharani, 66–67.

19.   Ghannoushi, "Participation in Non-Islamic Government," in *Liberal Islam*, ed. Kurzman, 91.

20.   Rida, "Al-Khilafa aw al-Imama al-'Uzma," in *Al -Dawla wa-l- Khilafa fi-l-Khitab al-'Arabi*, ed. Kawtharani, 67–68.

21.   Ibid., 68–70. These pages provide a general overview of the subject of *shūra*.

22. See Lewis, chap. 9 in *Islam*, vol. 1. This chapter offers a description of the myriad bases (whether from the Scriptures or the Prophetic Tradition) alleged by jurisprudents to justify the doctrine of Islamic state.

23. See Ashmawi, *Usul al-Shari'a*, 103, 172*ff.*

24. Walk, trans., http://www.altafsir.com.

25. Yusuf Ali, trans., http://www.altafsir.com.

26. Walk, trans., http://www.altafsir.com.

27. Yusuf Ali, trans., http://www.altafsir.com.

28. Arberry, trans., http://www.altafsir.com.

29. Yusuf Ali, trans., http://www.altafsir.com.

30. 'Uthmani, trans., http://www.altafsir.com.

31. See Enayat, chap. 2 in *Modern Islamic Political Thought*. This chapter provides an account of the polemics and discussions to which the abolition of the caliphate by the Turkish parliament following World War I gave rise.

32. Jabiri, *Ad-Din wa-d-Dawla*, 66ff.

33. Engineer, "Rational Approach to Islam," in *Islam in Transition* eds. Donohue and Esposito, 140.

34. See Qaradawi, *Al-Tatarruf al-'Ilmani,* 39. Here, Qaradawi advocates the need for a successor to the Prophet to take charge of the *umma* following his death, implying that an Islamic state structure is necessary for that purpose. He cites Qur'anic Verses 2:238 and 2:239 to demonstrate the implied requirement for leadership of the prayers and conclude to the duty of the state to create mosques for people to pray. However, the necessity to lead the prayer does not require the leader to be a successor to the Prophet or otherwise be the head of state.

35. Filali-Ansari, *L'Islam est-il Hostile à la Laicité*, 75, 101; D. Brown, *Rethinking Tradition in Modern Islamic Thought*, 69*ff.*

36. Sachedina, *The Islamic Roots of Democratic Pluralism*, 79.

37. See Qaradawi, *Al-Tatarruf al-'Ilmani*, 38–43. Qaradawi asserts that the Islamic State is a religious requirement to ensure the strict enforcement of religious requirements. He thus opposes secularism because it does not hold accountable those who openly abandon fundamental worship-related duties, or fail to enforce punishments against those who abandon prayer, abstain from paying zakat, or refuse to observe the fast of Ramadan (among other things). Bearing in mind that the Prophet was cautioned against enforcing the faith requirements, the reasons so advanced are precisely the right reasons to implement the secular nature of Islam.

38. Nonconforming believers are those who interpret the faith for themselves and do not subscribe to any "official" version of it.

39. See Barnavi, *Les Religions Meurtrières*, 25–31, 57. The identitarian perception of religion is not specific to Islamic tradition. It existed in Christian Europe until secularization of the political systems took root. It is also anchored in the Zionist movement which oversaw the founding of the state of Israel.

40. See Afghani and 'Abdu, *Al-'Urwa al-Wuthqa wa al-Thawra al-Tahririyya al-Kubra*, 10. Afghani and 'Abdu reject all forms of identities other than that of Islam; they consider all forms of racial, ethnic, or other identities as limitations on the reach of Islam.

41. Saleh, *Al-Islam Wa-l- Mujtama' al-'Asri*, 112; De Prémare, *Aux Origines du Coran*, 34.

42. A. Charfi, *La Pensée Islamique: Rupture et Fidélité*, 78.

43. In three of these forty-seven times, the term *umma* does not refer to any group of people. Instead, it refers to a time frame in Qur'anic Verses 11:8 and 12:45; and in Verse 16:120, it refers to one person—Prophet Abraham—and by implication, his community. It also appears twelve times in the plural form referring to unidentified groups of peoples, past and present (Qur'anic Verses 6:38, 6:42, 7:38, 7:160, 7:168, 11:48, 13:30, 16:63, 29:18, 35:42, 41:25, 46:18).

44. See Qur'an: 2:213, 4:41, 6:108, 7:34, 7:38, 7:164, 10:19, 10:47, 10:49, 13:30, 15:5, 16:36, 16:84, 16:89, 16:92, 22:67, 23:43, 23:44, 27:83, 28:23, 28:75, 35:24, 40:5.

45. See Qur'an 2:134, 2:141, 3:104 3:113, 5:48, 5:66, 7:159, 7:181, 11:118, 16:93, 22:34, 42:8, 43:22, 43:23, 43:33, 45:28.

46. See Qur'an 2:143, 2:128, 3:110.

47. See Qur'an 21:92, 23:52.

48. Talbi, *Plaidoyer pour un Islam Moderne*, 26–28. See also his discussion of various other meanings of the term *umma*, found throughout various sections of *Plaidoyer pour un Islam Moderne*.

49. Qur'an 21:67–92, 23:42–52.

50. Qur'an 21:92 (Walk, trans., http://www.altafsir.com).

51. Qur'an 23:52 (Muhsin, trans., http://www.quranexplorer.com/Quran/Default.aspx).

52. Bulaç, "The Medina Document," in *Liberal Islam*, ed. Kurzman, 174–175.

53. Kurzman, *Liberal Islam*, 171. This page provides the full text of the Constitution of Medina.

54. See Moussalli, *The Islamic Quest for Democracy, Pluralism and Human Rights*, 132. Moussalli calls it the Islamic *umma* of Medina, on grounds that Prophet Muhammad sought to establish peace among the feuding factions of Medina through an "Islamic dominance over Medina and among neighboring

tribes" using *dhimma* contracts with the Jews, pagans, and Christians of Medina. *Dhimma* contracts are different from the contract imposing the *dhimmī* status, and the Charter of Medina is a document entered into among equals and is not based on the inferior *dhimmī* status, developed at a later date.

55.   The English translation of the relevant section of the charter referred to above inadvertently stipulates, "[Among Jews, those who *submit to us* shall receive our assistance." This translation implies that Jews had inferior status. The correct translation is, "Among Jews, those who *follow us* shall receive our assistance." This rendition is more consistent with the equal status among the contracting parties.

56.   See Moussalli, *The Islamic Quest for Democracy, Pluralism and Human Rights*, 132. Moussalli believes the Medina community was a state that "enjoyed religious foundations" when in reality, it was not religiously founded. Initially, Medina was a multifaith society that did not enact Shariʿa law and instead recognized all religious and tribal laws. It was only when Medina later lost its non-Muslim components following the displacement of the Jews that it became the capital of Islamdom.

57.   An-Naiʿm, *Toward an Islamic Reformation*, 1. For another example of Islam being treated as an identity, see Rodinson, *L'Islam: Politique et Croyance*, 29–30, in which Rodinson asserts, "what is essential from a sociological perspective in Islam as in any other ideological movement, is that it has created…a new community which attributes to its adherents its own identity…"

58.   Maalouf, *Les Identités Meurtrières*.

59.   Soroush, *Reason, Freedom, and Democracy in Islam*, 24.

60.   Ramadan, *Mon Intime Conviction*, 55ff.

61.   Sachedina, *The Islamic Roots of Democratic Pluralism*, 4–9. Sachedina rightly observes that the adherents of a religion become more intolerant as politics become more associated with religion (in other words, as religion turns into an identity).

62.   See Talbi, *Plaidoyer pour un Islam Moderne*, 81. Here, Talbi distinguishes between *umma* and nation— boundaries being spiritual in the former, and geographic in the latter.

63.   Moussalli, "Islamic Democracy and Pluralism," in *Progressive Muslims*, ed. Safi, 289.

64.   T. Hussein, *Al-Fitna al-Kubra*. See Hussein's text for a detailed account of this event and its global implications.

65.   Marcia Hermansen, "How to Put the Genie Back in the Bottle? 'Identity' Islam and Muslim Youth Cultures in America," in *Progressive Muslims*, ed. Safi, 309.

66. Qur'an 5:48, 11:118, 16:93, 42:8.

67. Cook, chap. 2 in *Commanding Right and Forbidding Wrong in Islamic Thought*, pt. 1. Cook discusses the Qur'anic provisions providing for that command, observing that there was no well-defined framework for its meaning and scope.

68. Qur'an 2:178, 2:228, 2:229, 2:231-236, 2:240, 2:241, 4:6, 4:19, 4:25, 60:12, 65:2, 65:6. See also Ibn 'Ashour's exegesis of Qur'anic Verse 3:104 in *Al-Tahrir wa al-Tanwir*.

69. Qur'an 2:263, 4:5, 4:8, 31:15, 33:32, 47:21.

70. Qur'an 2:180, 4:114, 33:6.

71. Qur'an 5:79, 22:72.

72. Qur'an 16:90, 24:21, 29:29, 29:45.

73. See Tabari, *Jami' al-Bayan fi Tafsir al-Qur'an*; Zamakhshari, *Tafsir al-Kashshaf*; Razi, *Mafatih al-Ghayb*; Tabarsi, *Majma' al-Bayan fi Tafsir al-Qur'an*; Qurtubi, *Al-Jami' li-Ahkam al-Qur'an*. These works provide interpretations of Qur'anic Verses 3:104, 3:110, 3:114.

74. Qur'an 3:104, 3:110, 3:114, 7:157, 9:67, 9:71, 9:112, 22:41, 31:17.

75. Mahmassani, *Al-Da'a'im al-Khuluqiyya li-l-Qawa'ed al-Shar'iyya*.

76. Dawood, trans., *The Koran*, 336–337; Talbi, *Plaidoyer pour un Islam Moderne*, 94.

77. Sachedina, *The Role of Islam in the Public Square*, 16–17.

78. Mernissi, "Women's Rights in Islam," in *Liberal Islam*, ed. Kurzman, 116; Sachedina, *The Islamic Roots of Democratic Pluralism*, 109.

79. Talbi, *Plaidoyer pour un Islam Moderne*, 89.

80. See Zamakhshari, *Tafsir al-Kashshaf*; Razi, *Mafatih al-Ghayb*. These two exegeses offer interpretations of Qur'anic Verse 3:104.

81. See Cook, *Commanding Right and Forbidding Wrong in Islamic Thought*, 109–153. Cook provides a general synopsis of the manner in which the command was practiced in the early days of Islam, in politics and society. In politics, the command was exercised by people who had the courage to face the ruler and offer advice. In society, the command was often used to criticize and coercively change behaviors of others (especially with regard to drinking alcohol, prostitution, gambling, and music). Talbi (in *Plaidoyer pour un Islam Moderne*, 90–93) refers to the Takfir and Hijra extremist groups who have used the command to justify their zealous, antigovernment activities. See also H. Amin, *Dalil al-Muslim al-Hazin*, 127.

82. "Whoever witnesses an evil and can change it with his hands, let him do so; he may alternatively try with his tongue; and if not, then let him pray in his heart for it to change, and that is the minimum required under the faith," (Jassass,

Ahkam al-Qur'an; Suyuti, *Al-Jami' al-Saghir*, vol. 6, no. 8687; *Sunan Abi Daoud*, vol. 1, no. 1140; and *Sahih Muslim*, vol. 1, no. 78). There are also sayings imputed to the Prophet which seem to tone down the scope of the command, especially if the enforcer is likely to be exposed to risk (Cook, *Commanding Right and Forbidding Wrong in Islamic Thought*, 92*ff.*).

83. Qur'an 22:41, 31:17 (Khalidi, trans., *The Qur'an*, 270, 333). In her translation of this verse, Bakhtiar (*The Sublime Qur'an*, 289) provides a rendition of the last sentence— *"and with God is the ultimate end of the command"*—which is indicative of the need to withhold human enforcement of the command so as to respect God's exclusive prerogative to render judgment on peoples' behaviors. Qur'anic Verse 22:41 was revealed in order to remind the Companions of this as they had just regained Mecca and thought it was their duty to enforce the command. In that context, Meccans were returning, after having been forced out of their homes, to what was still a pagan environment. Most importantly, they were freeing the most sacred shrine of Islam from the deities which stood as an affront to monotheism and the glorification of God. In such an environment, enjoining good and forbidding evil meant freeing the shrine from fetishes and idols so that it could be dedicated to the worship of God. With respect to Qur'anic Verse 31:17, while the command takes the form of advice from Luqman to his son, it is equivalent to a command to all Muslims.

84. Qur'an 5:105 (Khalidi, trans., *The Qur'an*, 96).

85. Jassass, *Ahkam al-Qur'an*. See the comments by Jassass under *Sūrat al-Ma'ida*.

86. Khalidi, trans., *The Qur'an*, 52, 270. In each of these three verses, the emphasis is 'ours.'

87. Tabari, *Jami' al-Bayan fi Tafsir al-Qur'an*; Tabarsi, *Majma' al-Bayan fi tafsir al-Qur'an*; Ibn 'Ashour, *Al-Tahrir wa al-Tanwir*.

88. See Jabiri, *Fahm al-Qur'an al-Hakim*, 3:148.

89. Rida, "Al-Khilafa aw al-Imama al-'Uzma," in *Al-Dawla wa-l- Khilafa fi-l-Khitab al-'Arabi*, ed. Kawtharani, 65.

90. Zamakhshari, *Tafsir al Kashshaf*; Razi , *Mafatih al-Ghayb*; Qurtubi, *Al-Jami' li-Ahkam al-Qur'an*; Ibn 'Ashour, *Al-Tahrir wa al-Tanwir*.

91. Cook, *Commanding Right and Forbidding Wrong in Islamic Thought*, pt. 2–5. The command to enjoin good and forbid evil has been a hot subject of *fiqh*. Over time, each of the major schools of jurisprudence and their followers have commented on all aspects of its implementation. Cook's text provides a detailed discussion of the various views in the Islamic *fiqh* in Sunni and Shi'i Islam, and an account of the Islamic philosophy discourse.

92. Qur'an 3:114, 7:157, 9:71, 9:112.

93. Yusuf Ali, trans., http://www.altafsir.com.
94. Moussalli, *The Islamic Quest for Democracy, Pluralism and Human Rights*, 30, 105. Moussalli describes how the command to enjoin good and forbid evil got institutionalized through the *hisba* organization.
95. See Humayun Kabir, "Minorities in a Democracy," in *Liberal Islam*, ed. Kurzman, 150–151. Kabir discusses the importance of secularism in a country with large minorities (such as India).
96. Sachedina, *The Islamic Roots of Democratic Pluralism*, 5.
97. Qaradawi, *Fiqh al-Aqalliyyat al-Muslima*, 16, 17, 52, 98–100.
98. Mawardi, chap. 1 in *Al-Ahkam al Sultaniyya*, pt. 1; Rida, "Al-Khilafa aw al-Imama al-'Uzma," in *Al-Dawla wa-l- Khilafa fi-l- Khitab al-'Arabi*, ed. Kawtharani, 84.
99. Abou El Fadl, *The Place of Tolerance in Islam*, 20, 21.
100. See Mutwalli (*Mabadi' Nizam al-Hukm fi-l- Islam*, 493–550) for a comprehensive discussion of the arguments and counter-arguments regarding whether an Islamic state is necessary under Islam.
101. Traditional scholars generally agree that the Enlightened Caliphate embodies the Islamic form of government. However, their views diverge with respect to subsequent caliphates.
102. Qur'an 13:37.
103. Qur'an 2:113, 4:141, 6:62; 7:87, 13:41, 16:124, 21:112, 22:56, 22:69, 28:70, 28:88, 39:3, 39:46, 40:12.
104. Qur'an 12:40, 12:67.
105. Qur'an 2:188, 2:213, 4:35, 4:60, 5:44, 5:45, 5:47, 5:95, 21:78, 38:22.
106. Qur'an 4:65, 4:105, 5:42, 5:43, 5:48, 5:49, 24:48, 24:51.
107. Qur'an 3:79, 6:89, 12:22, 19:12, 21:74, 21:79, 26:21, 26:83, 28:14, 45:16.
108. Qur'an 5:50, 6:57, 6:114, 11:45, 12:80, 18:26, 60:10, 68:48, 76:24, 95:8.
109. Qur'an 6:136, 10:35, 16:59, 29:4, 37:154, 45:21, 68:34–39.
110. Muhsin, trans., http://www.quranexplorer.com/Quran/Default.aspx.
111. Qur'an 17:71, 36:12.
112. Qur'an 11:17, 15:79.
113. Qur'an 25:74.
114. Qur'an 2:124, 21:73, 32:24. These verses specifically reference the prophets of the Children of Israel, descended from Abraham.
115. Qur'an 9:12, 28:41. In the former verse, the leaders of evil are the Meccan pagan nobility. In the latter verse, the leader of evil is Pharaoh.
116. Qur'an 28:5, 28:6: "*And We wished to do a favour to those who were weak (and oppressed) in the land, and to make them rulers and to make them the inheritors (5), And to establish them in the land, and We let Fir'aun (Pharaoh)*

and Hâmân and their hosts receive from them that which they feared" (Muhsin, trans., http://www.quranexplorer.com/Quran/Default.aspx).

117. Qur'an 2:30, 6:165, 27:62, 35:39, 57:7.

118. Qur'an 6:133, 7:69, 7:74, 7:129, 7:169, 10:14, 10:73, 10:92, 11:57, 19:59, 24:55.

119. Qur'an 38:26.

120. Rida, "Al-Khilafa aw al-Imama al-'Uzma," in *Al-Dawla wa-l- Khilafa fi-l- Khitab al-'Arabi*, ed. Kawtharani, 67.

121. Qur'an 2:124: "*And remember that Abraham was tried by his Lord with certain commands, which he fulfilled: He said: 'I will make thee an Imām to the Nations.' He pleaded: 'And also (Imāms) from my offspring!' He answered: 'But My Promise is not within the reach of evildoers'*" (Yusuf Ali, trans., http://www.altafsir.com).

122. See Qur'an 4:1, 6:98, 7:189, 16:72, 39:6, 40:17.

123. Qur'an 49:13: "*O mankind, We created you male and female, and made you into nations and tribes that you may come to know one another. The noblest among you in God's sight are the most pious*" (Khalidi, trans., The Qur'an, 424).

124. See 'Abdul-Karim, *Shadw al-Rababa,* 3:129–131. 'Abdul-Karim cites several traditions imputed to Prophet Muhammad regarding the necessity to maintain the preeminence of *Quraysh*. He also mentions the great lengths the *fiqh* went to in order to sacralize the people of Quraysh, and Banu Hashim (from which Prophet Muhammad descends) in particular, citing for that purpose Ibn Taymiyya.

125. Rida, "Al-Khilafa aw al-Imama al-'Uzma," in *Al-Dawla wa-l- Khilafa fi-l- Khitab al-'Arabi*, ed. Kawtharani, 53, 67, 97, 104.

126. Ibid., 130.

127. 'Uthmani, trans., http://www.altafsir.com.

128. Rida, "Al-Khilafa aw al-Imama al-'Uzma," in *Al-Dawla wa-l- Khilafa fi-l- Khitab al-'Arabi*, ed. Kawtharani, 67.

129. Ibid., 104. Rida asserts that the *ijtihād* by the Imam is the only valid one, and no one may question his judgment with a different *ijtihād*.

130. Ibid. This is what Rida calls *iqāmat al din*.

131. Moussalli, *The Islamic Quest for Democracy, Pluralism, and Human Rights*, 32.

132. See Tabari (*Jami' al-Bayan fi Tafsir al Qur'an*) for an exegesis of Qur'anic Verse 3:159.

133. See Esposito and Mogahed, *Who Speaks for Islam*, 29. Esposito and Mogahed report that similar views are widely accepted in the West.

134. Enayat, *Modern Islamic Political Thought*, 135.
135. See Esposito and Voll, chap. 1 in *Islam and Democracy*. This chapter reviews and discusses the perception of democracy among relatively modern Muslim thinkers such as Abul A'la al-Mawdudi, Muhammad Iqbal, Fazlur Rahman, and others. Unfortunately, attempts are consistently made by other Muslim thinkers to prove that Islam can have democracy without calling it democracy (because 'democracy' is a product of the West). Concepts such as *shūra* (consultation), *ijmā'* (consensus), *ijtihād* (rational analysis) are consistently advanced as alternatives to Western democracy, when in reality each such concept has its own meaning and context, unrelated to nation building. See also Esposito, *The Islamic Threat*, 240–248. Esposito offers an expose on the behavior of Arab and Muslim regimes during the last few decades that attempted to avoid a system based on fully fledged democracy.
136. See Moussalli, *The Islamic Quest for Democracy*, 106. Moussalli offers a detailed description of the theoretical aspects of the constituency's rights to secure their legitimate general interests from the ruler in an Islamic state through the command in question, together with the positions of various schools of traditional and philosophical religious thought.
137. Ibid., 31*ff*.
138. Filali-Ansari, *L'Islam est-il Hostile à la Laïcité*, 27; Rida, "Al-Khilafa aw al-Imama al-'Uzma," in *Al-Dawla wa-l- Khilafa fi-l- Khitab al-'Arabi*, ed. Kawtharani, 74–77.
139. Wahidi, *Asbab an-Nuzul*.
140. See Bazergan, "Religion and Liberty," in *Liberal Islam*, ed. Kurzman, 77. Bazergan accuses the caliphs of unduly usurping a divine role to assert absolute sovereignty and autocracy.
141. Qur'an 4:64: "*All the messengers We sent were meant to be obeyed, by God's leave. If only [the hypocrites] had come to you [Prophet] when they wronged themselves, and begged God's forgiveness, and the Messenger had asked forgiveness for them, they would have found that God accepts repentance and is most merciful*" (Abdel Haleem, trans., The Qur'an, 56–57).
142. See Foda, *Al-Haqiqa al-Gha'iba*, 42–43. Foda applies this argument to justify Abu Bakr's fighting those who refused to pay zakat to the caliph as a secular political act.
143. One might assume that zakat could be collected as tax because Qur'anic Verse 9:60 provides that "monies for charitable purposes" can be dispensed to those who "work on it" (that is, those who administer those charities), and those whose loyalty was remunerated by the Prophet. However, the Prophet had a source of money (namely, God and the Prophet's share of the spoils of

war which are provided for in Qur'anic Verse 8:41) which he used for those purposes among others.

144. Tabari, *Jami' al-Bayan fi Tafsir al-Qur'an*.

145. Arberry, trans., http://www.altafsir.com.

146. While fighting to repel an aggression against the nation is sanctioned by the Qur'an, such fighting does not qualify as jihad, nor does it constitute a holy war as long as that aggression did not aim at obstructing the way of God of the aggressed party or at preventing their peaceful worship of God.

147. Wahidi, *Asbab an-Nuzul*; Tabari, *Jami' al-Bayan fi Tafsir al-Qur'an*; Mahalli and Suyuti, *Tafsir al-Jalalayn*.

148. Moussalli, "Islamic Democracy and Pluralism," in *Progressive Muslims* ed. Safi, 289*ff*. In these pages, Moussalli presents an overview of modern political thought on the issue.

149. Esposito and Mogahed, *Who Speaks for Islam*, 63.

150. Qur'an 5:48: *"To you We revealed the Book with the Truth, confirming previous Scriptures and witnessing to their veracity. So judge between them as God revealed and do not follow their whims, to turn you away from the truth revealed to you. For every community We decreed a law and a way of life. Had God willed, He could have made you a single community—but in order to test you in what He revealed to you. So vie with one another in virtue. To God is your homecoming, all of you, and He will then acquaint you with that over which you differed"* (Khalidi, trans., The Qur'an, 89).

151. Qur'an 2:188: *"And do not consume one another's wealth unjustly or send it [in bribery] to the rulers in order that [they might aid] you [to] consume a portion of the wealth of the people in sin, while you know [it is unlawful]"*; Qur'an 7:85: *"And to [the people of] Madyan [We sent] their brother Shu'ayb. He said, "O my people, worship Allah; you have no deity other than Him. There has come to you clear evidence from your Lord. So fulfill the measure and weight and do not deprive people of their due and cause not corruption upon the earth after its reformation. That is better for you, if you should be believers"* (Walk, trans., http://www.altafsir.com).

152. See Qurr'an 4:58: *"Verily! Allâh commands that you should render back the trusts to those, to whom they are due; and that when you judge between men, you judge with justice. Verily, how excellent is the teaching which He (Allâh) gives you! Truly, Allâh is Ever All¬Hearer, All¬Seer"* (Walk, trans., http://www.altafsir.com); Qur'an 4:135: *"O you who believe, be upholders of justice - witnesses for Allah, even though against (the interest of) your selves or the parents, and the kinsmen. One may be rich or poor, Allah is better caretaker of both. So do not follow desires, lest you should swerve. If you twist or avoid (the evidence), then, Allah is all-aware of what you do"* ('Uthmani, trans. http://

www.altafsir.com); Qur'an 5:8: "*O ye who believe! stand out firmly for Allah, as witnesses to fair dealing, and let not the hatred of others to you make you swerve to wrong and depart from justice. Be just: that is next to piety: and fear Allah. For Allah is well-acquainted with all that ye do*" (Yusuf Ali, trans., http://www.altafsir.com); Qur'an 16:90: "*Lo! Allah enjoineth justice and kindness, and giving to kinsfolk, and forbiddeth lewdness and abomination and wickedness. He exhorteth you in order that ye may take heed*" (Pickthall, trans. http://www.altafsir.com).

153. See Qur'anic Verses 49:10–12, which offer advice on achieving social peace. Qur'an 49:10: "*All believers are but brothers, therefore seek reconciliation between your two brothers, and fear Allah, so that you may be blessed with mercy*"; Qur'an 49:11: "*O you who believe, no men should ever scoff at other men. May be, the latter are better than the former. Nor should women (ever scoff) at other women. May be, the latter women are better than the former ones. And do not find fault with one another, nor call one another with bad nicknames. Bad is the name of sinfulness after embracing Faith. If anyone does not repent, then such people are the wrongdoers*"; Qur'an 49:12: "*O you who believe, abstain from many of the suspicions. Some suspicions are sins. And do not be curious (to find out faults of others), and do not backbite one another. Does one of you like that he eats the flesh of his dead brother? You would abhor it*" ('Uthmani, trans. http://www.altafsir.com).

154. Qur'an 9:60: "*Alms are for the poor and the needy, and those employed to administer the (funds); for those whose hearts have been (recently) reconciled (to Truth); for those in bondage and in debt; in the cause of God; and for the wayfarer: (thus is it) ordained by God, and God is full of knowledge and wisdom*" (Yusuf Ali, trans., http://www.altafsir.com).

155. Abou El Fadl, *Islam and the challenge of Democracy*, 5.

156. Foda, *Al-Haqiqa al-Gha'iba*, 11–38. See Foda's critique of calls to establish the Islamic state with Shari'a as constitution and law of the land.

CHAPTER 9: ISLAM AND SHARI'A

1. Akhtar, *A Faith for All Seasons*, 155.

2. Qaradawi, *Al-Tatarruf al-'Ilmani*, 23. This perception is often echoed by non-Muslims, such as Mark Cohen, "Another important contrast with Christendom is that traditional Islam knows no distinction between secular and religious law, between the law of the State and the law of the 'church.'" (Cohen, *Under Crescent and Cross*, 54).

3. See 'Ashmawi, *Usul al-Shari'a*, 175–176. 'Ashmawi assumes that upon the Prophet's hijra to Medina, the Qur'anic verses became legislative in nature in order to address the need for a body of laws that would organize day-to-day

life in that new community. In reality, only a few verses were revealed to address specific situations and assist the Prophet in arbitrating disputes; and the ratio of legislative verses to other verses revealed during the Medina phase remains very low, thereby removing any implication that God was revealing a legal system.

4.   Fyzee, "A Modern Approach to Islam," in *Islam in Transition*, eds. Donohue and Esposito, 151.

5.   See Filali-Ansari, *Réformer l'Islam*, 41–51; Berque, *Relire le Coran*, 79–103. These two references discuss the differences between the rule of law and Shari'a.

6.   We say "primarily" because in the early days, the 'ulama' had no other sources with which to work. Later on, however, the 'ulama' included additional sources in their jurisprudence—namely the *fiqh* of earlier scholars and then existing exegeses of the Qur'an.

7.   The Hanafi school of jurisprudence is the one officially adopted by the Ottoman Administration as a legal reference for all *fiqh*-related issues.

8.   Notable in this respect are the efforts of the Egyptian government, who entrusted then minister of justice, Qadri Pasha, to codify the Shari'a provisions that related to family law. The end product, commonly known as the Qadri Pasha Code, was adopted as legislation to be followed by the Shari'a courts in several other Arab countries. For further details on the practices of each Arab country regarding this legislation, see Mahmassani, *Al-Awda' al-Tashri'iyya fi-d-Dual al-'Arabiyya*, 209*ff*.

9.   A. Charfi, *La Pensée Islamique: Rupture et Fidélité*, 25, 67.

10. Ramadan, *Peut-on Vivre avec l'Islam*, 157.

11. 'Ashmawi, *Usul al-Shari'a*, 37–56. See these pages for a detailed analysis of the term Shari'a and its uses in Islam, Judaism, and Christianity.

12. A. Charfi, *La Pensée Islamique, Rupture et Fidélité*, 25n8.

13. Ali, "Progressive Muslims and Islamic Jurisprudence," in *Progressive Muslims*, ed. Safi, 167; Feldman, *The Rise and Fall of the Islamic State*, 9. For his part, Feldman asserts: "The true meaning of shari'a is, of course, law itself—and just not any law, but the divine Law that governed the Islamic state through the centuries of its success." In reality, Shari'a is divine, but it is not the "divine Law that governed the Islamic state." Instead, the governing law was a human law, devised by the *fiqh* schools and based on Shari'a.

14. By way of example, Article 2 of the Egyptian Constitution of 1980 declares that the principles of Islamic Shari'a constitute the principal basis and source for legislation. It does not, however, provide a definition of Shari'a. If Shari'a is the cumulative body of laws devised throughout history under the caption of *fiqh*, then such provision would be a major cause of confusion and instability

with regard to legislation. However, this problem disappears if Shari'a is understood to be the body of principles and commands set forth in the Holy Qur'an.

15. See Charfi, *L'Islam et Liberté*, 124: "Shari'a consists of a body of rules which, when considered by today's standards, would appear to be unjust"; Sachedina, *The Role of Islam in the Public Square*, 20–21: "The Sharia does not advance a concept of egalitarian citizenship…It simply divides the people into 'Muslim members' with full privileges, and 'non-Muslim minorities' with a protected status under its divinely ordained system…Herein lies the main cause for its incompatibility with the modern democratic system that conceives of its nationals as equal citizens, with equal rights and obligations." In these instances, Charfi and Sachedina were not referring to the divine Shari'a, but rather to 'legislative' Shari'a (or its equivalent in the Arabic language—*al-tashrī' al-Islami*—where the term *tashrī'* is derivative of shari'a, and where both terms derive from the same root—*shara'a*—and act as the human iteration of Shari'a). For commentary on the dangers of confusing Shari'a with Islamic Law, see Esposito, "Practice and Theory," in *Islam and the Challenge of Democracy*, ed. Abou El Fadl, 98–100.

16. Esposito, *The Islamic Threat*, 34.

17. See M. Charfi, *Islam et Liberté*, 113. Charfi asserts that the number of legalistic Qur'anic verses could be anywhere from two hundred to five hundred, and he points to the difficulty of distinguishing between verses containing legal commands and verses advocating moral principles. The fact that such confusion can exist—and that jurists can be divided over the categorization of individual Qur'anic Verses—constitutes proof that it was not God's intention to preempt his trustees (and prevent them from legislating for their own needs and lives) by providing a readymade code of law. See also Talbi, "Le Fait Coranique: Nature et Approches," in *Réflexions sur le Coran*, eds. Talbi and Bucaille, 24.

18. See 'Ashmawi, "Shari'a: The Codification of Islamic Law," in *Liberal Islam*, ed. Kurzman, 52–53.

19. See Amin, *Fajr Al-Islam*, 74*ff.* Amin observes that most of the Shari'a commands, which founded certain aspects of Islamic law, were actually offered as moral principles and were included within a context of enjoining morality and higher values. By way of illustration, Amin cites three Qur'anic Verses (2:177, 16:90, 7:199) that enjoin justice and the fulfillment of commitments, incorporated into the overall context of what constitutes righteousness, such as enjoining compassion, caring for kin, forgiveness, and other values within which justice and keeping one's own word fit.

20. See Esack, *Le Coran: Mode d'Emploi*, 136–137. Esack criticizes John Burton's theory (found in *The Collection of the Qur'an*) that strict adherence to the text of the Scriptures deprives Muslim jurists of all flexibility in legislation. Esack contributes the view that the Qur'an is a book of spiritual guidance, rather than a code of laws.

21. Jabiri, *Ad-Din wa-d-Dawla*, 194–195.

22. A term derived from the root word *shara'a* has been used in Qur'anic Verse 7:163 in a sense totally unrelated to our subject matter. On the issue of how the concept of Shari'a became a fully fledged body of Islamic law after integrating, over time, Prophetic Tradition, doctrinal exegeses, personal, legal, and religious opinions and judgments, see 'Ashmawi, "Shari'a: the Codification of Islamic Law," in *Liberal Islam*, ed. Kurzman, 50.

23. Khalidi, trans., *The Qur'an*, 89.

24. Walk, trans, http://www.altafsir.com.

25. Ibid.

26. Yusuf Ali, trans., http://www.altafsir.com. Yusuf Ali offers his understanding of the term Shari'a in an explanatory note following his rendition of Verse 45:18, "Shariat is best translated the 'right Way of Religion,' which is wider than the mere formal rites and legal provisions, which mostly came in the Madinah period, long after this Makkan verse had been revealed." This explanation is very pertinent because other translators rendered the term in question (in this particular context) to be a reference to divine law or to a legal system, and did so even before the first verse with a legal connotation had been revealed.

27. See Abou El Fadl, *Islam and the Challenge of Democracy*. Within this text, Muqtedar Khan and Abou El Fadl argue over whether or not Shari'a should be central in Muslim peoples' lives (Khan, 63–68; Abou El Fadl, 122–125). In the debate, Abou El Fadl criticizes Khan for dismissing Qur'anic literature, prophetic precedents, precedents of the Companions, and other doctrinal and historical sources (other than the Constitution of Medina) as being irrelevant, for according to Abou El Fadl, it is these sources that make Shari'a central to a Muslim's life. In reality, the truth lies somewhere between these two positions. First, Shari'a is divine, while *fiqh* is human. Second, divine will should not be searched for in the acts of humans (including the statements and precedents of the Prophet and his Companions). And third, reports regarding the Prophet's conduct—which remain important sources of guidance— cannot be considered historical and are anecdotal at best.

28. See Coulson, chap. 3, 4, 5 in *A History of Islamic Law*. Coulson's *Islamic Law* chronicles the rise of the major schools of *fiqh*. Chapter 3 covers the earlier Maliki and Hanafi schools in Medina and Kufa, respectively. Chapter 4 discusses the Shafi'i school and the particular role of its leader, Imam

Muhammad Ibn Idriss al-Shafiʻi. Chapter 5 explores the impact of Shafiʻi's theories and the rise of the Hanbali and Ẓāhiri schools.

29. See Amin, *Fajr Al-Islam*, 246–247. Amin discusses Goldziher's views (in *Le Dogme et la Loi dans l'Islam*) about the Islamic *fiqh* having adopted Roman laws either directly or through the Talmud. Amin resists this view on the grounds that laws often resemble each other due to the universality of certain principles. This is most likely the essence of the concept of *fiṭra* (natural right). The relationship between systems of law is based more on the methodology and process than on the individual rules. Roman law was based on statutes, whereas Islamic law is developed from case law. However, Amin does point to the fact that Islamic law may have benefited from Roman law when Islam spread to lands in which Roman law was applicable. Thus, Roman law solutions that were compatible with Shariʻa were considered to address specific issues for which Islamic law had not developed solutions.

30. Sachedina, *The Role of Islam in the Public Square*, 20–21.

31. Faruqi, *Women, Muslim Society and Islam*, 64: "The religious laws of personal status are therefore crucial to any understanding of Islamic marriage. It is in these laws that the most detailed enunciation of both the woman's and the man's rights and obligations is to be found. Complying with the fulfillment of those mutual responsibilities is therefore regarded as a religious obligation for both parties. The acquiescence or the failure to comply is regarded as an act carrying divine reward or punishment, and therefore is not a matter to be taken lightly." In this quotation, Faruqi makes no distinction between the divine Shariʻa and the human *fiqh* output. Additionally, in Islamic family law, marriage is a secular contract .

32. See Bellah, *Beyond Belief*, 151. Bellah points out the modernity of the principles brought about by the Qur'an and the early experiments which, following the end of the Enlightened Caliphate, were overshadowed by the return of many of the rules and principles that had been inherent in the tribal system.

33. Ebrahim Moosa, "The Debts and Burdens of Critical Islam," in *Progressive Muslims*, Safi, 123.

34. Walk, trans., http://www.altafsir.com .

35. Filali-Ansari, *L'Islam est-il Hostile à la Laïcité*, 103–123.

36. Ghannoushi, "Participation in Non-Islamic Government," in *Liberal Islam* ed. Kurzman, 91. Here, Ghannoushi refers to what he calls "the commandment to implement the law of God and not to resort to adopting laws other than His" and concludes that it is "a must for all Muslims…to obey God's commandments and establish His Governance." However, nowhere in the Qur'an are humans enjoined to establish the kingdom of God and impose His governance, for the

simple reason that God's governance exists by divine will and does not depend on human will and resolve. In addition, the Qur'an does not prohibit adopting laws other than the laws of God, as long as they do not contradict the guiding principles and values contained in the Shari'a.

37. See Novak, "Revealed Law and Democracy," in *Islam and the Challenge of Democracy*, ed. Abou El Fadl, 88. Here, Novak discusses what he considers to be the unresolvable contradiction between "the divine authority of revealed law and the human authority of popular sovereignty."

38. Saleh, *Al-Islam wa-l- Mujtama' al-'Asri*, 87.

39. Qur'an 5:44–49.

40. Qur'an 5:50: "*Do they truly desire the law of paganism? But who is fairer than God in judgment for a people firm of faith?*" (Khalidi, trans., The Qur'an, 90).

41. Ibid., 221.

42. See Qaradawi, *Al-Tatarruf al-'Ilmāni*, 44–45. Qaradawi objects to secularism because it takes legislative power away from God and instead gives it to society. In support of his claim, he cites a passage from Qur'anic Verse 7:54: "*Is it not His to create and to govern? Blessed be God, the Cherisher and Sustainer of the worlds!*" (Yusuf Ali, trans., http://www.altafsir.com). In reality, this passage—when placed back within the context of the verse in question, which describes God's creation of the Universe—reads as follows: "*Your Guardian-Lord is God, Who created the heavens and the earth in six days, and is firmly established on the throne (of authority): He draweth the night as a veil o'er the day, each seeking the other in rapid succession: He created the sun, the moon, and the stars, (all) governed by laws under His command. Is it not His to create and to govern? Blessed be God, the Cherisher and Sustainer of the worlds!*" This verse is about creation, and it reveals that God (who made that creation) will continue to look after His creation and govern it. The topic here is Divine Governance, exemplified in the laws of nature. This verse has nothing to do with legislation for day-to-day events .

43. 'Uthmani, trans., http://www.altafsir.com.

44. Ghaleb, "Nahnu fi-l-Asr," in *Islam Dod Islam*, ed. Nayhoum, 306.

45. Customs that freely evolve out of the day-to-day lives of people and are within the bounds of good ethics often acquire the force of law. God acknowledged that such customs—which are entirely the product of human interaction—were a potential source of law and order when he commanded His Prophet to heed the mandates of customs. That command came in Qur'anic Verse 7:199, in which the Prophet is enjoined to be guided by local customs when commanding people. Unfortunately, the term *'urf* (customs) has been misconstrued by the commentators to mean "what is right and kind."

46. See Qur'an 2:173, 5:3, 16:115, 16:118.

47. See Qur'an 2:275–280, 3:130–131.
48. See Qur'an 4:22–25.
49. See Qur'an 6:151–153.
50. See Qur'an 16:116.
51. See Qur'an 17:23–39.
52. See Qur'an 2:282–283, 5:106–108.
53. See Qur'an 5:90.
54. Qur'an 5:91: *"Satan seeks to stir up enmity and hatred among you by means of wine and gambling, and to keep you from the remembrance of God and from your prayers. Will you not abstain from them?"* (Dawood, trans., The Koran, 89)
55. See Talbi, *Plaidoyer pour un Islam Moderne*, 68.
56. Ramadan, *Peut-on Vivre avec l'Islam*, 121.
57. See Qaradawi, *Al-Halal wa-l-Haram*, 171. Here, Qaradawi presents arguments traditionally used to justify polygamy.
58. Hibri, *Islam, Law and Custom: Redefining Muslim Women's Rights*, 22–23. In the Hanafi school of jurisprudence, a man cannot even waive his so-called right to polygamy, and the clause of the marriage contract to that effect is null and void.
59. See Berque, *Quel Islam*, 31–32. In this work, Berque offers the view that: "Polygamy is tolerated, notwithstanding an express option for monogamy. What was nothing other than a concession to the then prevailing customs got interpreted by an archaic society as a right. The exegesis went even further. Neglecting the Qur'an's own suggestions, and wiping out its repeated invitations to pardon a spouse at fault, it insisted on the coercive aspects."
60. Qur'an 4:3: *"And if you have reason to fear that you might not act equitably towards orphans, then marry from among [other] women such as are lawful to you— [even] two, or three, or four: but if you have reason to fear that you might not be able to treat them with equal fairness, then [only] one— or [from among] those whom you rightfully possess. This will make it more likely that you will not deviate from the right course"* (Asad, trans., http://www.altafsir. com).
61. Qur'an 4:129: *"Ye are never able to be fair and just as between women, even if it is your ardent desire: But turn not away (from a woman) altogether, so as to leave her (as it were) hanging (in the air). If ye come to a friendly understanding, and practise self- restraint, God is Oft-forgiving, Most Merciful"* (Yusuf Ali, trans., http://www.altafsir.com).
62. During the period preceding the start of Divine Revelation, the tribal customs of the *jāhiliyya* society treated women as objects or chattels. In addition, the number of women that a man could marry was often unlimited. The Qur'an

adopted a gradual approach to this second issue—first tolerating a limited number of women that a man could marry while establishing monogamy as the standard.

63. Rahman, *Major Themes of the Qur'an*, 48. Here, Rahman observes that the Qur'an often offers a *ratio legis* for the rules it sets forth. When the rule in question is an exception to a more general rule, that exception becomes a tolerance until circumstances change and the reason for the exception ceases to exist.

64. Qur'an 4:36.

65. See M. Charfi, *Islam et Liberté*, 65. Charfi explains how institutions such as slavery—which God intended to eliminate but allowed to remain temporarily by way of tolerance—continued to exist for a long time as divinely recognized and regulated rights. Charfi blames the *fuqahā'* for transforming tolerances into codified rights.

66. See Jait, *Fi al-Sira al-Nabawiyya*, 2:52. Jait refers to a study conducted by orientalist Henri Lammens, in which he describes the institution of revenge as religiously sanctioned and even mandated, both individually and collectively.

67. Goldziher, *Muslim Studies*, 18.

68. Moussalli, *The Islamic Quest for Democracy*, 11; 'Awwa, "The Basis of Islamic Penal Legislation," in *The Islamic Criminal Justice System*, ed. Bassiouni, 127.

69. Bassiouni, "Sources of Islamic law and the Protection of Human Rights in the Islamic Criminal Justice System," in *The Islamic Criminal Justice System*, ed. Bassiouni, 13.

70. See Shahrour, *Al-Kitab wa-l- Qur'an*, 443*ff.* These pages offer a detailed analysis of the concept of *hudud*.

71. Yusuf Ali, trans., http://www.altafsir.com.

72. Arberry, trans., http://www.altafsir.com.

73. See Goldziher, *Islamic Studies*, 15.

74. Shahrour, *Al-Kitab Wa-l--Qur'an*, 568–569.

75. Ahmad Amin, *Fajr al-Islam*, 195*ff.*

76. Translations took time to appear on the market due to a fear of distorting the word of God.

77. Shahrour, *Al-Kitab wa-l--Qur'an*, 472, 579.

78. See Rahman, *Islam and Modernity*, 29–30. Rahman criticizes secularism and compares it to defeatism. He prefers preserving the integrity of Islamic law through frequent reformulations and expansion thereof. Perhaps Rahman is equating the divine Shari'a with the man-made Islamic law. In reality the failure to progress Islamic law is not the result of any secular defeatism, because Islam itself is secular. Instead it is the result of a human failure to

take full advantage, and make the best use, of the divine Shariʿa in secular legislations. Rahman further observes that a central purpose of Islam and the Qurʾan is to induce *taqwa,* which he defines as piety and fear of God. He concludes that secular law is tantamount to a rejection of *taqwa* because it renders the state indifferent to the obdience of God. This view ignores the freedom of faith and expression that God demands in his Message.

79. Asad, trans., http://www.altafsir.com.
80. Esposito and Mogahed, *Who speaks for Islam,* 23.
81. ʿAshmawi, *Usul al-Shariʿa,* 129.
82. See ʿAbdul-Karim, *Al- ʿArab wa-l- Marʾa,* 231-242. This book provides details on the condition of women in pre-Islamic Arabia.
83. Qurʾan 4:11, 4:12, 4:176.
84. Suyuti, *Al-Jamiʿ al-Saghir,* vol. 2, no. 1758; *Sahih al-Bukhari,* vol. 2, Book 59, chap. 6, no. 2596; and *Sunan al-Tirmidhi,* vol. 3, chap. 4, no. 2203. Note that the Shiʿite *fiqh,* following the Jaafari school of jurisprudence, allows the will to be made to any person whether a heir or not (Mahmassani, *al-Mabadiʾ al-Sharʿiyya wa-l-Qanuniyya,* 198; and Mughniyya, *al-Ahwal al-Shakhsiyya ʿala-l-Madhahib al-Khamsa,* 181).
85. See Qurʾan 4:8.
86. Yusuf Ali, trans., http://www.altafsir.com.
87. Ibid.
88. See Mahmassani, *Al-Mabadiʾ al-Sharʿiyya wa-l-Qanuniyya,* 311; Mughniyya, *Al-Ahwal al-Shakhsiyya ʿala-l-Madhahib al-Khamsa,* 227–230. The Shiʿite *fiqh* has correctly rendered the term *walad* to mean 'a male descendent.'
89. See Qurʾan 4:11: "*Allah directs you concerning* your children: *for a male there is a share equal to that of two females. But, if they are (only) women, more than two, then they get two-thirds of what one leaves behind. If she is one, she gets one-half. As for his parents, for each of them, there is one-sixth of what he leaves in case he has a child. But, if he has no child and his parents have inherited him, then his mother gets one-third. If he has some brothers (or sisters), his mother gets one-sixth, all after (settling) the will he might have made, or a debt. You do not know who, out of your fathers and your sons, is closer to you in benefiting (you). All this is determined by Allah. Surely, Allah is All-Knowing, All-Wise*" (Yusuf Ali, trans., http://www.altafsir.com). In Arabic, the word used for the highlighted term 'your children' is *awlāduqum,* which is the plural form of *walad.*
90. This injustice did not appear at the outset, but unfolded over time as tribal solidarity (which catered to the situation) faded out.
91. See Mahmassani, *Al-Mabadiʾ al-Sharʿiyya,* 339–340. This jurisprudence is that of Ibn Hazm al-Andalusi of the Al-Ẓāhiri school of jurisprudence.

92. The Egyptian law on wills of 24 June 1947 (Article 76); the Tunisian family law as amended by law No. 19 of 1959; and the Syrian family law of 1953. For an overview of the legislative systems in certain Arab countries, see Mahmassani, *al-Awda' al-Tashri'iyya fi-d-Dual al-'Arabiyya*, pt. 2.

93. Bellah, *Beyond Belief*, 154.

94. Mahmassani, *Turath al-Khulafa' al-Rashidin*, 205*ff*.

95. Walk, trans., http://www.altafsir.com.

96. Ibid.

97. Shahrour, *Al-Kitab wa-l-Qur'an*, 573*ff*.

98. Abdel Haleem, trans., *The Qur'an*, 21.

99. See Qur'an 6:164, 17:15, 35:18, 39:7, 53:38.

100. See Caratini, *Le Génie de l'Islamisme*, 73–74. In these pages, Caratini reviews the evolution, in tribal Arabia, through which the law of retaliation (an eye for an eye) was slowly replaced by a system of financial compensation, often referred to as *diyya*.

101. Asad, trans., http://www.altafsir.com.

102. See Goldziher, *Islamic Studies*, 6. Goldhizer provides an interesting depiction of the true purpose of the Islamic message.

103. Bhutto, "Politics and the Muslim Woman," in *Liberal Islam*, 109.

104. Cohen, *Under Crescent and Cross*, 79–90. The prohibition of usury is not specific to Islamdom—it was fully enforced in Christendom as well.

105. Several translators of the holy text have translated the term *riba* to mean interest, without further qualification.

106. Royal Aal al-Bayt Institute, trans., http://www.altafsir.com.

107. See Qur'an 4:160–161: "*Because of the wrongdoing of the Jews We forbade them good things which were (before) made lawful unto them, and because of their much hindering from Allah's way (160). And of their taking usury when they were forbidden it, and of their devouring people's wealth by false pretences, We have prepared for those of them who disbelieve a painful doom (161)*" (Pickthall, trans., http://www.altafsir.com).

108. Qur'an 2:280 is very indicative.

109. Walk, trans., http://www.quranexplorer.com.

110. Asad, trans., http://www.quranexplorer.com.

111. A. Charfi, *L'Islam entre le Message et l'Histoire*, 80*ff*; 'Ashmawi, *Usul al-Shari'a*, 142–150; 'Ashmawi, *Ma'alim al-Islam*, 376. In *Ma'alim al-Islam*, 'Ashmawi asserts that *riba* does not refer to the conventional interest collected by banks and other financial institutions—he withdraws the term from the realm of money lending and places it instead within the institution of barter.

112. See Gamal, *Islamic Finance*, 51. Gamal asserts that *riba* is not the same as interest.

113. Evidence of such intent is often found in the transaction documentation, where a variable rate lease payment or purchase installment payment is calculated by referencing the Libor, Bibor, Sibor, Euribor, or any other commonly used benchmark of variable rates of interest.

114. Saleh, *Al-Islam Wa-l-Mujtama' al-'Asri*, 98.

115. See Suyuti, *Al-Jami' al Saghir*, vol. 2, no. 2553; and *Sunan al-Tirmidhi*, vol. 2, chapter 4, no. 1259. Prophet Muhammad is reported to have said that any increase due solely to passage of time constitutes *riba*.

116. Qur'an 17:26–27: "*And give his due to the near of kin, as well as to the needy and the wayfarer, but do not squander [thy substance] senselessly (26). Behold, the squanderers are, indeed, of the ilk of the satans—inasmuch as Satan has indeed proved most ungrateful to his Sustainer (27)*" (Asad, trans., http://www.quranexplorer.com).

117. Saleh, *Al-Islam Wa-l-Mujtama' Al-'Asri*, 101.

118. See Qur'an 3:29, 5:99.

119. Gamal, *Islamic Finance*, xii.

120. See Hoffman, chap. 11, in *Al-Islam ka-Badil*. Hoffman provides an overview of the extended scope of do's and don'ts in the financial sector of the economy, including a new list of actions unnecessarily declared to be haram (strictly prohibited).

121. Saleh, *Al-Islam Wa-l-Mujtama' al-'Asri*, 10; Shaltut, "Political and Social Thought in the Contemporary Middle East," in *Islam in Transition*, eds. Donohue and Esposito, 79*ff*. Shaltut charts a socialist—almost communist—economic system, and attributes it to Islam. See also Taliqani, "The Characteristics of Islamic Economics," also in *Islam in Transition*, 229–235.

122. Saleh, *Al-Islam Wa-l-Mujtama' al-'Asri*, 39–47.

123. Ibid., 49.

124. Ibid., 64.

125. Mahmassani, *Arkan Huquq al-Insan*, 206–208; Mahmassani, *Al-Da'a'im al-Khuluqiyya li-l- Qawanin al-Shari'iyya*, 162–215.

126. See Saleh, *Al-Islam wa-l-Mujtama' al-'Asri*, 38. Saleh's extreme views deem the accumulation of wealth—the sole function of which is social—to be a sinful act, or haram, that is punishable by God..

127. See Qur'an 9:60; 30:38; 51:19, 70:24, 70:25; D. Brown, *Rethinking Tradition in Modern Islamic Thought*, 47. Brown notes that, aware of its own mandatory nature, the Qur'an purposefully did not establish the precise amount of zakat to be levied. In this way, the amount can be appropriately set in light of relevant circumstances.

128. Moosa, "The Debts and Burdens of Critical Islam," in *Progressive Muslims*, ed. Safi, 122–123.

129. Ibid., 120.
130. Ajijola, "The Problem of 'Ulama," in *Liberal Islam*, ed. Kurzman, 243; Faruqi, *Women, Muslim Society and Islam*, 14.
131. Rahman, *Islam and Modernity*, 156–157.
132. Abou al-Majd, *Ru'ya Islamiyya Mu'asira: I'lan Mabadi'*.
133. The manifesto's position on the condition of women does not go far enough towards complete gender equality. On the proposed forms of business activity in the economic sector, it appears to acknowledge restrictions derived from misconstrued Islamic concepts (*riba,* and risk and rewards).
134. See Abou El Fadl, *Islam and the Challenge of Democracy*, 18–38, 39n19. Abou El Fadl discusses the obligation that God imposed on his trustees to act justly and implement justice.

CHAPTER 10: HUMANISM AND INDIVIDUALISM IN ISLAM

1. Bidar, *Self-Islam*, 73.
2. See Esposito and Mogahed, *Who Speaks for Islam*, 100–118. Gallup conducted surveys of more than fifty thousand people in over thirty-five predominantly Muslim nations, following the September 11th terrorist attacks.
3. A. Charfi, *La Pensée Islamique: Rupture et Fidélité*, 62–65.
4. See Filali-Ansari, *L'Islam est-il Hostile à la Laïcité*, 96–97. Filali-Ansari cites the concurring views of Taha, Rahman, and Talbi.
5. Bearing in mind that *din* means "religion," and *dunia* means "this life," it would have been more accurate to describe the relationship as a religion encompassing this life and the hereafter—in other words, a *din* covering *dunia* and *ākhira* (life after death).
6. Qur'an 88:21.
7. See Qur'an 16:44: "…*anzalna 'alayka al-dhikr*…"
8. Izetbegović, *Islam between East and West*, 295–301. Izetbegović was the first president of the independent Republic of Bosnia and Herzegovina. He observes, "The person, male or female, who adheres to Islam does thereby join a community which has both social and political aspects, including material legal commitments as opposed to mere moral obligation." It is true that Islam, as a faith, places great emphasis on the importance of implementation. However, the Muslim community is not to be conflated with the state in which that community lives in order to assume that statelike legal commitments arise from becoming a Muslim. It is conceivable that a Muslim majority might impose a tax and call it zakat. However, such an act is a statutory act and entirely secular.
9. 'Uthmani, trans., http://www.altafsir.com.
10. Asad, trans., http://www.altafsir.com. These two verses are identical.

11. 'Uthmani, trans., http://www.altafsir.com. See also Qur'an 6:164, 35:18, 39:7.

12. Walk, trans., http://www.altafsir.com. See also Qur'an 41:46.

13. Qur'an 39:61.

14. Tahtawi, "Kitab al-Murshid al-Amin li-l-Banat wa-l-Banin," in Donohue and Esposito, *Islam in Transition*, 12.

15. Qur'an 32:6–8: "*That One is the All-knower of the Unseen and the seen, the All-Mighty, the Very-Merciful (6), who made well whatever He created, and started the creation of man from clay (7). Then He made his progeny from a drop of semen, from despised water (8)*" ('Uthmani, trans., http://www.altafsir.com).

16. Pickthall, trans., http://www.altafsir.com.

17. Yusuf Ali, trans., http://www.altafsir.com.

18. Ibid.

19. Ibid.

20. Asad, trans., http://www.altafsir.com.

21. 'Uthmani, trans., http://www.altafsir.com.

22. Ibid. See also Qur'an 35:39.

23. 'Uthmani, trans., http://www.altafsir.com. See also Qur'an 7:11, 17:61, 18:50, 20:116, 38:72.

24. See Akhtar, *A Faith for All Seasons*, 141; Qur'an 75:36–40: "*DOES MAN, then, think that he is to be left to himself, to go about at will? (36) Was he not once a [mere] drop of sperm that had been spilt, (37) and thereafter became a germ-cell— whereupon He created and formed [it] in accordance with what [it] was meant to be, (38) and fashioned out of it the two sexes, the male and the female? (39) Is not He, then, able to bring the dead back to life? (40)*" (Asad, trans., http://www.altafsir.com).

25. See Qur'an 4:28: "*And Allah wants to lighten for you [your difficulties]; and mankind was created weak*" (Walk, trans., http://www.altafsir.com); Qur'an 12:53: "*And I do not absolve my inner self of blame. Surely, man's inner self often incites to evil, unless my Lord shows mercy. Certainly, my Lord is the Most-Forgiving, Very-Merciful*" ('Uthmani, trans., http://www.altafsir.com); Qur'an 17:11: "*Man prays for evil like his prayer for good, and man is so hasty*" ('Uthmani, trans., http://www.altafsir.com); Qur'an 70:11: "*Indeed man is created weak in courage*" ('Uthmani, trans., http://www.altafsir.com).

26. Qur'an 95:4.

27. Qur'an 2:31.

28. See Bidar, *Self-Islam*, 132. Bidar strives to link Christianity and Islam by defining the two religions as iterations of the same divine message, continuing each other from different perspectives.

29. This additional extreme path was designed by Bidar in *L'Islam Sans Soumission*, which followed his first book, *Self-Islam*.

30. Bidar, chap. 2, 4 in *L'Islam Sans Soumission*.

31. Ibid., chap. 3.

32. Qur'an 3:180, 15:23, 28:58.

33. Qur'an 7:100, 7:128, 7:137, 7:169, 21:105, 33:27, 39:74, 44:28.

34. 'Uthmani, trans., http://www.altafsir.com.

35. Ibid.

36. See Qur'an 2:107, 2:116, 2:255, 2:284, 3:109, 3:129, 3:180. Countless Qur'anic verses (including the ones cited here) assert that God owns the earths, the skies, and everything He created therein.

37. Akhtar, *A Faith for All Seasons*, 137.

38. Qur'an 12:21: "*And the one from Egypt who bought him said to his wife, "Make his residence comfortable. Perhaps he will benefit us, or we will adopt him as a son." And thus, We established Joseph in the land that We might teach him the interpretation of events. And* Allah is predominant over His affair*, but most of the people do not know*" (Walk, trans., http://www.altafsir.com).

39. Akhtar, *A Faith for All Seasons*, 141.

40. See Lamont, *The Philosophy of Humanism*, 12–15. Lamont offers a definition of humanism which includes assumptions of an atheistic nature. However, humanism and religious faith are not inconsistent, and Islam is essentially secular and humanistic.

41. Qur'an 53:39–40: "*That man shall gain only what he endeavors (39); That his endeavour shall be noted (40)*" (Khalidi, trans., The Qur'an, 436). See also Qur'an 20:15, 76:22.

42. See Qur'an 2:178, 2:237, 3:134, 3:159, 5:13, 5:15, 7:199, 24:22, 42:40, 64:14.

43. See Qur'an 2:196, 2:264, 2:271, 2:276, 2:280, 4:92, 4:114, 5:45, 9:60, 9:79, 9:103–104, 12:88, 33:35, 57:18–19, 58:13.

44. See Qur'an 2:245, 5:12, 57:11, 57:18, 64:17, 73:20.

45. See Qur'an 2:25, 2:82, 2:277, 3:57, 4:57, 4:122, 4:173, 5:9, 5:93, 7:42, 10:4, Q11:23, Q13:29, 17:9, 18:2, 18:30, 18:88, 18:117, 19:60, 19:96, 20:82, 20:112, 21:94, 22:14, 22:23, 22:50, 22:56, 24:55, 26:227, 28:67, 28:80, 29:7, 29:9, 29:58, 30:15, 30:45, 31:8, 32:19, 34:4 43:37, 35:7, 38:24, 38:28, 40:40, 40:58, 41:8, 41:33, 42:22–23, 42:26, 45:21, 45:30, 47:2, 47:12, 48:29, 65:11, 84:25, 85:11, 95:6, 98:7, 103:3.

46. See Qur'an 2:25, 2: 82, 4:57, 4:122, 4:124, 10:9, 13:29, 14:23, 18:107–108, 19:60, 20:75–76, 22:14, 22:23, 22:56, 29:58, 30:15, 32:19, 40:40, 42:22–23, 45:30, 47:12, 64:9, 65:11, 85:11.

47. See Qur'an 25:70, 29:7.

48. See Qur'an 2:62, 5:69.

49. See Qur'an 30:44, 41:46.
50. See Qur'an 7:42.
51. See Qur'an 6:48, 24:5.
52. See Qur'an 3:134.
53. See Qur'an 2:83, 4:36, 6:151, 9:91, 16:90, 17:23, 29:8, 46:15.
54. See Qur'an 2:195, 2:236, 13:22.
55. See Qur'an 2:109, 2:178, 4:128, 4:149, 24:22, 64:14, 42:40.
56. See Qur'an 11:115, 12:90, 13:22, 39:10.
57. See Qur'an 13:22, 23:96, 41:34.
58. See Qur'an 2:112, 7:56, 7:161, 9:120, 11:115, 12:90, 16:30, 16:128, 18:30, 22:37, 29:69, 33:29, 37:80, 37:105, 55:60, 77:44.
59. See Qur'an 28:77.
60. See Qur'an 5:13, 5:93, 39:34.
61. See Qur'an 4:40, 6:160, 27:89, 28:84, 42:23.
62. See Qur'an 5:85, 10:26.
63. Soroush, *Reason, Freedom, and Democracy*, 92–93.
64. See Abou El Fadl, *Islam and the Challenge of Democracy*, 29. Abou El Fadl sums it up eloquently from the perspective of the divine sanctity of each individual, as God's creation.
65. See Ramadan, *Islam, the West and the Challenges of Modernity*, 33. Here, Ramadan discusses the importance of Islam's social function: "Islam is the carrier of a teaching which is entirely directed toward the collective and social dimension."
66. Rahman, *Major Themes of the Qur'an*, 19.
67. See Bidar, *Self-Islam*, 82; 'Ashmawi, *Al-'Aql fi-l-Islam*, 55. Bidar cites Qur'anic Verse 2:148 in support of his argument. 'Ashmawi advances the same argument—cautioning against abdicating the use of one's own mind and blindly following the flock.
68. See Talbi and Bucaille, *Réflexions sur le Coran*, 25–26. Talbi cites thirty-one Qur'anic verses in which that concept is cited.
69. Nasr, *The Heart of Islam*, 260; Rahman, *Major Themes of the Qur'an*, 64. For his part, Rahman considers jihad to be "a total endeavor, an all-out effort."
70. Abou El Fadl, *The Great Theft*, 220*ff*.
71. 'Uthmani, trans., http://www.altafsir.com.
72. Ibid.
73. Sachedina, *The Islamic Roots of Democratic Pluralism*, 82.
74. Talbi, *Al-Islam Hurriyya wa Hiwar*, 27.
75. Arberry, trans., http://www.altafsir.com. The underscored term is the English rendition of the verb derived from the term 'jihad.'

76. Walk, trans., http://www.altafsir.com. The underscored terms are the English rendition of the term 'jihad' and its derivatives.

77. Esposito and Mogahed, *Who Speaks for Islam*, 17*ff.*; Shahrour, *Tajfif Manabi' al-Irhab*. Shahrour devotes this entire book to clarifying the misconception of 'jihad' as being synonymous with 'fighting' (*qitāl*).

78. See Dousse, *Dieu en Guerre*; Burns, *War and its Discontents*. These works cover the potential interpretations of the perspectives of violence, pacifism, and quietism in the scriptures of the three Abrahamic religions.

79. Arberry, trans., http://www.altafsir.com. The underscored term is the English rendition of the verb derived from the term 'jihad.'

80. See Saleh, *Al-Islam Wa-l- Mujtama' al-'Asri*, 92. Saleh exemplifies the misconception of jihad (as a war for the sake of God) by asserting that its purpose is to "raise His word high…" He also notes, "The Shari'a has glorified that concept of jihad to the point of almost placing it among the pillars of Islam."

81. Shahrour, *Tajfif Manabi' al-Irhab*, 73–137.

82. Esposito, *Islam: The Straight Path*, 13. See also Qur'an 4:95: *"Those of the believers who sit still, other than those who have a (disabling) hurt, are not on an equality with those who strive in the way of Allah with their wealth and lives. Allah hath conferred on those who strive with their wealth and lives a rank above the sedentary. Unto each Allah hath promised good, but He hath bestowed on those who strive a great reward above the sedentary"* (Arberry, trans., http://www.altafsir.com).

83. Esposito and Mogahed, *Who Speaks for Islam*, 20. See also 'Ashmawi, *Al-Islam al-Siyasi*, 100*ff.* 'Ashmawi traces the evolution of the concept of jihad, which began as an individual worship-related endeavor in the early period of the Revelation and evolved into what he calls a "sacred defensive war" during the Medinan period.

84. M. Charfi, *Islam et Liberté*, 166–167.

85. See Qur'an 2:109, 2:178, 2:179, 2:195, 3:134, 5:45, 6:90, 6:160, 10:26, 13:22, 16:95, 16:128, 23:96, 24:22, 28:54, 42:40, 55:60, 64:14.

86. This study is limited to the discussion of issues based on the scriptures. It does not discuss fundamentalism from any political perspective (such as global imperialism or anti-Muslim fundamentalism against political Islam) because such perspectives are not religious perspectives but political perspectives which use and abuse religion for political purposes. See examples cited by Moussalli, in *The Islamic Quest for Democracy*, 113. For a global discussion of fundamentalism, as well as a history of its rise, see Meddeb, *The Malady of Islam*.

87. See Esposito and Mogahed, *Who Speaks for Islam*, 75*ff.* Esposito and Mogahed rightly observe that violence in religion is a general pattern that was followed and practiced by most religions throughout history (Judaism, Christianity, Hinduism, etc.), a fact that is often ignored by researchers.

88. See De Prémare, *Les Fondations de L'Islam*, 95. De Prémare confuses the terms *jihad* and *qitāl* (fighting) and asserts that they are synonymous and that their usage alternates freely in the Qur'an.

89. Lewis, *Cultures in Conflict*, 67; De Prémare, *Aux Origines du Coran*, 43; Morabia, *Le Gihad dans l'Islam Médiéval: Le combat sacre des origines au XIIe siècle*; Akhtar, *A Faith for all Seasons*, 231; Nabulsi, *As'ilat al-Hamqa fi al-Siyasa wa-l-Islam al-Siyasi*, 169. Nabulsi contends that jihad was ordained to spread and protect Islam, and to fight against the apostates. However, none of these purposes constitutes a valid justification for the use of force.

90. See Nasr, *The Heart of Islam*, 263. While Nasr gave the appropriate definition of jihad (as an attribute of humanism), he ended up equating jihad with permitted fighting to repel aggression, thereby prompting his question as to who may issue the call for jihad. In doing so, he gave the religious establishment an unwarranted say in government.

91. Arberry, trans., http://www.altafsir.com.

92. See translations of Qur'anic Verse 2:190 by Dawood, *The Koran*; Abdel Haleem, *The Qur'an*; Khalidi, *The Qur'an*; Asad, http://www.altafsir.com; Yusuf Ali, http://www.altafsir.com.

93. Amin, H, *Dalil al-Muslim al-Hazin*, 145.

94. See translations of Qur'anic Verse 2:190 by Pickthall, http://www.altafsir.com; Arberry, http://www.altafsir.com; 'Uthmani, http://www.altafsir.com; Walk, http://www.altafsir.com; Bakhtiar, *The Sublime Quran*; Mohsin, http://www.quranexplorer.com/Quran/Default.aspx; Royal Aal al-Bayt Institute, http://www.altafsir.com.

95. See Qur'an 3:121–124, 3:160, 22:38–39.

96. This is the plural form of the term *mu'min* (believer).

97. Dawood, trans., *The Koran*, 126.

98. Pickthall, trans., http://www.altafsir.com.

99. These two terms are forms of the plural term for *kāfir* (nonbeliever) and are used interchangeably in the Qur'an.

100. Christians and Jews have been declared by some as *kuffār* because they do not accept the Message of Prophet Muhammad or acknowledge his divine role and mission. Such labeling is inconsistent with the provisions of Qur'anic Verse 2:62: "*Surely, those who believed in Allah, and those who are Jews, and Christians, and Sabians—whosoever believes in Allah and in the Last Day,*

and does good deeds—all such people will have their reward with their Lord, and there will be no reason for them to fear, nor shall they grieve" ('Uthmani, trans., http://www.altafsir.com). This verse follows a series of verses in which God encourages the Jews to believe in the message of Prophet Muhammad, but also repels potential implications that their failure to do so will lead them to hell. This verse offers to Jews and Christians God's assurance of salvation so long as the essentials of the faith are present: belief in the unicity of God and the Final Day, coupled with the performance of good deeds. Qur'anic Verse 5:48 determines that Muhammad's message is a reminder of previous messages, each of which contains a valid path towards salvation.

101. See Qur'an 2:191, 2:193, 2:217, 4:90–91, 4:101, 8:38–40, 85:10.

102. See Qur'an 5:49, 9:48–49.

103. See Qur'an 2:191, 2:217.

104. See Qur'an 2:191, 8:39. See the early interpretations of these two verses by Tabari, Zamakhshari, Razi, Qurtubi, and Ibn Katheer, and the more recent interpretations by Ibn 'Ashour, Sha'rawi, and Qutb. Note however, that among the recent interpreters, Tantawi got closest to the true meaning of the expression, *al-din kulluhu lillāh.*

105. See Noorani, *Al-Jihad wa-l-Islam*, 75–84. Noorani points to certain misinterpretations of Qur'anic verses which support the perception that Islam promotes a culture of violence.

106. Abdullah Saeed and Hassan Saeed, *Freedom of Religion, Apostasy and Islam*, 77.

107. See Jabiri, *Fahm al-Qur'an al-Hakim*, 3:381*ff.*

108. 'Uthmani, trans., http://www.altafsir.com.

109. Jabiri, *Fahm al-Qur'an al-Hakim*, 3:390.

110. Ezzeddine, *Al-Haqiqa*, 143.

111. Although a large number of its verses became ineffectual upon completion of the Prophet's mission, the underlying lessons to be learned from *Sūrat al-Tawba* remain indefinitely and universally pertinent, as is the case with all the tales and stories of ancient peoples related in the Qur'an.

112. See Qur'an 33:10–20, 33:60–62.

113. See, by way of example, *Sūrat al-Anfal*, 8:12, 8:15, 8:45, 8:57, 8:65, and 8:66; *Sūrat Muhammad*, 47:4, 47:20 to 28, and 47:35; *Sūrat al-Fat'ḥ*, 48:16; *Sūrat al-Hadid*, 57:10; and *Sūrat al-Ṣaff*, 61: 3 and 61:4 .

114. Qur'an 2:154, 3:169, 4:74.

115. M. Charfi, *Islam et Liberté*, 28.

116. 'Uthmani, trans., http://www.altafsir.com.

117. Ibid.

118. Ibid.
119. Walk, trans., http://www.altafsir.com.
120. Asad, trans., http://www.altafsir.com. Asad adds his own explanation of the scope of the fighting permitted in this verse, observing that this verse is: "uncompromising with regard to ethical principles. The reference to 'those deniers of the truth who are near you' may arise from the fact that only 'those who are near' can be dangerous in a physical sense or, alternatively, that— having come from afar— they have already approached the Muslim country with an aggressive intent."
121. Tantawi, *Al-Wasit fi Tafsir al-Qur'an al-Karim.*
122. Witness to that fact is the practice of the Prophet with the regard to those called *al-mu'allafa qulūbuhum* (those whose hearts have been softened and pacified using funds from zakat).
123. Khalidi, trans., *The Qur'an,* 450.
124. Commentators have added their own interpretations by claiming that befriending pagans must (1) with respect to Verse 60:7, lead to their conversion to Islam; and (2) with respect to Verse 60:8, be preceded by a pact to be entered with them (Zuḥaylī, *Al-Mawsū'ah al-Qur'āniyyah al-Muyassarah,* 551). On their part, al-Mahally and al-Suyuti (*Tafseer al-Jalalayn*) believe that these verses have been abrogated and are no longer in effect. However, al-Tabari (*Jami'i al-Bayan fi Tafsir al-Qur'an*) refers to this controversy, but he concludes against abrogation because it does not befit divine justice and wisdom.
125. Based on these criteria, the Qur'an certainly permits resistance fighting for the purpose of repelling an aggressor or freeing one's homeland. However, such fighting does not constitute a religious duty, but rather a secular, national duty. Rida (in fatwa excerpts reproduced on page 42 of Donohue and Esposito's *Islam in Transition*) considers repelling any aggression toward the homeland to be "an imperative of Islam."
126. Royal Aal al-Bayt Institute, trans., http://www.altafsir.com.
127. Talbi, *L'Universalité du Coran,* 45.
128. 'Uthmani, trans., http://www.altafsir.com.
129. Asad, trans., http://www.altafsir.com.
130. See Qur'an 4:100.
131. See Qur'an 73:10.
132. Sachedina, *The Islamic Roots of Democratic Pluralism,* 118.
133. Ibid., 118, 130–131.
134. Qur'an 4:65, 5:42–49, 24:51. Although the Qur'an enjoins believers of all faiths to submit their disputes to the Prophet, the underlying principle is to

settle disputes among believers in a peaceful, civilized manner, by way of arbitration, through public institutions.

135. 'Uthmani, trans., http://www.altafsir.com.

136. Moussalli, *The Islamic Quest for Democracy*, 133.

137. Noorani, *Al-Jihad wa-l-Islam*, 70.

138. A. Charfi, *L'Islam entre le Message et l'Histoire*, 127.

139. See Abou El Fadl, "The Ugly Modern and the Modern Ugly," in *Progressive Muslims*, ed. Safi, 51. With regard to modern-day fundamentalism, Abou El Fadl deplores the fact that violence against both non-Muslims and Muslims has been glorified. (The glorification of such violence is a violation of express provisions in the Qur'an.)

140. Sachedina, *The Islamic Roots of Democratic Pluralism*, 55.

141. Asad, trans., http://www.altafsir.com.

142. 'Uthmani, trans., http://www.altafsir.com.

143. Pickthall, trans., http://www.altafsir.com.

144. Ibid.

145. This interpretation of the terms *fitna* (as *shirk*) and *al-din kulluhu lillāh* (as imposing the conversion to Islam by force), appears in most of the exegeses, old and more recent See, for example, the exegeses of al-Tabari, al-Zamakhshari, al-Tabarsi, al-Razi, and Ibn Kathir. However, the interpretation by Jabiri (in *Fahm al Qur'an al-Hakim*, vol. 3) refers the term *fitna* to attempts to dissuade the Prophet and his companions from the new religion.

146. See M. Charfi, *Islam et Liberté*, 165. Charfi refers to certain interpretations according to which the apparent restriction on the mission of the Prophet means that he is not responsible for the outcome of his performance.

147. In a note to his translation of Verse 2:193, Muhammad Asad explains the term *al-din kulluhu lillāh* as meaning: "and religion belongs to God [alone]" — i.e., until God can be worshipped without fear of persecution, and none is compelled to bow down in awe before another human being. (See also 22:40.) The term *dīn* in this context is more suitably translated as "worship," inasmuch as it comprises here both the doctrinal and the moral aspects of religion; that is to say, man's faith as well as the obligations arising from that faith."

148. Talbi, *Plaidoyer pour un Islam Moderne*, 90.

149. See M. Charfi, *Islam et Liberté*, 165.

150. 'Ashmawi, *Usul al-Shari'a*, 96–97.

151. A. Charfi, *L'Islam entre le Message et l'Histoire*, 128–129n116. In Note 116, Charfi refers to Al-Sarakhsi's "*Sharh Al-Syar al-Kabir*," Hayderabad, 1335 H, vol. 1, 125–126.

152. Al-Qurtubi, *Al-Jami' li Ahkam al-Qur'an* (exegesis of Verse 9:73).

153. 'Ashmawi, *Uṣool al-Shari'a*, 96–97.

154. Yusuf Ali, trans., http://www.altafsir.com; Hussain, "Muslims, Pluralism and Interfaith Dialogue," in *Progressive Muslims*, ed. Safi, 256. Hussain highlights the message of justice and amnesty in Islam.

155. Qur'an 22:38–41; Khalidi, trans., *The Qur'an*, 270.

156. These are mainly suras 33, 47, 48, 57 and 61, which were revealed in part in connection with the various wars that the Prophet had to fight in the latter part of his prophetic career.

157. See Sachedina, *The Islamic Roots of Democratic Pluralism*, 115–119. Sachedina rejects the concept of abrogation and discusses the issue of offensive jihad against the people of the Book according to Qur'anic Verse 9:29 on grounds of public order.

158. Qur'an 25:63; Yusuf Ali, trans., http://www.altafsir.com.

159. Dawood, trans., *The Koran*, 336–337.

160. See Qur'an 4:140–141.

161. Khalidi, trans., *The Qur'an*, 221.

162. Asad, trans., http://www.altafsir.com. Contrary to many claims, this is the verse which sets the tone for dealing with the people of the Book—not Qur'anic Verse 9:29.

163. Qur'an 48:4: "*It is He who sent down the Shechina (tranquility) into the hearts of the believers, that they might add faith to their faith*" (Arberry, trans., http://www.altafsir.com).

164. Nasr, *The Heart of Islam*, 221.

Part Three: The Progrssive Nature of Islam

1.   A. Charfi, *L'Islam entre le Message et l'Histoire*, 128.

2.   Esposito, *The Islamic Threat*, 36–37.

3.   A. Charfi, in *Mustaqbal al-Islam fi-l-Gharb wa-l-Sharq*, eds. Hoffman and Charfi, 67.

4.   It is the reverential fear arising from the perceived binding nature of what the Prophet, his companions, and succeeding caliphs reportedly did or said, as well as what the *fuqahā'* and clergy approved or disapproved.

5.   Hopwood, "The Culture of Modernity in Islam and the Middle East," in *Islam and Modernity*, eds. Cooper, Nettler, and Mahmoud, 3.

CHAPTER 11: THE CONCEPT AND SCOPE OF PROGRESSIVISM IN ISLAM

1.   Ramadan, *Islam, the West and the Challenges of Modernity*, 1.

2.   See Essack, "In Search of Progressive Islam Beyond 9/11," in *Progressive Muslims*, ed. Safi, 79. Some authors have attributed that sociopolitical connotation to the term 'progressive'.

3.   Shahrour, *Al-Kitab wa-l Qur'an*, 445*ff*.

4.   See Ajijola, in "The Problem of Ulama," in *Liberal Islam*, ed. Kurzman, 239. Ajijola criticizes modern-day clerics and learned *fuqahā'* who continue to look to the past, not realizing that past achievements cannot transcend the limitations of their time.

5.   See Esposito and Mogahed, *Who speaks for Islam*, 24–25. Esposito and Mogahed affirm Islamic civilization's role in exporting the Renaissance to Europe (contrary to prevailing views at the time). See also Viorst, "Puritanism and Stagnation," in *The Place of Tolerance in Islam*, ed. Abou El Fadl, 28–29.

6.   Caratini, *Le Génie de l'Islamisme*, xvii.

7.   Bidar, chap. 2 in *Un Islam pour Notre Temps*.

8.   Akhtar, *A Faith for All Seasons*, 11.

9.   See Safi, "Introduction: The Times They are a-Changin'—A Muslim Quest for Justice, Gender Equality, and Pluralism," in *Progressive Muslims*, ed. Safi, 17–18. Here, Safi discusses the meaning of progress, and quotes a pertinent statement (made by one of the other contributors to *Progressive Muslims*) which highlights the paradox between the inherent progressivism of Islam and the conservatism of many Muslims.

10.   See D. Brown, *Rethinking Tradition in Modern Islamic Thought*, 49. Brown explores this issue, and in doing so he cites the views of Syed Hussein Nasr and Mawdudi.

11.   Ibid., 44.

12.   See Madjid, "Islamic Thought and Religious Understanding," in *Liberal Islam*, ed. Kurzman, 288. Madjid translates the term *taqwa* as 'the fear of God'.

13.   Qur'an 4:7–8, 4:11–13.

14.   Qur'an 2:180; Suyuti, *Al-Jami' al-Saghir*, vol. 6, no. 9933.

15.   M. Charfi, *Islam et Liberté*, 116.

16.   See Safi, "The Times they Are a-Changin'—A Muslim Quest for Justice, Gender Equality, and Pluralism," in *Progressive Muslims*, ed. Safi, 3–6. This passage provides a more detailed discussion of these attempts.

17.   Talbi, *Plaidoyer pour un Islam Moderne*, 122–123.

18.   Talbi, *Universalité du Coran*, 41.

19.   Talbi, *Universalité du Coran*, 42. See also A. Charfi, *L'Islam entre le Message et l'Histoire*, 19; Talbi, "La Vocation de l'Homme," in *Réflexions sur le Coran*, eds. Talbi and Bucaille, 90–91. In his contribution to *Réflexions*, Talbi points to the universality of the Qur'an from the perspective of the purpose of the creation of humankind.

20.   See Kurzman, "Liberal Islam and its Islamic Context," in *Liberal Islam*, ed. Kurzman, 6. Kurzman proposes, "Instead, the liberal tradition argues that

Islam, properly understood, is compatible with—or even a precursor to—Western liberalism."

21. Abou El Fadl, *The Great Theft*, 13–15.

22. See Esposito, "Practice and Theory," in *Islam and the Challenge of Democracy*, ed. Abou El Fadl, 99. Esposito refers to the views of Abdurrahman Wahid regarding the secular nature of Islam as an engine of progress.

23. Ibid., 98. Esposito supports the views of Abou El Fadl.

24. See Rahman, *Islam and Modernity*, 30.

25. Safi, "The Times they Are a-Changin'—A Muslim Quest for Justice, Gender Equality, and Pluralism," in *Progressive Muslims*, ed. Safi, 7–8.

26. Moussalli, *The Islamic Quest for Democracy, Pluralism and Human Rights*, 3.

27. Abou El Fadl, "The Ugly Modern and the Modern Ugly," in *Progressive Muslims*, ed. Safi, 47.

28. This quote is from Talbi's *'Iyal Allah*, reproduced in Nettler, "Mohamed Talbi's Ideas and Politics: A Conception of Islam for the Modern World," in *Islam and Modernity*, eds. Cooper, Nettler and Mahmoud, 145.

CHAPTER 12: ISLAM AND THE MIND

1. Kabir, "Minorities in a Democracy," in *Liberal Islam*, ed. Kurzman, 149.

2. Qaradawi, *Al-Tatarruf al-'Ilmani*, 130; Zafar, "Accountability, Parliament, and *Ijtihad*," in *Liberal Islam*, ed. Kurzman, 70; Haykal, introduction to *Al-Faruq 'Umar*, vol. 1. Haykal refers to a certain negative attitude on the part of the Prophet (and later, 'Umar) towards those who argue theological matters. He attributes their negative attitude toward the use of the mind to the belligerence encountered in the early days of the revelation which took the form of sterile argumentation.

3. Hourani, *A History of the Arab Peoples*, 68.

4. Buti, "Hawla Tajdid Usool al-Fiqh," in *Ishkaliyyat Tajdid Usul al-Fiqh*, eds. Marzoogy and Buti, 155*ff.* See also page 191 of this work, where Marzoogy refutes Buti's view and asserts that the call for renewal of thought is a tribute to divine governance and the trusteeship to mankind enacted by God.

5. See Christmann, "Islamic Scholar and Religious Leader: Shaikh Muhammad Sa'id Ramadan al-Buti," in *Islam and Modernity*, eds. Cooper, Nettler and Mahmoud, 57–81. Christmann provides a comprehensive overview of Buti's thoughts on this matter.

6. Noorani, *Al-Jihad wa-l-Islam*, 138–142.

7. See Chebel, *L'Islam et la Raison*, 7*ff.* Chebel describes the tension—and hence the claims of incompatibility—between faith and Reason.

8. See Qur'an 4:164, 7:143, 42:51. Moses is the only prophet God spoke to directly.

9.   See Lassouad, *Islam al-Falasifa*, 7. "How were the Muslim philosophers able to combine two types of truths, one in which sovereignty is exclusively to the mind, and another which accepts nothing less than total submission to—and compliance with—its precepts." Here, Lassouad references the antagonistic attitudes toward, and persecution of, philosophers.

10.   Akhtar, *A Faith for all Seasons*, 25.

11.   Ibid., 26. Akhtar tends to support the view that certain provisions of the Qur'an—while not expressly forbidding philosophy—discourage argument on matters of faith in a manner that he describes as "deeply anti-intellectual," citing Qur'anic Verses 2:67 and 2:71 as evidence. In reality, these verses express God's extreme patience with people who, in their reluctance to believe, seek one proof after another. In chapter four of *Al-'Aql fi-l-Islam*, 'Ashmawi presents an overview of the various philosophical controversies surrounding basic religious topics that developed in the first few centuries of Islam. 'Ashmawi then devotes chapter five to discussing the views of Abu Hamid Al-Ghazali, and blames him for muzzling the mind with his theory that everything is created by God (including every thought and every action of every creature).

12.   Esack, *Le Coran Mode d'Emploi*, 304n5.

13.   'Aqqad, *Al-Tafkir Farida Islamiyya*, 42.

14.   'Abdu, *Al-Islam wa-l-Nasraniyya ma' al-'Ilm wa-l-Madaniyya*, 58.

15.   See Soroush, *Reason, Freedom and Democracy in Islam*, 178. Soroush cautions against scare tactics that function as a form of intellectual terrorism aimed at deterring questions that students of the religious universities raise.

16.   Gesink, "Madrasa Reform and Legal Change in Egypt," in *Islam and Education*, eds. Kadi and Billeh, 26.

17.   Talbi, *Universalité du Coran*, 33.

18.   Akhtar, *A Faith for all Seasons*, 66–69.

19.   See Bouthawry, *Maqasid al-Shari'a*, 110. Here, Bouthawry reports this perception of Fassi. See also 'Aqqad, *Al-Tafkir Farida Islamiyya*, 9–15, in which 'Aqqad reviews Qur'anic verses that incite mankind to use their mind on matters of faith.

20.   Shari'ati, *Ma'rifat al-Islam*, 82.

21.   Royal Aal al-Bayt Institute, trans., http://www.altafsir.com; Akhtar, "Islam and the Challenge of the Modern World," in *Liberal Islam*, ed. Kurzman, 319.

22.   See 'Abdul-Karim, *Shadw al-Rababa*, 1:67–69. 'Abdul-Karim recalls that Caliph 'Umar banned all arguments regarding provisions of the Qur'an. This episode, if true and justified by local circumstances, does not constitute a general precedent for people to follow.

23. Qur'an 6: 80–82 ('Uthmani, trans., http://www.altafsir.com).

24. Some verses, when taken out of context, seem to equate *kufr* (rejection of the faith) to 'arguing over the signs sent by God'. For example, Qur'anic Verse 40:4 states: "*None can dispute about the Signs of God but the Unbelievers. Let not, then, their strutting about through the land deceive thee!*" (Yusuf Ali trans., http://www.altafsir.com). In reality, this verse does not condemn rational argument. Instead, it condemns sterile argumentation intended to spoil the belief in the Messenger of God and thwart his efforts and mission. See also Qur'an 40:35, 40:56, 40:69.

25. Akhtar, *A Faith for All Seasons*, 29–30; Akhtar, "Islam and the Challenge of the Modern World," in *Liberal Islam*, ed. Kurzman, 319.

26. Jait, *Fi al-Sira al-Nabawiyya*, 2:203.

27. Akhtar, *A Faith for All Seasons*, 27.

28. Qur'an 17:85.

29. 'Abdu, *Al-Islam wa-l-Nasraniyya ma' al-'Ilm wa-l-Madaniyya*, 62; Soroush, *Reason, Freedom, and Democracy*, 127–128. Soroush discusses the necessary concordance between reason and Revelation.

30. Saleh, *Al-Islam wa-l-Mujtama' al-'Asri*, 183.

31. Talbi, *Plaidoyer pour un Islam Moderne*, 76; Sachedina, *The Islamic Roots of Democratic Pluralism*, 46.

32. Talbi, *Plaidoyer pour un Islam Moderne*, 42; Moussalli, *The Islamic Quest for Democracy, Pluralism, and Human Rights*, 89–90.

33. Moosa, "The Debts and Burdens of Critical Islam," in *Progressive Muslims*, ed. Safi, 112.

34. Suyuti, *Al-Jami' al-Saghir*, vol. 1, sec. *alif*.

35. Qur'an 20:114, 29:43, 39:9, 58:11, 96:1-5.

36. Izetbegović, *Islam Between East and West*, 84.

37. A. Charfi, *La Pensée Islamique: Rupture et Fidélité*, 61.

38. See Abdullah Saeed and Hassan Saeed, *Freedom of Religion, Apostasy and Islam*, 72. Here, Abdullah Saeed offers his interpretation of free will with respect to the choice to believe or not to believe (as well as what to believe in).

39. Mayer, *Islam and Human Rights*, 48.

40. See Sha'rawi, *Khawatir Muhammad Mutwalli Sha'rawi*. In this work Sha'rawi interprets Verse 24:51 in the sense of equating submission to God with relinquishing the freedom of rational argument in religious matters.

41. Iqbal, *The Reconstruction of Religious Thought in Islam*, 97.

42. Jabiri, *Al-Dimuqratiyya wa Huquq al-Insan*, 156–157; 'Ashmawi, *Al-'Aql fi-l-Islam*, 25–31.

43. Hoffman, *Al-Islam ka-Badil*, 96; 'Ashmawi, *Al-'Aql fi-l-Islam*, 20.

44. Esack, *Le Coran: Mode d'Emploi*, 158*ff*.

45. See A. Charfi, *L'Islam entre le Message et l'Histoire*, 204; Talbi, *Universalité du Coran*, 28. In *Universalité*, Talbi praises the way in which God appeals to the minds of humans by encouraging them to abandon convictions based solely upon miracles, and to replace magical thinking with more rational thinking.

46. See Watt and Bell, *An Introduction to the Qur'an*, 150–152. Watt and Bell provide examples of verses wrongly believed to support claims of divine arbitrariness and suppression of free will. This explains their conclusion that "the Quran simply holds fast to the complementary truth of God's omnipotence and man's responsibility without reconciling them intellectually."

47. Dawood, trans., *The Koran*, 207.

48. Qur'an 2:90: "*Vile is that [false pride] for which they have sold their own selves by denying the truth of what God has bestowed from on high, out of envy that* God should bestow aught of His favor upon whomsoever He wills of His servants*: and thus have they earned the burden of God's condemnation, over and over. And for those who deny the truth there is shameful suffering in store*" (Asad, trans., http://www.altafsir.com).

49. Qur'an 2:272: "*Not upon you, [O Muhammad], is [responsibility for] their guidance, but* Allah guides whom He wills. *And whatever good you [believers] spend is for yourselves, and you do not spend except seeking the countenance of Allah . And whatever you spend of good - it will be fully repaid to you, and* you will not be wronged" (Walk, trans., http://www.altafsir.com).

50. Qur'an 2:268–269: "*Satan promises you poverty, and bids you unto indecency; but God promises you His pardon and His bounty; and God is All-embracing, All-knowing (268).* He gives the Wisdom to whomsoever He will, *and whoso is given the Wisdom, has been given much good;* yet none remembers but men possessed of minds *(269)*" (Arberry, trans., http://www.altafsir.com).

51. Qur'an 6:111: "*If We had sent down to them the angels, and the dead had spoken to them, and (even if) We had gathered everything before them face to face, still, they were not to believe, unless Allah would have so willed. But, most of them adopt the way of ignorance*"
('Uthmani, trans., http://www.altafsir.com).

52. 'Uthmani, trans., http://www.altafsir.com.

53. See Jabiri (*Fahm al-Qur'an al-Hakim*, 2:161–180) for a discussion of the proper interpretation of the verses about God's option to either provide guidance or withhold it.

54. Qur'an 76:29–31 (Asad, trans., http://www.altafsir.com).

55. Qur'an 2:225: "*Allah will not take you to task for that which is unintentional in your oaths. But He will take you to task for that which your hearts have garnered. Allah is Forgiving, Clement*" (Pickthall, trans., http://www.altafsir.com).

56. Qur'an 29:10 ('Uthmani, trans., http://www.altafsir.com). See also Qur'an 3:29, 3:119, 3:154, 5:7, 8:43, 11:5, 27:74, 28:69, 35:38, 39:7, 40:19, 42:24, 57:6, 64:4, 67:13.

57. Qur'an 11:1 (Walk, trans., http://www.altafsir.com). A similar formula appears in twenty-three of the one hundred and fourteen suras of the Qur'an.

58. Qur'an 2:282–283.

59. Qur'an 4:103.

60. Qur'an 2:183.

61. Qur'an 2:216, 2:246, 4:66, 4:77.

62. Qur'an 2:180.

63. Qur'an 2:178, 5:45.

64. Qur'an 2:235, 4:127.

65. Qur'an 2:187.

66. Qur'an 4:24, 5:32

67. Qur'an 9:120–121, 21:94, 58:22.

68. Qur'an 3:53, 5:83.

69. Qur'an 7:156.

70. Qur'an 6:12.

71. Qur'an 6:54.

72. Qur'an 8:75.

73. Qur'an 4:81, 6:38, 10:21, 10:61, 17:13–14, 17:71, 18:49, 19:79, 22:70, 27:75, 69:19, 69:25, 78:29, 83:7, 83:9, 83:18, 83:20, 84:7, 84:10.

74. Qur'an 5:21, 13:43, 17:4, 17:58, 20:52, 21:105, 52:41, 58:21, 59:3, 68:47, 98:3.

75. Asad, trans., http://www.altafsir.com.

76. See the interpretations of Tabari in *Jami' al-Bayan*, and Razi in *Mafatih al-Ghayb, al-Tafsir al-Kabir*.

77. Qur'anic Verse 9:51 should be read in conjunction with Verses Q9:48 to 50, as follows: "*Indeed, even before this time have they tried to stir up discord and devised all manner of plots against thee, [O Prophet,] until the truth was revealed and God's will became manifest, however hateful this may have been to them (48). And among them there was [many a one] who said, 'Grant me permission [to remain at home], and do not put me to too hard a test!' Oh, verily, [by making such a request] they had [already failed in their test and] succumbed to a temptation to evil: and, behold, hell will indeed encompass all who refuse to acknowledge the truth (49)! Should good fortune alight on thee,*

[O Prophet,] it will grieve them; and should misfortune befall thee, they will say [to themselves], 'We have already taken our precautions beforehand!'—and will turn away, and will rejoice (50). Say: 'Never can anything befall us save what God has decreed! He is our Lord Supreme; and in God let the believers place their trust!' (51)" (Asad, trans., http://www.altafsir.com).

78. Qur'an 9:51. See the interpretations of this verse by Tabarsi in *Majma' al-Bayan fi Tafsir al-Qur'an*, and Ibn 'Ashour in *Al-Tahrir wa al-Tanwir*.

79. Asad, trans., http://www.altafsir.com.

80. 'Uthmani, trans., http://www.altafsir.com.

81. Ibn Kathir, *Tafsir al-Qur'an al-Karim*.

82. Asad, trans., http://www.altafsir.com.

83. 'Uthmani, trans., http://www.altafsir.com.

84. Asad, trans., http://www.altafsir.com.

85. M. Ghazali, *Al-Mahawir al-Khamsa fi-l-Qur'an al-Karim*, 31.

86. Most traditional commentators of the Qur'an (including Tabari, Zamakhshari, Qurtubi, Ibn Kathir, Razi) have opted for an interpretation based on the concept of predestination. Most contemporary commentators did the same except for Ibn 'Ashour, whose interpretation was based more closely on the concept of the laws of nature. Another modern-day thinker, Muhammad Shahrour, rejects the theory of predestination and brings attention to the laws of nature in order to rationally explain the verses which people misconstrued as predestination (Shahrour, *Al-Kitab wa-l-Qur'an,* 51*ff.,* 409*ff.*). 'Ashmawi also subscribed to the view that the term *kitab* is not a divine preordainment of day-to-day occurrences, but rather is about the preordained laws of nature which affect them ('Ashmawi, *Al-'Aql fi-l-Islam*, 129).

87. See Qur'an 74:36–38, 74:54–55.

88. Qur'an 4:40 (Abdel Haleem, trans., *The Qur'an*, 54). See also Verse 21:47.

89. Qur'an 3:108 (Yusuf Ali, trans., http://www.altafsir.com). See also Qur'an 5:39, 9:104, 20:82.

90. See Qur'an 2:217.

91. See Qur'an 14:51, 21:47, 99:7–8.

92. Arberrry, trans., http://www.altafsir.com.

93. 'Uthmani, trans., http://www.altafsir.com.

94. Walk, trans., http://www.altafsir.com.

95. Ibid. See also Qur'an 40:40. .

96. See Qur'an 11:123, 13:9, 16:77, 18:26, 23:92, 27:65, 32:6, 35:38, 39:46, 59:22, 64:18, 72:26.

97. Walk, trans., http://www.altafsir.com.

98. See Shahrour, *Al-Kitab wa-l Qur'an*, 385–394; Schuon, *Comprendre L'Islam*, 14. Shahrour organizes God's infinite knowledge of human activity into

two subcategories: knowledge of potential actions (all possible alternatives before an action occurs) and knowledge of actual occurrences (as and when they occur). Schuon offers an illustration of how divine omniscience can be confused with divine predestination.

99. See Abizaid, *Al-Tafkir fi Zaman al-Takfir*, 204, 259–260. Abizaid shares the philosophical arguments on predestination and free will of the Mu'tazila and Ash'ari schools of thought. For a more detailed overview of the Mu'tazila school of thought, see Chebel, *L'Islam et la Raison*, 36–58.

100. Abizaid, *Al-Tafkir fi Zaman al-Takfir*, 37–38; 'Aqqad, *Al-Tafkir Farida Islamiyya*, 18ff.

101. Goldziher, *Muslim Studies*, 19–20. This should explain people's natural inclination to readily accept the Prophet's warnings against *bid'a* (innovation in religion).

102. Jait, *Fi al-Sira al-Nabawiyya*, 1:12. Jait observes, "*Īmān*...is therefore a very strong feeling, that cannot be demonstrated by rational proofs, but requires divine inspiration and presence...this, of course, requires believing the Prophet and even treating him with sanctity."

103. See Hoffman, *Al-Islam ka-Badil*, 24. Hoffman attributes the mental stagnation of Muslim societies to a belief originating in the fourteenth century, according to which the good and pious Muslims of the early days, namely the 'ulama' and *fuqahā'*, did a comprehensive job in addressing, analyzing and resolving every single issue that anyone may ever think of, thereby leaving nothing for later people to waste their time on rethinking, other than to possibly summarize, imitate, and further explain.

104. Zafar, "Accountability, Parliament, and *Ijtihad*," in *Liberal Islam*, ed. Kurzman, 70.

105. *Sunan al Nissa'i*, vol. 3, no. 1.14; H. Amin, *Dalil al-Muslim al-Hazin*, 59.

106. See Hoffman, *Al-Islam ka-Badil*, 69–70. These pages provide an overview of the evolution of the concept of *bid'a*.

107. Goldziher, *Madhahib al-Tafsir al-Islami*, 73ff.

108. See Akhtar, *The Quran and the Secular Mind*, 40–46. Here, Akhtar discusses the concept of *bid'a*.

109. Wartani and Qammouri, *Islam 'Usur al-Inhitat*, 60–61.

110. Ibid., 63–68.

111. Ibid., 79–85.

112. See Étienne, *Les Questions qui Fachent*, 59–66. Étienne's *Les Questions* provides an overview of the period of enlightenment following Islam's expansion outside Arabia and interaction with other cultures, as well as its subsequent decline following closure of *ijtihād* and mounting pressures from European colonial intrusions.

113. See M. Ghazali, *Laysa min al-Islam*, 75–112. Ghazali's definition of *bid'a* offers an example of conditions, the observance of which is sufficient to deter any God-fearing person in good faith from ever attempting to use his or her mind in any sphere of religion.

114. Abizaid, *Al-Tafkir fi Zaman al-Takfir*, 138; Soroush, *Reason, Freedom and Democracy in Islam*, 31; Chebel, *L'Islam et la Raison*, 127–129. Soroush distinguishes between the divine truth of religion and the human understanding of it. Chebel decries the persecution of scientists and intellectuals in the name of religion which led to stagnation within Islamic nations.

115. Akhtar, *A Faith for All Seasons*, 34–38.

116. Berque, *Relire Le Coran*, 110.

117. Bucaille, "Préludes à un Examen du Coran à la Lumière des Connaissances Modernes," in *Réflexions sur le Coran*, eds. Talbi and Bucaille, 168.

118. Qur'an 27:1, Asad, trans., http://www.altafsir.com; Qur'an 4:174, Walk, trans., http://www.altafsir.com. See also Qur'an 3:184, 5:15, 12:1, 15:1, 26:2, 28:2, 36:69, 43:2, 43:3, 44:2.

119. Asad, trans., http://www.altafsir.com. See also Qur'an 13:37, 16:103, 26:195, 39:28, 41:3, 42:7, 43:3, 46:12.

120. Yusuf Ali, trans., http://www.altafsir.com. See also Qur'an 7:184, 15:89, 22:49, 26:115, 29:50, 38:70, 43:29, 46:9, 51:50–51, 67:26, 71:2. Note that the messages carried by Prophet Muhammad's predecessors are also denoted as being clear and accessible to the mind (as seen in Qur'anic Verses 11:25, 23:45, 40:23, 44:19, 51:38).

121. Asad, trans., http://www.altafsir.com.

122. See Qur'an 2:197, 2:269, 3:7, 3:190, 5:100, 12:111, 13:19, 14:52, 38:29, 38:43, 39:18, 39:21, 40:54, 65:10.

123. Qur'an 14:52: "*This is a clear message for mankind in order that they may be warned thereby, and that they may know that He is only One God, and that men of understanding may take heed*" (Pickthall, trans., http://www.altafsir. com).

124. Qur'an 38:29: "*[All this have We expounded in this] blessed divine writ which We have revealed unto thee, [O Muhammad,] so that men may ponder over its messages, and that those who are endowed with insight may take them to heart*" (Asad, trans., http://www.altafsir.com).

125. Qur'an 3:190: "*Surely, in the creation of the heavens and the earth, and in the alternation of night and day, there are signs for the people of wisdom*" ('Uthmani, trans., http://www.altafsir.com).

126. See Madjid, "Islamic Thought and Religious Understanding," in *Liberal Islam*, ed. Kurzman, 288. Madjid cites Qur'anic Verse 39:18, which defines *uli-l-albāb* as 'those who listen and then choose what is best'.

127. Asad, trans., http://www.altafsir.com.

128. Yusuf Ali, trans., http://www.altafsir.com. See also Qur'an 3:13, 38:45, 59:2.

129. Asad, trans., http://www.altafsir.com. See also Qur'an 2:73, 2:164, 2:170, 3:118, 6:151, 12:2, 13:4, 16:12, 16:67, 24:61, 26:28, 29:35, 30:24, 30:28, 40:67, 43:3, 45:5, 49:4, 57:17, 59:14.

130. Abdel Haleem, trans., *The Qur'an*, 87. See also Qur'an 6:65.

131. 'Uthmani, trans., http://www.altafsir.com. See also Qur'an 2:219, 2:266, 3:191, 7:176, 10:24, 13:3, 16:11, 16:44, 16:69, 30:21, 39:42, 45:13, 59:21.

132. Pickthall, trans., http://www.altafsir.com. See also Qur'an 2:221, 3:7, 6:152, 7:26, 7:57, 7:130, 7:201, 8:57, 11:114, 13:19, 14:25 14:52, 16:13, 16:90, 17:41, 20:44, 24:1, 24:27, 25:50, 25:62, 28:43, 28:46, 28:51, 38:29, 39:9, 39:27, 40:13, 44:58, 51:49, 51:55, 69:12, 80:10, 80:11.

133. 'Uthmani, trans., http://www.altafsir.com. See also Qur'an 2:269, 13:19, 14:52, 38:29, 39:9.

134. Asad, trans., http://www.altafsir.com. See also Qur'an 2:4, 2:118, 5:50, 6:75, 13:2, 26:24, 31:4, 32:12, 32:24, 44:7, 45:4, 51:20, 56:95, 69:51, 74:31, 74:47, 102:5, 102:7.

135. Asad, trans., http://www.altafsir.com.

136. 'Uthmani uses the term 'faith', while Asad uses the term 'inner certainty'. For a definition of the term *ghayb*, see Qur'anic Verse 16:77: "*And God's [alone] is the knowledge of the hidden reality of the heavens and the earth. And so, the advent of the Last Hour will but manifest itself [in a single moment,] like the twinkling of an eye, or closer still: for, behold, God has the power to will anything*" (Asad, trans., http://www.altafsir.com). See also Qur'an 31:34.

137. See Qur'an 2:44, 2:76, 2:171, 3:65, 5:58, 6:32, 10:16, 10:42, 10:100, 11:51, 12:109, 21:10, 21:67, 23:80, 28:60, 29:63, 37:138, 49:4.

138. See Qur'an 4:78, 8:65, 9:81, 9:87, 9:127, 17:44, 48:15, 59:13, 63:3, 63:7.

139. See Qur'an 6:50, 7:184, 30:8.

140. See Qur'an 6:80, 7:3, 9:126, 10:3, 11:24, 11:30, 16:17, 23:85, 27:62, 32:4, 37:155, 40:58, 45:23, 54:32, 54:40, 56:62, 69:42, 74:49.

141. See Qur'an 27:82, 30:60, 52:36.

142. This section does not address the countless verses which use the terms *āyas* and *amthāl* in a general sense, without referencing a specific topic. Examples include Qur'anic Verses 2:39, 2:99, 3:21, 6:126, 10:1, 11:1, 15:1, 15:81, 16:104–105, 24:1, 26:2, 28:2, 38:29, and 41:3.

143. Asad, trans., http://www.altafsir.com. See also Qur'an 17:89, 18:54, 30:58.

144. Because matters relating to *ghayb* are beyond full human comprehension or verification, translators Asad and Yusuf Ali use the term 'parables' to convey the meaning of the examples and signs offered by God (see Asad's note regarding Qur'anic Verse 39:27). Yusuf Ali offers the following explanation of Qur'anic parables: "Men can only understand high spiritual truths by parables and similitudes and these are given abundantly in the Qur-An. The object is not merely to tell stories but to teach lessons of spiritual wisdom."

145. Asad, trans., http://www.altafsir.com.

146. Ibid. See also Qur'an 6:101–105, 29:41–42, 39:52.

147. Asad, trans., http://www.altafsir.com. See also Qur'an 6:98, 21:30–33, 29:44, 39:42.

148. Asad, trans., http://www.altafsir.com.

149. Yusuf Ali, trans., http://www.altafsir.com.

150. Pickthall, trans., http://www.altafsir.com. See also Qur'an 27:82–86, 47:15.

151. 'Uthmani, trans., http://www.altafsir.com.

152. Qur'an 20:117–128.

153. See Qur'an 10:71, 23:30, 25:37, 29:15, 54:13–15.

154. See Qur'an 11:61–66, 17:59.

155. See Qur'an 15:58–75, 29:31–35.

156. See Qur'an 12:7.

157. See Qur'an 7:132, 7:133, 10:90–92.

158. See Qur'an 2:246–252.

159. See Qur'an 34:15.

160. See Qur'an 21:91, 23:50.

161. See Qur'an 18:17.

162. See Qur'an 3:49–51, 7:106-108, 20:17–23, 27:12, 27:13, 28:35, 28:36.

163. See Akhtar, *The Quran and the Secular Mind*, 225–230. Akhtar discusses the role of *āyas* (the signs of God) in the context of scientific development.

164. Yusuf Ali, trans., http://www.altafsir.com. See also Qur'an 13:2–4, 30:24, 30:46.

165. Asad, trans., http://www.altafsir.com. See also Qur'an 31:31, 42:32–33.

166. Yusuf Ali, trans., http://www.altafsir.com. See also Qur'an 36:33.

167. Yusuf Ali, trans., http://www.altafsir.com.

168. Arberry, trans., http://www.altafsir.com. See also Qur'an 22:4–5, 23:12–16.

169. Arberry, trans., http://www.altafsir.com. See also Qur'an 3:190, 10:6, 10:67, 10:101, 16:12, 17:12, 30:23, 36:37, 41:37.

170. Arberry, trans., http://www.altafsir.com.

171. Yusuf Ali, trans., http://www.altafsir.com. See also Qur'an 16:10, 16:11, 20:54, 40:13.

172. 'Uthmani, trans., http://www.altafsir.com.

173. Ibid.

174. Ibid.

175. Asad, trans., http://www.altafsir.com.

176. Yusuf Ali, trans., http://www.altafsir.com.

177. Arberry, trans., http://www.altafsir.com.

178. 'Uthmani, trans., http://www.altafsir.com.

179. Asad, trans., http://www.altafsir.com.

180. Ibid.

181. Dawood, trans., *The Koran*, 32.

182. Dawood, trans., *The Koran*, 285.

183. Yusuf Ali, trans., http://www.altafsir.com. See also Qur'an 2:257, 5:15, 5:16, 14:1, 14:5, 33:43.

184. 'Uthmani, trans., http://www.altafsir.com. See also Qur'an 2:129, 62:2.

185. See Talbi, "La Vocation de l'Homme," in *Réflexions sur le Coran*, eds. Talbi and Bucaille, 77*ff.* Talbi discusses the role of science in understanding the Qur'an. In light of the scriptural evidence on the importance of science offered in this article, the theory of evolution—which so far has been considered to clash with the theory of creation—becomes plausible and finds support in the divine scripture.

186. Qur'an 20:114.

187. Asad, trans., http://www.altafsir.com. See also Qur'an 6:104, 7:203, 51:20–21.

188. Royal Aal al-Bayt Institute, trans., http://www.altafsir.com. See also Qur'an 46:26–27.

189. 'Uthmani, trans., http://www.altafsir.com.

190. Asad, trans., http://www.altafsir.com. See also Qur'an 23:78.

191. Qur'an 29:43 ('Uthmani, trans., http://www.altafsir.com).

192. Yusuf Ali, trans., http://www.altafsir.com.

193. Qaradawi, *Al-Tatarruf al-'Ilmani*, 62.

194. 'Azm, *Naqd al-Fikr al-Dini*, 15.

195. Rahman, *Islam and Modernity*, 51; Jabiri, *Al-Dimuqratiyya wa Huquq al-Insan*, 156.

196. "*We have created man from an extract of clay (12), Then We made him a sperm-drop in a firm resting place (13), Then We turned the sperm-drop into a clot, then We turned the clot into a fetus-lump, then We turned the fetus-lump into bones, then We clothed the bones with flesh; thereafter We developed it into another creature. So, glorious is Allah, the Best of the creators (14)*" ('Uthmani, trans., http://www.altafsir.com).

197. 'Azm, *Naqd al-Fikr al-Dini*, 27–28.

198. Asad, trans., http://www.altafsir.com.

199. Rida, "Al-Khilafa aw al-Imama al-'Uzma," in *Al-Dawla wa-l-Khilafa fi-l-Khitab al-'Arabi*, ed. Kawtharani, 109–110.

200. See Qaradawi, *Al-Tatarruf al-'Ilmani*, 68; A. Charfi, *L'Islam entre le Message et l'Histoire*, 12. In *L'Islam*, Charfi criticizes the near-sacralization of human pronouncements.

201. Soroush, "The Evolution and Devolution of Religious Knowledge," in *Liberal Islam*, ed. Kurzman, 244–251; Shahrour, *Al-Kitab wa-l-Qur'an*, 185–191. Shahrour proposes that the Qur'an's *i'jāz*, or miraculous inimitability, is made manifest through its adaptability to reinterpretation in each time and place.

202. Hamza, *Islam al-Mujaddidin*, 41.

203. A. Charfi, *La Pensée Islamique: Rupture et Fidélité*, 80–81. This prophetic tradition is cited by Mahmassani on page 77 of *Falsafat Al-Tashrī Fi Al-Islām*. The conservative Maliki and Hanbali schools of jurisprudence rejected *ijmā'* as a source of Shari'a (except in certain cases for the *ijmā'* of the Prophet's companions). See also D. Brown, *Rethinking Tradition in Modern Islamic Thought*, 28.

204. A. Charfi, *L'Islam entre le Message et l'Histoire*, 180.

205. Shahrour, "Islam and the 1995 Beijing World Conference on Women," in *Liberal Islam*, ed. Kurzman, 141.

206. A. Charfi, *L'Islam entre le Message et l'Histoire*, 181; Abizaid, *Al-Tafkir fi Zaman al-Takfir*, 22. Abizaid observes that whenever *ijmā'* is restricted to the views of the few, sacralization starts and becomes a tool of regression.

207. Asad, trans., http://www.altafsir.com.

208. D. Brown, *Rethinking Tradition in Modern Islamic Thought*, 25–26.

209. Kurzman, "Liberal Islam and its Islamic Context," in *Liberal Islam*, ed. Kurzman, 7–8.

210. Soroush, "The Evolution and Devolution of Religious Knowledge," in *Liberal Islam*, ed. Kurzman, 244–251.

211. Suyuti, *Al-Jami' al-Saghir*, vol. 1, no. 565; *Sahih al-Bukhari*, vol. 4, chap. 99, no. 6919.

212. Qur'an 26:69–77 (Asad, trans., http://www.altafsir.com).

213. Mahmassani, *Arkan Huquq al-Insan*, 196.

214. See Wadud, *Qur'an and Woman*, 23; Soroush, *Reason, Freedom, and Democracy in Islam*, 100. Wadud observes that free choice was granted to humankind very early on after creation. Soroush recalls the tale of God's admonition of Moses, who feared the Pharaoh's sorcerers' threat to put a spell on peoples' rational faculties.

215. Filali-Ansari, *L'Islam est-il Hostile à la Laïcité*, 126.

216. Mahmassani, *Al-Da'a'im al-Khuluqiyya li-l-Qawanin al-Shar'iyya*, 93ff.

217. Pickthall, trans., http://www.altafsir.com.

218. See Mahmassani, *Al-Da'a'im al-Khuluqiyya li-l-Qawanin al-Shar'iyya*, 362. This principle found its way firmly into the first codification of civil law, known as Majallat al-Ahkam al-'Adliyya.

219. See Mahmassani, *Falsafat al-Tashrī Fi al-Islām*, 105*ff.* In this work, Mahmassani provides an overview of the treatment of this principle by the traditional jurisprudence. While there was unanimous agreement regarding this principle, there was no consensus over the details of its implementation.

220. Yusuf Ali, trans., http://www.altafsir.com.

221. In another example, Caliph 'Umar was allocating an estate among heirs who included a number of persons privileged with a minimum reserved share, together with siblings, some from both common parents and others from the mother's side only. Under the rules set forth in the Qur'an, the siblings from the mother's side get a reserved share, while the siblings from the same parents receive the estate remaining after distribution to those with reserved shares in their capacity as '*assabāt* descending from the male line. In this particular instance, the entire estate was exhausted by the reserved shares allocated to the maternal siblings and to other heirs entitled to reserved shares, leaving nothing for the siblings who descend from both common parents. In light of the unfairness arising from blind application of the stated rule, and because all siblings in the instance share the same mother, 'Umar decided to treat the siblings descending from common parents similarly to maternal siblings in the allocation of the reserved share. Thus, since promoting fairness is among the objectives of the Divine Message, Caliph 'Umar set the Qur'anic provision aside in the case where its implementation would otherwise result in unfairness.

222. See Qur'an 6:119, 6:145.

223. It is a codification of the rules applicable to obligations and contracts under the Hanafi doctrine, compiled by a committee of law and Shari'a experts designated by the Ottoman authorities. It was completed in the year 1876 A.D. See also a discussion of the principle of *al-darūrāt tubīhu-l-mahzūrāt* in Mahmassani, *Falsafat al-Tashrī Fi al-Islām*, 152–158.

224. See Qur'an 2:185, 22:78.

225. In support of their attachment to the technique of *qiyās*, the principals of the liberal School of Baghdad cite Qur'anic Verse Q29:43: "*We cite these examples for people, but no one understands them except the knowledgeable ones*" ('Uthmani, trans., http://www.altafsir.com.). In reality, it was not necessary to look in the Qur'an for a basis to apply that technique or any other rational technique which seeks to better implement, and fulfill the objectives

of, the Divine Message. For a discussion of the concept of *qiyās* from the *fiqh* perspective, see Mahmassani, *Falsafat al-Tashrī Fi al-Islām*, 79–83.

226. Qur'an 5:90–91: *"Believers, wine and games of chance, idols and divining arrows, are abominations devised by Satan. Avoid them, so that you may prosper (90). Satan seeks to stir up enmity and hatred among you by means of wine and gambling, and to keep you from the remembrance of God and from your prayers. Will you not abstain from them? (91)"* (Dawood, trans., The Koran, 89).

227. See Mahmassani, *Falsafat al-Tashrī Fi al-Islām*, 83–91. Mahmassani provides an overview of these concepts.

228. A. Charfi, *L'Islam entre le Message et l'Histoire*, 102.

229. See Soroush, *Reason, Freedom and Democracy in Islam*, 88*ff*.; Bazergan, "Religion and Liberty," in *Liberal Islam*, ed. Kurzman, 76–77. These works provide a comprehensive overview of the intimate relationship of reason and freedom.

230. Foda, *Al-Haqiqa al-Gha'ba*, 45–52.

231. Arkoun, "Rethinking Islam Today," in *Liberal Islam*, ed. Kurzman, 221; Soroush *Reason, Freedom, and Democracy in Islam*, 61. Arkoun and Soroush hold opposing viewpoints regarding the compatibly of religion and science.

232. Saleh, *Al-Islam Wa-l-Mujtama' al-'Asri*, 25.

233. Hamza, *Islam al-Mujaddidin*, 46.

234. Moosa, "The Debts and Burdens of Critical Islam," in *Progressive Muslims*, ed. Safi, 113.

235. Talbi, *Plaidoyer pour un Islam Moderne*, 191. See also Chebel, *Islam et Libre Arbitre*, 233; A. Charfi, *L'Islam entre le Message et l'Histoire*, 137.

236. Johns and Saeed, "Nurcholish Madjid and the Interpretation of the Qur'an," in *Modern Muslim Intellectuals and the Qur'an*, ed. Taji-Farouki, 79.

CHAPTER 13: ISLAMD AND 'OTHERS'

1. Kabir, "Minorities in a Democracy," in *Liberal Islam*, ed. Kurzman, 145–154. The 'others' may be a majority in a community in which the Muslims are a minority, or a minority in a community in which the Muslims are a majority.

2. See Sachedina, *The Islamic Roots of Democratic Pluralism*, 50–53; Abou El Fadl, "The Ugly Modern and the Modern Ugly: Reclaiming the Beautiful in Islam," in *Progressive Muslims*, ed. Safi, 50. Ibn Abdel Wahhab is the founder of the Wahhabi faith. Abou El Fadl offers an interesting account of Ibn Abdel Wahhab's rejection of pluralism.

3. Cohen, *Under Crescent and Cross*, 32.

4. Ramadan, *Mon Intime Conviction*, 20.

5.   Talbi, *Plaidoyer pour un Islam Moderne*, 172–173.

6.   Ibid., 69–74. While Talbi condemns violence and intolerance, he advocates for what he calls "the right to difference," or the freedom of each person to have his or her own reading and understanding of religion, no matter how different it may be from the readings and understandings of others.

7.   See Safi, "The Times They Are a-Changin'—A Muslim Quest for Justice, Gender Equality, and Pluralism," in *Progressive Muslims*, ed. Safi, 24. Safi cautions against reducing pluralism in Islam to mere tolerance. He advocates for a pluralistic society in which commonalities and differences are vehicles of interaction and mutual appreciation. See also Amir Hussain, "Muslims, Pluralism and Interfaith Dialogue," in *Progressive Muslims*, ed. Safi, 252.

8.   Sachedina, *The Islamic Roots of Democratic Pluralism*, 23.

9.   Ibid., 69.

10. Muhammad Natsir, "The Indonesian Revolution," in *Liberal Islam*, ed. Kurzman, 66.

11. Talbi, *Plaidoyer pour un Islam Moderne*, 75.

12. Asad, trans., http://www.altafsir.com.

13. See Ayoub, *A Muslim View of Christianity*, 37–38. Ayoub cites Qur'anic Verse 5:48 as evidence that the Qur'an projects a world view and a spirit which rejects any religious exclusivism.

14. Khalidi, trans., *The Qur'an*, 89.

15. Qur'an 6:108. This verse enjoins believers to behave with civility towards nonbelievers and abstain from reviling their deities, lest they revile God.

16. See Bidar, *Self-Islam*, 32–33. Bidar provides a good description of this aspect of Islam.

17. Ayoub, *A Muslim View of Christianity*, 15.

18. Boullata, "Fa-Stabiqū 'l-khayrāt: A Qur'anic Principle of Interfaith Relations," in *Christian-Muslim Encounters*, eds. Yvonne Haddad and Wadi Haddad, 44.

19. Talbi, *L'Universalité du Coran*, 38–39.

20. Dawood, trans., *The Koran*, 148, 285.

21. Asad, trans., http://www.altafsir.com.

22. Walk, trans., http://www.altafsir.com.

23. Asad, trans., http://www.altafsir.com.

24. Talbi, "Religious Liberty," in *Liberal Islam*, ed. Kurzman, 164.

25. Yusuf Ali, trans., http://www.altafsir.com.

26. See Saleh, *Al-Islam wa-l-Mujtama' al-'Asri*, 151–188. Saleh asserts that Prophet Muhammad's eternal message should help in the transition from "the state of the unity of the Muslim Umma to the unity of the entire human-kind," thereby refuting that pluralism is inherent in Islam.

27. Khalidi, trans., *The Qur'an*, 464.
28. Asad, trans., http://www.altafsir.com.
29. 'Uthmani, trans., http://www.altafsir.com.
30. Shahrour, "Islam and the 1995 Beijing World Conference on Women," in *Liberal Islam*, ed. Kurzman, 140.
31. See Moussalli, *The Islamic Quest for Democracy*, 143–153. Mousalli offers an overview of the radical views on freedom of faith and equality in plurality. He includes such radical thinkers as Qutb, Mawdudi, Mustapha, and Qaradawi.
32. Yusuf Ali, trans., http://www.altafsir.com.
33. Hussain, "Muslims, Pluralism, and Interfaith Dialogue," in *Progressive Muslims*, ed. Safi, 254–255.
34. Khalidi, trans., *The Qur'an*, 424.
35. See Sachedina, *The Islamic Roots of Democratic Pluralism*, 23ff. Sachedina discusses the unity of humankind under one God and the Qur'anic concept of religious pluralism.
36. Jabiri, *Al-Dimuqratiyya wa Huquq al-Insan*, 218.
37. M. Charfi, *Islam et Liberté*, 182–183.
38. Safi, "The Times They Are a-Changin'—A Muslim Quest for Justice, Gender Equality, and Pluralism," in *Progressive Muslims*, ed. Safi, 12; Sachedina, *The Islamic Roots of Democratic Pluralism*, 13.
39. Ayoub, *A Muslim View of Christianity*, 19.
40. See Qur'an 16:19, 60:1, 64:4.
41. The discord that occurred later between the Jews and the Muslims within that society was mostly politically motivated.
42. Talbi, *Plaidoyer pour un Islam Moderne*, 82–83; Gardet, *Les Hommes de l'Islam*, 44–45; Ramadan, *Islam, the West and the Challenges of Modernity*, 105.
43. Muhtadi Ghaleb, "Nahnu fi-l-Asr," in *Islam dodd Islam*, ed. Nayhoum, 310.
44. These views are expressed by several early interpreters of Qur'anic Verse 48:28, including Qurtubi in *Al-Jami' li Ahkam al Qur'an* and Tabari in *Jami' al-Bayan fi Tafsir al-Qur'an*. They are also expressed by modern-day commentators, including Tantawi, in *Al-Wasit fi Tafsir al-Qur'an al-Karim*, and Jabiri in *Fahm al-Qur'an al-Hakim*, 3:109. These views were recently reproduced by orientalists and others such as De Prémare in *Aux Origines du Coran*, 34; and Akeel Bilgrami' with "The Importance of Democracy," in *The Place of Tolerance in Islam*, ed. Abou El Fadl, 65. See also Esposito, *The Islamic Threat*, 24.
45. See Qur'an 9:5, 9:29. For exegeses of these verses, see Qurtubi, *Al-Jami' li Ahkam al-Qur'an*; Zamakhshari, *Tafsir al-Kashshaf*; Ibn 'Ashour, *Al-Tahrir wa al-Tanwir*; Tantawi, *Al-Wasit fi Tafsir Al-Qur'an al-Karim*.

46. See Berque, *Quel Islam*, 34–40. Berque offers some thoughts on the subject. Note, however, that 'Islamophobia' is often exaggerated beyond reasonable bounds. Bernard Lewis (*Cultures in Conflict*, 29) relates the following episode from the early days of seventeenth century Europe: "On 13 April 1602, a concerned citizen of Venice petitioned the republic against the proposal to establish the Fondaco dei Turchi on a regular basis. This institution, which provided board and lodging for visiting Turkish merchants, was, according to the petitioner, objectionable and dangerous for a number of reasons. The presence of large numbers of Turks in one place would inevitably lead to the building of a mosque and to the worship (the petitioner evidently knew little of the Islamic religion) of Muhammad. This would be an even greater scandal than that already caused by the presence of Jews and Protestant Germans."

47. Yusuf Ali, trans., http://www.altafsir.com.

48. These views were expressed by several early and modern-day commentators of the Qur'an, including Tabari, Razi, Qurtubi, Ibn Kathir, Suyuti, Mahalli, Ibn 'Ashour, Tantawi, and Sha'rawi.

49. Jabiri, *Fahm al-Qur'an al-Hakim*, 3:349. See also Zamakhshari (in *Tafsir al-Kashshaf*) who sees this verse as a reference to victory and prevalence over pagan religions and any divine religions which are distorted as to jeopardize the unicity of God.

50. See Qur'an 48:28 (Asad, trans., http://www.altafsir.com). In a note accompanying his translation of Qur'anic Verse Q48:28, Asad explains that the 'religion of God' should be interpreted as 'man's self-surrender unto God'.

51. See Qur'an 48:29: "*MUHAMMAD is God's Apostle; and those who are [truly] with him are firm and unyielding toward all deniers of the truth, [yet] full of mercy toward one another. Thou canst see them bowing down, prostrating themselves [in prayer], seeking favour with God and [His] goodly acceptance: their marks are on their faces, traced by prostration. This is their parable in the Torah as well as their parable in the Gospel: [they are] like a seed that brings forth its shoot, and then He strengthens it, so that it grows stout, and [in the end] stands firm upon its stem, delighting the sowers.. [Thus will God cause the believers to grow in strength,] so that through them He might confound the deniers of the truth. [But] unto such of them as may [yet] attain to faith and do righteous deeds, God has promised forgiveness and a reward supreme*" (Asad, trans., http://www.altafsir.com).

52. 'Uthmani, trans., http://www.altafsir.com.

53. Ibid.

54. Qutb, *Fi Dhilal al-Qur'an*. See Qutb's interpretation of Qur'anic Verse 9:29.

55. Pickthall, trans., http://www.altafsir.com. Among the translators, Khalidi (*The Qur'an*, 26) is the one who rendered the highlighted term for *fitna* as

'apostasy' which is most reflective of the context of Verse 2:193—namely that the idolaters were trying to push Muslims into reverting to their pagan religion, hence the need to fight them.

56.   'Uthmani, trans., http://www.altafsir.com.

57.   Yusuf Ali, trans., http://www.altafsir.com.

58.   Akhtar, *A Faith for all Seasons*, 199, 244n74.

59.   See A. Moussalli, *The Islamic Quest for Democracy, Pluralism, and Human Rights*, 112*ff.* In his discussion of radical exclusivism, Mousalli cites the views of those who allocate people into three categories: Muslims, infidels, or hypocrites (in which the 'Muslim' category excludes anyone who does not fully adhere to their brand of Islam).

60.   Qur'an 3:19. Several translators have rendered the term 'Islam' using its wider, generic meaning: "devotion to Him alone" (Abdel Haleem, *The Qur'an*, 35); Submission to the Will of God (Bakhtiar, *The Sublime Quran*, 58); Surrender to His Will and Guidance (Pickthall, http://www.altafsir.com); submission to His Will (Ali, http://www.altafsir.com); man's self-surrender unto Him (Asad, http://www.altafsir.com); Submission to the one God (Royal Aal al-Bayt Institute, http://www.altafsir.com).

61.   Yusuf Ali, trans., http://www.altafsir.com.

62.   Ahmad Amin, *Fajr al-Islam*, 70–71.

63.   'Uthmani, trans., http://www.altafsir.com.

64.   See A. Charfi, *La Pensée Islamique: Rupture et Fidélité*, 217. Charfi observes that the alleged abrogation of the messages of Moses and Jesus by Muhammad's message is nowhere to be found in the Qur'an. See also Abou El Fadl, *The Place of Tolerance in Islam*, 100–101.

65.   See Ayoub *A Muslim View of Christianity*, 3.

66.   See Ayoub, *A Muslim View of Christianity*, 44. The Prophet is reported to have said, "Whoever died in the faith of Jesus, and died in Islam before he heard of me, his lot shall be good. But whoever hears of me today and yet does not assent to me, he shall surely perish." This tradition must have been wrongly attributed to the Prophet by the early commentators. Prophet Muhammad could not have said it because it contradicts the Qur'anic verse that considers each revelation to be a valid path toward salvation. More importantly, this tradition contradicts the verses which specifically tell the Prophet that his revelation confirms the previous ones.

67.   See Fattal, *Le Statut Legal des Non-Musulmans en Pays d'Islam*; Cohen, *Under Crescent and Cross*; Lewis and Churchill, *Islam: the Religion and the People*, 51–60. These works provide a global account of the 'legal' status of *dhimmīs* in the early Islamic period following the death of the Prophet.

68.   A. Amin, *Duha al-Islam*, 1:22*ff.*

69. Lewis, *Cultures in Conflict*, 16–17.
70. See Coulson, *A History of Islamic Law*, 27. Coulson asserts that the *dhimmī* status may have been adopted from the fides status of noncitizens under Roman law.
71. This section does not purport to provide a comprehensive presentation of the *dhimmī* status. It discusses it in general terms only to determine if Islam mandates an inferior status for the People of the Book.
72. The *dhimmī* status—developed and practiced following the death of the Prophet—was sparingly applied to non-Muslims by the Prophet. For example, the Jews of Bahrain were not charged any *jizya* head tax, whereas some Jews of Medina surrendered their belongings, and others at a later time were charged with the *jizya* (see Haykal, chap. 21, 27 in *Hayat Muhammad*). For the text of the first *dhimma* pact issued by the Prophet, see Rabbath, *Mahomet Prophète Arabe et Fondateur d'État*, 496–498.
73. M. Talbi, "Religious Liberty," in *Liberal Islam*, ed. Kurzman, 165.
74. Sachedina, *The Islamic Roots of Democratic Pluralism*, 64–97.
75. Jabiri, *Al-Dimuqratiyya wa Huquq al-Insan*, 249.
76. See Rabbath, *Les Chrétiens dans l'Islam des Premiers Temps*, vol. 1–4; Gardet, *Les Hommes de l'Islam*, 96–100. These works provide a detailed history of the *dhimmī* status.
77. Talbi, *Plaidoyer pour un Islam Moderne*, 82–83; Sachedina, *The Islamic Roots of Democratic Pluralism*, 81.
78. 'Uthmani, trans., http://www.altafsir.com.
79. Rabbath, *Mahomet Prophète Arabe et Fondateur d'État*, 361ff.
80. See Abou El Fadl, *The Place of Tolerance in Islam*, 21. Abou El Fadl observes that "when the Qur'an was revealed, it was common inside and outside of Arabia to levy poll taxes against alien groups." The Byzantines and the Sassanids imposed such a tax on Christians and Jews in return for protection; however, in that instance, the tax did not indicate any permanent inferior status.
81. See De Prémare, *Les Fondations de l'Islam*, 377. De Prémare cites instances in which the governor appointed by Omayyad Caliph Walid I levied the *jizya* on Egypt's Christian Copts following their conversion to Islam.
82. Bidar, *Self-Islam*, 34.
83. Filali-Ansari, *l'Islam est-il Hostile à la Laïcité?*, 90.
84. Talbi, *Plaidoyer pour un Islam Moderne*, 184–185.
85. Elmessiri, *Toward a New Islamic Discourse*.
86. Abou El Fadl, "The Ugly Modern and the Modern Ugly: Reclaiming the Beautiful in Islam," in *Progressive Muslims*, ed. Safi, 41.

87. See M. Talbi, *Plaidoyer pour un Islam Moderne*, 111. Talbi deplores the fact that the manuscripts of Arab and Muslim authors can be commonly found in Western libraries whereas the reverse is not true. He blames this lack of interest in Western authors on a lack of free thought in Muslim countries.

88. Soroush, *Reason, Freedom, and Democracy in Islam*, 168.

89. Caratini, *Le Génie de l'Islamisme*, xvi, 611*ff*.; Waldron, "Democracy and Conflict," in *Islam and the Challenge of Democracy* ed. Abou El Fadl, 55.

90. See Ahmad Amin, chap. 1, 6 in *Duha al-Islam*, vol. 1. In chapter one, Amin describes the cultural diversity of the Arabo-Islamic Empire, and how the civilizations that existed in that geographical area coalesced to create the Islamo-Arab civilization. In chapter six, Amin discusses how, in the plural society of the first Abbasid Period, several different cultures—Greek, Arab, Indian, and Persian, among others— fused together to produce a brilliant Muslim culture. See also Lapidus, *A History of Islamic Societies*, 81–97.

91. Iqbal, *The Reconstruction of Religious Thought in Islam*, 97.

92. Soroush, *Reason, Freedom, and Democracy in Islam*, 162–170.

93. Abou El Fadl, "The Ugly Modern and the Modern Ugly: Reclaiming the Beautiful in Islam," in *Progressive Muslims*, ed. Safi, 45.

94. See details in chapter 16 of this book (titled "Reflections on Human Rights in Islam"), section entitled "Muslim Nations' Perception of Universal Human rights."

95. Karamustafa, "A Civilizational Project in Progress," in *Progressive Muslims*, ed. Safi, 109.

96. Kabir, "Minorities in a Democracy," in *Liberal Islam*, ed. Kurzman, 153.

97. Qur'an 2:143, 5:48, 10:19, 10:40-41, 10:99, 11:118, 16:93, 30:22, 42:8, 49:13.

98. See Saleh, *Al-Islam wa-l-Mujtama' al-'Asri*, 260; Iqbal, *The Reconstruction of Religious Thought in Islam*, 188–189. Iqbal points out the risks of substituting nationalism for global religious sentiment. In reality, political concepts of nationalism and identity should not be confused with religious universalism. Nationalism is neither incompatible nor inconsistent with the concept of the universal Umma.

99. Hamza, *Islam al-Mujaddidin*, 41.

100. Sachedina, *The Islamic Roots of Democratic Pluralism*, 70.

101. See Bellah, *Beyond Belief*, 150–151. Bellah provides a comparative description of the social environments in which each of the three major Abrahamic monotheisms appeared.

102. Abdullah Saeed and Hassan Saeed, *Freedom of Faith, Apostasy and Islam*, 21.

103. 'Abdu, *Al-Islam wa-l-Nasraniyya ma' al-'Ilm wa-l-Madaniyya*, 54.

104. See Étienne, *Les Questions qui Fachent*, 46–54. Étienne offers an expose of the respective contexts of the relations of Islam to Christianity and Judaism.

105. Izetbegović, *Islam between East and West*, 271.
106. 'Ashmawi takes the origin of the Abrahamic Faith all the way back to the ancient Egyptian religion and draws powerful parallels between the ancient Egyptian religion and Judaism (as well as Christianity and Islam, in part through Judaism). For example, the prohibition of eating pork in Judaism and Islam is linked to a similar prohibition in the ancient Egyptian religion. For a detailed discussion of 'Ashmawi's views on this matter, see Fluehr-Lobban, *Against Islamic Extremism*, 42*ff.* See also Esposito, *Islam: The Straight Path*, 17–18.
107. Asad, trans., http://www.altafsir.com.
108. De Prémare, *Aux Origines du Coran*, 37–39. De Prémare highlights similarities between *sūrat Al-Rahman* and certain Biblical themes.
109. Dawood, trans., *The Koran*, 11.
110. Walk, trans., http://www.altafsir.com.
111. 'Uthmani, trans., http://www.altafsir.com.
112. Khalidi, trans., *The Qur'an*, 81.
113. See the views of 'Ashmawi on this subject in Fluehr-Lobban, *Against Islamic Extremism*, 54. .
114. Qur'an 5:48. Khalidi, trans., *The Qur'an*, 89.
115. Qur'an 2:62 (Yusuf ali, trans., http://www.altafsir.com). Zuḥaylī, *Al-Mawsū'ah al-Qur'āniyyah al-Muyassarah*, 120; Tabari, *Jami' al-Bayan fi Tafsir al-Qur'an*; Tabarsi, *Majma' al-Bayan fi Tafsir al-Qur'an*; Qurtubi, *Tafsir al-Jami' li Ahkam al-Qur'an*; Ibn Kathir, *Tafsir al-Qur'an al-Karim*; Qur'an 5:68: "*Say, "O people of the Book, you have nothing to stand on, unless you uphold the Torah and the Injīl and what has been sent down to you from your Lord." What has been sent down to you from your Lord will certainly make many of them more persistent in rebellion and disbelief. So, do not grieve over the disbelieving people*" ('Uthmani, trans., http://www.altafsir.com). The commentators cited above interpret this verse to mean that it is insufficient for Jews and Christians to believe solely in their respective scriptures, but that they must also believe in the Qur'an. (Zamakhshari, Razi, and Jabiri did not advance this view). However, this interpretation is disproved by Qur'anic Verse 5:69, which unequivocally confirms that Jews, Sabeans, and Christians will be saved if they believe in God and the Day of Judgment, and perform good deeds. There is no implication that belief in Prophet Muhammad's mission and Message is a mandatory precondition of salvation.
116. Boullata, "Fa-stabiqū 'l-khayrāt: A Qur'anic Principle of Interfaith Relations," in *Christian-Muslim Encounters*, eds. Yvonne Haddad and Wadi Haddad, 45.
117. Yusuf Ali, trans., http://www.altafsir.com.
118. Akhtar, *A Faith for All Seasons*, 199; Bidar, *Self-Islam*, 75–77.

119. Dawood, trans., *The Koran*, 126.
120. 'Uthmani, trans., http://www.altafsir.com.
121. Qur'an 22:40, 24:36.
122. Qur'an 2:113: *"Furthermore, the Jews assert, "The Christians have no valid ground for their beliefs," while the Christians assert, "The Jews have no valid ground for their beliefs"— and both quote the divine writ! Even thus, like unto what they say, have [always] spoken those who were devoid of knowledge; but it is God who will judge between them on Resurrection Day with regard to all on which they were wont to differ"* (Asad, trans., http://www.altafsir.com).
123. Ayoub, *A Muslim View of Christianity*, 10.
124. See the introduction by Hamid Dabbash to the Aldine Edition of Goldhizer, *Muslim Studies*, xxiii–xxv.
125. Esack, *Le Coran, Mode d'Emploi*, 220.
126. Walk, trans., http://www.altafsir.com.
127. Ibid. This theme is similar to the theme of Qur'anic Verses 3:84–85.
128. Arberry, trans., http://www.altafsir.com.
129. Ibid.
130. See for example, the exegeses of Tabari, Zamakhshari, Tabarsi, Razi, and Ibn Kathir. For his part, Qurtubi focuses on the favors that were granted to each of the prophets. He stresses those prophetic traditions in which Prophet Muhammad cautioned against attributing to him any preferences over the other prophets and messengers of God. See also Esack, *Le Coran, Mode d'Emploi*, 222.
131. Wadud, *Qur'an and Woman*, 69.
132. See the translations of Pickthall, Arberry, Walk, 'Uthmani, Asad, Khalidi, and Dawood.
133. See the translations of Yusuf Ali and Abdel Haleem.
134. Makarian, *Le Choc Jésus Mahomet*, 115, 129. Despite the clear content to the contrary evident in Qur'anic Verses 2:253 and 17:55, Makarian insists that Islam does not recognize that God spoke to Moses.
135. Makarian, *Le Choc Jésus Mahomet*, 175. Pointing to the duality of language in the Holy Qur'an relating to Jews and Chirstians, Makarian observes— without considering the respective contexts of the relevant provisions— that it is disconcerting to find calls for the praise and tolerance of Jews and Christians, and then also encounter provisions which call for their expulsion and exclusion.
136. Qur'an 2:75, 2:79, 3:78, 4:46, 5:13.
137. Qur'an 4:150, 5:66, 5:68, 57:28, 57:29.

138. Qur'an 2:109, 2:120, 2:217, 3:69, 3:100; 'Abdul-Karim, *Shadw al-Rababa*, 3:81–84, 85–87, 89–94. 'Abdul-Karim offers an account of the early deterioration of relations between Jews and Muslims. Pages 81–84 cover the behavior of the Jews of Banu Qainuqa'; pages 85–87 deal with behavior of the Jews of Banu al-Nadir who attempted to kill Prophet Muhammad; and pages 89–94 discuss the behavior of the Jews of Banu Qurayza, in connection with the al-Khandaq battle.

139. See Haykal, chap. 11–14, 16, 18 in *Hayat Muhammad*. These chapters offer a comprehensive account of the relationship between Jews and Muslims during that period. See also Jabiri, *Fahm al-Qur'an al-Hakim*, 3:159–162. (Part of that period is also accounted for in Qur'anic Verses 3:69–109.)

140. Esposito, *Islam: The Straight Path*, 15.

141. Qur'an 2:47–61, 7:137–141, 16:118–124, 20:80–82, 27:15, 44:30–33.

142. Caratini, *Le Génie de l'Islamisme*, 151–153. See also Qur'anic Verses 59:2–4, which provide a short description of how the Banu al-Nadir tribe was expelled from Medina for conspiring with Meccan idolaters against the Prophet and his companions (actions which violated the Charter of Medina).

143. 'Abdul-Karim, *Shadw al-Rababa*, 3:71–112.

144. See Cohen, *Under Crescent and Cross*; Lewis, *The Jews of Islam*. These works offer a comprehensive account of Jewish communities that have lived in predominantly Muslim areas throughout history.

145. Qur'an 3:59–63.

146. See Haykal, *Hayat Muhammad*, 251–253. Haykal discusses the interaction between Prophet Muhammad and the Christian delegation from Najran. See also Jabiri, *Fahm al-Qur'an al-Hakim*, 3:160.

147. *Sūrat Maryam* of the Qur'an (19), and Verses 3:33–63, 5:110, 66:12.

148. Akhtar, *A Faith for All Seasons*, 192.

149. Watt and Bell, *Introduction to the Quran*, 156. Watt and Bell include a sequence from the polemical dialogue in question. See also Akhtar, chap. 9 in *A Faith for All Seasons*.

150. Ayoub, *A Muslim View of Christianity*, 42; Haykal, *Al-Siddiq Abou Bakr*, 43–44.

151. Qur'an 2:121, 3:75–78, 3:113–115, 3:199, 5:12–13, 5:82–83, 7:159, 45:16–17, 57:26–27. In Qur'anic Verse 5:13, God guides the Prophet to pardon certain ill-advised actions. Contrary to certain claims, this verse was not abrogated by the so-called 'Verse of the Sword' (Qur'an 9:29), which only condones the use of violence when repelling an aggressor.

152. Qur'an 3:20, 29:46.

153. Qur'an 2:139, 2:163, 3:64, 22:34, 29:46, 41:6, 42:15.

154. Qur'an 48:29.
155. Qur'an 3:28: *"LET NOT the believers take those who deny the truth for their allies in preference to the believers—since he who does this cuts himself off from God in everything—unless it be to protect yourselves against them in this way. But God warns you to beware of Him: for with God is all journeys' end"* (Asad, trans., http://www.altafsir.com); Qur'an 3:118: *"O YOU who have attained to faith! Do not take for your bosom-friends people who are not of your kind. They spare no effort to corrupt you; they would love to see you in distress. Vehement hatred has already come into the open from out of their mouths, but what their hearts conceal is yet worse. We have indeed made the signs [thereof] clear unto you, if you would but use your reason"* (Asad, trans., http://www.altafsir.com); Qur'an 5:51: *"O YOU who have attained to faith! Do not take the Jews and the Christians for your allies: they are but allies of one another—and whoever of you allies himself with them becomes, verily, one of them; behold, God does not guide such evildoers"* (Asad, trans., http://www.altafsir.com); Qur'an 5:57: *"O you who have attained to faith! Do not take for your friends such as mock at your faith and make a jest of it—be they from among those who have been vouchsafed revelation before your time, or [from among] those who deny the truth [of revelation as such]—but remain conscious of God, if you are [truly] believers"* (Asad, trans., http://www. altafsir.com); Qur'an 4:140: *"And, indeed, He has enjoined upon you in this divine writ that whenever you hear people deny the truth of God's messages and mock at them, you shall avoid their company until they begin to talk of other things— or else, verily, you will become like them. Behold, together with those who deny the truth God will gather in hell the hypocrites"* (Asad, trans., http://www.altafsir.com); Qur'an 6:68: *"NOW, whenever thou meet such as indulge in [blasphemous] talk about Our messages, turn thy back upon them until they begin to talk of other things; and if Satan should ever cause thee to forget [thyself], remain not, after recollection, in the company of such evildoing folk"* (Asad, trans., http://www.altafsir.com). Ayoub (*A Muslim View of Christianity*, 19–21) asserts that the aforementioned verses have been misinterpreted. He contends that Qur'anic injunctions which call for peaceable relations between Muslims and non-Muslim faithfuls have been repeatedly overshadowed.
156. Cohen, *Under Crescent and Cross*, 95.
157. Khalidi, trans., *The Qur'an*, 459.
158. 'Uthmani, trans., http://www.altafsir.com.
159. Bidar, *Self-Islam*, 51.
160. Yusuf Ali, trans., http://www.altafsir.com.

161. This prophetic tradition is cited by Razi in *Mafatih al-Ghayb al-Tafsir al-Kabir* (under Qur'anic Verse 9:28).

162. See Moosa, "The Debts and Burdens of Critical Islam," in *Progressive Muslims*, ed. Safi, 126. The Holy Mosque and the Ka'ba were previously used to house the deities of the various tribes of the Arabian Peninsula. These tribes traveled to Mecca each year during the sacred months of the hajj season in order to worship, do business, and engage in cultural exchange.

163. Tabari, *Jami' al-Bayan fi Tafsir al-Qur'an*.

164. Akhtar, *A Faith for all Seasons*, 165.

165. Haykal, *Al-Faruq 'Umar*, 2:204–205.

166. Yusuf Ali, trans., http://www.altafsir.com.

167. Shamiyyeh, *Al-Islam: Hal Yuqaddim li-l-'Alam Nazariyya li-l-Hukm*, 48–50.

168. Sachedina, *The Islamic Roots of Democratic Pluralism*, 45.

CHAPTER 14: THE RIGHT TO EQUALITY

1.   A. Charfi, *L'Islam entre le Message et l'Histoire*, 125.

2.   Jabiri, *Al-Dimuqratiyya wa Huquq al-Insan*, 209.

3.   Asad, trans., http://www.altafsir.com.

4.   Khalidi, trans., *The Qur'an*, 424.

5.   Yusuf Ali, trans., http://www.altafsir.com.

6.   Asad, trans., http://www.altafsir.com.

7.   See Wadud, *Qur'an and Woman*, 65–74. Wadud discusses the seemingly discriminatory concepts of 'divine degrees' (*darajāt*) and 'preferences' (*tafḍīl*), with regard to gender relations.

8.   Qur'an 6:132, 9:20, 17:21, 46:19.

9.   Jabiri, *Al-Dimuqratiyya wa Huquq al-Insan*, 226–231.

10. Arberry, trans., http://www.altafsir.com.

11. Khalidi, trans., *The Qur'an*, 436.

12. 'Uthmani, trans., http://www.altafsir.com.

13. Yusuf Ali, trans., http://www.altafsir.com.

14. Dawood, trans., *The Koran*, 385. See also Qur'an 39:9.

15. See Ben Salama, *Naqd al-Thawabit*, 61–68. While some Muslim nations have taken steps toward greater gender equality, much more still needs to be done. Salama's text describes Tunisia's progress to date on this issue.

16. Abdel Haleem, trans., *The Qur'an*, 50.

17. Asad, trans., http://www.altafsir.com.

18. Ibid.

19. Barlas, *Believing Women in Islam*, 106–136.

20. A. Charfi, *L'Islam entre le Message et l'Histoire*, 120.

21. Enayat, *Modern Islamic Political Thought*, 125–132.

22. *Sunan Abi Daoud*, vol. 3, no. 2911. "No inheritance among people belonging to different confessions."

23. Mahmassani, *Al-Mabadi' al-Shar'iyya wa-l-Qanuniyya*, 300.

24. Qur'an 2:221: "*Do not marry polytheistic women unless they believe. A female slave, who is a believer, is better than a polytheistic woman, even if winning your admiration. Do not give in marriage to polytheists unless they believe. A male slave who is a believer is better than a polytheistic man, even if winning your admiration.* These people will lead you to the Fire, *but God leads you to the Garden and forgiveness, by His leave. He makes clear His signs to mankind; perhaps they will remember and reflect*" (Khalidi, trans., The Qur'an, 30). The highlighted phrase is the operative reason.

25. 'Uthmani, trans., http://www.altafsir.com.

26. Hibri, *An Introduction to Women's Muslim Rights*, 68–69. Hibri suggests that such discrimination might be reconsidered if circumstances were to change and the non-Muslim husband was no longer considered to be a threat to the faith of his Muslim wife.

27. Qaradawi, *Fi Fiqh al-Aqalliyyat al-Muslima*, 91–104.

28. See Hassan al-Turabi's statements, originally made in a public conference and then reported in *Al-Sharq Al-Awsat*, no. 9994, April 9, 2006.

29. Mahmassani, *Al-Mabadi' al-Shar'iyya wa-l-Qanuniyya*, 302.

30. 'Uthmani, trans., http://www.altafsir.com. See also Qur'an 6:152.

31. Suyuti, *Al-Jami' al-Saghir*, vol. 2, no. 6368.

32. *Sahih Muslim*, vol. 5, 114.

33. Suyuti, *Al-Jami' al-Saghir*, vol. 2, no. 7684.

34. Mahmassani, *Arkan Huquq al-Insan*, 265.

35. See Marzoogy, *Human Rights in Islamic Law*, 167–168n2. The Prophet is said to have pronounced this principle in the farewell address that he delivered during his final pilgrimage to Mecca. Margoozy's book provides the full text of that address, including the text of the cited tradition.

36. See Mayer, *Human Rights in Islam*, 115–120. Despite Qur'anic principles to the contrary, gender inequality based on religious grounds remains prevalent. Mayer summarizes the views of thinkers like Tabandeh and Mawdudi, who oppose gender equality.

37. Arkoun, *Al-Fikr al-Islami*, 125–130.

38. See Q. Amin, introduction to *The Liberation of Women*; Meddeb, *The Malady of Islam*, 35; S. 'Uthmani, *Qadiyyat al-Mar'a wa Nafsiyyat al-Istibdad*, 5–8, 48. Instead of redressing the injustices affecting women without regard to traditions, many authors (with the exception of Qassim Amin) blame traditions

for the condition of women. The same authors then turn to other traditions to determine what rights women may claim, and to what extent the powers of men may be curbed. See also Faruqi (*Women, Muslim Society and Islam*, 13) who believes that women are to blame for their own inferior condition because they have abdicated their rights.

39. Hibri, "Legal Reform: Reviewing Human Rights in the Muslim World," *Harvard International Review* (June 22, 1998).

40. Hoffman, chap. 16 in *Al-Islam ka-Badil*.

41. Suyuti, *Al-Jami' al-Saghir*, vol. 2, no. 2560; *Sunan Abi Daoud*, vol. 2, no. 236.

42. Suyuti, *Al-Jami' al-Saghir*, vol. 3, no. 4102.

43. Ibid., vol. 3, no. 3642.

44. Ouzon, *Jinayat al-Bukhari*, 113–129. Ouzon offers additional examples of traditions that are demeaning to women and have been wrongly attributed to the Prophet.

45. Suyuti, *Al-Jami' al-Saghir*, vol. 6, no. 7482.

46. Suyuti, *Al-Jami' al-Saghir*, vol. 5, no. 7871; *Sahih al-Bukhari*, vol. 3, no. 4808.

47. Suyuti, *Al-Jami' al-Saghir*, vol. 1, no. 1117; *Sahih Muslim*, vol. 2, no. 3069.

48. A. Charfi, *Mustaqbal al-Islam fi-l-Gharb wa-l-Sharq*, eds. Hoffman and Charfi 78–80; Stowasser, "Gender Issues and Contemporary Quran Interpretation," in *Islam, Gender and Social Change*, eds. Haddad and Esposito, 30–44. Stowasser's work explores perceptions of gender status in Islam among the early commentators and more recent reformists and modernists.

49. Rida, "Al-Khilafa aw al-Imama al-'Uzma," in *Al-Dawla wa-l- Khilafa fi-l-Khitab al-'Arabi*, ed. Kawtharani, 117. Here, Rida argues that women must be placed under continuous male guardianship.

50. Qur'an 4:117, 43:16, 52:39, 53:21. See commentary on these verses from Tabari (*Jami' al-Bayan fi Tafsir al-Qur'an*), Qurtubi (*Al-Jami' li Ahkam al-Qur'an*), and Ibn Kathir (*Tafsir al-Qur'an al-Karim*).

51. See Ahmed, chap. 1, 2 in *Women and Gender in Islam*. Ahmed describes the condition of women in Mesopotamia and the Mediterranean Middle East during the pre-Islamic period.

52. 'Uthmani, trans., http://www.altafsir.com. See also Qur'an 43:17–19.

53. Qaradawi, *Markaz al-Mar'a fi-l-Hayat al-Islamiyya*, 34. Tabari, Qurtubi, Ibn Kathir, Sayyid Qutb, Mahalli, and Suyuti are among the commentators who offered a similar interpretation.

54. Asad, trans., http://www.altafsir.com.

55. The wife of 'Imran had previously prayed that God give her an offspring. She vowed that if her prayer was answered, and she delivered a male, she would

devote that child to the worship and service of God in the temple. See Qur'an 3:35: *"(Remember) when 'Imrān's wife said: 'O my Lord, I have vowed that what is in my womb will be devoted exclusively for You. So, accept (it) from me. You, certainly You, are the All-Hearing, the All-Knowing'"* ('Uthmani, trans., http://www.altafsir.com).

56. Among those who have translated the Qur'an into English, Asad is one who noted the true intent of this controversial clip (namely that it is an interjection uttered by God pointing to the importance of the newborn female) and incorporated it in his translations. A few of the early and later commentators also understood the true meaning of this clip (including Zamakhshari, Razi, Ibn 'Ashour, Sha'arawi, and Jabiri). For a comprehensive overview of the exegeses of this verse, see Ayoub, *The Qur'an and its Interpreters*, 2:93–99.

57. Asad, trans., http://www.altafsir.com.

58. Qur'an 9:71: *"The Believers, men and women, are protectors one of another: they enjoin what is just, and forbid what is evil: they observe regular prayers, practise regular charity, and obey God and His Apostle. On them will God pour His mercy: for God is Exalted in power, Wise"* (Asad, trans., http://www.altafsir.com).

59. Khalidi, trans., *The Qur'an*, 219.

60. Yusuf Ali, trans., http://www.altafsir.com.

61. Walk, trans., http://www.altafsir.com. See also Qur'an 33:72–73, 40:40, 4:124, 57:12–13.

62. 'Uthmani, trans., http://www.altafsir.com.

63. Qur'an 5:38: *"NOW AS FOR the man who steals and the woman who steals, cut off the hand of either of them in requital for what they have wrought, as a deterrent ordained by God: for God is almighty, wise"* (Asad, trans., http://www.altafsir.com).

64. Qur'an 24:2: *"The woman and the man guilty of adultery or fornication, flog each of them with a hundred stripes: Let not compassion move you in their case, in a matter prescribed by God, if ye believe in God and the Last Day: and let a party of the Believers witness their punishment"* (Yusuf Ali, trans., http://www.altafsir.com).

65. Qur'an 2:178–179: *"You who believe, fair retribution is prescribed for you in cases of murder: the free man for the free man, the slave for the slave, the female for the female. But if the culprit is pardoned by his aggrieved brother, this shall be adhered to fairly, and the culprit shall pay what is due in a good way. This is an alleviation from your Lord, and an act of mercy. If anyone then exceeds these limits, grievous suffering awaits him (178). Fair retribution*

saves life for you, people of understanding, so that you may guard yourselves against what is wrong (179)" (Abdel Haleem, trans., The Qur'an, 20).

66. See Qur'an 4:92. This verse ordains compensation payment and the freeing of a slave in the case of unintentional homicide. The verse does not indicate that the payment amount should vary depending on the gender of the slain person (in line with the principles of gender equality discussed above). However, most early *fiqh* concluded that the share for a slain female should be one-half that of a slain male (following reported precedents by the Caliphs 'Umar and 'Ali and the Companion Ibn Mass'oud). See the commentaries of Razi (*Mafatih al-Ghayb al-Tafsir al-Kabir*) and Ibn 'Ashour, (*Tafsir al-Tahrir wa al-Tanwir*).

67. Qaradawi, *Markaz al-Mar'a fi-l-Hayat al-Islamiyya*, 27–30; Cherif Bassiouni, "Qisas Crimes," in *The Islamic Criminal Justice System*, ed. Bassiouni, 209.

68. See Abizaid, *Al-Mar'a fi Khitab al-Azama*, 76. Abizaid criticizes religious discourse that defends apparent gender inequalities in the Qur'an instead of refuting noncontextual misinterpretations that fail to grasp the underlying Qur'anic message that rejects—and even aims to reverse—prevailing inequalities.

69. Even certain modern-day advocates of gender equality may have taken such prejudices as givens. Wadud (*Qur'an and Woman*, 9–23) observes, "The Qur'an seems to have remained neutral [toward the practices of] social patriarchy, marital patriarchy, economic hierarchy, the division of labor between males and female within a particular family." She concludes, "Part of Allah's original plan in the creation of humankind was for man to function as a khalif (trustee) on earth." In reality, the role of trusteeship (*khalīfa*) was not assigned exclusively to men and not to women; nor has the Qur'an remained neutral with regard to practices relating to patriarchy, and the like. Those who have concluded otherwise have done so because they have interpreted the verses without taking into account the relevant context (*bi ẓāhir al-nass*, according to *fiqh* jargon). Faruqi (*Women, Muslim Society and Islam*, 25) also subscribes to the concept of "division of labor along sex lines" and considers it as "generally beneficial to all members of the society."

70. The *Memorandum on Human Rights in Islam and Their Implementation in the Kingdom of Saudi Arabia*, presented by the delegation of the Kingdom of Saudi Arabia to the participants in a colloquium on human rights in Islam held in Paris, 2 November 1974 (*Colloques de Riyad, de Paris, du Vatican, de Genève et de Strasbourg sur le Dogme Musulman et les Droits de l'Homme en Islam*, 51) states, "Islam has proclaimed that women are the sisters of men; it admitted men and women to the enjoyment of equal rights except for such

rights as have been recognized to man in his capacity as head of family, and because man is more able to carry the heavy responsibilities that only his strong physical constitution allows him to perform for the good of society as a whole. In reality there are only charges which were imposed on man and of which the woman was released without any prejudice to her dignity or any of her rights which remain equal to those of man: such provisions constitute the highest expression of justice between the two genders." Yet, we find that all the abuse and discrimination to which women were subjected was justified under the umbrella of the prerogatives of the male chief of the family.

71. Asad, trans., http://www.altafsir.com.

72. Mahalli and Suyuti, *Tafsir al-Jalalayn*.

73. See Ali, "Progressive Muslims and Islamic Jurisprudence," in *Progressive Muslims*, ed. Safi, 173. Ali reports what a professor of Shari'a describes as the inferior mental and physical aptitudes of women. Similarly, Soroush (*Reason, Freedom, and Democracy in Islam*, 181) decries some clergymen's depiction of women as beasts, with only the appearance of a human being.

74. 'Uthmani, trans., http://www.altafsir.com.

75. This order of priority could vary due to age considerations, the existence of a will left by a legal guardian, or the discretion of the overseeing judge, among other circumstances.

76. Islamic law has developed an order of priority among male kin in the attribution of the burden of providing guidance and financial support to women, based on the so-called *'aṣaba* relationship, that is, the male kinship in which no female intercedes vertically in the relevant relationship. For example, there is no female intermediate relationship between the father and his son or daughter, or between the brother and his sister (the links being first upward to the father, then downward to reach the sister) and so on.

77. See Hibri, *An Introduction to Muslim Women's Rights*, 53. Hibri calls the concept of patriarchal superiority "Satanic Logic." In another study (*Divine Justice and Human Order*, 240–241), Hibri traces this idea to A. H. al-Ghazali.

78. Guardianship is exercised over two aspects of a person's life. With regard to personal matters (*al-wilāya 'ala-l nafs*), guardianship powers include raising, educating, teaching, disciplining, and marrying off the person under guardianship. With respect to financial matters (*al-wilāya 'ala-l-māl*), the guardian has the duty to preserve the financial assets of the person under guardianship, and the power to invest those assets and spend from them in order to provide for all the financial needs of the person in question. For further details on the treatment, under Islamic law, of guardianship in general and guardianship over females in particular, see Mahmassani, *Al-Mabadi' al-Shar'iyya wa-l-Qanuniyya*, 77–150.

79. See Qaradawi, *Markaz al-Mar'a fi-l-Hayat al-Islamiyya*, 74–89. Qaradawi recalls ancient, long- forgotten tribal customs and declares that the guardian has no power to sell females who are under his guardianship or conclude 'back-to-back marriages,' which is when marriage of a female is consented to by the guardian, and in return a female kin of the groom agrees to marry either the guardian or one of his male kin, and dowries owed to each bride are offset against each other. Qaradawi finds such practice reprehensible because the guardian's power does not include the right to waive the female's entitlement to the dowry. In reality, this practice is reprehensible in the first place because it ignores the female's freedom of choice.

80. This is the position of the Ottoman Family Law, based on the Hanafi school of jurisprudence (see Mahmassani, *Al-Mabadi' al-Shar'iyya wa-l-Qanuniyya*, 79.) The law gives a *de facto* veto power to the father, as the judge is required to confirm that the father has no objection to his daughter's marriage. The Sunni Maliki and Shi'i Jaafari schools of jurisprudence consider the condition requiring the groom to match the social and financial standing of the bride repulsive to Islam, under which all people are equal. For a discussion of the concept of the eligibility of the groom, see Hibri, "Islam, Law and Custom: Redefining Muslim Women's Rights," 16*ff.*

81. Mughniyya, *Al-Ahwal al-Shakhsiyya*, 38.

82. See Abou El Fadl, *Speaking in God's Name*, 209*ff.* Abou El Fadl offers an account of "faith-based assumptions and determinations demeaning to women." He provides countless examples of subservience to husbands, based on responsa citing traditions imputed to the Prophet.

83. Yusuf Ali, trans., http://www.altafsir.com.

84. 'Abdul-Karim, *Al-Judhur al-Tarikhiyya li-l-Shari'a al-Islamiyya*, 41–51.

85. Mayer, *Human Rights in Islam*, 112.

86. See the exegeses of Qur'anic Verse 4:34 by Tabari, Razi, Qurtubi, Ibn Kathir, Sha'rawi, and Tantawi.

87. That same term is used in Qur'anic Verses 4:127, 4:135, and 5:8 to describe the extent to which believers are determined to stand for justice and witness the truth before God.

88. See *Al-Tahrir wal Tanwir*. See also Shahrour, *Al-Kitab wa-l-Qur'an*, 620.

89. Talbi, *L'Universalité du Coran*, 48.

90. Bakhtiar, *The Sublime Quran*, 94.

91. Shahrour, *Al-Kitab wa-l-Qur'an*, 621–622.

92. Asad, trans., http://www.altafsir.com.

93. Dawood, trans., *The Koran*, 64.

94. See Talbi, *Plaidoyer pour un Islam Moderne*, 63.

95. The Ottoman Family Law (*Qanūn Huqūq al 'Ā'ila al-'Uthmāni*) continues to govern family relations and the rights of the Sunni Muslim community in Lebanon and other Arab countries.

96. The Ottoman Family Law, art. 73.

97. Moussalli, *The Islamic Quest for Democracy, Pluralism, and Human Rights*, 155.

98. Wadud, *Qur'an and Woman*, 78*ff.*

99. Such toleration was justified in part because of prevailing social circumstances, wherein war casualties increased the number of widows and orphans in need of marital and paternal support.

100. See M. Hussein, *Penser le Coran*, 120*ff.* Hussein identifies other reprehensible tribal customs that the Qur'an sought to reverse.

101. Qur'an 2:227: "*but if they are determined to divorce, remember that God hears all and knows all*" (Abdel Haleem, trans., *The Qur'an*, 25).

102. Qur'an 2:228: "*And the divorced women shall undergo, without remarrying, a waiting-period of three monthly courses: for it is not lawful for them to conceal what God may have created in their wombs, if they believe in God and the Last Day. And during this period their husbands are fully entitled to take them back, if they desire reconciliation;* but, in accordance with justice, the rights of the wives [with regard to their husbands] are equal to the [husbands'] rights with regard to them, *although men have precedence over them [in this respect]. And God is almighty, wise*" (Asad, trans., http://www.altafsir.com). The preference given to men in this verse refers to the dowry that the groom advanced at marriage. Upon termination of the marriage, the entitlement to that dowry depends on who initiates the separation. Therefore, the preference in question, if any, is not attributable to the sole power of man to pronounce the repudiation, as suggested by Wadud (Qur'an and Woman, 79). For his part, Tarif Khalidi, unlike other translators, attributes to the term *daraja* the sense of added responsibility on the husband.

103. Qur'an 4:128: "*And if a woman has reason to fear ill-treatment from her husband, or that he might turn away from her, it shall not be wrong for the two to set things peacefully to rights between themselves: for peace is best, and selfishness is ever-present in human souls. But if you do good and are conscious of Him—behold, God is indeed aware of all that you do*" (Asad, trans., http://www.altafsir.com).

104. Qur'an 4:35: "*And if you have reason to fear that a breach might occur between a [married] couple, appoint an arbiter from among his people and an arbiter from among her people; if they both want to set things aright, God may bring about their reconciliation. Behold, God is indeed all-knowing, aware*" (Ibid.).

105. Qur'an 30:21.

106. See Arkoun, *Al-Fikr al-Islami*, 125*ff.* Arkoun discusses the role and condition of women in Islam from a sociological perspective.

107. This is the general principle, with a few exceptions—for example, when the respective shares of the mother and father of the deceased person are, under certain circumstances, equal.

108. Shahrour, *Al-Kitab Wa-l-Qur'an*, 602–603. See also Abizaid, *Dawa'ir al-Khawf*, 228–235.

109. *Sahih Al-Bukhari*, vol. 4, chap. 88, sec. 8, no. 6356; *Sahih Muslim*, vol. 3, chap. 23, sec. 1, no. 1615.

110. Qur'an 33:6: "*The Prophet is more worthy of the believers than themselves, and his wives are [in the position of] their mothers. And those of [blood] relationship are more entitled [to inheritance] in the decree of Allah than the [other] believers and the emigrants, except that you may do to your close associates a kindness [through bequest]. That was in the Book inscribed*" ('Uthmani, trans., http://www.altafsir.com).

111. For a comprehensive discussion of this issue, see Mughniyya, *Al-Ahwal al-Shakhsiyya*, 222*ff.*

112. See Hibri, *Islam, Law and Custom: Redefining Muslim Women's Rights*, 13–25. Hibri reviews the stipulations that a woman can impose in a marriage contract under the various schools of jurisprudence.

113. Ali, "Progressive Muslims and Islamic Jurisprudence," in *Progressive Muslims*, ed. Safi, 164. However, see also L. Faruki (*Women, Muslim Society and Islam*, 7, 27, 72) who says it is a blessing that the unilateral repudiation that the man exercises is revocable.

114. *Sahih Al-Bukhari*, vol. 4, chap. 81, sec. 8, no. 5634.

115. *Sunan Al-Nissa'i*, vol. 6, no. 11. This tradition is also reported at times under jihad and under *ihsān*, at others because the Prophet considered caring for a mother to be an act of jihad and *ihsān*.

116. *Sahih Al-Bukhari*, vol. 4, chap. 81, sec. 2, no. 5626; *Sahih Muslim*, vol. 4, chap. 45, section 1, no. 2548.

117. Suyuti, *Al-Jami' al-Saghir*, vol. 3, no. 3642.

118. Yusuf Ali, trans., http://www.altafsir.com. See also Qur'an 29:8.

119. Asad, trans., http://www.altafsir.com. See also Qur'an 46:15.

120. See Yamani, "The Political Competence of Women in Islamic Law," in *Islam in Transition*, eds. Donohue and Esposito, 175–177. Yamani cites examples of women who held public roles of responsibility in the early periods of Islam.

121. Ahmed, chap. 3 in *Women and Gender in Islam*.

122. Ahmed, chap. 4, 5 in *Women and Gender in Islam*.

123. See Qaradawi, *Markaz al-Mar'a fi-l-Hayat al-Islamiyya*, 9*ff*. Qaradawi challenges those who blame Islam for the inequality of men and women and asserts that equality together with the freedom of women to work and participate in public life, etc. However, he also attributes innate qualities and rights to men and innate weaknesses, duties, and functions to women (all having presumably been ordained by God) and justifies the *fiqh*-based rights of men over women, and restrictions on women's ability to participate in public life. See also M. al-Ghazali, *Raka'iz al-Iman*, 219*ff*.

124. Mawdudi, "Islam: Its Meaning and Message," in *Islam in Transition*, eds. Donohue and Esposito, 265.

125. Suyuti, *Al-Jami' al-Saghir*, vol. 5, no. 7393; *Sahih Al-Bukhari*, vol. 4, bk. 96, No. 6683; *Sunan Al-Tirmidhi*, vol. 3, chap. 64, no. 2365.

126. Mernissi, "Women's Rights in Islam," in *Liberal Islam*, ed. Kurzman, 114.

127. Qaradawi, *Markaz al-Mar'a fi-l-Hayat al-Islamiyya*, 147–148.

128. Yusuf Ali, trans., http://www.altafsir.com.

129. See Mahmassani, *Arkan Huquq al-Insan*, 298. Mahmassani refutes the arguments (based on the grounds of religion or of physical or mental inferiorities) that would ban women from political office.

130. Abizaid, *Al-Mar'a fi Khitab al-Azama*, 35.

131. Qaradawi, *Markaz al-Mar'a fi-l-Hayat al-Islamiyya*, 158. See also the words of Ghannoushi (*Al-Mar'ah Bayn al-Qur'an wa-Waqi' al-Muslimin*), quoted in Y. Haddad, "Islam and Gender: Dilemmas in the Changing Arab World," in *Islam, Gender and Social Change*, eds. Yazbeck and Esposito, 9.

132. For a sample of such qualifications, see Qaradawi, *Markaz al-Mar'a fi-l-Hayat al-Islamiyya*, 147–149.

133. Hibri, "Legal Reform: Reviewing Human Rights in the Muslim world."

134. Suyuti, *Al-Jami' al-Saghir*, vol. 1, no. 1111.

135. Qaradawi, *Markaz al-Mar'a fi-l-Hayat al-Islamiyya*, 143.

136. See Zakaria, *Al-Haqiqa wa-l-Wahm fi-l-Haraka al-Islamiyya al-Mu'asira*, 30. Here, Zakaria comments on the perception of women as sex symbols, and their association with evil behavior.

137. For a critique of so-called 'Islamic clothing' from the perspective of the dignity of women, see Ben Salama, *Naqd al-Thawabit*, 11–17. See also Barlas, *Believing Women in Islam*, 53–58.

138. Abizaid, *Al-Mar'a fi Khitab al-Azama*, 27. See also commentary by Stowasser (*Women in the Qur'an, Traditions, and Interpretation*, 127–131) on the significance of the veil from the perspective of traditions.

139. Asad, trans., http://www.altafsir.com.

140. 'Uthmani, trans., http://www.altafsir.com.

141. Abdel Haleem, trans., *The Qur'an*, 271.

142. For a debate over the potential significance and scope of the three verses in question, see Babès and Oubrou, *Loi d'Allah, Loi des Hommes*, 181–219.

143. See the *Memorandum on Human Rights in Islam and Their Implementation in the Kingdom of Saudi Arabia (Colloques de Riyad, de Paris, du Vatican, de Genève et de Strasbourg sur le Dogme Musulman et les Droits de l'Homme en Islam*, 181ff.). In that memorandum, Qur'anic Verse 7:26 is presented as the prime verse enjoining both men and women to wear decent clothing that covers their private parts, followed by the assertion, not found in the Qur'an, that the private parts of a woman consist of her entire body with the exception of her face, hands, and feet.

144. Talbi, *L'Universalité du Coran*, 48–49.

145. There is a consensus among the early commentators (including Tabari, Zamakhshari, Qurtubi, and Ibn Kathir) regarding restrictive interpretation—an approach that was then adopted and perpetuated by modern-day interpreters (such as Ibn 'Ashour, Sayyid Qutb, Tantawi, and Sha'rawi).

146. Ouzon, *Laffaqa al-Muslimun idh-Qalu*, 176–177.

147. In Qur'anic Verse 33:53, people are instructed to abstain from talking to the wives of the Prophet, except from behind a curtain (or a veil, or *hijāb*). Whether the separation referred to in that verse is a veil or a curtain, the fact remains that this provision is exclusively limited to wives of the Prophet. The stipulations regarding the Prophet's wives cannot be extended to include other women. (Note also that this stipulation only existed to protect the Prophet's wives, and Qur'anic Verse 33:32 specifically declares that the Prophet's wives are unlike any other women.)

148. See Mernissi, "Women's Rights in Islam," in *Liberal Islam*, ed. Kurzman, 126. Mernissi expresses her outrage that the *ḥijāb* (the veil that women are required to wear) has become a symbol of Muslim identity, when in reality it is nothing other than a symbol of the "jāhiliyya mentality that Islam was supposed to annihilate." L. Faruqi (*Women, Muslim Society and Islam*, 13) traces the origin of the veil in Muslim society to the expansion of the Muslim Empire and the contact that Arabian Muslim peoples had with the sedentary, urban Persian and Byzantine societies, although the veil existed in the *jāhiliyya* as a mark of distinction between free and slave women.

149. Abou El Fadl, "The Ugly Modern and the Modern Ugly," in *Progressive Muslims*, ed. Safi, 37.

150. Ahmed (chap. 8, in *Women and Gender in Islam*) observes that non-Muslim thinkers perceive the wearing of the veil to be a sign of inferior status more than Muslim thinkers do. She asserts that Q. Amin's attacks against the veil

are motivated by a sense of glorification of the West. For an overview of the evolution of Islamic clothing since the Revelation, see Ben Salama, *Naqd al-Thawabit*, 29–45.

151. Qur'an 33:33: *"And abide quietly in your homes, and do not flaunt your charms as they used to flaunt them in the old days of pagan ignorance; and be constant in prayer, and render the purifying dues, and pay heed unto God and His Apostle: for God only wants to remove from you all that might be loathsome, O you members of the [Prophet's] household, and to purify you to utmost purity"* (Yusuf Ali, trans., http://www.altafsir.com). Wadud (*Qur'an and Woman*, 98) tried in vain to justify the relevance of this verse to all women by reference to the circumstances at the time of the Revelation, while it was exclusively addressed to the women in the household of the Prophet.

152. Qur'an 2:282: *"O you who believe, when you transact a debt payable at a specified time, put it in writing, and let a scribe write it between you with fairness. A scribe should not refuse to write as Allah has educated him. He, therefore, should write. The one who owes something should get it written, but he must fear Allah, his Lord, and he should not omit anything from it. If the one who owes is feeble-minded or weak or cannot dictate himself, then his guardian should dictate with fairness. Have two witnesses from among your men, and if two men are not there, then one man and two women from those witnesses whom you like, so that if one of the two women errs, the other woman may remind her. The witnesses should not refuse when summoned. And do not be weary of writing it down, along with its due date, no matter whether the debt is small or large. That is more equitable in Allah's sight, and more supportive as evidence, and more likely to make you free of doubt. However, if it is a spot transaction you are effecting between yourselves, there is no sin on you, should you not write it. Have witnesses when you transact a sale. Neither a scribe should be made to suffer, nor a witness. If you do (something harmful to them), it is certainly a sin on your part, and fear Allah. Allah educates you, and Allah is All-Knowing in respect of everything"* ('Uthmani, trans., http://www.altafsir.com).

153. See the exegeses of Qur'an 4:15 by Tabari (*Jami' al-Bayan fi Tafsir al-Qur'an*), Razi (*Mafatih al-Ghayb, al-Tafsir al-Kabir*), Qurtubi (*Al-Jami' li Ahkam al-Qur'an*), Mahalli and Suyuti (*Tafsir al-Jalalayn*), and Tantawi (*Al-Wasit fi Tafsir al-Qur'an al-Karim*).

154. See, for example, the translations of Qur'anic Verse 5:106 by Yusuf Ali, Pickthall, Arberry, Walk, Abdel Haleem, Dawood, and Khalidi.

155. Qaradawi, *Markaz al-Mar'a fi-l-Hayat al-Islamiyya*, 18.

156. See Wadud, *Qur'an and Woman*, 85–86; Rahman, *Major Themes of the Qur'an*, 48–49; Jabiri, *Al-Dimuqratiyya wa Huquq al-Insan*, 181–182.

157. See Esack, *Le Coran, Mode d'Emploi*, 265. Esack refers to a common misunderstanding when he observes, "[i]n general, we perceive a very strong tendency toward egalitarianism when the Qur'an deals with the ethical and religious responsibilities and the retribution of believers, and a discriminatory tendency when it comes to social and legal obligations of women." Such a misunderstanding is indicative of a reliance on verses taken out of context, and a lack of distinction between scripture and tradition, social and legal, and injunction and tolerance.

158. Ben Salama, *Naqd al-Thawabit*, 43. See also Mayer, chap. 5, 6 in *Islam and Human Rights*. Mayer discusses what she sees to be the Qur'an's contribution to the elevation of Islamic women's dignity.

159. For an account of the progressive nature of Qur'anic provisions regarding women, see Abou El Fadl, chap. 12 in *The Great Theft*.

160. Ramadan, *Radical Reform*, 224–232.

161. Asad, trans., http://www.altafsir.com.

162. Yusuf Ali, trans., http://www.altafsir.com.

163. Ibid.

164. It is the category of *Mu'allafa Qulūbuhum*—those with weak faith whose personal apostasy could lead to the apostasy of a large number of their followers. The allocation of zakat subsidy monies to them was intended to prevent obstacles to the spread of Islam in the early days.

165. Yusuf Ali, trans., http://www.altafsir.com.

166. Ibid.

167. Walk, trans., http://www.altafsir.com.

168. Yusuf Ali, trans., http://www.altafsir.com.

169. See Qur'an 2:271, 4:114, 33:35, 57:18.

170. Mahmassani, *Arkan Huquq al-Insan*, 221*ff.*; Marzoogy, *Human Rights in Islamic Law*, 297*ff.*

171. Abdel Haleem, trans., *The Qur'an*, 372.

172. Khalidi, trans., *The Qur'an*, 156.

173. 'Uthmani, trans., http://www.altafsir.com.

174. Suyuti, *Al-Jami' al-Saghir*, vol. 2, no. 1290.

175. Ibid., vol. 2, no. 1873.

176. Ibid., vol. 2, no. 1861.

177. Ibid., vol. 1, no. 1164.

178. *Sunan Ibn Majah*, vol. 1, Book 8, chap. 25, no. 1836.

179. For a brief discussion on the protection of personal property, and the conditions of its acquisition and holding, see Ramadan, *Islam, the West and the Challenges of Modernity*, 147–150.

180. Dawood, trans., *The Koran*, 64. The personal integrity referred to in this verse includes the prohibition of murder and suicide. See also Qur'anic Verse 2:188, which cautions against enlisting the help of a judge to cheat someone out of his or her property.

181. Asad, trans., http://www.altafsir.com. See also Qur'an 7:85, 26:183.

182. See Qur'an 2:177, 3:76, 5:1, 6:152, 7:85, 16:91, 17:34–35, 26:181.

183. Khalidi, trans., *The Qur'an*, 235.

184. Pickthall, trans., http://www.altafsir.com.

185. Asad, trans., http://www.altafsir.com. See also Qur'an 2:267, 5:87, 7:31–32, 28:77, 40:64; Jabiri, *Al-Dimuqratiyya wa Huquq al-Insan*, 212.

CHAPTER 15: THE RIGHT TO FREEDOM

1.   'Uthmani, trans., http://www.altafsir.com.

2.   Asad, trans., http://www.altafsir.com.

3.   Ibid.

4.   Ibid.

5.   Ibid.

6.   Dawood, trans., *The Koran*, 64.

7.   See Abou El Fadl, *Islam and the Challenge of Democracy*, 29. About El Fadl asserts that the Qur'an does not discriminate between believers and nonbelievers when it comes to the sanctity of human life and the universal right to life.

8.   Qur'an 42:40.

9.   Walk, trans., http://www.altafsir.com.

10. Suyuti, *Al-Jami'i al-Saghir*, vol. 2, no. 2575; Suyuti, *Al-Jami'i al-Saghir*, vol. 6, no. 9173.

11. Nayhoum (*Al-Islam fi-l-Asr*), calls for recreating the role of the mosque as an alternative to a democratic representative system where people (instead of parliaments) get the opportunity to participate in running their affairs through attendance of mosque functions.

12. Suyuti, *Al-Jami' al-Saghir*, vol. 2, no. 1246; *Sunan Abi Daoud*, vol. 2, chap. 36, sec. 17, no. 4345; *Sunan Ibn Maja*, vol. 2, chap. 36, no. 4011, 4012.

13. Mahmassani, *Arkan Huquq al-Insan*, 144.

14. Esack, *Le Coran Mode d'Emploi*, 260.

15. See Watt and Bell, *Introduction to the Qur'an*, 166; Haykel, "Popular Support First," in *Islam and the Challenge of Democracy*, ed. Abou El Fadl, 79–80. See also 'Abdul-Karim (*Al-Judhur al-Tarikhiyya li-l-Shari'a al-Islamiyya*, 79) who criticizes 'Abbas Mahmoud Al-'Aqqad's views on slavery in Islam and insists that Islam condones slavery, thereby ignoring the context of the relevant Qur'anic verses that deal with this issue.

16. See A. Charfi, *L'Islam entre le Message et l'Histoire, 118–119.* Charfi observes that the Qur'an does not directly or indirectly mention a single circumstance under which a human being can be enslaved.

17. Mahmassani, *Arkan Huquq al-Insan,* 105.

18. Walk, trans., http://www.altafsir.com.

19. 'Uthmani, trans., http://www.altafsir.com.

20. Qur'an 24:33: *"Let those who find not the wherewithal for marriage keep themselves chaste, until God gives them means out of His grace. And if any of your slaves ask for a deed in writing (to enable them to earn their freedom for a certain sum), give them such a deed if ye know any good in them: yea, give them something yourselves out of the means which God has given to you. But force not your maids to prostitution when they desire chastity, in order that ye may make a gain in the goods of this life. But if anyone compels them, yet, after such compulsion, is God, Oft-Forgiving, Most Merciful (to them)"* (Yusuf Ali, trans., http://www.altafsir.com).

21. Qur'an 49:13.

22. 'Uthmani, trans., http://www.altafsir.com.

23. Walk, trans., http://www.altafsir.com. See also Qur'an 9:60.

24. See Qur'an 4:3, 5:89.

25. See Qur'an 58:3.

26. Qur'an 4:92, 5:89.

27. Zein-ed-Dine, "Unveiling and Veiling," in *Liberal Islam,* ed. Kurzman, 104.

28. Talbi, *L'Universalité du Coran,* 7. See also Talbi (*Al-Islam: Hurriyya wa Hiwar,* 83*ff.*) who discusses the various components of the freedom of faith.

29. Asad, trans., http://www.altafsir.com .

30. Bulaç, "The Medina Document," in *Liberal Islam,* ed. Kurzman, 177.

31. Sachedina, *The Role of Islam in the Public Square: Guidance or Governance,* 14.

32. Asad, trans., http://www.altafsir.com.

33. See Nissaburi, *Asbab an-Nuzul.* See also 'Abdul-Karim, *Shadw al-Rabab,* 2:76–77.

34. Urvoy, *Les Penseurs Libres dans l'Islam Classique,* 25.

35. 'Uthmani, trans., http://www.altafsir.com.

36. In his exegesis of Qur'anic Verse 109:6, Ibn Kathir (*Tafsir al-Qur'an al-Karim*) refers to the fact that this verse was used by the Shafi'i and Hanbali schools of jurisprudence to justify the prohibition of inheritance among people of different faiths (including Christians, Jews, and Muslims). Aside from the fact that such a prohibition ignores the commonality of the Abrahamic faiths, it exemplifies the distortion that may arise when a verse is taken out of context. Instead, that prohibition is based on a Prophetic Tradition according to which

the Prophet ruled that "people from different faiths cannot inherit from each other" (Mahmassani, *al-Mabadi' al-Shar'iyya wa-l-Qanuniyya*, 300).

37. Khalidi, trans., *The Qur'an*, 221.

38. Yusuf Ali, trans., http://www.altafsir.com. In a note to his translation, Yusuf Ali provides further commentary on this verse: "The Apostles are not sent to cancel man's limited free-will. They are sent to preach and teach, to preach hope to the repentant ("good news"), and to warn the rebellious of the Wrath to come."

39. Abdel Haleem, trans., *The Qur'an*, 314.

40. Ibid., 419.

41. 'Uthmani, trans., http://www.altafsir.com.

42. The abrogation is mentioned in Tabari's *Jami' al-Bayan fi Tafsir al-Qur'an*, and Razi's *Mafatih al-Ghayb, al-Tafsir al-Kabir*.

43. Abdel Haleem, trans., *The Qur'an*, 419. See also Sachedina, *The Islamic Roots of Democratic Pluralism*, 95.

44. Walk, trans., http://www.altafsir.com. In this verse, and in addition to the clarification related to the role of the Prophet, a noble principle is set forth wherein aid to the needy is offered not only to Muslims but to non-Muslims, as well. Needy people should be helped not because they are Muslims but because it pleases God. This is yet another illustration of the universal nature of Islam.

45. See Moussalli, *The Islamic Quest for Democracy, Pluralism, and Human Rights*, 132. Here, Mousalli discusses Prophet Muhammad's response to accusations made by Ibn Ubayy. In addition, Qur'anic Verse 49:12 cautions against being suspicious of other people's intentions, because only God is capable of knowing what is inside a person's mind: "*O you who believe, abstain from many of the suspicions. Some suspicions are sins. And do not be curious (to find out faults of others), and do not backbite one another. Does one of you like that he eats the flesh of his dead brother? You would abhor it*" ('Uthmani, trans., http://www.altafsir.com.).

46. See Qaradawi (*Al-Tatarruf al-'Ilmani*, 39) who objects to secularism partly because it does not allow for the punishment of those who openly abandon worship-related duties (such as prayer, fasting at Ramadan, or payment of zakat, all of which is required by the *'ulamā'* who consider the abandonment of worship duties to be idolatry).

47. Throughout history, rulers have at times used *takfir* (the act of accusing someone of weak faith, idolatry, or an untrue declaration of faith) to justify the use of the death penalty, and have been aided in such determinations by the religious establishment. See also Jamal, *Al-Islam al-Sunni*, 43.

48. Talbi, *Al-Islam: Hurriyya wa Hiwar*, 95. Talbi cites Qur'an 2:109 in support of his argument.

49. 'Uthmani, trans., http://www.altafsir.com.

50. Sachedina, *The Role of Islam in the Public Square: Guidance or Governance*, 15.

51. Qaradawi, "Extremism," in *Liberal Islam*, ed. Kurzman, 199.

52. See 'Abdu, *Al-Islam wal-Nasraniyya ma' al-'Ilm wa-l-Madaniyya*, 63. 'Abdu asserts that no one may be accused of *kufr* if even the slightest doubt exists.

53. Asad, trans., http://www.altafsir.com.

54. 'Uthmani, trans., http://www.altafsir.com.

55. Ibid.

56. Qaradawi, *Al-Sahwa al-Islamiyya Bayna-l-Ikhtilaf al-Mashru' wa al-Tafarruq al-Madhmum*, 25.

57. Cohen, *Under Crescent and Cross*, 61.

58. A. Saeed in *Freedom of Religion, Apostasy and Islam*, eds. Abdullah Saeed and Hassan Saeed, 15–16.

59. A. Charfi, *L'Islam entre le Message et l'Histoire*, 76; Talbi, *Al-Islam: Hurriyya wa Hiwar*, 90–96. For a debate regarding differing perceptions of the punishment of apostasy, see Babès and Oubrou, *Loi d'Allah Loi des Hommes*, 40–63.

60. A. Saeed in *Freedom of Religion, Apostasy and Islam*, eds. Abdullah Saeed and Hassan Saeed, 35*ff*. A. Saeed devotes all of chapter three to exploring the various concepts and actions that qualify as apostasy and are punishable by the death penalty.

61. *Musnad al-Imam al-Shafi'i*, vol. 2, no. 284; al-Muttaqi al-Hindi, *Kanz al-'Ummal*, vol. 1, no. 394.

62. This tradition of the Prophet is cited by A. Saeed in *Freedom of Religion, Apostasy and Islam*, eds. Abdullah Saeed and Hassan Saeed, 59.

63. Mahmassani, *Al-Awza'i*, 123. See also Abdullah and Hassan Saeed, *Freedom of Religion, Apostasy and Islam*, 59–64, wherein A. Saeed comments on instances in which the Prophet is said to have dealt with cases of apostasy.

64. Mahmassani, *Turath al-Khulafa' al-Rashidin*, 246.

65. 'Uthmani, trans., http://www.altafsir.com.

66. See Abdullah and Hassan Saeed, *Freedom of Religion, Apostasy and Islam*, 78*ff*. A. Saeed discusses the punishment of apostasy only in the hereafter.

67. Yusuf Ali, trans., http://www.altafsir.com.

68. Ibid.

69. See the exegeses of Qur'anic Verse 3:86 by Tabari (*Jami' al-Bayan fi Tafsir al Qur'an*) and Zamakhshari (*Tafsir al-Kashshaf*). See also Jabiri, *Fahm al-Qur'an al-Hakim*, 3:144–145nn21–22.

70. Yusuf Ali, trans., http://www.altafsir.com.
71. Qur'an 4:116: "*Indeed, Allah does not forgive association with Him, but He forgives what is less than that for whom He wills. And he who associates others with Allah has certainly gone far astray*" (Walk, trans., http://www.altafsir.com). The principle set forth in this verse also appears in Qur'anic Verse 4:48.
72. The repentance denied in this verse is that of sins other than apostasy, because Verse 3:89 expressly reserves the option of repentance, and Verses 3:85 and 91 condition the punishment on dying while in idolatry, prior to repentance. Muhammad Asad, in his translation of Verse Q3:90, makes that clarification about the nonacceptance of repentance [*of other sins*].
73. Asad, trans., http://www.altafsir.com.
74. Tabari, *Jami' al-Bayan fi Tafsir al-Qur'an*; Zamakhshari, *Tafsir al-Kashshaf*; Razi, *Mafatih al-Ghayb al-Tafsir al-Kabir*; Qurtubi, *Al-Jami' li Ahkam al-Qur'an*; Ibn Kathir, *Tafsir al-Qur'an al-Karim*.
75. Bearing in mind that the earliest exegesis was written approximately two hundred and fifty years after the end of the Revelation, it is understandable that the commentators may have found the Abu Bakr wars of Ridda to be an easy interpretation of Qur'anic Verse 5:54, which they placed in the realm of the advance *ghayb*—foretelling about that which is yet to come.
76. Yusuf Ali, trans., http://www.altafsir.com.
77. See Qur'an 39:7: "*If you disbelieve, then, Allah does not need you at all, however He does not like for His servants to be disbelievers; and if you are grateful, He will like it for you. No one will bear the burden of someone else. Then, to your Lord is your return; so He will tell you about what you used to do. He is aware of whatever lies in the hearts*" ('Uthmani, trans., http://www.altafsir.com); Qur'an 49:17: "*They impress on thee as a favour that they have embraced Islam. Say, 'Count not your Islam as a favour upon me: Nay, God has conferred a favour upon you that He has guided you to the faith, if ye be true and sincere*'" (Yusuf Ali, trans., http://www.altafsir.com).
78. Ibn 'Ashour, *Al-Tahrir wa al-Tanwir*.
79. Asad, trans., http://www.altafsir.com.
80. Abizaid, *Al-Tafkir Fi Zaman al-Takfir*, 272. See also A. Saeed (in Abdullah Saeed and Hassan Saeed, *Freedom of Religion, Apostasy and Islam*, 100–108), who relates episodes of misuse and abuse of the concept of apostasy, wherein the term is used against intellectuals (such as Saadawy, Ashmawy, Hanafi, Abdel Raziq, the late Farag Foda, among others), politicians (including the President Atatürk of Turkey, President Bourguiba of Tunisia, Prime Minister Benazir Bhutto of Pakistan, and political activist Mahmoud Taha of Sudan), journalists (such as Said Mekbel and Zine-Eddine Aliou-Salah of Morocco), and others in various Arab and Muslim countries.

81. Talbi, *Plaidoyer pour un Islam Moderne*, 112; Filali-Ansari, *L'Islam est-il Hostile à la Laïcité?*, 99.

82. A. Saeed in *Freedom of Religion, Apostasy and Islam*, eds. Abdullah Saeed and Hassan Saeed, 90–93; Mayer, chap. 8 in *Islam and Human Rights*; 'Ashmawi, *Usul al-Shari'a*, 163. See also Saleh, *Al-Islam wal Mujtama' al-'Asri*, 262.

83. A. Saeed in *Freedom of Religion, Apostasy and Islam*, eds. Abdullah Saeed and Hassan Saeed, 93–98. Saeed offers a comprehensive round-up of modern thought on the freedom to change faith.

84. M. Charfi, *L'Islam et Liberté*, 79*ff*. In this work, Charfi relates Shaykh Muhammad al-Ghazali's testimony before an Egyptian court in the trial of the assassin of Farag Foda. In his testimony, Ghazali asserts that the assassination is the religious obligation of each Muslim person whenever the state fails to fulfill its duty in this respect. See also an account of the modernist views of Johns and Saeed, "Nurcholich Madjid and the Interpretation of the Qur'an," in *Modern Muslim Intellectuals*, ed. Farouki, 84–88.

85. 'Uthmani, trans., http://www.altafsir.com.

86. For more details on the Wars of Ridda waged by Caliph Abu Bakr, see Rabbath, *La conquête Arabe sous les quatre premiers califes*, 1:43*ff*.; A. Saeed in *Freedom of Religion, Apostasy and Islam*, eds. Abdullah Saeed and Hassan Saeed, 65*ff*.; Haykal, *Al-Siddiq Abou Bakr*, 95*ff*.; T. Hussein, *Al-Shaykhan*, 54ff.

87. Foda, *Al-Haqiqa al-Gha'iba*, 44. See also Talbi (*Al-Islam: Hurriyya wa Hiwar*, 91) who defines potential cases of capital punishment for apostasy that the Prophet or any of his successors may have enforced as self-defense against armed aggression (assuming that those apostates had turned violent against the Muslims following their defection).

88. Moussalli (*The Islamic Quest for Democracy*, 92) observes that Abu Bakr saw the movement to challenge the state's right to collect zakat as a mass-desertion of religious duty that lead to apostasy. Abu Bakr presumably drew these conclusions without ever confirming that the people involved had actually rejected Islam as a faith. Moussalli further observes that even the Companions were hesitant to approve Abu Bakr's move. See also Moussalli, "Islamic Democracy and Pluralism," in *Progressive Muslims*, ed. Safi, 286*ff*., in which Mousalli addresses the need to distinguish between Islam (a divine religion) and the Islamic state (a human political system). See Filali-Ansari, *L'Islam est-il Hostile à la Laïcité?*, 69.

89. See Jabiri, *Al-Dimuqratiyya wa Huquq al-Insan*, 178–179. Jabiri supports his views regarding the continued relevance of repressing apostasy as a crime against society and the state by drawing a parallel with modern criminal law, which does not excuse treason against the state or conspiracy with the enemy

under freedom of expression and human rights. That parallel is not relevant here because religion and state are not likes. Above all, Islam is secular, and freedom of faith is a pillar of Islam.

90. *Memorandum on Human Rights in Islam and Their Implementation in the Kingdom of Saudi Arabia (Colloques de Riyad, de Paris, du Vatican, de Genève et de Strasbourg sur le Dogme Musulman et les Droits de l'Homme en Islam*, 57).

91. For more on the interdependence of freedom and justice, see Soroush, *Reason, Freedom, and Democracy*, 97.

92. Mohsin, trans., http://www.quranexplorer.com/Quran/Default.aspx.

93. Qur'an 2:283.

94. 'Uthmani, trans., http://www.altafsir.com.

95. See Qur'an 4:22–23, 5:95.

96. Asad, trans., http://www.altafsir.com.

97. Ibid.

98. 'Uthmani, trans., http://www.altafsir.com.

99. See the position of the Saudi delegation at the colloquium held in Riyadh on 23 March 1972, as described in the summary of the minutes appearing in *Colloques de Riyad, de Paris, du Vatican, de Genève et de Strasbourg sur le Dogme Musulman et les Droits de l'Homme en Islam*, 22.

100. See Qur'an 6:164, 17:15, 35:18, 39:7, 53:38.

101. See Mahmoud, *Quest for Divinity*, 197–204. Mahmoud summarizes the views of Taha, who defends all aspects of corporeal punishment under Shari'a-based criminal law.

102. Marzoogy, *Human Rights in Islamic Law*, 453.

103. Qur'an 2:178.

104. Qur'an 5:38.

105. Qur'an 4:15, 24:2.

106. Qur'an 24:4.

107. Qur'an 5:33.

108. The Qur'an does not provide for the jailing of defaulting debtors. In fact, Qur'anic Verse 2:280 indicates that a debtor should be given ample time to repay, that is, enough time for his financial condition to improve. This verse also suggests that the debtor may be relieved of his debt by way of charity: "*If the debtor is in a difficulty, grant him time Till it is easy for him to repay. But if ye remit it by way of charity, that is best for you if ye only knew*" (Yusuf Ali, trans., http://www.altafsir.com).

109. A. Charfi, *L'Islam entre le Message et l'Histoire*, 93.

110. 'Alayli, *Ayna-l-Khata'*, 86.

111. Khalidi, *The Qur'an*, 64.

112. Yusuf Ali, trans., http://www.altafsir.com.
113. See Hammami, *Islam al-Fuqaha'*, 93–99.

CHAPTER 16: REFLECTIONS ON HUMAN RIGHTS IN ISLAM

1. Esposito and Mogahed, *Who Speaks for Islam*, 130.
2. Moussalli, *The Islamic Quest for Democracy*, 127; Mayer, *Islam and Human Rights,* 64; Bassiouni, "Sources of Islamic law and the Protection of Human Rights," in *The Islamic Criminal Justice System*, ed. Bassiouni.
3. Chebel, *Islam et Libre Arbitre*, 159*ff.*
4. For a discussion on how religion has been used to justify repressive regimes and oppression, see Mayer, chap. 1 in *Islam and Human Rights*.
5. Jabiri, *Al-Dimuqratiyya wa Huquq al-Insan*, 208. See also Natsir, "The Indonesian Revolution: Harmony of Life! Freedom of Religion! Unity of the Nation," in *Liberal Islam*, ed. Kurzman, 64.
6. Soroush, *Reason, Freedom, and Democracy in Islam*, 63.
7. Kurzman, "Liberal Islam and its Islamic Context, a Sourcebook," in *Liberal Islam*, ed. Kurzman, 20.
8. Paragraph (f) of the Preamble to the Universal Islamic Declaration of Human Rights, proclaimed by the Islamic Council's meeting in Paris, 19 September 1981, www.alhewar.com/ISLAMDECL.HTML.
9. See Gardet, *Les Hommes de l'Islam*, 83. Gardet speaks of the duty to defend the rights of God.
10. Jabiri, *Al-Dimuqratiyya wa Huquq al-Insan*, 150–151, 160–163.
11. Asad, trans., http://www.altafsir.com.
12. When Adam was first created he did not yet have descendants.
13. Abou El Fadl, *Islam and the Challenge of Democracy*, 28.
14. Saleh, *Al-Islam wa-l-Mujtama' al-'Asri*, 181–182.
15. Moussalli, *The Islamic Quest for Democracy, Pluralism and Human Rights*, 127.
16. Sachedina, *The Role of Islam in the Public Square*, 9.
17. See Abizaid, *Dawa'ir al-Khawf*, 129–130. Abizaid challenges the claim that Islam recognized human rights prior to the modern-day universal declarations of human rights. He observes, "We need to remember that the person honored by religion and to whom rights are guaranteed is the person who belongs to one or the other religion...bearing in mind that the person who remains outside the sphere of a given religion is in the eyes of that religion a 'lost' person with no rights whatsoever, even though he may be a person with full rights in the eyes of his or her religion." In reality, from Islam's universal perspective, all human beings—regardless of creed or lack thereof—share the same human dignity and the same rights in this life.
18. Jabiri, *Al-Dimucratiyya wa Huquq al-Insan*, 167–171.

19. Qur'an 32:9: "*Then He gave him a proportioned shape, and breathed into him of His spirit. And He granted you the (power of) hearing and the eyes and the hearts. Little you give thanks*" ('Uthmani, trans., http://www.altafsir.com).

20. Qur'an 2:30: "*Behold, thy Lord said to the angels: 'I will create a vicegerent on earth.' They said: 'Wilt Thou place therein one who will make mischief therein and shed blood? whilst we do celebrate Thy praises and glorify Thy holy (name)?' He said: 'I know what ye know not.'*" (Yusuf Ali, trans., http://www.altafsir.com).

21. Qur'an 31:20: "*ARE YOU NOT aware that God has made subservient to you all that is in the heavens and all that is on earth, and has lavished upon you His blessings, both outward and inward? And yet, among men there is many a one that argues about God without having any knowledge [of Him], without any guidance, and without any light-giving revelation*" (Asad, trans., http://www.altafsir.com); Qur'an 45:13: "*And He has made subservient to you, [as a gift] from Himself, all that is in the heavens and on earth: in this, behold, there are messages indeed for people who think!*" (Ibid.).

22. Qur'an 32:9: "*Then He gave him a proportioned shape, and breathed into him of His spirit. And He granted you the (power of) hearing and the eyes and the hearts. Little you give thanks*" ('Uthmani, trans., http://www.altafsir.com).

23. Qur'an 95:4: "*We have certainly created man in the best of stature*" (Walk, trans., http://www.altafsir.com); Qur'an 64:3: "*He created the heavens and earth in truth and formed you and perfected your forms; and to Him is the [final] destination*" (Walk, trans., http://www.altafsir.com); Qur'an 40:64: "*Allah it is Who appointed for you the earth for a dwelling-place and the sky for a canopy, and fashioned you and perfected your shapes, and hath provided you with good things. Such is Allah, your Lord. Then blessed be Allah, the Lord of the Worlds!*" (Mohsin, trans., http://www.quranexplorer.com/Quran/Default.aspx).

24. Qur'an 38:71–72: "*Behold, thy Lord said to the angels: 'I am about to create man from clay (71): When I have fashioned him (in due proportion) and breathed into him of My spirit, fall ye down in obeisance unto him'. (72)*" (Yusuf Ali, trans., http://www.altafsir.com). See also Qur'an 2:34, 17:61.

25. Qur'an 17:70: "*NOW, INDEED, We have conferred dignity on the children of Adam, and borne them over land and sea, and provided for them sustenance out of the good things of life, and favoured them far above most of Our creation*" (Asad, trans., http://www.altafsir.com).

26. Yusuf Ali, trans., http://www.altafsir.com. God's role in further endowing humankind with knowledge is discussed in Qur'anic Verses 55:2–4, 96:1–5.

27. Qur'an 39:9: "*Is one who worships devoutly during the hour of the night prostrating himself or standing (in adoration), who takes heed of the Hereafter,*

and who places his hope in the Mercy of his Lord - (like one who does not)? Say: 'Are those equal, those who know and those who do not know? It is those who are endued with understanding that receive admonition'" (Yusuf Ali, trans., http://www.altafsir.com).

28. Qur'an 58:11: *"God will elevate to high ranks those who have faith and knowledge among you"* (Abdel Haleem, trans., The Qur'an, 385).

29. Mahmassani, *Arkan Huquq al-Insan*, 196–198.

30. See the presentation by the Saudi delegation to the colloquium held in the Vatican on 25 October 1974 on the subject of human cultural rights in Islam (*Colloques de Riyad, de Paris, du Vatican, de Genève et de Strasbourg sur le Dogme Musulman et les Droits de l'Homme en Islam*, 126).

31. Kabir, "Minorities in a Democracy," in *Liberal Islam*, ed. Kurzman, 149. Upon the advent of Islam, Judaism still restricted the teaching of the Bible to the chosen people. When Christ arrived, the Jewish religious establishment opposed him because he shared his Biblical teachings with the *goim* (the common people). By doing so, the Jewish religious establishment was attempting to intercede between humankind and God. Islam addresses itself to all people (not just Muslims and believers) and seeks to remove all intermediaries and barriers that exist between humanity and divine knowledge.

32. Jabiri, *Al-Dimuqratiyya wa Huquq al-Insan*, 144; A. Charfi, *Islam et Liberté*, 75.

33. Mayer, *Islam and Human Rights*, 73.

34. Shari'a is the body of general principles that governs relations among people. However, over time, the system of law derived from Shari'a by the Islamic jurisprudents (the *fiqh*) also became commonly known as Shari'a law and Islamic law. See our discussion on terminology in Chapter 9 of this book.

35. A. Saeed in *Freedom of Religion, Apostasy and Islam*, eds., Abdullah Saeed and Hassan Saeed, 10–19.

36. For a critique of this attitude of Muslim nations, see Ben Salama, *Naqd al-Thawabit*, 18.

37. The Cairo Declaration of Human Rights in Islam, Resolution 49/19-P, adopted by the Nineteenth Islamic Conference of Foreign Ministers (Session of Peace, Interdependence and Development), held in Cairo, 31 July to 5 August 1990.

38. This definition is derived from the Explanatory Notes to the Universal Islamic Declaration of Human Rights, 19 September 1981, prepared by the Islamic Council in London (www.alhewar.com/ISLAMDECL.html; last accessed 30 November 2013). A. Saeed (A. and H. Saeed, *Freedom of Religion, Apostasy and Islam*, 17–18) points to certain significant discrepancies between the Arabic and English versions of this declaration.

39. For a discussion of the arts in Islam from a conservative perspective, see Nasr, *The Heart of Islam*, 222–235.
40. Qaradawi, *Al-Halal wa-l-Haram*, 90–91.
41. 'Uthmani, trans., http://www.altafsir.com.
42. Qaradawi, *Markaz al-Mar'a fi-l-Hayat al-Islamiyya*, 40–41.
43. Mahmassani, *Falsafat Al-Tashrī' fi Al-Islām*, 119*ff.*
44. Soroush, *Reason, Freedom, and Democracy*, 89.
45. Ibid., 92.
46. Mayer, *Islam and Human Rights*, 1.
47. Moussalli, *The Islamic Quest for Democracy, Pluralism and Human Rights*, 5.
48. For a discussion of the perceived relationship between human rights and religion, see Soroush, *Reason, Freedom, and Democracy in Islam*, 128–130.
49. Bazergan, "Religion and Liberty," in *Liberal Islam*, ed. Kurzman, 84.

CONCLUSION: RECOVERING THE MESSAGE: REFORMING OUR PERCEPTION OF GOD

1. Abou El Fadl, "*The Search for Beauty in Islam*, vii.
2. See A. Charfi in *Mustaqbal al-Islam fi-l-Gharb wa-l-Sharq*, eds. Hoffman and Charfi, 47–57. Here, Charfi discusses the role of rituals in worship.
3. See Qaradawi, *Al-'Ibada fi-l-Islam*. Qaradawi devotes the entire first chapter to defining the term *'ibāda* (with particular focus on subservience, humiliation, and guilt).
4. Verse 86:4 states: "*There is no soul but has a protector over it*" (Yusuf Ali, trans., http://www.altafsir.com). According to prominent exegeses by Tabari (*Jami' al-Bayan fi Tafsir al-Qur'an*), Qurtubi (*Al-Jami' li Ahkam al-Qur'an*), Mahalli and Suyuti (*Tafsir al-Jalalayn*), this has been interpreted as meaning that God has placed an angel over each person's shoulders to collect and record all good and bad deeds that a person commits in his or her lifetime to serve as documentation for the Day of Judgment. In reality, the term ḥafaẓa appearing in this verse may mean either to memorize or to protect. Closer to the true meaning of this verse, Ibn Kathir (in *Tafsir al-Qur'an al-Karim*) correctly interprets it as meaning that God has placed angels to protect a person from the dangers of everyday life.
5. Qur'an 3:31, 5:54, 11:90, 85:14; Nasr, *The Heart of Islam*, 209–210. In contrast, Makarian (*Le Choc Jésus Mahomet*, 120–123) describes the God of Islam as being inaccessible to humankind and asserts that the concept of love does not appear in the Qur'an.
6. Asad, trans., http://www.altafsir.com.

7. The root term *'abd* and words derived from it are used two hundred and seventy times throughout the Qur'an (one hundred forty-three times in the verb form: 'to worship and adore').

8. The term *'ibād* is used to refer to all people, without distinction between believers and nonbelievers, because humankind was created in the first place for the sole purpose of adoring and worshiping God. The term *'ibād* reflects the innate tendency of all people (atheists included) to admire and appreciate that which is beautiful and perfect, and that transcends humanity. *'Ibād and its derivatives—used for adoration and worship—* is used ninety-eight times throughout the Qur'an. In contrast, the term *'abeed*—a plural term generally used to refer to slaves—appears only five times in the Qur'an, and in the same recurrent phrase, "*God does not do injustice to His 'abeed.*" When used in this way, *'abeed* has the more general meaning, 'subjects of God' (see Qur'an 3:182, 8:51, 22:10, 41:46, 50:29).

9. See Rahman, *Major Themes of the Qur'an*, 3. Rahman stresses the importance of the served-servant relationship between humankind and God. In reality, even when the term *'abd* is used in the singular form (which occurs twenty-five times throughout the Qur'an), it is used almost invariably in the sense of 'someone who worships and loves God.' There are only three specific instances in which 'slavery' is clearly intended (other than in the relations of humankind with God): Qur'an 2:178, 2:221, and 16:75. In Qur'anic Verse 16:75, the term 'owned' was added to the term *'abd* to clarify that the intended meaning was 'slave', because the context did not otherwise render that meaning obvious. Finally, the term *'ibād* is used only once in the sense of slavery (Qur'an 24:32), but then only in the relations among humans and not in their relations with God.

10. Shahrour, Tajfif Manabi' al-Irhab, 138.

11. This is our own translation, because all other accessible translations have rendered the term *'ibād* to mean 'servants' or 'slaves'.

12. See 'Abdu, *Risalat al-Tawhid*, 129. Even some of the most liberal modern-day revivalists (such as Imam Muhammad 'Abdu) have described Islam as a religion characterized by *istslām* (surrender) and *'ubūdiyya* (subservience and slavery) to God.

13. See Rahman, *Major Themes of the Qur'an*, 8. "The purpose of man is to 'serve' God."

14. See Makarian, *Le Choc Jésus Mahomet*, 139–140. Makarian ignores all evidence to the contrary when he asserts that Islam calls for humankind to become slaves to God, devoid of any dignity.

15. See Qur'an 2:255: "*To Him belongs all that is in the heavens and all that is on the earth.*" ('Uthmani, trans., http://www.altafsir.com). Ibn Kathir (*Tafsir al-Qur'an al-Karim*) interprets this verse as follows: "This is a notification that all people are His slaves, subject to His sovereignty, and they all fall under his oppression and might."

16. Yusuf Ali, trans., http://www.altafsir.com.

17. Asad, trans., http://www.altafsir.com.See also Qur'an 29:6, 39:7.

18. Qur'an 29:45 (Asad, trans., http://www.altafsir.com).

19. Qur'an 2:153 (Asad, trans., http://www.altafsir.com).

20. See Qur'an 17:7, 17:15, 27:40, 27:91–92, 31:12, 35:18, 39:41, 41:46, 45:15.

21. A. Charfi, *L'Islam entre le Message et l'Histoire*, 75.

22. Throughout the Qur'anic translations, there are countless examples of poorly selected, fear-inducing terms that grant God an aura of terror and awe. For example, Qur'anic Verse 2:40 provides as follows: "*Believe in that which I have [now] bestowed from on high, confirming the truth already in your possession, and be not foremost among those who deny its truth; and do not barter away My messages for a trifling gain; and* of Me be conscious!" (Asad, trans., http://www.altafsir.com). The term 'of Me be conscious' is Asad's rendition of the Arabic term *irhabūni*. However, all other translations that we have consulted have rendered *irhabūni* to mean 'fear' or 'awe'. In reality, the term *irhabooni* derives from the root term *rahaba* which means 'to display a reverential attitude deriving from consciousness of the importance and might toward the other'. With the exception of only a few (such as Zamakhshari and Razi), most exegetes have opted for the 'fear and awe' interpretation.

23. See Qur'an 5:8: "*O ye who believe! stand out firmly for Allah, as witnesses to fair dealing, and let not the hatred of others to you make you swerve to wrong and depart from justice. Be just: that is next* to piety: *and* fear *Allah. For Allah is well-acquainted with all that ye do.*" (Yusuf Ali, trans., http://www.altafsir.com). The highlighted terms are renditions of the term *taqwa* and its verb derivative, respectively.

24. Barlas, *Believing Women in Islam*, 143.

25. Walk, trans., http://www.altafsir.com.

26. Qur'an 17:109, 21:90, 23:2, 57:16.

27. See Qur'an 20:2–3, 23:57, 24:52, 50:33.

28. See Ahmad Amin, *Fajr al-Islam*, 176. Here, Amin describes life in Mecca and Medina during the early days of Islam where the more light-hearted enjoyment of life's pleasures coexisted with the serious atmosphere of religious life. The first four caliphs did not prohibit arts, singing, or music. They were even present in the Hijaz during the hajj period. See also Hoffman, chap. 13 in *Al-Islam ka-Badil*.

29. Esack, *Le Coran Mode d'Emploi*, 245.
30. Esack, *Le Coran Mode d'Emploi*, 246. Esack also cites Qur'anic Verses 27:60, 32:7, 40:64 which exalt the beauty in God's creation. The beauty in God's creation of the universe is also referenced in Qur'anic Verses 2:117, 15:16, 18:7, 37:6, 50:6.
31. Asad trans., http://www.altafsir.com.
32. Walk, trans., http://www.altafsir.com.
33. See Fuehr-Lobban, *Against Islamic Extremism*, 6. "In the humanistic view, there is no punishing or vengeful God; the notion of a vengeful God is not appropriate to this era in human history, according to al-'Ashmawi."
34. Qur'an 35:45.
35. Qur'an 25:70–71.
36. Qur'an 2:160, 4:17, 4:110, 4:146, 7:153, 9:102–104, 42:25, 66:8.
37. See Qur'an 5:39, 24:5, 25:68–71.
38. Kurzman, "Liberal Islam and its Islamic Context, a Sourcebook," in *Liberal Islam*, ed. Kurzman, 47. Kurzman cites Taleqani's views on divine mercy (which he expressed in his last sermon). See also De Saint Bon and Khiari, *Catholique/Musulman*, 131
39. See Qur'an 4:48, 4:116.
40. Nasr, *The Heart of Islam*, 203.
41. All but one of the one hundred and fourteen surasof the Qur'an start with that caption. The only exception is *Sūrat Al-Tawba* (the Repentance).
42. See Qur'an 17:20, 20:76–82, 33:43, among many others.
43. Qur'an 39:53 (Arberry, trans., http://www.altafsir.com). See also Qur'an 15:56.
44. Qur'an 6:54: *"And when those who believe in Our messages come unto thee, say: 'Peace be upon you. Your Sustainer has willed upon Himself the law of grace and mercy—so that if any of you does a bad deed out of ignorance, and thereafter repents and lives righteously, He shall be [found] much-forgiving, a dispenser of grace'"* (Asad, trans., http://www.altafsir.com). See also Qur'an 6:12.
45. Qur'an 2:186.
46. Arberry, trans., http://www.altafsir.com.
47. Watt and Bell, *Introduction to the Quran*, 122–123.
48. Arkoun, *Al-Fikr al-Islami*, 53.
49. The call to trust in God by way of *tawakkul* appears countless times in the Qur'an, including Verses 3:159–160, 4:81, 5:11, 8:49, 9:48–51, 9:128–129, 10:71, 11:88, 11:123, 12:67, 14:11–12, 16:42, 16:98–99, 25:58, 26:217, 27:78–79, 29:58–59, 33:48, 42:10, 42:36, 58:9–10, 65:2–3, 67:29, 73:9.

50. Ghannoushi, "Participation in Non-Islamic Government," in *Liberal Islam*, ed. Kurzman, 90.

51. Arslane, "Our Decline and its Causes," in *Islam in Transition*, eds. Donohue and Esposito, 47.

52. See Bazergan, "Religion and Liberty," in *Liberal Islam*, ed. Kurzman, 74. Here, Bazergan accuses the religious establishment of cultivating a culture of *ittikāl* (reliance).

53. Ayoub, *A Muslim View of Christianity*, 94.

54. The mere fact that a tradition is brought by Abu Hurayra is prima facie evidence that it is fabricated because he was a young teenager when Prophet Muhammad died, and could not possibly have heard the Prophet say, or witnessed the Prophet do, all of the traditions reportedly attributed to him.

55. Qur'an 3:169, 3:195, 22:58.

56. In witness to the original scope of martyrdom, the verses dealing with the subject matter were referring to the companions of the Prophet who died fighting for their right to maintain their faith and proceed on the way of God.

57. See Ayoub, *A Muslim View of Christianity*, 85. Ayoub cites a prophetic tradition (reported by Malik Ibn Anas) in which Prophet Muhammad said that the only person who might still want to return to life following an experience in paradise is the martyr so that he may further experience the pleasures of martyrdom. Ayoub also cites another tradition wherein the Prophet presumably said, "The door of paradise is under the glittering swords."

58. Akhtar, *A Faith for all Seasons*, 180.

59. See Akhtar, *A Faith for All Seasons*, 130–135.

60. Some of the attributes of God appear to be negative when read out of context. Of the ninety-nine attributes of God, these six may appear questionable: *al-mākir* (the cunning), as seen in Qur'anic Verses 3:54 and Q8:30; *al-mudhill* (the humiliator) in Verse 3:26; *al-qahhār* and *al-qāhir* (the subduer) in Verses 6:18, 6:61, 12:39, 13:16, 14:48, 38:65, 39:4, 40:16; *al-mutakabbir* (the haughty) in Verses 59:23; *al-muntaqim* (the revengeful or avenger) in Verses 3:4, 5:95, 14:47, 39:37; and *al-jabbār* (the compeller, oppressor, or tyrant) in Verse 59:23. Taken out of context, these titles could perpetuate a perception of God that does not reflect His true image. However, the titles acquire an entirely different meaning when considered contextually. The verses in which these terms are used appear amid descriptions of (and responses to) the belligerent attitude of the *Quraysh* pagans and other enemies of the Prophet. Thus, when God describes Himself in such a seemingly negative way, He does so in response to those who would fight Him and His adherents. Certain Qur'anic commentators have contributed to the misperception of God's nature that sometimes occurs as a result of these seven attribute titles.

In their interpretation of Qur'anic Verse 59:23—in which God is described as *al-jabbār* (the compeller, oppressor, or tyrant) and *al-mutakabbir* (the haughty)—Zamakhshari, Razi, and Tabarsi explain that these titles refer to a God who subdues His creatures and forces upon them what He pleases. In another example, God describes Himself countless times throughout the Qur'an as *al-'azīz*. That adjective was deemed by some commentators to be an attribute of divine, revengeful pride, when in reality *al-'azīz* means someone who commands *al-'azza* (meaning 'grandeur and magnanimity'). That said, one can set aside negative perceptions of God's nature by simply recalling that of the ninety-nine Beautiful Names of God, only the seven names mentioned above are questionable, and they are only used fifteen times. By contrast, the other ninety-two names are used more than nine hundred times throughout the Qur'an, and of *those* occurrences, the adjectives compassion, justness, generosity, and kindness are used to describe God more than three hundred and fifty times. That does not include the openings of the suras, which echo the attributes of compassion and mercy.

61. Chebel, *Islam et Libre Arbitre*, 175
62. "Rethinking Islam Today," in *Liberal Islam*, ed. Kurzman, 206.
63. D. Brown, *Rethinking Tradition in Modern Islamic Thought*, 113.
64. For a general discussion of culture and identity, see An-Na'im, *Islam and the Secular State*, 33*ff.*
65. Filali-Ansari, *Reformer l'Islam*; Bidar, *Un Islam pour Notre Temps*.

Glossary of Arabic Terms

*'abd (*pl. *'abīd):*	servant or slave
*'ābed (*pl. *'ibād):*	a worshiper, from the verb and root term *'abada*
'adāla:	integrity and virtue
'adhāb al-qabr:	the fright of the grave
'adl:	justice
'afuw:	forgiveness
ahādīth al-shafā'a:	Prophetic Tradition related to intercession
ahl al-hadith:	the adherents to the schools of jurisprudence and thought which give prominence to sunna and hadith over *ijtihād* and reason, as sources of law
ahl al-hall wa-l-'aqd:	literally, those who hold the authority to bind and release (i.e. a select group of people who are vested with the authority to speak for and make decision on behalf of the *umma*)
ahl al-kitāb:	the People of the Book, a reference in the Holy Qur'an to the Christians and Jews
ahl al-ra'y:	the adherents to the schools of jurisprudence and thought which give prominence to *ijtihād* and reason over sunna and hadith, as sources of law
(al-) ākhira:	life in the hereafter or after death
'ālamīn:	all people of all times and places
Allah:	God
Allah *rabbul-'ālamīn:*	God is the sole and unique deity of all people of all times and places
Allah-u-ghālibun:	God is predominant

alladhīna ūtu-l-'ilm:	those who have been given knowledge
(al-)'amal al-ṣāliḥ:	performing good deeds
(al-) Amīn:	the trusted or trustworthy, a reference to Prophet Muhammad
amr:	command
(al-) amr bi-l-ma'rūf:	the command to enjoin the good
amthāl:	examples
anṣār:	the Muslim community of Medina, as opposed to the Muslims of Mecca who accompanied the Prophet on the hijra from Mecca
'aql:	mind, brain
'aṣaba:	male descendence and ascendance of a person in which no female intercedes, namely the father, the children, the grandfather, the grandchildren, and the paternal uncles and their male descendants, by order of priority
asbāb an-nuzūl:	the circumstances that occasioned the revelation of certain verses of the Holy Qur'an, as set out in a book carrying the same name by al-Wahidi al-Nisaburi (See Bibliography)
'aṣabiyya:	blood-based tribal relations and bond
Ash'aris:	the adherents to the philosophical school *al-Ash'ariyya*
Ash'ariyya:	a philosophical school which advocated, among other things, that the Qur'an was eternal as opposed to being created
al-'awal:	a rule of *fiqh* whereby when the allocations of shares in an estate exceed 100 percent of that estate, all allocations are reduced on a pro-rata basis

āya:	revealed sign, an example or proof provided by God in the Holy Qur'an; the term is also used to mean a verse of the Holy Qur'an
(al-) 'azīz:	someone who commands *al-'azza*, namely grandeur and magnanimity
(al-) baghiy:	prostitution
ba'l:	a name traditionally attributed to male Phoenician divinities
balāgh:	conveying a message
(al-) balāgh al-mubīn:	the clear message
Banu Isrā'īl:	the sons of Israel
bāṭin:	intrinsic secret meaning
bay'a:	the pledge of allegiance of a preselected nominee for the position of caliph so that his appointment can acquire legitimacy
bayt al-māl:	the public treasury of the caliphate
bid'a:	innovation
Bilād al-Shām:	Levant of the Byzantine Empire, made up of the lands bordering the eastern seashore of the Mediterranean Sea
(al-) birr:	righteousness
Bismillahi-r-Raḥmāni-r-Raḥīm:	in the name of God, the Compassionate, the Merciful
caliph:	literally means successor (i.e. the successor of the Prophet Muhammad); this term is used as a reference to the head of the caliphate, the Islamic state
caliphate:	the institution of state administration established following the death of the Prophet and whose chief is the caliph

ḍalāla:	error and strayance from the right path
dār al-ḥarb:	the abode of war, or the enemy
dār al-Islam:	the abode of Islam, or the Islamic state
ḍaraba:	to stand firm in rejecting a belligerent attitude; also means to beat
darajāt:	degrees
al-ḍarūrāt tubīḥu-l- maḥzūrāt:	the necessities legitimize actions that are otherwise prohibited, equivalent to the modern-day concept of force majeure
dhimma or dhimmī system:	the status recognized to the non-Muslim believers among the category of the People of the Book under the caliphate pursuant to which those non-Muslim believers would be granted most of the freedoms recognized for Muslim believers against the payment by them to the state treasury of a head tax called *jizya* in return for the promise by the state to provide them protection
dhimmī:	a non-Muslim believer living under the *dhimmī* system
dīn al-fiṭra:	religion of simplicity because it relies on values that are innate, inherent to human creation
al-dīn kulluhu li-l-lāh:	literally it means "so that religion will be entirely for God"; however, when placed in the appropriate context, it means the principles set out in the Qur'an, which contains the "religion of God," should at all times prevail, namely the freedom of faith and worship for all, with the only exception of the Holy Ḥaram of Mecca, in which the worship of God only, and no other deity, may be performed

dīn wa dawla:	religion and state, an expression often used to describe the wide-ranging scope of Islam from the political perspective
dīn wa dunia:	religion and day-to-day life, an expression often used to describe the wide-ranging scope of Islam from the social perspective
dīn wa shari'a:	religion and legal system, an expression often used to describe the wide-ranging scope of Islam from the legal perspective
diyya:	blood money
al-dunia:	the day-to-day life in this world as opposed to the afterlife
faḍḍalna:	we have favored or provided a favor; this word comes from the root term *faḍl*, which may also be used to indicate a preference, depending on the context
faḍl:	see the term *faḍḍalna*
(al-) fāḥisha:	shameful acts, including adultery
faqīh (pl. *fuqahā'*):	Muslim jurisprudent
fatana:	to sway and pervert
faṭara:	to create
fatwa:	opinion of a *faqīh* on issues of religious law, the equivalent of a legal opinion in a secular legal system
fī sabīl-il-lāh:	in the way or path of God
fiqh:	Islamic jurisprudence
fitna:	public discord; a term also used for persecution, temptation and perversion
fiṭra:	the innate attributes inherent to creation; this term is also used for simplicity of

	understanding
fuqahā':	see *faqīh*
gharar:	a transaction involving uncertainty, where the obligations of one party are well defined and the other party's obligations are not so defined
(al-) ghayb:	the occult or unknown, that which is in the exclusive domain of God
ghazuw:	tribal raids
ḥadd (pl. *ḥudūd*):	limit, namely upper and lower limits in the application of certain provisions of the Shari'a, more particularly in connection with punishment of criminal acts, and determination of inheritance shares; *fiqh*, however, has interpreted that term to mean a straight criminal penalty, namely by reference to the punishments prescribed in the Qur'an for offenses which fall within the scope of divine public order
hadith:	the traditions of Prophet Muhammad represented by his sayings and pronouncements
ḥafīẓ:	guardian
hajj:	the pilgrimage to the Holy sanctuary of Mecca, as one of the five pillars of Islam
al-Ḥakīm:	an attribute of God, the Wise
halal:	anything which is not specifically designated as haram
ḥanīf:	a person who is neither Jewish nor Christian, but yet believes in one deity and an afterlife
ḥanīfism:	this term has two meanings: (a) the religion of Abraham, according to the Qur'an; and (b)

	the changing nature of matter
haram:	things that are prohibited *erga omnes* by God
Hijaz:	the geographic region in the Arabian peninsula in which the cities of Mecca and Medina, the birthplace of Islam, are located
hijra:	the migration of the Prophet and his companions from Mecca to Medina
ḥikma:	wisdom
ḥubb:	love
(al-) huda:	God's guidance
ḥudūd:	see *ḥadd*
ḥujja:	proof
ḥukm:	governance and judgment
al-ḥukm bima anzala-l-Lāh:	to judge by what God has revealed
'ibād:	worshippers (this term has been wrongly used as a reference to servants); in the term *'ibādi*, the suffix "i" is the equivalent of the possessive pronoun "my" (see *'ābed*)
'ibāda:	an act of worship
'ibādāt:	plural of *'ibāda*; it is also the branch of *fiqh* which deals with the worship requirements
ibn:	a son; it is also used to refer to spiritual affiliation as opposed to physical offspring
iftā':	the act of issuing fatwas; it is also used to refer to the institution or official vested with the authority to issue fatwas
iḥrām:	the special clothing worn in preparation for performing the hajj or *'Imra* pilgrimage
iḥsān:	an act of goodwill performed by one person

toward another involving the renunciation of a right; as such it taps into the highest human virtues of compassion, such as charity and generosity, forgiveness, patience, etc.

ijāra: a leasing transaction

i'jāz: the act of producing a miracle or something which is inimitable

ijmā': general consensus, referring to the rules of Islamic jurisprudence derived by the *fuqahā'* from the general consensus of the people, the companions or the learned, as the case may be

ijmā' sukūti: implied consensus

ijtihād: the process of identifying or creating rules or, as the case may be, solutions by way of rational thinking and argumentation

'ilm muṣṭalaḥ al-hadith: the science of Prophetic Tradition aimed at ascertaining the accuracy and reliability of Prophetic Tradition through the critical analysis of compiled and recorded traditions

'ilmāniyya: secularity

imam: in Sunni Islam, it means the cleric who leads the prayer; also used to refer to the caliph or head of state, as the ultimate religious authority or leader

(al-) imāma al-'uẓma or

(al-) imāma al-kubra: the supreme leadership of the *umma*, equivalent to the post of head of state

imamate the institution headed by the Imam

īmān: faith

'iqāb: punishment

irhabūni: from the root term *rahaba*, to feel a reverential

	attitude deriving from consciousness of the importance and might toward the other
irth:	inheritance
iṣlāḥ:	reforming what is evil or sinful
Islam:	the religion contained in the divine message brought by Prophet Muhammad; it is also the global religion represented by the Abrahamic faith and encompassing the messages of Moses, Jesus, and Muhammad. Islam also means submission to, and trust, in God
'iṣma:	infallibility
al-istidlāl or istiṣḥāb al-ḥāl:	a method of *ijtihād* adopted by the Shafi'i and Hanbali schools of jurisprudence, respectively, pursuant to which solutions may be based on the equivalent in modern law of the presumption
istiḥsān:	a method of *ijtihād* devised by the Hanafi school of jurisprudence to select a solution among others which serves best the public interest
istislām:	the act of surrender
'Iṣyān:	rebellion and resistance
(al-) ithm:	a sin
ittikāl:	reliance
(al-) jabbār:	the one who compels or oppresses the others
jāhiliyya:	the period preceding the start of Divine Revelation, announcing the advent of Islam
jihad:	the process of personal endeavor by a Muslim in the path of God
jihad *bi-l-māl*:	the jihad which takes the form of a financial endeavor

jihad *bi-n-nafs*:	the jihad through the human physical and spiritual endeavor
jizya:	the head tax
kāfirūn:	synonym of *kuffār*
kataba:	to write; when that term is used in connection with an action by God, it means a divine order
kataba 'ala nafsihi:	he took it upon himself
khalīfa:	a caliph; it also means successor and, in the context of the role of mankind assigned pursuant to Divine Governance, it means a trustee.
khawārij:	a political-religious sect that rose in the final days of the last Enlightened Caliph, 'Ali, who adopted an extremist, puritanical interpretation of Islam and perceived all those who claimed to lead the community as heretics deserving capital punishment
khilāfa:	caliphate, it also means succession
(al-) khulafā' al-rāshidūn:	the Enlightened Caliphs
khushū' and *khishiya*:	the reverential fear imbued with love and piety
kitāb:	book or record; it is also a reference to the Holy Qur'an
(al-) kitāb al-mubīn:	the clear and comprehensive book
kitābann mu'ajjalann:	a time-bound destiny
kuffār:	plural of *kāfir*, the unbelievers who do not believe in all or some of the basic creeds of the faith as set out in anyone of the divine messages brought by God's messengers
kufr:	rejection of the faith

kutiba 'alaykum:	it has been ordained upon you
(al-) lawḥ al-maḥfūẓ:	God's preserved tablet
Laylat-ul-Qadr:	the sacred night of the 27th day of the month of Ramadan in which the Holy Qur'an was descended and Revelation commenced
ma'rūf:	literally, what is generally accepted; it is also used as a reference to the "good deed"
madhāhib:	plural of *madhhab*, a reference to the major schools of jurisprudence in Islam; it can also mean a religious sect
madrasa:	Qur'anic school
Majalla:	it is the short name for *Majallat al-Aḥkām al-'Adliyya*, the semi-official civil code adapted from Shari'a, and commissioned by the Ottoman administration
(al-) mākir:	the one who is cunning
mansūkh:	the abrogated verse (see also *naskh* and *nāsekh*)
(al-) maṣāliḥ al-mursala:	it is a method of *ijtihād* devised by the Maliki school of jurisprudence in which the public interest or public order serves as basis of necessary solutions
mīrāth:	inheritance, a synonym of *irth*
(al-) mīzān:	the balance of justice
(al-) Mourji'a:	a philosophical school which tried to bridge the gap between the Mu'tazila and the *Ash'aris* by advocating that it was fruitless to fight over whether the Qur'an was created or eternal, but that the matter should instead be postponed to be considered by God on the Day of Judgment
(al-) mu'allafa qulūbuhum:	literally, those whose hearts have been softened and pacified; in the Holy Qur'an, this term refers to influential tribal leaders

	whose goodwill the Prophet bought in an effort to convert them to Islam and avoid violence
mu'āmalāt:	transactions among people; it is also the branch of *fiqh* which deals with civil and commercial transactions
mubāya'a:	the process of soliciting and attributing the *bay'a*
mubīn:	clear
muḍāraba:	a transaction which substantially replicates quasi-equity investments
mudhakkir:	an adjective attributed in the Holy Qur'an to Prophet Muhammad by reference to the part of his mission involving reminding people of previous messages sent by God
(al-) mudhill:	the one who humiliates others
mufti:	a person, usually a cleric, vested with the authority to issue fatwas (rulings and opinions on religious matters)
muḥkamāt:	an adjective used in the Qur'an in reference to verses whose meanings are firmly established
muḥram:	a person whom a woman cannot marry due to proximity of kin relations
mujtahid:	a scholar qualified to practice *ijtihād*
mulla:	a term more commonly used in Turkey and Iran to designate a Muslim priest or religious learned person
mu'minūn:	the believers, plural of *mu'min*
Munāfiqūn:	the hypocrites, a term used in the Qur'an as a reference to those who professed their adherence to the message of Islam without truly believing and worked discreetly to discredit the Messenger

munkar:	literally, what is not generally accepted, a term also used as a reference to evil
(al-) muntaqim:	the revengeful or avenger
muqallid:	a person who is not qualified to practice *ijtihād*, for whom the only option is to follow the imitation approach (*taqlīd*)
murābaha:	a purchase and sale agreement in which the purchase price is paid in installments
(al-) Muṣḥaf al-'Uthmāni:	also known as *al-Muṣḥaf al-Imam*, it is the official vulgate, or compilation, of the Holy Qur'an ordered and then adopted by the third Enlightened Caliph, 'Uthman
mushrikūn:	plural of *mushrik*, those who associate other deities with God
(al-) mutakabbir:	the one who displays a haughty attitude toward others.
mutashābihāt:	an adjective used in the Qur'an in reference to verses whose meanings are uncertain; this term also means similar, perhaps a reference to verses with similar meanings.
Mu'tazila:	a philosophical school which advocated, among other things, that the Qur'an was created as opposed to being eternal
(an-) nahiy 'ani-l-munkar:	the command to prevent the evil
naskh:	the abrogation of one verse of the Holy Qur'an by another verse (see also *nāsekh* and *mansūkh*)
nāsekh:	the abrogating verse (see also *naskh* and *mansūkh*)
(al-) nās:	the people
natlu:	the verb to recite or to tell, in the first person of the plural (see also *tilāwa*)

nushūz:	typically, it is a form of belligerent attitude on the part of a woman with some reluctance and lack of interest on her part toward her husband; in the context of Islamic family law, that term has been interpreted as the disobedience of a woman to her husband, an attitude which they equated to an act repulsive to God
qaḍā':	God's decision or decree
(al-) qahhār and *(al-) qāhir*:	the one who subdues others
qāniṭāt:	see *qunūṭ*
qānūn ḥuqūq al-'ā'ila:	the family law code enacted by the Ottoman administration
qawmin ya'aqilūn:	those who are receptive with their minds and can reason
qawmin yafqahūn:	those who understand and grasp
qawmin yatadhakkarūn:	those who heed and remember the lessons
qawmin yatafakkarūn:	those who reflect and ponder over a message after having understood it
qawmin yuwqinūn:	those who seek to achieve inner conviction and certainty after having read and understood a message and then reflected over it
al-qawwāma:	the authority of the husband over his wife under Islamic law; but in reality that term means the determination to provide support without gender-related allocation of the duty (a derivative term is *qawwāmūn*, those determined to provide support)
qiṣāṣ	it is the category of punishments, for offences other than those that attract *ḥudūd*, which are imposed in the interest of the victim, and which can therefore be replaced by monetary compensation or even be forgiven by the victim or its heirs

qist:	literally, the balance, a term generally used for exact, measured and balanced justice
qitāl:	fighting
qiyās:	syllogism
qunūt:	devotion to God; *qānitāt* (derived from this term) refers to women who are devout in their worship of God and are obedient to God
Qur'an:	the Holy Scripture of Islam, as revealed to Prophet Muhammad and containing the Divine Message in its entirety
Quraysh:	name of the tribe of which Prophet Muhammad is a descendant
qurrā':	plural of *quāri'*, those who read the Qur'an, primarily from memory
rabbu-l-'ālamīn:	the god of the entire humanity
rabbu-l-mu'minīn:	the god of all the believers
(al-) radd:	a rule of *fiqh* whereby when the allocations of shares in an estate fall below 100 percent of that estate, all allocations are increased on a pro-rata basis
al-rāsikhūna fi-l-'ilm:	those who are firmly grounded in knowledge
riba:	usury
(al-) ridda:	apostasy
sabīl-il-lāh:	the way of God (see *fi sabīl-il-lāh*)
ṣadaqāt:	charitable acts
sadd al-dharā'i':	by way of precaution, a concept used by *fiqh* to restrict rights, in particular to avoid certain potential perceived non-physical dangers
ṣaḥāba:	companions of Prophet Muhammad
Ṣaḥīḥ:	a compendium of Prophetic Tradition

	recognized as solid and accurate by reference to the rules developed by *fiqh* in *'Ilm muṣṭalaḥ al-hadith*
salat:	the prayer, as one of the five pillars of Islam
salat *al-jamā'a*:	collective prayer
ṣawm:	the fasting of the month of Ramadan, as one of the five pillars of Islam
shafā'a:	intercession
shahāda:	the act of witnessing an occurrence; *al-Shahāda* refers to the statement of faith professed by each Muslim "There is no god but Allah; and Muhammad is the prophet of Allah." Used in a different context, it means martyrdom
shara'a:	to ordain a way or path; it is the root term for Shari'a and is used for the verb "to legitimate"
Shari'a:	a structured path leading to a certain objective, namely the right path; the term is also used by the Holy Qur'an for the body of general principles which carry a legal connotation or which edict moral values serving as basis for legal provisions
shaykh:	an elderly person; that term is more commonly used to designate a Muslim priest
shiqāq:	quarrel and obstruction
shirk:	the sin of associating other deities with God
shur'a:	charter, also used to mean path
shūra:	consultation process
sijn:	prison
sīra:	in relation to the Prophet, means the biography of the Prophet

(al-) ṣirāt al-mustaqīm:	the straight path
sunna:	the traditions of Prophet Muhammad represented by his sayings and acts, express and implied; under certain *fiqh* teachings, traditions of the first four caliphs who succeeded the Prophet have been treated as part of sunna
sunna *fi'liyya*:	the traditions of the Prophet consisting of the acts performed by the Prophet
sunna *qawliyya*:	the traditions of the Prophet consisting of what the Prophet said or uttered, i.e. hadith
sunna *taqrīriyya*:	the traditions of the Prophet consisting of what the Prophet implied by keeping silent in reaction to specific occurrences, in terms of consent or otherwise, depending on the relevant context
sura or *sūrat*:	a chapter of the Holy Qur'an
ṭā'a:	obedience and submission
ta'āruf	knowing and interacting with one another
ta'zīr:	the penalties prescribed for misdemeanors which are not provided for in the Qur'an
tafḍīl:	See *faḍl*
tafsīr:	exegesis
tajdīd:	Renewal approach.
Takfir:	the act of accusing someone of weak faith, idolatry or of untrue declaration of faith
taqlīd:	imitation approach
taqwa:	piety and righteousness
(al-)tashrī' al-Islami:	Islamic law

tawakkul:	the trust in God
tawḥīd:	believing in the unicity of God
tha'r:	revenge
thawāb:	divine reward
tilāwa:	recitation, telling
'ubūdiyya:	subservience and slavery
uḍrubūhunna:	see *ḍaraba*
'ulama':	plural of *'ālim*, a learned person, also used to refer to religious scholars
uli-l-abṣār:	those with vision
uli-l-albāb:	those who are endowed with reason and wisdom, and are selective after careful consideration
umma:	the community, also used to mean nation
ummi (pl. *ummiyyūn*):	from the common people; it is also used to mean illiterate
(al-) Wadūd:	an attribute of God, as being kind and loving
wakala:	to trust; it is the root term for *tawakkul*, *ittikāl*, *wakīl*, among others
wakīl:	agent or taskmaster; when used as an attribute of God it means the trustworthy
walad:	a child of any gender
waratha:	to inherit
wilāya:	a power or mandate to exercise authority, as the case may be
(al-) wilāya 'ala-l-māl:	the guardianship with respect to financial matters; it includes the duty to preserve the financial assets of the person under guardianship, including the power to invest

	those assets and spend from them in order to provide for all the financial needs of the person in question, namely for his or her education, sustenance, medical expenses, etc
(al-) wilāya 'ala-n-nafs:	the guardianship with respect to personal matters; it includes the power to raise, educate, teach, discipline and marry the person under that guardianship
ya'budūni:	to worship me
ya ayyuha-l-mu'minūn:	o you believers
ya'qilūn:	see *qawmin ya'qilūn*
yafqahūn:	see *qawmin yafqahūn*
yatadhakkarūn:	see *qawmin yatadhakkarūn*
yatafakkarūn:	see *qawmin yatafakkarūn*
ya ayyuha-n-nās:	o you people
yas'alūnaka:	they ask you
yastaftūnaka:	they seek your learned opinion
yuḥakkimūka:	verb derived from the root term *taḥkīm* which means "to designate you as an arbitrator"
yuwqinūn:	see *qawmin yuwqinūn*
zakat:	the funds and/or goods that Muslims are mandated to distribute, each according to his or her means, to those entitled to receive it, as one of the five pillars of Islam
ẓāhir:	apparent and conspicuous meaning
ẓihār:	a form of repudiation (divorce) pronounced by the husband frivolously

Bibliography

Qur'ānic Sources

The Holy Qur'ān

In Arabic

Al-Qur'an al-Karim. Damascus: Dar al-Muṣḥaf, 1979.

In English, by translator

Abdel Haleem, M. A. S. *The Qur'an*. New York: Oxford University Press, 2005.

Ali, Abdullah Yusuf. http://www.altafsir.com.

Arberrry, Arthur J. http://www.altafsir.com.

Asad, Muhammad. http://www.altafsir.com.

Bakhtiar, Laleh. *The Sublime Quran*. Chicago: Kazi Publications, 2007.

Dawood, N. J.: *The Koran*. London: Penguin Books 1999.

Khalidi, Tarif. *The Qur'an*. New York: Viking Penguin, 2008.

Mohsin, Muhammad Khan. http://www.quranexplorer.com/Quran/Default.aspx.

Pickthall, Marmaduke. http://www.altafsir.com.

Royal Aal al-Bayt Institute, Amman, Jordan. http://www.altafsir.com.

'Uthmani, Muhammad Taqi (Mufti). http://www.altafsir.com.

Walk, Ibrahim. http://www.altafsir.com.

Traditional Arabic Language Exegeses of the Qur'ān

http://www.altafsir.com

Ibn 'Ashour, Muhammad al-Tahir. *Al-Tahrir wa al-Tanwir* [Liberation and enlightenment].

Ibn Kathir, Aboul Fida' 'Imadeddine Ismail bin 'Umar. *Tafsir al-Qur'ān al-Karim* [Exegesis of the Holy Qur'an].

al-Baydawi, Nasireddin Abdullah bin 'Umar. *Anwar al-Tanzil wa Asrar al-Ta'wil* [The lights of Revelation and the secrets of interpretation].

al-Mahally, Jalal al-Din, and Jalal al-Din al-Suyuti. *Tafsir al-Jalalayn* [Exegesis of the two Jalals].

al-Qattan, Ibrahim. *Taysir al-Tafsir* [Simplification of interpretation].

al-Qurtubi, Abu Abdullah Muhammad Bin Ahmad. *Al-Jami' li-Ahkam al-Bayan* [The comprehensive interpretation of the rules].

Qutb, Sayyid. *Fi Zilal al-Qur'an* [In the shades of the Qur'an].

al-Razi, Abu Abdullah Muhammad bin 'Umar. *Mafatih al-Ghayb, al-Tafsir al-Kabir* [The keys to the unseen, the great exegesis].

al-Sha'rawi, Muhammad Mutawalli. *Khawatir Muhammad Mutawalli al-Sha'rawi* [The thoughts of Muhammad Mutawalli al-Sha'rawi].

al-Tabari, Muhammad bin Jarir. *Jami' al-Bayan fi Tafsir al-Qur'an* [The comprehensive exegesis of the Qur'an].

al-Tabarsi, Abu 'Ali al-Fadl bin Hasan. *Majma' al-Bayan fi Tafsir al-Qur'an* [The compendium of Qur'anic exegesis].

al-Tantawi, Muhammad Sayyid. *Al-Wasit fi Tafsir al-Qur'an al-Karim* [The intermediate exegesis of the Holy Qur'an].

al-Wahidi al-Nisaburi, Abul Hasan 'Ali bin Ahmad. *Al-Wajiz* [The succint exegesis].

al-Zamakhshari, Abul Qasim Jar Allah Mahmoud Bin 'Umar. *Tafsir al-Kashshaf* [Al-Kashshaf exegesis].

Prophetic Tradition

Compendia referenced

http://www.muhaddith.org/cgi-bin/e_optns.exe

Al-Hafiz al-'Iraqi's *Takhrij Ahadith al-Ihya'*
Malik's *al-Muwatta'*
Musnad al-Imam al-Shafi'i
Musnad al-Imam Ibn Hanbal
al-Muttaqi al-Hindi's *Kanz al-'Ummal*
Sahih al-Bukhari
Sahih Muslim
Sunan Abi Daoud
Sunan al-Tirmidhi
Sunnan al-Nassa'i
Sunan Ibn Maja
al-Suyuti's *al-Jami' al-Saghir*

Islamic and Religious Scholarship and Commentary

'Abdel Baqi, Muhammad F. *Al-Mu'jam al-Mufahras li Alfaz al-Qur'an al-Karim* [An alphabetical Index of Qur'anic terms]. Beirut: Jamal Publishing.

'Abdel Raziq, 'Ali. *Al-Islam wa Usul al-Hukm* [Islam and the principles of government]. Beirut: Al-Takween Publications, 2005.

'Abdessalam, Mahmud. *Tasa'ulat Islamiyya* [Raising Islamic questions]. Cairo 2001.

'Abdu, Muhammad (Sheikh). *Al-Islam wa-l-Nasraniyya ma' al-'Ilm wa-l-Madaniyya* [Islam and Christianity: knowledge and civilization]. 2d ed. Cairo: Al-Manar Printers, 1905.

———. *Risalat al-Tawhid* [The Message of Unicity]. Cairo: Publications of Muhammad Ali Sabeeh and Sons, 1965.

———. *Ma'alim al-Islam fi Risalat al-Tawhid* [The basic concepts of Islam in the message of unicity], Edited by Abdul Hamid al-Bohsali, with commentaries by Muhammad Rashid Rida. Beirut: al-Insaf Press, 1965.

'Abdul-Karim, Khalil. *Dawlat Yathrib: Basa'ir fi 'Am al-Wufud* [The state of Yathrib: perspectives on the year of the delegations]. Cairo: Sinai Publishing, 1999.

———. *Fatrat al-Takwin fi Hayat al-Sadik al-Amin* [The period of formation in the life of the honest and trustworthy]. Cairo: Merit Publishing, 2001.

———. *Al-Judhur al-Tarikhiyya li-l-Shari'a al-Islamiyya* [The historical roots of the Islamic Shari'a]. 2d ed. Cairo: Sinai Publishing, 1997.

———. *Quraysh Minal-Qabila ila al-Dawla al-Markaziyya* [Quraysh, from tribe to centralized state]. 2d ed. Cairo: Sinai Publishing, 1997.

———. *Shadw al-Rababa Bi Ahwal Mujtama' al-Sahaba* [The tune of al-Rababa on the Conditions of the society of the companions]. Vol. 1, *Muhammad wa-l-Sahaba* [Muhammad and the companions]. 2d ed. Cairo: Sinai Publishing, 1998.

———. *Shadw al-Rababa* [The Tune of al-Rababa]. Vol. 2, *Al-Sahaba wa-l-Sahaba* [The companions and the companions]. Cairo: Sinai Publishing, 1997.

———. *Shadw al-Rababa* [The Tune of al-Rababa]. Vol. 3, *Al-Sahaba wa-l-Mujtama'* [The companions and society]. Cairo: Sinai Publishing, 1997.

Abizaid, Nasr Hamid. *Daw'ir al-Khawf: Qira'at fi Khitab al-Mar'a* [The areas of fear: a reading on the subject of women]. 3d ed. Beirut: Arab Cultural Center Publications, 2004.

———. *Mafhum al-Nass: Dirasa fi 'Ulum al-Qur'an* [The concept of scripture: a study of Qur'anic science]. 6th ed. Beirut: Arab Cultural Center Publications, 2005.

———. *Al-Mar'a fi Khitab al-Azama* [Women in the crisis discourse]. Cairo: Nusus Publications, 1994.

———. *Al-Tafkir fi Zaman al-Takfir* [Thinking in the age of accusations of unbelief]. Cairo: Sinai Publications, 1995.

Abou El Fadl, Khaled M. *The Great Theft: Wrestling Islam from the Extremists*. San Francisco: HarperSanFrancisco, 2005.

————. *Islam and the Challenge of Democracy.* Princeton: Princeton University Press, 2004.

————. *The Place of Tolerance in Islam.* Boston: Beacon Press, 2002.

————. *The Search for Beauty in Islam: A Conference of the Books.* Lanham: Rowman and Littlefield, 2006.

————. *Speaking in God's Name: Islamic Law, Authority and Women.* Oxford: Oneworld Publications, 2007.

Abou al-Majd, Ahmad Kamal. *Ru'ya Islamiyya Mu'asira: I'lane Mabadi'* [A contemporary vision of Islam: a declaration of principles]. Cairo: Dar al-Shuruq Publications, 1991.

Abu-Sahlieh, Sami A. Aldeeb. *Les Musulmans Face aux Droits de l'Homme* [The Muslims in the face of human rights]. 2d ed. Charleston: Createspace, 2013.

el-Affendi, Abdel Wahab. *Who Needs an Islamic State?* 2d ed. Peterborough: Malaysia Think Tank London, 2008.

al-Afghani, Jamaluddin, and Muhammad (Sheikh) Abdu. *Al-'Urwa al-Wuthqa wa-l-Thawrah al-Tahririyya al-Kubra* [The trustworthy handhold and the great revolution for freedom]. 3d ed. Cairo: Dar al-Arab Publishing, 1993.

Ahmed, Leila. *Women and Gender in Islam.* New Haven: Yale University Press, 1992.

Akhtar, Shabbir. *A Faith for All Seasons: Islam and the Challenge of the Modern World.* Chicago: Ivan R. Dee, 1991.

————. *The Quran and the Secular Mind: A Philosophy of Islam.* New York: Routledge, 2008.

al-'Alayli, Abdullah. *Ayna-l-Khata': Tashih Mafahim wa Nazrat Tajdeed* [Where is the error: correcting certain concepts and an attempt of renewal]. Beirut: Dar al-'Ilm li-l-Malayin, 1978.

'Amara, Muhammad. *Al-Islam wa Usul al-Hukm li-'Ali 'Abdel Raziq: Dirasat wa Wathaeq* [Islam and the principles of government of 'Ali 'Abdel Raziq: commentary and documents]. Beirut: Arab Institute for Studies and Publications, 2000.

————. *Qasim Amin: Tahrir al-Mar'a wa-l-Tamaddun al-Islami* [Qasim Amin: women's liberation and Islamic modernization]. Beirut: Dar al-Wihda, 1985.

al-Amin, 'Ali. *Al-'Ilmāniyya wa-l-Mumana'a al-Islamiyya: Muhawarat fi-l-Nahda wa-l-Hadatha* [Secularism and Islamic reaction: debates on revival and modernity]. Beirut: As-Saqi, 1999.

Amin, Ahmad. *Duha al-Islam* [The forenoon of Islam]. 3 vols. 10th ed. Cairo: Maktabat Annahda al-Masriyya, 1933 to 1936.

————. *Fajr al-Islam* [The dawn of Islam]. 14th ed. Cairo: Maktabat Annahda al-Arabiyya, 1933.

————. *Zu'ama' al-Islah fi-l-'Asr al-Hadith* [The leaders of reform in the modern age]. 5th ed. Cairo: Maktabat Annahda al-'Arabiyya, 1989.

Amin, Hussein A. *Dalil al-Muslim al-Hazin* [The guide of the sad Muslim]. 4th ed. Kuwait: Dar Su'ad al-Sabbah, 1992.

Amin, Qasim. *The Liberation of Women:The New Woman*. Translated from the Arabic by Samiha Sidhom Peterson. 4th ed. Cairo: The American University in Cairo Press, 2005.

Andrae, Tor. *Les Origines de l'Islam et le Christianisme* [The origins of Islam and Christianity]. Translated from the German by Jules Roche. Paris: Éditions Jean Maisonneuve, 1955.

al-'Aqqad, Mahmoud 'Abbas. *Al-Tafkir Farida Islamiyya* [Thinking is an Islamic duty]. Beirut: Al-Maktaba al-'Asriyya, 2006.

Arkoun, Mohammed. *Ayna Huwa al-Fikr al-Islami al-Mu'asir?* [Where is modern Islamic thought?]. Translated from the French by Hashim Salih. Beirut: Dar al-Saqi, 1990.

————. *Al-Fikr al-Islami: Naqd wa Ijtihad* [Islamic thought: criticism and Ijthad]. Translated from the French by Hashim Salih. 2d ed. Beirut: Dar Al Saqi, 1992.

'Ashmawi, Muhammad Sa'id. *Al-'Aql fi-l-Islam* [The mind in Islam]. 2d ed. Beirut: Al-Intishar al-'Arabi, 2004.

————. Hisad al-'Aql [Harvest of the mind]. 3d ed. Beirut: Al-Intishar al-Arabi, 2004.

————. *Al-Islam al-Siyasi* [Political Islam]. 3d ed. Cairo: Sinai Publishing, 1992.

————. *Al-Khilafa al-Islamiyya* [The Islamic caliphate]. 5th ed. Beirut: Al-Intishar al-'Arabi, 2004.

————. *Ma'alim al-Islam* [The features of Islam]. 2d ed. Beirut: Al-Intishar al-'Arabi, 2004.

————. *Usul al-Shari'a* [The sources of Shari'a]. 5th ed. Beirut: Al-Intishar al-'Arabi, 2004.

Ayoub, Mahmoud. *A Muslim View of Christianity: Essays on Dialogue*. Edited by Irfan A. Omar. Maryknoll: Orbis Books, 2007.

————. *The Qur'an and its Interpreters*. Vol. 1. Albany: State University of New York Press, 1984.

————. *The Qur'an and its Interpreters*. Vol. 2, *The House of 'Imran*. Albany: State University of New York Press, 1992.

al-'Azm, Sadeq Jalal. *Naqd al-Fikr Al-Dini* [A critique of religious thought]. 9th ed. Beirut: Dar Attali'a, 2003.

————. *Dhihniyyat al-Tahrim* [The mentality of prohibition]. 3d ed. Beirut: Al-Mada House, 2003.

Babès, Leïla, and Tareq Oubrou. *Loi d'Allah, Loi des Hommes: Liberté, Égalité et Femmes en Islam* [Law of God, law of men: freedom, equality, and women in Islam]. Paris: Albin Michel, 2002.

Bar-Zeev, Hai. *Une Lecture Juive du Coran* [A Jewish reading of the Qur'an]. Paris: Berg International, 2005.

Barlas, Asma. *"Believing Women" in Islam: Unreading Patriarchal Interpretations of the Qur'an*. 5th ed. Austin: University of Texas Press, 2006.

Barnavi, Élie. *Les Religions Meurtrières* [The murderous religions]. Bruxelles: Flammarion, 2006.

————., Monseigneur Jean Michel di Falco, and Tariq Ramadan. *Faut-il Avoir Peur des Religions?* [Should one fear religions?]. Paris: Mordicus, 2008.

Bassiouni, M. Cherif. *The Islamic Criminal Justice System*. New York: Oceana Publications, 1982.

Bellah, Robert N. *Beyond Belief: Essays on Religion in the Post-Traditional World*. London: University of California Press, 1991.

Ben Salama, Raja'. *Naqd al-Thawabit: Ara' fi-l-'Unf wa-l-Tamyiz wa-l-Musadara* [Critique of constants: views on violence, discrimination, and confiscation]. Beirut: Dar al-Tali'a, 2005.

Benzine, Rachid. *Les Nouveaux Penseurs de l'Islam* [The new thinkers of Islam]. Paris: Albin Michel, 2004.

Berque, Jacques. *Quel Islam?* [Which Islam ?]. Arles: Actes Sud, 2003.

————. *Relire Le Coran* [Rereading of the Qur'an]. Paris: Albin Michel, 1993.

Bidar, Abdennour. *L'Islam Sans Soumission: Pour un Éxistentialisme Musulman* [Islam without submission: for a Muslim existentialism]. Paris: Albin Michel, 2008.

————. *Un Islam pour Notre Temps* [An Islam for our time]. Paris: Éditions du Seuil, 2004.

————. *Self-Islam* [Self-Islam]. Paris: Éditions du Seuil, 2006.

Bouhindi, Mustapha. *Al-Ta'thir al-Masihi fi Tafsir al-Qur'an* [The Chrisitian influence on the interpretation of the Qur'an]. Beirut: Dar Attali'a, 2004.

Bouthawry, Noureddine. *Maqasid al-Shari'a: Al-Tashri' al-Islami bayna Tumuh al-Mujtahid wa Qusur al-Ijtihad* [The purposes of Sharia'a: contemporary Islamic law between the ambitions of the jurisprudent and the failings of Ijtihad]. Beirut: Dar Attali'a, 2000.

Brown, Daniel W. *Rethinking Tradition in Modern Islamic Thought*. New York: Cambridge University Press, 2003.

Brown, Laurence. *God'ed? The Case for Islam as the Completion of Revelation*. BookSurge Publishing, 2008.

Bucaille, Maurice. *La Bible, le Coran et la Science* [The Bible, the Qur'an and science]. Paris: Seghers, 1976.

Caratini, Roger. *Le Génie de L'Islamisme* [The genius of Islamism]. Paris: Michel Lafon, 1992.

Charfi, Abdelmajid. *Al-Islam wa-l-Hadatha* [Islam and modernity]. 2d ed. Tunis: al-Dar al-Tunisiyya li-l Nashr, 1991.

———. *L'Islam entre le Message et l'Histoire* [Islam between the Message and history]. Paris: Albin Michel, 2004.

———. *La Pensée Islamique: Rupture et Fidélité* [Islamic thought: rupture and loyalty]. Paris: Albin Michel, 2008.

Charfi, Mohammed. *Islam et Liberté: Le Malentendu Historique* [Islam and freedom: The historic misunderstanding]. Paris: Albin Michel, 1998.

Chebel, Malek. *Dictionnaire Encyclopédique du Coran* [Encyclopedic dictionary of the Qur'an]. Paris: Fayard Publishing, 2009.

———. *Islam et Libre Arbitre? La Tentation de l'Insolence* [Islam and free will? The Temptation of Insolence]. Paris: Dervy, 2003

———. *L'Islam et la Raison: Combat des Idées* [Islam and reason: the conflict of ideas]. Paris: Perrin, 2006.

Christmann, Andreas. *The Qur'an, Morality and Critical Reason: The Essential Muhammad Shahrour*. Leiden: Brill, 2009.

Cohen, Mark R. *Under Crescent and Cross*. Princeton: Princeton University Press, 1996.

Colloques de Riyad, de Paris, du Vatican, de Genève et de Strasbourg sur le Dogme Musulman et les Droits de l'Homme en Islam [Colloquia of Riyadh, Paris, the Vatican, Geneva and Strasburg on the Islamic dogma and human rights in Islam]. Beirut: Dar al-Kitab Allubnani.

Cook, Michael. *Al-Amr bil Ma'arūf wa-l-Nahiy 'ani-l-Munkar fi-l-Fikr al-Islami* [Commanding right and forbidding wrong in Islamic thought]. Translated from the English by Radwan al-Sayyid, Abdul Rahman al-Salemi, and 'Ammar al-Jalassi. Beirut: Arab Network for Research and Publishing, 2009.

Cooper, John, Ronald Nettler, and Mohamad Mahmoud. *Islam and Modernity: Muslim Intellectuals Respond*. New York: I. B. Tauris, 2000.

Coulson, Noel J. *A History of Islamic Law*. Edinburgh: Edinburgh University Press, 1971.

Donohue, John J., and John L. Esposito, eds. *Islam in Transition*. New York: Oxford University Press, 2007.

Dousse, Michel. *Dieu en Guerre: La Violence au Coeur des Trois Monothéismes* [God at war: violence at the heart of the three monotheisms]. Paris: Albin Michel, 2002.

Elmessiri, Abdel-Wahab. *Towards a New Islamic Discourse*. http://nawaat.org/
portail/2006/01/23/towards-a-new-islamic-discourse/.

Enayat, Hamid. *Modern Islamic Political Thought*. New York: I. B. Tauris, 2005.

Esack, Farid. *Coran, Mode d'Emploi* [The Qur'an: a user's guide]. Translated
from the English by Jean-Louis Bour. Paris: Albin Michel, 2004.

―――. *The Islamic Threat: Myth or Reality?* 3d ed. New York: Oxford
University Press, 1999.

Esposito, John L., ed. *The Oxford Encycolpedia of the Modern Islamic World*, ed.
New York: Oxford University Press, 2001.

―――. *Islam: The Straight Path*. 3d ed. New York: Oxford University Press,
2005.

Esposito, John L., and Mogahed, Dalia. *Who Speaks for Islam*. New York: Gallup
Press, 2007.

Esposito, John L., and John Voll. *Islam and Democracy*. New York: Oxford
University Press, 1996.

Étienne, Bruno. *Les Questions qui Fachent* [Anger provoking issues]. Paris:
Bayard, 2003.

Ezzeddine, Niazi. *Din al-Sultan: Al-Burhan* [The religion of the sultan: the proof].
Beirut: Bissane 1997.

―――. *Din al-Rahman: Al-Madkhal ila-l-Haqiqa* [The religion of the
compassionate: introduction to the truth]. Beirut: Bissane 1998.

―――. *Al-Haqiqa: Min Haqa'iq al-Qur'an al-Maskut 'Anha* [The truth:
Qur'anic truths that are ignored]. Beirut: Bissane, 2000.

―――. *Indhar min al-Sama': Al-Nazariyya.* [Warning from the sky: the theory].
Beirut: Bissane, 1996.

al-Faruqi, Lamya. *Women, Muslim Society and Islam*. Plainfield, Ill.: American
Trust Publications, 1994.

Fattal, Antoine. *Le Statut Légal des non-Musulmans en Pays d'Islam* [The legal
status of non-Muslims in Islamdom]. Beirut: Imprimerie Catholique, 1958.

Fawzi, Ibrahim. *Tadween al-Sunna* [The documentation of prophetic tradition].
London: Riad El-Rayyes Books, 1994.

Feldman, Noah. *The Fall and Rise of the Islamic State*. Princeton: Princeton
University Press, 2008.

Filali-Ansari, Abdou. *L'Islam Est-il Hostile à la Laïcité?* [Is Islam hostile to
secularism?]. Arles: Actes Sud, 2002.

―――. *Réformer l'Islam? Une Introduction aux Débats Contemporains*
[To reform Islam? An introduction to contemporary debates]. Paris: La
Découverte, 2003.

Fluehr-Lobban, Carolyn. *Against Islamic Extremism: The Writings of Muhammad Sa'id al-'Ashmawy.* Gainesville: University Press of Florida, 2001.

Foda, Farag. *Al-Haqiqa al-Gha'iba* [The Absent Truth]. 3d ed. Cairo: Dar Al-Fikr li-l-Dirasat, 1988.

———. *Hatta la Yakun Kalaman fi-l-Hawa'* [So that they not remain words in the air]. 3d ed. Alexandria: Al-Mustaqbal, 2005.

Gallez, Édouard-Marie. *Le Méssie et son Prophète: Aux Origines de l'Islam* [The Messiah and his Prophet: searching for the origins of Islam]. Vol. 1, *De Qumran à Muhammad* [From Qumran to Muhammad]. Versailles: Éditions de Paris, 2005.

———. *Le Méssie et son Prophète* [The Messiah and His Prophet]. Vol. 2, *Du Muhammad des Califes au Muhammad de l'Histoire* [From Muhammad of the caliphs to Muhammad of history]. Versailles: Éditions de Paris, 2005.

el-Gamal, Mahmoud A. *Islamic Finance: Law, Economics, and Practice.* New York: Cambridge University Press, 2009.

Gardet, Louis. *Les Hommes de l'Islam* [The Men of Islam]. Brussels: Éditions Complexe, 1989.

———., and M. M. Anawati. *Introduction à la Théologie Musulmane: Essai de Théologie Comparée* [Introduction to Muslim theology: essay on comparative theology]. Paris: Librairie Philosophique J. Vrin, 1948.

Ghanem, Muhammad Salman. *Allah wal Jama'a: Min Haqa'ek al-Qur'an* [God and the collectivity: realities of the Qur'an]. Beirut: Dar al-Farabi, 2007.

al-Ghazali, Abu Hamid. *Al-Mustasfa fi 'Ilm al-Usul* [The essence of legal theory]. http://www.mohamedrabeea.com/books/book1_2638.pdf .

al-Ghazali, Muhammad. *Laysa min al-Islam* [Not part of Islam]. Cairo: Dar Al-Shuruq, Cairo 1998.

———. *Al-Mahawir al-Khamsa Li-l-Qur'an al-Karim* [The five axes of the Holy Qur'an]. Cairo: Dar Al-Shuruq, Cairo 1997.

———. *Raka'iz al-Iman: Bayna-l-'Aql wa-l-Qalb* [The bases of faith: between mind and heart]. Cairo: Dar Al-Shuruq, 1997.

Goldziher, Ignaz. *Muslim Studies.* Edited by S. M. Stern. Translated from the German by C. R. Barber and S. M. Stern. New Brunswick: Transaction Publishers, 2006.

———. *Madhahib al-Tafsir al-Islami* [Schools of Islamic commentators]. Translated from the German by Abdel Haleem al-Najjar. ed. Beirut: Dar Iqra', 1983.

Golliau, Catherine, ed. *L'Islam: Avicenne, Averroès, Al-Ghazali, Ibn Khaldoun— Les Textes Fondamentaux Commentés* [Islam: Avicenna, Al-Ghazali, Ibn Khaldoun—basic texts]. Paris: Éditions Tallandier, 2005.

Haddad, Yvonne Y., and John L. Esposito, eds. *Islam, Gender, and Social Change*. New York: Oxford University Press, 1998.

Haddad, Yvonne Y., and Wadi Z. Haddad, eds. *Christian-Muslim Encounters*. Gainesville: University Press of Florida, 1995.

Hadith. See Prophetic Tradition.

Hafez, Ziad. *La Pensée Religieuse en Islam Contemporain* [Religious thought in modern-day Islam]. Paris: Gueutner, 2012.

Hammami, Nader. *Islam al-fuqaha'* [The Islam of jurisprudents]. Beirut: Dar Attali'a, 2006.

Hamza, Muhammad. *Islam al-Mujaddidin* [The Islam of modernizers]. Beirut: Dar Attali'a, 2007.

Haykal, Muhammad Hussain. *Al-Faruq 'Umar* [The caliph 'Umar], vol. 1. Cairo: Annahda al-'Arabiyya Bookstore, 1963. and vol. 2, 1964.

———. *Hayat Muhammad* [The life of Muhammad]. 11th ed. Cairo: Dar al-Ma'arif, 1971.

———. *Al-Siddiq Abu Bakr* [The caliph Abu Bakr]. 11th ed. Cairo: Dar Al-Ma'arif, 1990.

Hippler, Jochen, and Andrea Lueg. *The Next Threat: Western Perceptions of Islam*. Boulder: Pluto Press, 1995.

al-Hibri, Aziza. *An Introduction to Muslim Women's Rights*. http://www.karamah. org/wp-content/uploads/2011/10/An-Introduction-to-Muslim-Womens-Rights.pdf .

———. *Divine Justice and the Human Order: An Islamic Perspective*. http:// karamah.org/wp- content/uploads/2011/09/Divine-Justice-and-the-Human-Order.pdf.

———. *Islam, Law and Custom: Redefining Muslim Women's Rights*. http:// www.karamah.org/ wp-content/uploads/2011/10/Islam-Law-and-Custom-Redefining-Muslim-Womens-Rights.pdf.

———. Legal Reform: Reviewing Human Rights in the Muslim World. *Harvard International Review* (June 22, 1998).

Hitti, Philip K. *History of the Arabs*. 10th ed. New York: St. Martin's Press, 1991.

———. *Tarikh Souriya, wa Lubnan wa Falastine* [The history of Syria, Lebanon, and Palestine], Vol. 1. Translated from the English by George Haddad and Abdel Karim Rafik. Beirut: Dar al-Thaqafa.

Hodgson, Marshall G. S. *The Venture of Islam: Conscience and History in a World Civilization*. Vol. 1, *The Classical Age of Islam*. Chicago: University of Chicago Press, 1977.

———. *The Venture of Islam*. Vol. 2, *The Expansion of Islam in the Middle Periods*. Chicago: University of Chicago Press, 1977.

————. *The Venture of Islam*. Vol. 3, *The Gunpowder Empires and Modern Times*. Chicago: University of Chicago Press, 1974.

Hoffman, Murad. *Al-Islam ka-Badil* [Islam as an alternative]. Translated from the German by Gharib M. Gharib. Munich: Bavaria Verlag, 1993.

Hoffman, Murad, and Abdelmajid Charfi. *Mustaqbal al-Islam fi-l-Gharb wa-l-Sharq* [The future of Islam in the east and the west]. Damascus: Dar al-Fikr al-Mu'asir, 2008.

Holy Bible. New International Version. Grand Rapids: Zondervan, 2005.

Hourani, Albert. *Arabic Thought in the Liberal Age (1798–1939)*. London: Cambridge University Press, 1991.

————. *A History of the Arab Peoples*. New York: Warner Books, 1992.

————. *Al-Islam Fi-l-Fikr al-Oroppi* [Islam in European thought]. Beirut: Al-Ahliyya, 1994.

Hussein, Taha. *Al-Fitna al-Kubra* [The great discord]. Vol. 1, *'Uthman Ibn 'Affan*. Beirut: Dar Al-Kitab Al-Lubnani, 1973.

————. *Al-Fitna al-Kubra* [The great discord]. Vol. 2, *'Ali Ibn Abi Talib*. Beirut: Dar Al-Kitab Al-Lubnani, 1973.

————. *Al-Shaykhan* [The two patriarchs]. Beirut: Dar Al-Kitab Al-Lubnani, 1973.

Hussein, Mahmoud. *Al-Sira: Le Prophète de l'Islam Raconté par ses Compagnons* [The Sira: the Prophet of Islam told by his companions]. Paris: Grasset and Fasquelle, 2005.

————. *Penser le Coran* [Pondering the Qur'an]. Paris: Grasset and Fasquelle, 2009.

Ibn Ḥazm al-Andalusi, Ali Bin Ahmad. *Al-Ihkam li Usul al-Ahkam* [The perfection of the principles of fiqh]. Cairo: Dar al-Hadith, 1983.

Ibn Qayyim al-Jawziyyah, Shamshuddin Abu 'Abdullah al-Dimishqi. *Muftah Dar al-Sa'ada* [The Key to the Abode of Happiness]. http://www.almeshkat.net/books/open.php?cat=26&book=493.

Ibn Taymiyya, Taqiyy ad-Din Ahmad. *Al-Siyasa al-Shar'iyya fi Islah al-Ra'i wa-l-Ra'iyya* [The Shari'a Politics of Reforming Ruler and Ruled]. http://www.feqh.al-Islam.com/Loader.aspx?pageid=277&BookID=71&TOCID=1.

Iogna-Prat, Dominique, and Gilles Veinstein. *Histoires des Hommes de Dieu dans l'Islam et le Christianisme* [Tales of God's men in Islam and Christianity]. Paris: Flammarion, 2003.

Iqbal, Muhammad. *The Reconstruction of Religious Thought in Islam*. Lahore: Ashraf Printing Press, 1982.

Izutsu, Toshihiko. *Allah wal Insan fi-l-Qur'an: 'Ilm Dalalat al-Ru'ya al-Qur'aniyya li-l-'Alam* [Man in the Qur'an: semantics of the Qur'anic weltanschaung]. Translated from the English by Hilal Muhammad al-Jihad. Beirut: Center for Studies on Arab Unity, 2007.

Izetbegović, Alija. *Al-Islam bayna al-Sharq wa-l-Gharb* [Islam between east and west]. Translated from the English by Muhammad Yusuf Adas. Munich: Bavaria Verlag and Handel, 1994.

al-Jabiri, Muhammad 'Abed. *Al-Dimuqratiyya wa Huquq al-Insan* [Democracy and human rights]. 3d ed. Beirut: Center for Studies on Arab Unity, 2004.

———. *Ad-Din wa-d-Dawla wa Tatbiq al-Shari'a* [Religion and state and the application of Shari'a]. 2d ed. Beirut: Center for Studies on Arab Unity, 2004.

———. *Fahm al-Qur'an al-Hakim: Al-Tafsir al-Wadih Hasab Tartib al-Nuzul* [Comprehending the judicious Qur'an: a clear exegesis according the sequence of revelation], vol. 1. Beirut: Center for Studies on Arab Unity, 2008.

———. *Fahm al-Qur'an al-Hakim* [Comprehending the judicious Qur'an], vol. 2. 2d ed. Beirut: Center for Studies on Arab Unity, 2009.

———. *Fahm al-Qur'an al-Hakim* [Comprehending the judicious Qur'an], vol. 3. Beirut: Center for Studies on Arab Unity, 2009.

———. *Madkhal ila-l-Qur'an al-Karim* [Introduction to the Holy Qur'an]. Vol. 1, *Fi-l-Ta'rif bi-l-Qur'an* [Presenting the Qur'an]. 2d ed. Beirut: Center for Studies on Arab Unity, Beirut 2007.

al-Jabiri, Muhammad 'Abed, and Hasan Hanafi. *Hiwar al-Mashriq wa-l-Maghrib* [Dialogue of the east and west]. 4th ed. Cairo: Ru'ya Publishing, 2005.

Jait, Hisham. *Fi al-Sira al-Nabawiyya* [The life of the Prophet]. Vol. 1, *Al-Wahiyy wal Qur'an wal Nubuwwa* [Revelation, Qur'an and Prophecy]. 3d ed. Beirut: Dar Attali'a, 2007.

———. *Fi al-Sira al-Nabawiyya* [The life of the Prophet]. Vol. 2, *Tarikhiyyat al-Da'wa al-Muhammadiyya fi Makka* [Historicity of the Muhammedan Call to the Faith in Mecca]. Beirut: Dar Attali'a, 2007.

———. Al-Fitna: *Jadaliyyat al-Din wa-l-Siyasa fi-l-Islam al-Mubkir* [The discord: the dialectic of religion and politics in early Islam]. 5th ed. Beirut: Dar Attali'a, 2005.

al-Jamal, Bassam. *Al-Islam al-Sunni* [Sunni Islam]. Beirut: Dar Attali'a, 2007.

al-Jassas, Abu Bakr Ahmad bin 'Ali al-Razi. *Ahkam al-Qur'an* [Principles of the Qur'an]. http://www.feqh.al-Islam.com.

Jeffery, Arthur. *The Foreign Vocabulary of the Qur'an*. Hertford: Oriental Institute Baroda, 1938.

Kadi, Wadad, and Victor Billeh, eds. *Islam and Education: Myths and Truths*. Chicago: University of Chicago Press, 2007.

Kawtharani, Wajih. *Al-Dawla wa-l-Khilafa Fi-l-Khitab al-Arabi Ibbana al-Thawrah al-Kamaliyya fi Turkiya* [The state and the caliphate in Arab discourse during the Kemalist revolution in Turkey]. Beirut: Dar Attali'a, 1996.

Khairallah, Shawqi Ibrahim. *Al-Injeel al-Khamis* [The fifth evangel]. Beirut: Bissan, 2004.

Khalayfi, Abdullah. *Al-Islam al-'Arabi* [Arab Islam]. Beirut: Dar Attali'a, Beirut 2007.

Kurzman, Charles, ed. *Liberal Islam: A Source Book*. New York: Oxford University Press, 1998.

Lamont, Corliss. *The Philosophy of Humanism*. 8th ed. Amherst, N.Y.: Humanist Press, 1997.

Lapidus, Ira. *A History of Islamic Societies*. New York: Cambridge University Press, 1994.

Lassouad, Munji. *Islam al-Falasifa* [The Islam of the philosophers]. Beirut: Dar Attali'a, 2007.

Lawrence, Bruce. *Shattering the Myth: Islam beyond Violence*. Princeton: Princeton University Press, 1998

Lewis, Bernard. *Cultures in Conflict: Christians, Muslims and Jews in the Age of Discovery*. New York: Oxford University Press, 1996.

———. *Islam: From the Prophet Muhammad to the Capture of Constantinople*. Vol. 1, *Politics and War*. New York: Oxford University Press, 1987.

———. *Islam: From the Prophet Muhammad to the Capture of Constantinople*. Vol. 2, *Religion and Society*. New York: Oxford University Press, 1987.

———. *The Jews of Islam*. Princeton: Princeton University Press, 1987.

Lewis, Bernard, and Buntzie E. Churchill. *Islam: The Religion and the People*. Upper Saddle River: Wharton School Publishing, 2009.

Lings, Martin. *Muhammad, His Life Based on the Earliest Sources*. 2d ed. Rochester: Inner Traditions, 2006.

Luxenberg, Christoph. *The Syro-Aramaïc Reading of the Koran: A Contribution to the Decoding of the Language of the Koran*. Berlin: Verlag Hans Schiler, 2007.

Maalouf, Amine. *Les Identités Meurtrières*. Paris: Grasset, 1998.

Madelung, Wilferd. *The Succession to Muhammad: A Study of the Early Caliphate*. Cambridge: Cambridge University Press, 1997.

Mahmassani, Sobhi. *Arkan Huquq al-Insan* [Basic concepts of human rights: A Comparative Study in Islamic, Lebanese and International Law]. Beirut: Dar al-'Ilm li-l-Malayin, 1979.

————. *Al-Awda' al-Tashri'iyya fi-d-Dual al-'Arabiyya: Madiha wa Hadiruha* [Legal systems in the Arab sates: past and present]. 4th ed. Beirut: Dar al-'Ilm li-l-Malayin, 1981.

————. *Al-Awza'i wa Ta'alimuhu al-Insaniyya wal-Qanuniyya* (Al-Awza'i and his humanistic and legal teachings]. Beirut: Dar al-'Ilm li-l-Malayin, 1978.

————. *Al-Da'a'im al-Khuluqiyya li-l-Qawanin al-Shar'iyya* [The moral pillars of Islamic jurisprudence]. Beirut: Dar al-'Ilm li-l-Malayin, 1973.

————. *Falsafat Al-Tashrī fi al-Islām* [The philosophy of jurisprudence in Islam]. Translated from the Arabic by Farhat Ziadeh. Leiden: E. J. Brill, 1961.

————. *Al-Mabadi' al-Shar'iyya wa-l-Qanuniyya fi-l-Hajr wa-n-Nafaqat wa-l-Mawarith wa-l-wasiyya* [Principles of Islamic law relating to incapacitiy, alimony, inheritance, and wills]. 7th ed. Beirut: Dar al-'Ilm li-l-Malayin, 1981.

————. *Turath al-Khulafa' al-Rashidin fi-l-Fiqh wa-l-Qada'* [The legal and judicial heritage of the Orthodox caliphs]. Beirut: Dar al-'Ilm li-l-Malayin, 1984.

Mahmoud, Mohammed A. *Quest for Divinity: A Critical Examination of the Thought of Mahmud Muhammad Taha*. Syracuse: Syracuse University Press, 2007.

Makarian, Christian. *Le Choc Jésus Mahomet* [The Jesus Muhammad clash]. Paris: J. C. Lattès, Paris 2008.

Manji, Irshad. *The Trouble with Islam: A Muslim's Call for Reform of Her Faith*. New York: St. Martin's Press, 2003.

Manna, Haytham. *Human Rights in the Arab-Islamic Culture*. Translated from the Arabic by Wassim Wagdy. Cairo: Cairo Institute for Human Rights Studies.

al-Marzoogy, Abu Ya'rub, and Muhammad Sa'id Ramadan Al-Buṭi. *Ishkaliyyat Tajdid Usul al-Fiqh* [The problematic of renewal of the principles of jurisprudence]. Damascus: Dar al-Fikr, 2006.

al-Marzoogy, Ibrahim Abdullah. *Huquq al-Insan fi-l-Islam* [Human rights in Islamic law]. Translated from the English by Muhammad Hussein Mursi. Abu Dhabi: Cultural Foundation, 1997.

al-Mawardi, Abul Hassan 'Ali Bin Muhammad. *Al-Ahkam al-Sultaniyya* [Rules governing the sultanate]. http://www.feqh.al-Islam.com/Loader. aspx?pageid=277&BookID=55&TOCID=1.

Mayer, Ann Elizabeth. *Islam and Human Rights: Tradition and Politics*. Boulder: Westview Press, 1991.

Meddeb, Abdel Wahab. *The Malady of Islam*. Translated from the French by Pierre Joris and Ann Reid. New York: Basic Books, 2003.

Monneret, Jean-Luc. *Les Grands Thèmes du Coran* [The major themes of the Qur'an]. Paris: Dervy, 2003.

Morabia, Alfred, and Ariel Morabia. *Le Gihad dans l'Islam Medieval: Le combat Sacré des Origines au XIIe Siècle* [Jihad in medieval Islam: the sacred combat from the origins until the 12th century]. Paris: Albin Michel, 1993.

Moussalli, Ahmad. *The Islamic Quest for Democracy, Pluralism, and Human Rights*. Gainesville: University Press of Florida, 2003.

Mughniyya, Muhammad Jawad. *Al-Ahwal al-Shakhsiyya 'ala-l-Madhahib al-Khamsa: Al-Ja'fari, al-Hanafi, al-Maliki, al-Shafi'i, al-Hanbali* [Family law under the five schools of jurisprudence, Ja'fari, Hanefi, Maliki, Shafi'i and Hanbali]. Beirut: Dar al-'Ilm li-l-Malayin, 1964.

Muhammad, Yahia. *Mushkilat al-Hadith* [The controversy over prophetic tradition]. Beirut: Al-Intishar al-'Arabi, 2007.

Muir, William. *The Caliphate: Its Rise, Decline and Fall*. Beirut: Khayats, 1963.

———. *The Life of Muhammad from Original sources*. Lexington: Elibron Classics, 2011.

Munawwar, Muhammad. *Iqbal and Quranic Wisdom*. Lahore: Islamic Book Foundation, 1981.

Mutwalli, Abdul Hamid. *Mabadi' Nizam al-Hukm fi-l-Islam* [Principles of government system in Islam]. Cairo: Dar al-Ma'arif, 1966.

al-Nabulsi, Shaker. *As'ilat al-Hamqa fi al-Siyasa wa-l-Islam al-Siyasi* [Questions of the fools on politics and political Islam]. 2d ed. Beirut: Arabic Studies Institute, 2006.

an-Na'im, Abdullahi A. *Islam and the Secular State: Negotiating the Future of Shari'a*. Cambridge: Harvard University Press, 2008.

———. *Toward an Islamic Reformation: Civil Liberties, Human Rights, and International Law*. Syracuse: Syracuse University Press, 1996.

Nasr, Seyyed Hossein. *The Heart of Islam: Enduring Values for Humanity*. New York: Harper Collins, 2004.

al-Nayhoum, Al-Sadiq. *Islam Dod Al-Islam* [Islam versus Islam]. London: Riad el-Rayyes Books, 1994.

———. *Al-Islam fi-l-Asr: Mann Saraqa al-Jami' wa ayna Dhahaba Yawmu-l-Jumu'a* [Islam in confinement: who stole the mosque and where did Friday—day of prayers—disappear?]. 3d ed. London: Riad El-Rayyes Books, 1995.

Nöldeke, Theodore. *Tarikh al-Qur'an* [History of the Qur'an]. Translated from the German by George Tamer. Beirut: Konrad-Adenauer Stiftung, 2004.

Noorani, A. J. *Al-Jihad wa-l-Islam: Al-Tahayyuz fi Muwajahat al-Waqe'* [Islam and jihad: prejudice versus reality]. Translated from the Hindi by Riad Hassan. Beirut: Dar al-Farabi, 2007.

Ouzon, Zakaria. *Jinayat al-Bukhari: Inqadh al-Din min Imam al-Muhaddithin* [Al-Bukhari's crime: saving religion from the guru of prophetic tradition]. Beirut: Riad el-Rayyes Books, 2004.

———. *Jinayat al-Shafi'i: Takhlis al-Umma min Fiqh al-A'imma* [Al-Shafi'i's crime: saving the umma from the scholarship of the ulema]. Beirut: Riad el-Rayyes Books, 2005.

———. *Laffaqa al-Muslimun idh-Qalu* [Muslims spun when they said]. Beirut: Riad el-Rayyes Books, 2008.

Patout Burns, J., ed. *War and Its Discontents: Pacifism and Quietism in the Abrahamic Traditions.* Washington, D.C.: Georgetown University Press, 1996.

Prémare, Alfred-Louis de.. *Aux Origines du Coran: Questions d'Hier, Approches d'Aujourd'hui* [At the origins of the Qur'an: yesterday's questions, today's approaches]. Paris: Tétraèdre 2004.

———. *Les Fondations de l'Islam: entre Écriture et Histoire* [The foundations of Islam: between scripture and history]. Paris: Éditions du Seuil, 2002.

Qaradawi, Yusuf (Shaykh). *Al-'Aql wa-l-'Ilm fi-l-Qur'an al-Karim* [The mind and knowledge in the Holy Qur'an]. Cairo: Maktabat Wahba, 1996.

———. *Fi Fiqh al-Aqalliyyat al-Muslima: Hayat al-Muslimin Wasat al-Mujtama'at al-Ukhra* [Principles of Islamic law applicable to Muslim minorities: the life of Muslims amidst other societies]. Cairo: Dar al-Shuruq, Cairo 2001.

———. *Al-Halal wa-l-Haram* [The permitted and the illicit]. 28th ed. Cairo: Maktabat Wahba, 2004.

———. *Al-'Ibada fi-l-Islam* [Worship in Islam]. 24th ed. Cairo: Maktbat Wahba, 1996.

———. *Kaifa Nata'amalu Ma'al-Sunna al-Nabawiyya* [How do we deal with prophetic tradition]. Cairo: Dar al-Shuruq, 2002.

———. *Ma' A'immat al-Tajdid wa Ru'ahum Fi-l-Fikr wa-l-Islah* [With the Leaders of Renewal and Their Views on Thought and Reform]. http://www.eltwhed.com/vb/showthread.php?28842-%E3%DA-%C3%C6%E3%C9-%C7%E1%CA%CC%CF%ED%CF-%E6%D1%C4%C7%E5%E3-%DD%ED-%C7%E1%DD%DF%D1-%E6%C7%E1%C5%D5%E1%C7%CD.

———. *Markaz al-Mar'a fi-l-Hayat al-Islamiyya* [The status of women in Islamic life]. Cairo: Maktabat Wahba, 1996.

————. *Al-Sahwa al-Islamiyya bayna-l-Ikhtilaf al-Mashru' wa al-Tafarruq al-Madhmum* [The Islamic awakening: between legitimate disagreement and hated dispersion]. Cairo: Dar al-Shuruq, 2001.

————. *Al-Tatarruf al-'Ilmani fi Muwajahat al-Islam* [Secular extremism in the face of Islam]. Cairo: Dar al-Shuruq, 2001.

Qassem, Assaad Wahid. *Azamat al-Khilafa wa Atharuha al-Mu'asira* [The crisis of succession and its effects]. http://www.shiaweb.org/books/khelafa/index.html.

al-Qumni, Sayyid Mahmoud. *Al-Ustura wa al-Turath* [Myth and heritage]. 2d ed. Cairo: Sinai Publications, 1993.

Rabbath, Edmond. *Les Chrétiens dans l'Islam des Premiers Temps* [Christians in the 'Islam of the early days]. Vol. 1, *L'Orient Chrétien à la Veille de l'Islam* [The Christian Orient on the eve of Islam]. Beirut: Lebanese University Publications, 1989.

————. *Les Chrétiens dans l'Islam des Premiers Temps* [Christians in the Islam of the early days]. Vol. 2, *Mahomet: Prophète Arabe et Fondateur d'État* [Muhammad: Arab prophet and state founder]. Beirut: Lebanese University Publications, 1989.

————. *Les Chrétiens dans l'Islam des Premiers Temps* [Christians in the Islam of the early Days]. Vol. 3, *La Conquête Arabe Sous les Quatre Premiers Califes* [Arab conquest under the first four caliphs]. Beirut: Lebanese University Publications, 1985.

Rahman, Fazlur. *Islam and Modernity: Transformation of an Intellectual Tradition*. Chicago: University of Chicago Press, 1984.

————. *Islamic Methodology in History*. Islamabad: Islamic Research Institute, 1964.

————. *Major Themes of the Qur'an*. 2d ed. Minneapolis: Bibliotheca Islamica, 1994.

Ramadan, Tariq. *Islam, the West and the Challenges of Modernity*. Translated from the French by Sa'id Amghar. Markefield: Islamic Foundation, 2001.

————. *Mon Intime Conviction* [My intimate conviction]. Paris: Presses du Châtelet, 2009.

————. *Peut-on Vivre avec l'Islam* [Can one live with Islam]. Lausanne: Éditions Favre, 2004.

————. *Radical Reform: Islamic Ethics and Liberation*. New York: Oxford University Press, 2009.

Rodinson, Maxime. *L'Islam: Politique et Croyance* [Islam: politics and creed]. Paris: Fayard, 1993.

al-Rusafi, Ma'ruf. *Kitab al-Shakhsiyya al-Muhammadiyya aw Hall al-Lughz al-Muqaddas* [The book on the Muhammedan personality or solving the sacred mystery]. Köln: Al-Kamel Verlag, 2002.

Sachedina, Abdulaziz. *The Islamic Roots of Democratic Pluralism.* New York: Oxford University Press, 2001.

————. *The Role of Islam in the Public Square: Guidance or Governance?* Leiden: Amsterdam University Press, 2006.

Saeed, Abdullah, and Hassan Saeed. *Freedom of Religion, Apostasy and Islam.* Burlington: Ashgate Publications, 2005.

Safi, Omid, ed. *Progresive Muslims on Justice, Gender, and Pluralism.* Oxford: Oneworld Publications, 2005.

Saint-Bon, Henri de, and Saad Khiari. *Cahtolique/Musulman: Je te Connais, Moi Non Plus* (Catholic/Muslim: I know you! Neither do I]. Paris: Éditions François-Xavier de Guibert, 2006.

al-Saleh, Sobhi. *Al-Islam wa-l-Mujtama' Al-'Asri* [Islam and modernity]. 2d ed. Beirut: Dar al-Adab, 1983.

Sawma, Gabriel. *The Qur'an Misinterpreted, Mistranslated, and Misread: The Aramaic Language of the Qur'an.* Plainsboro: Adibooks, 2006.

al-Sayyid, Radwan. *Al-Jama'a wa-l-Mujtama'a wa al-Dawla: Sultat al-Ideologiyya fi-l-Majal al-Siyasi al-'Arabi al-Islami* [The collectivity, society, and the state: authoritative ideology in Arab-Islamic politics]. Beirut: Dar al-Kitab al-'Arabi, 1997.

Schacht, Joseph. *An Introduction to Islamic Law.* London: Oxford at the Clarendon Press, 1967.

————. *Muhammadan Jurisprudence.* London: Oxford at the Clarendon Press, 1966.

Schuon, Frithjof. *Comprendre l'Islam* [Understanding Islam]. Paris: Éditions du Seuil, 1976.

Sfar, Mondher. *In Search of the Original Koran: The True History of the Revealed Text.* Translated from the French by Emilia Lanier. Amherst, N.Y.: Promotheus Books, 2008.

al-Shafi'i, (Imam) Muhammad bin Idriss. *Al-Risala* [The Message]. Realization and commentary by Ahmad Muhammad Shaker. Beirut: Dar al-Kutub al-'Ilmiyya.

Shahrour, Muhammad. *Al-Kitab wa-l-Qur'an: Qira'a Mu'asira* [The Book and the Qur'an: a contemporary reading]. 4th ed. Damascus: Al-Ahali, 1992.

————. *Nahwa Usul Jadida li-l-Fiqh al-Islami: Fiqh al-Mar'a* [Toward new foundations for Islamic jurisprudence: jurisprudence relating to women]. Damascus: Al-Ahali, 2000.

————. *Tajfif Manabi' al-Irhab* [Draining the sources of terrorism]. Damascus: Al-Ahali, 2008.

Shalabi, Ahmad. *Mawsu'at at-Tarikh al-Islami* [Encyclopedia of Islamic history]. 10 vols. Cairo: Annahda Bookstore, 1958 to 1990.

————. *Mawsuat al-Hadara al-Islamiyya* [Encyclopedia of Islamic civilization]. 10 vols. Cairo: Annahda Bookstore, 1954 to 1978.

Shamiyyeh, Jubran. *Al-Islam: Hal Yuqaddim li-l- 'Alam Nazariyya li-l-Hukm* [Islam: does it offer the world a theory of state]. Sinn el-Fil: Research and Publishing House, 1990.

Shari'ati, 'Ali. *Ma'rifat al-Islam* [The knowledge of Islam]. 2d ed. Beirut: Dar al-Amir, 2007.

al-Shawwaf, Munir Muhammad Tahir. *Tahafut "al-Qira'at al-Mu'asira"* [The rush to "contemporary reading"]. Limassol, Cyprus: Al-Shawwaf Publishers, 1993.

Soroush, Abdolkarim. *Reason, Freedom and Democracy in Islam*. Translated from the Farsi, edited, and with a critical commentary by Mahmoud and Ahmad Sadri. New York: Oxford University Press, 2002.

Stowasser, Barbara F. *Women in the Qur'an: Traditions and Interpretation*. New York: Oxford University Press, 1994.

Sunna—See Prophetic Tradition.

Suyuti, Jalal al-Din al-. *Al-Itqan fi 'Ulum al-Qur'an* [The perfection of Qur'anic science]. http://www.altafsir.com/MiscellaneousBooks.asp.

Taha, Mahmoud. *Al-Risala al-Thaniya min al-Islam* [The second message of Islam]. http://www.alfikra.org/books_a.php.

Taji-Farouki, Suha, ed. *Modern Muslim Intellectuals and the Qur'an*. New York: Oxford University Press, 2006.

Talbi, Mohamed. *Al-Islam: Hurriyya wa Hiwar* [Islam: freedom and dialogue]. Translated from the French by Husni Zina. Beirut: Dar Annahar, 1999.

————. *Plaidoyer pour un Islam Moderne* [Plea for a modern Islam]. Paris: Éditions de l'Aube, 2004.

————. *Universalité du Coran* [Universality of the Qur'an]. Paris: Actes Sud, 2002.

Talbi, Mohamed, and Maurice Bucaille. *Réflexions sur le Coran* [Thoughts on the Qur'an]. Paris: Seghers, 1989.

Tibi, Bassam. *Islam and the Cultural Accommodation of Social Change*. Translated from the German by Clare Krojzl. Boulder: Westview Press, 1991.

Urvoy, Dominique. *Les Penseurs Libres dans l'Islam Classique* [The free thinkers of classical Islam]. Paris: Flammarion, 1996.

al-'Uthmani, Saadeddine. *Qadiyyat al-Mar'a wa Nafsiyyat al-Istibdad* [Women's issue and the mentality of abuse]. 2d ed. Al-Rabat: Top Press, 2004.

Wadud, Amina. *Qur'an and Woman: Rereading the Sacred Text from a Woman's Perspective.* New York: Oxford University Press, 1999.

al-Wahidi al-Nisaburi, Abul Hasan 'Ali bin Ahmad. *Asbab An-Nuzul* [The circumstances of the revelation]. http://www.altafsir.com/AsbabAlnuzol. asp?SoraName=1&Ayah=0&img= A&LanguageID=1.

al-Wartani, Hala, and Abdul Basit Qammouri. *Islam 'Usur al-Inhitat* [Islam druing the periods of decline]. Beirut: Dar Attali'a, 2007.

Watt, W. Montgomery, and Richard Bell. *Introduction to the Qur'an.* Edinburgh: Edinburgh University Press, 2003.

Wellhausen, J. *The Arab Kingdom and its Fall.* Beirut: Khayat Publishing, 1963.

Zakaria, Fouad. *Al-Haqiqa wa-l-Wahm fi-l-Haraka al-Islamiyya al-Mu'asira* [Truth and myth about the contemporary Islamic movement]. 2d ed. Cairo: Dar Al-Fikr li al-Dirasat, 1986.

Zaman, Muhammad Qasim. *The 'Ulama in Contemporary Islam: Custodians of Change.* Princeton: Princeton University Press, 2002.

al-Zuhaylī, Wahba, and others. *Al-Mawsū'ah al-Qur'āniyyah al-Muyassarah* [Easy Qur'anic encyclopedia]. 2d ed. Damascus: Dar al Fikr, 2002.

al-Zurayqi, Balqis. *Al-Islam fi-l-Madina* [Islam in al-Madina]. Beirut: Dar Attali'a, 2007.

Index of Subjects